Encountering Children's Literature

An Arts Approach

Jane M. Gangi

Sacred Heart University

With a foreword by Joseph Bruchac

PEARSON

Boston   New York   San Francisco
Mexico City   Montreal   Toronto   London   Madrid   Munich   Paris
Hong Kong   Singapore   Tokyo   Cape Town   Sydney

For Peter, Caryn, Devin, Sarah, and Robyn;

for Joyce and her family, especially the grandchildren;

and

in memory of Jonah Thomas Surratt (1987–2001)

Series Editor: Aurora Martínez Ramos
Editorial Assistant: Katie Freddoso
Senior Marketing Manager: Elizabeth Fogarty
Production Editor: Michelle Limoges
Editorial-Production Service: Denise Botelho, Colophon
Compositor: Omegatype Typography, Inc.
Composition and Prepress Buyer: Linda Cox
Manufacturing Buyer: Andrew Turso
Interior Designer: Denise Hoffman
Cover Designer: Kristina Mose-Libon

For related titles and support materials, visit our online catalog at www.ablongman.com.

Between the time Website information is gathered and then published, it is not unusual for some sites to have closed. Also, the transcription of URLs can result in typographical errors. The publisher would appreciate notification where these errors occur so that they may be corrected in subsequent editions.

Library of Congress Cataloging-in-Publication Data

Gangi, Jane M.
    Encountering children's literature : an arts approach / Jane M. Gangi.
      p. cm.
    Includes bibliographical references and index.
    ISBN 0-205-39240-7 (alk. paper)
    1. Children's literature, American—History and criticism. 2. Children's literature, English—History and criticism. 3. Children's literature—Study and teaching. I. Title.

CURR PS490.G36 2004
    809'.89282–dc21

                  2003046387

Printed in the United States of America

10 9 8 7 6 5 4 3 2 1   HAM 08 07 06 05 04 03

Contents

Chapter 7
Folklore:
A Global Legacy   *131*

Chapter 8
Informational Books:
Finding the Aesthetic   *164*

Chapter 9
Integrated Historical
Literature: The
Human Dimension   *180*

Chapter 13
Celebrations and Commemorations: Understanding Our World   243

Foreword

The Journey Is the Destination
Joseph Bruchac

During the course of the last few decades I've sometimes found myself in the position of comparing the traditional American Indian way of teaching with that most common to the western world, the way that has dominated American education, the way that a good many critics have said our country needs to get back to in order to "preserve our competitive edge." That western model is, put into a single word, didacticism. The teacher tells you what you need to hear, what you need to read, what you need to do. Then you do it just that way. We're talking, of course, about the basics: reading, writing, and arithmetic. (Which are *not,* unless we are encouraging bumptious illiteracy, three words that begin with the seventeenth letter of the alphabet.) Taking it a little further, this model operates within a system in which each aspect of education is neatly cut out of the herd, corralled, and then dissected. (Have you ever noticed how dead something is after it has been dissected? About as dead as the eyes of a classroom full of children reduced to mindless repetition.) If you think you detect a bit of animosity on my part toward the more militant form of this sort of cerebral laundering, blame it on those Sisyphean years of my own childhood when I suffered, snored, and retreated into my imagination while being forced to roll the rock of rote up that endless hill. (However, I must hasten to add that the memory of the Promethean intellects of at least two of my grade school teachers—Mrs. Monthony in second grade and Miss McTygue in fourth— will always be there to remind me that the best teachers can find a way to get through to their students no matter what system they labor under.)

The American Indian model of education, an experiential model that my grandfather Jesse Bowman showed me without ever breathing a word about teaching, could not be more different. It is, quite simply, learning by doing. Whenever he did something, he always made sure that I knew he needed my help doing it. It made me wonder, at times, how he had ever gotten as old as he was without knowing how to do such things as straighten a nail or float a line down to a trout or walk quietly in the forest or take the bark off a piece of willow to make a whistle. It was lucky I was there to help him, I used to think. Sometimes, when we were fishing, he'd even start to forget to say "Thank you" when we caught a fish. But I would remind him. I realize now, years later, just how much he taught me—including the fact that the journey itself is just as important and rewarding as "getting somewhere."

In western education, if you want to learn about something, you study it in a classroom. In American Indian education, you just do it—usually in the presence of someone who knows so well how something is done that they can sometimes draw you into the doing of it without your hardly even noticing. Moreover, there are things that happen in the learning that may seem, to a strictly western mind, to have little or nothing to do with the real thing. A Pomo Indian basket maker teaching a workshop in basket making to a group of Anglo women began by telling them they had to learn a certain song. "But we just want to learn how to make a basket," one woman said. "No, you don't," was the reply she got. In American Indian cultures and communities, the so-called "arts" have never been separated from the rest of life or seen as a part of the "curriculum" that could be sacrificed because we need to emphasize the "Real Basics."

Of course, lines between cultures and ways of learning are not that strict nor that easily drawn. There are and always have been places where they come together. Life, after all, is a messy business and one thing is always spilling out of its container and contaminating something else. Let's, in fact, substitute the word "enriching" for "contaminating." Of late, things have been enriching the western approach to education in ways that bring it closer to that old native model. There is the recent awareness of the several different types of intelligence with which we are blessed that go far beyond mathematical and linguistic abilities. Modern studies of the working of the brain have proved that music study develops areas that are also needed for mathematical aptitude. And, to my delight, storytelling is becoming a regular part of the curriculum at many grade levels. (Storytelling, I should add, although it consists of no more than the voice and presence of the storyteller, is not at all the same as a lecture. A good story transports the listener, making the world of the story as real as any personal experience can be. Thus I classify storytelling as an experience of the imagination and the spirit, an engagement of all the senses, rather than a mere reiteration.)

Bringing things together, as you can see, has always been important to me. It is one reason, apart from my own obvious interest in American Indian literature, why I have been a strong advocate of multicultural literature (by the way, "multicultural" is *not* a codeword for either "inferior" or "exclusionary"). I celebrate books that help shape a wider awareness of the world, especially when they are for young readers. The marvelously inclusive approach of this book is one reason why I was delighted to be asked to write these few prefatory words.

But there is more. I do not know of another book that has both undertaken and succeeded so well at the task shouldered by this text, the important job of bringing the arts—in the fullest and most glorious sense of the word—into the study, the experience, the celebration of the best literature available for children. Both teachers and students have reason to be grateful for the scholarship, the dedication, and the pure enjoyment that this book brings us. Get ready to learn and do, to listen and be transported.

Enjoy the journey.

Preface

Encountering Children's Literature: An Arts Approach is designed for preservice and in-service teachers of kindergarten through grade six. The book can serve as the primary text for a children's literature course or as a supplement to a reading and language arts course. It has been field-tested on both the graduate and undergraduate levels by six instructors of children's literature during the past five years. Although primarily written for education students and practicing teachers, students of children's literature in English departments, librarians, and parents will benefit: The book unlocks the potential of the arts for engaged learning and provides inclusive, up-to-date bibliographies for discovering children's literature.

The experiential, arts-based approach helps future and practicing teachers develop their abilities, and gives them a range of strategies to share with elementary school children. The book is brief enough to ensure that more time is spent reading children's books than reading a textbook.

Organization and Features

Each chapter begins with an encounter session that actively engages the class. All of the encounters have been successfully field-tested, not only in higher education, but also with elementary school children in urban, suburban, and rural settings. The research base that supports this way of sharing literature with children is woven into every chapter. **About the Encounters,** found at the beginning of Chapter 1, provides more practical details, and the **Suggested Activities** section at the end of the chapters includes other arts-based encounters with literature. Each chapter contains a **chapter overview.**

Chapter 1 provides a rationale for integrating the arts in the education of teachers, including strong evidence that the arts enhance student achievement in other academic areas. Educators of color, who describe artistic teaching practices that help all children learn, are introduced.

Chapter 2 gives a brief overview of genre and its appearance in the history of children's literature. Historical aspects are further considered in succeeding chapters in time-lines and/or short narrative sections.

Chapter 3 provides guidelines for selecting and evaluating literature, especially multicultural literature, which is critical to address people of color in the curriculum. Multicultural awards and websites are provided at the end of this chapter to guide individual reading journeys.

Chapter 4, on the picture book, begins with the creation of an artistic product in the style of children's illustrator-author Donald Crews. The chapter introduces the elements, styles, and media of the visual arts, including a table for viewing the visual aspects of children's picture books.

Chapter 5, on poetry, introduces the elements of figurative language, and performances of choral readings reveal the power—and fun—of words.

Chapter 6, on drama, takes a closer look at the elements of literature, and a readers theater piece is the encounter. Understanding the visual, poetic, and literary elements and styles at the beginning of the study of children's literature will help readers see and hear more keenly literature in subsequent chapters.

Chapter 7 introduces the oral tradition, the root of the world's literature, anonymously authored by the community of tellers. There are two encounters for this chapter: a storytelling workshop that potentially includes all categories of folklore, and creative movement and tableaux based on a myth.

High-quality informational books are the subject of **Chapter 8.** This chapter is particularly attentive to ways teachers can address the wide range of abilities present in elementary classrooms.

Chapter 9, in tandem with the interdisciplinary approach found in the bibliography of recommended books in Appendix C, integrates literature from several genres—historical fiction (primarily), biography, autobiography, and other informational books—to illuminate life in previous eras. The rationale for including various genres in connection with history is as follows:

- It helps preservice teachers pass Praxis II and other national teacher exit exams that require evidence of interdisciplinary learning.

- Through stories, facts are brought to life. Literature provides the emotional appeal needed to help students care about historical events.

- Boys are more likely to choose nonfiction; girls, fiction. Grouping genres around historical topics validates more reading choices.

- Such interdisciplinary learning is reflected in national standards.

Literature circles, based on reader response theory, are the encounter for this chapter.

Chapter 10 further considers biography, autobiography, and memoir with a focus on the life stories of accomplished individuals from all walks of life. The elementary school years offer an unparalleled opportunity to help children develop a sense of purpose and persistence. By analogy, teachers can provide mentors and role models through books, helping to create a school culture in which persons of all ethnicities see themselves as capable of high achievement. An oral interpretation workshop is the encounter.

Contemporary realism is the subject of **Chapter 11.** Current issues, including censorship, are explored. Role-playing selections from realistic fiction and transforming outcomes are interactively shared.

Chapter 12 looks at the ways fantasy and science fiction delight and amuse, while probing deep philosophical questions. Metaphors enrich thinking about fantasy.

Finally, in **Chapter 13,** the various genres are brought together with a focus on literature about celebrations and commemorations, both secular and religious. To ignore religious literature is to leave out a huge portion of the world's literature and, based on the number of followers of the world's religions, our children are more likely to meet religious than nonreligious persons throughout their lives. This literature can promote understanding and respect in the midst of diversity. In the college classroom, Jews, Muslims, Christians, Hindus, Buddhists, and those of other faiths share children's books they love from their religious traditions. The encounter is a story dramatization.

Primarily for teacher educators, **Appendix A** contains reproducible assessments. Reflecting national standards, open-ended performance tasks invite self-selection and student contributions that evoke higher order thinking, creativity, and collaboration. Experts in performance-based learning assisted in their development:

- Maggie Sneed, Elementary Coordinator at Alverno College (Alverno College has been the leader of performance-based learning for several decades.)
- Catherine Oleksiw, former Title II Project Director at the Connecticut State Department of Education
- Jeff Cain, Director of Writing Across the Curriculum (WAC), and Jack DeGraffenreid, both of Sacred Heart University

Preservice and inservice teachers will also find the assessments of interest. They must assess elementary schoolchildren's learning and can modify these examples for the K–6 schools.

Appendix B offers more professional resources.

Appendix C contains an abbreviated version of the extensive bibliographies of children's literature, placed together so that readers of this book can easily take them on their reading journeys in libraries and bookstores. (You can find a detailed version of this appendix at http://faculty.sacredheart.edu/gangij) Infused throughout with multicultural and international literature, and developed in consultation with over a dozen experts, these bibliographies provide a framework for exploring the full spectrum of reading choices. Sampling these books will help readers gain competence in judging quality. Because teachers need multiple ways of organizing books, the bibliography is ordered as follows:

- Picture books include biographies, contemporary realism, fantasy, historical fiction, and concept books, thus introducing readers early on to a range of genres.
- Poetry includes anthologies, collections, single editions, and poetry by children.
- Drama, rarely included in children's literature textbooks, provides plays elementary schoolchildren can enjoy as literature or as a performance venue.
- Folklore is organized by continent and country, offering opportunities for interdisciplinary teaching, especially of geography and the social studies.
- Informational books are by subject (archeology, architecture, calligraphy, and so on), which can help readers find their passions.

- Historical literature is topical and chronological, allowing for integrated learning (Slavery and the Underground Railroad, the Civil War, and so on).
- The genres of biography, autobiography, and memoir are considered again by career and vocation (athletes, scientists, mathematicians, and so on). Because of their special significance to children and teachers, books about authors and illustrators of children's books are highlighted in this bibliography.

Weaving nonfiction through three bibliographies (Chapters 8, 9, and 10) can redress the imbalance of genre in the schools. Gender studies show that girls prefer fantasy and boys prefer nonfiction. Not surprisingly, because women make up about 90 percent of the elementary teaching profession, fantasy receives the greater emphasis, especially in read-alouds.

- Contemporary realism is arranged thematically and topically (immigration, mysteries, sports, and so on).
- Fantasy and science fiction includes a range of fantastical literature, from high fantasy to futuristic fiction.
- Celebrations and commemorations integrate genres and correspond to the lunar and Gregorian (January, February, and so on) calendars.

In the full Appendix C on the website, the consultants who contributed are introduced at the beginning of each section, and connections are made to national standards. Readers are also cued into underrepresented authors and illustrators, who are often cultural insiders.

To help readers find literature by diverse artists, **Appendix D** lists multicultural and international authors and illustrators.

National Council for the Accreditation of Teacher Education (NCATE), International Reading Association (IRA), and National Council of Teachers of English (NCTE) A word about standards: At their worst, they further overwhelm already overwhelmed educators. At their best, they articulate best practices in the field of education, much like standards in the medical profession articulate best practices in the medical field. I include them for teacher educators and preservice and inservice teachers because, practically speaking, we need to know the standards to maintain accreditation (in teacher preparation programs) and attain and/or maintain teacher licensure (in the K–12 schools). I also wanted to make the connection that standards do not mean more worksheets and drills. In fact, the standards support the approach taken in this book: active learning, higher order thinking, and using a range of strategies to help all children learn. NCATE standards are considered throughout all chapters: Both IRA/NCTE standards and NCATE standards are further considered in Appendix A.[1]

Endnotes During field tests of this manuscript, some students did not like the endnotes; others did. The latter group vehemently did not want to see the endnotes removed, because they looked forward to reading professional books on their own. Besides cueing readers in to all kinds of high-quality children's literature, an additional goal of the book is to introduce future and practicing teachers to professional literature that will enhance teacher development. To save space, if a reference is in the endnote, I have usually not included it in the For Further Reading section at the end of each chapter. Reading and language arts expert Regie Routman recommends, *"Set aside time each week for professional reading. . . .* If I were involved in hiring a new teacher, I would be sure to ask candidates, 'What are you reading professionally and/or what have you read recently? How has that reading impacted you as a learner?' Any teacher who could not answer those questions would not have my vote."[2]

Websites at the end of each chapter give resources for further learning. This book is a practical resource that readers continue to use long after the college course ends.

Information Not Included

Readability and Leveling Helpful work exists elsewhere. Thomas Gunning, Irene Fountas and Gay Su Pinnell, and others have already published important work on leveling books.[3] Language arts expert Lucy Calkins advises leveling one third of the classroom library. However, teachers may need to do some of this work on their own because book lists often do not contain enough authentic or appropriate multicultural books. The concept of leveling books challenges the tradition of readability. Previously, readability addressed a calculation that required counting sentence length, the number of syllables in a passage, or the number of high-frequency words to determine a grade level equivalent. This technique did not account for student background, interest, or development. Today we know that a student's grade placement does not make all texts written for that audience comprehensible. A second grader is a student who has probably been in school for three years but his stage of reading development could be emergent, early, or fluent. All students are developmentally different, so no single text can serve all third graders. It is the challenge to classroom teachers to match readers to multiple texts that allow for individual differences, interests, and backgrounds.

This book highlights the childhood favorites of creative and productive people. These cherished books sometimes challenge current notions of what is regarded developmentally appropriate. For example, as an elementary school-age child, Maya Angelou loved selections not typically found in elementary schools: Samuel Butler's *Erewhon,* William Shakespeare's plays and poetry, and the work of Harlem Renaissance poets. Explaining the impetus of the standards and outcomes assessment movement in education, Mary Diez, a leader in the field of teacher education, says, "[C]hildren are capable of much more development than we have sometimes given them credit for."[4] Childhood reading experiences, often detailed in biographies and autobiographies, support this tenet. Rigid adherence to developmental levels in helping children select literature can restrict growth.

Plot Summaries There are many sources for these; see, especially, Appendix B. Assessments in Appendix A show how to structure the class so that shared book reviews create a collaborative learning environment in which students take responsibility for their own and their classmates' learning by providing each other with summaries, reviews, and reflections.

Acknowledgments

Without my students, who are all preservice and inservice teachers, there would be no book. They have shared with me their joys (and, sometimes, their sorrow) in their transactions with the art form of children's literature. Good-heartedly, they have participated in the encounters during class time. Outside of class, they have written their own children's books (sometimes coauthored by one of their own children), designed stunning dust jackets, created newsletters with graphics, adapted their own readers theater pieces, composed poetry, told stories to children, created *papel picado* styled after Carmen Lomas Garza's work, drafted and painted maps (for books like *Island of the Blue Dolphins*), designed travel brochures (for *The Phantom Tollbooth*), created dreamcatchers (like the one in *Grandmother's Dreamcatcher*), written memoirs, and crafted origami in response to *Sadako and the Thousand Paper Cranes.* Their insights, humor, suggestions, enthusiasm, and the meanings they bring to literature and the arts are reflected throughout this book. To all my past and present students: Thank you, thank you.

The Sacred Heart University Research and Creativity Grant provided support during Summer 1999 and again during Summer 2001, including Allison Trowbridge's invaluable help as a research assistant.

To my colleagues, I owe much. Edward Murray, designer of the highly successful Comer School Development Essentials of Literacy project, has opened many doors for me. To my other colleagues in the department of education, thank you for your continual support. I would also like to thank Thomas Forget, Academic Vice President of Sacred Heart University, for his understanding and support, and for making the connection between Mary Jackson Scroggins and me. To Dean Patricia Walker and Chair Ed Malin, thank you for supporting my sabbatical. Thanks, also, to Beverly Birch, Kathy Olsen, Emily Burgos, Jimi Dennis, and Ingrid Wagner, who provided support at work, and to Mary and Bob Korin, Ellen and Clay Hines, and my mother, Mary McBrayer, who provided support at home. Thanks to former Sacred Heart University students Alice Hutchinson, Toby Elberger, and Jennifer Crawley, who provided much assistance, and to undergraduate Kristen Olsen. Bill Morris at HarperCollins was also especially generous and helpful.

My longtime association with the Connecticut Storytelling Center and its founder, Barbara Reed, has enriched my life and my thinking about oral literature. Lot Therrio, Peg O'Sullivan, Rosalind Hinman, J. G. Pinkerton, Ann Shapiro, and Lorna Stengel, in addition to being lots of fun, are true friends with generous hearts.

From New York University, Nellie McCaslin provided both encouragement and help, for five years. Julie Cummins and Candy Warren aided me with the visual arts aspect of this book, and Rebecca Abbott, creator of the television documentary, *Designing Minds: The Arts in Education,* and Scott Shuler, the arts consultant for the Connecticut State Department of Education, kept me up-to-date on the arts-in-education world. And, always, my husband, Robyn Gangi, inspires me by his work in music education.

My gratitude is also extended to those who reviewed the manuscript and/or the bibliographies: Librarians Gabriella Kaye and Mary Gilbert; editors Lynn Taylor, Jane Garry, and Gayle Sergel; reviewers Mike Cadden, Missouri Western State College; Thomas A. Caron, Marshall University Graduate College; Marilyn Carpenter, Eastern Washington University; Janice A. DeLong, Liberty College; Catherine Kurkjian, Central Connecticut

State University; Meggin McIntosh, University of Nevada, Reno; and Jill Potts, Gustavus Adolphus College; and writers Laurie Brooks, Karen Young, Brad Seidensticker, Susanna Reich, and Joseph Bruchac. Thank you, also, to those teachers, principals, and language arts consultants in the elementary schools who read and commented on the manuscript: Lois Smith, Lori Ercoli, Jackie Norcel, Tami Priestley, Stephanie Neborsky, Nayda Rodriguez, Kate Lunnie, Yolanda Trowbridge, Jeanette Bosch, Lynn Ellis, Mary Misevich, Marcia Van Hise, and Cheryl McCain. I offer my thanks to teacher educators Maggie Sneed of Alverno College, Barbara Goodwillie of Central Connecticut State University, Connie Rockman of University of Bridgeport, and Lois Libby, Sondra Melzer, Dan Christianson, Karen Waters, Terry Neu, Toni Bruciati, Jeanne Peloso, Karl Lorenz, and Edward Murray of Sacred Heart University. I also benefited from conversations with Seymour Sarason, Yale University professor emeritus, who has written extensively about teacher education.

Thank you to those professors of children's literature who field-tested the manuscript: Edward Murray and Connie Rockman with undergraduates, Tami Priestley and Jason McKinnon with graduates, and Stephanie Neborsky who used parts of it with her graduate classes.

Thanks to those who helped develop performance-based assessments: Maggie Sneed, Jeff Cain, Jack DeGraffenreid, and Catherine Oleksiw.

Thank you to Sacred Heart University librarians Cheryl Mitchell and Kim Macomber, and to Bethel Public Library librarian Sheila Moore, who provided much assistance. Interlibrary loan librarians Sachi Spohn at Sacred Heart and Lorna Rhyins in Bethel ordered hundreds—more likely thousands—of books for me during the past several years, spending many, many hours on this project. Thank you; thank you both. Sherry Earle and Eilene Bertsche, thank you. To Aurora Martinez, my editor at Allyn and Bacon, thank you for seeing the value of a new approach to the teaching of children's literature. Katie Freddoso, Michelle Limoges, Denise Hoffman, Denise Botelho, and Cat Ohala, you are terrific.

Clearly, a great many people have been involved in this work. However, there are three individuals who have contributed on a number of levels. Mary Jackson Scroggins became my sounding board, writing teacher, companion in a labor of love, and new friend. In addition to her guidance on the bibliographies, Lyn Miller-Lachmann thoroughly read the manuscript twice and especially contributed to its conceptual design. Connie Rockman read and reread. It would be impossible for me to provide the details of our many conversations, emails, and telephone calls. Suffice it to say, her contribution, along with Lyn's and Mary's, has been immense.

—*Jane M. Gangi*

notes

1. NCATE standards can be found at www.ncate.org/ standard/elemstds.pdf, and IRA/NCTE standards can be found at www.ncte.org/standards/standards. shtml

2. Regie Routman, *Conversations: Strategies for Teaching, Learning, and Evaluating* (Portsmouth, NH: Heinemann, 1999), p. 11.

3. Irene C. Fountas and Gay Su Pinnell, *Matching Books to Readers: Using Leveled Books in Guided Reading, K–3* (Portsmouth, NH: Heinemann, 1999); Thomas Gunning, *Creating Literacy Instruction for All Children* (Boston: Allyn and Bacon, 2000); Julia Chamberlain and Dorothy Leal, "Caldecott Medal Books and Readability: Not 'Just' Picture Books," *The Read-* *ing Teacher 52.8* (1999): 898–902; and Dorothy J. Leal and Julia Chamberlain–Solecki, "Newbery Medal-Winning Combination: High Student Interest Plus Appropriate Readability Levels," *The Reading Teacher 51.8* (1998): 712–715. See the Leveling Books Sites: 204.98.1.2/isu/langarts.bklst.html-guide, and www.leveledbooks.com.

4. Lucy Calkins, *The Art of Teaching Reading* (New York: Longman, 2001), p. 119.

5. Linda Darling-Hammond, et al. "The Role of Standards and Assessments: A Dialogue." In: *Changing the Practice of Teacher Education: Standards and Assessment as a Lever for Change,* Mary E. Diez, ed. (Washington, DC: AACTE Publications, 1998), p. 17.

Credits

Text Credits

Chapter 5

"Colors Crackle. Colors Roar" from *Confetti: Poems for Children* by Pat Mora. Permission arranged with LEE & LOW BOOKS Inc., 95 Madison Ave., New York, NY 10016.

"Morning Horses" by Basho from IN THE EYES OF THE CAT: Japanese Poetry for All Seasons, selected and illustrated by Demi, translated by Tze-si Huang. Copyright, © 1992 by Demi. Reprinted by permission of Henry Holt and Company, LLC.

"Pull Hitter" by R. Gerry Fabian. Reprinted with permission from R. Gerry Fabian, Raw Dog Press, Doylestown, PA.

Chapter 6

"Brer Tiger and the Big Wind" adapted by permission of Marie Brown Associates, Copyright © 1993 by the Estate of William J. Faulkner.

Chapter 10

"Chocolates" from BOY by Roald Dahl. Copyright © 1984. Reprinted by permission of Farrar, Straus and Giroux, LLC.

Chapter 11

From THE SHIMMERSHINE QUEENS by Camille Yarbrough, copyright © 1989 by Camille Yarbrough. Used by permission of G. P. Putnam's Sons, an imprint of Penguin Putnam Books for Young Readers, a division of Penguin Putnam Inc. All rights reserved.

Chapter 13

From OUTCAST OF REDWALL by Brian Jacques, copyright © 1995 by The Redwall Abbey Company, Ltd., text. Used by permission of Philomel Books, an imprint of Penguin Putnam Books for Young Readers, a division of Penguin Putnam Inc. All rights reserved.

Excerpt from THE LITTLE PRINCE by Antoine de Saint-Exupery, copyright © 1943 by Harcourt, Inc. and renewed 1971 by Consuelo de Saint-Exupery, English translation copyright © 2000 by Richard Howard, reprinted by permission of Harcourt, Inc.

Illustration Credits

Chapter 1

Cover illustration copyright © 1998 by Aliki Brandenberg from *Miranthe's Story Two: Spoken Memories,* text by Aliki. Used by permission of HarperCollins Publishers.

Cover illustration copyright © 2000 by Cornelius Van Wright and Ying-Hwa Hu from *Jingle Dancer* by Cynthia Leitich Smith. Used by permission of HarperCollins Publishers.

Illustrations copyright © 1996 by Denver Museum of Natural History from *Dia's Story Cloth* by Dia Cha, stitched by Chue and Nhia Thao Cha. Permission arranged with LEE & LOW BOOKS Inc., 95 Madison Ave., New York, NY 10016.

Chapter 2

Cover illustration copyright © 1968, 1986 by Donald Crews from *Ten Black Dots,* text by Donald Crews. Used by permission of HarperCollins Publishers.

Cover illustration copyright © 1997 by Javaka Steptoe from *In Daddy's Arms I Am Tall: African Americans Celebrating Fathers.* Permission arranged with LEE & LOW BOOKS Inc., 95 Madison Ave., New York, NY 10016.

Chapter 3

Chapter 4

Chapter 5

Chapter 6

Chapter 7

Tradition by Jewell Coburn. Reprinted with permission from Shen's Books.

Cover illustration copyright © 1990 by Michael Lacapa from *The Flute Player: An Apache Folktale,* text by Michael Lacapa. Courtesy of Northland Publishing/Rising Moon.

Cover illustration copyright © 1996 by Colectivo Callejero from *The Story of Colors* by Subcomandante Marcos. Reprinted with permission of Cinco Puntos Press.

Cover illustration copyright © 2000 by Kiva Publishing, Inc. from *Coyote Tales* retold by William Morgan and adapted in English by Hildegaard Thompson. Reprinted with permission from Kiva Publishing, Inc.

Jacket illustration copyright © 1999 by Jean and Mou-Sien Tseng from *White Tiger, Blue Serpent* by Grace Tseng. Used by permission of HarperCollins Publishers.

Cover illustration copyright © 1992 by Deborah Nourse Lattimore from *The Winged Cat: A Tale of Ancient Egypt,* text by Deborah Nourse Lattimore. Used by permission of HarperCollins Publishers.

Cover illustration copyright © 1995 by Kris Waldherr from *The Book of Goddesses,* text by Kris Waldherr. Reprinted with permission from Beyond Words Publishing.

THE MIDAS TOUCH Text copyright © 1999 Jan Mark; Illustrations Copyright © 1999 Juan Wijngaard. Reproduced by permission of the publisher Candlewick Press, Inc., Cambridge, MA, on behalf of Walker Books Ltd., London.

Chapter 8

Cover illustration copyright © 1990 by Robert Vavra from *I Love Nature More.* Used by permission of HarperCollins Publishers.

Cover illustration copyright © 1992 by Kristin Pratt from *A Walk in the Rainforest.* Reprinted with permission from Dawn Publications.

Talking Walls by Margy Burns Knight. Illustrated by Anne Sibley O'Brien. Tilbury House, Publishers, 1992.

Cover illustration copyright © 1999 by Sheila Hamanaka from *In Search of the Spirit: The Living National Treasures of Japan.* Used by permission of HarperCollins Publishers.

Cover illustration copyright © 1997 by Hongbin Zhang from *D Is for Doufu: An Alphabet Book of Chinese Culture* by Maywan Shen Krach. Reprinted with permission from Shen's Books.

Cover photograph courtesy of The Image Bank/Garry Gay from *Earthquakes* by Seymour Simon copyright © 1991. Used by permission of HarperCollins Publishers.

Chapter 9

Cover from *The Midwife's Apprentice* by Karen Cushman. Copyright © 1995 by Karen Cushman. Used by permission of HarperCollins Publishers.

Cover from *Red Scarf Girl: A Memoir of the Cultural Revolution* by Ji-li Jiang. Copyright © 1997 by Ji-li Jiang. Used by permission of HarperCollins Publishers.

Cover illustration from *The Endless Steppe* by Esther Hautzig. Copyright © 1968 by Esther Hautzig. Used by permission of HarperCollins Publishers.

Cover from *Dragon's Gate* by Laurence Yep. Copyright © 1993 by Laurence Yep. Used by permission of HarperCollins Publishers.

Cover illustration copyright © 1984 by Marc Simont from *In the Year of the Boar and Jackie Robinson* by Bette Bao Lord. Used by permission of HarperCollins Publishers.

Cover illustration copyright © 1986 by Eric Velasquez from *Journey to Jo'burg: A South African Story* by Beverly Naidoo. Used by permission of HarperCollins Publishers.

Chapter 10

Cover illustration copyright © 2000 by Elizabeth Ann Kelly from *John Muir: My Life with Nature* by Joseph Cornell. Reprinted with permission from Dawn Publications.

Reprinted with permission of the publisher, Children's Book Press, San Francisco, CA. Overall book project copyright © 1997 by Harriet Rohmer. Individual self-portraits copyright © 1997 by JoeSam, © 1997 by Nancy Hom, © 1997 by Maya Christina Gonzalez, © 1997 by George Littlechild.

Jacket art for *Just Like Me: Stories and Self-Portraits by Fourteen Artists* reprinted with permission of the publisher.

Cover illustration copyright © 1997 by Kathryn Hewitt from *Lives of the Athletes: Thrills, Spills (and What the Neighbors Thought)* by Kathleen Krull. Jacket used with permission of Harcourt, Inc. All Rights Reserved.

Cover photograph copyright © 1998 by Walter Chinn from *Savion: My Life in Tap* by Savion Glover and Bruce Weber. Copyright © 2000 by Bruce Weber and Savion Glover/Maniactin, Inc. Used by permission of HarperCollins Publishers.

Cover illustration copyright © 1996 by David Diaz from *Wilma Unlimited: How Wilma Rudolph Became the World's Fastest Woman* by Kathleen Krull. Jacket used with permission of Harcourt, Inc. All Rights Reserved.

Cover photograph courtesy of NASA from *Black Stars in Orbit: NASA's African American Astronauts* by Kephra Burns and William Miles, copyright © 1995. Jacket used with permission of Harcourt, Inc. All Rights Reserved.

Cover photographs copyright © 1999 by United States Forest Service, Los Angeles Country Fire Department, and Karen Wattenmaker from *Fire in Their Eyes: Wildfires and the People Who Fight Them* by Karen Magnuson Beil, copyright © 1999. Jacket used with permission of Harcourt, Inc. All Rights Reserved.

Chapter 11

Cover from *Dear Mr. Henshaw* by Beverly Cleary. Copyright © 1983 by Beverly Cleary. Used by permission of HarperCollins Publishers.

Cover from *The Pinballs* by Betsy Byars. Copyright © 1977 by Betsy Byars. Used by permission of HarperCollins Publishers.

Cover from *Walk Two Moons* by Sharon Creech. Copyright © 1994 by Sharon Creech. Used by permission of HarperCollins Publishers.

Chapter 12

Cover illustration copyright © 1982 by Bear Run Publishing, Inc. from *Alice's Adventures in Wonderland* by Lewis Carroll. Jacket used with permission of Harcourt, Inc. All Rights Reserved.

Cover from *The Little Prince* by Antoine de Saint-Exupéry. Copyright © 1943, 2000 by Harcourt, Inc. Jacket used with permission of Harcourt, Inc. All Rights Reserved.

Cover from *The Hero and the Crown* by Robin McKinley. Used by permission of HarperCollins Publishers.

Cover from *The Borrowers* by Mary Norton. Copyright © 1953 by Mary Norton. Jacket used with permission of Harcourt, Inc. All Rights Reserved.

Chapter 13

Cover illustration from *Children's Prayers for America: Young People of Many Faiths Share Their Hopes for Our Nation* edited by Karlynn Keyes Lee, copyright © 2001. Courtesy of Northland Publishing/Rising Moon.

Cover illustration copyright © 1995 by Junko Morimoto from *One Hand Clapping: Zen Stories for All Ages*. Reprinted with permission from Junko Morimoto.

Cover illustration copyright © 1996 by Juan Wijngaard from *Esther's Story* by Diane Wolkstein. Used by permission of HarperCollins Publishers.

Jacket art copyright © 1995 by Erwin Printup, Jr., from *Giving Thanks: A Native American Good Morning Message* by Chief Jake Swamp. Permission arranged with LEE & LOW BOOKS Inc., 95 Madison Ave., New York, NY 10016.

Cover illustration copyright © 1997 by Michael Chiago from *Sing Down the Rain* by Judi Moreillon. Reprinted with permission from Kiva Publications, Inc.

Cover illustration copyright © 1995 by Cornelius Van Wright and Ying-Hwa Hu from *Sam and the Lucky Money* by Karen Chinn. Permission arranged with LEE & LOW BOOKS Inc., 95 Madison Ave., New York, NY 10016.

Teaching Children's Literature

*A*rt as a civilizing influence, art as source of the self-understanding that refines our capacity for understanding the neighbors with whom we share this planet—this, I believe, is the case we must take to the American people. This is the message we must carry to our communities. This is the message we must see that Congress hears. And this is the message we need to promulgate at every college and university that prepares the teachers who will prepare the students of tomorrow for life within our shrunken world.

—MARY HATWOOD FUTRELL[1]

1.1 About the Encounters

Although drama, the visual arts, music, film, storytelling, and dance are disciplines with distinctive content knowledge and processes, they simultaneously offer inviting pedagogical possibilities to help literature come alive. The encounter sessions in this book are

- Narrative pantomime in Chapter 1
- A read-aloud in Chapter 2 (genre and history)
- The storytelling shawl in Chapter 3 (selection and evaluation)
- Visual art in Chapter 4 (picture books)
- Choral readings in Chapter 5 (poetry)
- Readers theater in Chapter 6 (drama)
- Story theater, also in Chapter 6
- Storytelling workshop in Chapter 7 (oral tradition)
- Music, movement, and tableaux, also in Chapter 7
- Discovering patterns in Chapter 8 (informational books)
- Literature circles in Chapter 9 (historical literature)
- Oral interpretation in Chapter 10 (biography)
- Role playing in Chapter 11 (contemporary realism)
- Metaphorical thinking in Chapter 12 (fantasy)
- Story dramatization in Chapter 13 (celebrations and commemorations)

Like ornaments on a tree, these encounters with literature can just as easily hang on another branch. For example, readers theater and literature circles (the art of conversation) are appropriate for all genres of literature, and story dramatizations are effective for any story with a strong plot, action, and interesting characters. Working with different media of art, and interpreting literature through movement and music, are possible in response to most genres. These encounter sessions are "hung" as models. Once you have experienced them, you can design your own, then lead similar endeavors in your work with K–6 children. All of the encounters are easy to facilitate.

In a children's literature course, the encounters immediately get everyone involved. Studies in higher education repeatedly affirm the benefits of experiential learning. Actively participating in the encounters energizes the college classroom, ensuring learning that lasts.[2] Another benefit is collaborative effort, in which it is important for preservice and inservice teachers to gain competence. Teaching has historically been called *the lonely profession*—between thirty to fifty percent leave annually.[3] Shared group experiences in the arts create a vital learning community that lasts well after the course is over. The class itself becomes a place to develop collegiality—each person developing skills and knowledge while contributing to each other's growing expertise.

About "note to leader": Typically the leader is the professor. However, professors who teach courses with large enrollments may assign student-leaders to lead smaller sections. Practicing teachers are also leaders, who can lead the encounters with elementary school children. Instructors, of course, use their discretion—the encounters can be used at any time during a session, and it may not be possible to use all the encounters—I don't. Instead, I select what seems to be appropriate for the group I have, following student interest when I can. I have placed the encounters at the beginning of each chapter because I often use them at the beginning of class, but not always.

For most of the encounters, all the materials you need are in this book. Other materials are listed and are easy to obtain, usually at libraries or through interlibrary loan.

1.2 *Encountering Literature*
through narrative pantomime

Materials Needed

> A copy of *Andy and the Lion* by James Daughtery or *Jonathan and His Mommy* by Irene Smalls–Hector

First, either read the story aloud to the class or at least summarize the plot, sharing the pictures. Then, have the whole class perform narrative pantomime simultaneously. As the leader expressively reads the story, partners nonverbally enact what is being read.

For *Andy and the Lion,* find a partner and find *one* chair or desk for the two of you. Make sure you can get around the chair and that you are not too close to other partners. Decide which one of you will pantomime Andy and which one of you will pantomime the lion.

Rehearse the following: In the story the lion does some roaring so, as a class, practice roaring *without making a sound.* Andy does some shouting; practice shouting without making a sound. In the part of the story when the lion licks Andy's face—you will not literally do that.

There are three parts to the story during which your chair will make several transformations: In the first part, your chair is the library, then it transforms into Andy's dining room table, then his bed. In the second part, the chair becomes a rock. In the third part, it becomes the stands at a circus. If you are the lion, you are not in part I, so take a step back and let the narrative pantomime begin.

After the pantomime, share with each other your responses to the story and to its enactment. What thoughts and feelings did you have as you pantomimed the story with your partner? What did you think of having the whole class involved simultaneously? What questions do you have about classroom management?

n o t e   t o   l e a d e r :   This activity is great fun and starts a first session in a nonthreatening and supportive tone. I stand on a chair to narrate and watch a room full of Andys and lions enact the story: running and running around the rock (a chair or desk), and dancing for joy when they meet up again in part III. Having participated together in narrative pantomime generates feelings of warmth and goodwill, and helps create the low-anxiety setting necessary for experiences in the arts. For a practical purpose in a college course, all the Andys and lions can then become buddies—the person to call if one is sick or must miss a class.

Expressively read the story, pausing when appropriate, and introduce parts I, II, and III as found in *Andy and the Lion.* I edit out the word "queer," replacing it with "strange," because the connotations of the word have changed since 1938. I also edit out some of the description—for example, the sun and the dog. I add in some action: "Andy reached way up to the top shelf for the most exciting book he could find."

If you use *Jonathan and His Mommy* by Irene Smalls–Hector, a warm-up is for the whole class to practice walking in space (desks pushed out of the way): slowly, quickly, backward, diagonally, and in curves. In *Andy and the Lion,* partners can run in place; however, *Jonathan and His Mommy* invites moving through space.

When using this with children, instruct them to walk without touching each other or the furniture. Praise those who keep equidistant from others; in some cases, children may need you to speak quietly to them about not bumping into others or the furniture. If the problem persists, you can ask them to sit out for a moment or two. Children are usually eager to rejoin the class.

After hearing the story read aloud, decide which partner will play Jonathan and which will play his mom. Then the leader expressively reads aloud the story, giving time for partners to pantomime the action.

When your group has gained some experience working with partners, you may want to try pantomiming with an ensemble—for example, Jonathan London and Lanny Pinola's retelling of *Fire Race: A Karuk Coyote Tale.* For more suggestions of literature suitable for narrative pantomime, see Ruth Beall Heinig's *Creative Drama for the Classroom Teacher,* 4th ed. (Englewood Cliffs, NJ: Prentice–Hall, 1993).

1.3 *A Passion for Reading*

When Heidi, the orphan girl in Johanna Spyri's 1880 novel called *Heidi,* learns to read at age eight, "People suddenly became alive and stepped out of the black letters and took part in wonderful stories."[4] Mari, an immigrant girl in Aliki's *Miranthe's Story One and Two* (Figure 1.1), has a similar experience: "Slowly, like clouds lifting, things became clearer. Sticks and chicken feet became letters. Sputters and coughs became words. And the words had meanings.[5] "Based on a true story, Pat Mora's *Tomás and the Library Lady* poignantly depicts the tender bond that develops between a migrant boy and a librarian. Because Tomás does not have a home address and therefore cannot obtain a library card to check out the books he loves, the librarian invites him to use her card. Another child in fiction, Andy (in James Daughtery's 1938 picture book *Andy and the Lion*) is fascinated by lions, and through reading and listening to storytelling, he satisfies his passion. The exhilaration of moments like these, when children no longer see reading as an arduous task but as an exciting way of participating in the unexpected and unknown, can transform learning and lives.

Mari, Tomás, Heidi, and Andy epitomize what educators want for all children: To catapult over and through incomprehensible line configurations to the engaging experi-

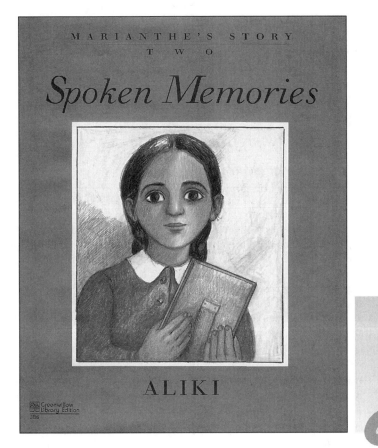

Figure 1.1 Based on her experience as an immigrant from Greece, Aliki, in *Miranthe's Story One: Painted Words* and *Miranthe's Story Two: Spoken Memories,* tells the story of a young girl who discovers the adventures of art and reading.

ence of stories that touch their hearts and minds. How can children share Heidi's and Mari's adventures in literature? How can we evoke in our students hunger and longing for books like Tomás's? How can we find ways for children who, like Andy, unself-consciously read and read and read some more?

Literature opens up worlds—social, emotional, spiritual, imaginative, intellectual, cultural, and aesthetic. Through reading we gain multiple perspectives to help make sense of our lives. Not only do books—all kinds—expand outward knowledge, but vicariously encountering people and places through stories shapes and deepens our inner lives as well. Whether reading silently, or listening to stories read aloud or retold, literature invites us to envision images for ourselves. In the process, we bring our own unique life story to the reading or telling event. This transaction nurtures our interior landscapes, helping us learn to enjoy our own companionship. Because we live in an age when the mass media constantly accords outward and often sensationalized entertainment, imaginative engagement with literary works and other art forms is vitally important.

At the beginning of the twenty-first century, the controversial question of how to teach reading continues to rage on national, state, and local levels. Federal and state legislators have begun to mandate how teachers should teach, sometimes passing legislation based on a very small and questionable research base.[6] Although no one will argue that children must learn skills, if they are taught in a fragmented, mechanistic fashion, children's lives are deadened to the joys of literature. There is simply no evidence—anywhere—that endlessly filling out worksheets improves learning. Quality children's literature must be the centerpiece of any effective reading program, and children who *want* to read is key (see Table 1.1).

Table 1.1 **Children's Literature at the Center of the Reading Program**

Researchers	*Research Findings*
Catherine E. Snow is a researcher and professor of education at Harvard University, and M. Susan Burns is a researcher and professor of education at George Mason University. With Peg Griffin, they were part of the National Research Council Committee.	They say, "As in every domain of learning, motivation is crucial. Although most children begin school with positive attitudes and expectations for success, by the end of the primary grades and increasingly thereafter, some children become disaffected." By having access to quality children's literature, "children begin to appreciate stories in which characters use language to deceive or pretend, to understand the point of fables and other texts that include metaphors and other figurative devices, and to grasp the difference between narrative, expository, poetic, and other variety of texts that books contain." From *Preventing Reading Difficulties in Young Children* (Washington, DC: National Academy Press, 1998, pp. 5, 49, and 231).
Louise Spear–Swerling is professor of special education at Southern Connecticut State University, and Robert Sternberg is professor of psychology at Yale University.	They say, "Children must indeed acquire accurate and automatic word-recognition skills in order to progress in reading acquisition . . . but their engagement with text and their interest in reading also push forward their decoding skills . . . children become 'hooked' not on phonics, but on stories, books, and ideas." From *Off Track: When Poor Readers Become "Learning Disabled"* (New York: Westview Press, 1996, p. 174).
Sean A. Walmsley is professor of reading at the State University of New York at Albany, and Richard L. Allington is professor of education at University of Florida.	They say, "Children need to value reading and writing as pleasurable and enriching experiences. The desire to read is as important as the act of reading. Reading to relax, to satisfy curiosity, and to gain new information are important benefits. A love of books, enthusiasm for reading and writing, and a positive attitude, if established at a very early age, greatly facilitate literacy development. In their encounters with reading and writing, children's emotions are engaged and their imaginations stirred and stretched. If children are to develop lifelong reading and writing habits, they must experience the excitement and personal fulfillment that print brings to them." From *No Quick Fix: Rethinking Literacy Programs in America's Elementary Schools* (New York: Teachers College Press and International Reading Association, 1995, p. 39).

You would not pursue the helping profession of teaching if you did not want to enhance the life chances of the children with whom you work. The power to express and understand language effectively is the primary prerequisite for participation in political, economic, and democratic life. As teachers, we bear the great responsibility—and privilege—of helping children achieve their personal and professional potential, and to become active participants in civic and community life. Children who are excited about reading will have more opportunities in life than those who aren't.

One way to stir this excitement in children is for the teachers who teach them to possess it themselves. To awaken a passion for literature is, first, the purpose of this book. A framework is set for *you to have your own encounter* with literature and the sister art forms. Like Tomás, Mari, Heidi, and Andy, it is hoped that you fall in love, or fall in love again, with literature by learning to see and hear more keenly and through becoming experientially engaged in the various symbols of art—literature, visual art, drama, dance, music, and film.

Experiences in the arts prepare teachers to provide students in the K–6 schools with similar inviting and participatory learning. Endorsed by the National Council for the Accreditation of Teacher Education (NCATE), a recent policy report concludes, "This study indicates that the most effective classroom practices involve conveying higher order thinking skills and engaging in hands-on learning activities."[7] Such undertakings are found in abundance here, helping to meet the NCATE standard, "Active engagement in learning—Candidates use their knowledge and understanding of individual and group motivation and behavior among students at the K–6 level to foster active engagement in learning, self motivation, and positive social interaction and to create supportive learning environments."[8] See Table 1.2 for recent studies that acknowledge the importance of active learning.

The encounter sessions are beginning experiences in the arts that can be strengthened by working with an arts specialist or by inviting someone in your community with expertise in the arts to work with your class. In the curriculum, the arts move horizontally, as a dynamic pedagogy, and vertically, as a discipline. Each of the arts has its own traditions, conventions, and processes, and is an inexhaustible source for further learning.

1.4 Diversity and an Arts Approach in Teacher Education

Probably no professional licensing programs are under greater scrutiny than those that prepare teachers. In the new millennium, what must teachers know and be able to do? What kind of preparation will best serve an increasingly diverse K–6 student body? The children of the twenty-first century need to attain sophisticated levels of literacy and understanding to survive and thrive in a technological and global environment, and they must make connections between an escalating number of disciplines. How can teachers address these challenges?

To answer these questions, we will look at research from several domains and we will especially listen to what educators of color tell us will help children of color succeed.

Table 1.2 **The Importance of Active Learning for Diverse Children**

Educators and Researchers	*On the Benefits of Active Learning*
Ofelia B. Miramontes, Adel Nadeau, and Nancy L. Commins, *Restructuring Schools for Linguistic Diversity: Linking Decision Making to Effective Programs* (New York: Teachers College Press, 1997)	"Knowledge is best acquired when learners actively participate in meaningful activities that are constructive in nature and appropriate to their level of development. . . . An orientation toward active, participatory, and meaning-centered instruction can be situated within a range of approaches." (pp. 37–38)
Geneva Gay, *Culturally Responsive Teaching* (New York: Teachers College Press, 2000)	Culturally responsive teaching "uses a wide variety of instructional strategies that are connected to different learning styles." (p. 29)
Donna M. Gollnick and Philip C. Chinn, *Multicultural Education in a Pluralistic Society,* 4th ed. (New York: Merrill, 1994)	Teacher effectiveness and multicultural education show that good teachers have a wide repertoire of approaches to teaching. (p. 299)
Karen Swisher and Donna Deyhle, "Adapting Instruction to Culture." In: *Teaching American Indian Students,* Jon Reyhner, ed. (Norman, OK: University of Oklahoma Press, 1992)	To help American Indian children succeed in school, teachers should offer "multisensory instruction." (p. 92)
Linda Darling–Hammond, *The Right to Learn: A Blueprint for Creating Schools That Work* (San Francisco: Jossey-Bass, 1997)	In schools that work, children have opportunities to develop deep understanding, which has "at least three features: it requires the use of higher-order cognitive functions, taking students beyond recall, recognition, and reproduction of information to evaluation, analysis, synthesis, and production of arguments, ideas and performances. It asks students to apply these skills and ideas in meaningful contexts, engaging them in activities they have real reason to want to undertake." (pp. 109, 331)

Even with long-overdue recruiting efforts, the face of this nation's teaching force for the next decade fits the following description: "The typical graduate of the American education school is female, is of Anglo descent, is about 21 years of age, speaks only English, travels less than 100 miles to attend college, was raised in a small town or a suburban or rural setting, and expects to teach in a school whose demographics are similar to her own."[9] The number of teachers of color has steadily declined in recent decades. This crisis is occurring as the number of students of color is growing.[10] About one in three students is a child of color, and that percentage is expected to continue to rise. Equity and social justice require that teachers seek diverse literature, both children's and professional, and the kinds of strategies that will help all children learn.

White teachers *can* teach children of color. Geneva Gay, professor of curriculum and instruction at the University of Washington, reminds us that to assume that teachers of

European descent cannot successfully teach children of different ethnic backgrounds disregards research to the contrary and "that knowledge and use of the cultural heritages, experiences, and perspectives of ethnic groups in teaching are far more important to improving student achievement than shared group membership."[11] One way to support successful teachers is to identify and learn from those who are effectively working with diverse schools and children.

Throughout this book you will meet Elaine Aoki, Sonia Nieto, Janice E. Hale, Johnny Saldaña, Mary Hatwood Futrell, and other educators of color. A common thread found in this diverse group is support for artistic teaching practices and active, experiential learning. Futrell, the Dean of the Graduate School of Education at the George Washington University, writes,

> If future teachers are to have what it takes to prepare students for this new world, I know of nothing that can help them more than intensive study in the arts. What I am suggesting is that the future of global studies and of artistic intelligences may depend decisively on restructuring teacher preparation programs. . . . I have no doubt that teacher education has nothing to lose and everything to gain if it grants a privileged position to those disciplines whose subject is the human spirit and whose goal is the ennoblement of that spirit.[12]

Bringing about this vision will require a retreat from the chalk-and-talk method that dominates the pedagogy found in many schools. This method comes from a flawed philosophy of education that assumes teachers, textbooks, and workbooks transmit knowledge to students, who sit passively like blank slates or empty buckets to receive it. Not surprisingly, teachers teach the way they were taught, and it is more likely than not that the teachers who currently teach elementary school children were themselves brought up on this static, teacher-as-disseminator-of-information model. If schools are to improve, today's teachers must *experience for themselves* engaging, interactive, and dynamic ways of learning. Gay writes, "Since the achievement of many students of color is dependent on their ethnic and cultural differences being embraced in the classroom, teachers cannot be allowed or enticed to think that culturally responsive teaching is anything other than an obligatory and necessary part of the professional preparation and performance."[13] Gay's challenge to preservice and inservice teachers is a serious one. The process, however, of meeting her challenge can be pleasurable (the encounter sessions exemplify some of what Gay describes), and can help you develop your capacities and discover abilities you didn't know you had.

Using the children's literature bibliographies in Appendix C may help fill gaps in learning. Carl Grant, a multicultural education scholar, writes that teachers need "course work that introduces them to the histories and the literature of many cultures and that provides them with a range of pedagogical knowledge and skills to teach diverse learners effectively."[14] These goals are addressed simultaneously in this book.

So that all children can experience success, part of the role of the teacher is to create the circumstances in which a range of strengths and abilities can emerge. Fostering a variety of artistic expressions can help accomplish this (see Figure 1.2). Although

Figure 1.2 In *Jingle Dancer* by Cynthia Leitich Smith (Muscogee) and illustrated by Cornelius Van Wright and Ying-Hwa Hu, Jenna celebrates the art of jingle dancing from her Muscogee and Ojibway heritage.

sometimes the best response to a good book or story is silence, children can be encouraged to write, draw, act, tell, sing, dance, and play in response to literature.

1.5 An Arts Approach in a Technological Society

Facilitating active modes of learning becomes more challenging the further we move into the electronic age. Although there are many benefits to technology for all kinds of groups, especially those with special needs, children are surrounded by electronic media—satellite television, computers, hand-held video games, cinema, videotapes, and the Internet—to an extent far beyond what any of us thought possible during the 1950s, 1960s, and 1970s. One risk of a highly technocratic society is that we become consumers who passively receive art forms and entertainment from others, instead of being active agents who create, compose, sing, dance, tell, improvise, and enact for ourselves. This dependence on the producers of mass media and computer programmers to create imagined worlds for us has implications for our development as individuals confident in our inventive and expressive powers. Technology may take away time for shared communal, live, and unmediated engagement with art forms.

How can we motivate children to fashion their thoughts and feelings through the varying symbols of art? How can we motivate ourselves into more active, responsive, creative, and engaged modes of expression? How can we create community through shared art forms and shape our culture with our own voices? How can we use technology as an expressive art, and how can technology support response to literature in creative ways? The process of answering these questions will help us see that we can create, shape, and change our culture.

1.6 Responding to Literature: An Arts Approach to Achieve Engaged Reading

With this book as a guide, the time you spend in your college classroom will not be primarily lecture and note taking (although there may be some). Instead, you will be involved with each other in the crafting and producing of art forms in response to literature. Outside of class time, try new responses to the literature you are reading. Here are some suggestions from which to choose:

- Write a letter to an author or a fictional character.
- Imagine you are a particular character from a story and write a diary entry from her point of view.
- Write and/or illustrate your own children's book (which can be simply bound with two holes, a stick, and a rubber band).
- Compose a poem in response to a piece of literature.
- Experiment with computer graphics.
- Explore the visual arts by creating a map of a real or imaginary land.
- Design a travel brochure for a literary fantasy world.
- Illustrate a chapter book or create an illustration the artist left out of a picture book.
- Create puppets for a story (marionettes, paper bag, stick, or sock).
- Create a mask or work with plasticene.
- Invent background music for a favorite piece of literature.

Keep a response journal for what you are reading. Possible entries are

- What you like and/or dislike
- What the story reminds you of
- The thoughts and feelings you have as you read
- A time when you were in a similar situation

- What the literature makes you wonder about
- What surprises you while you are reading
- Something in the book you have never thought about
- Characters in the story who are like people you have known
- The things you are confused by
- The questions you have after reading
- The things you would do differently if you were one of the characters
- What would happen if you could step into one of the illustrations in a picture book
- The changes you would make if you were the author or the changes you would make if you were the illustrator

These prompts are based on reader response theory—a theory that sees reading as a *transaction* between the reader and the text. Readers imagine what the author left out—the gaps in the text. Louise Rosenblatt, in 1935, was one of the first to conceptualize reading in this way. When reading, the reader adopts a stance that falls along the continuum of efferent and aesthetic reading. Rosenblatt defines efferent reading as when we focus on the information that we will carry away with us—the kind of reading we do when using a technical manual to put together a model rocket. In contrast, in aesthetic reading,

> [T]he reader seeks a story, a poem, a play, [then] attention will shift inward, will center on what is being created *during* the actual reading. A much broader range of elements will be allowed to rise into consciousness, not simply the abstract concepts that the words point to, but also what those objects or referents stir up of personal feelings, ideas, and attitudes. The very sound and rhythm of words will be attended to. Out of these ideas and feelings, a new experience, the story or poem, is shaped and lived through.[15]

It is this quality of living through that characterizes encountering the arts. Everyone experiences reading, viewing, acting, and listening differently, bringing his or her own complex background of memories and associations to the artistic event. Like a prism, great art possesses complexity and can be interpreted in more than one way. It can be revisited over time and can be understood at different levels.

However, transactional responses to literature do not happen automatically. Not all children are flung into a world beyond what they know through reading. To become lost in reading, children have to be able to *imagine*. The arts cultivate the imagination, providing segues into engaged, enjoyable reading. In his case study, Jeffrey Wilhelm writes,

> I became convinced that for most of my student readers, engagement with literature through the aesthetic stance did not occur naturally or spontaneously. Rosenblatt, like many literary theorists, seems to assume an Ideal situation versus the Real situation of the classroom. Despite free reading and reading workshops, journals, literary letter exchanges, and a variety of response activities, many of my students did not seem to improve as readers, and many more continued to resist reading.[16]

By experimenting with arts approaches, Wilhelm observed students who previously found reading boring become enthusiastic about reading. He describes using the arts as "a way of bringing the invisible secrets of engaged readers out into the open, where they could be observed and shared and tried on by other readers. Drama and art naturally engender involvement and a sense of ownership, which I wished to develop in my less engaged readers."[17] If you did not experience this approach to reading yourself in your own school days, experiment with it now. Do what we sometimes ask children to do; you may discover you are capable of more than you thought.

Existentialist philosopher and teacher educator Maxine Greene notes that in a highly technocratic society it is "extremely difficult to feel ourselves active participants." She exhorts teacher preparation programs to evoke in teachers "wide-awakeness," which can be attained by an enlargement of landscapes through aesthetic and artistic experiences. Ultimately, through engagement in the arts as active readers, viewers, and producers, teachers can discover their expressive powers and their ability to transcend the habitual through viewing or reading works of art. Greene says,

> To look at Cezanne paintings, to read Tolkien or Melville, to listen to Mozart or Copeland or jazz, to attend to *Romeo and Juliet* or *Colored Girls* or *The Cherry Orchard,* to watch *Swan Lake* or an Alvin Ailey ballet, to memorize a poem or to write a poem, to weave a rug, to shape a pot, or to watch a sculptor shape some clay: all these are undertakings that demand our being there in person, that cannot—on some level—but open up new possibilities in our experiences, even as they confront us with ourselves.[18]

1.7 Research in the Arts

The past several decades have been tremendously exciting in the fields of cognitive psychology, human development, special education, second language learning, brain-based learning, and reading. A common area of research from these domains is the arts and their contributions to human learning.

Cognitive Psychology Begun in 1967 by Nelson Goodman, Harvard University's Project Zero has generated a number of studies in the arts. Called Project Zero because Goodman saw that there was virtually zero research in the arts, its initiatives have included Arts PROPEL, an integrated approach to teaching and assessment that focuses on developing the "artist within."[19] Howard Gardner's publication of *Frames of Mind* in 1983 validated spheres of intelligence in the arts: musical–rhythmic, bodily–kinesthetic, interpersonal–social, intrapersonal–introspective, and visual–spatial, in addition to those already recognized in schools—verbal–linguistic and logical–mathematical. The ways of human knowing and learning are many and varied, and to appeal to multiple intelligences, teachers must know how to recognize and tap into the strengths children bring with them to school.

Human Development Mihaly Csikszentmihalyi, a professor at the University of Chicago, has contributed much to our understanding of flow experiences; that is, when we step out of our mundane existence into a playfulness where our attention is focused for sustained periods. We experience flow when we participate in activities for the sheer joy of them, losing our sense of time, and when the doing of them are their own reward. This kind of experience is especially available in the arts and is the antithesis of the passivity of television viewing. Engaging in artistic production and/or aesthetic appreciation requires complex, active, and constructive involvement; we develop competence through multiple experiences.

Special Education In today's schools, a child of European descent is far more likely to be identified as gifted than children outside the dominant culture: African American, Latino, and American Indian children are left out of gifted programs at appalling rates.[20] African American educators assert that opportunities in the arts could be a means of identifying and programming for gifted children of color.[21] Furthermore, more opportunities in the arts can be a way of keeping children *out* of other areas of special education. Currently, African American children are twice as likely as their counterparts to be labeled seriously emotionally disturbed, often *before the third grade.* Arts approaches, theater in particular, have the potential of decreasing the number of children negatively labeled.[22]

Second Language Learning Currently, about 2.1 million children of 47.2 million in the nation's schools are English Language Learners (ELLs).[23] The arts have great potential in second language acquisition. A preliminary report on Project All in Los Angeles, which uses the performing and visual arts with children with limited English proficiency, shows measurable gains in reading and math.[24] ELLs are considered again in later chapters. See Table 1.3 for brief summaries of other research.

Brain-Based Learning Renate Nummela Caine and Geoffrey Caine continue to publish their findings in this area, especially the social and emotional connections to learning.[25] All children need to belong. Better they tap into the arts community than to let their belonging needs lead them into gangs and violence. Caine and Caine recommend, "Participating in debates, telling stories, role-playing historical figures, reenacting historical events, and generating 'expert panel' solutions to social and medical or other scientific problems are only a few of the intellectually challenging behaviors that involve our need for social belonging and interaction."[26]

Reading A four-year study of more than 600 students in a Dallas, Texas, elementary school demonstrated conclusively that integrating arts experiences into the curriculum results in dramatically higher language arts achievement. And, because reading is fundamental to all disciplines, the study has positive implications for math, science, and social studies as well.[27] Specialists in the education of American Indians regard abilities in the arts as part of developing critical literacy—analytical and creative thinking.[28] Other studies on reading and the arts are described throughout this book.

Comprehensive Arts Research Experimentation in arts-based learning is occurring internationally and includes HOT Schools (higher order thinking through the arts) that integrate the arts into the curricula.[29] For example, if the social studies unit is on Egypt, in language arts the students read and participate in Egyptian literature, in art they create

Table 1.3 The Arts and Academic Achievement: What Research Says

Researchers	Population	Impact
Kent Seidel, a professor and researcher at the University of Cincinatti, (www.aaae.org/research.html)	All children	After reviewing hundreds of studies published since 1983, Seidel concluded, "Participation with the arts helps students develop methods and habits of mind that help them succeed in many areas. . . . [W]hen connected with other subjects, they can make learning easier and more meaningful." (Association for the Advancement of Arts website)
Edward B. Fiske, *Champions of Change: The Impacts of Arts on Learning* (Washington, DC: The Arts Education Partnership and the President's Committee on the Arts and Humanities, 1999)	All children	The study concluded, "[I]nvolvement with the arts is the most powerful factor to success in and out of school." (p. iv)
Geneva Gay, *Culturally Responsive Teaching: Theory, Research and Practice* (New York: Teachers College, 2000)	Children of color	In her review of successful programs, many include the arts, particularly "readers theater, choral reading and reading aloud, personal response to literature, and dramatic interpretation." (p. 155)
Robert Colwell, "The Arts," In *Handbook of Research on Improving Student Achievement,* Gordon Cawelti, ed. (Arlington, VA: Educational Research Service, 1995)	Children with special needs	"Among special education students, production experience in the arts (such as singing, playing, drawing and painting, acting, and dancing) enhances motivation and self concept and improves attitude toward school." (p. 38)
Virginia G. Allen, "Teaching Bilingual and ESL Children," In *Handbook of Research on Teaching the English Language Arts,* James Flood, Julie M. Jensen, Diane Lapp, and James R. Squire, eds. (New York: Macmillan, 1991)	English Language Learners	The arts can help create the low-anxiety setting second language learners need; high anxiety sets up a filter that negatively affects children's abilities to learn. (p. 357)
Elizabeth Murfee, *Eloquent Evidence: Arts at the Core of Learning* (Washington, DC: National Assembly of State Arts Agencies, 1995)	All children	The academic, interpersonal, and creative impact of the arts is described. For example, those who participate in the arts for four or more years score significantly higher on the SATs.
Ellin Oliver Keene and Susan Zimmerman, *Mosaic of Thought: Teaching Comprehension in a Reader's Workshop* (Portsmouth, NH: Heinemann, 1997)	All children	Multiple forms of response—a "mosaic of thought"—enhances reading comprehension. (pp. 137–138)

products in the style of Egyptian art, and so on. This way of working offers the possibility of greater meaning because students are not asked to take tests on unrelated facts. Simply put, the arts provide more hooks for engaged learning.

The arts, it seems, simultaneously address both arts and academic outcomes. Success builds upon success—for both elementary school children and their teachers. Positive, achieving classes create a feedback loop—motivating their teachers to keep growing and learning. Each generation of adults must answer anew for the rising generation the perennial philosophical question: What's worth knowing? In today's climate, when teachers are expected to cover vast amounts of material, it is helpful to know *not* to eliminate the arts, which can be two-for-the-price-of-one.

However, Stanford University teacher educator Elliott Eisner cautions against looking too much to the arts to achieve nonarts outcomes and, instead of justifying their use in the curriculum for reasons extrinsic to the arts, asks us to consider what is intrinsic to the arts. They

- Help us realize that not all problems have single, correct answers, encouraging divergent (in contrast with convergent) thinking
- Teach us that form and content are integrally related, and can give us an aesthetic awareness in both art and life
- Help us see that the serendipitous has as much to offer as fixed objectives
- Are not only expressive, but lead us to the discovery of possibilities
- Help us realize our capacities to feel, to imagine, and to take risks[30]

The arts, Eisner argues, should not be part of the curriculum because of what they do for math and reading anymore than the athletics department should have to justify its existence because of what basketball does for academic subjects.

In this age of information, there is a danger that fragmentation and isolated facts overwhelm and alienate youth. The late Ernest Boyer, former President of the Carnegie Foundation for the Advancement of Teaching, said, "I am convinced that students at all levels need to see connections. And I believe that finding patterns across separate disciplines can be accomplished through the arts. . . . I'm suggesting that the arts give us a language that cuts across disciplines, help[ing] us to see connections and bring[ing] a more coherent meaning to our world."[31]

Other arts outcomes include persistence, flexibility, and motivation, helping children *want* to attain background knowledge that otherwise is often force-fed through tests and lectures. The arts help us gain insight and understanding into cultures and ethnicities not our own, creating unity while celebrating diversity (see Figure 1.3). And, as Greene says, the arts help us imagine things otherwise; that is, things as they might be: "[I]magination is what, above all, makes empathy possible."[32]

Business leaders look to what the arts can provide for future employees: the ability to brainstorm and arrive at creative ideas, moving easily between different symbol systems and disciplines; the ability to collaborate and communicate well with others; and the ability to tolerate ambiguity. The arts are a significant force in the health of the economy, contributing close to $37 billion annually.[33]

Figure 1.3 The Hmong people share the artistic heritage of embroidered story cloths, as seen in *Dia's Story Cloth: The Hmong People's Journey of Freedom* by Dia Cha, and stitched by Chue and Nhia Thao Cha.

Today, teachers face a challenge of balance. Although advancements in technology continue to improve the lives of many students, teachers, administrators, and members of boards of education frequently must choose between funding for technology or funding for the arts and, too often, technology is chosen and the arts are phased out.[34] The arts enhance cognitive, creative, and emotional development by offering enjoyment, providing glimpses into lives and experiences not our own, and giving shape and form to life's often incomprehensible experiences.

1.8 Theory into Practice: Approaching Performance

What happens when a course in children's literature takes an arts approach? Because there are multiple points of entry, not everyone has the same experience. Each class is unique, and what happens during a semester depends on the interests, personalities, and temperaments of the individuals who are a part of the class. Products do not have to look alike: Some students experiment more with the visual arts, others with music, others with drama and storytelling. There is no one right way to grow and develop in what you know and are able to do.

Although there may be a core of books we all read, each literature journey is different. If there is one thing we know about reading, it is that children must have some choice in what they read, and how they respond to what they read. So, too, with adult learners.

What have my students done with this approach? To answer this question in depth would require a second book. Some of my students have made presentations at regional conferences about their successes in the K–6 schools when they have used the encounters, and some of my students' stories are woven into this book.[35]

Performance Approach The creation of art occurs within the context of culture. Knowledge of what has gone before contributes to the ability to craft artistic products. Csikszentmihalyi, in his path-breaking study, affirms that creative persons must immerse themselves in their cultural heritages.[36] Gardner also supports the view that domain knowledge, along with its conventions, precedes invention: "Creativity has a lot more to do with getting to know the subject in great detail, and being willing to take that knowledge and use it in new kinds of ways. . . ."[37] Throughout this book I try to balance historical traditions and arts conventions with the process of art.

Controversy exists in most disciplines regarding whether to emphasize process or content. Too much emphasis on content and form causes boredom and lack of connection to the subject matter. Too much emphasis on process deprives students of background knowledge they need. Although Keith Swanwick is describing music, include literature and the other fine arts when reflecting on this passage:

> Instruction without encounter, analysis without intuition, artistic craft without aesthetic pleasure; these are recipes for educational disaster. Meaningless action is worse than no activity at all and leads to confusion and apathy, whereas meaning generates its own models and motivation and in so doing frees the student from the teacher. Thus we take charge of our own learning; there is no other way. . . . The ultimate educational ambition remains the same—that music comes increasingly to be seen by students as a significant symbolic form. This is the ultimate heart of musical knowing, opening up the possibility of important changes of disposition and attitude that may significantly affect our lives, like the day we fell in love with someone. . . . This is not the same as being told about the delights of love . . . but rather experiencing it ourselves; that expressive and structural elements relate to the way we feel and think and lead us on into new realms of understanding.[38]

The art of teaching, whether in university or elementary classrooms, means continually traversing the continuum of encounter and instruction, and embracing the creative and dynamic tension between the two.

When exploring the performative arts suggested in this book—pantomime, choral reading, readers theater, storytelling, creative movement, oral interpretation, and story dramatization—your instrument is yourself. Uppermost in my mind when I lead my students in the performative arts is the inspiring work of Kristin Linklater, Nancy King, and Sanford Meisner.

Developing the ability to use your body and voice effectively is beneficial to artistic performances and to carrying out the day-in, day-out realities of teaching: Teachers spend much of their lives orally communicating with others (students, parents, administrators, and members of boards of education). Linklater's work in freeing the natural voice has great significance not only for artists but also for teachers. She writes, "The objective is a voice in direct contact with emotional impulse, shaped by the intellect but not inhibited by it. . . . The natural voice is transparent—revealing, not describing, inner impulses of emotion and thought, directly and spontaneously. The person is heard, not the person's voice. To free the voice is to free the person, and each person is indivisibly mind and body."[39] Physical relaxation and awareness are essential to this process, and are explored especially in the storytelling workshop in Chapter 7.1.

In all performances, bring yourself and the connections you make with literature. To use a musical analogy: Until singers and/or instrumentalists bring themselves and their unique interpretations to a musical work, the notes arranged by the composer are lifeless black marks on a page. So, too, with literature: Until you and your class bring yourselves and your bodies, minds, and voices to *interpret* a literary work, the words are lifeless symbols on a page. This is the beauty of the performative arts; although ephemeral and quickly gone, they are powerfully alive, vital, communal, and uniquely in the present moment. Your primary focus in performance is, as the great acting teacher Sanford Meisner said, to live "truthfully under imaginary circumstances."[40] Do not give a performance—let the performance give you. Although conventions and technique are important in the development of artistic form, if they become the sole focus, and the performer's transaction with the literary work is underemphasized, the result may be more harmful than beneficial.

Seymour Sarason, Louis Rubin, and others have written about the potential the arts have in teacher education.[41] The analogy of the theater, especially, can help teachers enliven learning in their classrooms. Sound and silence, movement and stillness, light and dark are dramatic elements that can inform much teaching practice.

Although the encounters are meant for you to experience, they are also intended for your eventual use in elementary schools with diverse children. What follows may not apply to all children of color, but is nevertheless helpful in understanding different cultural orientations.

Johnny Saldaña observes that Latino children may not wish to stand out, and many Asian children are taught not to draw attention to themselves. Although American Indian children enjoy participating in the arts, teachers should know that controlling emotional expression is sometimes, in their cultures, a sign of maturity.[42] Simultaneous, ensemble, or parallel playing, like the narrative pantomime at the beginning of this chapter, creates low-anxiety opportunities.

African American children, says Janice Hale, bring high degrees of sensitivity and sophistication toward nonverbal communication. To dignify and to enhance the strengths of African American children, teachers need to open up the curriculum and instructional time to include kinesthetic experiences. Doing so, Hale believes, will help many African American children feel more welcomed and comfortable in schools, thus facilitating their success. Not to do so often means that children find teachers oppressive, and the downward institutional cycle begins. The mismatch between black children's culture and life in many classrooms causes children to "psychologically shut down."[43] Experiential learning in the arts provides alternatives.

1.9 Conclusion

Educators, parents, and employers increasingly recognize the value of the arts in education. National and state standards for the visual and performing arts are now expected of elementary teachers: "Candidates know, understand, and use—as appropriate to their own understanding and skills—the content, functions, and achievements of dance, music, theater, and the several visual arts as primary media for communication, inquiry, and insight among elementary students."[44] When teacher preparation programs emphasize the arts, candidates can tap into their creative potentialities and heighten their aesthetic sensibilities. Having experienced both creating and responding to art, they can then bring artistry into the teaching profession. African American educator Janice E. Hale writes,

> Artistic teachers identify ways to unlock the potential of every child, provide more human contact in the classroom, enhance the spirituality of the classroom, and incorporate arts in all aspects of instruction. . . . Children should be given multidisciplinary exposure to the curriculum so that they are able to develop their interests and talents in the process of mastering information and skills.[45]

Suggested Activities

1. After reading *Andy and the Lion* or *Tomás and the Library Lady* or *Miranthe's Story One: Painted Words,* get together in groups to share books or orally told stories that transported you to new worlds when you were children.

   note to leader: I start each semester off this way, grouping the books by genre as my students report their favorites. I assign each genre a number, according to the session. Because I teach thirty-six hours over twelve sessions, my groupings look like this:

   > 2nd week: Picture books
   > 3rd week: Poetry
   > 4th week: Drama and folklore—fables and folktales
   > 5th week: Folklore—fairy tales (this is the session during which I conduct the storytelling workshop, so there is more process than content)
   > 6th week: Folklore—myth, legends, tall tales, and epics
   > 7th week: Informational literature
   > 8th week: Historical literature with a focus on historical fiction

9th week: Biography and autobiography with a focus on career and vocation

10th week: Contemporary realism

11th week: Fantasy

12th week: Celebrations and commemorations

Before revealing the genre—or topic—I ask students to identify commonalities; they usually can identify some of the genres. This exercise helps elicit what they already know about children's literature and helps them see they already have some expertise. Furthermore, they get to know each other and I begin to get to know them.

To begin thinking about some of the issues in children's literature, I also ask students to look at their favorite books to see how many people of color appear in them— *Corduroy* by Don Freeman is usually the only one. Are there authors of color? What is the ratio of male and female protagonists? Which genres are the most popular?

2. In addition to the responses to literature suggested in Section 1.6, consider other written responses: letter writing, diary entries, journalistic writing (editorials, obituaries, sports, and so on), websites, and advertising.

for further reading and viewing

Abbott, Rebecca. 1999. *Designing Minds: The Arts in Education.* Documentary video. Hartford, CT: Connecticut Public Television.

Arnheim, Rudolf. 1989. *Thoughts on Art Education.* Occasional paper 2. Santa Monica, CA: The Getty Center for Education in the Arts.

Buchbinder, Jane. 1999. "The Arts Step Out from the Wings." *Harvard Education Letter,* 15.6., 1–7.

Caine, Renate Nummela, and Geoffrey Caine. 1997. *Education on the Edge of Possibility.* Alexandria, VA: Association for Supervision and Curriculum Development.

Calogero, Joanna. 2002. "Integrating Music and Children's Literature." *Music Educators Journal,* March: 23–30.

Cawelti, Gordon, ed. 1995. *Handbook of Research on Improving Student Achievement.* Arlington, VA: Educational Research Service.

The Center for Arts in the Basic Curriculum, Inc. 1995. *The Balanced Mind: An Educational and Societal Imperative.* Hingham, MA: CABC.

Csikszentmihalyi, Mihaly. 1990. *Flow: The Psychology of Optimal Experience.* New York: HarperCollins.

Dewey, John. 1934. *Art as Experience.* New York: Putnam's.

Dobbs, Stephen Mark. 1992. *The DBAE Handbook: An Overview of Discipline-Based Art Education.* Los Angeles, CA: The Getty Center for Education in the Arts.

Gardner, Howard. 1991. *The Unschooled Mind: How Children Think and How Teachers Should Teach.* New York: Basic Books.

———. 1990. *Art Education and Human Development.* Occasional paper 3. Los Angeles: The Getty Center for Education in the Arts.

———. 1983. *Frames of Mind.* New York: Basic Books.

———. 1982. *Art, Mind, and Brain: A Cognitive Approach to Creativity.* New York: Basic Books.

Greene, Maxine. 2001. *Variations on a Blue Guitar: The Lincoln Center Institute Lectures on Aesthetic Education.* New York: Teachers College Press.

———. 1995. *Releasing the Imagination: Essays on Education, the Arts, and Social Change.* San Francisco: Jossey-Bass.

———. 1978. *Landscapes of Learning.* New York: Teachers College Press.

Hotvedt, Rebecca. 2001. "In the Arts Spotlight." *Educational Leadership,* October: 70–73.

Iser, Wolfgang. 1978. *The Act of Reading: A Theory of Aesthetic Response.* Baltimore: The Johns Hopkins University Press.

Rosenblatt, Louise. 1983 [1935]. *Literature as Exploration.* 4th ed. New York: The Modern Language Association.

———. 1978. *The Transactional Theory of the Literary Work.* Carbondale: Southern Illinois University Press.

Sloan, Douglas. 1983. *Insight-Imagination: The Emancipation of Thought and the Modern World.* Westport, CT: Greenwood.

Smith, Ralph A., and Alan Simpson. 1991. *Aesthetics and Arts Education.* Chicago: University of Illinois Press.

Sternberg, Robert, ed. 1988. *The Nature of Creativity: Contemporary Psychological Perspectives.* New York: Cambridge University Press.

Welch, Nancy, and Andrea Greene. 1995. *Schools, Communities, and the Arts: A Research Compendium.* Tempe, AZ: Morrison Institute for Public Policy, Arizona State University. Available online at http://artsedge.kennedy-center.org/db/kc/aae-npub.html

websites on the arts

Arts Education Partnership, One Massachusetts Ave., NW, Washington, DC 20001-1431; 202-326-8693:

www.aep-arts.org

Arts PROPEL:

www.pz.harvard.edu/research/PROPEL.htm

ARTSEDGE, The John F. Kennedy Center for the Performing Arts, Washington, DC 20566; 202-416-8000:

www.artsedge.kennedy-center.org/artsedge.html

Getty Education Institute for the Arts, 1200 Getty Center Dr., Los Angeles, CA 90049; 310-440-7300:

www.artsednet.getty.edu

Kennedy Center Alliance for Arts Education Network (KCAAEN):

kennedy-center.org/education/kcaaen/

Lincoln Center Institute:

www.lincolncenter.org/

National Arts Education Association, 1916 Association Dr., Reston, VA 20191-1590; 703-860-8000:

www.naea-reston.org

National Endowment for the Arts:

www.arts.endow.gov

The President's Committee on the Arts and Humanities, 1100 Pennsylvania Ave., NW, Suite 526, Washington, DC 20506; 202-682-5409:

www.pcah.gov

SUAVE, California State University, San Marcos, 333 S. Twin Oaks Valley Rd., San Marcos, CA 92096-4000:

www.csusm.edu/SUAVE

notes

1. Mary Hatwood Futrell, "The Challenge of Implementation." In: *Artistic Intelligences: Implications for Education,* William Moody, ed. (New York: Teachers College Press, 1990), p. 48.

2. See Marcia Mentkowski et al., *Learning That Lasts: Integrating Learning, Development, and Performance in College and Beyond* (San Francisco: Jossey-Bass, 2000), p. 224; Susan Sellman Obler, Julie Stark, and Linda Umdenstock, "Classroom Assessment." In: *Making a Difference: Outcomes of a Decade of Assessment in Higher Education,* Trudy W. Banta et al., eds. (San Francisco: Jossey-Bass, 1993), p. 216; and Michael Fullan, *Change Forces: Probing the Depths of Educational Reform* (London: Falmer, 1993), pp. 28–29.

3. Harry K. Wong and Rosemary T. Wong, *The First Days of School: How to Be an Effective Teacher* (Mountain View, CA: Harry K. Wong Publications, 1998), p. v.

4. Johanna Spyri, *Heidi* (Racine, WI: Whitman, 1945 [1880]), p. 123.

5. Aliki, *Miranthe's Story One: Painted Words* (New York: Greenwillow, 1998), n.p.

6. See Gerald Coles, *Misreading Reading: The Bad Science That Hurts Children* (Portsmouth, NH: Heinemann, 2000) and Denny Taylor, *Beginning to Read and the Spin Doctors of Science: The Political Campaign to Change America's Mind about How Children Learn to Read* (Urbana, IL: National Council of Teachers of English, 1998).

7. Harold Wenglinsky, *How Teaching Matters: Bringing the Classroom Back Into Discussions of Teacher Quality* (Princeton, NJ: Milken Family Foundation and Educational Testing Service, 2000), p. 32.

8. National Council for Accreditation of Teacher Education, *Program Standards for Elementary Teacher Preparation*, 3d.

9. Nancy L. Zimpher, "Right-Sizing Teacher Education: The Policy Imperative." In: *Teachers for the New Millennium: Aligning Teacher Development, National Goals, and High Standards for All Students*, Leonard Kaplan and Roy A. Edelfelt, eds. (Thousand Oaks, CA: Corwin Press, 1996), p. 51.

10. June A. Gordon, *The Color of Teaching* (London: Routledge, 2000).

11. Geneva Gay, *Culturally Responsive Teaching: Theory, Research and Practice* (New York: Teachers College, 2000), p. 205.

12. Futrell, "The Challenge of Implementation," p. 49.

13. Gay, *Culturally Responsive Teaching*, p. 204.

14. Carl A. Grant, "The Influence of Agencies on Teacher Preparation: Social Justice in the New Millennium," In: *Teachers for the New Millennium: Aligning Teacher Development, National Goals, and High Standards for All Students*, Leonard Kaplan and Roy A. Edelfelt, eds. (Thousand Oaks, CA: Corwin Press, 1996), p. 77.

15. Louise Rosenblatt, "The Literary Transaction: Evocation and Response." In: *Journeying: Children Responding to Literature*, Kathleen E. Holland, Rachael A. Hungerford, and Shirley B. Ernst, eds. (Portsmouth, NH: Heinemann, 1993), p. 7.

16. Jeffrey D. Wilhelm, *"You Gotta BE the Book": Teaching Engaged and Reflective Reading with Adolescents* (New York: Teachers College Press and National Council of Teachers of English, 1997), p. 22.

17. Wilhelm, *"You Gotta BE the Book,"* p. 85.

18. Maxine Greene, *Landscapes of Learning* (New York: Teachers College Press, 1978), pp. 22, 84–85.

19. www.praxis.org/profdvlp/tools/artsprop.html

20. Robert T. Jiménez, Luis Moll, Flora Rodríguez–Brown, and Rosalinda Barrera, "Conversations: Latina and Latino Researchers Interact on Issues Related to Literacy Learning," *Reading Research Quarterly*, 34.2 (1999): 219.

21. James M. Patton and Joy L. Baytops, "Identifying and Transforming the Potential of Young, Gifted African Americans: A Clarion Call for Action." In: *Effective Education of African American Exceptional Learners*, Bridgie Alexis Ford, Festus E. Obiakor, and James M. Patton, eds. (Austin, TX: pro-ed, 1995), pp. 27–68.

22. Mary Gresham Anderson and Gwendolyn Webb–Johnson, "Cultural Contexts, the Seriously Emotionally Disturbed, and African American Learners." In: *Effective Education of African American Exceptional Learners*, Ford et al., eds. pp. 151–183.

23. http://nces.ed.gov/pubs2002/digest2001/chl.asp and http://nces.ed.gov/fastfacts/display.asp?id-96.

24. www.inner-cityarts.org

25. For a cautionary statement on the limits of brain-based research, see John T. Bruer, "Education and the Brain: A Bridge Too Far," *Educational Researcher*, 26.8 (1997): 4–16.

26. Renate Nummela Caine and Geoffrey Caine, *Making Connections: Teaching and the Human Brain* (Alexandria, VA: Association of Supervision and Curriculum Development, 1991), p. 59.

27. www.naesp.org/com/p0398c.htm

28. Ricardo L. Garcia and Janet Goldenstein Ahler, "Indian Education: Assumptions, Ideologies, Strategies." In: *Teaching American Indian Students*, Jon Reyhner, ed. (Norman, OK: University of Oklahoma Press, 1992), p. 19.

29. See the Connecticut Commission on the Arts web page, www.ctartsconnected.org

30. Elliot W. Eisner, *The Kind of Schools We Need: Personal Essays* (Portsmouth, NH: Heinemann, 1998), pp. 77–102.

31. Ernest Boyer, "The Arts, Language and the Schools," *Basic Education*, 2.4 (Summer 1987). ERIC ED286806.

32. Maxine Greene, *Releasing the Imagination: Essays on Education, the Arts, and Social Change* (San Francisco: Jossey-Bass, 1995), pp. 3, 16, 34.

33. *Educating for the Workplace through the Arts, The Getty Education Institute for the Arts and Business Week* (28 October 1996), pp. 1–16.

34. Todd Oppenheimer, "The Computer Delusion," *The Atlantic Monthly*, 280.1 (1997): 46.

35. Jane M. Gangi, Anne Alpert, Ann Shapiro, and Marni Carrom, *Storytelling and Reading: What Happens When Children Become Storytellers?* Paper presented at the Connecticut Reading Association's 49th Annual Reading Conference, "Literacy: Legacy for a Lifetime," Waterbury, CT, 28 October 2000. Jane M. Gangi, Savannah Metcalf, and Maureen Niestemksi, *Extending the Extensions: How a Course in Children's Literature Promotes Active Learning for Diverse Schools*. Paper presented at Connecticut Reading Association's 47th Annual Reading Conference, Waterbury, CT, 17 October 1998.

36. Mihaly Csikszentmihalyi, *Creativity: Flow and the Psychology of Discovery and Invention* (New York: HarperCollins, 1996), p. 23.

37. Howard Gardner, "Multiple Intelligences: Implications for Art and Creativity." In: *Artistic Intelligences: Implications for Education,* William Moody, ed. (New York: Teachers College Press, 1990), p. 21.

38. Keith Swanwick, *Musical Knowledge: Intuition, Analysis and Music Education* (London: Routledge, 1994), pp. 159, 163–164.

39. Kristin Linklater, *Freeing the Natural Voice* (New York: Drama Book Publishers, 1976), pp. 1–2.

40. Sanford Meisner and Dennis Longwell, *Sanford Meisner on Acting* (New York: Random House, 1987), p. 87.

41. See Seymour Sarason's *Teaching as a Performing Art* (New York: Teachers College Press, 1999) and Louis Rubin's *Artistry in Teaching* (New York: McGraw Hill, 1985).

42. Johnny Saldaña, *Drama of Color: Improvisation with Multiethnic Folklore* (Portsmouth, NH: Heinemann, 1995), p. 26.

43. Janice Hale, *Unbank the Fire: Visions for the Education of African American Children* (Baltimore: Johns Hopkins University Press, 1994), p. 160.

44. National Council for Accreditation of Teacher Education, *Program Standards for Elementary Teacher Preparation,* Curriculum Standard 2f.

45. Hale, *Unbank the Fire,* p. xxii.

chapter 2

An Introduction to Genre and to the History of Children's Literature

No one single playwright, but the sum of the playwrights of all ages can reflect an approximately satisfactory picture of this world.[1]

—FRIEDRICH DURENMATT

Encountering Literature

through reading aloud

Materials Needed

Favorite books to read aloud

Throughout your careers as elementary teachers, you will frequently read books aloud to children. Most reading programs include daily read-alouds. To develop competence in reading aloud, practice with your classmates in small groups. Select a short passage from a novel or read a short picture storybook. Keep in mind the approach to performance discussed in Chapter 1.8, giving attention to the following:

- The way you hold the book. Can all members see the pictures?

- Nonverbal communication—posture, breath, gesture, eye contact. These will be explored again in Chapter 7.1.

- Verbal communication—vocal variety, pitch, volume, rate, articulation, projection. These will be explored again in Chapter 5.1.

- Characterization. How do characters express themselves differently?

- Tone. Should the text be read whimsically? Enthusiastically? Seriously?

When each member has had a turn, discuss what was most effective in reading aloud.

Experts in reading see reading aloud as a cornerstone in best reading practice. Lucy Calkins says, "Above all, we support fluency by giving children many opportunities to hear beautiful texts read aloud—and read well."[2]

note to leader: You may wish to model reading aloud. In connection with the content of this chapter, you could choose favorite passages from several genres, demonstrating the characteristics of genres. Or, you could choose a passage from one of the early books in children's literature, such as *Robinson Crusoe* or *Gulliver's Travels*.

2.2 Genre: Spreading the Feast

During this journey into children's literature on which you are about to embark, there is plenty of room to follow your interests. What do you like to read? What do you want to learn more about? Look at the bibliographies in Appendix C for suggestions of books to begin with, or consult the websites listed at the ends of chapters on genres.

Although some books can comfortably fit into more than one category, the following genres are on the shelves of libraries and bookstores, waiting for you to read:

- Picture books
- Poetry

- Drama
- Folklore from the oral tradition
- Informational books
- Historical fiction
- Biography
- Contemporary realism
- Fantasy and science fiction

As part of your professional preparation, explore each of these genres, reading widely and deeply.

Because art refuses exact definition, there will be shades of gray and overlap; a book can sometimes fit the characteristics of more than one category. For example, is Dr. Seuss's *Green Eggs and Ham* a picture storybook, or poetry, or fantasy, or all three? Is Irene Smalls–Hector's *Jonathan and His Mommy* a poem or realistic fiction? How do you categorize David Macaulay's *Black and White* for which you are invited to create your own meaning? While guarding against the tendency to overcategorize, the following definitions are offered as a framework.

The *picture book* is an umbrella term that includes a variety of categories: concept books (alphabet, counting, manners, and so on), wordless books, and contemporary realistic books. The *picture storybook* is a form of children's literature in which the visual image and the written word are both essential to the artistic import of the work. In this book, *picture books* are the focus of Chapter 4. However, picture storybooks also appear in the chapters on poetry, folklore, informational books, and celebrations. Picture books are often, but not exclusively, written for children in the lower elementary grades (K–3). These slender volumes—usually thirty-two pages in length and between 1,000 and 1,500 words—are generally not divided into chapters. Examples are

- *Biography picture books: Duke Ellington: The Piano Prince and His Orchestra* written by Andrea Davis Pinkney and illustrated by Brian Pinkney. This book tells the story of one of the greatest jazz musicians of all time.
- *Fantasy picture storybooks: The Goat in the Rug* written by Charles Blood and Martin Link and illustrated by Nancy Winslow Parker. This Navajo story about the process of rug weaving is told from the point of view of the goat (improbable, but convincing).
- *Historical fiction picture storybooks: Peppe the Lamplighter* written by Elisa Bartone and illustrated by Ted Lewin. This is the story of an Italian immigrant family during the early 1900s in the United States—a time of massive immigration, transition, and adjustment.
- *Realistic picture storybooks: Family Farm* written and illustrated by Thomas Locker. Children's farming efforts stave off the family's financial difficulties.
- *Wordless or textless picture storybooks: Zoom* illustrated by Istvan Banyai. Without words Banyai tells a remarkably original story that challenges human perspective.
- *Concept picture books: Ten Black Dots* by Donald Crews (see Figure 2.1). Such books teach the colors, months, and other concepts.

Figure 2.1 *Ten Black Dots,* by Donald Crews, is an example of a counting concept book—one that invites creative responses.

Illustrated books, longer than picture storybooks, contain illustrations to heighten interest, like Diane Stanley's beautifully illustrated biographies. *Easy readers* are written with beginning readers in mind; the vocabulary is controlled, the point size is large with brief paragraphs on each page, and the books are as long as sixty-four pages with as many as 2,000 words. Arnold Lobel's *Frog and Toad* series is an example of this form. After meeting the challenge of easy readers, children often seek *transition books* that are slightly more difficult and are divided into brief chapters. See, for example, Patricia Reilly Giff's *Polk Street School* series. Giff's books, and others like them, then become the bridge to novels and chapter books.

Poetry can be found in picture book form as well as in collections. It is a type of literature patterned into lines and rhythms of either metric verse or free verse. Poetry does not have to rhyme. Its use of imagery and figurative language is often more richly concentrated than in prose forms. The following are categories of poetry:

- Lullabies
- Mother Goose and nursery rhymes
- Lyric poems
- Narrative poetry (ballads, story poems, romances, sea chanties)
- Haiku (Japanese verse)
- Ca dao (Vietnamese verse)

- Rap (which originated in the African American community)
- Free verse
- Humorous and nonsense verses
- Songs and finger poems
- Playground games

We can think of individual poets, like Nikki Grimes and Gary Soto, but must remember that much poetry comes out of the oral tradition, authored anonymously for generations, for example, ballads, sea chanties, and the Mother Goose and nursery rhymes. Some collections are organized around a theme, like Javaka Steptoe's *In Daddy's Arms I Am Tall* (see Figure 2.2). And there are collections of poetry written by children, such as Davida Adedjouma's edited volume *The Palm of My Heart* (see Figure 2.3).

In the genre of *drama,* actors, evoking imaginary worlds, perform for, or sometimes with, an audience. Playwrights may provide a script; when unscripted, the actor, or ensemble, essentially becomes the playwright. At its most essential, drama involves an actor and a space; however, scene, costume and light designers, directors, and others may be involved. A versatile art, forms of drama include pantomime, readers theater, story theater, story dramatization, and improvisation.

Figure 2.2 Javaka Steptoe's mixed-media collage conveys both tenderness and strength in the themed poetry collection *In Daddy's Arms I Am Tall: African Americans Celebrating Fathers.*

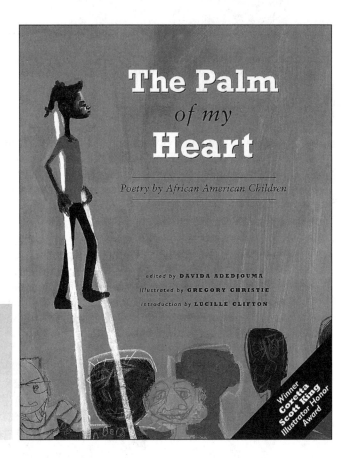

Figure 2.3 *The Palm of My Heart: Poetry by African American Children,* edited by Davida Adedjouma, is illustrated by Gregory Christie, winner of the Coretta Scott King Illustrator Honor Award, who uses acrylic and pencils in an expressionistic style.

Folklore is an umbrella term that encompasses fables, folk tales, fairy tales, myths, legends, tall tales, and epics. These oral narratives—or spoken stories—have been handed down from one generation to the next, in contrast with the single-author literary compositions found in the modern picture book and other genres. *Where the Wild Things Are* is a fantasy picture storybook written and illustrated by Maurice Sendak. *The Magic Hummingbird* (see Figure 2.4) comes out of Hopi traditional stories *retold* by Michael Lomatuway'ma. Folklore is an art form shared by an intergenerational community and, in recent centuries, has been written down in both picture books and collections. The following are categories of folklore:

- *Fables* are short, moralistic tales whose animal characters represent abstractions, like greed or dishonesty.
- *Folk tales* deal with the problems of life and survival, and encompass the following subcategories:
  - Cumulative or formula tales
  - Pourquoi tales

Figure 2.4 *The Magic Hummingbird: A Hopi Folktale* is collected and translated by Ekkehart Malotki and narrated by Michael Lomatuway'ma (Hopi). Southwestern pottery and basketry influence the illustrations by Michael Lacapa (Apache/Tewa/Hopi).

- Noodlehead stories
- Animal tales
- Trickster stories
- Realistic tales
- Wisdom tales

- *Fairy tales* are tales of enchantment that include extraordinary, transformational, and supernatural happenings.

- *Myths* explain origins and creation of natural phenomena, humans, and animals, and are often part of religious beliefs.

- *Legends* are greatly elaborated stories based on probable historical figures.

- *Epics,* originally composed orally in poetic form, are usually about the acts of heroic national figures.

- *Tall tales* seem to be indigenous to the United States and often humorously describe the deeds of the superheros of the common folk.

There are many single-author *literary fairy tales,* like those by Hans Christian Andersen and Oscar Wilde, which are included in Chapter 7, along with parodies and fractured fairy tales like John Scieszka and Lane Smith's *The True Story of the Three Little Pigs.* It is sometimes difficult to determine whether stories stem from the oral tradition or whether they are single-author literary fairy tales. A way to distinguish folklore from literary tales is to watch for the words "retold," "collected," and "adapted," and to look at the first page after the title page of a book for clues. Retellers, collectors, and adapters, out of respect for the culture from which the story comes, should provide notes on the original source for their stories.

Informational books, an exploding market in recent years, is that category of children's literature that conveys information about disciplinary subjects—for example, science, history, and mathematics. Although these books are often expository in style, they sometimes blend genres by combining narration and exposition: *The Magic School Bus* series depicts fantastical voyages while conveying information about topics like the human body. When reading informational books, the reader usually takes an efferent stance (which was discussed in Chapter 1.6). However, today's informational books often have appealing aesthetic qualities.

Although you will find fantasy, historical fiction, biography, and contemporary realism in picture book form, these genres also appear in chapter books, called *novels* and *novellas. Historical fiction* is realistic fiction that pictures life in previous eras, drawn from diaries, letters, and reports about historical events. An example is Irene Hunt's *Across Five Aprils,* set in the time of the Civil War. Hunt, a contemporary author, researched historical documents and places to write her book accurately. According to Constantine Georgiou, a professor of children's literature, *historical realism* refers to books written more than seventy-five years ago that also picture life during a previous era.[3] Although seventy-five is an arbitrary dividing line, it is useful to help us think about authors *who lived during the time in which they wrote.* Louisa May Alcott published *Little Women* in 1868. Alcott, unlike Hunt, did not have to investigate old letters and diaries, nor read history about the Civil War—she *lived* during that time; Hunt did not live during the Civil War. Works like Alcott's are often called *classics* because, despite their age, they have held the enduring interest of generations of children. Classics can also be found in fantasy (*Alice's Adventures in Wonderland* by Lewis Carroll) and biography (*Invincible Louisa* by Cornelia Miegs).

Biography portrays the life of a single individual. For example, Patricia and Frederick McKissack, contemporary authors, have written a biography called *Sojourner Truth: Ain't I a Woman?* about the great abolitionist. *Autobiography* is a written work about one's own life span, whereas *memoir* usually focuses on a specific period of one's life with the emphasis on people and events of one's time. Esther Hautzig wrote *The Endless Steppe,* an autobiography that focuses on her experiences as a Polish Jew exiled to Siberia in World War II. Beverly Cleary wrote *My Own Two Feet: A Memoir,* a sequel to her autobiography *The Girl from Yamhill,* in which she focuses on the beginning of her career as a writer.

Contemporary realism is a story based in modern life that is not true in a factual sense but is plausible enough that it could happen. Humorous stories, stories about school, friends, family, and other themes and topics emerge in this category of literature. Katherine Paterson explores themes of death and friendship in the Newbery-winning *Bridge to Terabithia.*

Fantasy calls forth imaginative and fantastical happenings that are plausible in the worlds in which they exist: Children fly about on broomsticks playing quidditch, as in the *Harry Potter* books; animals talk, as in *The Wind in the Willows;* time has no boundaries, as in *A Wrinkle in Time;* and magical worlds are called into being as in J. R. R. Tolkien's *Lord of the Rings* trilogy. Although sharing similarities with the fairy tales from traditional literature, a single author (instead of a community of tellers) writes these volumes, and they are often more sophisticated in thought, character, and style than folklore. Fantasy can also *cross* genres, as in Robert Lawson's *Ben and Me,* a book in which Benjamin Franklin and a mouse become acquainted, blending fantasy with informational literature. *Science fiction,* often involving advanced technology, visualizes the possibilities and dangers in future societies. Profoundly moral, science fiction often asks philosophical questions in narrative form.

Beginning in Chapter 4 with the picture book, we will look more closely at these genres, ending with Chapter 12 on fantasy. Chapter 13, then, integrates the genres around celebrations and commemorations.

2.3 Approximating a Picture of the World: Classroom Libraries

Knowledge of genre is indispensable for the classroom teacher. Edward Murray, designer of the Essentials of Literacy Reading Room in the Comer School Development Project, believes classrooms should resemble libraries—lots of books in lots of genres. Murray's inspiring success with urban remedial readers, highlighted in James Comer's book, *Waiting for a Miracle,* is based in part on this metaphor of classroom as library, affording children extensive self-selection and exposure to hundreds of books.[4]

Although Murray's work is with remedial readers, the classroom-as-library metaphor is beneficial for all children. Barbara Clark, an expert in gifted education, comments on the importance of availability of a wide range of genres for advanced readers: "[A]ge-in-grade grouping and the reluctance to provide acceleration or experiences outside of the regular classroom [are] obstacles to appropriate programming for gifted readers. Allowing children to read widely, creatively, critically, and with an excellent and motivated teacher is suggested as part of the solution to providing more appropriate language arts instruction."[5] Today's teachers must be prepared to offer instruction and guidance to children who possess a range of learning abilities. Although it is not developmentally appropriate to expect children to do what is overly frustrating, it is also not developmentally appropriate to hold back those capable of higher reading levels.

The classroom-as-library metaphor implies balance and representation of all genres, leading to better reading *and* writing. Discussing the needs of children for whom English is a second language, Kathryn Au points out that "a variety of genres enhances their ability to do literary writing."[6] Other reading experts agree: "At the very minimum, the literacy curriculum for all children should include reading skills and the reading of full-length material. This full-length material should include books, magazines, newspapers, and documents. In each of these categories, students . . . should sample the full range of fiction and nonfiction genres (from myths and folk tales to historical and contemporary fiction, from newspapers to biographies)."[7] As a matter of equity, the International Reading Association has recommended that there are at least seven books for every one child in a classroom. Too often, low-income children do not have the range of reading materials in schools that middle-income children have.[8]

Teachers who discover the fullness of literature will have an easier time making connections with the children they teach. In our professional preparation, we need to stretch beyond books we already know to what we do not know. Our reading discoveries may be the very books children in our classrooms need to find meaning and significance, thus helping them to become independent readers and writers.

2.4 The Emergence of Genre in the History of Children's Literature

Children's literature is young in comparison with other art forms. Music, dance, drama, storytelling, the visual arts, and poetry have existed for thousands of years in diverse cultures, shared with intergenerational audiences. Radical changes in the media of communication shaped what has become the art form of children's literature. These communication shifts include the invention of phonetic writing around the eighth century BCE; the invention of movable type, and the invention of electronic forms, beginning with Samuel Morse's telegraph in the nineteenth century and continuing into the current digital age. What follows is a history of the various genres as they emerged in the context of the media of communication, informing and shaping the development of children's literature.

Before literacy, before the alphabet, there were stories, told orally, sung, danced, and performed. In sound and movement, *folklore* expressed the wisdom, insights, and values of diverse cultural groups, and provided entertainment. Before printing and paper, the rhythmic and mnemonic nature of *poetry*, one of the oldest genres, helped tellers to memorize their cultural expressions then pass them on to the next generation. With the invention of writing came the possibility of capturing ephemeral, oral performance in print. A scholar of studies in media, Walter Ong writes, "Moving into the exciting world of literacy means leaving behind much that is exciting and deeply loved in the earlier oral world."[9] Oral cultures are more communal, providing a greater sense of belonging to those who live in them. Recapturing the qualities of earlier, oral cultures requires participation in collective events, such as storytelling, that can foster a sense of belonging in our contemporary individualistic and sometimes alienated world.

Drama existed in the form of rituals perhaps more than 30,000 years ago when the Egyptians dramatically enacted myths. The advent of the phonetic alphabet made it further possible to blend orality and literacy, as demonstrated in the Greek plays of the third and fourth centuries BCE. Playwrights drew on the oral epics for plots and heroic characters; audiences of children and adults viewed them.

During the centuries commonly called the Dark Ages, while literacy stayed within the confines of the wealthy and religious classes, the oral tradition was alive and well, and shared by young and old. In Europe, monk-scribes created a manuscript culture in which they elegantly transcribed literary works by hand on vellum (animal skins). St. Aldhelm, the English abbot and bishop (640–709 CE), wrote lessons for children using the question-and-answer approach on the mystical number seven, but with few exceptions children were not considered, at this time, a distinct group for whom to write.

Informational books have their origin during the medieval period, when the first encyclopedias and dictionaries appeared. Around 1440, small wooden paddles called *hornbooks* (see Figure 2.5) taught children the alphabet and the Lord's prayer, linking literacy with religious instruction.

Prior to 1450, printing existed in varying degrees of efficiency and use in different cultures. The Minoans developed printing around 1700 BCE, and the Chinese experimented with forms of printing from about the second century CE, attaining enough sophistication by 868 to print books. The Chinese are also credited with inventing paper, probably during the first or second century BCE. The alchemist Pi Sheng used movable type by around 1041 in China, and a Korean inventor improved this invention by using cast-bronze type by 1403.[10] In 1450 in Europe, Gutenberg's improvements with movable type made mass production possible. Thus, for the first time in history, widespread literacy became feasible. Sounding the end of scribal culture, print set off the "gunpowder of the mind"[11] — books fixed in print, scattered about to wide and unknown audiences. Opposing viewpoints could be placed side by side, generating multilayered meanings and perspectives.

Elizabeth Eisenstein, a scholar of the history of print, suggests that the effects of the printing press included deepening introspection, heightened individuality, and a growing sense of nationalism that, perhaps, led to the conception of democracy itself.[12]

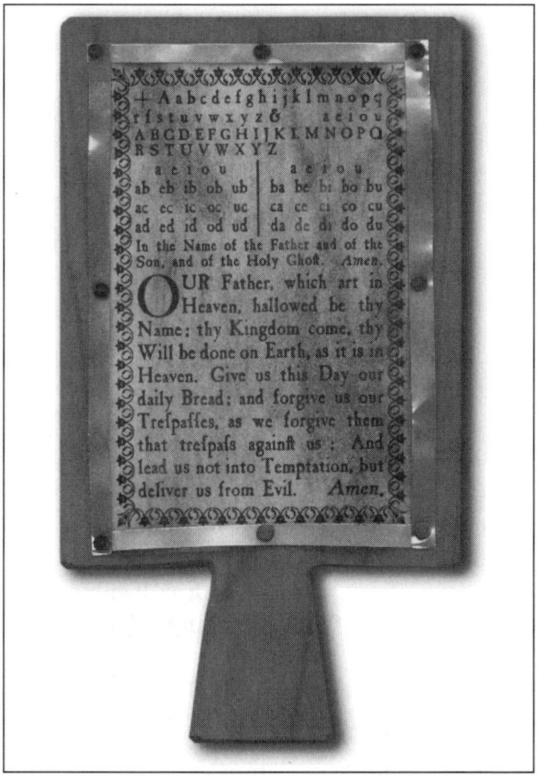

Figure 2.5 Hornbooks taught children the alphabet and the Lord's prayer. Note the patterned borders.

These changes propelled the collection of folklore in the nineteenth century. The folk who created folklore came to be seen as sources of wisdom. Another effect of the printing press was a growing awareness that children could be an audience separate from adults. As Phillipe Aries points out, distinct delineations between childhood and adulthood were not common in the Middle Ages.[13]

Shortly after Gutenberg's invention, the publisher William Caxton began his long and prolific career, publishing the *Book of Curtasye* in 1477 (in which servants were taught their manners; and nobility, the pattern of behavior suitable to that class), followed by The *Historye of Reynart the Foxe* and *The Book of the Subtyle Historyes and Fables of Esope* (1483). Because of cost, these books were read mostly by the upper classes. In 1548, primers espoused Henry VIII's interpretation of religion, exemplifying adults' assumptions that written materials could be used to indoctrinate children into preapproved beliefs. Foxe's *Book of Martyrs* (1563), for example, was an anti-Catholic tract intended for Protestants. For 300 years after the invention of the printing press, literature published for children—with few exceptions—was confined to teaching religion, the alphabet, and manners. Children's literature scholar Francelia Butler observes, "children's literature began as an exploitation of children—threatening them with death if they did not behave."[14] The intent was to induct children into the existing status quo.

Puritanical Influence   During the seventeenth century, children and adults read and enjoyed John Bunyan's allegory, *A Pilgrim's Progress* (1628). Under the influence of the Puritans, the prevailing conception of children was that they were naturally more inclined to evil than to good. A popular primer, the prototype for today's alphabet book, stated, "A–In Adam's fall/We sinned all./Thy Life to mend,/This Book attend." The first American publication for children was John Cotton's *Spiritual Milk for Boston Babies in Either England Drawn from the Breast of Both Testaments for their Soul's Nourishment* (1656); the title leaves little to explain. Other publications included *Day of Doom,* which described the terrible things that awaited sinful children in hell, and *A Token for Children,* which told thirteen stories in which all the child protagonists die. *The New England Primer* (available from about 1680 and for nearly the next 200 years) sold close to three million copies, second to the Bible in sales. Despite their rigid, moralistic stance, because they wanted their children to read the Bible, the Puritans encouraged literacy, perhaps not foreseeing the day when their children would choose to read secular works.

Education was conceived of as transmission, when content is simply transferred from the mind of the teacher to the mind of the pupil. The printing press itself provided a metaphor for this type of education. The Moravian bishop Comenius (1592–1671) called the pupil the blank paper, the voice of the teacher the ink, and the discipline of school the printing press. Comenius also wrote the first basal reader for boys—not girls—*Orbis Pictus,* which was 150 chapters long. The contemporary Orbis Pictus awards are named for Comenius's book, and are made for outstanding informational books written for children.

Despite the literature of the time—which emphasized morality, manners, and religion—more subversive and more appealing literature emerged in the form of chapbooks sometime during the sixteenth century. These predecessors to the picture book and the illustrated book recaptured old tales from the oral tradition in cheap, low-quality renditions: *Robin Hood, Dick Whittington, Tom Thumb,* and *Jack the Giant Killer.* Children, of course, preferred chapbooks over the didactic books set on ferreting out their sins.

The Enlightenment Gradually, the conception of the child began to change. During the Enlightenment of the eighteenth century, John Locke's philosophy of education was influential: He thought of the child as an empty slate that could be formed and shaped as adults saw fit. Like Horace in ancient Rome, Locke thought educational materials should both teach and delight. The focus during the Enlightenment was on the moral tale, thus the popularity of the fable during that time. The novel was also gradually gaining in popularity and recognition. Daniel Defoe's *Robinson Crusoe* (1719), considered the first survival story, Sir Walter Scott's works of *historical fiction,* like *Ivanhoe,* and Jonathan Swift's *fantasy, Gulliver's Travels* (1726), attracted intergenerational audiences.

John Newbery, generally considered the father of children's literature, built on the success of the chapbooks with his publication of *A Little Pretty Pocket-Book* in 1744. In contrast with previous didacticism, starting with Newbery's publication, many more books simultaneously provided both entertainment and instruction. Initiated by Frederic Melcher in 1921, the Newbery Award is given annually to the author who has made the most distinguished contribution to children's literature.

Romanticism The Romantic movement of the late eighteenth and early nineteenth centuries further spurred development of children's literature as a distinct art form. Rejecting the puritanical assumption that children are innately wicked, Jean Jacques Rousseau published his romantic treatise *Emile* in 1762, which speculated that, provided a natural environment with minimal adult guidance and out from under the evil influence of institutions, children would manifest goodness. Although this view is naive, it was a refreshing alternative to the Puritan's overly negative view of children. Slowly, publications for children began to change, becoming less frightening and more attractive, picturing children in idyllic and romantic settings. Romanticism in children's literature had the tendency to glorify children, because they had so recently emanated from God, as dwelling on a higher plane of spirituality than adults and, therefore, were more vulnerable to death and hardship.

Although St. Augustine's *Confessions* in the fourth century is considered the first known autobiography, the genre did not flourish until the nineteenth century. Scholars think that the effects of literacy over time resulted in a growing interiorization in which attention to one's inner life gained in importance.

During the nineteenth century in America, the Cherokee leader Sequoyah became fascinated with the books brought by European settlers—"talking leaves," he called them—inspiring him to create the first alphabet for an Indian language and opening up the possibility of encoding aspects of Cherokee culture in print.

In England, the Victorian period gave birth to what is often called the *golden age of literature.* Children's authors continually explored the lost childhood that adults, presumably, would do well to recover. Many of these books were illustrated, and in the 1860s, Edmund Evans made advances in color printing that greatly contributed to the development of *picture books.* The publication of Randolph Caldecott's *The Diverting History of John Gilpin* in 1878 is considered the beginning of the modern picture book.

Although a welcome development in the history of literature, it must be noted that children's literature has historically, primarily been written for children of European descent. In fact, since its inception, many publications for children have been blatantly racist, which in addition to demeaning children of color, has an insidious effect on white children. Children's literature scholar Donnarae MacCann writes,

> The myth of white superiority was introduced into each successive generation's social conditioning, and the very act of passing down white supremacist attitudes to children tells us much about the importance of this myth to the child-raisers. There was little reason for the European American child to doubt his or her racial superiority because the storybooks, periodicals, schools, churches, and government authorities were all sending the same signal. Racial bias has reached White children through books, and also by way of the institutions that constantly impinged on their lives. The Black child, on the other hand, was treated in the publishing world as a legitimate target of derision.[15]

MacCann gives the following example from the popular nineteenth century children's magazine, *St. Nicholas:* An "editor tells readers they will 'split' with laughter over the poem 'Ten Little Niggers' ('Ten little nigger boys went out to dine/One choked his little self and then/there were nine. . . .')."[16] When children of color were not being derided in children's literature, they were simply omitted. These historical injustices have left a legacy that we will look at more closely in the next chapter.

2.5 Conclusion

A knowledge of genres and an awareness of their emergence in the history of literature will help you better plan for your classroom library. An NCATE program standard states: "Candidates know, understand, and use the central concepts, tools of inquiry, and structures of content for students across the K–6 grades and can create meaningful learning experiences that develop students' competence in subject matter and skills for various developmental levels."[17] Understanding genre and the history of genre in children's literature helps develop competence in these areas.

Suggested Activities

1. Edward Murray urges, for your future or current classroom library, that you record books on tape. Purchase fifteen- to twenty-minute-long blank tapes for picture books (longer blank tapes for chapter books) and a few favorite books. Tape yourself reading aloud, stopping to ask an imaginary child questions, and commenting on your own enjoyment of the story. Place the tape and the book inside a sealable bag.

   To be able to see and to hear words as they read builds on the strengths of auditory learners and gives opportunities for children to read and hear the same story a number of times. We would not expect children to perform in a piano recital without having practiced their piece numerous times, yet in reading we often expect them to achieve proficiency without practice. There are on the market paperback/cassette packages.

2. In your class, what are your favorite genres? Why? Do preferences run along gender lines?

for further reading

Allen, Marjorie N. 1996. *100 Years of Children's Books in America: Decade by Decade.* New York: Facts on File.

Avery, Gillian. 1975. *Childhood's Pattern: A Study of the Heroes and Heroines of Children's Fiction, 1770–1950.* London: Hodder and Stoughton.

Carpenter, Humphrey. 1985. *Secret Gardens: A Study of the Golden Age of Children's Literature.* Boston: Houghton Mifflin.

Carpenter, Humphrey, and Mari Prichard. 1984. *The Oxford Companion to Children's Literature.* Oxford: Oxford University Press.

MacLeod, Anne Scott. 1994. *American Childhood: Essays on Children's Literature of the Nineteenth and Twentieth Centuries.* Athens: University of Georgia Press.

———. 1975. *A Moral Tale: Children's Fiction and American Culture, 1820–1860.* Hamden: Archon.

Mortenstern, John. 2001. "The Rise of Children's Literature Reconsidered." *Children's Literature Association Quarterly, 26.2:* pp. 64–73.

Murray, Gail Schmunk. 1998. *American Children's Literature and the Construction of Childhood.* New York: Twayne.

Nikolajeva, Maria, ed. 1995. *Aspects and Issues in the History of Children's Literature.* Contributions to the study of world literature, no. 60. Westport, CT: Greenwood.

Pollack, Linda. 1983. *Forgotten Children: Parent-Child Relations from 1500–1900.* Cambridge: Cambridge University Press.

Richardson, Selma, ed. 1980. *Research about Nineteenth Century Children and Books: Portrait Studies.* Urbana-Champaign, IL: University of Illinois.

Summerfeld, Geoffrey. 1983. *Fantasy and Reason: Children's Literature in the Eighteenth Century.* Athens: University of Georgia Press.

websites

Nijmegen University's The History of Education and Childhood:

www.socisci.kun.nl/ped/whp/histeduc/readme.html

San Antonio College LitWeb has landmarks in the history of children's literature:

www.accd.edu/sac/english/bailey/childlit.htm

Vandergrift's Children's Literature Page has a link to the history of children's literature:

www.scils.rutgers.edu/ ~ kvander /HistoryofChildLit/

awards

Caldecott Award:

www.ala.org/alsc

Children's Literature Awards:

www.literature-awards.com/ childrens_literature.htm

Newbery Award:

www.ala.org/alsc/nmedal.html

U.S. Children's Book Awards:

www.ucalgary.ca/ ~ dkbrown/usawards.html

notes

1. Friedrich Durenmatt, *Writings on Theatre and Drama* (London: Jonathan Cape, 1976), p. 135.

2. Lucy Calkins, *The Art of Teaching Reading* (New York: Longman, 2001), p. 172.

3. Constantine Georgiou, *Children and Their Literature* (Englewood Cliffs, NJ: Prentice-Hall, 1988), p. 305.

4. The 1999 training videotape *Essentials of Literacy Process Facilitator Guide* can be ordered through the Yale Child Study Center, School Development Project, 55 College Street, New Haven, CT 06510-3208. See also James Comer, *Waiting for a Miracle: Why Schools Can't Solve Our Problems—and How We Can* (Dutton, 1997), pp. 228–229.

5. Barbara Clark, *Growing Up Gifted* (Columbus, OH: Merrill, 1988), p. 338.

6. Kathryn H. Au, *Literacy Instruction in Multicultural Settings* (San Diego: Harcourt Brace, 1993), p. 165.

7. Sean A. Walmsley and Richard L. Allington, "Redefining and Reforming Instructional Support Programs for At-Risk Students." In: *No Quick Fix: Rethinking Literacy Programs in America's Elementary Schools,* Richard L. Allington and Sean A. Walmsley, eds. (New York: Teachers College Press and International Reading Association, 1995), p. 31.

8. Susan B. Neuman and Donna Celano, "Access to Print in Low-Income and Middle-Income Communities: An Ecological Study of Four Neighborhoods," *Reading Research Quarterly, 36.1* (2001): 25; and Jill Fitzgerald and Jim Cummins, "Bridging Disciplines to Critique a National Research Agenda for Language–Minority Children's Schooling," *Reading Research Quarterly, 34.3* (1999): 384.

9. Walter Ong, *Orality and Literacy: The Technologizing of the Word* (London: Routledge, 1983), p. 15.

10. Jared Diamond, "Invention is the Mother of Necessity: Gutenberg Didn't Invent the Printing Press and Other Surprises from 1,000 Years of Ingenuity," *The New York Times Magazine* (18 April 1999): 142.

11. David Riesman, "The Oral and Written Traditions." In: *Explorations in Communication: An Anthology,* Edmund Carpenter and Marshall McLuhan, eds. (Boston: Beacon Press, 1960), p. 110.

12. Elizabeth Eisenstein, *The Printing Press as Agent of Change: Communications and Cultural Transformations in Early-Modern Europe* (Cambridge: Cambridge University Press, 1979).

13. Phillipe Aries, *Centuries of Childhood: A Social History of Family Life,* Robert Baldick, trans. (New York: Vintage, 1962), p. 411.

14. Quoted in Gillian Adams, "The Francelia Butler Watershed: Then and Now," *Children's Literature Association Quarterly, 25.4* (2001): 184.

15. Donnarae MacCann, *White Supremacy in Children's Literature: Characterizations of African Americans, 1830–1900* (New York: Garland, 1998), p. 233.

16. MacCann, *White Supremacy in Children's Literature,* p. 201.

17. National Council for Accreditation of Teacher Education, *Program Standards for Elementary Teacher Preparation,* Curriculum 2a.

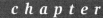

chapter **3**

Selecting and Evaluating Children's Literature

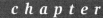

overview

*W*hat has happened to us in this country? If we study our own history we find that we have always been ready to receive the unfortunates from other countries, and though this may seem a generous gesture on our part, we have profited a thousandfold by what they have brought us.[1]

—ELEANOR ROOSEVELT

41

3.1 Encountering Literature
with the storytelling shawl

Materials Needed

A shawl

A multicultural book such as Nicholasa Mohr's autobiography, *Growing Up Inside the Sanctuary of My Imagination*. I suggest a multicultural book in connection with the content of this chapter; however, most genres work well with the storytelling shawl.

note to leader: Read aloud passages from the book—for example, the passage when Nicholasa's eighth-grade guidance counselor discourages her from going to a college preparatory high school (she'd be taking someone else's spot) and coaxes her instead to become a seamstress because that's where Puerto Ricans supposedly excel (pp. 104–105). Or, the passage in which Nicholasa describes her love of reading; however, she notices early on that teachers do not use and she cannot find books about her and her family; it is as if Latinos do not exist (p. 62).

I learned about the storytelling shawl from Constance Borab in *Teaching African American Literature*, who learned it from Michael Cremonini at a Shakespeare and Company Summer Institute.[2] Taking turns, participants hold the shawl, become a character or an inanimate object in the story, or the author, and speak from that person's or object's point of view. This continues in a round. When everyone has had a turn, the round may continue if people want second turns or the story can come to an end. In a large class, this can be done in small groups.

For example, based on *Growing Up Inside the Sanctuary of My Imagination,* participants can become Nicholasa's guidance counselor or the Puerto Rican seamstress who makes the guidance counselor's clothes or a window in the room.

Trying to tell the story without the shawl does make a difference in how the telling goes. It seems the shawl gives confidence and security, much like puppets can for some children who otherwise hesitate to perform. Once participants have tried this encounter, they usually want to try it again with other books.

3.2 Defining Children's Literature

To help you explore the possibilities of children's literature on your own, this chapter introduces you to several criteria for selection and evaluation. But first, how do we define children's literature? How does it differ from literature written for adults? There are not as many defining characteristics as might be expected. In fictional prose narratives, the protagonists are usually children who live through some aspect of growing up, however funny or painful. In poetry, the subjects generally address the interests of children, like popcorn, swings, and shadows, but adults take pleasure in these topics too. Children enjoy folklore, which has always been intergenerationally shared. Good informational literature written for children has a clear, usually well-researched and informative style that is sometimes the quickest way for adults to find out what they want to know. Furthermore, some informational books are works of art that elicit aesthetic responses—for example, David Macaulay's *Cathedral* or Walter Wick's *A Drop of Water*. Books like *Treasure Island, The Wind in the Willows,* and *The Little Prince,* which are seen as children's books, have readability levels higher than most adult novels listed on the *New York Times Bestseller List.* Some elementary school-age children have loved novels written for adults, like *Oliver Twist* and *Jane Eyre*. Clearly, the boundaries are blurred. Perhaps children's literature is simply good literature that appeals to the needs and interests of children. Much of it could be called *literature for all ages*. Most likely, you, as adults, will enjoy many—if not most—of the books you read from the children's literature bibliographies found in Appendix C.

While exploring books in libraries and bookstores, you will find much that is memorable, humorous, deeply moving, and profoundly wise. You will also find varying degrees of quality, from the artistic and imaginative to the trite and banal. Keep in mind that even junk reading can be beneficial. Anthropologist Margaret Mead's mother thought her daughter's series and pulp fiction reading helped her to recognize high-quality literature when she found it. But, children generally find low-quality books on their own. Teachers can introduce them to books they may not find on their own. Jessica Olson, a kindergarten teacher, wrote in her log:

> I learned that there are plenty of bad children's books out there. I became fiercely protective of my log, very reluctant to enter books that, in my mind, did not attain a certain standard. As a result, I have probably read twice the books that were required for this course, but was inspired to record only a select few. (personal communication)

Schools are places where children can have experiences they are not likely to have elsewhere. For seven hours a day, five days a week, and 180 days a year, teachers can provide children with books that take them beyond what they currently know, think, and feel. But with approximately 127,000 children's books in print and about 5,000 new titles annually, where do teachers begin?[3] How can teachers build high-quality collections of children's books for their classrooms? What criteria are used to make these very important choices? With limited budgets, how can teachers provide children—and themselves—with the very best? To explore these questions we will consider the commercialization of literature, gender and diversity issues, and literary elements and criticism.

3.3 Mass Media and the Commercialization of Children's Literature

Children's literature has been a commercial endeavor since at least the eighteenth century. However, commercialization and consumerism have invaded children's lives to a degree unknown several centuries ago. Since television's inception, children have been market segments for advertisers, who know that middle- and upper-class children, especially, have tremendous buying power. The primary purpose of much of the media is to cultivate consumers. Indeed, some argue that from the time they are toddlers, children are inducted into a culture that purposefully addicts them to material goods, making them become "commodity dependent."[4]

The commercial aspect of our culture permeates too much of the field of children's literature. Joel Taxel writes,

> While thankful for the growing number of marvelously innovative authors and illustrators who are encouraged by bold and innovative editors willing to take chances, I am deeply troubled by the remarkable amount of junk published that reflects the desire to play it safe, to appeal to the lowest common denominator, to capitalize on the latest fads, to publish sequels or copies of somebody else's best seller, and so on that has become generic to television and films. The skyrocketing price of books also threatens to make purchase of the best of children's literature impossible for an increasingly large portion of the public.[5]

When selecting books, teachers can, like Jessica Olson, think about what *not* to select. *Mass-market books* are created for the consumer market, and *trade books* are created primarily for schools and libraries. The sole purpose of mass-market books is to create and maintain customers. Corporations seek to license characters in books, who are then used to sell toy lines and material goods—sheets, wallpaper, toothbrushes, pajamas, and so on. When licensed characters are in books, telling a story is secondary to the overriding purpose of selling sheets and wallpaper and toothbrushes. Although books about mass-market characters may have entertainment value, there is no reason to have them in classrooms; children will most certainly see them elsewhere.

Another consideration when selecting children's books is the quality of second-hand books. Most teachers are on tight budgets and must visit tag sales and flea markets to supplement their classroom libraries. Bargains can be found, but too often teachers settle for poor-quality literature. Teachers should ask: Is a large quantity of poor-quality literature better than a small quantity of higher quality books?

3.4 Gender and Children's Literature

Although the women's movement has helped bring about improvement in career options for girls, images of girls in the media, and what is considered aesthetically beautiful, has drastically narrowed in recent decades. In 1950, the White Rock mineral girl was 5'4" tall and typically weighed 140 pounds. Today she is 5'10" and weighs 110 pounds. Our daughters are growing up in the "cult of thinness."[6] They are also growing up in an environment that infantilizes them. In numerous ads they are so slight, sexualized, and nonassertive that they can be "knocked over with a feather."[7]

Boys have historically outnumbered girls in representation: A study of the Caldecott winners and honors books between 1967 and 1971 showed a ratio of 11:1. When animals of obvious identities are included, the ratio was 95:1.[8] Video games are equally limited: Ninety-two percent of video games do not include females and, of the eight percent of the games that do include females, six percent are helpless and/or victimized; only two percent of the female characters have active roles.[9] The gender of the author even impacts the sales of books: J. K. Rowling did not use her first name as author of the *Harry Potter* books. Instead, the initials "J. K." led buyers to believe she might be a man, which her publisher thought would increase the sales of the book.

Boys are in as much need as girls for balanced role models in literature. James Garbarino, who has studied why some adolescent boys become violent, writes,

> Boys are routinely taught to ignore or deny their feelings by parents and others who are training them to be men in a culture that demands male stoicism. It is no secret that boys and men in many societies, including our own, are encouraged to put their emotions in boxes, to keep them out of consciousness, and to regard the expression of powerful feelings of pain and sorrow as a highly dangerous activity. We call this *compartmentalization,* and it is dissociation's first cousin.[10]

Boys should have the experience of reading about boys and men who are sensitive, caring, expressive, and nurturing, just as girls should have the experience of reading about girls and women who are adventurous, courageous risk takers (see Figures 3.1 and 3.2).

Figure 3.1 In Karen Romano Young's *The Beetle and Me: A Love Story,* Daisy defies female stereotypes by fixing cars.

Figure 3.2 In *Allie's Basketball Dream* by Barbara E. Barber and illustrated by Darryl Ligasan, Allie moves toward her dream of becoming a professional basketball player.

At the end of Mem Fox's picture storybook, *Tough Boris* (see Figure 3.3), children see a pirate cry over the loss of his parrot. In Laurie Brooks's play, *Devon's Hurt,* a boy meaningfully works through his desire to separate himself from his feelings to a place of wholeness and integration. Both girls and boys benefit from literature that encourages a rich emotional life (see Figure 3.4). Mem Fox asks,

> Boys can do anything . . . and be anything, and feel anything. . . . Why is it, then, that they aren't allowed to cry? Why is it that ballet dancing and painting are seen as less fit occupations for them than being machine gunners, for example, or baseball players? Why should they live, as most of them do, with the idea that it is, in the main, *their* crippling responsibility to provide for a family when they become grown-up boys? Don't boys and men need liberating, too? Could children's literature be partly to blame for trapping males in a frightful emotional prison and demanding intolerable social expectations of them?[11]

Although there has been improvement in the field of children's literature, content analyses of the most prestigious awards, the Caldecott and Newbery Medals, reveal that even in these fine, well-written books, stereotypes of men and women prevail.[12] Newberys and Caldecotts can and should be used, but teachers can help children see their limitations, and can seek other award-winning books.

Figure 3.3 Mem Fox's *Tough Boris* tells the story of a fearless pirate who cries when his parrot dies. Illustrated in watercolors by Kathryn Brown.

The billions of dollars spent annually on advertising demonstrate that advertisers, despite their protestations to the contrary, know that they can shape and thus influence spending habits around what is considered beautiful. Donnarae MacCann writes,

> A society's conceptions of beauty are among its most enduring features. They do not lend themselves to easy revision, even when history has moved into a new phase and a people's traditional aesthetic is glaringly inadequate. A multicultural approach to aesthetics is particularly imperative when intense struggles are underway between cultural groups. The dominant power is in a position to produce an array of artistic objects in support of its cause. It has the means for controlling the gatekeeping and tastemaking institutions and can indoctrinate its population with self-serving conceptions of beauty.[13]

With computer retouching, advertisers promote a standard of beauty that does not exist.[14]

Ethnic groups outside the mainstream can lead us toward a broader, more attainable, inclusive aesthetic. For instance, in his books, Jan Carew says, "I attempt to bring back a kind of African Aesthetic about age and beauty to counter the Western idea that all beauty must be young, have a toothpaste smile, high bosom, long legs, blonde hair. When you get older they fade you out. Whereas in Africa the tradition was for the aged

Figure 3.4 In 1972, Charlotte Zolotow's *William's Doll,* illustrated by William Pène du Bois, broke away from the stereotypical thinking about toys for boys.

to acquire more status and respect."[15] When evaluating and selecting children's literature, attributes like these can be considered.

3.5 Diversity and Children's Literature

For much of its history, children's literature has been primarily white authors writing for white children. Some exceptions occurred during the Harlem Renaissance when Arna Bontemps and others wrote books that had African Americans as protagonists; however, these books were not usually published by mainstream publishers and quickly went out of print. In 1920 the great sociologist and intellectual W. E. B. Du Bois started a monthly magazine for "children of the sun" called *The Brownies' Book.* In 1932 Laura Adams Armer won the Newbery for her book *Waterless Mountain,* about the Navajo with whom she lived and worked. Augusta Baker, storyteller and coordinator of children's services at the New York Public Library, shaped the list "Books about Negro Life for Children," which appeared in 1946 and continued until 1961. Part of the problem stemmed from publishers who were reluctant to publish books by unknown authors or by authors of color; commercial success could not be guaranteed.

In the 1950s and 1960s, Ezra Jack Keats and Don Freeman challenged the status quo by writing picture storybooks that had children of color as protagonists. Other white authors followed their lead; however, some of these books were *universal*—that is, they could have applied to either a white child or a child of color. Peter, an African American boy in *The Snowy Day*, could easily be replaced by a white child (see Figure 3.5).

In 1965, Nancy Larrick published a seminal article, "The All-White World of Children's Books," in which she directed the public's attention to the near invisibility of children of color. Despite Larrick's wake-up call, almost forty years later, people of color are still underrepresented in children's literature.

European Americans in the United States have historically been the dominant group. With the exception of the indigenous peoples who first inhabited this country, all of us have come from somewhere else. Yet despite the immigrant status most of us (or our ancestors) share, many groups remain underrepresented. These groups are generally African Americans or persons of African-Caribbean descent, American Indians, Asian Americans, Asian Pacific Americans (including Vietnamese, Thais, Laotians, Cambodians, Filipinos, Japanese, Chinese, and Koreans), Pacific Islanders (Native Hawaiians and those from other islands in the Pacific), and Latino Americans, an umbrella term for those of Cuban, Puerto Rican, Caribbean, and Central and South American origins (areas originally colonized by Spain). Because of their large population and distinctiveness,

Figure 3.5 John Steptoe's 1969 publication of *Stevie* was a seminal contribution to children's literature because of its authentic depiction of an African American protagonist.

Mexican Americans have resisted the label *Latino,* choosing *Mexicano* instead. As Beverly Tatum helpfully points out in her book on race, "[T]hese groups are not mutually exclusive. . . . The politics of racial categorization has served to create artificial boundaries between groups with shared ancestry."[17] Intermarriage among many ethnic groups has created a large population that can claim several ethnic heritages.

Some groups came to this country voluntarily; others are involuntary immigrants—that is, they were coerced into coming to America.[18] Examples are the transportation through the Middle Passage of millions of Africans, who were then sold as slaves in the Americas. Europeans conquered the indigenous peoples of the Americas, whose estimated numbers at the time of Columbus could have been ten to twelve million in North America alone.[19] Mexican Americans, too, were conquered, and Puerto Ricans and Filipinos were annexed under colonialization.

The literature of these groups has not had adequate representation in the elementary curriculum. Two recent surveys conducted by the National Education Association have alarming results: The top 100 favorite books used most by teachers in 1999 contain less than ten multicultural books, written mostly by cultural outsiders (those who do not share the same cultural group about whom they write), and there are only three authors of color. The list also includes several books that have been heartily criticized because of their demeaning treatment of people of color—for example, Lynn Reid Banks's *The Indian in the Cupboard.* Despite the fact that there are 6.3 million Latino children in this country, there is not one book representative of this group.[20] One year later, the top 100 favorite books named by children had similar results. There are only four books that could be considered multicultural, and none are by an author of color.[21] It is not surprising children's choices reflect, to some extent, teachers' choices; teachers often introduce children to literature or decide what fills classroom libraries. It is not surprising that elementary teachers continue to omit multicultural literature. Reviewing the textbooks that teach the teachers shows that, despite the efforts of some textbook writers, multicultural literature is still woefully underutilized in current children's literature and reading and language arts textbooks—even textbooks published in the twenty-first century.[22]

One effect of underrepresentation is that these groups become invisible. The anthropologist Edward Hall wrote, "Culture hides more than it reveals and what it hides, it hides most effectively from its own participants."[23] To the dominant groups, the invisibility of other groups is hidden and seems natural. Privileged groups rarely recognize the extent to which their advantages exist at the expense of others who are, as critical theorist Peter McLaren puts, "detachable appendages of other people's dreams and desires."[24]

Schools may bring out some multicultural literature during Hispanic History Month in October or Black History Month in February. Unfortunately, this emphasis lasts only for a month. The great abolitionist, Sojourner Truth, said in the nineteenth century: "We have been a source of wealth to this republic. . . . Our nerves and sinews, our tears and blood have been sacrificed on the altar of this nation's avarice. Our unpaid labor has been a stepping stone to its financial success. Some of its dividends must surely be ours."[25] Surely one of those dividends is having ample books by and about African Americans throughout the year and not only during Black History Month. There should also be books by and about Latinos and American Indians and Asian Americans in *all* classrooms from September to June, not just during designated months.

To achieve this infusion of multicultural literature we must learn to see invisible groups. In the early 1990s, of the 5,000 children's books published each year, between one and two percent featured African Americans.[26] Of the 40,000 children's books published between 1983 and 1991, just nineteen featured Puerto Ricans, the second largest Latino group in the country. There are about fourteen million Mexican Americans, who are also underrepresented in children's literature.[27] In the year 2000, of the approximately 5,500 published children's books, ninety-six were by African Americans, fifty-four were by and about Asian Pacific and Asian Pacific Americans, thirty-nine were by and about American Indians, and forty-two were by and about Latinos.[28]

Lack of representation and visibility are of continuing concern in the Asian Pacific American community. This group also often experiences the forever foreign syndrome, meaning that no matter how many generations their families have lived in the United States, people assume they have just arrived.[29] Confirmation of one's existence is one of the most humanizing experiences; lack of confirmation of one's existence is one of the most dehumanizing experiences. Unequivocally, all our children deserve visibility and affirmation.

We have a long way to go. In 1999, a teacher in Illinois, when previewing a standardized test her students were about to take, was pleased to see a selection from Ann Cameron's *More Stories Julian Tells*. Because her class had been using the book and thus were familiar with it, the teacher felt confident that her students would do well on the test. However, as the test taking began, one youngster, deeply upset, pointed out that the illustrations in the test were of a *white* child, not an African American child. The illustrator for the test company had altered the illustrations from the original. When the teacher reported this to the test makers, it was revealed that more than 100 adults had reviewed the test before publication, and not one had noticed the change of an African American child in Cameron's books to a white child on the test.[30] Although it must be noted that Cameron's books, like Keats's, are universal rather than culturally specific, the degree of invisibility of children of color demonstrated in this incident is appalling.

Finding authentic books about American Indians poses a different set of problems from that of other ethnic groups outside the mainstream. Mary Gloyne Byler writes, "If anything, there are too many children's books about American Indians. There are too many books featuring painted, whooping befeathered Indians closing in on too many forts, maliciously attacking 'peaceful' settlers or simply leering menacingly from the background; too many books in which white benevolence is the only thing that saves the day for the incompetent, childlike Indian . . . "[31] In an analysis of 600 children's books about native people, Byler mostly found "depersonalization, ridicule, derision, inauthenticity and stereotyping."[32] Learning to weed out demeaning images of American Indians can be a challenge for teachers, who must realize that there are more biased books than books that treat American Indians with dignity and respect.[33]

Another problem is that of amalgamating about 400 recognized Indian nations, each with its own unique culture, into one generic group. Out of respect, writers whose subjects are members of various ethnic groups should aim for cultural specificity and authenticity. Imagine an American Indian writing and illustrating a picture book that featured a European American character simultaneously wearing a Scottish kilt, French beret, and Spanish bolero.[34] This example shows how silly—and insulting—white artists seem to American Indians when they depict a Navajo in Great Plains regalia.

When selecting literature, Abenaki author Joseph Bruchac suggests we ask whether the book debases or lessens the humanity of others. He writes, "Some of the popular stories of the American frontier in which bloodthirsty Indians are killed as if they were vermin or the tales told in the pre-Civil War South of lazy and ignorant African slaves are strikingly similar to the Nazi portrayal of the Jews. Ethnic caricatures and sexist 'humor' are further examples of the way certain stories can debase and lessen the humanity of others."[35] The impact of stereotypes on children is undeniable. Tatum cites a study carried out by one of her students. A group of three- and four-year-olds who had no first-hand experience with American Indians were asked to draw pictures of American Indians. They complied, and the result was feathers, knives, and tomahawks. "Though I would not describe three-year-olds as prejudiced," writes Tatum, "the stereotypes to which they have been exposed become the foundation for the adult prejudices so many of us have."[36]

Coupled with the legacy of the Indian Boarding School experience, which lasted from 1870 to the early 1930s, this exploitation of the Indian in literature has made schools seem inhospitable to Indian children. Multicultural educator Gary Howard writes, "Although most Indian families want the same positive educational outcomes for their children as other parents do, the emotional legacy of cultural genocide is not easily overcome. . . . it will take much work on the part of educators to regain their trust."[37]

Another aspect to consider when choosing children's books is how a book about one marginalized group refers to another marginalized group. How is the second group presented? Caroline Binch Hoffman's *Amazing Grace* depicts a black girl who, defying the odds, plays the role of Peter Pan. There is a scene, however, when Grace stereotypes behavior of an American Indian. An African American teacher of children's literature, Violet J. Harris, "decided to 'give it up' as a favorite because she believes it wrong to celebrate one culture at the expense of another."[38]

Children with Disabilities and Social Diversity

Another group that tends to be invisible is the disabled. About one in ten children have a disability at some time during their school careers. Progress has been made in the field of children's literature during the last few decades in picturing more and more disabled children, although gaps remain. There are few books about children of color who have disabilities. Children in regular education must be helped to see that children with disabilities did nothing to deserve their situation—a concept known as *immanent justice*—and that a disability is not contagious. All children must be helped to see that disabled children also have many abilities that contribute to their families and communities.

Literature collections should reflect the number of children growing up in nontraditional families. More than 100 years ago, Johanna Spyri's *Heidi* depicted families in which there was not a single nuclear family arrangement (father, mother, brother, and sister). Heidi, an orphan, lived first with her aunt, then with her grandfather, and then with Clara, whose mother had died and whose father was often away. Her friend on the Alps, Peter, whose father had died, lived with his mother and grandmother.[39] Throughout history, children have had to find, because of circumstances beyond their control, family and a sense of belonging with people who were not their birth parents. Literature can help children see that a sense of family can emerge from all kinds of arrangements. Louise Erdrich's *The Birchbark House,* a work of historical fiction about the Ojibwas, movingly portrays a child who, after her own parents die from the smallpox epidemic that killed many American Indians, is lovingly raised by another family and other tribal members.

3.6 Teaching with Diverse Literature

All children need to see themselves in literature and to learn about the contributions their ancestors have made. Too often, however, teachers do not have this knowledge base because the textbooks from which most of us learned when we were children included little about the history and contributions of people of color. In the movie *Stand and Deliver,* based on a true story, Jaime Escalante's knowledge of the Latino influence on mathematics became a powerful motivator for adolescents in the Los Angeles barrio. Baffling the authorities, these youngsters achieved passing scores on the Advanced Placement calculus exam. Those of us who are teachers were ourselves often not taught—because of invisibility—about these contributions and so will have to seek this information continually for ourselves. Kathleen T. Horning and Ginny Moore Kruse of the University of Wisconsin write, "It is now clear that a devastating lack of information and insight about cultures (other than their own and the dominant culture) was provided to professionals through formal education or through incidental exposure to the images within society."[40] Those who enter the teaching profession will have to take the initiative to make up for that deficiency, seeking out multicultural and international books. Vivian Yenika–Agbaw from Cameroon especially asks Americans to consider the difficulties African authors and illustrators have getting published and to try, when possible, to support their work. Major publishing houses tend to publish known authors, unwilling to risk publishing new artists.[41]

Teachers, young and old, often have no idea how much authority children vest in them. If teachers do not choose literature in which people of color, children who come from nontraditional families, and children who have disabilities appear in respectful ways, these groups are more likely to internalize this to mean that *something is wrong with who they are,* rather than question the teacher's judgment and biases, which are often unconscious. Regardless of whether you realize it, when you are a teacher you are an extremely powerful person in children's lives. Seymour Sarason makes the very important point that there is no evidence that university professors have greater influence or make greater contributions to students' development than elementary school teachers.[42] Even though K–6 teachers do not—currently—have the status of professors, if such studies were done, we might find that elementary school teachers have *more* power and influence on children than any other group of educators. Inspiring, knowledgeable, and caring teachers have the potential to help students in positive ways that last a lifetime. Uninspired, uncaring, and unknowledgeable teachers have the capacity to bring lasting harm.

The National Research Council's Committee on the Prevention of Reading Difficulties in Young Children defines one of society's greatest challenges: "Failure to learn to read adequately for continued school success is much more likely among poor children, among nonwhite children, and among nonnative speakers of English. Achieving educational equity requires an understanding of why these disparities exist and efforts to redress them."[43] Greater visibility in the curriculum is part of the solution, with a caution that it is a mistake to assume that large groups of people who share the same ethnicity are homogeneous. The many areas of disagreement within European American groups are an example of just how heterogeneous people who share the same skin color can be.

Based on extensive research, reading experts have reached a consensus on at least some of the features of excellent reading instruction. Good teachers of reading know that they must explicitly teach

- About schema—Children use prior knowledge and background to make connections with what they read.
- About visualizing—Good readers visually imagine as they read, creating pictures in their minds (like a movie).
- About inferring, asking questions, synthesizing, and discriminating between what is important and what is not.[44]

If children of color do not see themselves in books, they will not have as many opportunities as white children to utilize these strategies. *Max Found Two Sticks* by Brian Pinkney is more likely to activate the prior knowledge of an African American child to a far greater degree than *Family Farm* by Thomas Locker. Should both books be shared with children? Of course. Currently, however, because multicultural books are underutilized, white children have many more opportunities to activate their prior knowledge and to develop competence in other reading strategies than children of color.

3.7 *Guidelines for Selection*

When analyzing the classroom library for visibility and voice for those who have often been invisible and voiceless, today's teachers must listen to cultural insiders' perspectives. I have developed the following questions from the books and articles listed found in the For Further Reading section of this chapter. I encourage you to familiarize yourself with at least some of these works.[45] Recalling the classroom-as-library metaphor used earlier, apply the following questions for building a classroom collection:

Thinking about Children of Color
- Is there a plethora of books that represent racial, ethnic, and cultural diversity?
- Are there people or children of color who are the protagonists? Or do a few children of color appear as tokens, hanging mostly in the background?
- Are whites mostly or all of the characters?
- Are there books in which children and adults of varying races and ethnicities work together?
- Are people of color portrayed as unique individuals or are they portrayed stereotypically?

- Are they dependent on white individuals or do they act independently?
- Are they portrayed on equal footing with those of the white race?
- Are people of color portrayed in urban, suburban, and rural settings?
- Do people of color emerge from every socioeconomic class?
- If the standard code of English is not used, is the code authentic and respectful?
- Is understanding and respect conveyed in the tone of the book?

Thinking about African Americans or African Caribbeans

- Are they confined to the realms of sports and music?
- Do the books depict slavery only, without recognizing the many positive accomplishments in a variety of endeavors?

Thinking about Asian Americans

- Are they portrayed as all looking alike, as in Claire Bishop's *The Five Chinese Brothers*? (Avoid this.)
- Are they portrayed as being yellow skinned, as in Marjorie Flack's *The Story about Ping*? (Avoid this.)
- If they are successful, why are they successful? Does success depend on accepting the status quo?
- Are they stereotyped as super human beings?
- Are the varied Asian Pacific cultures represented and distinct: Chinese, Japanese, Vietnamese, Korean, Cambodian, and others?

Thinking about Latinos

- Are the Puerto Ricans portrayed as living in New York City only?
- Are Latinos stereotyped as illegal immigrants?
- Is the diversity of this group represented, including Spain, Central and South America, Mexico, the Dominican Republic, Puerto Rico, and Cuba?

Thinking about American Indians

- Are offensive terms like *squaw, papoose, savage,* or *buck* used?
- Do they have human names or are they compared with members of the animal kingdom?
- Is the uniqueness of the individual or nation portrayed? Or are Indian nations represented generically—like putting a European character into French, Scottish, and Spanish clothing?
- Is the nation specified?
- Are most of the books folkloric? If so, seek a balance; it is important for today's children to see American Indians in contemporary settings.

Gender and Social Diversity

- Are there girls and women pictured as being brave, taking risks, and having adventures?
- Are there boys and men pictured in roles in which they are kind, nurturing, and sensitive, valuing relationships with others?
- Are nontraditional lifestyles represented?
- Are there children with disabilities?

These questions are a place to begin. However, simply having more literature about people of color, and balancing representation of boys and girls and nontraditional families is not all there is to the matter. A book still must have literary value.

3.8 *Literary Elements and Criticism*

"You can't harangue people," says Hazel Rochman, "into reading, however worthy the cause. There has to be the pleasure of story, character, passionate conflict, and language if you're going to grab readers and make them want to read on."[46] When evaluating literature, knowledge of the following elements serve as a basis: *plot, character, theme, setting,* and *style.* It is the unified and harmonious integration of these elements that leave readers with the sense that they have encountered a literary work of art.

Style reflects the artistic choices of the author—*how* the writer tells the story. *Setting* is the environment authors choose to place characters whose stories unfold. Because they were first introduced in western aesthetics in Aristotle's *Poetics,* a work on drama, *plot, character,* and *theme* are discussed in greater detail in Chapter 6.4 on drama. Literary critics in the western tradition have used Aristotle's seminal work to evaluate much of literature.

However, other traditions value different characteristics. For example, the plot structures of Asian Pacific literature, unlike the linear structure in western literature, are often *episodic* and do not have a definable beginning, middle, and end. Similarly, an American Indian story may begin in the present, leap back into the past (*flashback*), go forward again, then backward, and finally, "having made a complete circle, [end] at its own beginning."[47] Aesthetics are culturally bound. Western aesthetics find beauty in places other traditions do not; other aesthetic traditions may find beauty elsewhere. Describing Japanese aesthetics, Elaine Aoki makes the contrast: "[The Western narrative . . . is about overcoming, changing, hope, and promise while the Japanese narrative is about conforming, renewing and continuing."[48] Teachers ought to know of several approaches to aesthetics.

Two other aspects of which to be aware when evaluating literature are *sentimentality* and *sensationalism. Sentimentality* disproportionately exaggerates feeling in a stock or trite manner, often purposefully aiming to manipulate readers' emotions. This manipulation is sometimes tied to commercial outcomes—influencing consumers to buy certain products. *Sensationalism* in literature occurs when an author includes gratuitous violence or so crowds a plot with action and incident that it becomes too contrived or too implausible.

When evaluating fiction, the following general questions can be posed:

- Are the characters both memorable and consistent? Is character development believable?
- Does the plot, intertwined with character development, make sense?
- Is the setting appropriate for the plot and characters?
- Is the style of the author, in diction (word choice) and scope, unique and illuminating?

Chapter 8.7, on informational books, contains further criteria for evaluating nonfiction. When looking over your classroom collection, ask the following questions:

- Are there books that pose questions to readers?
- Are there books that widen the interpretive frames of children?
- Are there books that give them alternate ways of making sense of the world?
- Are there books that appeal to thought, emotions, and the senses?
- Would the books be enjoyable to reread for both adults and children?

3.9 Cultural Studies and Children's Literature

Analyzing children's literature from the perspective of cultural studies requires that we look at oppression and marginalization of groups of people and that dominant groups become aware of their privileges. Teachers who assume these responsibilities become agents of change, helping to create a more just society. Based on Clar Doyle's work in drama education, the following questions can be asked of most literature:

- What values and beliefs are assumed and/or promoted?
- What symbols and images are being used for what purpose?
- What cultures are being affirmed or ridiculed? Whose voices are not heard?
- Whose truth is represented?
- Whose interests are served?[49]

With questions like these, art becomes a space for changing societal injustices.

The immensely popular rags-to-riches novels of the late nineteenth and early twentieth centuries promoted the values and interests of the robber barons, who assumed that anyone (the poorer, the better) in a meritocracy could attain great wealth by persistence and hard work. Andrew Carnegie, most noticeably, eventually recanted this belief. Rags-to-riches oversimplified the causes of the accumulation of wealth, minimizing the complexity of poverty. This is not to say that persistence and hard work are not necessary; however, there are many who work hard and persist but, because of the color of their skin or because of their gender, do not reap the rewards that others do.

Seeing the positive implications of yet another theory of literature, Harris observes that it can enhance aesthetic approaches, "Literature is not immune to the intellectual currents of the day. Consider, for example, how exhilarating it was to discover that a poem or text could have multiple meanings. This shift in thought occurred gradually. Similarly, one might expect the eventual acceptance of criticism that emphasizes racial or ethnic identity, gender relations, or class issues."[50]

3.10 Conclusion

As grounding for culturally responsive teaching, explore a wide variety of multicultural children's literature, thus expanding your own knowledge base. To meet an NCATE standard, teachers "are . . . familiar with, able to use, and recommend to students many reading materials based on different topics, themes, and a variety of situations and consisting of different types. . . ."[51] Gary Howard writes,

> If we as white educators are not deeply moved and transformed, there is little hope that anything else will significantly shift. We must assume that we will be changed in the process of engagement and dialogue. We cannot help our students overcome the negative repercussions of past and present racial dominance if we have not unraveled the remnants of dominance that still lingers in our minds, hearts, and habits. As Malcolm X reminded us years ago, 'We can't teach what we don't know, and we can't lead where we won't go.'[52]

Using the resources found at the end of this chapter and in Appendix C, go beyond the familiar. Then you can lead where you have been and teach what you know. As you develop expertise, share it with your colleagues—most of them have entered the helping profession because they want to help all children.

All teachers are change agents. As Michael Fullan, a scholar of educational leadership, suggests, change is "too important to leave to the experts."[53] Part of your role, as an agent of change, may be retiring books that are culturally insensitive, inauthentic, and demeaning. Or using them with upper grade elementary children to discuss why such books are offensive.

When answering the question, "What should our research agenda for reading teacher education look like?" in the new millennium, reading educators James Hoffman and P. David Pearson write,

> *Place issues of diversity at the top of our priority list for research* . . . it may be the most challenging issue we face, but it is also the most important. It is simply unacceptable that a vastly disproportionate number of minority students fail to learn to read. . . . It is even more unacceptable that so many majority teachers possess so little knowledge about cultural and linguistic diversity. We may not be the sole source of the problem, but we can and must become part of the solution.[54]

To remain ignorant of other cultures and their experiences in this country is a "luxury," says Howard, white people have that people of color do not have.[55] High-quality, multi-faceted books that appeal to all kinds of interests must be made available in the classroom. Teachers share with the family the responsibility—and the remarkable opportunity—of introducing children to their very first experiences in literature. Only the best is good enough.

Suggested Activities

1. Inquire at bookstores in your area: Do they offer a discount for educators? Do they give assistance to teachers who are beginning to develop their own collections of children's literature?

2. Check with national teachers' organizations and regional branches of these organizations. Are there grants for which you can apply to update and expand classroom libraries?

3. Imagine you are a group of archaeologists 2,000 years in the future. You have come upon an archaeological site, it just so happens, in your class. Examine literature and other forms of contemporary print and nonprint media (newspapers, children's magazines, children's games, comics, videos, video games, radio stations, and so on).

   Describe the artifacts: How many male and female characters can you find? How many characters of color? What roles do you see the male and female characters taking? What roles do the characters of color have?

   Analyze the society on which you have stumbled. Based on the artifacts, how many men and how many women would you estimate lived in this society? How many people of color would you estimate lived in this society? What were the prescribed roles for men, women, and people of color?

for further reading

Bishop, Rudine Sims, ed. 1994. *Kaleidoscope: A Multicultural Booklist for Grades K–8.* Urbana, IL: National Council of Teachers of English.

Corliss, Julia Candace. 1998. *Crossing Borders with Literature of Diversity.* Norwood, MA: Christopher-Gordon.

Council on Interracial Books for Children. 1980. *Guidelines for Selecting Bias-Free Textbooks and Storybooks.* New York: Council on Interracial Books for Children.

Day, Frances Ann. 1999. *Multicultural Voices in Contemporary Literature: A Resource for Teachers.* Rev. ed. Portsmouth, NH: Heinemann.

——. 1997. *Latina and Latino Voices in Literature for Children and Teenagers.* Portsmouth, NH: Heinemann.

De Cortés, Oalia Garza. 1999. "Justice in the Publishing Field: A Look at Multicultural Awards for Children." *MultiCultural Review,* June: 42–48.

Freeman, Evelyn B., and Barbara A. Lehman. 2001. *Global Perspectives in Children's Literature.* Boston: Allyn and Bacon.

Harris, Violet J., ed. 1997. *Using Multiethnic Literature in the K–8 Classroom.* Norwood, MA: Christopher-Gordon.

——. 1993. *Teaching Multicultural Literature in Grades K–8.* Norwood, MA: Christopher-Gordon.

Hirschfelder, Arlene, Paulette Fairbanks Molin, and Yvonne Wakin. 1999. *American Indian Stereotypes in the World of Children: A Reader and Bibliography.* 2nd ed. Lanham, MD: Scarecrow Press.

Li, Marjorie H., and Peter Li, comps., eds. 1990. *Understanding Asian Americans: A Curriculum Resource Guide.* New York: Neal-Schuman Publishers.

Lindgren, Merri V., ed. 1991. *The Multicolored Mirror: Cultural Substance in Literature for Children and Young Adults.* Fort Atkinson, WI: Highsmith.

Miller–Lachmann, Lyn. 1992. *Our Family, Our Friends, Our World: An Annotated Guide to Significant Multicultural Books for Children and Teenagers.* New Providence, NJ: R. R. Bowker.

Odean, Kathleen. 1998. *Great Books for Boys: More Than 600 Books for Boys 2 to 14.* New York: Ballantine.

———. 1997. *Great Books for Girls: More Than 600 Books to Inspire Today's Girls and Tomorrow's Women.* New York: Ballantine.

Rand, Donna, and Toni Trent Parker. 2001. *Black Books Galore! Guide to Great African American Children's Books about Girls.* New York: Wiley.

———. 2001. *Black Books Galore! Guide to Great African American Children's Books about Boys.* New York: Wiley.

Rand, Donna, Toni Trent Parker, and Sheila Foster. 1999. *Black Books Galore! Guide to Great African American Children's Books.* Stamford: Wiley.

Rochman, Hazel. 1993. *Against Borders: Promoting Books for a Multicultural World.* Chicago: American Library Association.

Slapin, Beverly, and Doris Seale, eds. 1998 [1987]. *Through Indian Eyes: The Native Experience in Books for Children.* Los Angeles, CA: University of California.

Smith, Henrietta M., ed. 1999. *The Coretta Scott King Awards Book: 1970–1999.* Chicago: American Library Association.

Stott, Jon C. 1995. *Native Americans in Children's Literature.* Phoenix, AZ: Oryx Press.

Tomlinson, Carl, ed. 1998. *Children's Books from Other Countries: United States Board on Books for Young People.* Lanham, MD: Scarecrow Press.

Young, Josephine Peyton, and William G. Brozo. 2001. "Boys Will Be Boys, or Will They? Literacy and Masculinities." *Reading Research Quarterly,* 36.3:316–325.

review journals for multicultural literature

How are busy, well-intentioned teachers to find high-quality multicultural literature for their students? How do you evaluate new books? How do you keep up with an ever-changing knowledge base? Because multicultural reviews are sometimes not published as frequently as other general sources, it is best to wait for a year and read several reviews before buying a book that will become part of a permanent classroom collection. Although not all reviewers have to share the same ethnicity as an author of a book, having cultural sensitivity is a prerequisite. See the discussion in Chapter 9.6 on the controversial reviews of *My Heart Is on the Ground* by Ann Rinaldi. Cultural outsiders gave it glowing reviews; cultural insiders reviewed it negatively. The following are recommended sources for finding reviews of multicultural books. More review journals are listed in Appendix B.

Blackberry Express: All About African American's Children's Books Newsletter
Kids Cultural Books
PO Box 16822
Stamford, CT 06905
A new publication, *Blackberry* focuses on African Americans.

Bookbird
The Ohio State University at Mansfield
1680 University Drive
Mansfield, OH 44906
This is an excellent source for international books.

Booklist
American Library Association
50 E. Huron Street
Chicago, IL 60611

Booklist seeks out multiethnic reviewers and has published during the last several years reviews by African Americans, American Indians, Asian Americans, Latin Americans, Arab Americans, and Jewish Americans. Hazel Rochman, who has considerable expertise in multicultural literature as the author of *Against Borders* is on staff. *Booklist* welcomes qualified reviewers of color.

MultiCultural Review
Greenwood Publishing Group, Inc.
The Goldman Group
14497 N. Dale, Mabry Highway, Suite 205-N
Tampa, FL 33618
www.mcreview.com
Reviewers for *MultiCultural Review* include librarians, teachers, academics, and writers of children's books. About half the reviewers are cultural insiders, and all reviewers have expertise in the areas that they review.

The New Advocate
1502 Providence Highway, Suite 12
Norwood, MA 02062
www.ed.arizona.edu/DEPARTS/LRC_old/
advoc.htm
This is a scholarly journal that also reviews books. Violet J. Harris is the editor, with Rosalinda Barrera and Sarah McCarthy as associate editors—a multiethnic team.

Skipping Stones
PO Box 3939
Eugene, OR 97403
www.efn.org/ ~ skipping/honors_98.htm
Skipping Stones is a multicultural magazine for children who make contributions along with parents, teachers, and librarians. The staff is ethnically diverse and each book is reviewed by several reviewers before a review is published. Great care is taken to consult cultural insiders. The summer issue includes the year's best multicultural and environmental books and teaching resources.

Other sources for multicultural books are

Cooperative Children's Book Center
CCBC Choices
Friends of the CCBC, Inc.
Box 5288
Madison, WI 53705

and

Children's Book Council
12 West 37th Steet, 2nd floor
New York, NY 10018-7480
Telephone: 212-966-1990
Fax: 212-966-2073
www.cbcbooks.org
Email: features@cbcbooks.org

multicultural websites

Africa Access:
 filemaker.mcps.k12.md.us/aad/

American Indians:
 Oyate, www.oyate.org
 www.nativechild.com/resources.html

Anti-Defamation League:
 www.adl.org

Disabilities:
 www.kidsource.com/NICHCY/literature.html

Gallaudet (hearing impaired):
 www.aslp.gallaudet.edu/as;[wel/business/

Japanese Americans Citizens League:
 www.jacl.org

Kids cultural books:
 www.blackbooksgalore.com

Latino bibliography:
 www.latino.sscnet.ucla.edu/Latino_
 Bibliography.html

Notable Books for a Global Society, International Reading Association's Children's Literature and Special Interest Group:

www.csulb.edu/org/childrens-lit/proj/nbgs.html

Pacific children's literature website:

www.uog.edu/cor/paclit/index.htm

The Tomás Rivera Mexican American Children's Book Award:

www.education.swt.edu/rivera/mainpage.html

University of Pittsburgh:

www.pitt.edu/ ~ lmitten/ailabib.htm

University of Wisconsin:

www.soemadison.wisc.edu/ccbc

For a synthesis of websites on children's literature, see www.indiana.edu/ ~ eric_rec/comatt/childlit.html

m u l t i c u l t u r a l   a w a r d s

African Studies Association Children's Book Award:

www.uflib.ufl.edu/cm/africana/award.htm

Children's Africana Book Awards:

www.africanstudies.org/asa_childbook.html

Consortium of Latin American Studies Programs (CLASP) Americas Award for Children's and Young Adult Literature:

www.uwm.edu/Dept/CLA/final97.htm

Coretta Scott King Award and Honor Books:

www.ala.org/srrt/csking/html/

Lee & Low Books, New Voices Award:

www.leeandlow.com/editorial/voices.html

Pura Belpré Award:

www.ala.org/alsc/belpre.html

Skipping Stones Award:

www.efn.org/ ~ skipping/

p u b l i s h e r s   o f   m u l t i c u l t u r a l   c h i l d r e n ' s   b o o k s

For small presses owned and operated by people of color, see www.soemadison.wisc.edu/ccbc/pclist.htm

See also www.lights.com/publisher/ for listings of most publishers.

n o t e s

1. Quoted in Russell Freedman, *Eleanor Roosevelt: A Life of Discovery* (New York: Clarion, 1993), p. 128.
2. Constance Borab, "Freeing the Female Voice." In: *Teaching African American Literature: Theory and Practice,* Maryemma Graham, Sharon Pineault–Burke, and Marianna White Davis, eds. (New York: Routledge, 1998), p. 87.
3. www.soemadison.wisc.edu/ccbc
4. Jerry Mander, *In the Absence of the Sacred: The Failure of Technology and the Survival of the Indian Nations* (San Francisco: Sierra Club Books, 1991), p. 84.
5. Joel Taxel, "Cultural Politics and Writing for Young People." In: *Battling Dragons: Issues and Controversy*

in *Children's Literature,* Susan Lehr, ed. (Portsmouth, NH: Heinemann, 1995), p. 164.
6. Mary Pipher, *Reviving Ophelia: Saving the Selves of Adolescent Girls* (New York: Ballantine Books, 1994), p. 184.
7. George Gerbner, *Television as a Shaper of Cultural Values: "Telling All the Stories,"* Paper presented at the Media, Children and Culture Conference, Quinnipiac University, Hamden, CT, 21 October 2000.
8. Lenore Weitzman, Deborah Eifler, Elizabeth Hokada, and Catherine Ross, "Sex-Role Socialization in Picture Books for Preschool Children," *American Journal of Sociology* 77 (1972): 1125–1150.

9. Eugene F. Provenzo, *Video Kids: Making Sense of Nintendo* (Cambridge, MA: Harvard University Press, 1991), p. 61.

10. James Garbarino, *Lost Boys: Why Our Sons Turn Violent and How We Can Save Them* (New York: Simon & Schuster, 1999), p. 86.

11. Mem Fox, *Radical Reflections: Passionate Opinions on Teaching, Learning, and Living* (San Diego: Harcourt Brace, 1993), p. 153.

12. Shirley B. Ernst, "Gender Issues in Books for Young Children." In: *Battling Dragons: Issues and Controversy in Children's Literature,* Susan Lehr, ed. (Portsmouth, NH: Heinemann, 1995), p. 164. Nancy A. Schubert, "Sex-Role Stereotyping in Caldecott Award Books," *ERIC,* 1980 ED220870.

13. Donnarae MacCann, *White Supremacy in Children's Literature: Characterizations of African Americans, 1830–1900* (New York: Garland, 1998), p. 228.

14. Jean Kilbourne, *Effects of Advertising on Children and Adolescents,* Paper presented at the Media, Children and Culture Conference, Quinnipiac University, Hamden, CT, 21 October 2000.

15. Jan Carew, quoted in Maureen Wamer–Lewis, "Jan Carew Interviewed by Maureen Wamer–Lewis, Prague 1984," *Journal of West Indian Literature 2* (1987): 39.

16. Nancy Larrick, "The All-White World of Children's Books," *Saturday Review* (11 September 1965): 63–65, 84–85.

17. Beverly Daniels Tatum, *"Why Are All the Black Kids Sitting Together in the Cafeteria?" and Other Conversations about Race* (New York: Basic Books, 1999), p. 222.

18. John Ogbu, "Beyond Language: Ebonics, Proper English, and Identity in a Black-American Speech Community," *American Educational Research Journal, 36.2* (1999): 153.

19. James W. Loewenn, *Lies My Teacher Told Me: Everything Your American History Textbook Got Wrong* (New York: Simon and Schuster, 1995), p. 85.

20. "NEA Spotlights 100 Books to Grow On," *Reading Today: The Bimonthly Newspaper of the International Reading Association* (April/May 1999): 10.

21. "NEA Poll Spotlights Kids' Favorite Books," *Reading Today: The Bimonthly Newspaper of the International Reading Association* (April/May 2000): 14.

22. Jane M. Gangi, *Forty Years After Civil Rights: A Look at Ethnicity in Children's Literature.* Paper presented at "Color, Hair, and Bone—The Persistence of Race into the 21st Century," Bucknell University, Lewisburg, PA, 27 September 2002.

23. Edward Hall, *The Silent Language* (Greenwich, CT: Fawcett Publications, 1966), p. 30.

24. Peter McLaren, "A Pedagogy of Possibility: Reflecting Upon Paulo Freire's Politics of Education," *Educational Researcher, 28.2* (1999): 50.

25. Patricia McKissack and Frederick McKissack, *Sojourner Truth: Ain't I A Woman?* (New York: Scholastic, 1992), p. 156.

26. Rudine Sims Bishop, "Evaluating Books by and about African Americans." In: *The Multicolored Mirror: Cultural Substance in Literature for Children and Young Adults,* Merri V. Lindgren, ed. (Fort Atkinson, WI: Highsmith Press, 1991), p. 34.

27. Rosalinda D. Barrera, Olga Liguori, and Loretta Salas, "Ideas a Literature Can Grow On: Key Insights for Enriching and Expanding Children's Literature About the Mexican-American Experience." In: *Teaching Multicultural Literature in Grades K–8,* Violet J. Harris, ed. (Norwood, MA: Christopher-Gordon, 1993), p. 207.

28. www.soemadison.wisc.edu/ccbc/pcstats.htm

29. Sandra S. Yamate, "Asian Pacific American Children's Literature: Expanding Perceptions About Who Americans Are." In: *Using Multiethnic Literature in the K–8 Classroom,* Violet J. Harris, ed. (Norwood, MA: Christopher-Gordon, 1997), p. 97.

30. Joan Slater, *Multicultural Matters: Writing for ALL Readers.* Paper presented at the Children's Literature and Reading Special Interest Group 3, International Reading Association 45th Annual Convention, "Reading the New World," Indianapolis, IN, 2 May 2000.

31. Mary Gloyne Byler, "Taking Another Look." In: *Through Indian Eyes: The Native Experience in Books for Children,* Beverly Slapin and Doris Seale, eds. (Philadelphia, PA: New Society Publishers, 1992), p. 81.

32. Robert B. Moore and Arlene B. Hirschfelder, "Feathers, Tomahawks and Tipis: A Study of Stereotyped 'Indian' Imagery in Children's Picture Books." In: *American Indian Stereotypes in the World of Children: A Reader and Bibliography,* 2nd ed., Arlene Hirschfelder, Paulette Fairbanks Molin, and Yvonne Wakin, eds. (Lanham, MD: Scarecrow Press, 1999), p. 58.

33. Donnarae MacCann, "Native Americans in Books for the Young." In: *Teaching Multicultural Literature in Grades K–8,* Violet J. Harris, ed. (Norwood, MA: Christopher-Gordon, 1993), p. 140.

34. Joseph Bruchac, as quoted by Pat Cummings, *Multicultural Matters: Writing for ALL Readers.* Paper

presented at Children's Literature and Reading, Special Interest Group 3, International Reading Association Annual Convention, Indianapolis, IN, 2 May 2000.

35. Joseph Bruchac, *Roots of Survival* (Golden, CO: Fulcrum, 1996), p. x.

36. Tatum, *"Why Are All the Black Kids Sitting Together in the Cafeteria?"*, p. 4.

37. Gary R. Howard, *We Can't Teach What We Don't Know: White Teachers, Multiracial Schools* (New York: Teachers College Press, 1999), p. 44.

38. Debbie Reese, "Native Americans in Children's Literature." In: *Using Multiethnic Literature in the K–8 Classroom,* Violet J. Harris, ed. (Norwood, MA: Christopher-Gordon, 1997), p. 161.

39. I thank Nancy Larocca for this insight.

40. Kathleen T. Horning and Ginny Moore Kruse, "Looking into the Mirror: Considerations behind the Reflections." In: *The Multicolored Mirror: Cultural Substance in Literature for Children and Young Adults,* Merri V. Lindgren, ed. (Fort Atkinson, WI: Highsmith, 1991), p. 7.

41. Vivian Yenika–Agbaw, *The Invisibility of African Children's Cultural Experiences, and the Publishing Industry.* Paper presented at the Children's Literature Association and the International Research Society for Children's Literature Joint Meeting, "Children's Literature and the *Fin de Siècle,"* Calgary, Canada, 6 July 1999.

42. Seymour Sarason, *Teaching as a Performing Art* (New York: Teachers College Press, 1999), p. 133.

43. Catherine E. Snow, M. Susan Burns, and Peg Griffin, eds. *Preventing Reading Difficulties in Young Children* (Washington, DC: National Academy Press, 1998), pp. 17–18.

44. Stephanie Harvey and Anne Goudvis, *Strategies That Work: Teaching Comprehension to Enhance Understanding* (Portland, ME: Stenhouse, 2000), pp. 10–12. Debbie Miller, *Reading with Meaning: Teaching Comprehension in the Primary Grades* (Portland, ME: Stenhouse, 2002), p. 8. Michael W. Smith and Jeffrey D. Wilhelm, *"Reading Don't Fix No Chevies": Literacy in the Lives of Young Men* (Portsmouth, NH: Heinemann, 2002), p. 86. Ellin Oliver Keene and Susan Zimmerman, *Mosaic of Thought: Teaching Comprehension in a Reader's Workshop* (Portsmouth, NH: Heinemann, 1997), pp. 22–23.

45. Although almost thirty years old, "10 Quick Ways to Analyze Children's Books for Racism and Sexism" by the Council on Interracial Books for Children is still pertinent. For a reprint of this brief article, see *Rethinking Our Classrooms: Teaching for Equity and Social Justice.* In: Bill Bigelow, Linda Christensen, Stan Karp, Barbara Miner, and Bob Peterson, eds. (Milwaukee, WI: Rethinking Schools, Ltd., 1994), pp. 14–15.

46. Hazel Rochman, *Against Borders: Promoting Books for a Multicultural World* (Chicago: American Library Association, 1993), p. 24.

47. Bruchac, *Roots of Survival,* p. 205.

48. Elaine Aoki, "Turning the Page: Asian Pacific American Children's Literature." In: *Teaching Multicultural Literature in Grades K–8,* Violet J. Harris, ed. (Norwood, MA: Christopher-Gordon, 1993), p. 118.

49. Clar Doyle, *Raising Curtains of Education: Drama as a Site for Critical Pedagogy* (Westport, CT: Bergin & Garvey, 1993), p. 30.

50. Violet J. Harris, "Applying Critical Theories to Children's Literature," *Theory into Practice, 38.*3 (1999): 153–154.

51. National Council for Accreditation of Teacher Education, *Program Standards for Elementary Teacher Preparation,* Supporting Explanation, 2b.

52. Howard, *We Can't Teach What We Don't Know,* p. 4.

53. Michael Fullan, *Change Forces: Probing the Depths of Educational Reform* (London: Falmer, 1993), p. 22.

54. James Hoffman and P. David Pearson, "Reading Teacher Education in the Next Millennium: What Your Grandmother's Teacher Didn't Know That Your Granddaughter's Teacher Should," *Reading Research Quarterly, 35.*1 (2000): 41.

55. Howard, *We Can't Teach What We Don't Know,* p. 59.

The Picture Book
Linking Word and Image

*I*t would please me if my pictures served in some measure to spur an interest in the magnificent art from which I have drawn.[1]

—PAUL ZELINSKY

4.1 Encountering Literature
through the visual arts

Materials Needed

Ten Black Dots by Donald Crews or *Bembo's Zoo: An Animal ABC Book* by Roberto de Vicq de Comptich or *The Alphabeast Book: An Abecedarium* by Dorothy Schmiderer

Blank paper

Markers

Dots, if Crews's book is used (available in most school supply sections in stores)

Read aloud *Ten Black Dots* by Donald Crews. Then, using paper, markers, and dots, create your own transformations. Modeling Crews's work, come up with your own ideas for the dots; whether you use one, or two, or ten is up to you.

Other books that provide a springboard into similar divergent undertakings are *Bembo's Zoo: An Animal ABC Book* by Roberto de Vicq de Compitch and *The Alphabeast Book: An Abecedarium* by Dorothy Schmiderer. Like Crews's dots, letters are transformed into animals or other phenomena.

After sharing your pictures with each other—perhaps creating your own book—look again at the pictures: What moves you? What is exciting? What is your favorite? How does Crews (or de Vicq de Compitch or Schmiderer) use line? Space? Color? Perspective? Shape?

Guided by philosopher and teacher educator Maxine Greene, Lincoln Center Institute asks teachers, when they are looking at art, to think about and to discuss the following questions:

- What in this work do I personally find most striking?
- What makes this a compelling work of art?
- What do we think students will notice about this work?
- What can we do to help students notice more about this work?
- What can we draw their attention to that will fundamentally change their experiences as viewers?[2]

As you view picture books, these questions can guide your aesthetic experience.

4.2 History of the Picture Book

Although exact dates in oral cultures are hard to come by, since the beginning of recorded time diverse peoples have created narratives that simultaneously combine linguistic and visual sign systems—word and shape. Using a variety of media, groups as disparate as Australian aborigines and the Navajo of the American Southwest sculpted their stories—and dreams—in sand. Indigenous Alaskan women, using knifelike whalebone, drew their stories in snow in the winter and mud in the summer. North American Plains Indians used buffalo hide to record their tales, whereas Mayans carved their stories in tree bark. The Chinese recorded symbols in wood and bamboo. In parts of Africa, as well as in the Pacific, storytellers in oral cultures have traditionally used string and vine as symbols of specific stories. Cultures with pictographic forms of communication, such as Japan, have many traditional storytelling chants accompanied by picture drawing.

The cave paintings of Lascaux, circa 15,000 BCE, give further historical evidence of the human impulse to express stories in images. The hieroglyphs of Mesopotamia, from 2700 BCE, were carved in heavy clay. The Egyptians invented papyrus from the pith of the papyrus plant, which led to the development of scrolls, which were lighter than clay tablets. As early as 1310 BCE, the Egyptians recorded in images their fables, astronomy, satire, and stories, mostly about the afterlife. The Greeks visited Egypt, where they learned about papyrus; it did not hold up as well in Greece's moist climate. An alternative was parchment, the skin of goats and sheep, first developed by the Persians, which became the media of communication that lasted for centuries in Europe.

The Chinese invented paper during the Han Dynasty (202 BCE–220 CE), which they used for bureaucratic and religious purposes. They kept the papermaking process a carefully guarded secret for centuries. However, it was eventually introduced to Japan through Korea during the rise of Buddhism in the seventh century. Paper was used to copy sutra, the sacred Buddhist sayings.[3]

The rise of Islam as a major world religion during the seventh century led to a significant increase in the decorative arts. Islam forbade the representation of humans and animals in religious art, thus artists channeled their creative abilities to produce an exquisite and distinctive style of geometric design and plant forms. This Islamic style influenced monks in European scriptoriums. The Lindisfarne Gospels appeared in about 690 CE, and the Book of Kells in 800. These manuscripts, along with the Utrecht Psalter, existed in a largely illiterate population. Their significance to children's picture books is that they introduced the idea of art for art's sake rather than art for a didactic purpose.[4] *Rubricators,* who most certainly were familiar with the geometric patterns characteristic of Islamic art (numerous monks had arrived on Ireland's shores from the Iberian peninsula) decorated fancy initial letters in gospel manuscripts. *Illuminators* laid precious gold paint on vellum, achieving a stunning, three-dimensional effect. *Miniaturists* painted flowers, landscapes, and insects that sometimes seemed irrelevant to the gospel text. It was not uncommon to find ladybugs and strawberries surrounding a gruesome biblical story—for example, John the Baptist's decapitated head. Scribal art, especially borders and miniatures, continue to influence contemporary illustrators such as Jan Brett and Trina Schart Hyman.[5]

In 800, Charlemagne brought the educator Alcuin to Europe. Because of his influence, the beautiful and legible Carolingian alphabet eventually replaced the more abstruse Gothic alphabet. In 1410, paper and wood block printing expanded the range of media available to visual artists. When Gutenberg refined movable type in 1450, his contemporaries predicted that his awkward, poor-quality letters would eventually die out, paltry competition for the elegantly styled manuscripts of the time.

Woodcuts were the primary illustrations of the fifteenth century, as seen in William Caxton's many publications. In 1823, George Cruikshank illustrated the first English translation of the Grimms' fairy tales. Edmund Evans's invention of color printing in 1860 further expanded the media possibilities for visual artists. In 1878, Randolph Caldecott, often considered the father of the modern picture book and for whom the Caldecott Medal is named, illustrated *The Diverting History of John Gilpin* by William Cowper. Kate Greenaway also illustrated picture books during this time. Today, in the United Kingdom, the Kate Greenaway Medal is comparable with the Caldecott.

In America, Jessie Wilcox Smith's paintings, in particular, gave form to romantic notions of childhood first introduced by Rosseau's *Emile.* In addition to children's books, illustrated children's magazines were also flourishing. The *Horn Book Magazine* was first published in 1924. Even in popular culture, the idea of children as an audience distinct from adults had come of age, and the picture book was an important genre.

Classic Picture Books In this book, classic refers to those books that have enduring value for generations of children, and rarely go out of print. Although published more than 100 years ago, Beatrix Potter's watercolor picture storybooks are examples of classic books; they have not lost their appeal. Children continue not to want to follow their mother's instructions *exactly*, continue to find their siblings too officious, continue to want to be completely forgiven when they have not asked permission, and continue to want their scrapes with life to meet up with comfort at the end of the day. Peter Rabbit returns home in the evening, after having a series of near-death experiences during the day, to drink hot and soothing chamomile tea prepared by his mother. Children from every generation can identify with Peter.

In 1928, Wanda Gág published *Millions of Cats,* generally considered the first major publication of a children's picture storybook in the United States. First rejected by more than twenty publishing houses, Dr. Seuss (pseudonym for Theodore Geisel) began his long and inimitable career with the publication of the fantasy *And To Think That I Saw it on Mulberry Street* in 1937, followed by *The 500 Hats of Bartholomew Cubbins* in 1938. About twenty years later, in response to schools glutted with less than engaging basal readers, Dr. Seuss accepted a publisher's challenge to use less than 300 words when writing *The Cat in the Hat,* thus originating the *easy reader* picture book.

Other children's picture books that are classics, enjoyed just as much by today's children as they were years ago, are the following:

1930	*The Little Engine That Could,* originally by Mabel Caroline Bragg;
	Angus and the Ducks by Marjorie Flack
1934	*The Little Auto* by Lois Lenski
1935	*The Story of Ferdinand* by Munro Leaf, illustrated by Robert Lawson
1938	*Andy and the Lion* by James Daughtery
1939	*Madeline* by Ludwig Bemelmens,
	Mike Mulligan and His Steam Shovel by Virginia Lee Burton,
	Caps for Sale by Esphyr Slobodkina,
	The Noisy Book by Margaret Wise Brown, illustrated by Leonard Weisgard

1941	*Make Way for Ducklings* by Robert McCloskey,
	Curious George by H. A. Rey
1942	*The Runaway Bunny* by Margaret Wise Brown,
	The Little House by Virginia Lee Burton
1944	*Many Moons* by James Thurber, illustrated by Louis Slobodkin
1945	*The Carrot Seed* by Ruth Kraus, illustrated by Crockett Johnson;
	Georgie by Robert Bright
1947	*Goodnight Moon* by Margaret Wise Brown, illustrated by Clement Hurd;
	It Looked Like Spilt Milk by Charles G. Shaw
1948	*Blueberries for Sal* by Robert McCloskey
1951	*Madeline's Rescue* by Ludwig Bemelmans
1952	*A Hole Is to Dig* by Ruth Kraus, illustrated by Maurice Sendak
1955	*Harold and the Purple Crayon* by Crockett Johnson
1956	*Madeline and the Bad Hat* by Ludwig Bemelmans
1957	*The Cat in the Hat* by Dr. Seuss,
	Time of Wonder by Robert McCloskey

Colors were limited in these early books. Artists had to preseparate colors to prepare for printing, painting the different colors on separate overlays. During the 1980s, improvements in technology rendered the time-consuming preseparation process unnecessary, and increased the visual possibilities of the children's picture book.

It is important for preservice teachers to be aware of these books. Practically speaking, they sometimes appear on teacher licensure exit exams. Acquainting yourself with them will help you learn to recognize quality. These early picture storybooks spurred the creation of thousands more picture books, expanding from the genres of realism and fantasy during the early days to biography, historical fiction, and wordless and concept books.

Multicultural *biography picture books* can help children gain ethnic pride, as well as build respect for the cultures of others. Children see both adults and children in choice-making situations, and see that we can, to some extent, shape our lives and our culture. Marie Bradby's *More Than Anything Else,* sensitively illustrated by Chris Soentpiet, movingly portrays Booker T. Washington's intense desire to learn to read.

Contemporary realism found in *picture storybooks* can delight, amuse, and enlighten; it can also help young elementary school-age children know they are not alone when facing the inevitable difficulties of life. Adoja Burrowes's *Grandma's Purple Flowers* validates children's feelings of loss when a grandparent dies. *My Little Island* by Frané Lessac portrays a multiethnic friendship in which one of the boys shares with his friend his birthplace in the Caribbean.

Fantasy has a special place in the realm of the child: imaginative, funny, but also asking what if? Arthur Dorros's *Abuela,* illustrated by Elisa Klevin, is an intergenerational example of fantasy. *Historical fiction* pictures life in previous eras. Angela Shelf Medearis's *Dancing with the Indians,* illustrated by Samuel Byrd portrays the relationship between

African Americans and the Seminole Indians. During slavery, the Seminoles welcomed runaway slaves. After the deportation of the Seminoles from Florida to Oklahoma, African Americans have continued to the present time to join the Seminoles in powwows.

Wordless or *textless* picture books have found receptive audiences in recent decades. Although without words, they tell a story, like David Wiesner's humorous *Tuesday*. *Concept books* are didactic in nature; their primary purpose is to teach. Sometimes the teaching of a concept is embodied in a story, as in Marilyn Burns's delightful *The Greedy Triangle*. Alphabet books must, in particular, be scrutinized for stereotypes. The illustrations surrounding "I is for Indian" are demeaning to Americans Indians, who are often pictured brandishing tomahawks, befeathered, and buckskinned (many Indians did not and do not possess tomahawks, feathers, and buckskins).

4.3 The Picture Book and the Teaching of Reading

First and foremost, children learn to read when they are excited about the world of ideas, thoughts, and feelings they know words will unlock. Children rely on three cueing systems to construct meaning when reading: semantic (knowledge of the world), syntactic (knowledge of language), and graphophonic (knowledge of print).[6]

In the Essentials of Literacy program, for ninety minutes to two hours daily, remedial readers visit the reading room, designed by Edward Murray, where they move through six reading stations, manned by trained volunteers and overseen by one classroom teacher. An essential aspect of the experience is listening to stories, available from volunteers who read aloud to children, and on audiotape. Murray believes children need to hear at least a thousand stories to develop the schema for proficient reading. His remedial students are saturated with stories, four or five a day, and are required to take home at night books recorded on audiotape. Hearing stories read aloud appeals to the *aural* aspects of reading, giving children opportunities to build on strengths beyond the visual; children can often comprehend more through listening than when reading.[7] Teachers should read to children, throughout their elementary years, literature that is beyond their grasp as readers but within their grasp as listeners.

The picture storybook can help children with that aspect of reading called *graphic awareness,* which deals with visual aspects of phonics—the alphabet, concepts of print, left to right, orientation, and spaces between words. The wordless picture book also helps to develop a sense of left to right. Alphabet books reinforce the idea that the twenty-six incomprehensible, squiggly shapes called letters have meaning, and are symbols for words, thoughts, and ideas; alphabetic insight is essential to the process of learning to read. Even upper elementary school children who are still nonalphabetic readers can benefit from alphabet books, especially sufficiently sophisticated concept books like Stephen Johnson's *Alphabet City* and Graeme Baese's *Animalia.*

Picture books as a whole continually reinforce concepts of print as well as spatial concepts: The spaces in between words are meaningful too. Denise Fleming's work in particular contributes to this aspect of reading.

4.4 Criticism and Evaluation of the Picture Book

The success of the picture book can be evaluated by the quality of the integration of word and image. When evaluating the picture book, librarian Kathleen Horning suggests the following:

> Beyond judging the quality of the illustrations themselves . . . think about how well they complement the story. Has the artist tried to give a sense of the place and culture from which the tale comes and, if so, has he or she succeeded? Does the style the artist used blend well with the tone of the story? What details has the artist added to expand characterization or define setting? Does the artist add a personal interpretation to the story through the use of mood or symbols?[8]

These important questions deal with the literary and aesthetic aspects of reading. However, today's teachers must also exercise cultural sensitivity. Several negative examples are discussed to help teachers know what to avoid.

A popular book on the market is Bill Martin and John Archambault's *Knots on a Counting Rope.* Teachers often believe they are choosing a multicultural book when they share it with children. However, reviewers Beverly Slapin and Doris Seale call it "repulsive, in its deliberate pandering to the romantic mythology about 'Indians' in the minds of a certain kind of white adult purchaser."[9] Although the story appears to take place within the Navajo, or Diné, culture, it is instead a generic composite of the author's and illustrator's misconceptions and amalgamations of Indian nations. In actuality, Indian children do not, like the blind boy in *Knots on a Counting Rope,* interrupt their elders during storytelling and, unlike the grandfather in this tale, grandparents patiently repeat their stories when children request them. The counting rope is itself deceptive; no such artifact exists within the Navajo culture. Books like *Knots on a Counting Rope* that are inauthentic and not culturally specific should be avoided. This is especially challenging for new teachers because many reading and language arts specialists, unaware of criticism from a cultural perspective, continue to recommend *Knots on a Counting Rope* in their books and articles.

Another widely embraced book is Susan Jeffers's stunningly illustrated *Brother Eagle, Sister Sky.* Well-intentioned teachers again often think they are choosing multicultural literature when they select this book, and its strong ecological message is a positive one. However, Jeffers has permuted a Squamish Indian from the Northwest into a Plains Indian, and sanitized Chief Seathl's original speech, which "despaired of the survival of his people."[10] The concept of sister sky is unknown to American Indians, and the book promotes a stereotype—that of the noble, disappearing Indian. Again, it is a challenge for new teachers to address the criticism of this book, when even literature experts recommend it. Maurice Sendak's *Alligators All Around* and Virginia Grossman's *Ten Little Rabbits* also promote demeaning images of American Indians—the feather-wearing, tomahawk-brandishing savage.

Stereotypes from other cultures include those found in *The Story about Ping* by Marjorie Flack, illustrated by Kurt Wiese. The skin of the Chinese is yellow, and the family members look very much alike. Stereotypical portrayals of African Americans in such books as Helen Bannerman's *Little Black Sambo* and in Margot Zemach's *Jake and Honeybunch Go to Heaven* should also be avoided. These books have the potential to hurt and alienate children of color while perpetuating negative stereotypes among white children. Some have been effectively rewritten for today's audiences. For example, Fred Marcellino's *The Story of Little Babaji* is a fine retelling of *Little Black Sambo.*

To discuss these issues with upper grade elementary students, you can bring in some of these books and, before reading them aloud, ask students what might be wrong with them. Then, false representations of cultures can be discussed.

4.5 The Elements, Styles, and Media of the Visual Arts

To help the students we teach fulfill their potential as producers of knowledge, creators of art, and shapers of their culture, we need to share with them what has come before. In her award-winning essay on creativity, Sharon Bailin writes, "Truly creative innovation, change which is effective, useful, and significant is not a product of arbitrary novelty, of uninformed intuition, but emerges, rather, out of a profound understanding of the nature of tradition and of its principles."[11] As stated in Chapter 1.8, Howard Gardner and other researchers share this view of creativity. Both children and their teachers can benefit from examining what preceded them.

Linking the visual arts of children's literature with cultural forms serves especially those persons who are adept at what Gardner calls *spatial intelligence,* which does not necessarily mean they will become artists in their adult life.[12] Providing opportunities for spatial intelligence to emerge in the study and production of the visual arts can benefit all walks of life. A theorist in the visual arts, Rudolf Arnheim says,

> Artists spend their professional lives on the study of visual structures. They are the experts on what one might call the resources of visual language. It is sensible, therefore, to conclude that the study of art should be an indispensable part of the training in any other field of knowledge. . . . A practical acquaintance with the principles of artistic form and the ways of conveying meaning by way of these principles contribute . . . directly to the training of productive thinking in any field.[13]

One way of helping children to explore their cultural heritage is to see for yourselves the range of artistic forms through looking at the elements, styles, and media of art available in picture storybooks. To assist you in better seeing the elements, styles, and media of art, I have placed a table at the end of this chapter that you can use in your visits to libraries and go to http://faculty.sacredheart.edu/gangij for other tables. See the Guide for Responding to the Visual Arts in Appendix A on the way this kind of knowledge might be assessed.

Elements of Art   Illustrators of children's picture books artistically mold their ideas and thoughts by choosing from the following elements:

Shape spans the continuum of symmetry and asymmetry. Objects tend to be linear whereas animals and humans tend to be curved. However, human forms are sometimes presented in geometric form: square, rectangular, triangular. Proportion may either be realistic or expressive. Although shape in picture books is two-dimensional, some picture books have a three-dimensional feel to them—for example, the work of Chris Van Allsburg. Patricia Polacco's innovative use of contrasts in shape create the feeling that the characters are about to walk off the pages and into our lives.

Texture depicts the sensory quality of illustrations. Barry Moser, whether through the media of paint or woodcuts, often creates pictures rich in texture that appeal to our sense of touch.

Line is the way an illustrator encloses and opens space. Line may be bold or receding; horizontal, vertical, diagonal, curved or linear, continuous or broken, or some combination of all these. Crockett Johnson's *Harold and the Purple Crayon* is almost completely stated in line, and Brian Pinkney's scratchboard illustrations are fine examples of artistic use of line.

Color emerges from the spectrum of the rainbow—black to white—and all the combinations thereof (light and dark, bright and dull). Floyd Cooper makes use of a broad range of lush colors in his paintings. Limiting color can be equally effective, as seen in the work of Arnold Lobel. *Monochromatic coloration* explores one color. Depending on the text and the artist's intent, black and white, or achromatic colors, can be as effective as bright, vivid coloration.

Space is the way the artist foregrounds and backgrounds the various elements. Some picture books are deliberately flat—no attempt is made to create depth to capture a particular style of art, like folk art. The use of space spans a continuum, from minimalist art to the more baroque. Graeme Baese fills his pictures up to the brim. Demi, Barbara Cooney, Peter Spier, and Clement Hurd often alternate pages that provide contrasts in the use of space.

Perspective is the choice illustrators make in shaping their work from a variety of points of view—for example, aerial or linear, small to large, and large to small.

Styles of Art World cultures have historically contributed a variety of styles in the visual arts; these styles are comparable with styles in literature, theater, music, and dance. Lucy Micklethwait's *I Spy: An Alphabet In Art* is an excellent source to view the many styles of art.

Although *Asian* art often has a delicate, nonrepresentational style, distinctions can be made between *Japanese* art, such as the illustrations in Taro Yashima's *Crow Boy* or Keizaburō Tejima's Japanese woodcuts in *Owl Lake,* and *Chinese* art emanating from different historical time periods, which also have distinct styles. The distinctiveness and contributions of the geometric, patterned designs of *Islamic* art have already been mentioned, especially its influence on the manuscript illuminations and rubrications. The *Mithila* style of mural art is the highly stylized, symbolic art of India.

Western art includes the *frescoes* of Minoan art, the *mosaics* and *stained glass* of Early Christian art, and the rounded and massive shapes of *Romanesque* art, which evolved during the eleventh and twelfth centuries. *Medieval* art spanned from 400 to 1400. Angela Barrett's illustrations in *Joan of Arc* by Josephine Poole are an example, especially of the rubrications and illuminations, based on manuscript art. Tony Parillo's *Michaelangelo's Surprise* is in the style of the *Italian Renaissance* (1420–1600). Arthur Geisert's *Pigs A to Z* is in the *classical etching* style, also from the Renaissance, whereas Emily Arnold McCully's *Mirette on the High Wire* is reflective of a technique that emerged during this same period called *chiaroscuro*, which dramatically uses light and dark through levels of gradation.

Romanticism as a movement lasted from 1740 to 1853. The twentieth century illustrator Jessie Wilcox Smith is in this tradition. *Realism* and *naturalism* as movements began in the midnineteenth century. Thomas Locker's oil paintings are *realistic*, in the style of the *Hudson River School*. *Representational art* seeks to recreate reality; *presentational art* does not try to portray phenomena realistically, but instead expresses unique or abstract qualities.

John Goodall's wordless books are in the *Victorian* style (1837–1901). French *Impressionism* lasted as a school from 1874 through the early part of the twentieth century, with its emphasis on the diffusion of light and inherent quality (as opposed to capturing minute, realistic details). Bijou LeTord's biographical picture book, *A Blue Butterfly: A Story about Claude Monet*, gives us a sense of impressionistic art in children's books. Brian Wildsmith's work is reflective of a movement called *Expressionism* (late nineteenth through early twentieth century) in which art does not try to portray its subject realistically, but instead expresses something about the artist's inner feelings. The prolific work of Jacob Lawrence, an African American artist, exemplifies the expressionistic style and can be found in Walter Dean Myers's biography of Toussaint L'Ouverture. *Fauvism*, also expressionistic, playfully and impulsively distorts traditional forms and explores nontraditional uses of colors. Giselle Potter's contemporary illustrations capture this lightheartedness.

Surrealism evolved from the new twentieth century discipline of psychology, propelled by Freud's emphasis on dreams and the subconscious, and exemplified by such artists as René Magritte and Salvador Dali. The cover of Micklethwait's book is Magritte's surrealistic painting, *The Great War* (see Figure 4.1). *The Grey Lady and the Strawberry Snatcher* by Molly Bang and *The Wild Bunch* by Dee Lillega, illustrated by Rex Barron, are also in the surrealistic style.

As a result of the new field of anthropology, nonwestern art made an impact on western art around the beginning of the twentieth century. *Africanist* art appeared during the late nineteenth century, and Paul Gauguin brought art from the Pacific to a western audience around the same time. S. D. Nelson's stunning work in *Crazy Horse's Vision* (see Figure 4.2) by Joseph Bruchac is based on *ledger art*, developed by imprisoned American Indians during the nineteenth century. Captured by white soldiers, they were jailed for the crime of fighting for their own land. While in jail, they created art using ledger books, despite their desperate circumstances.

The *Mexican mural renaissance*, especially the murals of Diego Rivera, his wife Frida Kahlo, and Jose Clemente Orozco, has influenced American illustrators such as Tomie dePaola. *Cubism*, as exemplified in the work of Pablo Picasso and Piet Mondrian, emphasizes harmony, balance, and order, rather than realistic presentation. Other styles followed: *modernism, pointillism, constructivism, minimalism, pop and op art, abstract*

Figure 4.1 Lucy Micklethwait's *I Spy! An Alphabet In Art* is not only an alphabet book but also an introduction to the world and styles of the visual arts. René Magritte's surrealistic painting, *The Great War,* is the jacket art.

art, photorealism, and *art deco.* Using the tables at the end of the chapter and on the website, or in your own journeys, watch for examples of the many styles of art.

Folk art reflects the simple and stylized art of the folk, which varies from region to region. The use of color is often vivid, and perspective is not used. *In My Family/En mi familia* by Carmen Garza is an example of Mexican folk art; Garza often uses *papel picado*—paper cutouts. *My Little Island* by Frané Lessac is an example of Caribbean folk art, and *Ox-Cart Man* by Donald Hall, illustrated by Barbara Cooney, is an example of early American folk art.

Cartoon styles are popular with children, as found in Mercer Mayer's and Peggy Rathmann's books, including her Caldecott-winning *Officer Buckle and Gloria,* or in the 2001 Caldecott winner, *So You Want to Be President?* by Judith St. George and illustrated by David Small. An illustrator of Mexican American Gary Soto's books, Susan Guevara effectively uses the cartoon style, as seen in the *Chato* books.

Figure 4.2 Lakota illustrator S. D. Nelson draws in the style of Native American ledger art in *Crazy Horse's Vision,* text by Joseph Bruchac (Abenaki).

A new style that could be termed *digital age* is highly graphic, intense, and nonlinear, and word and image are often indistinguishable. Eliza Dresang describes this recent phenomena: "The new relationships between words and pictures that have emerged . . . can be summarized as synergy: words become pictures and pictures become words. In the most radical form of synergy, words and pictures are so much a part of one another that it is almost impossible to say which is which."[14] Picture books by Carlos Encinas (see Figure 4.3), Chris Raschka, and Henrik Drescher exemplify this new style that has emerged from the age of the computer.

Picture books used in the classroom ought to reflect a range of styles in art. Even preschoolers and six-year-olds, Gardner reports, can attend to differences in styles of art. He says,

[I]n the absence of supporting cultural context, it is unlikely that anyone could become an artistic connoisseur. Under proper guidance, one could probably become a connoisseur at a young age. The great art historian Kenneth Clark was apparently able to remember with great fidelity any painting he had ever seen; this fact makes it a bit easier to understand how he came to be appointed head of the National Gallery in London at the age of twenty-nine![15]

Figure 4.3 Mexican American illustrator-author Carlos Encinas experiments with computer-generated artwork in *The New Engine/La maquina nueva,* a historical story in which the new technology of trains at first threatens unemployment.

As teachers, you have the opportunity to open up to children the possibilities of art; perhaps some of your pupils will include a child with the proclivities of Kenneth Clark. Early creative work often means imitating various styles of art to discover one's own style.

Media of Art

Developing connoisseurship in children's book illustrations also means looking at the varied media of art. Hopefully you will experiment with some of these media for yourself. Some media are more accessible to teachers than others—for example, collage and watercolor. See the table at the end of the chapter and on the website for the incredible variety of media that illustrators of children's books use. The wider the vocabulary of the teacher in describing these books, the greater the impact on children's vocabularies, and their ability to name and shape their world.

Book Forms

Variations on the standard form of picture books—pages bound by hard or soft covers—include the paper mechanics, for example, *Moving Pictures* by the Victorian artist Ernest Nister, and contemporary artist Robert Sabuda's *The 12 Days of Christmas.* For preschool children there are board books and pop-up books. Endpapers and dust jackets are also worth examining for their artistic import.

4.6 Conclusion

The study of children's literature provides a venue both to view and to create art. Teacher educator and philosopher Maxine Greene says,

> [T]hose who can attend to and absorb themselves in particular works of art are more likely to effect connections in their own experiences than those who cannot. They are more likely to perceive the shapes of things as they are conscious of them, to pay heed to qualities and appearances ordinarily obscured by the conventional and routine. I believe that we can release people for this kind of seeing if we ourselves are able to recover—and help our students to discover—the imaginative mode of awareness that makes paintings available, and poetry, and sculpture, and theatre, and film.[16]

Having experienced it for yourself will make it easier for you to attain with children the NCATE standard, "Candidates know, understand, and use . . . the visual arts as primary media for self-expression, communication, inquiry, and insight among students."[17]

The visual aspects of children's literature delights the eye. The next chapter presents a genre that delights the ear: poetry.

Suggested Activities

1. Visit an art museum. The Getty Institute for the Arts found that collaborations between schools and museums have positive effects on the sophistication and understanding of the arts.[18]

2. *Mike Mulligan and His Steam Shovel* by Virginia Lee Burton can stimulate a discussion on the changes technology brings.

3. In response to picture books,
   • Write the words for a wordless book
   • Create your own toy book (paper engineering)
   • Create a book jacket for a favorite book
   • Illustrate parts of the story the illustrator left out
   • Write a newsletter on a picture book; consider using graphics
   • Create a piece of art in the style and media of a favorite book—for example, the collage of Eric Carle
   • Create a paper bag story with setting, author, title, characters, and theme
   • Create a comic strip

for further reading

Bader, Barbara. 2001 [1976]. *The World in 32 Pages: One Hundred Years of American Picture Books.* Delary Beach, FL: Winslow Press.

Benedict, Susan, and Lenore Carlisle, eds. 1992. *Beyond Words: Picture Books for Older Readers and Writers.* Portsmouth, NH: Heinemann.

Cianciolo, Patricia J. 1997. *Picture Books for Children.* 4th ed. Chicago: American Library Association.

Cummins, Julie, ed. 1992, 1996. *Children's Book Illustration and Design, Volumes 1 & 2.* New York: Library of Applied Design, PBC International.

Giorgis, Cyndi, and Nancy L. Johnson. 2001. "Creativity." *The Reading Teacher, 54.6:* 632–640.

Hindley, Joanne. 1995. *In the Company of Children.* Stemmer, ME: Stenhouse. (See Chapter 6, The Power of Picture Books: A Whole-Class Genre Study.)

Lacy, Lyn Ellen. 1986. *Art and Design in Children's Picture Books: An Analysis of Caldecott-Award Winning Illustrations.* Chicago: American Library Association.

Lima, Carolyn W., and John A. Lima. 2001. *A to Zoo: Subject Access to Children's Picture Books.* 6th ed. Westport, CT: Bowker-Greenwood.

Meyer, Susan E. 1983. *A Treasury of the Great Children's Book Illustrators.* New York: Abrams.

Mitchell, Florence S. 1990. "Introducing Art History Through Children's Literature." *Language Arts, 67* (December): 839–846.

Nodelman, Perry. 1988. *Words about Pictures: The Narrative Art of Children's Picture Books.* Athens, GA: University of Georgia Press.

Schwarcz, Joseph H., and Chara Schwarcz. 1991. *The Picture Book Comes of Age: Looking at Childhood through the Art of Illustration.* Chicago: American Library Association.

Spitz, Ellen Handler. 1999. *Inside Picture Books.* New Haven: Yale University Press.

Stewig, John Warren. 1995. *Looking at Picture Books.* Fort Atkinson, WI: Highsmith.

Yenawine, Philip. 1995. *Key Art Terms for Beginners.* New York: Abrams.

websites

National Center for Children's Illustrated Literature: www.nccil.org/exhibit/index.html

Many illustrators maintain websites; check the Web by using their names.

awards

Caldecott Award:
www.ala.org/alsc

Carnegie Medal:
www.ala.org/alsc/carnegie.html

The Charlotte Zolotow:
www.soemadison.wisc.edu/ccbc/zolotow.htm

Ezra Jack Keats Award:
www.nypl.org/press/keats02.html

The Kate Greenaway Medal:
www.lahq.org.uk/directory/medals_awards/medals_pastkate.html

the picture book: elements, styles, and media of art

Elements of Art

For examples of excellence:　**See:**

Line　　*Jalani and the Lock* by Lorenzo Pace

Color　　*Aunt Flossie's Hats (and Crab Cakes Later)* by Elizabeth F. Howard, illustrated by James Ransome

For examples of excellence:	See:
Space	*Miss Rumphius* by Barbara Cooney
Perspective	*Abuela* by Arthur Dorros, illustrated by Elisa Kleven *Round Trip* by Ann Jonas
Shape	*In the Small, Small Pond* by Denise Fleming
Texture	*Make Way for Ducklings* by Robert McCloskey

Styles of Art

Multiple	*I Spy: An Alphabet in Art* by Lucy Micklethwait
Medieval	*Joan of Arc* by Josephine Poole, illustrated by Angela Barrett
Renaissance	*Michaelangelo's Surprise* by Tony Parillo
Classical etching style	*Pigs A to Z* by Arthur Geisert
Chiaroscuro	*Mirette on the High Wire* by Emily Arnold McCully
Victorian	*Moving Pictures* by Ernest Nister (also paper mechanics)
Realism	*Family Farm* by Thomas Locker (Hudson River School)
Ledger art	*Crazy Horse's Vision* by Joseph Bruchac, illustrated by S. D. Nelson
Folk	*The Little House* by Virginia Lee Burton *A Peaceable Kingdom: The Shaker Abcedarius* by Alice and Martin Provensen
Expressionism	*Li'l Sis and Uncle Willie* by Gwen Everett, illustrated by William H. Johnson *Smoky Night* by Eve Bunting, illustrated by David Diaz
Surrealism	*The Grey Lady and the Strawberry Snatcher* by Molly Bang *The Wild Bunch* by Dee Lillega, illustrated by Rex Barron
Art deco	*Little Nino's Pizzeria* by Karen Barbour
Cartoon	*The Adventures of Sparrowboy* by Brian Pinkney *There's a Nightmare in My Closet* by Mercer Mayer
Photorealism	*Alphabet City* by Stephen T. Johnson

Media of Art

Batik	*The Horrendous Hullabaloo* by Margaret Mahy, illustrated by Patricia McCarthy
Carbon pencil	*The Garden of Abdul Gasazi* by Chris Van Allsburg
Charcoal	*Moja Means One: Swahili Counting Book* by Muriel Feelings, illustrated by Tom Feelings
Clay figures	*Josefina* by Jeanette Winter
Collage	*The Very Hungry Caterpillar* by Eric Carle *Numblers* by Suse MacDonald and Bill Oakes
Colored paper	*Little Blue and Little Yellow* by Leo Lionni

For examples of excellence:	See:
Colored pencil	*The Relatives Came* by Cynthia Rylant, illustrated by Stephen Gammell
Colored pencil and crayon	*Miranthe's Story One: Painted Words* and *Miranthe's Story Two: Spoken Memories* by Aliki
Computer graphics	*The New Engine/La maquina nueva* by Carlos Encinas, *Mr. Lunch Takes a Plane Ride* by J. Otto Siebold
Conté pencil and conté dust	*Jumanji* by Chris Van Allsburg
Crayons	*Come Away from the Water, Shirley* by John Burningham
Cut paper	*Pablo's Tree* by Pat Mora, illustrated by Cecily Lang
Cut paper and collage	*Chicka Chicka Boom Boom* by Bill Martin and John Archambault, Jr., illustrated by Lois Ehlert
Digital and traditional techniques	*Allie's Basketball Dream* by Barbara E. Barber, illustrated by Darryl Ligasan
Gouache	*Brian Wildsmith's ABC* by Brian Wildsmith
Gouache and airbrush	*Flying* by Donald Crews
Gouache, inks, and pencil/pen	*Less Than Half, More Than Whole* by Kathleen and Michael Lacapa
Ink and spot coloring overlay	*Andy and the Lion* by James Daughtery
India ink line over tempera	*Where the Wild Things Are* by Maurice Sendak
Lithographic crayon on zinc plates	*Make Way for Ducklings* by Robert McCloskey
Paint	
Acrylic	*Storm in the Night* by Mary Stoltz, illustrated by Pat Cummings; *Sky, Sea, the Jetty, and Me* by Leonard Everett Fisher
Acrylic and pastel	*Roxaboxen* by Alice McLerran, illustrated by Barbara Cooney
Acrylic, pastel, and spray paint layered on museum board	*Malcolm X: A Fire Burning Brightly* by Walter Dean Myers, illustrated by Leonard Jenkins
Acrylic on museum rag	*Doesn't Fall Off His Horse* by Virginia Stroud
Acrylic on wood	*Gift Horse* by S. D. Nelson
Oil	*Home Run* by Robert Burleigh, illustrated by Mike Wimmer;
Oil on gesso	*Brave Women* by Betsy Hearne, illustrated by Behane Andersen
Pastels	*Sister Anne's Hands* by Marybeth Lorbiecki, illustrated by K. Wendy Popp
Pen and ink	*Ben's Dream* by Chris Van Allsburg; *Hildilid's Night* by Cheli D. Ryan, illustrated by Arnold Lobel; *Blueberries for Sal* by Robert McCloskey

For examples of excellence:	See:
Pen and ink/watercolor	*Julius, the Baby of the World* by Kevin Henkes
Pencil and watercolor	*The Patchwork Quilt* by Valerie Flournoy, illustrated by Jerry Pinkney
Photography	*Daddy and Me: A Photo Story of Arthur Ashe and His Daughter Camera* by Jeanne Moutonoussamy–Ashe
	Tana Hoban's concept books
Plasticene	*The New Baby Calf* by Edith Chase, illustrated by Barbara Reid
Poster color and silhouettes	*Harriet and the Promised Land* by Jacob Lawrence
Preseparated art	*Truck* by Donald Crews
	Rosie's Walk by Pat Hutchins
Scratchboard	*Duke Ellington: The Piano Prince and His Orchestra* by Andrea Davis Pinkney, illustrated by Brian Pinkney
Stencils	*Mama Cat Has Three Kittens* by Denise Fleming (cotton fiber poured through hand-cut stencils)
Story quilt	*Tar Beach* by Faith Ringgold
Textile art	*Dia's Story Cloth: The Hmong People's Journey to Freedom* by Dia Cha, stitched by Chue and Nhia Thao Cha
Trompe l'oeil	*Anno's Alphabet* by Mitsumasa Anno
Watercolor	*Virgie Goes to School with Us Boys* by Elizabeth Fitzgerald Howard, illustrated by E. B. Lewis
	Tuesday by David Wiesner
	The Tale of Peter Rabbit by Beatrix Potter
Watercolor collage	*Eating the Alphabet* by Lois Ehlert
Watercolor and collage	*Uptown* by Bryan Collier
Watercolor, gouache, pastels, and charcoal	*City by Numbers* by Stephen T. Johnson
Watercolor and pencil	*Mei-Mei Loves the Morning* by Margaret Holloway Tsubakiyama, illustrated by Cornelius Van Wright and Ying-Hwa Hu
Watercolor and rubber stamps	*I Need a Lunch Box* by Jeannette Caines, illustrated by Pat Cummings
Woodcut	*The Farmer's Alphabet* by Mary Azarian

Tables for poetry, folklore, and celebrations books are posted at http://faculty.sacredheart.edu/gangij.

notes

1. Paul Zelinsky, *Rapunzel* (New York: Dutton, 1997), n. p.
2. Carol Shookhoff, *Background Paper*. Paper presented at the Lincoln Center Institute Conference, "Aesthetic Education at Lincoln Center: Ongoing Inquiry," New York, NY, 2–3 March 1996.
3. Sophie Dawson, *The Art and Craft of Papermaking* (New York: Sterling, 1992), pp. 9–10.
4. Barbara Kiefer, *The Potential of Picturebooks: From Visual Literacy to Aesthetic Understanding* (Englewood Cliffs, NJ: Prentice–Hall, 1995), p. 76.
5. Kiefer, *The Potential of Picturebooks*, p. 72.

6. Mem Fox, *Radical Reflections: Passionate Opinions on Teaching, Learning, and Living* (San Diego: Harcourt, 1993), p. 45.

7. Louise Spear–Swerling and Robert Sternberg, *Off Track: When Poor Readers Become "Learning Disabled"* (New York: Westview Press, 1996), p. 176.

8. Kathleen T. Horning, *From Cover to Cover: Evaluating and Reviewing Children's Books* (New York: HarperCollins, 1997), p. 65.

9. Beverly Slapin and Doris Seale, *Through Indian Eyes: The Native Experience in Books for Children* (Philadelphia, PA: New Society Publishers, 1992), p. 181.

10. John Stott, *Native Americans in Children's Literature* (Phoenix, AZ: Oryx, 1995), pp. 18–22.

11. Sharon Bailin, *Achieving Extraordinary Ends: An Essay on Creativity* (Norwood, NJ: Ablex, 1994), p. 126.

12. Howard Gardner, "Multiple Intelligences: Implications for Art and Creativity." In: *Artistic Intelligences: Implications for Education,* William Moody, ed. (New York: Teachers College Press, 1990), p. 19.

13. Rudolf Arnheim, *Thoughts on Art Education,* occasional paper 2 (Santa Monica, CA: The Getty Center for Education in the Arts, 1989), p. 41.

14. Eliza Dresang, *Radical Change: Books for Youth in a Digital Age* (New York: H. W. Wilson), p. 88.

15. Howard Gardner, *Art Education and Human Development* (Los Angeles, CA: Getty Center for Education in the Arts, 1990), pp. 13–14.

16. Maxine Greene, "Imagination and Aesthetic Literacy," *Art Education 30.6* (1977): p. 15.

17. National Council for Accreditation of Teacher Education, *Program Standards for Elementary Teacher Preparation,* 2f.

18. Brent Wilson, *The Quiet Evolution: Changing the Face of Arts Education* (Los Angeles: Getty Trust Publications, 1997), p. 13.

Poetry
The Music of Language

*P*oetry is above all a verbal pleasure. In 548 BC Simonedes of Ceos remarked that poetry is vocal painting as painting is silent poetry. Recently a child said to me, 'When you read it outloud, it understands itself better.'[1]

— EVE MERRIAM

5.1 Encountering Literature
through choral reading

Materials Needed

Highlighters

To extend the choral reading experience beyond what is contained in this chapter, you could bring short poems that are enlarged in font and are double spaced.

After trying *The Snowman* and *John Henry*, create in small groups your own interpretation of choral readings of poetry. Poems that work well are

- Stanzas from *I Hear America Singing* by Walt Whitman
- *The Guitar* by Federíco Garcia Lorca, found in *Call Down the Moon: Poems of Music*, selected by Myra Cohn Livingston
- *Juke Box Love Song* by Langston Hughes, also found in *Call Down the Moon: Poems of Music*, selected by Myra Cohn Livingston
- *The Drum* by Nikki Giovanni, found in *My Song Is Beautiful: Poems and Pictures in Many Voices*, selected by Mary Ann Hoberman
- *Sun, Moon, Stars*, from an Omaha Ceremony for the Newborn, found in *Dancing Teepees: Poems of American Indian Youth*, collected by Virginia Driving Hawk Sneve

  Some volumes of poetry are already set up for choral reading:

- "Sunny Market Song" and "Nativity Play Plan" in *When I Dance* by James Berry
- *Side by Side: Poems to Read Together* by Lee Bennett Hopkins
- *I Am a Phoenix: Poems for Two Voices, Joyful Noise: Poems for Two Voices*, and *Big Talk: Poems for Four Voices*, all by Paul Fleischman

Warm-ups Prepare for reading poetry aloud by playing around with the following warm-ups.

Tongue Twisters In small or large groups, take turns saying these tongue twisters as quickly as you can, three times each:

Lemon liniment.

Strange strategic statistics.

She sells seashells by the seashore.

Unique New York.

Much whirling water makes the mill wheel work well.

Odd birds always gobble green almonds in the autumn.

A box of biscuits, a box of mixed biscuits, and a biscuit mixer.

The big black bug bled black blood.

Round and round the rugged rocks the ragged rascal ran.

Shave a cedar shingle thin.

Purple pickle percolator.

She makes a proper cup of coffee in a copper coffee pot.

Double bubble gum bubbles double.

Six thick thistle sticks.

Watch the whacky wristwatch.

For more tongue twisters, see Joanna Cole and Stephanie Calmenson's *Six Sick Sheep*.

Onomatopoeic Words In large or small groups or in pairs, say the following onomatopoeic words as expressively as possible. There is no right or wrong way; there is simply interpretation. *Play* with these sounds:

BOOM	SPLAT	CLASH	DRIP
COUGH	SIGH	WOW	POW
SNEEZE	CRACKLE	BONK	COO
GROWL	GURGLE	PING	POP
SHOUT	POUT	BAM	SNAP
CHUCKLE	SWISH	SMASH	BUZZ
BOING	CHOP	GASP	THIN
GULP	SPLASH	PANT	ROAR
SPUTTER	COOL	DROP	BANG
TINKLE	MURMUR	CRASH	HUM
GRUNT	CLANG	BUBBLE	CRY
WHEEZE	BOO!	BONG	

Choral Reading Poetry presented orally in groups is called *choral reading*. When interpreting poetry, *play* with these musical ideas:

- *Sound and silence.* In the dynamics in choral reading, silence can be as effective as sound; create a space for silence in your interpretation. Sound carries musical gradations: The human voice can whisper (no voice); and speak softly (pianissimo), moderately, loudly, and very loudly (crescendo).

- *Rate.* You can vary the rate: slowly, moderately, and quickly.
- *Pitch.* The color of the voice ranges from high timbres to tonal depth.

To avoid a sing-song presentation, read for the meaning of the line, *which does not mean stopping at the end of every sentence.* In choral reading the musicality of poetry emerges without deliberately stressing it.

Conventions of Choral Reading Consider using the following combinations of the human voice:

- *Solo.* One person reads a stanza alone; male and female voices, child and adult voices, can alternate.
- *Unison.* Whole-group reading can carry gradations of sound.
- *Line around.* Interpreters take turns reading one line each. This differs from solo reading in that a soloist usually reads an entire stanza.
- *Cumulative.* One by one or two by two (or three by three, and so on), interpreters read one line, and keep on reading, as other voices join gradually, line by line. This crescendos at the last line of the stanza, or at a climactic line, perhaps all in unison.
- *Reverse cumulative.* Starting off in unison, one by one or two by two (or more), choral readers drop out until the last line of a stanza is read by a solo voice.
- *Antiphonal.* Groups read a designated stanza in unison. Males and females, adults and children, or mixed groups can read antiphonally.
- *Obligato.* A group repeats the same phrase throughout—for example, "Rum pum pum . . ." or "Heigh ho, heigh ho . . . "
- *Musical instruments* are useful for emphasis or improvisation. Draw on the talents in your classroom community: Does anyone play guitar? Flute? Some other instrument?

The entire poem can be first read aloud, then roles assigned. Review the approach to performance statement in Chapter 1.8. Try out *The Snowman* and *John Henry.*

Note double-spacing. Large point size, easily accomplished with a word processing program, facilitates ease in reading, thus making an aesthetic experience more likely. Participants should use highlighters to mark their individual roles. *Italicized* words are stage directions, not to be read aloud.

The Snowman
Anonymous

Cumulative	Once
	Once
	Once there was
Unison (*loudly*)	Once there was a snowman

Line Around	Stood outside the door.
	Thought he'd like to come inside
	And run
	run
	run
	around the floor;
Solo	Thought he'd like to warm himself
	By the firelight red.
	Thought he'd like to climb
	Upon the big white bed;
Antiphonal I	So he called the North Wind,
Antiphonal II	"Help me now I pray,
	I'm completely frozen
	Standing here all day."
Reverse Cumulative	(*Many voices*) So the North Wind came along
	(*Fewer voices*) And blew him in the door—
	(*Very few voices, slowly*) Now there's nothing left of him
	(*One or two voices, very slowly*) But a puddle on the floor.

Permission to reproduce from *Encountering Children's Literature: An Arts Approach* by Jane M. Gangi.

John Henry

From the Oral Tradition[2]

Narrator	John Henry told his Captain,
John Henry	"Well, a man ain't nothin' but a man,
	And before I let that steam drill beat me down,
	I'll die with a hammer in my hand,
Unison, with John Henry	I'll die with a hammer in my hand."
Narrator	Well, the Captain says to John Henry,
Captain	"Gonna bring that steam drill around,
	Gonna take that steam drill out on the job,
	Gonna whop that steel on down,
Unison, with Captain	Gonna whop that steel on down."

Female, Cumulative	*1st speaker:* John Henry had a little woman,
	1st and 2nd speaker: And her name was Polly Ann,
	1st, 2nd and 3rd speaker: When John Henry took sick and couldn't work one day,
	1st, 2nd, 3rd and 4th speaker: Polly Ann drove steel like a man,
Female, Unison	Polly Ann drove steel like a man.
Narrator	John Henry said to his shaker,
John Henry	"Shaker, why don't you sing?
	I'm throwin' twelve pounds from my hips on down,
	Just listen to that cold steel ring,
Unison, with John Henry	Just listen to that cold steel ring."
Narrator	Well, the Captain says to John Henry,
Captain	"I believe this mountain's cavin' in."
Narrator	John Henry said to the Captain,
John Henry	"'Tain't nothin' but my hammer suckin' wind, 'Tain't nothin' but my hammer suckin' wind."
Male, Reverse Cumulative	*Unison:* The man that invented the steam drill
	1st, 2nd, 3rd and 4th speaker: Thought that he was mighty fine;
	1st, 2nd and 3rd speaker: John Henry made his fourteen feet,
	1st and 2nd speaker: While the steam drill it made only nine,
	1st speaker: While the steam drill it made only nine.
Narrator	John Henry, O John Henry,
	Blood am runnin' red,
	Falls right down his hammer to the ground, Says,
John Henry	"I've beat him to the bottom but I'm dead."

Unison, with John Henry	Says, "I've beat him to the bottom but I'm dead."
Narrator	John Henry had a little woman, And the dress she wore was red, She said,
Polly Ann	"I'm goin' down the railroad track, I'm goin' where John Henry fell dead,
Unison, with Polly Ann	I'm goin' where John Henry fell dead.
Line Around	*1st speaker:* They took John Henry to the buryin' ground, *2nd speaker:* And they buried him in the sand; *3rd speaker:* And every locomotive come roarin' round
Unison	Says, "There lies a steel-drivin' man."
Unison (*softly whispering*)	Says, "There lies a steel-drivin' man."

The interpretation of *The Snowman* and *John Henry* are offered as models. Once you experience the approach and learn the possibilities inherent in the conventions, you can chorally interpret poems on your own.

5.2 Choral Reading and Culturally Responsive Teaching

Fun, enjoyment, and laughter let children know that schools are safe and worthwhile places. Using choral reading gets children involved. It also is congruent with diverse cultural styles. For example, a communication style of call–response is common among many African Americans. Geneva Gay describes this highly interactive style as one, in which listeners offer "encouragement, commentary, compliments, and even criticism to speakers as they are talking."[3] The interactive nature of choral reading taps into this cultural background. Educators of American Indians also encourage such interactive approaches to poetry: "Rhymes, limericks, tongue twisters, and jokes" ease the difficulty of mastering new sounds, and create a merrier classroom climate.[4] Sandra Fox, an Oglala Lakota educator, says, "Primary students need an environment rich in oral literature: songs, singing games, poetry, storytelling and oral play."[5] ELLs also benefit from choral reading; see the For Further Reading section in this chapter for research in this area.

5.3 The Poetry Genre

Poetry paints musically. With intensified, sensuous language, poets shape words like painters choose colors and sculptors shape clay. As the child quoted in the epigraph intuitively knew, poetry is meant to be both visualized and *heard*. When read aloud expressively, poetry captures the musicality of language while sparking children's visual imagination.

Young children naturally engage with poetry and the wonderful possibilities of words. However, the entrenched school practice of requiring children to find the *right* meaning renders boring what once delighted. And, the mistaken belief that all poetry must rhyme or be read in a sing-song manner further deadens delight. The result is that, with each passing year, poetry is less used than other genres.[6]

This decline in the use of poetry in schools may be an effect of the increase of electronic media, a form more suited to and therefore dominated by the styles of realism and naturalism. An acute observer of the media environment, sociologist Jacques Ellul writes,

> Beginning in 1930, experts noticed that language was becoming impoverished because of the development of telegraphic style and basic English. Both of these reduce the construction of a sentence to its utilitarian elements, eliminating inflection and embellishment. Computer language completes this process.[7]

Another analyst of our media culture, Julian Jaynes, shares this view, writing that the "grinding tides of irreversible naturalism" have swept away "literary languages."[8] Hearing poetry read aloud well, and the communal sharing of poetry through choral reading, can reengage lost learners, spurring them to discover other forms and types of poetry.

5.4 History of Poetry and Poetry Timeline

The poetry of the oral epics probably preceded all other literary genres and existed in many ancient cultures, often the sources of mythology. These heroic tales were created by the community and told orally. Adults and children together received them through the ear (not the eye) for centuries. The phrasing, parallel structure, and repetitions of epics helped tellers remember through speech or song. The invention of writing then allowed transcription, as Homer transcribed the *Iliad* and the *Odyssey* sometime during the eighth or seventh century BCE.

c. 3000 BCE	*Gilgamesh*, the Sumerian epic of Mesopotamia
c. 1700–1200 BCE	Rigvedic hymns of the Vedic Aryan civilization of Northern India
c. 1200 BCE	The *Iliad* and the *Odyssey*. In Greece *aidoi*, or traveling bands of poets, orated these epics.
7th cent. BCE	Sappho, lyric poetess of Lesbos

c. 1000–600 BCE	The *Mahabharata* and the *Ramayana* of the Brahmanic Age of Northern India
1st cent. BCE	*Metamorphoses,* a literary epic by Ovid; a romanized version of Greek mythology
1st cent.	*The Bhagavad-Gita* of India
618–907	The T'ang Dynasty's Golden Age of China, famous for its poetry
700	*Beowulf,* in England
13th cent.	*Prose Edda.* Probably centuries old, Sturluson collected this poem in Iceland.
1387	*Canterbury Tales,* the only extant piece of literature from this time
1600s	Basho, a Japanese poet
16th cent.	Spirituals, or sorrow songs. Enslaved Africans created poetry and song that emphasized those parts of the Bible that deal with oppression and release, like the Jews' captivity in and deliverance from Egypt. These songs both gave expression to their pain and offered comfort to those who suffered injustices from white owners.
	Shuangqing, a peasant woman poet of the Qing Dynasty, China
	Sonnets by Shakespeare
1686	*A Book for Boys and Girls: Country Rhimes for Children* by John Bunyan
1715	*Divine and Moral Songs for Children* by Isaac Watts. A refreshing change from other previously published religious works, the songs reflected a different picture of God—not the Puritan's God of vengeance but, instead, a more merciful and loving God.
1773	*Poems on Various Subjects, Religious and Moral* by Phillis Wheatley. Because of her status as an enslaved African, American publishers refused to accept her work, which was subsequently published in London.
1775	Emily Dickinson
1789, 1794	*Songs of Innocence* and *Songs of Experience* composed and illustrated by William Blake. Maurice Sendak, 200 years later, acknowledged Blake as the one who influenced his art the most.[9]
1804	*Original Poems for Infant Minds* by Ann and Jane Taylor (origin of *Twinkle, Twinkle, Little Star*)
1807	*The Butterfly's Ball and the Grasshopper's Feast* by William Roscoe published in the United States
1823	*A Visit from St. Nicholas* by Clement C. Moore

1835	*Kalevala,* Finnish legends in poetic form, compiled by Elias Lönnrot
1842	*The Pied Piper of Hamelin* by Robert Browning, illustrated by Kate Greenaway in 1888
1846	*A Book of Nonsense* by Edward Lear
1865	*The House That Jack Built* by Walter Crane, engraved by Edmund Evans
1872	*Sing-Song* by Christina Rossetti
1885	Robert Louis Stevenson's *A Child's Garden of Verses,* illustrated by Jesse Wilcox Smith
1912	Rabindranath Tagore (1861–1941), Hindu poet, awarded the Nobel prize for literature
1913	*Peacock Pie* by Walter de la Mare
1924	*When We Were Very Young* by A. A. Milne, illustrated by Ernest Shephard
1932	*The Dreamkeepers and Other Poems* by Langston Hughes

In addition to Hughes, the Harlem Renaissance engendered the poetry of James Weldon Johnson, Countee Cullen, Arna Bontemps, and others. As devastating as slavery was, children of all colors should be helped to see that the oppression of slavery is not the *only* heritage African Americans have. During this time, a blues aesthetic developed that exposes injustices and celebrates victories.[10] Because of the link between aural and musical forces, Trudier Harris suggests bringing in blues records or recordings of Langston Hughes when sharing poetry from this time.[11] Connections between his poetry and jazz form can be made.

5.5 Poetry, Creativity, and Memorization

Csikszentmihalyi's study on creativity, in which he and his associates interviewed more than ninety highly creative people, verified the importance of learning the "symbolic information" of the discipline. Successful poets reported having memorized the poems of others before finding their own voice and their own style.[12] In response to the meaningless rote learning required by most public schools at the end of the nineteenth century, and the harsh punishment that often accompanied it, humane progressive educators moved away from recitation and rote learning. Today, with the exception of the multiplication tables, few teachers emphasize memorization of any kind. However, in light of Csikszentmihalyi's research, perhaps educators can rethink memorization in nonoppressive ways.

In her biography, Nien Ching describes her suffering through six and a half years of solitary confinement during Mao's cultural revolution—a desperate time when she barely survived because of poor health and lack of food. Nothing was allowed in her dark cell except for the writings of Chairman Mao. To endure her misery, hunger, and depression, Ching found solace in poetry. She writes,

> I turned . . . to the Tang dynasty poetry I had learned as a schoolgirl. It really amazed me that I was able to dig out from the deep recesses of my brain verses that had lain dormant for decades. Trying to remember poems I thought I had forgotten was a joyful occupation. Whenever I managed to piece together a whole poem, I felt a sense of happy accomplishment. The immortal words of the great Tang poets not only helped me to improve my memory but also transported me from the grim reality of the prison cell to a world of beauty and freedom.[13]

Hopefully, none of our children will undergo such ordeals. Teachers who emphasize poetry, however, may not ever know the powerful contribution they make, which only emerges in their pupils' later years. Celebrated Chicago-based educator, Marva Collins, tells her mostly African American students, "You will memorize a poem every week so that you can train your mind to remember things."[14] Such concentration can nurture imagination.

Johan Huizinga, in his path-breaking *Homo Ludens,* makes the observation that most civilized and artistic forms grew out of the human impulse to play. He says, "The affinity between poetry and play is not external only; it is also apparent in the structure of the creative imagination itself. In the turning of a poetic phrase, the development of a motif, the expression of a mood, there is always a play element at work."[15] Playfulness and creativity go hand in hand; keeping alive a sense of play is vital in creative work of any kind.

As an elementary school-age child, author Maya Angelou loved the poetry of Paul Lawrence Dunbar, Langston Hughes, and James Weldon Johnson. Growing up in poverty-stricken Stamps, Arkansas, during the Depression, Maya Angelou describes falling in love with sonnets by William Shakespeare before adolescence. She admired other classical writers, she says, but Shakespeare was the one who wrote "When in disgrace with fortune and men's eyes"—this line, written more than 300 years before, expressed how Angelou often felt.[16] Offering a full palette of poetry by diverse poets, including poetry not typically found in elementary classrooms, ensures that all children have the possibility of finding something meaningful, based on their past experiences, tastes, and abilities.

Because we learn best through analogy, the teacher who emphasizes poetry may give the greatest gift of all. Imagination is central in the process of reading and writing: "We cannot know through language what we cannot imagine," says Elliott Eisner. "The image—visual, tactile, auditory—plays a crucial role in the construction of meaning through text. Those who cannot imagine cannot read."[17] Debbie Miller, Denver first-grade teacher extraordinaire, explicitly models this crucial reading strategy, using poetry to help children gain competence in visualizing and imagining.[18]

5.6 *The Elements of Poetic Language*

In the previous chapter, the elements, styles, and media of the visual arts were introduced. In this chapter, the elements of figurative and poetic language are introduced. Although there are many excellent picture books of poetry, the emphasis in poetry is the linkage between word and music, in contrast with the word and visual art as in picture books. Illustrated versions can be used, of course, but teachers must create spaces in the curriculum for children to *hear* poetry read aloud—without the pictures—so that children can visualize for themselves the imagery and feel the full effect of the musical sound of language.

An awareness of the elements of poetic language will help you to recognize them more keenly when you encounter them in prose genres, even the expository language of nonfiction.

Before exploring the elements of poetic language, first read Pat Mora's poem, *Colors Crackle, Colors Roar* (see Figure 5.1):

> Red shouts a loud, balloon-round sound.
> Black crackles like noisy grackles.
> *Café* clickety-clicks its wooden sticks.
> Yellow sparks and sizzles, tzz-tzz.
> White sings, *Ay,* her high, light note.
> *Verde* rustles leaf-secrets, swhish, swhish.
> *Gris* whis-whis-whispers its kitten whiskers.
> Silver ting-ting-a-ling jingles.
> *Azul* coo-coo-coos like *pajaritos* do.
> Purple thunders and rum-rum-rumbles.
> *Oro* blares, a brassy, brass tuba.
> Orange growls its striped, rolled roar.
> Colors Crackle. Colors roar.

Referring back to Mora's poem, we'll explore the elements.

Imagery is the evocation of sensuous mental pictures through the concrete language of smelling, touching, hearing, tasting, or seeing. Mora's poem is rich in images that appeal to the senses, for example, the line "*Verde* rustles leaf-secrets . . . " appeals to both smelling and hearing: When leaves rustle, there is often a scent of the woods.

Figurative Language   *Metaphor* is a direct comparison between two distinctly different things: "*Gris* whis-whis-whispers its kitten whiskers." Here she compares the color gray with the whiskers of a kitten.

Simile is an explicit comparison between two distinctly different things by using the words *like* or *as:* "*Azul* coo-coo-coos like *pajaritos* do."

Personification is a metaphor in which inanimate or nonhuman things are described as if they were human or animal: "Red shouts . . . / White sings. . . ./ Orange growls . . . " To find other examples of personification, see *Dirty Laundry Pile,* selected by Paul Janeczko, a collection of poems written in the voices of inanimate objects and animals.

Allusion refers to the way literature refers to earlier works of literature: "Silver ting-ting-a-ling jingles" might call to mind the song *Jingle Bells.*

Sounds of Poetry   *Rhythm* is the recognizable pattern, or the beat, of the poem and shares with music patterned sound (called *cadence* when found in prose): "*Café*

Figure 5.1 *Confetti: Poems for Children* by Pat Mora features "Colors Crackle, Colors Roar." Acrylic illustrations are by Enrique O. Sanchez.

clickety-clicks its wooden sticks" has a distinct rhythm. The poetry picture book, *Bein' with You This Way,* exudes rhythm (see Figure 5.2).

Rhyme is the repetition of similar speech sounds, often, although not always, placed on the last stressed vowel in a line. In "Red shouts a loud, balloon-round sound," the rhyme is *within* the line, whereas in this anonymous poem, rhyming words are at the *end* of the line:

One two three
Father caught a flea:
Put him in the teapot
To make a cup of tea.

Melody refers to sounds arranged in such a way to evoke a musical effect. Some poems are especially suitable for singing, either a cappella or with a musical instrument—for example, Tom Paxton's *Going to the Zoo.* Recording artists Ella Jenkins, the King's Singers, and Raffi are other excellent sources.

Figure 5.2 W. Nikola–Lisa's *Bein' with You This Way*, illustrated in watercolor and pencil by Michael Bryant, is a rhythmic, multiethnic celebration of all the colors people are.

Alliteration is the repetition of similar speech sounds with initial consonants in a group of words: "Colors Crackle, Colors Roar." Mora's title includes alliterative sounds— the *k, k, k* of the first three words.

Consonance is the repetition of consonants throughout a grouping of words, usually the ending of words:

There were three *ghostesses*
Sitting on *postesses*
Eating buttered *toastesses*
And greasing their *fistesses*
Right up to their *wristesses.*
Weren't they *beastesses*
To make such *feastesses!*

If you read this chorally, take advantage of the dramatic possibilities inherent in the "-esses."

Assonance refers to repeated speech sounds that are vowels and, because of their soothing effect, are often found in lullabies. Tongue twisters emphasizing assonance are

Willy Wombat watched Wally worth wallow with warblers.
Around the rugged rock, the ragged rascal ran.
Amos asked Aaron about Amy.

Here, the emphasis is placed on the "aaahhh" sounds.

Onomatopoeia refers to words that sound like what they mean. Again, from Mora's poem: "crackles," "grackles," "clickety-clicks," and "whis-whis-whispers."

5.7 Forms of Poetry

Form in poetry—the way the words are arranged on the page—is tied to its meaning. For example, *Pull Hitter* by R. Gerry Fabian:

> At
> the
> CRACK
> of the bat
> a l o n g drive
> c
> u
> r
> v
> i
> n
> g
> Foul![19]

Paul Janeczko's *A Poke in the I: A Collection of Concrete Poems* illustrated by Chris Raschka, and Michael Rosen's *The Kingfisher Book of Children's Poetry* have other examples of form in poetry. Children can respond to this type of poetry by creating their own forms.

5.8 Types of Poetry

Lullabies, or cradlesongs, seem to be universal in cultures. Parents and other caretakers everywhere sing or chant words to lull children to sleep. A number of lullabies are included in the poetry bibliography in Appendix C.

Mother Goose and Nursery Rhymes are short, rhymed poems for the littlest ones. They come to us from the oral tradition, shaped and reshaped by generations of retellers. They address the young child's most pressing needs and interests, like falling down and getting up, and eating, and, often, address their fears, such as in "Miss Muffet."

Some of the rhymes might have originated in tragedies centuries ago: *Ring-a-ring o'roses,* it has been speculated, was created during an outbreak of the bubonic plague. The rosy signaled infection, the posies were superstitiously used for protection. The bodies fell so quickly there was little time for burial, and so were burned.[20] Young children, in response to what they saw and experienced, may have created their own cultural forms of expression.

Because of electronic media, today's children are not as familiar with nursery rhymes and playground games as previous generations were. Preschool children watch significant amounts of television, which displaces time that might have been spent hearing nursery rhymes. Called *phonological awareness,* familiarity with these rhymes brings children a richer knowledge of language and the possibilities of sounds, and repetition helps develop a sense of prediction crucial to becoming proficient readers. Nursery rhymes can be found throughout the bibliography, including the illustrated versions of timeless artists like Kate Greenaway, Jessie Wilcox Smith, and Arthur Rackham. More modern renditions include Shelly Gill's *The Alaska Mother Goose* and Susan Jeffers's Caldecott honor book, *Three Jovial Huntsmen.*

Lyric poetry has its roots in ancient Greece, referring to short poems accompanied by the lyre, and written in first person. The lyrical poem focuses on one aspect of life or nature and usually evokes an intensified mood. William Blake's verse—"To see the world in a grain of sand, and eternity in an hour"[21]—best describes the effect of the lyric poem. The poet helps us step outside of time and see in the small thing far more than we usually see in our daily lives. One of the world's greatest lyric poets was Christina Rossetti:

Who has seen the wind?
  Neither I nor you;
But when the leaves hang trembling
  The wind is passing through.
Who has seen the wind?
  Neither you nor I;
But when the trees bow down their heads
  The wind is passing by.[22]

Lyric poems often crystallize some perception, thought, and feeling about *nature.* A fine collection of lyric poetry is Barbara Rogasky's *Winter Poems.*

Human experience and the *everyday world* is another popular subject in lyric poetry—for example, Robert Louis Stevenson's *A Child's Garden of Verses.*

The *sonnet,* a type of lyric poem, has differing rhyming schemes depending on the type of sonnet, and is fourteen lines long. Shakespeare's sonnets are some of the most famous.

Narrative poetry, in contrast with lyric poetry, which focuses on singular incidents or phenomena, tells a story in poetic form (see Figure 5.3). Subgenres of narrative poetry are epics, ballads, story poems, and romances. *Ballads,* including *sea chanties,* tell stories in song, often accompanied by a chant or repetition. There are usually places for audiences to participate in the singing and chanting. Many ballads come to us from the oral tradition and have entertained the common folk for centuries. Because each singer performs the poem differently, there are many variants of ballads. Examples are *Greensleeves,* and *The Fox Went Out on a Chilly Night* retold by Peter Spier, and *Mommy Buy Me a China Doll* retold by Harve and Margot Zemach.

Story poems vary in length, and follow the Aristotelian structure of a clear beginning, middle, and end (see Figure 5.4). The plot of the story poem usually builds to a climactic moment. Still-cherished story poems from the nineteenth and early twentieth century are Clement C. Moore's *A Visit from St. Nicholas,* Christina Rossetti's *Goblin Market,* Alfred Noyes's *The Highway Man,* Robert Browning's *The Pied Piper,* and Ernest Thayer's *Casey at the Bat.* Gustave Doré's engravings found in Samuel Taylor Coleridge's narrative poem, *The Rime of the Ancient Mariner,* influenced the contemporary children's illustrator Paul

Figure 5.3 Navajo Luci Tapahonso's *Songs of Shiprock Fair* is a narrative poem, illustrated in the style of Navajo folk art and the medium of acrylic by Navajo illustrator Anthony Chee Emerson.

Galdone. The veterinarian James Herriott found titles in Coleridge's poem for his autobiographical accounts of veterinary practice in rural England—for example, *All Creatures Great and Small*. Literature and art evoke more literature and art. Examples of contemporary story poems are *Songs of Shiprock Fair* by Luci Tapahonso, illustrated by Anthony Chee Emerson; and *Meet Danitra Brown* by Nikki Grimes, illustrated by Floyd Cooper.

Rap as poetic form emerged out of urban areas in the 1970s. It is characterized by a rhythmic background beat that serves as a counterpoint for improvised wording. *I See the Rhythm* by Toyomi Igus and illustrator Michele Wood is a history of African American music, including rap, blues, ragtime, jazz, swing, bebop, gospel, and funk, and lends itself well to the inclusion of these types of music. Eloise Greenfield's *Nathaniel Talking* gives examples of rap, and David Vozar's *Yo! Hungry Wolf!* and *Rapunzel: A Happenin' Rap* set folktales in the style of rap. In her book *Other People's Children: Cultural Conflict in the Classroom*, Lisa Delpit highlights teacher Amanda Branscombe who utilized her students' expert knowledge of rap as a segue into a study of grammar and Shakespeare.[23] This exemplifies what it means to recognize and draw on students' strengths, and to build on their cultural knowledge.

Vietnamese *ca dao* are short, lyrical poem-songs from the oral tradition. John Balaban audiotaped some of these poems in 1980, and comments that, for the Vietnamese, these poems are like the architecture of the West. The annual monsoons made lasting architectural structures almost impossible. Instead, the Vietnamese monuments to civilization reside in its songs and poems.[24]

Haiku, a highly structured Japanese form of poetry, offers western children a different kind of aesthetic experience, inviting yet another way to perceive beauty. In this elegantly simple poetic form, less is more. Japanese aesthetics place value on the single moment, the quiet innuendo that has the possibility of opening up a universe of beauty.

MEET
DANITRA
BROWN

N I K K I   G R I M E S
I L L U S T R A T E D   B Y
F L O Y D   C O O P E R

Figure 5.4 Nikki Grimes's lyrical verse creates a story poem about friendship in *Meet Danitra Brown,* illustrated by Floyd Cooper.

A single flower is as beautiful, to the Japanese, as a huge bouquet of flowers. This focus on beauty found in simplicity is an alternative message for our materialistic society. Usually nonrhyming, haiku has three lines and seventeen syllables. Five syllables in the first line create the setting, seven syllables in the second line show the action, and five syllables in the third line indicate an overall feeling or insight (the exact number of syllables do not always translate into English):

Morning Horses by Basho (1644–1694)

O look!
See the horses
In the morning snow![25]

Free verse, although it is similar to other forms of poetry because it is expressed in short lines, is not organized by meter and does not rhyme. Examples include Walt Whitman's *Leaves of Grass,* Langston Hughes's *Mother to Son,* and *Brown Honey in Broomwheat Tea* by Joyce Carol Thomas.

Humorous and nonsense verses should be a part of every child's experience. To laugh and play with words feeds both the imagination and the developing schema by which children become more sophisticated readers. These rhymes make light of the human condition, and are often nonsensical and whimsical, like this anonymous verse:

> Way down South where bananas grow,
> A grasshopper stepped on an elephant's toe.
> The elephant said, with tears in his eyes,
> "Pick on somebody your own size!"

Nonsense verses are common in children's *playground games* and *jump rope chants:*

> Cinderella dressed in yella
> Went downstairs and kissed a fella
> She made a mistake
> And kissed a snake
> How many doctors did it take? 5, 10, 15, 20, 25 . . .

See Francelia Butler's *Skipping Around the World* and "Jump Rope Rhyme" in Nikki Grimes's *Meet Danitra Brown.*

Limericks have five lines: The first, second, and fifth lines rhyme with each other, and the third and fourth lines rhyme. For examples, see Edward Lear, Ogden Nash, and Lewis Carroll. The latter's *Jabberwocky* particularly invites interpretation through dance and movement. Humorous verse can be found in Laura Richards's *Tirra Lirra* (especially "Eletelephony") and Bruce Lansky's *Kids Pick the Funniest Poems.* Shel Silverstein and Jack Prelutsky, both humorists, are the most common poets found in elementary classrooms. A former teacher of children's literature, Barbara Reed says Silverstein "made poetry possible for children," but she hopes that children broaden their explorations to other poets.[26]

Songs and finger poems are either lyrical or narrative in form, and are accompanied by motion. An example is the old finger song:

> (*Hands behind your back*) Where is Thumbkin?
> Where is Thumbkin?
> (*Bring out one thumb*) Here I am.
> (*Bring out the other thumb*) Here I am.
> (*As if one thumb were talking to the other*) How are you today, sir?
> Very well, I thank you.
> (*One thumb returning behind back*) Run away.
> (*Other thumb behind back*) Run away.

Poetry by children should also be shared in classrooms. Excellent collections are Davida Adedjouma's *The Palm of My Heart: Poetry by African American Children,* Miriam Morton's *The Moon Is Like a Silver Sickle: A Celebration of Poetry by Russian Children,* and the St. Paul Community Programs in the Arts and Science's *Angwamas Minosewag Anishinabeg—Time of the Indian.*

There are a number of *bilingual* poetry collections, like *Laughing Out Loud I Fly: Poems in English and Spanish* by Juan Felipe Herrera (see Figure 5.5), available to help with ELLs. In Appendix C, double titles, or subtitles like Herrera's that specifically mention the two languages, will cue you into such books.

Figure 5.5 Karen Barbour's folk art decorates Juan Felipe Herrera's lyric poems in *Laughing Out Loud, I Fly: Poems in English and Spanish.* Note the artist's strong sense of line.

5.9 *Poetry and the Teaching of Reading*

Although picture storybooks help with the visual aspects of reading through graphic awareness, conceptions of left-to-right, alphabetical insight, and so on, poetry is crucial to the *aural* aspects of reading—that of phonological awareness. To stay on the path toward proficient reading, children must *hear* sounds as much as they need to see words encoded through writing. By listening to rhymes, rhythms, and alliterative repetitions, children hear the patterns of language. Phonological awareness is a characteristic of good readers, and lack of it can indicate where poor readers have gone off track.[27] However, Linda Hoyt and other reading educators find it disadvantageous that what should be a joyful, playful exploration of words is sometimes reduced to worksheets: "Phonemic awareness is not phonics. It is a function of the ear, not the eye."[28]

Through rhyming activities children become aware of word families, or analytic phonics (i.e., tan, man, fan), and are then better able to use whole-word strategies when decoding words. Although "not a magic wand," say reading experts Spear–Swerling and Sternberg, two of the phonological awareness tasks—rhyming and alliteration—"may be developed . . . by reading poetry and nursery rhymes to children, by playing word games, and by singing songs."[29]

In choral reading, struggling readers who need repetition can both hear and see the words. All levels of readers can simply enjoy the process. "Shared reading of poetry," writes reading expert Regie Routman, "particularly when it includes rhythm and rhyme, is one of the best ways I know for promoting confidence and competency in developing readers of any age."[30]

5.10 Conclusion

Poetry nurtures many aspects of our lives—imaginative, aural, linguistic, intellectual, and emotional. Although beneficial to all children, activities such as choral reading help you attain the NCATE standard that addresses ELLs: "Teachers need access to the growing knowledge that exists about how to teach these learners . . . effectively."[31]

As an old man, scientist Charles Darwin wrote,

> My mind seems to have become a kind of machine for grinding general laws out of large collections of facts, but why this should have caused the atrophy of that part of the brain alone, on which the higher tastes depend, I cannot conceive. . . . If I had to live my life again, I would have made a rule to read some poetry and listen to some music at least once every week; for perhaps the parts of my brain now atrophied would thus have been kept active through use. The loss of these tastes is a loss of happiness, and may possibly be injurious to the intellect, and more probably to the moral character, by enfeebling the emotional part of our nature.[32]

Hopefully, in this new century, poetry will be restored to its once honored place in the curriculum.

Suggested Activities

1. In a field experience, try choral reading with elementary school children.

2. David McCord's poem *Mug and Jug* can be a springboard for improvising the dialogue of inanimate objects set on a table moments before the family meal.[33] Throw a sheet on the floor for a tablecloth and allow students to identify and set themselves: I am the candelabra, I am the gravy, and so on. After improvising in this way, using personification in writing becomes easier.

3. Using poetry as a model, write your own riddles, jokes, and limericks in poem form. Children might involve their parents in this activity.

4. Design a baseball card based on *Casey at the Bat* by Ernest Lawrence Thayer. Or, create a narrative pantomime of the same poem—many of the sports poems included in the bibliography in Appendix C are suitable for narrative pantomime.

5. The poem Maya Angelou most loved as a child was William Shakespeare's Sonnet 29, reprinted here. First, read the poem, taking the time to register your own associations and response to the poem. (See Chapter 1.6 for reader response prompts.) Then, analyze the poem for its figurative and poetic language:

Sonnet 29
When, in disgrace with fortune and men's eyes,
I all alone beweep my outcast state,
And trouble deaf heaven with my bootless cries,
And look upon myself, and curse my fate,
Wishing me like to one more rich in hope,
Featured like him, like him with friends possessed,
Desiring this man's art and that man's scope,
With what I most enjoy contented least;
Yet in these thoughts myself almost despising,
Haply I think on thee—and then my state,
Like to the lark at break of day arising
From sullen earth, sings hymns at heaven's gate;
For thy sweet love remembered such wealth brings
That then I scorn to change my state with kings.[34]

Where do you find *imagery? Metaphor? Simile? Personification? Rhythm? Alliteration? Consonance? Assonance? Onomatopoeia?*

for further reading

Allen, Virginia G. 1991. "Teaching Bilingual and ESL Children." In: *Handbook of Research on Teaching the English Language Arts*. James Flood, Julie M. Jensen, Diane Lapp, and James R. Squire, eds. New York: Macmillan.

Bauman, James F., and Edward J. Kameenui. 1991. "Research on Vocabulary Instruction: Ode to Voltaire." In: *Handbook of Research on Teaching the English Language Arts*. James Flood, Julie M. Jensen, Diane Lapp, and James R. Squire, eds. New York: Macmillan.

Butler, Francelia. 1989. *Skipping Around the World: The Ritual Nature of Folk Rhymes*. New York: Ballantine.

Cunningham, Patricia M., and Richard L. Allington. 1999. *Classrooms That Work: They Can All Read and Write*. 2nd ed. New York: Longman.

Copeland, Jeffrey S. 1993. *Speaking of Poets: Interviews with Poets Who Write for Children and Young Adults*. Urbana, IL: National Council of Teachers of English.

Hadaway, Nancy L., Sylvia M. Vardell, and Terrell A. Young. 2001. *Literature-based Instruction with English Language Learners*. New York: Allyn & Bacon Longman.

———. 2001. "Scaffolding Oral Language Development Through Poetry for Students Learning English." *The Reading Teacher, 54.8:* 796–806.

McCauley, Joyce K., and Daniel S. McCauley. 1992. "Using Choral Reading to Promote Language Learning for ESL Students." *The Reading Teacher, 45.7:* 526–533.

Opie, Iona, and Peter Opie, eds. 1955. *The Oxford Nursery Rhyme Book*. Oxford: The Clarendon Press.

Perfect, Kathy A. 1999. "Rhyme and Reason: Poetry for the Heart and Head." *The Reading Teacher, 52.7:* 728–737.

Smith, John A. 2000. "Singing and Songwriting Support Early Literacy Instruction." *The Reading Teacher, 53.8:* 646–649.

Thomas, Edna. 1997. "Postcards of the Hanging: 1869 African American Poetry, Drama, and

Interpretation." In: *Dreamseekers: Creative Approaches to the African American Heritage*. Anita Manley and Cecily O'Neill, eds. Portsmouth, NH: Heinemann, pp. 47–58.

Williams, Joan A. 2001. "Classroom Conversations: Opportunities to Learn for ESL Students in Mainstream Classrooms." *The Reading Teacher, 54.8:* 750–757.

websites

Choral Speaking and Readers Theater:
   www.loiswalker.com/choralsp.html

Environmental Art and Poetry contest:
   http://riverofwords.org

Type in the poet's name. Many poets have their own websites—for example, Joan Graham:

www.joangraham.com

awards

Lee Bennett Hopkins Promising Poet Award:
   www.reading.org/awards/Lee.html

National Council of Teachers of English Award for Excellence in Poetry for Children:
   www.ncte.org/elem/poetry/

Signal Poetry Award:
   www.uni-leipzig.de/ ~ angl/signalpoetry.htm

notes

1. Eve Merriam, "Out Loud: Centering the Narrator in the Sound." In: *The Voice of the Narrator in Children's Literature: Insights from Writers and Critics,* Charlotte F. Otten and Gary D. Schmidt, eds. (New York: Greenwood Press, 1989), p. 231.
2. Variations of the ballad by *John Henry* can be found in B. A. Botkin, *A Treasury of American Folklore* (New York: Crown, 1944) and Margaret Bradford Boni, sel. and ed., *Fireside Book of Folk Songs* (New York: Simon & Schuster, 1947). The author was unable to track down original source of this ballad and would appreciate any assistance in doing so.
3. Geneva Gay, *Culturally Responsive Teaching: Theory, Research and Practice* (New York: Teachers College, 2000), p. 91.
4. Edwina Hoffman, "Oral Language Development." In: *Teaching American Indian Students,* Jon Reyhner, ed. (Norman, OK: University of Oklahoma Press, 1992), p. 136.
5. Sandra Fox, "The Whole Language Approach." In: *Teaching American Indian Students,* Jon Reyhner, ed. (Norman, OK: University of Oklahoma Press, 1992), p. 168.

6. Nancie Atwell, *In the Middle* (Portsmouth, NH: Heinemann, 1998), p. 416. See also Kathy A. Perfect, "Rhyme and Reason: Poetry for the Heart and Soul," *The Reading Teacher, 52.7* (1999): 731.
7. Jacques Ellul, *The Humiliation of the Word* (Grand Rapids, MI: Eerdmans, 1985), p. 161.
8. Julian Jaynes, *The Origin of Consciousness in the Breakdown of the Bicameral Mind* (Boston: Houghton Mifflin), p. 378.
9. Nicholas A. Basbanes, "Call of the Wild: Finding Inspiration in Books, Opera and the Terrors of Childhood," *Civilization* (December 1997/January 1998): 57.
10. Nancy D. Tolson, " 'Brutal Honesty and Metaphorical Grace': The Blues Aesthetic in Black Children's Literature," *Children's Literature Association Quarterly, 25.1* (2000): 56.
11. Trudier Harris, "Lying Through Our Teeth." In: *Teaching African American Literature: Theory and Practice,* Maryemma Graham, Sharon Pineault–Burke, and Marianna White Davis, eds. (New York: Routledge, 1998), p. 220.

12. Mihaly Csikszentmihalyi, *Creativity: Flow and the Psychology of Discovery and Invention* (New York: HarperCollins, 1996), pp. 251–252.

13. Nien Ching, *Life and Death in Shanghai* (New York: Penguin, 1993), p. 204.

14. Marva Collins and Civia Tamarkin, *Marva Collins's Way* (New York: Putnam's, 1990), p. 22.

15. Johan Huizinga, *Homo Ludens: A Study of the Play Element in Culture* (Boston: Beacon Press, 1950), p. 132.

16. Maya Angelou, *I Know Why the Caged Bird Sings* (New York: Bantam, 1969), p. 11.

17. Elliott Eisner, *The Kind of Schools We Need: Personal Essays* (Portsmouth, NH: Heinemann, 1998), p. 15.

18. Debbie Miller, *Reading with Meaning: Teaching Comprehension in the Primary Grades* (Portland, ME: Stenhouse, 2002), pp. 74 ff.

19. Lillian Morrison, comp., *At the Crack of the Bat: Baseball Poems* (New York: Hyperion, 1992), n.p.

20. Iona and Peter Opie, eds., *The Oxford Dictionary of Nursery Rhymes* (London: Oxford, 1951), p. 365.

21. William Blake, "Augeries of Innocence."

22. Christina Rossetti, *Sing-song: A Nursey Rhyme,* 1872.

23. Lisa Delpit, *Other People's Children: Cultural Conflict in the Classroom* (New York: New Press, 1995), pp. 32–33.

24. John Balaban, *Ca Dao Vietnam* (Greensboro, NC: Unicorn Press, 1980), p. 14.

25. Demi, *In the Eyes of the Cat: Japanese Poetry for All Seasons* (New York: Holt, 1992), n.p.

26. Jane M. Gangi, "Barbara Reed: Visionary Storyteller and Dramatist," *Stage of the Art, 4* (Summer 2000): 22.

27. Louise Spear–Swerling and Robert J. Sternberg, *Off Track: When Poor Readers Become "Learning Disabled"* (New York: Westview Press, 1996), p. 23.

28. Linda Hoyt, *Snapshots: Literacy Minilessons Up Close* (Portsmouth, NH: Heinemann, 2000), pp. 75–76.

29. Spear–Swerling and Sternberg, *Off Track,* p. 192.

30. Regie Routman, *Conversations: Strategies for Teaching, Learning, and Evaluating* (Portsmouth, NH: Heinemann, 1999), p. 36.

31. National Council for Accreditation of Teacher Education, *Program Standards for Elementary Teacher Preparation,* Introduction.

32. Quoted in Douglas Sloan, *Insight-Imagination: The Emancipation of Thought and the Modern World* (Westport, CT: Greenwood, 1983), p. 220.

33. David McCord, *Every Time I Climb a Tree* (Boston: Little, Brown, 1999), p. 10.

34. Irving Ribner and George L. Kittredge, eds., *The Complete Works of Shakespeare* (Waltham, MA: Ginn, 1971), p. 1696.

Drama
The Art of the Present

*T*heater . . . takes the student into many areas of human knowledge—literature, art, music, politics, economics, philosophy, science, invention—practically exploring all of man's activities and ideas. The study of the theatre can be and ideally is the most 'liberalizing' of all the liberal arts. Certainly . . . [it] is the most rewarding field of study for those insatiable people who desire to know 'all about everything.'[1]

—VERA MOWRY ROBERTS

6.1 Encountering Literature
through readers theater

Materials Needed

Highlighters

If you wish, you can use stools, a rope, and musical instruments.

Readers theater is a staged performance by two or more readers whose goal is to interpret and recreate a literary work expressively. Like singers who, with the human voice as an instrument, reveal the meanings they bring to the composer's notations, so do performers of readers theater bring their own interpretation to what an author has written. The relationship with the audience differs from traditional theater; the style of readers theater is suggestive rather than demonstrative. The performers guide the audience to visualize imaginatively the work of literature. Readers stay on stage for the entirety of the performance and, although movement and gesture may be used, readers generally remain stationary, sitting on stools or chairs, or standing. Almost any genre can be transformed into readers theater—novels, plays, and biography (chorally reading poetry is a form of readers theater). It is appropriate to edit selections and to provide connecting narration. Scripts are not memorized but rather are held unobtrusively by the performer.

Warm-ups Those warm-ups found in the previous chapter on poetry can be used, or the leader can simply begin by telling or reading the story *Brer Tiger and the Big Wind*. Then, as a group, rehearse improvising sounds that will be made in the performance. Have tigers practice growling, and the creatures practice making hurricane sounds. The leader uses an arrow, or some other indicator, that turns the noise up when appropriate, and then turns the noise down.

Staging can be simple: The Creatures can take their places to one side of the classroom stage, Brer Tiger can stay close to the center on the other side of the Creatures, and Brer Rabbit can sit on a stool between the Creatures and the Tiger, swiveling between the Creatures to Brer Tiger, facing whomever the dialogue implies. Prepare scripts by using highlighters for each character. The size of the group does not matter because everyone can be Creatures. One group could pantomime the story while another group reads the script.

After the readers theater event, participants can discuss what they enjoyed, what they thought was effective, what they thought could be improved, and any questions they have on classroom management. The political and economic context of the story can be discussed: Like Brer Tiger, slave owners cornered the resources and, like the Creatures, enslaved Africans were constantly faced with finding the resources they needed to survive, which they often did with subtlety and cleverness. See Responding to Drama in 6.9 of this chapter for other response questions.

Note double-spacing. Large point size, easily accomplished with a word processing program, facilitates ease in reading, thus making an aesthetic experience more likely.

Individual characters should use highlighters to mark their individual roles. When using readers theater with children, keep the highlighted set in your classroom (which will be ready for use in succeeding years). For those children who want to take copies home, keep extra copies for that purpose. *Italicized* words are stage directions, not to be read aloud.

Brer Tiger and the Big Wind
(retold by William Faulkner as told to him by a former slave)

A Readers Theater Piece

Characters

NARRATOR(S): *Several narrators may be used, depending on the number of children available.*

BRER TIGER: *Stays on stage by the tree throughout.*

BRER RABBIT

CREATURES

Brer Bear	Brer Turkey Buzzard
Brer Alligator Cooter	Brer Racoon and family
Brer Eagle and big fowls	Brer Squirrel
Sis Possum and little ones	Brer Otter
Brer Muskrat	
Birds	

The number of Creatures may be modified, depending on the number of interpreters available.

Presentation:

Narrator(s) can sit on stage left (if two are used, stage left and stage right).

The tree can be imagined—center stage.

Props and Instruments:

Musical instruments (drums, tambourines, bells) can be used to help make hurricane noise. Rope to tie Tiger can be imagined. If real rope is used, it should be gently and carefully wound around Tiger, with adult supervision (for children).

NARRATOR: In the olden days, the creatures used to plow in the fields and plant their crops the same as menfolks. When the rains came, the crops were good. But one year no rain came, and there was famine in the land. The sun boiled down like a red ball of fire. All the creeks and ditches and springs dried up. All the fruit on the trees shriveled, and there was no food and no drinking water for the creatures. It was a terrible time.

But there was one place where there was plenty of food and a spring that never ran dry. It was called Clayton Field. And in the field stood a big pear tree, just hanging down with juicy pears, enough for everybody. So the poor hungry creatures went over to the field to get something to eat and something to drink. But a great Bengal tiger lived under the pear tree, and when the creatures came nigh, he rose up.

BRER TIGER: Wumpf! Wumpf! I'll eat you up. I'll eat you if you come here. *Until the hurricane noises,* BRER TIGER *sleeps center stage, next to the tree. His sleep can be restless; but not so restless as to detract from the other actors.*

NARRATOR: All the creatures backed off and crawled to the edge of the woods and sat there with misery in their eyes, looking at the field. They were so starved and so parched that their ribs showed through their hides and their tongues hung out of their mouths.

Just about that time, along came Brer Rabbit, just a-hopping and a-skipping, as if he'd never been hungry or thirsty in his life.

BRER RABBIT: Say, what's the matter with you creatures?

CREATURES: We're hungry and thirsty and can't find any food or water—that's what's the matter with us. And we can't get into Clayton Field because Brer Tiger said he'd eat us up if we came over there.

BRER RABBIT: That's not right. It's not right for one animal to have it all and the rest to have nothing. Come here. Come close. I'm going to tell you something. BRER RABBIT *improvises whispering noisily.* CREATURES *improvise excited agreement.*

BRER RABBIT: Now, you-all be at your posts in the morning; everyone be there before sunup. CREATURES *and* BRER RABBIT *freeze in sleeping mode (tableau).*

NARRATOR: The first animal to get to his post was Brer Bear. Before daybreak, he came toting a big club on his shoulder and took his place along side an old hollow log. The next creature to arrive was Brer Alligator Cooter who crawled in the hollow log. Then Brer Turkey Buzzard and Brer Eagle and all the big fowls of the air came a-sailing in and roosted in the tops of the tall trees. Next to arrive were the tree-climbing animals, like Brer Raccoon and his family and Sis Possum and all her little ones. They climbed into the low trees. Then followed the littler creatures, like Brer Squirrel, Brer Muskrat, Brer Otter, and all kinds of birds. They all took their posts and waited for Brer Rabbit. Pretty soon, along came Brer Rabbit down the big road.

BRER RABBIT *holds a rope, either pantomimed or real.*

BRER RABBIT: Oh, Lord, oh, Lord, there's a great big wind that's a-coming through the woods, and it's going to blow ALL the people off the earth!

NARRATOR: A powerful noise broke out in the woods.

CREATURES *make shaking and blowing noises, as if a hurricane.* BRER TIGER *slowly arouses from sleep.*

BRER TIGER: What's going on out there, huh? What's going on out there?

CREATURES: Tie me! Please, sir, tie me!

BRER RABBIT: There's a great big cyclone a-coming through the woods that's going to blow all the people off the earth!

CREATURES: Tie me, Brer Rabbit. Tie me.

BRER TIGER: Brer Rabbit, I want you to tie me. I don't want the big wind to blow me off the earth!

BRER RABBIT: I don't have time to tie you, Brer Tiger. I've got to go down the road to tie those other folks to keep the wind from blowing them off the earth. Because it sure looks to me like a great big hurricane is a-coming through these woods.

CREATURES *make distant hurricane noises.*

BRER TIGER: Look-a-here, I've got my head up against this pine tree. It won't take but a minute to tie me to it. Please tie me, Brer Rabbit. Tie me, because I don't want the wind to blow me off the face of the earth.

BRER RABBIT: Brer Tiger, I don't have time to bother with you. I have to go tie those other folks; I told you.

BRER TIGER: I don't care about those other folks. I want you to tie me so the wind won't blow me off the earth. Look, Brer Rabbit, I've got my head here against this tree. Please, sir, tie me.

BRER RABBIT: All right, Brer Tiger. Just hold still a minute, and I'll take out time to save your striped hide.

CREATURES *make louder and louder hurricane noises.* BRER RABBIT *ties* BRER TIGER. BRER TIGER *pulls back and forth and believes the rope is too loose.*

BRER TIGER: Tie me a little tighter, because I don't want the big wind to blow me off the earth.

BRER RABBIT *ties* BRER TIGER *tighter while the* CREATURES *continue hurricane noises.*

BRER RABBIT (*to the* CREATURES):
Hush your fuss, children. Stop all of your crying. Come down here. I want to show you something. Look, there's our great Brer Tiger. He had all the pears and all the drinking water and all of everything, enough for everybody. But he wouldn't give a bite of food or a drop of water to anybody, no matter how much they needed it. So now, Brer Tiger, you just stay there until those ropes drop off you. And you, children, gather up your crocus sacks and water buckets. Get all the pears and drinking water you want, because the Good Lord doesn't love a stingy man. He put the food and water here for all His creatures to enjoy.

NARRATOR: After the animals had filled their sacks and buckets, they all joined in a song of thanks to the Lord for their leader, Brer Rabbit, who had shown them how to work together to defeat their enemy, Brer Tiger.

6.2 *Definitions*

Dramatic art is an umbrella term that encompasses all aspects of drama, from informal classroom improvisations to the more formal theatrical performances. *Drama* can refer to either literature for the theater, or to activities in which the participants have no audience in mind.

Creative drama, or playmaking, according to Nellie McCaslin, is "informal drama that is created by the participants. As the term *playmaking* implies, the activity goes beyond dramatic play in scope and intent. It may make use of a story with a beginning, a middle, and an end. It may also explore, develop, and express ideas and feelings through dramatic reenactment. It is, however, always improvised drama."[2]

Process drama, says Cecily O'Neill, "evokes an immediate dramatic world bounded in space and time, a world that depends on the consensus of all those present for its existence."[3] It is scriptless and improvised, and may or may not evolve from a story.

Other aspects of dramatic art are found throughout this book: *narrative pantomime* in Chapter 1.2, *choral reading* in Chapter 5.1, *readers theater* at the beginning of this chapter, *story theater* at the end of this chapter, *oral interpretation* (the solo form of readers theater) in Chapter 10.1, *role playing* in Chapter 11.1, and *story dramatization* in Chapter 13.1.

Puppetry and *masks* are natural extensions to and are often incorporated in dramatic art. Some children express themselves with more freedom when manipulating a hand, stick, or string puppet that represents animal or human characters. Similarly, wearing a mask can be a freeing experience for children, and mask making is an art and craft in many cultures. *Mother Mother I Feel Sick Send for the Doctor Quick Quick Quick,* published in 2001 by Remy Charlip and Burton Spree, is ideal for shadow puppetry, and many of the folktales listed in Appendix C, Chapter 7, are suitable for both mask making and puppetry.

6.3 *Drama Timeline*

"For as far back into history as we can know," says theater scholar David Hornbrook, "human beings have stepped out before others in a prescribed space to portray aspects of an imagined reality. Ghosts, spirits, kings, citizens and fools have been made substantial as performers and audience connive in that profoundly satisfying act of pretense we recognize as drama."[4] Through dialogue and action, theater performances tell stories as if they were happening in the present, in contrast with narrative stories that happened in the past. Ranging from the spectacularly embellished to the minimum of four boards, an actor, and a space, theater calls on the audience to interact and to imagine with actors in the exploration of some aspect of the human experience. In contrast with visual art forms, theater exists only for a brief duration of time. Like the musical event, spontaneity and an immediate group experience are part of its appeal. The artistic import of theater is created by the collective effort of director, actors, playwright, costumers, and set and light designers, thus tapping into a range of intellectual and artistic abilities. The boundaries between dance, drama, musical theater, and other performative art forms are often fluid. Drama, it seems, has almost always been part of the human experience.

8000 BCE	Mesopotamia fertility rituals probably included dramatic enactment
c. 2800 BCE	The Pyramid Texts of Egypt. These may have been enacted.
2500–550 BCE	Abydos Passion Play in Egypt
1500 BCE	The dramatic rituals during the Shang Dynasty in China

1500–1000 BCE	In India, the *Rigveda, Mahabharata,* and *Ramayana.* These literary epics provided material for Sanskrit dramatists.
1100–800 BCE	The tales of gods and goddesses in Aegean civilizations. Centuries later, in Greece, *aidoi* (traveling bands of poets) orated the *Illiad* and the *Odyssey,* which were later transcribed by Homer.
c. 8th century	Probably the time of the invention of the Phoenician alphabet. Alphabetic writing (as opposed to pictographic writing) led to playwrighting in Greece.
5th century	The tragedies and comedies of Aeschylus, Sophocles, Euripides, and others. Two forms of communication—speech and writing—collided and resulted in the dramas of the Golden Age. The plots were often drawn from the *Iliad* and the *Odyssey.*
c. 300 BCE	Aristotle's *Poetics.* This first work to examine the structure of tragedy in Greece described the elements: plot (exposition, complication, climax, denouement), thought (or theme), characters, diction, melody, and spectacle.
254–184 BCE	In Rome, Plautus's humorous, metrically arranged plays
c. 195–159 BCE	Also in Rome, Terence's complex plays, which combined Greek stories. He developed the following devices: double plots, street scenes, and eavesdropping.
c. 100 BCE	The Roman playwright Seneca's sentimental and sensational plays. He further developed theatrical devices by including asides and confidants in the unfolding dramatic story.
206 BCE–221 CE	A flowering of art and literature during the Han Dynasty in China
2nd century	In India, the appearance of the *Nāyashāstra.* Translated as *The Art of the Theater,* this volume describes for actors the physical language of gesture.
275 BCE	The *fibula Atellena,* predecessor to the *commedia dell'arte* of the Italian Renaissance. This form emerged in southern Italy, and introduced stock characters: Bucco the braggart, Pappus an old man, Maccus the glutton, and Dossenus the hunchback.
4th–5th cent.	In India, the Sanskrit drama *Sakuntala*
622 CE	The rise of Islam. Theater was forbidden; actors funneled their creative energies into puppetry and storytelling instead.
618–904	The music, dance, dialogue, and acrobatics of the T'ang Dynasty in China
923	Liturgical drama in Europe. Although long banned in most Christian circles, theater, beginning with the Easter trope, came into being as a way of teaching the gospel to illiterate parishioners.

c. 965	Ethelwold, the Bishop of Winchester, wrote *Regularis Cordia*
10th cent.	Hrosvitha, the first-known female playwright. She wrote six plays based on Terence; her plays circulated for more than 500 years.
1300s	The mystery cycles of Europe. A community endeavor organized around occupations/guilds performed the cycles: Shipbuilders dramatized the Biblical story of Noah's ark, goldsmiths dramatized the story of the Magi, and so on. The *Second Sheperd's Play* appeared around this time.
1400s	The Noh Theater and the comic Kyogen plays. In Japan, these two new forms appeared. In Europe, morality plays flourished, leading up to the publication of *Everyman* in 1500. In France, Molière brilliantly perfected French farce.
1500s	Japanese Bunraku included storytelling, puppetry, and music; India's *Kathakali* dance–drama
1512	*Ralph Roister Doister* and *Gammer Gurton's Needle.* At St. Paul's School in England, boys performed these plays in Latin.
1600s	William Shakespeare, one of the greatest dramatists of all time. He wrote plays in poetic form, thus infusing the appeal of poetry with the appeal of drama.
1400–1700	*Commedia dell'arte.* This form flourished in Italy for centuries and has influenced contemporary children's writers such as Tomie dePaola (*The Clown of God*) and Aurand Harris (*Androcles and the Lion*).
1731	With Lillo's *London Merchant.* This introduced plays about the middle class, a rising group in eighteenth century economic structures.
1806	Charles and Mary Lamb's adaptation, *Tales from Shakespeare*
1813–1883	German Romanticism. Richard Wagner sought through theatrical opera to create in hearers an ecstatic, sensual, mystical state.
1898	The Moscow Art Theater in Russia. Anton Chekhov (1860–1904) was its primary playwright, and Stanislavski, its great director. Stanislavski's "magic if" approach to acting is still an important metaphor when working creatively with children.
1904	J. M. Barrie's *Peter Pan.* Still performed today, this play that idealizes childhood must be sensitively handled in regard to its treatment of Indians.
1930s	Karamu House of Cleveland, an African American theater. The Works Progress Administration supported the Federal Theater Project during this time.

Like picture books and poetry, drama manifests itself in a variety of forms and styles. In fact, the development of a new style is often in reaction to the limitations of a previous style. For example, Bertolt Brecht created a new form called *epic theater,* in which he deliberately tried to get the audience to respond with detachment. Brecht thought the Stanislavskian and Wagnerian performances of his time were too overpowering, reducing the audience's ability to act politically or to seek change in society. Instead of trying to get his audiences to suspend disbelief, Brecht interspersed mimicry, narrative, and other devices to keep the audience from losing themselves in the play. Deliberately interrupting the drama, actors made side comments to and asked questions of the audience. Brecht thought that art, by making the routine and commonplace seem strange, could heighten perceptive powers and help the audience move out of mundane existences. Interestingly, long before multiculturalism became a movement, Brecht looked to ethnic theaters for inspiration. Asian theater, because of its nonrealistic, presentational style, especially attracted Brecht, who adapted masks and other devices to break the audience's suspension of disbelief.

Brecht's work, because it invites audience criticism, has implications for children who grow up in the electronic age. Because film and television are best calibrated to *realism* and *naturalism,* today's children already get heavy doses of these two styles in their media world, which unconsciously shapes preferences. In the visual arts, Howard Gardner observes that several studies have verified that elementary teachers "prefer realistic, representational works."[5] Yet, presentational styles have at least as much to offer as realism and naturalism—perhaps more, because they invite more participation from the audience. "How did the medieval drama succeed without any stage equipment?" asks director Vsevelod Meyerhold—"Thanks to the lively imagination of the spectator."[6]

To counterbalance a media bias toward realism, today's children can be introduced to other styles. A *minimalist* style, ideal for classrooms, requires more imagination from the audience and thus can be a more satisfying aesthetic experience than realism with all of its props, sets, and costumes.

6.4 *The Elements of Drama/Literature*

One of the first literary critics, Aristotle, in his *Poetics* wrote the *elements of tragedy,* which became foundational in the understanding of western literary form. Although the differences between western aesthetics and the aesthetics of other cultures should be remembered from the discussion in Chapter 3.8, the following can help us not only in the evaluation of drama, but in other literature as well:

- *Plot* refers to the arrangement of events and actions in the unfolding of the play (or story) that reveal character.
- *Character,* inseparably tied to the incidents of the story, is the distinct personality of the human beings—or, in fantasy, animals—revealed to the reader or viewer through action, dialogue (both what is said by and about the characters), and thought. The choices characters make reveal or solidify the qualities of their character.
- *Thought* or *theme* is the big idea or general concept the writer captures in an imaginative work.

- *Language* refers to the arrangement of words, ranging from the elevated to the commonplace to the humorous to the absurd.

- *Melody* can be partial or continually interwoven in the unfolding of the play.

- *Spectacle* includes the props, costumes, scenery, and ensemble work. Aristotle considered it the least artistic of the elements. Although it has its place, spectacle is not necessary for aesthetic enjoyment.

The latter two apply to dramatic literature that is performed; the first four apply to narrative text.

6.5 Classroom Drama: Philosophical Foundations

Most major philosophers of education, despite their other areas of disagreement, agree that the arts, and drama in particular, are essential to the curriculum. The progressivist philosopher John Dewey recommended that schools freely use "dramatizations, plays, and games."[7] He said, "Literature and the fine arts are of peculiar value because they represent appreciation at its best—a heightened realization of meaning through selection and concentration."[8] Learning by doing, thought Dewey, promoted growth, and he supported both formal and informal approaches to drama. Improvisation (informal) allows for self-expression and creativity, and playmaking (formal) can expand children's perceptions while providing the opportunity to solve problems as a group, which Dewey thought was the best preparation for participation in democracy. He had little patience for schools that emphasized process and children's inner guidance to the exclusion of content and teacher intervention: "It is impossible to understand why a suggestion from one who has larger experience and a wider horizon should not be at least as valid as a suggestion arising from one more or less accidental source."[9]

The rational humanist (or perennialist) philosopher Mortimer Adler takes a formal approach: "The best way to understand a play is to act in it, or at least to read it out loud. . . . Participation in the creation of works of art is as important as viewing, listening to, and discussing them. All children should have such pleasurable experiences" (see Figure 6.1).[10] In the *paideian* framework, like the Socratic seminar, the arts serve to enlarge understanding.

Focusing more on process, critical theorists look to the arts to contribute to empowering the oppressed through the development of the imagination and intuition. Critical theorist Peter McClaren writes, "[R]evolutionary critical pedagogy needs to be a *creative process* by incorporating elements of popular culture (i.e., drama, music, oral history, narratives) as educational tools to politicize and revolutionize working-class consciousness."[11] Educational reconstructionist Jonathan Kozol highlights a theater course as a significantly richer offering to students in poverty than the back-to-the-basics approach so often found in blighted urban schools.[12] E. D. Hirsch, who aligns himself mostly with an essentialist philosophy, calls drama "demonstrably effective classroom teaching," and recommends the combination of skills and drama.[13]

WOLF CHILD:
THE CORRECTION OF JOSEPH

by Edward Mast

Figure 6.1 Always a fascinating topic for children, Edward Mast's *Wolf Child: The Correction of Joseph* explores the legendary children raised by animals.

Throughout history the educative potential of theater has been recognized, even when disliked. For example, Goethe's father strongly disapproved of his young son's fascination with puppetry and theater (introduced to him by his grandmother)—"until he found that it was teaching young Goethe to speak French faster than any tutor."[14] Contemporary educators who work with students for whom English is a second language are discovering what Goethe's father meant (see the For Further Reading section in this chapter).

6.6 Drama as Culturally Responsive Teaching

Educators of color recognize drama as a potentially powerful way to learn what marginalized children most need to know, easing the cultural mismatch that often impedes their learning experiences. For children to participate successfully in economic and democratic life, they must learn to read and speak standard English. However, as James Comer observes (paraphrased by Janice Hale), "upward mobility for a poor, inner-city, African American child means that he must learn to speak differently and behave differently from everyone who has raised him, known him, and loved him."[15] When helping children attain the standard English they need to succeed in the larger society, teachers tend to overcorrect children who speak a different dialect. The constant threat of being corrected by the teacher negatively charges the classroom atmosphere, creates high anxiety, and makes it harder to learn. To eliminate denigration, educator Lisa Delpit suggests: "[M]emorizing parts for drama productions will allow students to 'get the feel' of speaking Standard English while not under the threat of correction. . . . Playing a role eliminates the possibility of implying that the *child's* language is inadequate, and suggests, instead that different language forms are appropriate in different contexts."[16] Drama educators are ambivalent about formal approaches to theater, which includes the memorization of lines. However, given a nonthreatening context, Delpit's suggestion could be beneficial with upper grade elementary school children.

Marva Collins—who has written several books about her teaching successes in Chicago and about whom a film starring Cecily Tyson has been made—infuses literature often deemed too advanced for elementary school children into her curriculum, including the plays of William Shakespeare.[17] Some educators worry about the appropriateness of such material; they are correct that not all children can make a connection with Shakespeare. This does not mean, however, that all elementary school children should be denied access to difficult work. Such works may become the sacred memory of childhood that enriches them throughout their lives. British author Richard Adams credits the Greek plays that he performed during his own school years as shaping his writing of the award-winning and beloved fantasy *Watership Down.*[18] Collins herself reports that she was enthralled with *Macbeth* when she was nine years old. In her school she has successfully used *Twelfth Night, A Midsummer's Night Dream, Hamlet, Romeo and Juliet, The Merchant of Venice, Julius Caesar,* and *King Lear.*[19] And Phyllis Aldrich reports that a Board of Cooperative Educational Services (BOCES) Young Scholars program in a rural area successfully used such classics as *Medea* with verbally advanced fifth- and sixth-grade students.[20]

Kathryn Au insists that quality literacy instruction in both monolingual and bilingual classrooms include creative dramatics as part of a range of strategies.[21] Describing multicultural, constructivist classrooms, Au recommends both the improvisational acting out of scenes from stories as well as the more formal putting on of plays.[22] Either project contributes to a positive classroom atmosphere because children can be engaged, collaborative learners. Drama and puppetry are also recommended for American Indian children so as "to enhance students' total physical and mental involvement in the language-learning process."[23] Angel Vigil's *¡Teatro! Hispanic Plays for Young People* helps fill the dearth of contemporary Hispanic dramatic literature; theater has strong historical roots in the American Southwest. Teachers can build, especially, on Mexican American children's knowledge of *Las Posadas,* traditional reenactments of the Christmas story for nine days during that holiday. Readers theater is an excellent segue into Latino traditional literature.[24] The participatory, interactive qualities of drama create dynamic and hospitable classrooms.

6.7 Research on Drama and Academic Achievement

Under the auspices of Harvard University, in 2000, Ellen Winner, a professor at Boston College, and Lois Hetland completed an enormous research undertaking. They reviewed more than 11,000 articles claiming evidence of enhanced academic achievement for those students who participate in arts programs. Using stringent—perhaps too stringent—scientific criteria, Winner and Hetland threw out many of the studies. However, of all the arts in the study, participation in drama was clearly a beneficial factor in student learning. Their findings are so important that I quote them at length:

> Based on 80 reports . . . a causal link was found between classroom drama (enacting texts) and a variety of verbal areas. Most were of medium size (oral understanding/recall of stories, reading readiness, oral language, writing), one was large (written understanding/recall of stories), and one was small and could not be generalized to new studies (vocabulary). In all cases, students who enacted texts were compared to students who read the same texts but did not enact them. Drama not only helped children's verbal skills with respect to the texts enacted; it also helped children's verbal skills when applied to new, non-enacted texts. *Thus drama helps to build verbal skills that transfer to new materials. Such an effect has great value for education; verbal skill is highly valued, adding such drama techniques costs little in terms of effort or expense, and a high proportion of students are influenced by such curricular changes.*[25] [emphasis added]

In 2001, Kent Seidel also reviewed hundreds of studies on the arts published since 1983. He concluded, "Having students work with creative drama and theatre in . . . earlier grades gives them a great advantage in their capacity for developing language skills, reading, writing, and verbal and interpersonal skills."[26]

So far, while reading this textbook, you may have participated in a narrative pantomime of *Andy and the Lion* or *Jonathan and His Mommy,* a choral reading of *The Snowman* and *John Henry,* and a readers theater performance of *Brer Tiger and the Big Wind.* Other dramatic forms will be introduced in later chapters: oral interpretation, improvisational role playing, and story dramatization. All of these dramatic experiences are strongly supported in a growing research base that we can ill afford to neglect.

Louise Spear–Swerling and Robert Sternberg use the analogy of piano practice: Prior to a recital, one piece of music is played many times; yet, in reading, we often expect children to get it after reading material once or twice. They and other reading researchers agree that children need multiple readings of texts as much as piano players need repetition in practice. But, as classroom teachers know, boredom sets in after several readings. However, couched in terms like *rehearsal* and *performance,* children are motivated to read and reread and reread. Then they can gain competence in fluency, automaticity, and other reading skills. The National Research Council Committee on the Prevention of Reading Difficulties final report recommends that teachers dedicate classroom time for dramatizations throughout the elementary school years.[27]

Brain-based researchers Renate and Geoffrey Caine describe a practical application. A second-grade teacher, frustrated that no matter how she presented it, her students could not grasp punctuation, took her students outside for this enactment:

> She told them, "I am going to read to you and I want you to walk around in a circle. When I say 'comma' I want you to sloooow down, whenever I say 'period' I want you to stop dead in your tracks, and when I say 'exclamation mark' I want you to jump up and down. Do you understand?" She tried this for five minutes with perfect success. When they went back inside and read, all of them slowed down at the commas, paused at the periods, and used emphasis at exclamation marks.[28]

This kind of utilitarian treatment of drama may disturb some drama educators. Although it is hoped that students can enact more than commas and exclamation marks during their school careers, if it helps children learn, it should be a legitimate strategy for teachers.

Shirley Brice Heath's classic work established that reading is more of a group process in African American communities than an individual process, as it is in most European American communities:

> Reading was a public group affair for almost all members of Trackton from the youngest to the oldest. Miss Lula sometimes read her Bible alone, and Annie Mae would sometimes quietly read magazines she brought home, but to read alone was frowned upon, and individuals who did so were accused of being anti-social. . . . Long before school, their language and culture at home has structured for them the meanings which will give shape to their experiences in classrooms and beyond.[29]

Using drama in your classroom can enhance the achievement of all children.

6.8 Drama in the Twenty-first Century: A Venue to Develop

Despite historical, philosophical, and broad-based support, drama is vastly underutilized in elementary classrooms. To strengthen understanding of its possibilities in helping children more quickly attain the knowledge and skills we want them to have will require interdisciplinary collaboration. Reading researchers, teacher educators, and teachers need to become aware of the remarkable research base that demonstrates drama's value for children, helping them to succeed. Elementary teachers must develop the skill to lead simple drama activities, ranging from formal to informal approaches. As pointed out in Chapter 1.4, we tend to teach the way we were taught and, for most of us, drama was not part of what we experienced in our own schooling.

Both formal and informal approaches to drama have their place in the classroom. Performance is more common in the upper elementary grades; however, if the suggestion comes from the children, performance may be appropriate for younger children. As Roberts observes in the epigraph, theater is by nature interdisciplinary. Students with varying abilities can fulfill varying roles, whether onstage or behind the scenes—a multiple intelligence fest.

Although you cannot be expected to have expertise in all aspects of the theater, there are ways for you to implement it easily in the classroom; you can find suggestions in the bibliography at the end of this chapter. You can also build on what already exists in the community: Actors, playwrights, and others with theater expertise can be invited to share their talents. Hopefully, there are drama specialists with whom you can work in your school.

In our work with children, we must go beyond the representational, Eurocentric styles of realism and naturalism. Multicultural dramatic forms tend to be more presentational. Sita Brahmachari writes, "The absence of culturally diverse dramatic forms of expression in the drama classroom confirms students' perception that naturalism, seen daily on our television screens, is the only form of dramatic expression of any interest." The Jamaican Jonkonnu, a masked performance, for example, can augment the curriculum. Further supportive of interdisciplinary work, Brahmachari says,

> Another obstacle to a genuinely multicultural drama curriculum is the historical compartmentalisation of the arts in European culture. For most world cultures, drama is the place where dance, music and text unselfconsciously meet. Forms of artistic expression—drama, dance, poetry, music, painting, or combinations of them—are intertwined and deeply rooted in the cultures from which they spring. Understanding this aesthetic unity will be essential for students embarking on an investigation of the dramatic function, structure and content of world drama.[30]

Too often children merely mimic what they see on television. Jonathan Levy asks us to resist trying to compete with electronic media, which tend to cram together a series of crises. Rather than appealing to the nervous system, says Levy, theater can appeal to the imagination.[31] A classroom does not have to be perceived as bereft of theatrical equipment. Instead, the fewer props, the more children will have to use their imaginations. Readers theater, story theater, and puppetry are presentational in style.

The creating and making of plays for elementary children is a challenge for the future. "Where," asks Scott Copeland, "are the contemporary plays for the younger set—and I am talking four to seven years of age here—that dramatize the conflicts of contemporary childhood for contemporary children?"[32] Laurie Brooks's play, *Devon's Hurt*, already highlighted in Chapter 3.4 because of its compassionate treatment of boys and their feelings, offers a wonderfully sensitive and humorous contribution to the dramatic literature for elementary school children.

All of the following are new plays, featuring casts of mostly children of color. Belinda Acosta's *3 Girls and Clorox* depicts multiethnic friendships at a private school, where the African American protagonist, Thayon, resorts to bleaching her hair so she can look like the white girls trying out for the cheerleading team. Her Latino friend, Lydia, helps her learn what it means to be herself and to belong. Joseph Bruchac's *Pushing Up the Sky:*

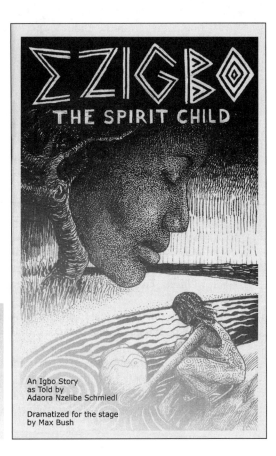

Figure 6.2 *Ezigbo: The Spirit Child,* an Igbo story as told by Nigerian storyteller Adaora Nzelibe Schmiedl to playwright Max Bush, explores the tension an Ogbanje child experiences in straddling the real world, where her beloved mother lives, and the spirit world, where her companions live. Cover art by John S. Douglas.

Seven Native American Plays for Children theatrically explores the traditional tales of American Indians. And Max Bush's dramatization of an Igbo story, *Ezigbo: The Spirit Child* (Figure 6.2), retold by the Nigerian storyteller Adaora Nzelibe Schmiedl, is a gripping play about an Ogbanje child, a child who has been born to die but who, nevertheless, is still close at hand. While bringing much joy to her human mother, Ezigbo eventually decides to rejoin her Ogbanje playmates. Schmiedl explains that the high child mortality rate in countries like Nigeria influence the creation of such tales; however, this story is also much like the transformation tales that occur in many cultures, like the selkie of Ireland. *The Yellow Boat* by David Soar chronicles the tragedy of a boy who becomes infected with AIDS.

When ordering multiple sets of books for children's literature response groups, teachers should not forget to order multiple sets of plays as well.

6.9 Responding to Drama

Whether engaging in informal or formal drama, a model, as developed by David Hornbrook, of making, performing, and responding is a helpful way to structure the enterprise.[33] Making would involve planning, writing, and thinking through. Performing is the actual dramatic event, and responding offers the opportunity to criticize, in the most positive sense of the word, what has been made and performed. According to Winnifred Ward and Nellie McCaslin, the following questions can be asked:

- Was the story or scene clear? Would someone who had not read the story understand the characters and plot? Did the players tell the story?
- Were the characters believable? How did the players use their imaginations to interpret the characters?
- Was there enough action? Too much?
- Was the dialogue true to the characters? Did it carry the story forward?
- Comment on the teamwork of the players: Did they listen and respond to each other?
- Was there anything important left out?
- Can you think of anything that would improve it when we play it again?[34]

For older children at a more sophisticated level, the following questions, based on David Hornbrook's application of semiotics, are also appropriate for the responding mode:

- To what extent has your initial response been modified?
- On reflection, what did the play most make you think about?
- Was the performance an interpretation? If so, how successful was it?
- If you had been the director, what would you have done differently?
- What are the differences between your interpretation of what you saw and others you have read or heard?
- What have you learned about drama from the production?
- In what medium would you most like to express your thoughts and feelings about the play?[35]

Semiotics, based on the science of signs, describes the processes by which meaning is attributed to cultural artifacts. It is important for children to have access to different models of response; each has its limitations that can be counterbalanced by multiple offerings. The responding mode is especially important in an age of mass media because of its potential in helping children develop a critical vocabulary, so they can then evaluate their many media experiences. Asking students to think aloud, and with each other, helps them articulate what they see, what they hear, what they comprehend, and how they understand their environment.

6.10 Conclusion

Preservice and inservice teachers who expand their knowledge and skills in drama can make tremendous contributions to the lives of the children they teach, drawing from a repertoire of instructional strategies, and enhancing their own abilities to communicate. Furthermore, all aspects of dramatic art can have positive effects on student learning. NCATE urges you to make connections among the standards "to motivate elementary students, build understanding, and encourage the application of knowledge, skills, tools, and ideas to real world issues."[36] Connecting the arts and literacy standards are a natural fit, well supported by research: Readers theater, story dramatization, and choral reading provide artistic and aesthetic experiences while enhancing reading.

6.11 Encountering Literature
through story theater

A small group can perform for the class a story theater piece. *Story theater,* as developed by Paul Sills, is a flexible dramatic form in which there may be a narrator who dictates the action and events that the actors perform. The narrating links are sometimes in the dialogue itself, spoken by the actors, giving the performance a Brechtian effect. Costuming may or may not be used. In this, and in all classroom drama, actors can play with the elements of the theater: *sound and silence, light and dark,* and *movement and stillness.* They can also play with the conventions of choral reading introduced in the poetry chapter. Offstage drums and tambourines can be used for dramatic effect. A good beginning experience is to use folklore found in Chapter 7, Appendix C.

In theater, use of space is also part of the art. Beginners tend to flock DC (down center) and can be helped to gain an awareness of the other eight areas. Also, beginners tend to turn their backs to audiences and may need some guidance in stage positioning. With all the performing arts, audibility can be a problem—"Share your voice" is a positive way of encouraging students to speak louder.

Stage space

UP RIGHT (UR)	UP CENTER (UC)	UP LEFT (UL)
RIGHT (R)	CENTER (C)	LEFT (L)
DOWN RIGHT (DR)	DOWN CENTER (DC)	DOWN LEFT (DL)

After the performance, evaluate the work by sharing what was effective.

Suggested Activities

1. Adapt a scene from a favorite book for readers theater.

2. Create a dialogue between interesting characters from any genre.

3. Create masks for a story then dramatize the story. *Who's in Rabbit's House?* retold by Verna Aardema, is a good place to start, or *Where the Wild Things Are* by Maurice Sendak.

4. Create puppets for a story then dramatize it.

for further reading

Drama and Reading

Bidwell, Sandra. 1992. "Ideas for Using Drama to Enhance Reading Instruction." *The Reading Teacher, 45*: 653–654.

de La Cruz, Rey E., Ming-Gon John Lian, and Lanny E. Morreau. 1998. "The Effects of Creative Drama on Social and Oral Language Skills of Children with Learning Disabilities." *Youth Theatre Journal, 12*: 89–95.

DuPont, Sherry. 1992. "The Effectiveness of Creative Drama as an Instructional Strategy to Enhance the Reading Comprehension Skills of Fifth-Grade Remedial Readers." *Reading Research and Instruction, 31.3*: 41–52.

Forsythe, Sheri J. 1995. "It Worked! Readers Theatre in Second Grade." *The Reading Teacher, 49.3*: 264 ff.

Freedman, Martha C. 1990. "Readers Theater, An Exciting Way to Motivate Reluctant Readers." *The NERA, Autumn*: 9–12.

Galda, Lee. 1982. "Playing About a Story: Its Impact on Comprehension." *The Reading Teacher, 36*: 52–55.

Hoyt, Linda. 1999. *Revisit, Reflect, Retell: Strategies for Improving Reading Comprehension.* Portsmouth, NH: Heinemann. (See the chapter called Showtime! A Celebration of Oral Reading.)

Larkin, Barbara. 2001. "'Can We Act It Out?'" *The Reading Teacher, 54.5*: 478–479.

Lindquist, Judy. 1991. "'No, Mother, I Don't Speak Japanese': Learning to Teach in an ESL Classroom." *Insights into Open Education, 24.4*: 2–7.

Martinez, Miriam. 1993. "Motivating Dramatic Story Reenactments." *The Reading Teacher, 46.8*: 682–688.

Martinez, Miriam, Nancy L. Roser, and Susan Strecker. 1999. "I Never Thought I Could Be a Star: A Readers Theatre Ticket to Fluency." *The Reading Teacher, 52.4*: 326–337.

McMaster, Jennifer Catney. 1998. "Doing Literature: Using Drama to Build Literacy Classrooms: The Segue for a Few Struggling Readers." *The Reading Teacher, 51.7*: 574–584.

Morado, Carolyn, Rosalie Koenig, and Alice Wilson. 1999. "Miniperformances, Many Stars: Playing with Stories." *The Reading Teacher, 53.2*: 116–123.

Richards, Maeribethe. 2000. "Be a Good Detective: Solve the Case of Oral Reading Fluency." *The Reading Teacher, 53.7*: 534–539.

Rinehart, Steven D. 1999. "'Don't Think for a Minute That I'm Getting Up There': Opportunities for Readers' Theater in a Tutorial for Children with Reading Problems." *Journal of Reading Psychology, 20*: 71–89.

Routman, Regie. 1999. *Conversations: Strategies for Teaching, Learning, and Evaluating.* Portsmouth, NH: Heinemann. (See p. 73 for readers theater.)

Shepard, Aaron. 1994. "From Script to Stage: Tips for Readers Theatre." *The Reading Teacher, 48.2*: 184–186.

Smith, J. Lea, and J. Daniel Herring. 2001. *Dramatic Literacy: Using Drama and Literature to Teach Middle-Level Content.* Portsmouth, NH: Heinemann.

Smolen, Lynn Atkinson, and Victoria Ortiz-Castro. 2000. "Dissolving Borders and Broadening Perspectives through Latino Traditional Literature," *The Reading Teacher, 53.7*: 566–578. (There are better selections than John Bierhorst's *Doctor Coyote,* which the authors recommend.)

Wagner, Betty J. 1991. "Imaginative Expression." In: *Handbook of Research on Teaching the English Language Arts.* James Flood, Julie M. Jensen, Diane Lapp, and James R. Squire, eds. New York: Macmillan.

Wolf, Shelby A. 1998. "The Flight of Reading: Shifts in Instruction, Orchestration, and Attitudes through Classroom Theatre." *Reading Research Quarterly, 33.4*: 382–415.

———. 1993. "What's in a Name? Labels and Literacy in Readers Theatre." *The Reading Teacher, 46.7*: 540–545.

Classroom Drama

Bolton, Gavin. 1999. *Acting in Classroom Drama: A Critical Analysis.* Portsmouth, NH: Heinemann.

Caruso, Sandra, with Susan Kosoff. 1998. *The Young Actor's Book of Improvisation: Dramatic Situations from Shakespeare to Spielberg, Volume I: Ages 7–11.* Portsmouth, NH: Heinemann.

Chapman, Gerald. 1991. *Teaching Young Playwrights.* Portsmouth, NH: Heinemann.

Grady, Sharon. 2000. *Drama and Diversity: A Pluralistic Perspective for Educational Drama.* Portsmouth, NH: Heinemann.

Heinig, Ruth Beall. 1993. *Creative Drama for the Classroom Teacher.* 4th ed. Englewood Cliffs, NJ: Prentice-Hall.

———. 1992. *Improvisation with Favorite Fairy Tales: Integrating Drama into the Reading/Writing Classroom.* Portsmouth, NH: Heinemann.

Hornbrook, David, ed. 1998. *On the Subject of Drama.* London: Routledge.

———. 1991. *Education in Drama: Casting the Dramatic Curriculum.* London: Falmer.

King, Nancy. 1995. *Playing Their Part: Language and Learning the Classroom.* Portsmouth, NH: Heinemann.

Korty, Carol. 2000. *Writing Your Own Plays.* Studio City, CA: Players Press.

Manley, Anita, and Cecily O'Neill, eds. 1997. *Dreamseekers: Creative Approaches to the African American Heritage.* Portsmouth, NH: Heinemann.

McCaslin, Nellie. 2000. *Creative Drama in the Classroom and Beyond.* 7th ed. New York: Longman.

O'Neill, Cecily. 1995. *Drama Worlds: A Framework for Process Drama.* Portsmouth, NH: Heinemann.

Saldaña, Johnny. 1995. *Drama of Color: Improvisation with Multiethnic Folklore.* Portsmouth, NH: Heinemann.

Sklar, Daniel Judah. 1991. *Playmaking: Children Writing and Performing Their Own Plays.* New York: Teachers & Writers Collaborative.

Spolin, Viola. 1986. *Theatre Games for the Classroom: A Teacher's Handbook.* Evanston, IL: Northwestern University Press.

———. 1985. *Theater Games for Rehearsal: A Director's Handbook.* Evanston, IL: Northwestern University Press.

Stewig, John, and Carol Buege. 1994. *Dramatizing Literature in Whole Language Classrooms.* 2nd ed. New York: Teachers College Press.

Swartz, Larry. 1995. *Dramathemes: A Practical Guide to Teaching Drama.* Portsmouth, NH: Heinemann.

Wagner, Betty Jane. 1998. *Educational Drama and Language Arts: What the Research Shows.* Portsmouth, NH: Heinemann.

Wilder, Roz. 1977. *A Space Where Anything Can Happen.* Charlottesville, VA: New Plays.

websites

Institute for Readers Theatre:
www.readers-theatre.com

Suzanne Barchers:
www.storycart.com

Aaron Shepard:
www.aaronshep.com

Lois Walker:
www.loiswalker.com

awards

www.aate.com/AWP.htm

notes

1. Vera Mowry Roberts, *On Stage: A History of the Theatre* (New York: Harper, 1962), p. vi.
2. Nellie McCaslin, *Creative Drama in the Classroom and Beyond*, 7th ed. (New York: Longman, 2000), p. 8.
3. Cecily O'Neill, *Drama Worlds: A Framework for Process Drama* (Portsmouth, NH: Heinemann, 1995), p. xiii. O'Neill's claim that process drama exemplifies the "aesthetic" end and creative dramatics the "efferent" end of Louise Rosenblatt's reader stance continuum is insupportable, and ignores the expanding research base that describes the effectiveness of creative drama, especially with diverse children.
4. David Hornbrook, "Drama and Education." In: *On the Subject of Drama,* David Hornbrook, ed. (London: Routledge, 1998), p. 6.
5. Howard Gardner, *Art Education and Human Development,* occasional paper 3 (Los Angeles: Getty Center for Education in the Arts, 1990), p. 22.
6. Quoted in Susan Bennett, *Theatre Audiences: A Theory of Production and Reception* (London: Routledge, 1990), p. 5.
7. John Dewey, *Democracy and Education* (New York: Macmillan, 1916), pp. 61–62.
8. Dewey, *Democracy and Education,* p. 249.
9. John Dewey, *Experience and Education* (New York: Macmillan, 1938), p. 71.
10. Mortimer Adler, *The Paideia Proposal* (New York: Collier, 1982), p. 31.
11. Peter McClaren, *Life in Schools: An Introduction to Critical Pedagogy in the Foundations of Education,* 4th ed. (Boston: Allyn & Bacon, 2003), p. xvii.
12. Jonathan Kozol, *Savage Inequalities: Children in America's Schools* (New York: Crown, 1991), p. 79.
13. E. D. Hirsch, *The Schools We Need and Why We Don't Have Them* (New York: Doubleday, 1996), p. 174.
14. Phil Coggin, *Drama and Education: An Historical Survey from Ancient Greece to the Present Day* (London: Thames and Hudson, 1956), p. 171.
15. Janice Hale, *Unbank the Fire: Visions for the Education of African American Children* (Baltimore: The Johns Hopkins University Press, 1994), xviii.
16. Lisa Delpit, *Other People's Children: Cultural Conflict in the Classroom* (New York: New Press, 1995), p. 53; and Lisa Delpit. "Ebonics and Culturally Responsive Teaching: What Should Teachers Do?" In: *Rethinking Our Classrooms, vol. 2,* Bill Bigelow, Brenda Harvey,

Stan Karp, and Larry Miller, eds. (Milwaukee, WI: Rethinking Schools, 2001), p. 23.
17. Marva Collins and Civia Tamarkin, *Marva Collins's Way* (New York: G. P. Putnam's, 1990), p. 12.
18. Richard Adams, "To the Order of Two Little Girls: The Oral and Written Versions of *Watership Down.*" In: *The Voice of the Narrator in Children's Literature: Insights from Writers and Critics,* Charlotte F. Otten and Gary D. Schmidt, eds. (New York: Greenwood Press, 1989), pp. 116–119.
19. Collins and Tamarkin, *Marva Collins's Way,* pp. 42, 159.
20. Phyllis W. Aldrich, "Evaluating Language Arts Materials." In: *Developing Verbal Talent: Ideas and Strategies for Teachers of Elementary and Middle School Students,* Joyce VanTassel-Baska, Dana T. Johnson, and Linda Neal Boyce, eds. (Needham Heights, MA: Allyn & Bacon, 1996), p. 221.
21. Kathryn H. Au, *Literacy Instruction in Multicultural Settings* (San Diego: Harcourt Brace, 1993), p. 151.
22. Au, *Literacy Instruction in Multicultural Settings,* pp. 43, 76.
23. Edwina Hoffman, "Oral Language Development." In: *Teaching American Indian Students,* Jon Reyhner, ed. (Norman, OK: University of Oklahoma Press, 1992), p. 133.
24. Lynn Atkinson and Victoria Ortiz-Castro, "Dissolving Borders and Broadening Perspectives Through Latino Traditional Literature," *The Reading Teacher, 53.7* (2000): 566–578.
25. Ellen Winner and Lois Hetland, "The Arts and Academic Achievement: What the Evidence Shows," Executive Summary of Project REAP, 2000, available at http://pzweb.harvard.edu/Research/REAP.htm.
26. www.aaae.org/artsbro/arts_bro.htm
27. M. Susan Burns, Peg Griffin, and Catherine E. Snow, *Starting Out Right: A Guide to Promoting Children's Reading Success* (Washington, DC: National Academy Press, 1999), pp. 74, 115, 118–119.
28. Renate Nummela Caine and Geoffrey Caine, *Making Connections: Teaching and the Human Brain* (Alexandria, VA: ASCD, 1991), pp. 109–110.
29. Shirley Brice Heath, *Ways with Words: Language, Life, and Work in Communities and Classrooms* (Cambridge: Cambridge University Press, 1983), pp. 191, 368.

30. Sita Brahmachari, "Stages of the World." In: *On the Subject of Drama,* David Hornbrook, ed. (London: Routledge, 1998), p. 20.

31. Jonathan Levy, *A Theatre of the Imagination: Reflections on Children and Theatre* (Charlottesville, VA: New Plays, 1987), p. 6.

32. Scott Copeland, "Foreword." In: *Devon's Hurt,* Laurie Brooks (Woodstock, IL: Dramatic Publishing, 2001), p. 5.

33. David Hornbrook, "Can We Do Ours, Miss? Towards a Dramatic Curriculum," *The Drama/Theatre Teacher, 4:2* (1992): 19.

34. McCaslin, *Creative Drama in the Classroom and Beyond,* p. 152; Winnifred Ward, *Stories to Dramatize* (New Orleans, LA: Anchorage, 1981 reprint of 1952 edition), p. 13.

35. David Hornbrook, *Education in Drama: Casting the Dramatic Curriculum* (London: Blackwell, 1991), p. 111. For another semiotic approach, see Dan Urian, "On Being an Audience: A Spectator's Guide," Naomi Paz, trans. In: *The Subject of Drama,* David Hornbrook, ed. (London: Routledge, 1998), pp. 133–150.

36. National Council for Accreditation of Teacher Education, *Program Standards for Elementary Teacher Preparation,* 2i.

Folklore
A Global Legacy

The stories that we tell ourselves and our children function to order our world, serving to create both a foundation upon which each of us constructs our sense of reality and a filter through which we process each event that confronts us every day. The values we cherish and wish to preserve, the behavior that we wish to censure, the fears and dread that we can barely confess in ordinary language, the aspirations and goals that we dearly prize—all of these things are encoded in the stories that each culture invents and preserves for the next generation, stories that, in effect, we live by and *through*.[1]

—HENRY LOUIS GATES, JR.

7.1 Encountering Literature
in a storytelling workshop

Before participating in the storytelling workshop, choose a story, perhaps from your cultural heritage. Read it over several times—do not memorize it—learning to tell stories is more about visualization and internalization than memorization. During the workshop, the focus is on *process,* not performance. At the end of the workshop, some of you may want to perform for the group, others may want to wait until a later time, or tell stories in a different setting, perhaps to a group of elementary schoolchildren.

By attending, almost annually, the Connecticut Storytelling Festival for the past twenty years and participating in workshops myself, I gleaned various components of the storytelling workshop from Heather Forest, Laura Simms, Jackie Torrance, Penninah Schram, Diane Ferlatte, and other professional storytellers. I have used this workshop for many years and can guarantee that almost everyone will come out of the workshop confident and capable of telling a story. The workshop is as effective with children as it is with adults.

The group's stories should be similar in length. For beginning storytellers, a three- to five-minute story is about right. To approximate the length, read it aloud while timing yourself. If you choose a longer story, the leader may sometimes interrupt your processes because others in the group are finished and ready to move on.

note to leader: If preferred, instead of having participants preselect and read a story, you can distribute copies of short stories or fables to read at the beginning of the workshop. See the oral interpretation workshop in Chapter 10.1 for strategies for participants to familiarize themselves quickly with a short piece. Arnold Lobel's *Fables* are suitable, as are Aesop's, La Fontaine's, and tales from the *Jataka.* Or, consider Heather Forest's *Wisdom Tales from Around the World.* During the workshop, model each direction to help participants understand what is expected.

Materials Needed

> Blank paper and markers
>
> Audiorecording of adagio music—for example, the soundtrack of *Out of Africa*
>
> Drum or tambourine

Physical Warm-up When sounded, the drum (or tambourine) means participants should stop, stand still, and listen for the next direction. Beginning with physical work, which brings about "relaxed alertness," this next section is based on Kristin Linklater's *Freeing the Natural Voice.*[2] See Chapter 1.8 for the philosophy that undergirds this approach.

- Relaxation and breathing: Stand with your feet slightly apart, knees slightly bent. Imagine strings from your sternum and the top of your head; this helps you find the posture that will best support vocal work. Imagine strings gently pulling toward the ceiling at both elbows (pause), at the wrists (pause), and at the fingertips (pause). Feel your body's weight and temperature; keep your shoulders down. Imagine the strings are cut at your fingertips (pause), at your wrists (pause), and at your elbows (pause). Allow your head and arms to roll slowly toward the floor, stopping to hang from the waist at a comfortable stretch point. Shake your head yes (pause); shake your head no (pause). Picturing one vertebrae at a time, slowly resume a standing position. Repeat.

- Movement based on *Theatre Movement: The Actor and His Space* by Nancy King: Find your personal space where your arms can stretch without touching others, the furniture, or walls. In that space, stretch out your limbs (pause), swing (pause), shake (pause), bounce (pause), glide (pause), pull (pause), and push (pause).[3]

- Walk through the classroom space, keeping equidistant from each other, without touching others or the furniture. Walk more quickly, then slowly, in curves, diagonally, and so on. Explore as many ways of walking as time permits.

- If you do not know the mirror game, practice it, because the mirror game is used in the workshop. Adagio music is helpful here, such as the soundtrack from *Out of Africa.* Two partners stand facing each other, without touching. One is the leader, looking into his or her reflection in the mirror. The other is the mirror, reflecting the leader's movement. This works best if partners look each other in the eye, following movements out of their peripheral vision. The leader periodically calls "Change," at which time the follower becomes the leader. Best results occur when the leader says, "When I am watching you, I should not be able to tell who is the leader and who is the follower." This encourages partners to slow down and work together.

A Process of Visualization and Internalization   A story is a work-in-progress, and it grows each time it is told. Storytellers make choices—all artists do. The purpose of the workshop is to brainstorm ideas from which to choose and to help you internalize your story through a variety of exercises. After the workshop is over, reflect on what you want to incorporate into your story. During the workshop, no one will be made to perform in front of others. All the explorations take the form of simultaneous, parallel playing; no one is spotlighted.

1. With a partner, take turns pantomiming your story to each other. Focus on the main events without too much attention to detail. Then, take turns telling each other what you *thought* was going on in your partner's story. It is not necessary that you are correct, nor that your partner explains any misconceptions. Do not *tell* your story to your partner and do not correct your partner's misconceptions; rather, listen to how he responds, taking in his impressions. Allow about two to three minutes for each partner.

2. Find a new partner. Verbally summarize your story to your partner, allowing about one minute for each partner.

3. Find a new partner. Nonverbally, mirror the beginning, the middle, and the end of your story. Remember, storytellers make choices; choose what you want from the beginning, the middle, and the end. When you have finished, your partner, who has

mirrored you, makes one statement about what she thought or felt. Again, do not correct your partner's misconceptions; just listen. Allow two to three minutes for each partner.

4. Working by yourself, walk around the room, telling your story to yourself in your mind. To landscape your story better, brainstorm descriptive words. When the leader flicks the lights, stop and turn to the person closest to you, describing who or what he is in your story. Then, let him tell you who or what you are in his story. (Example: "You are part of a large, golden field of wheat, waving in the wind . . . " or "You are great, big hairy man, with teeth as sharp as daggers and eyes as round as saucers . . . "). When the lights flick, resume walking, telling your story in your mind. When the lights flick again, repeat the landscaping process. (The leader will flick the lights on and off for about eight to ten minutes.) When you are finished with your story, move to the perimeter of the room, which will indicate to the leader how much more time is needed.

5. Working by yourself, draw a map of your story. Use stick figures and symbols; avoid too much detail. After about five minutes, holding your map in front of you, walk around the room, sharing with others. There is still no need to tell your story.

6. Find a new partner. Create and share paralinguistic sounds for the beginning, the middle, and the end of your story. ("C-r-r-r-eeeeek" for the sound of a door, and so on.)

7. Find a new partner. Take turns telling your story as if it was the juiciest piece of gossip you have ever heard.

Take time to share your responses to the workshop. What was effective? What helped you? Were you surprised by anything in the process?

Guidelines for Storytelling   Teaching by storytelling, although receiving more attention in recent years, is not common practice in elementary schools. Hopefully, in the twenty-first century, this untapped potential will flourish, as it did centuries ago in many cultures. Barbara Reed, founder of the Connecticut Storytelling Center, notes: If you learn to tell one story a year, in ten years, you will have ten stories (personal communication).

One obstacle to becoming storytellers is that we are far more self-conscious in front of groups than any previous generation. Well into the age of the electronically transmitted image, video cameras show us what we look like going in and out of the bank, the grocery store, and other public places. From our earliest years we are exposed to unattainable standards of (so-called) beauty. These barriers should not keep us from doing what would benefit children—learning to tell stories.

Teacher storytellers should find and develop storytelling styles with which they are comfortable. No two tellers have the same style, nor should they. The current revival in storytelling, found in places like the National Storytelling Festival in Jonesborough, Tennessee, features all kinds of tellers, many of them dramatic in their presentations. Beginning tellers should not feel threatened by theatrical storytellers, nor feel that they have to have the same style. The quiet, still teller has as much to contribute to the imaginations of children as professionally trained tellers.

During the early part of the twentieth century, storytelling experienced a revival among librarians, some of whom disparaged a dramatic style. In 1924 Sara Cone Bryant wrote, "[A]lways *remain suggestive rather than illustrative. . . .* The storyteller is not playing the parts of his stories: he is merely arousing the imagination of his hearers to picture the scenes for themselves."[4] In the 1950s, Ruth Tooze said, "[T]ell your story simply, directly, sincerely, using few gestures. . . . Storytelling is not dramatization. It is shared vital experience in which words are the means of communication. There are not specific gestures anyone can teach you to use in expressing joy or sorrow or anger. Your face will show what you feel."[5] In the long run, more children will hear more stories if you do not pressure yourself to give a dramatic performance, unless that is part of who you are and it is your style. "I now know what at first I refused to believe," says Reed, "that the meaningful story, quietly told to quiet listeners, is the true heart of storytelling."[6]

The process of the storytelling workshop should free you from the need to memorize your story because you have opportunities during the workshop to visualize and internalize. There may be a chant or chorus that must be committed to memory. When telling stories myself, I sometimes use an index card with the stanza on it to prompt my memory. It may be necessary to memorize sequence, for example: "The cat began to eat the rat; the rat began to gnaw the rope; the rope began to hang the butcher . . . " from *The Old Woman and Her Pig.* Some tellers bring a *storyteller's bag* with objects; objects can be arranged to prompt the memory of the teller.

Your audience *wants* you to succeed. Find a few friendly faces and let their energy give you confidence. When telling stories in your college class, remember all the adults present were once children; tell the story to the child within them.

In *tandem storytelling,* two tellers take responsibility for different parts of the story. This approach is yet another culturally responsive way of teaching. Kathryn Au describes the use of "talk story," a cultural form of Native Hawaiian students during which two or more children interactively tell a personal story together.[7] The participation and interaction of talk stories is similar to the African American practice of call and response, described in Chapter 5.2 on Poetry.

When selecting a story, professional storyteller Nancy Schimmel advises: "[T]ell stories you like to tell."[8] Internationally acclaimed storyteller Jackie Torrance suggests you peruse the tales found in the 398.2 section of your library. As suggested by this chapter and in the chapter on poetry, there are thousands of tellable tales, anonymously created for us by our ancestors. In addition to this rich heritage, there are also stories from oral history; for example, those stories told by immigrants who came through Ellis Island, or the narratives of formerly enslaved Africans and collected by scribes. Personal stories are another venue for storytelling.

Stories can be linked to material objects; for example, nesting dolls, origami, sand, line drawings, a pouch containing an object that helps the teller remember the tale (as used by the Seneca), and story vines or string (as used by the Lega of Zaire or the Sambui of Angola). Although not required, sound effects, such as a drumbeat, may be effective.

Some American Indians sit in a circle when telling a story, symbolizing its shared nature. In some cultures, both tellers and listeners close their eyes when telling. This is sometimes uncomfortable for people of European descent for whom eye contact is, usually unconsciously, highly valued. The Irish are the exception to this. Because many of the tellers were blind, both listeners and seeing tellers are accustomed to closing their eyes during tellings. If you are especially self-conscious, consider closing your eyes and asking your audience to close their eyes while you are telling your story. You may sit on a stool, on a chair, or stand. If you stand, take care not to wander aimlessly. See the Storytelling Guide in Appendix A for further guidelines.

When telling a story with a chant, have the audience rehearse the chant and any accompanying action prior to the telling, thus facilitating their easy participation. Consider how you will begin and end your story. The Abenaki keep their listeners focused by occasionally interrupting the tale to ask "Ho?" to which the listeners respond with "Hey!" Dianne Wolkstein describes the Haitian practice of the teller calling "Cr-r-r-ric?" to begin a story; the audience answers, "Cr-r-r-rac!" Seneca tellers ask, "Hanio!" and must hear the response, "Hah!," before beginning a tale. This allows your audience to acclimate themselves to you, and to get ready for the story transaction.

7.2 The Meaning of Folklore

Why does folklore have value for those who live in the twenty-first century? At the risk of oversimplification, the following is a brief outline of several perspectives.

Some folklorists consider the tales as concrete representations of spiritual beliefs and longings. Reflecting romanticist beliefs, Wilhelm Grimm considered them "the remains of an ancient faith extending far back into the oldest times, in which spiritual things are expressed in a figurative manner."[9] The Jewish storyteller, Penninah Schram, when analyzing her own process of selecting a story, describes the levels of spiritual understanding of story in the cabala: "[I]t is said that there are four levels of comprehending a story: *pshat,* or earth, meaning understanding of the plot; *remez,* water, or deductive, getting the lesson; *drosh,* air, inductive, asking questions; and *sod,* fire—knowing the secret that transcends all levels. When I find a story that hits me on that level, I know I have to tell it."[10] (See Figure 7.1 for an example of a story from the cabala.)

To Joseph Campbell the myths testified to an invisible reality far more real than the visible one. Additionally, he accepted the classical philosophy of India that held that the stories reflected "the ends for which men strive." There are three: *kama* (pleasure and love), *artha* (success and power), and *dharma* (lawful order and moral virtue).[11] Thus in all stories one or more of these ends are addressed.

Psychological explanations include Jungian and Freudian interpretations. Bruno Bettelheim, in *The Uses of Enchantment,* developed his post-Freudian theory, postulating that the tales help children, often overwhelmed by the intensity of their feelings, feel less alone in the world by showing characters who undergo similar extremes in feeling and action. Folklore should not be taken literally; instead, it is symbolic of human passions, fears, and desires. One of the great tasks of achieving maturity is to find ourselves—a self

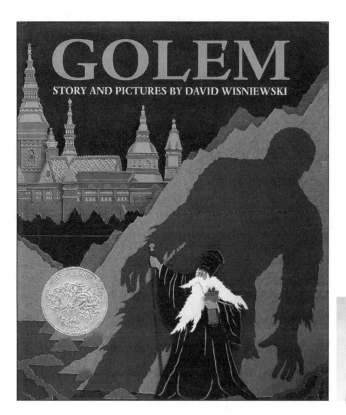

Figure 7.1 David Wisniewski's exquisite papercuttings for *Golem* won him the Caldecott. As he explains in the source notes, the story has its roots in the cabala.

that is not degraded by the perceived callous treatment most of us receive, at some time or other, during our lives. Bettelheim believed that the stories offer children the means to achieve inner integration. Children know they have selfish desires and aggressive tendencies, intermingled with their moral and ethical concerns for the larger community. Without the tales, children are left to believe that they are the only ones who are trying to manage such complexity. Through the tales, children can transcend the narrow confines of their self-centered existence. Bettelheim thought children's greatest need was also their most difficult achievement—to find meaning in life. The tales are, ultimately, hopeful; persistence in the face of difficulty is worth the effort:

> Fairy tales intimate that a rewarding, good life is within one's reach despite adversity—but only if one does not shy away from the hazardous struggles without which one can never achieve true identity. These stories promise that if a child dares to engage in this fearsome and taxing search, benevolent powers will come to his aid, and he will succeed. The stories also warn that those who are too timorous and narrow-minded to risk themselves in finding themselves must settle down to a humdrum existence—if an even worse fate does not befall them.[12]

The latter part of his book is devoted to specific analyses of stories—for example, *The Three Little Pigs* and the pleasure principle, and the *Arabian Nights* and the intricacy of psychological problems.

Parents, librarians, and teachers have sometimes suppressed folklore, often because of its violence. Bettelheim warns against taking the violence in the tales too literally. Most children understand that the tales are fictional. The violence symbolizes their intense feelings, which are often far out of proportion to actual events. *Cinderella*, Bettelheim posits, is not about finding a mate. Rather, it is about sibling rivalry. Children *feel* that their parents dote upon their siblings, while they are relegated to the ash heap. (See Figures 7.2 through 7.4 for examples of Cinderella tales.)

From a Jungian perspective, different characters in the tales represent aspects of ourselves. Like the Freudians, Jungians do not see *Cinderella* as a tale about marriage, but rather about becoming known to others for who we truly are—a *very* difficult task. Marrying the prince symbolizes the integration of the "gifted inner Prince"—accepting and developing one's innate abilities and capacities.[13]

In *Hansel and Gretel,* the wicked witch and wicked stepmother are dark sides of the same person—the good mother, who is symbolized by the candy house, always sweet, giving, and nurturing. Most women *are* the good mother—for a while. As time goes on

Figure 7.2 *Mufaro's Beautiful Daughters,* a Cinderella variant retold and illustrated by John Steptoe, is a wonderful choice for a storyteller. After telling the story and letting your audience imagine their own pictures, share Steptoe's illustrations, which he spent two and a half years to create.

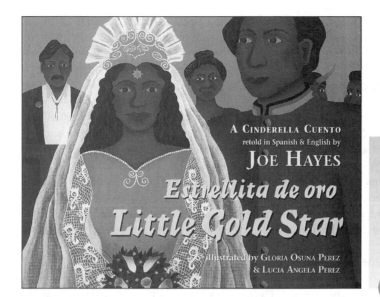

Figure 7.3 *Little Gold Star/Estrella de oro,* retold by Joe Hayes, is a southwestern Cinderella variant. When her mother became terminally ill, Lucia Angela Perez finished, under her mother's guidance, the acrylic Mexican folk paintings.

Figure 7.4 There are hundreds of variants of the Cinderella story, like *Domitíla: A Cinderella Tale from the Mexican Tradition,* adapted by Jewell Reinhart Coburn and illustrated in oil by Connie McLennan.

and children grow up mothers cannot, physically and emotionally, continue to carry out such a demanding level of involvement as caring for a newborn requires, although children would like them to. Unfortunately, some mothers and fathers recede too much from their children's lives. *Hansel and Gretel* represents children's intense feelings of deprivation and abandonment. However, children may negatively interpret any recession from their lives.

Jungian analyst Jacqueline Schectman believes *Hansel and Gretel* is ultimately an optimistic tale, for its philosophy is "that which most frightens us brings us our greatest opportunities. Hansel and Gretel are survivors, children with the hermetic capacity to catch a fur cap as a mouse runs across the room [the last line of the tale]. They exemplify the miraculous resiliency of the psyche, the capacity to transcend early deprivation and abandonment and still find precious jewels contained within the pain." While some children are, indeed, resilient, the more stressors in the child's life, the more difficult it is to overcome difficulties. Schectman, of course, would not defend child abuse; however, in the normal development of children, sometimes mothers *seem* wicked and this perceived wickedness is, in fact, positive:

> Still for all the dangers they present, these doubly Dark Mothers are psychological necessities. Children do more than survive their indulgence and rejection: *they grow through them.* The woodcutter's wife surely fosters independence, the move toward personal autonomy. The Witch's House is shelter for those moments when deep regression, a return to the matrix of our being, is the necessary path of healing. As long as there are Needy Children, there will be Stepmothers there to push and pull, to take us in and put us out.

When the Good Mother steps out, the wicked Stepmother steps in. Most mothers—and their children—are familiar with this continual dance of stepping in and stepping out.[14]

Others speak to the benefits of folklore. Drama critic Martin Esslin makes the point that, in comparison with today's gratuitous media violence, folklore at least is "accompanied by fine language, poetic imagery, and an underlying tenderness absent from today's cartoon fare."[15] J. R. R. Tolkien thought that the tales should not be illustrated; children would then imagine only those images that would not threaten them. Mary and Herbert Knapp think the tales help children take their place in society: "Folklore helps people to cope with the here and now in three ways. It helps them to escape from the unsatisfactory present into fantasy, consoles them by reminding them that their troubles aren't unique, and by virtue of its formal, traditional nature, provides a safe, accepted means of expressing social hostility. Thus folklore helps relieve individual frustration without destroying the *status quo.*"[16] In *Talk That Talk: An Anthology of African-American Storytelling,* Pearl Primus describes the teaching value of the tales: "Children sitting in the shadows of the house are learning that greed, laziness, dishonesty, arrogance and theft are all negative values that their society will not tolerate. The tales fill the time, teach, amuse, bring members of family close together."[17]

Folklore and feminist scholar Jack Zipes thinks the tales both "affirm the dominant social values" and "reveal the necessity to change them" depending on the social and political context.[18] Zipes's criticism also focuses on modern-day media distortions of the tales.

In the electronic age, the stories might offer yet another purpose. Even though Norbert Wiener made major contributions to cybernetics, on which computer technology is based, he was concerned about a society that saw technology only as progress. As a scientist, he knew there are disadvantages to technology, and believed all children in a technological society should be exposed to myth to help them develop a tragic sense of life. Knowing that there are two sides to every story could help them understand both the benefits and dangers of technology. Wiener analyzes the myth of Prometheus for modern times: "The Greeks regarded the act of discovering fire with very split emotions. On the one hand, fire was for them, as for us, a great benefit to all humanity. On the other, the carrying down of fire from heaven to earth was a defiance of the Gods of Olympus, and could not but be punished by them as a piece of insolence towards their pejoratives." Wiener thought myths could give us the wisdom we need to use technology wisely and for the good. Without such wisdom, we might transfer too much power to machines, abdicating the *human* responsibility of choosing good over evil.[19]

Like all the arts, the traditional tales are a form of play, which Johan Huizinga believed is the source of civilization itself. The playfulness of the story, says Huizinga, creates order, *is* order. "Into an imperfect world and into the confusion of life it brings a temporary, a limited perfection."[20] We need stories to make coherent the story of our own lives, and we need connection with others to lessen the isolation we often feel. Walter Kerr, commenting on the "truth" found in the traditional stories, says, "A good fairy tale is always a . . . fantastic mirror of the way things are. It may be advisable to try and bring the mirror more sharply into focus; it is never advisable to break it. That 'if' of the fairy tale is an 'if' that haunts all of us, day and night. 'What happens next?' is a permanent whisper inside us."[21]

There is an oft-repeated story of the mother who approached Albert Einstein to ask what she could do to help her son become a scientist. "Read to him the fairy tales." Yes, and then what, after that, asked the mother? "Read them to him again. It is imagination that is most needed."

7.3 The Oral Tradition and the Education of Children

"Schools days, school days . . . readin' and writin' and 'rithmetic taught to the tune of the hickory stick" goes the old song, describing the traditional tasks of the school. Although the hickory stick is currently against the law in most states, paper-and-pencil tasks continue to be carried out by young bodies struggling to keep in their seats. Yet, almost 2,500 years ago, the philosopher Plato observed that the young *cannot* keep still; they must be in motion, leaping, skipping, dancing, shouting, and making noises of joy.

Plato's insight can help us explore the oral tradition, which was physically and kinesthetically embodied long before it was ever a book experience. Not attributable to single authors, traditional tales—the fables, folk tales, fairy tales, epics, myths, legends, and tall tales—come to us from antiquity and from all cultures, preserved through oral retellings, reshaped by the community of tellers from one generation to the next. For centuries, the

Middle Eastern *rawls;* the Mexican *vaqueros;* the African *griots;* the Greek *aidoi;* the European troubadours, jongleurs, and minstrels; the English bards; the Irish *seanachies;* the Scandanavian *skalds;* spinners at their wheels; the *sages femmes*—storytellers all—kept folklore alive, often accompanied by instruments, movement, pantomime, dance, songs, and chants. In contrast with earlier oral and print-based cultures, our current electronic age moves us farther and farther away from this legacy.

A professor at Simon Fraser University with a long-time interest in the potential of the arts, Kieran Egan writes, "I think one can plausibly argue that Western schools' relatively poor achievement in teaching literacy is due in significant part to the failure to recognize and stimulate the development of a rich orality in the first place, and then to use the capacities of orality to teach literacy."[22] Orality and aurality are crucial in learning to read.

Teachers in the United States who use folklore and the telling of it can be sure they are practicing an inclusive pedagogy. Both the indigenous people in the Americas, as well as the immigrants from all over the globe who later arrived on these shores, value stories and storytelling. Pulitzer prize winner N. Scott Momaday cherishes the Kiowa stories his father told him when he was a child "These were many times more exciting than anything I found at school; they, more than the grammars and arithmetics, nourished the life of my mind."[23] Educator Edwina Hoffman writes, "Children worldwide respond to storytelling. American Indian children are no less enthusiastic in their enjoyment of narrative tales. Storytelling is quite consistent with Indian oral traditions."[24]

Sonia Nieto suggests that the oral tradition is so strong among Latinos that it shapes the kinds of artistic and literary contributions Latino authors make: "Latino children's literature has revolved around folklore, legends, riddles, games, poetry, and stories in the oral tradition rather than specifically on the childhood or adolescent experience."[25] Mexican Americans have historically intertwined temporal performance and print: "[T]he oral tradition has been an integral part of the Mexican-American community throughout its existence . . . teachers ought to consider the oral tradition which is an important part of many cultures, including the Mexican-American culture, and make the oral literary heritage and oral literature of the Mexican-American community a part of the literature curriculum."[26]

Those of African descent brought with them through the Middle Passage stories that comforted and kept them alive—a heritage they carried with them throughout the African diaspora. Educators should honor this heritage by tapping into cultural strengths. African American children, says Janice Hale, have "a preference for oral/aural modes of communication, in which both speaking and listening are treated as performances and in which oral virtuosity—the ability to use alliterative, metaphorical, and graphic forms of spoken language—is emphasized and cultivated."[27]

In the United States, exclusive private schools that mostly white upper class children can afford to attend promote the active, arts-based learning often missing in public schools. In the international Waldorf schools, teachers are, first and foremost, storytellers; there are no texts in the elementary grades. Through the elementary school years children hear from their teacher storytellers the tales of the world, beginning with fairy tales and fables through world mythology. The Waldorf approach is particularly effective with children with learning disabilities (LD), who may eventually prove that the LD label stands for learning differently. Hale views the Waldorf schools as exemplary models that are "highly compatible with . . . Afrocentric instructional strategies."[28] In the United States there are currently public schools experimenting with the Waldorf approach in several cities.

Including oral forms of learning in the curriculum stands to benefit all children. Although the contemporary feast of single editions and collections of picture books should be offered to elementary school children, so, too, should the opportunity for them to have a qualitatively different kind of aesthetic experience—that of storytellers and story listeners. Instead of having the visual image created for them by an illustrator, through storytelling children create their own pictures in their own minds by quietly listening—or actively participating through chants, dances, and responses—to their teacher storyteller. Although the process is generally initiated and modeled by the teacher, children can, with positive coaching, become tellers themselves. These experiences can help children find their own voices.

7.4 Storytelling in the Reading Program in the Digital Age

No matter their race or ethnicity, all children have one thing in common the media. Weekday television viewing amounts to about 100 hours per month.[29] Most of us are familiar with the profile of today's child, who spends fewer hours in school—about 14,000 hours—than in front of television—about 16,000 to 20,000 hours. Children who live in poverty spend considerably more time watching television than their middle and upper class peers. Lack of money and concerns about safety curtail their access to after-school activities and other nonelectronically mediated forms of entertainment. Latinos, African Americans, and American Indians are overrepresented in this group.[30]

The storytelling event invites children to participate, not as consumers, but as cocreators of an artistic transaction. In centuries past, storytelling was a primary form of pedagogy, a way of inducting the rising generation into the mores, values, symbols, and aesthetic field of the culture. The art of the folk fostered participation and fun—storytelling, dancing, singing, and dramatizing—a very different experience than that of the young who sit in front of monitors and screens. Storytelling contributes to the development of an interior landscape, a place of one's own within oneself, while simultaneously creating a sense of community as tellers and listeners collaborate in the creation of an artistic event. Feelings of belonging, warmth, and connection are characteristic of the storytelling audiences. The realization—by both children and their teachers—that there is a vast literature authored by the *community,* in contrast to the literature that is written by a single, individual author or mass media programs produced by a relatively small group who work in television and film, is especially significant in the context of our media environment, which works against community in a local and regional sense. Although book reading is not emphasized in all the homes our children come from, nevertheless, parents and others may have shared different kinds of literacy experiences with their children. Sonia Nieto draws on her past, "I remember sitting around our kitchen table listening to stories in Spanish of Juan Bobo or of the 'jíbaros' (greenhorns or peasants newly arrived from Puerto Rico), or tall tales of family exploits. . . . These too were literacy experiences, and although they generally were not known or acknowledged by my schools, they could have been used to extend my learning."[31]

Storytelling should be part of the reading program. Storytelling, like poetry as discussed in Chapter 5.5, stimulates the visualization of images, which is an essential reading strategy that must be taught. Such opportunities positively impact learning in all areas.

7.5 Definitions and Categories of Folklore

Folklore is an umbrella term that includes all literature from the oral tradition. In Chapter 5 on poetry, we looked at some of that heritage—rhymes, ballads, and songs. The English words defining the various categories of folklore, however, are not universal to all people and cannot be translated into all languages. For example, American Indians call the oral stories *traditional narratives* or, simply, *the teachings.* The following is offered to make distinctions in the enormous variety found in the oral tradition:

Fables are short tales that provide moral or spiritual instruction for young and old. Animals, the most common characters in fables, usually represent abstractions—for example, greed or pride or honesty or selfishness. Fables tend to be simplistic: They are either very naive, very selfish, or very cunning. The moral is usually clearly stated at the end of the tale.

Folk tales (see Figure 7.5) are stories that deal with the problems of life, survival, and/or accomplishing tasks. These tales are usually of an adventurous, comic, or romantic nature. The characters are stock, the plots usually simple, and good is most often

Figure 7.5 Michael Lacapa draws on his Apache heritage to retell and illustrate *The Flute Player: An Apache Folkale.*

rewarded. *Subcategories* of folk tales are cumulative or formula stories, pourquoi tales, noodlehead stories, animal tales, trickster tales, realistic tales, and wisdom tales.

In *cumulative* or *formula tales,* the accumulation of incidents is central to the plot. Besides the entertainment value for the audience, who can actively participate through rhythmic prediction, cumulative tales demonstrate the formulaic devices—distinctive to the oral tradition—helpful to the storyteller's memory. Examples of formula tales are Alma Flor Ada's retelling of *The Rooster Who Went to His Uncle's Wedding* from Latin America, or the Cuban tale *The Bossy Gallito,* retold by Lucía González, or Nonny Hogrogrian's retelling of an Armenian tale, *One Fine Day.* These are also examples of predictable text, which is helpful to beginning readers.

Pourquoi tales explain the phenomena of nature—why things are the way they are—and can often be amusing (see Figure 7.6). *How Racoons Got Their Masks,* found in Norma Livo's *Joining In,* and Danile Moreton's *La Cucaracha: A Caribbean Folktale,* are examples of pourquoi tales.

Noodlehead stories, or *droll stories,* present people acting foolishly and making nonsensical decisions. The Chelm stories from the Jewish oral tradition are representative,

Figure 7.6 In *The Story of Colors,* Mazatecan illustrator Domitila Domínguez uses oil with marble dust to illustrate this pourquoi tale. Retold by Subcomandante Marcos (Zapatista).

as are the versions of *The Three Sillies* in European tales. This category of folklore is particularly enjoyable to children as they observe, in their all too willing imaginations, adults behave in slapstick fashion.

In *animal tales,* our fears and concerns are played out as characters, who resemble humans, venture into the unknown (*Goldilocks and the Three Bears*), survive by delaying gratification (*The Three Pigs*), or stave off starvation (*The Three Billy Goats Gruff*).

Trickster tales can be found in the oral traditions of countries throughout the world: Coyote, Iktomi, and Raven of the American Indians, Campriano of Italy, Anansi of the Ashanti, Juan Bobo from Latino countries, Till Ulenspiegel from Scandanavia, Reynard from Europe, Brer Rabbit of the American South, and Jack from England and Appalachia (see Figure 7.7). Tricksters are also sometimes shape shifters.

Realistic tales are also a category of folk tales, dealing with the day-to-day responsibilities familiar to the common folk. *The Cow on the Roof* is an example of a realistic tale; Wanda Gág's single-edition picture book *Gone Is Gone* is based on a story that describes what happens when husband and wife switch roles for the day.

Wisdom tales address the hard realities of life common to all families—for example, old age, illness, and premature death. Although usually didactic in nature, these tales are often profoundly beautiful. In *The Old Man and His Grandson,* found in Atelia Clarkson and Gilbert Cross's *World Folktales,* an old man's table manners, which have deteriorated because of old age, repulse his son and daughter-in-law. They build a trough for the old man to eat his meals outside. Later, the husband and wife see their young son constructing something with wood and ask what it is for. The boy innocently replies that he is building a trough for them when they are old. This statement causes them to look at themselves—often a function of art—and bring the old man back to the table.

Thus, folk tales encompass a large variety of stories: cumulative, pourquoi, noodlehead, animal, trickster, realistic, and wisdom tales.

Fairy tales, sometimes called *marchen* or *wonder tales,* include extraordinary and supernatural happenings: Slippers are mysteriously worn out every night, as in *The*

Figure 7.7 The use of the element of line contributes to a strong sense of action in Andrew Tshinahjinnie's (Navajo) illustrations of *Coyote Tales,* a collection of trickster tales retold by William Morgan and adapted in English by Hildegaard Thompson.

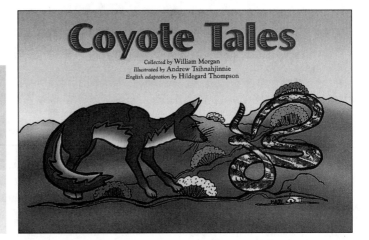

Twelve Dancing Princesses (retold and illustrated by Ruth Sanderson); all manner of enchantments are seen, as in *Beauty and the Beast;* or transformations are encountered, as in the Irish selkie tales. Fairy tales are also infused with magical figures, such as the Arabic djins; the Mexican American pichilinguis; the Norse tometens; the Scottish water kelpies; the Cornish dinkies; the Northern European brownies, pixies, fairies, and elves; the Irish lepracauns and Daoine Sidhe; the Mikumwesuk from the Abenaki nation; and other assorted imps, giants, wizards, magicians, sorcerers, witches, and devils.

The meaning of these enchanted personages differs from culture to culture. Thomas Cahill suggests the little people tales of Ireland may reflect Celtic guilt over the enslavement of the Tuatha De Danaan, who were more artful than themselves, as expressed in the awe-inspiring barrows and tumuli still remaining in Ireland today.[32] Elaine Aoki speaks of Asian Pacific American children's literature (see Figure 7.8) as "grounded in symbols and creatures of folklore and myth. Dragons, demons, and 'Ausangs' (spirits from the Phillipines) are so central to much of the Asian Pacific literature that Asian Pacific American authors run the risk of 'overt censorship' . . . "[33] Conservative and fundamentalist groups may regard such literature suspiciously, taking too literally their symbolic and metaphorical function.

As with most categories, there is overlap between the fairy tale and the folk tale. However, if the emphasis is primarily on survival (eating, building a house), the tale is

Figure 7.8 Jean and Mou-sien Tseng draw on their Chinese heritage to illustrate Grace Tseng's retelling of *White Tiger, Blue Serpent.*

probably a folk tale; if the emphasis is on enchantment, transformation, and magical happenings, it is probably a fairy tale. Also, most fairy tales, because of their more complicated plots, are longer than folk tales.

There are more than 1,000 variants of the Cinderella tale. The earliest variant was recorded in China during the T'ang Dynasty (618–907 CE). The version best known in the West, Perrault's version on which the Disney film is based, is probably one of the least interesting and most narrowing in terms of the role of women. John Steptoe's *Mufaro's Beautiful Daughters* and Virginia Hamilton's retelling of *Catskinella* in *Her Stories* provide stimulating contrasts to Perrault's version, as do Jewell Reinhart Coburn's *Domítíla* and Joe Hayes's *Little Gold Star*.

Literary fairy tales are written in the folkloric style by single authors—for example, Hans Christian Andersen, Oscar Wilde, and Rudyard Kipling (see Figure 7.9). *Fractured fairy tales* delight today's children (and adults). These books poke fun at the old tales and can inspire children to write their own.

Myths explain origins and creation of natural phenomena, humans, and animals. Religious in nature, myths embody belief systems, dealings between gods and heroic human beings, gods and other gods (see Figure 7.10 and 7.11). The study of mythology

Figure 7.9 Deborah Nourse Lattimore used original Egyptian sources to create her literary tale, *The Winged Cat: A Tale of Ancient Egypt,* which features a courageous young girl.

enhances literary appreciation because much of the world's literature contains mythological allusions. Care and sensitivity must be taken; what is myth to one group holds religious truth for another.

When she was barely eighteen years old and seeking to publish her first volume of poetry, Phillis Wheatley stood before a Boston tribunal who questioned her because they thought that she, of African descent, must have plagiarized her poetry. Henry Louis Gates writes,

> We can only speculate on the nature of the questions posed to the fledgling poet. Perhaps they asked her to explain for all to hear exactly who were the Greek and Latin gods and poets alluded to so frequently in her work. . . . Or perhaps they asked her to recite from memory key passages from the texts of Milton and Pope, the two poets by whom the African claimed to be most directly influenced.[34]

At the end of the interrogation, she was declared qualified. Nevertheless, because of the color of her skin, Wheatley could not find an American publisher; she had to go to London to find one instead.

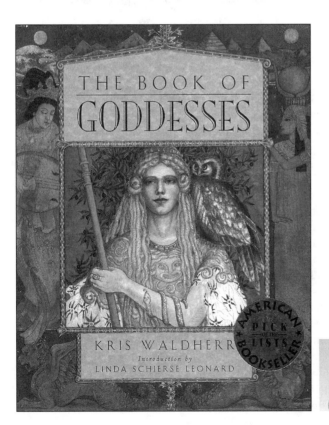

Figure 7.10 Kris Waldherr's *The Book of Goddesses* depicts women from world mythologies.

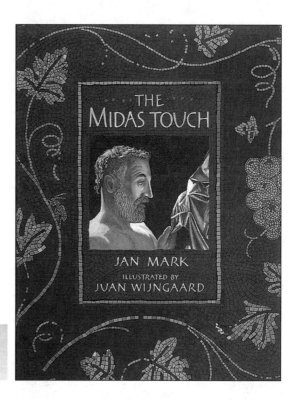

Figure 7.11 Juan Wijngaard's illustrations for
The Midas Touch make use of mosaics.

Epics like *Gilgamesh* from Sumeria (now Iraq, Iran, and Lebanon), the *Tain* of Ireland, the *Ramayana* and the *Mahabharata* of India, the *Kalevala* from Finland, the *Iliad* and the *Odyssey* of Greece, *Beowulf* of England, and the *Walum Olum* of the Lenape People were originally composed in oral cultures. They are episodic narrative poems, heroic in nature and often a source of mythic stories. Epics have successfully been used with verbally advanced fifth and sixth graders.[35]

The wisdom encompassed in these stories has implications for us today. In them, phenomena are recorded that shed light on issues we face. For example, *Gilgamesh* is "the earliest recorded story of downstream siltation and desertification caused by the extensive destruction of forestlands."[36]

Legends are based on persons who actually lived in the past, greatly elaborated. In England, Arthur, and in Spain, El Cid, were real people who lived in ancient times about whom numerous legends have sprung. Charlotte Spivak and Roberta Staples remind us of the intrinsic orality of the legends surrounding Arthur, made evident by inconsistency in spelling: "[W]e can well appreciate the readers' confusion over Guenevere and Guinevere, Kay and Cei, Mordred and Medraut and Gwydion. . . . We must remember that the gloriously imaginative reign of King Arthur flourished without a dictionary, and for that matter, without much literacy."[37] Like the Arthurian legends, the legends of other countries continue to have appeal: Children's author Alma Flor Ada reports having read *El Cid* by the time she was in the upper elementary grades.[38]

Tall tales are a distinctly American category of the folklore genre. The optimism characteristic of many of the immigrants who came to America looking for a better place to live and the confidence that enabled them to rise to the occasion by overcoming their fears and uncertainties are evident in these superhero stories. The hero is courageous, good, and/or clever: Sally Ann Thunder Ann, Paul Bunyan, John Henry, and Pecos Bill. The expansive terrain of this nation may have contributed to these larger-than-life and often hilarious tales. Tall tales featured the common folk, or working class, in contrast to the heroes of mythology and the nobility of the characters in legends. Children particularly enjoy tall tales because of their slapstick humor. To redress the balance—there are more tall tales about men than women—see Anne Isaac's modern literary tall tale, *Swamp Angel,* brilliantly illustrated by Paul Zelinsky with oils on cherry, maple, and birch veneer, which captures its folk art feeling.

The myths, legends, and tall tales of old continue to influence the development of literature in the present. To write *The Hobbit* and *The Lord of the Ring* series, J. R. R. Tolkien drew heavily on Norse mythology. Readers of C. S. Lewis's *The Chronicles of Narnia* will see the ways he drew on the oral tradition in his fantasy work.

7.6 *History of Folklore Collection*

During the late eighteenth and early nineteenth centuries, the Romantic movement propelled folklore collection on a large scale. Romanticism holds the view that beyond the natural world there exists a spirituality that can be glimpsed by experiencing any part of creation. The artist is the visionary who can provide guidance to others, transcending the duality of body and soul. Inherent in romanticism was a growing nationalism, which spurred collectors to seek out regional storyteller artists whose stories recalled simpler, purer times.

Although thankful for these collectors who transcribed what otherwise might have been lost, the early collectors also exercised censorship by leaving out, perhaps unconsciously, stories about women who were brave, adventurous risk takers, highlighting passive, sacrificial women. During the nineteenth century, women, for various cultural and political reasons, did not fulfill preconceived and diminished notions of what a woman could do and who she could become. Briefly, based on the organization of folk and fairy tales in Appendix C:

Jewish diaspora—Pogroms, wars, and immigration resulted in the Jews, with their rich folklore, migrating to most of the continents where the tales continue to be transcribed.

Africa—The African diaspora carried tales, mostly to the Americas and the Caribbean. European missionaries began transcribing the tales in the nineteenth century.

Arctic/Antarctic—John Bierhorst and others began an early collection of these tales.

Asia—The *Panchatantra* appeared in Kashmir around 200 BCE, and during the second to third centuries BCE, the *Jatakas,* a collection of teaching fables, were carved on shrines.

Caribbean—Anansi, or Aunt Nancy, the spider stories originally from Africa symbolized the struggle of enslaved peoples.

Europe—In the United Kingdom, Joseph Jacobs and Andrew Lang were the major nineteenth century collectors. In France, Charles Perrault published the *Contes de ma Mère l'Oye* (*The Tales of Mother Goose*) in 1697. In Germany, Jacob and Wilhelm Grimm collected tales in the nineteenth century, especially from Frau Viehmann, the story wife. Per Christian Asbjørsen and Jørgen E. Moe together collected Norwegian tales.

Central America—Victor Montejo's recent retelling of *Popol Vuh,* the Quiché Mayan mythological cycle, is a significant contribution to published folklore.

Middle East—Arab philogists began collecting Middle Eastern tales as early as the eighth century.

North America—The more than 400 Native groups have a staggering body of oral literature, first collected by Henry Rowe Schoolcraft and George Bird Grinnell in the nineteenth century. Joel Chandler Harris published the stories of enslaved Africans in *Uncle Remus: His Songs and His Sayings* in 1880, the first book for nonupper class folk. Harris's tone toward Africans was patronizing; Julius Lester's interpretation of the tales are better sources of the stories for today's children.

Oceania—Kate Langlole Parker collected aboriginal tales in 1896, the *Australian Legendary Tales.*

South America—Charles Finger published *Tales from Silver Lands* in 1924.

7.7 Cross-cultural Distortions of Folklore

Outsiders' renditions of stories from cultures other than their own risk inauthenticity and lack of specificity. For example, although Jean Fritz and Tomie dePaola had no intention of insulting the Wampanoags, their book *The Good Giants and the Bad Puckwudgies* (1982) is a "distortion" say Beverly Slapin and Doris Seale.[39] Similarly, Claire Bishop's retelling of *The Five Chinese Brothers* reinforces stereotypes of Asian Pacific Americans and, given more recent publications, is outdated. Elaine Aoki asks, "Standards for Asian Pacific American literature have been established by authors such as José Aruego, Yoshiko Uchida, and Laurence Yep. Why then do we continue to use *The Five Chinese Brothers*?"[40]

Not only do the tales have different meanings to individuals, the telling of the tales has different meanings between varying cultures. The people of the Ivory Coast believe that storytellers who know how to tell 100 tales will be blessed with children. The Mbiti of Kenya insist that all children of the people are present for the telling of the tales. The Xhosa children are expected not only to listen to stories but to learn to tell them as well. The Navajo believe if their children do not hear stories they will become bad people.[41]

Before telling stories from cultures not our own, it is important to learn about the culture and the meaning of the story within that culture. Although most American Indians do not object to non-Indians telling their stories, they do expect tellers to understand how the story is used. Joseph Bruchac says, "respect implies responsibility." The traditional stories usually teach the interdependence of cooperation and survival, and autonomy while "working for the good of all."[42] Certain stories are only appropriate during certain seasons and times of day. Bruchac counsels prospective tellers to participate in the life of the people, listen with patience, and, if the story's use or origin is not understood, don't tell it.

There is great variation within the many nations of American Indians. Lenore Keeshig–Tobias, an Ojibwa writer and reteller, describes the role of storytelling within her culture: "Storytelling is never done for sheer entertainment; for the stories were and are a record of proud nations confident in their achievements and their way of life. Stories contain information about tribal values, patterns of the environment and growing seasons, ceremonial or religious details, social roles, geographical formations, factual and symbolic data, animal and human traits."[43]

Bruchac describes the role of storytelling among the Haudenosaunee (Iroquois):

> Storytelling . . . has always served *at least* two major functions. One of those functions is to entertain. It is important that a story is entertaining, even entrancing, for a number of reasons. An interesting story is easier to remember. An entertaining story takes one out of the present moment into something which might be called the eternal or the mythic. (I use these terms which do not exist in Iroquois or most other Native languages because, in English, they may make some sense to the reader . . .). When you consider the fact that these stories were told during the cold months of the year when life may have been very difficult for the people, it may be easier to recognize the value of being taken out of the present moment, not so much to escape as to be given new energy or understanding with which to face that present moment when the story has been told.[44]

Expressing a cultural value of noninterference, many American Indians will, when observing a child—or even an adult—who is acting more in his own self-interest than in the interests of the group, offer a story instead of a reprimand.

Survival is at the heart of the meaning of storytelling for those of West African descent; West Africa was where most enslaved Africans were captured.[45] Hale says cultural values "have been transmitted intergenerationally through the oral tradition, a key feature of West African life and culture. It is critical that parents and teachers of African American children understand these cultural values and continue the tradition of transmitting them, because they have played a key role in the survival and sense of self of African American children."[46] Not only did the tales entertain, they offered comfort and hope to the community. Hale further advocates using folktales to help children see the "importance of faith and perseverance" and that "they can achieve power in the midst of a powerless community."[47] Ubiquitous, violent media have too often displaced the role of folklore—for example, stories that expressed feelings of pain. Historian Carl Nightingale, who spent several years living and working in urban Philadelphia, says,

> As I and a number of other historians and writers have suggested, many of the African-American folkloric forms that flourished before the mass-media onslaught were devised as a means of identifying hurt and expressing it imaginatively. Black folklore from the

rural South has been similarly filled with expressive forms, as have been its even more ancient African roots. The Afrocentric educational movement would do much service to the poorest of African-American children by emphasizing the rediscovery of these forms—from communal ceremonies and drumming, to ring shouts and expressive worship, to the blues and evocation of vulnerability, to the toasts, and perhaps most importantly, to the performance of rap—and adding to the creative but limited efforts to integrate those traditions into the country's culture of emotional self-awareness.[48]

Nicholasa Mohr explains another difference in the meaning of storytelling within cultures. Writing about her Puerto Rican heritage, she describes storytelling as a source of comfort when faced with life's problems. Stories helped those in her community transcend pain.[49]

Thomas Cahill explains that Irish stories are often fraught with themes of kidnapping because, during the time of St. Patrick, who was kidnapped himself, kidnapping was the order of the day: "The fear of such kidnapping still finds echoes in the lost children and loathsome adults who haunt the deep wood of European fairy tales." In fact, the word *shepard* connotes "trafficker in children."[50] Finding out the meanings tales have within cultures gives insight into the telling of them.

Stories in Asian cultures often teach values: respect for ancestors, the good of the group, and persistence in the face of difficulty. The Confucian and Buddhist influences are explored further in Chapter 13.

7.8 Criticism and Evaluation of Folklore

European stories often emphasize the success of the individual instead of social cooperation for mutually beneficial goals, as is more often found in Asian stories. Those of European descent must recognize that individualism, reflected in widely accepted theories of psychology, is not shared by all cultures. For example, Abraham Maslow's hierarchy of needs elevates self-actualization as the quintessential goal. Many cultures prize, instead, the greater good of the group. Recognizing differences in values can promote stimulating discussions in today's pluralistic classrooms.

Although she is contrasting African American values, Violet J. Harris's following guidelines can be adapted for use with other cultures as well:

- Discuss the motifs that appear, for example, the use of magic or enchantment, transformation, flying, and so forth.
- Determine the values, beliefs, or behaviors that are promoted by the tales. Are these universal or particularly African American?
- Discuss whether the tales include references to African American culture and history. Identify those elements that do.
- Note the use of humor.
- Discuss the variation of language styles in each book and the effects the variation produces.[51]

When choosing folklore, look to see if retellers have cited their source. Betsy Hearne, a professor of library and information science at the University of Illinois, describes the model source note, which should be found in the front or end matter of the book: "[It] cites the specific source(s), adds a description for cultural context, *and* describes what the author has done to change the tale, with some explanation of why. This delivers all the essential information to harried lay readers and leaves room for scholars to verify its accuracy or make a study of picture-book adaptations . . . "[52] Thus, print editions of oral stories can maintain the integrity of the cultures from which they come.

7.9 Conclusion

Folklore has much to offer today's children. Combining it with interactive, participatory approaches, such as storytelling and tableaux—the two encounters for this chapter—makes them accessible to children. An NCATE standard states, "Candidates understand and use a variety of teaching strategies that encourage elementary students' development of critical thinking, problem solving, and performance skills."[53] The encounters for this chapter provide ways of addressing this standard.

7.10 Encountering Literature
through music, movement, and tableaux

Materials Needed

Adagio music, such as the second movement of *Tubular Bells* by Mike Oldfield

Flocking I learned this from dance educator Sara Ingram more than twenty years ago. Here I use it as a warm-up for an interpretation of the myth of Icarus.

Get into groups of four and shape yourselves into a diamond, with all groups facing the windows (or some other designated point in the room). Like the mirror game that you tried in the storytelling workshop (7.1), follow the movement—this time three of you following the back of a leader instead of two of you face-to-face as in the mirror game—as you explore the theme of flight. However, leadership changes hands nonverbally as you move through space with adagio music accompanying you. To change leadership, the leader simply turns to her right and, while maintaining the shape of the diamond, the person on the right becomes the leader. All four members of each group should pass the leadership several times.

Narrative Pantomime Like *Andy and the Lion* in Chapter 1.2, pantomime the myth of Icarus. The background for the story is that King Minos of Crete, enraged that Daedalus helped Athenians escape the labyrinth for the Minotaur, has imprisoned Daedalus and his son Icarus in the labyrinth. Even though Daedalus was the architect who designed the labyrinth, so brilliant was his invention that even he could not find his way out.

The Narrative Pantomime Begins: Together, Daedalus and Icarus slide their hands along the twisting walls of the labyrinth, reaching high (*pause*) and bending low (*pause*) in search of an exit. In the darkness, they hear the monstrous roar of the Minotaur. They hasten their search, frantically running their hands along the walls. Suddenly, Daedalus stops, gazes upward and reaches out to catch feathers drifting from a flock of birds flying overhead. He urges Icarus to help him, and together they assemble two pairs of wings. Eager to fly, Icarus tries out his wings, but Daedalus pulls him back, warning him that he must not fly too close to the sun; that he must stay near the sea. Gently, slowly, quietly, the two rise above the labyrinth. At first they fly together, father and son. As Icarus feels the power and joy of flight, he soars higher. Daedalus pleads for him to come back to his side. Icarus disregards his father, ascending higher and higher. As he approaches the sun, Icarus's wings disintegrate, and he spirals into the sea. Daedalus, in his anguish, can only watch, and continue to fly, as the waters of the sea swallow his son.[54]

Tableaux   This form is also called *body sculpturing* or *still pictures*. Create tableaux for the beginning, the middle, and the end of *Icarus*. The leader softly and slowly counts from one to ten for each of the three parts. When the leader reaches ten, hold your shape in a still picture. Then, as best as possible, moving only your heads, look around to see how others interpreted the beginning of *Icarus*. Repeat for the middle and the end. This exercise may be conducted either verbally or nonverbally when the leader is counting from one to ten; however, when ten is reached, the group should maintain both silence and stillness.

Share your responses to flocking and tableaux. Then, consider the kinds of thinking skills you used to create tableaux. What did you have to do to create still picture? When you and your partner created tableaux for the beginning, middle, and end of the story, you were in the realm of higher order thinking. As set out by education researcher Benjamin Bloom in 1956, the lower order thinking skills are knowledge and comprehension; the higher order thinking skills are application, analysis, synthesis, and evaluation.[55] You had to analyze (take apart) the components of the myth, then apply what you comprehended about the characters and the plot. By the time the leader reached ten, you synthesized (put together) your knowledge to create your interpretation of the myth. You also had to evaluate; you decided what to attend to when selecting visual ideas to highlight in the still picture.

How would the experience have been different if, instead of creating tableaux, you had been asked instead to take a quiz on your reading of the myth and on that quiz were the following questions:

• Who were the characters? (Daedelus and Icarus)

• Where were they? (In the Minotaur's labyrinth)

• What happened? (They gathered bird feathers, attached them to their arms, and flew away to escape the Minotaur. Next, Icarus flew too close to the sun, and dropped to his death while his father could only watch.)

These questions require only retrieval skills—knowledge and comprehension—both lower order thinking. Although important, when retrieval is overemphasized and higher order thinking is underemphasized, students become bored and disinterested. Mythology (or any other subject) seems dull when children are asked to focus on knowledge and comprehension to the exclusion of more engaging types of thinking. Teachers who aim for higher order thinking skills can still assess knowledge and comprehension, without asking overt questions. To create tableaux, students have to know who the characters are and what happens (lower order). Their motivation does not disappear, as it does when they have to take a quiz. Endorsed by NCATE, a recent policy report states, "While both lower-order and higher-order thinking skills undoubtedly have a role to play in any classroom, much of the qualitative research asserts that the students of teachers who can convey higher-order thinking skills as well as lower-order thinking skills outperform students whose teachers are only capable of conveying lower-order thinking skills."[56] Tableaux are one way of offering a rich, high-quality experience in the schools.[57]

Culturally Responsive Teaching Geneva Gay discusses the large research base that convincingly demonstrates those in lower tracks are repeatedly subjected to "rote drill and memorization of facts, simplistic workbook exercises, filling out application forms, and memorizing facts and other low-level comprehension skills."[58] Commenting on the work of Jeannie Oakes, John Goodlad, and other researchers, Gay says it is "particularly disturbing because of the overrepresentation of Latinos, African Americans, and Native Americans in low-track curriculum and low-status classes. These 'emotionally flat' and 'intellectually dull' classrooms result from instructional strategies that emphasize teacher dominance, didactic and large-group teaching, a narrow range of learning activities, workbook assignments, and very little interactive dialogue."[59] To interact with each other as partners and create still pictures is far more effective than having students fill out an *Icarus* worksheet. *All* children deserve access to challenging and engaging learning.

    Tableaux also tap into the kinesthetic intelligence described by Howard Gardner's multiple intelligence theory. Constance Borab, an educator of color, writes "Body sculpturing and storytelling are two pedagogical techniques that tap into students' bodily–kinesthetic intelligence. I like these 'get on your feet/get up and make it happen' moments in the curriculum because they require students to become actively involved in their learning. These methods also require students to work together to negotiate meaning and achieve consensus."[60] Although published almost fifty years ago, Bloom's taxonomy has not found the place in the curriculum it deserves. Knowledge and comprehension questions—the two lowest skills—are still the most frequent kinds of questions asked in schools. In a study involving 7,300 third and fourth graders, only twenty-two percent of the questions teachers asked required interpretation, analysis, synthesis, and evaluation; seventy-eight percent elicited the least engaging, less challenging knowledge and comprehension questions.[61] Teachers who find ways to expand higher order thinking skills will be rewarded with motivated, engaged learners, which benefit teachers: Motivated, engaged students contribute to motivated, engaged teachers.[62]

    After experiencing it in her graduate children's literature course, Michelle Amaranto, a teacher in the city of Bridgeport, Connecticut, led flocking and tableaux with her fourth graders. Afterward, her students begged her, "When can we do it again?" Finding it a tool to engage students and to allow their identities to emerge, Michelle says, "They were learning the content, but at the same time they were learning cooperative techniques. They learned to respect each other, and each other's spaces." Calling tableaux and flocking a "lyrical approach," she notes the calming effect of the music, and that "no one was making fun of anyone else" as they explored expressive movement. Michelle also noted the powerful effect for all twenty-seven of her fourth graders of accomplishing something in unison (personal communication).

Suggested Activities

1. Although the emphasis is on storytelling in this chapter, sharing video and audio recordings based on the oral tradition should not be overlooked. Great composers, directors, and choreographers have adapted the tales to the art forms of opera, film, and ballet. Ingmar Bergman's delightful film *The Magic Flute* can be shared with elementary school children, as can the music and film of *Swan Lake*. Michèle Lemieux's illustrations can accompany a recording of Sergei Prokofiev's orchestral work *Peter and the Wolf*, which he wrote to introduce children to the orchestra. *William Tell*, the opera by Rossini, can be shared with Margaret Early's retelling in a picture storybook by the same name. Other adaptations are listed at the end of this chapter.

2. Watch for folklore especially good for story dramatization, like Patricia Compton's retelling of the Japanese tale *The Terrible EEK* or Ellin Greene's retelling of the Hungarian tale *The Little Golden Lamb*. (The Encounter for Chapter 13 is story dramatization.)

3. In your reading, watch for stories especially good for storytelling.

4. Invite a professional storyteller to your class. Most state departments can make recommendations, or check the Internet for storytellers in your area.

5. After reading or telling *Stone Soup*, prepare the soup (each person is responsible for one item).

6. Using John Scieszka's *The True Story of the Three Little Pigs* as a model, write your own stories from the point of view of a minor, or threatening, character from folklore.

7. Like Arnold Lobel, write your own fables (as can K–6 children).

8. In your reading of folklore, note other tales that could be explored through creative movement and tableaux.

for further reading and listening

Storytelling and Reading

Au, Kathryn H. 1993. *Literacy Instruction in Multicultural Settings.* Fort Worth, TX: Harcourt Brace College Publishers.

Colasent, Rita. 1996. "The Power of True Expression." *The Reading Teacher*, 49.5: 378 ff.

Dewey, Elizabeth J. 1994. "Come Alive Stories." *The Reading Teacher*, 48.4: 365 ff.

Hoyt, Linda. 1999. *Revisit, Reflect, Retell: Strategies for Improving Reading Comprehension.* Portsmouth, NH: Heinemann.

Morrow, Lesley Mandel, and Ellen M. O'Connor. 1995. "Literacy Partnerships for Change with 'At-Risk' Kindergarteners." In: *No Quick Fix: Rethinking Literacy Programs in America's Elementary Schools.* Richard Allington and Sean A. Walmsley, eds.

New York: Teachers College Press/International Reading Association.

Nelson, Olga. 1989. "Storytelling: Language Experience for Meaning Making." *The Reading Teacher, 42.6:* 386 ff.

Peck, Jackie. 1989. "Using Storytelling to Promote Language and Literacy Development." *The Reading Teacher, 43.2:* 38 ff.

Pinnell, Gay Su, and Angela M. Jaggar. 1991. "Oral Language: Speaking and Listening in the Classroom." In: *Handbook of Research on Teaching the English Language Arts.* James Flood, Julie M. Jensen, Diane Lapp, and James R. Squire, eds. New York: Macmillan.

Roney, Craig. 1989. "Back to the Basics with Storytelling." *The Reading Teacher, 42.7:* 520 ff.

Strickland, Dorothy S., and Lesley Mandel Morrow. 1989. "Oral Language Development: Children as Storytellers." *The Reading Teacher, 43.3:* 260 ff.

Tyson, Cynthia. 1997. "Meeting 'Hattie.'" In: *Dreamseekers: Creative Approaches to the African American Heritage.* Anita Manley and Cecily O'Neill, eds. Portsmouth, NH: Heinemann.

Storytelling in the Classroom

Barton, Bob, and David Booth. 1990. *Stories in the Classroom: Storytelling, Reading Aloud and Roleplaying with Children.* Portsmouth, NH: Heinemann.

Bauer, Carolyn. 1993. *New Handbook for Storytellers: With Stories, Poems, Magic and More.* Illustrated by Lynn Gates Bredeson. Chicago: American Library Association.

Bruchac, Joseph. 1997. *Tell Me a Tale: A Book About Storytelling.* New York: Harcourt.

Collins, Rives, and Pamela J. Cooper. 1997. *The Power of Story: Teaching through Storytelling.* 2nd ed. Scottsdale, AZ: Gorsuch Scarisbrick.

Dailey, Sheila. 1994. *Tales as Tools.* Jonesborough, TN: National Storytelling Association.

Greene, Ellin. 1996. *Storytelling: Art and Technique.* 3rd ed. Westport, CT: Bowker-Greenwood.

Herman, Gail. 1986. *Storytelling: A Triad in the Arts.* Mansfield Center, CT: Creative Learning Press.

Kraus, Joanna. 1980. *Sound and Motion Stories.* Charlottesville, VA: New Plays.

Lipke, Barbara. 1996. *Figures, Facts and Fables: Telling Tales in Science and Math.* Portsmouth, NH: Heinemann.

Lipman, Doug. 1995. *The Storytelling Coach.* Little Rock, AK: August House.

Livo, Norma J., and Sandra A. Rietz. 1987. *Storytelling Activities.* Littleton, CO: Libraries Unlimited.

———. 1986. *Storytelling: Process & Practice.* Littleton, CO: Libraries Unlimited.

MacDonald, Margaret Read. 1993. *The Storyteller's Start-Up Book: Finding, Learning, Performing, and Using Folktales.* Little Rock, AK: August House Publishers.

Maguire, Jack. 1991. *Creative Storytelling: Choosing, Inventing, and Sharing Tales for Children.* Cambridge, MA: Yellow Moon Press.

———. 1995. *The Storytelling Handbook: Storytelling Tips for Young People.* New York: Simon & Schuster.

Pellowski, Anne. 1977. *The World of Storytelling.* New York: R. R. Bowker.

Sawyer, Ruth. 1942. *The Way of the Storyteller.* New York: Penguin.

Schimmel, Nancy. 1982. *Just Enough to Make a Story.* 2nd ed. Berkeley, CA: Sister's Choice Press.

Shedlock, Marie. 1951. *The Art of the Storyteller.* New York: Dover.

Torrance, Jackie. 1998. *Jackie Tales: The Magic of Creating Stories and the Art of Telling Them.* New York: Avon.

The Meaning of the Tales

Bauman, Richard. 1986. *Story, Performance, and Event: Contextual Studies of Oral Narrative.* Cambridge: Cambridge University Press.

———. 1977. *Verbal Art as Performance.* Rowley, MA: Newbury House Publishers.

Bettelheim, Bruno. 1977. *The Uses of Enchantment: The Meaning and Importance of Fairy Tales.* New York: Vintage.

Bottigheimer, Ruth B., ed. 1986. *Fairy Tales and Society: Illusion, Allusion, and Paradigm.* Philadelphia: University of Pennsylvania Press.

———. 1976. *An Encyclopedia of Fairies: Hobgoblins, Brownies, Bogies and Other Supernatural Creatures.* New York: Pantheon.

Briggs, Katharine. 1978. *The Vanishing People: Fairy Lore and Legends.* New York: Pantheon.

Bruchac, Joseph. 1996. *Roots of Survival.* Golden, CO: Fulcrum.

Campbell, Joseph. 1968. *Hero with a Thousand Faces.* 2nd ed. Princeton, NJ: Princeton University Press.

Coles, Robert. 1989. *The Call of Stories: Teaching and the Moral Imagination.* Boston: Houghton.

Cook, Elizabeth. 1969. *The Ordinary and the Fabulous.* Cambridge: Cambridge University Press.

Degh, Linda. 1994. *American Folklore and the Mass Media.* Bloomington, IN: Indiana University Press.

Finnegan, Ruth. 1977. *Oral Poetry: Its Nature, Significance, and Social Function.* Cambridge: Cambridge University Press.

Fox, Carol. 1993. *At the Very Edge of the Forest: The Influence of Literature on Storytelling by Children.* London: Cassell.

Jung, Carl. 1964. *Man and His Symbols.* Garden City, NY: Doubleday.

Li, Suzanne D. 2000. "Beyond Mulan: Rediscovering the Heroines of Chinese Folklore," *The New Advocate,* 13.2: 143–155.

Opie, Iona, and Peter Opie. 1959. *The Lore and Language of Schoolchildren.* London: Oxford University Press.

Spivak, Charlotte, and Roberta Staples. 1994. *The Company of Camelot: Arthurian Characters in Romance and Fantasy.* Westport, CT: Greenwood.

Zipes, Jack. 1979. *Breaking the Magic Spell: Radical Theories of Folk and Fairy Tales.* London: Heinemann.

Storytelling Audio Recordings

Compiled with the assistance of Ann Shapiro, Executive Director of the Connecticut Storytelling Center, and Joseph Bruchac.

Ballard, Louis. 1973. *Indian Music for the Classroom.* Phoenix, AZ: Canyon Records. 4143 North 16th St. Phone: 602–266–4823. (four audiocassettes)

Bruchac, Joseph. 1990. *Gluskabe Stories.* Cambridge, MA: Yellow Moon Press.

———. 1988. *Iroquois Stories.* Greenfield Center, NY: Good Mind Records.

Callinan, Tom, and Ann Shapiro. 1999. *I'm Gonna Tell: Stories Told In-Tandem.* Clinton, CT: Crackerbarrel Entertainments. 168 Shore Rd.

Connecticut Storytelling Center (CSC). 1995. *The Listening Tree.* Available from CSC at www.connstorycenter.org/

Davis, Donald. 1993. *Jack's First Job.* Little Rock, AK: August House.

deBeer, Sara. 1991. *Seven Stories* and *Women of Wisdom, Women of Faith.* New Haven, CT: Recorded by the author.

Ferlatte, Diane. 1997. *Knick-knack Paddy Whack.* Oakland, CA: Self-published.

———. 1991. *Favorite Stories.* Oakland, CA: Self-published.

———. 1991. *Sapelo Time Is Winding Up: Tales from a Georgia Sea Island.* Oakland, CA: Self-published.

Hinman, Rosalind. 1990. *Three Hairs from the Devil's Beard.* Guilford, CT: American Melody. PO Box 270.

Lacapa, Michael. 1995. *Antelope Woman.* Flagstaff, AZ: Northland Publishing.

McQuillan, Synia, and Jeff McQuillan. 1991. *Tales from the First World.* Guilford, CT: American Melody. PO Box 270.

Red Wing, Narraganset Princess. 1986. *What Cheer Netop.* South Casco, ME: Mary L. Benjamin.

Ross, Gayle. 1986. *To This Day Native American Stories.* Fredericksburg, TX: Self-published.

———. 1982. *Twelve Moons.* Dallas, TX: Twelve Moons Storytellers.

Thomason, Dovie. 2001. *Fireside Tales: More Lessons from the Animal People.* Cambridge, MA: Yellow Moon.

———. 1996. *Lessons from the Animal People.* Cambridge, MA: Yellow Moon.

Torrence, Jackie. 1994. *Brer Rabbit Stories.* Weston, CT: Weston Woods.

———. 1994. *Traditions: A Potpourri of Tales.* Cambridge, MA: Rounder Records.

Audio Recordings of Ballet, Opera, and Orchestral Works

Compiled with the assistance of choral director and music educator Robyn Gangi.

Gluck. 2001. *Orphee and Eurydice.* Label: EMI Classics.

Hoffman. 1994. *Coppélia.* Composed by Léo Delibes. Performed by Royal Opera House Orchestra. Label: Conifer Classics. See Margot Fonteyn's book by the same name.

Humperdinck. 1997. *Hansel und Gretel.* Label: Decca Grand Opera Series. See Lisbeth Zwerger's *Hansel and Gretel.*

Mozart. 1997. *Die Zauberflote (The Magic Flute).* Performed by the Berlin Philharmonic Orchestra. Label: DG The Originals. See the film by Ingmar Bergman by the same name and the picture storybook *The Magic Flute* retold by Margaret Greaves and illustrated by Francesca Crespi.

Prokofiev. 2001. *Peter and the Wolf.* Levine, Cher, et al. Label: DG Deutsche Grammophon. See Michèle Lemieux's illustrated version of the book by the same name.

———. 2000. *Cinderella.* Performed by WDR Symphony Orchestra. Label: CPO. There are many versions of this story in the bibliography in Appendix C.

Stravinsky, Igor. 2001. *Firebird Suite.* Label: DG Panorama (includes other works by Stravinsky). See *The Firebird and Other Russian Fairy Tales,* edited by Jacqueline Onassis and illustrated by Boris Zvorykin.

Tchaikovsky. 1995. *The Sleeping Beauty.* Label: Philips Duo. See the picture storybooks *Sleeping Beauty,* retold by Monika Laimgruber, and *The Sleeping Beauty,* retold by Trina Schart Hyman.

———. 1992. *Swan Lake.* Label: Decca. See the picture storybook *Swan Lake,* retold by Anthea Bell, illustrated by Chihiro Iwasaki.

Verdi. *Aida.* Label: Decca. See Leontyne Price's retelling of the story by the same name.

websites

American Indian Storytellers:
www.uconsultus.com/
www.usindianstorytellers.com/resources.html
and www.wordcraftcircle.org

Black Storytellers Alliance:
www.blackstorytellers.com

Jewish Storytelling Coalition:
www.ultranet.com/ ~ jewish/story.html

LANES Storyteller Links:
www.lanes.org/links.html

Latino Storytellers:
http://clnet.ucr.edu/library/bplg/program.htm

National Association of Black Storytellers:
http://www.nabsnet.org/

National Storytelling Festival:
ww.storytellingfestival.org

National Storytelling Network:
www.storynet.org
(Publishes *Storytelling Magazine,* 116½ West Main St., Jonesborough, TN 37659)

Storytellers and Story Educators for Peace:
www.storytellingcenter.com/resources/
articles/neile4.htm

The Storytelling Home Page:
http://members.aol.com/storypage
1-800-525-4514m email: nsn@naxs.net

Websites for storytelling:
www.storynet.org

awards

Anne Izard Storytellers' Choice Award:
www.westchesterlibraries.org/owls/eligibility.html

The Children's Folklore Section of the American Folklore Society:
www.ucalgary.ca/ ~ dkbrown/aesop.html

notes

1. Henry Louis Gates, Jr., "Introduction." In: *Talk That Talk: An Anthology of African-American Storytelling,* Linda Goss and Marian E. Barnes, eds. (New York: Simon & Schuster, 1989), p. 17.

2. Based on Kristin Linklater, *Freeing the Natural Voice* (New York: Drama Book Publishers, 1976).

3. Based on Nancy King, *Theatre Movement: The Actor and His Space* (New York: Drama Book Specialists, 1971).

4. Sara Cone Bryant, *How to Tell Stories to Children* (Detroit: Reprinted by Gale Research, 1973 [1924]), p. 102.

5. Ruth Tooze, *Storytelling* (Englewood Cliffs, NJ: Prentice-Hall, 1959), p. 37.

6. Jane M. Gangi, "Barbara Reed: Visionary Storyteller and Dramatist," *Stage of the Art, 4* (Su 2000): 21.

7. Kathryn H. Au, *Literacy Instruction in Multicultural Settings* (San Diego: Harcourt, 1993), p. 114.

8. Nancy Schimmel, *Just Enough to Make a Story,* 2nd ed. (Berkeley, CA: Sister's Choice Press, 1982), p. 3.

9. Quoted in Jacqueline Simpson, *European Mythology* (New York: Peter Bedrick, 1987), p. 12.

10. Quoted in Claudia Wischner, *The Storytelling Experience: How Selected Contemporary Storytellers Perceive Their Art* (New York: New York University, Unpublished dissertation, 1990), p. 55.

11. Joseph Campbell, *The Masks of God: Primitive Mythology* (New York: Viking, 1959), pp. 465–467.

12. Bruno Bettleheim, *The Uses of Enchantment: The Meaning and Importance of Fairy Tales* (New York: Random House, 1975), p. 24.

13. Jacqueline M. Schectman, *The Stepmother in Fairy Tales: Bereavement and the Feminine Shadow* (Boston: Sigo Press, 1993), p. 91.

14. Schectman, *The Stepmother in Fairy Tales,* pp. 76–77.

15. Martin Esslin, *The Age of Television* (San Francisco: Freeman, 1982), p. 48.

16. Mary Knapp and Herbert Knapp, *One Potato, Two Potato . . . : The Secret Education of American Children* (New York: Norton, 1976), p. 161.

17. Quoted in Linda Goss and Marian Barnes, eds. *Talk That Talk: An Anthology of African-American Storytelling* (New York: Simon & Schuster, 1989), p. 11.

18. Jack Zipes, *Breaking the Magic Spell* (New York: Metheun, 1979), p. 5.

19. Norbert Wiener, *The Human Use of Human Beings: Cybernetics and Society* (New York: DaCapo Press, 1954), p. 270.

20. Johan Huizinga, *Homo Ludens* (Boston: Beacon Press, 1950), p. 10.

21. Walter Kerr, *How Not to Write a Play* (New York: Simon & Schuster, 1955), pp. 139–140.

22. Kieran Egan, "Literacy and the Oral Foundations of Education," *Harvard Education Review 57.4* (1987): 445–472.

23. N. Scott Momaday, *The Names: A Memoir* (Tucson: University of Arizona Press, 1976), p. 88.

24. Edwina Hoffman, "Oral Language Development." In: *Teaching American Indian Students,* Jon Reyhner, ed. (Norman, OK: University of Oklahoma Press, 1992), p. 134.

25. Sonia Nieto, "We Have Stories to Tell: A Case Study of Puerto Ricans in Children's Books." In: *Teaching Multicultural Literature in Grades K–8,* Violet J. Harris, ed. (Norwood, MA: Christopher-Gordon, 1993), p. 181.

26. Rosalinda B. Barrera, Olga Liguori, and Loretta Salas, "Ideas a Literature Can Grow On: Key Insights for Enriching and Expanding Children's Literature about the Mexican-American Experience." In: *Teaching Multicultural Literature in Grades K–8,* Violet J. Harris, ed. (Norwood, MA: Christopher-Gordon, 1993), pp. 220, 233.

27. Janice Hale, *Unbank the Fire: Visions for the Education of African American Children,* (Baltimore: Johns Hopkins University Press, 1994), pp. 3, 203.

28. Hale, *Unbank the Fire,* p. 208.

29. Edward L. Palmer, *Television and America's Children: A Crisis of Neglect* (New York: Oxford University Press, 1989), p. 12.

30. Aletha C. Huston, et al., *Big World, Small Screen: The Role of Television in American Society* (Lincoln, NE: University of Nebraska Press, 1992), p. 131.

31. Sonia Nieto, *The Light in Their Eyes: Creating Multicultural Learning Communities* (New York: Teachers College Press, 1999), p. 7.

32. Thomas Cahill, *How the Irish Saved Civilization: The Untold Story of Ireland's Heroic Role from the Fall of Rome to the Rise of Medieval Europe* (New York: Doubleday, 1995), p. 80.

33. Elaine Aoki, "Turning the Page: Asian Pacific American Children's Literature." In: *Teaching Multicultural Literature in Grades K–8,* Violet J. Harris, ed. (Norwood, MA: Christopher-Gordon, 1993), p. 119.

34. Henry Louis Gates, *Loose Canons: Notes on the Culture Wars* (New York: Oxford University Press, 1992), p. 52.

35. Phyllis W. Aldrich, "Evaluating Language Arts Materials." In: *Developing Verbal Talent: Ideas and Strategies for Teachers of Elementary and Middle School Students,* Joyce Van Tassel–Baska, Dana T. Johnson, and Linda Neal Boyce, eds. (Needham Heights, MA: Allyn & Bacon, 1996), p. 221.

36. Thom Hartmann, *The Last Hours of Ancient Sunlight: Waking Up to Personal and Global Transformation* (New York: Harmony Books, 1999), p. 86.

37. Charlotte Spivak and Roberta Staples, *The Company of Camelot: Arthurian Characters in Romance and Fantasy* (Westport, CT: Greenwood Press, 1994), xi–xii.

38. Alma Flor Ada, *Under the Royal Palms: A Childhood in Cuba* (New York: Atheneum, 1998), p. 69.

39. Beverly Slapin and Doris Seale, *Through Indian Eyes: The Native Experience in Books for Children* (Philadelphia, PA: New Society Publishers, 1992), p. 158.

40. Aoki, "Turning the Page: Asian Pacific American Children's Literature," p. 116.
41. Anne Pellowski, *The World of Storytelling* (New York: Bowker, 1977), pp. 44–49.
42. Joseph Bruchac, "Storytelling and the Sacred: On the Uses of Native American Stories," *Through Indian Eyes: The Native Experience in Books for Children* (Philadelphia, PA: New Society Publishers, 1992), p. 92.
43. Quoted in Joseph Bruchac, *Roots of Survival* (Golden, CO: Fulcrum, 1996), p. 74.
44. Bruchac, *Roots of Survival,* pp. 54–55.
45. V. P. Franklin, "Foreward." In: *Unbank the Fire: Visions for African American Children,* Janice E. Hale (Baltimore: The Johns Hopkins Press, 1994), p. xii.
46. Hale, *Unbank the Fire,* p. 135.
47. Hale, *Unbank the Fire,* p. 150.
48. Carl Nightingale, *On the Edge: A History of Poor Black Children and Their American Dreams* (New York: Basic Books, 1993), p. 193.
49. Nicholasa Mohr, *Growing Up Inside the Sanctuary of My Imagination* (Englewood Cliffs, NJ: Julian Messner, 1994), p. 45.
50. Cahill, *How the Irish Saved Civilization,* p. 36.
51. Violet J. Harris, "Contemporary Griots and Word Sorcerers." In: *Teaching Multicultural Literature in Grades K–8,* Violet J. Harris, ed. (Norwood, MA: Christopher-Gordon, 1993), p. 98.
52. Betsy Hearne, "Cite the Source: Reducing Cultural Chaos in Picture Books, Part One," *School Library Journal* (July 1993): 22.
53. National Council for Accreditation of Teacher Education, *Program Standards for Elementary Teacher Preparation,* 3c.
54. Adapted from Edith Hamilton, *Mythology: Timeless Tales of Gods and Heroes* (New York: New American Library, 1969), pp. 139–140.
55. Benjamin Bloom, *Taxonomy of Educational Objectives: The Classification of Educational Goals* (New York: David McKay, 1956). For an update on Bloom's work that synthesizes research findings from cognitive psychology and other domains since 1956, see Robert J. Marzano, *Designing a New Taxonomy of Educational Objectives* (Thousand Oaks, CA: Corwin, 2001).
56. Harold Wenglinsky, *How Teaching Matters: Bringing the Classroom Back Into Discussions of Teacher Quality* (Princeton, NJ: Milken Family Foundation and Educational Testing Service, 2000), p. 12.
57. For further activities like tableaux, see Frans Rijnbout, "Between Drama and Dance: The Use of Movement in Theatre Education," *Stage of the Art,* 10.2 (1999): 8–11.
58. Geneva Gay, *Culturally Responsive Teaching: Theory, Research and Practice* (New York: Teachers College, 2000), pp. 67–68.
59. Gay, *Culturally Responsive Teaching,* p. 57.
60. Constance Borab, "Freeing the Female Voice: New Models and Materials for Teaching." In: *Teaching African American Literature: Theory and Practice,* Maryemma Graham, Sharon Pineault–Burke, and Marianna White Davis, eds. (New York: Routledge, 1998), p. 83. See also Jacqueline Jordan Irvine, *Black Students and School Failure* (New York: Greenwood Press, 1990), p. 89.
61. Aldrich, "Evaluating Language Arts Materials," p. 222.
62. For a more detailed explanation of Bloom, see Harry K. Wong and Rosemary T. Wong, *The First Days of School: How To Be an Effective Teacher* (Mountain View, CA: Harry K. Wong Publications, 1998), p. 218.

Informational Books
Finding the Aesthetic

Schools generally fail to teach how exciting, how mesmerizingly beautiful science or mathematics can be; they teach the routine of literature or history rather than the adventure.[1]

—MIHALY CSIKSZENTMIHALY

8.1 Encountering Literature
through discovering patterns

Advance Preparation

Prior to this session, in response to an informational book, construct enrichment materials for children that reveal something exciting—or mesmerizing—about a discipline (math, science, and so on). For example, bring in pinecones, sunflowers, and other manifestations of Fibonacci's rule as explained in *Math Wizardry for Kids* by Margaret Kenda and Phyllis S. Williams. Then, read *Math Curse* by John Scieszka and Lane Smith, highlighting the math teacher's name, Mrs. Fibonacci. Fibonacci's rule is an example of, in Csikszentmihalyi's words in the epigraph, how mesmerizing math and science can be.

In-Class Sharing Bring the aforementioned materials to share with your classmates. They should be sturdy enough to withstand use in the elementary classroom (consider laminating them). Besides inviting students into the excitement of disciplinary knowledge, construction of these materials can help teachers plan for those inevitable children who finish assigned work before others. New teachers are often surprised at the range of abilities apparent in elementary classrooms. A fourth-grade teacher may have students whose reading levels fall between the first or second grade to high school and above. Abilities in math also greatly vary. Informational books in particular can address differentiation in the curriculum. Using resources in math, science, social studies, and other disciplines, teachers can design challenging, hands-on activities, kept in centers or learning stations, that provide meaningful work for students with a wide range of ability and achievement. Harry and Rosemary Wong, in their helpful book *The First Days of School: How to Be an Effective Teacher*, profile the procedures, including a wall chart entitled "What Do I Do Next? Activities," that create a positive and productive classroom atmosphere.[2]

8.2 The Information Genre

The expository writing found in many informational books is distinct from poetry, drama, folklore, and the prose writing of narrative fiction. The propositional, exact language of science contrasts with the literary and poetic, although today, as we will see, nonfiction writers frequently blend genres. Because standardized testing emphasizes expository passages, teachers are often asked to help students improve their comprehension of informational material; reading in the content areas refers to reading in math, science, history, and other domains. As the epigraph expresses, mesmerizing teaching of disciplinary knowledge is a challenge. Recurring patterns are found in most disciplines—science, mathematics, anthropology, and architecture to name a few. It is the discovery of these patterns that can evoke interest and awe. If we can see, as the progressive philosopher John Dewey did, that there are aesthetic qualities in everyday experience, then our approach to our subject matter in our classrooms will be dynamic, perhaps artistic.

As discussed in Chapter 1, Louise Rosenblatt describes the reader's stance as falling along a continuum between the aesthetic and the efferent. Depending on the purposes of the reader and the writer, the reading event may, primarily, convey information, but this type of reading event may also have aesthetic qualities. Likewise, with aesthetic reading, it may have "referential or cognitive elements."[3] The reader's stance when reading informational literature is usually on the efferent side of the continuum. However, with high-quality, well-designed nonfiction books, the potential exists for teachers to support aesthetic reading. For example, Walter Wick's *A Drop of Water: A Book of Science and Wonder,* although conveying through text and photographs information about water, is also a work of art. Similarly, all of David Macaulay's exquisitely rendered books on architecture, in the media of pen and ink, invite aesthetic responses: *Cathedral, City, Castle,* and *Mill.* Robert Vavra in *I Love Nature More* (see Figure 8.1), a tribute to the aesthetics of the natural world, photographs patterns in nature—the skins of animals, the nautilus, the feathers of birds, among other phenomena. Photographed by Kjell Sandved, the rubrications—the initial letters on each page—are from none other than photographs of butterfly wings.

Figure 8.1 Robert Vavra's *I Love Nature More* invites aesthetic reading while providing mesmerizingly beautiful scientific knowledge.

8.3 *History of Informational Literature*

It was not until Francis Bacon articulated the scientific method in the early 1600s that systematic study of nature and human events began. However, as early as the fourteenth century BCE, Egyptians recorded astronomy, and monolithic structures like Stonehenge and those on Easter Island in the Pacific show that humans around the world have closely observed their environment. However, written informational documents for the child audience are meager until the twentieth century. What follows is a record of the major contributions to the informational genre.

Between 673 and 735, the Venerable Bede, a teacher and historian at an English monastery, wrote in Latin *De Natura Rerum,* a tract about natural science and stars. *De Natura Rerum* circulated for hundreds of years and was translated from Latin to Old English in the tenth century. In about 800, Alcuin, a scholar and advisor to Charlemagne, wrote grammar and lesson books. Around 1000, Aelfric, an English abbot, wrote a dictionary that was used for the next four centuries. Anselm, the Archbishop of Canterbury, wrote *Elucidarium,* a type of encyclopedia, around 1100.

The Moravian bishop John Comenius wrote *Orbis Pictus* around 1657—the first picture book and basal reader so boys (not girls) could see things for themselves. Since 1990, the National Council of Teachers of English has offered the Orbis Pictus Award for Outstanding Nonfiction for Children. The first Newbery Award was awarded to Henrik Willem Van Loon in 1921 for his book *The Story of Mankind.*

Twentieth century interest in informational publications was spurred by developments in the former U.S.S.R. "Any consideration of informational books," says Barbara Bader, "must begin with the Russians who, with a whole nation to educate after the Revolution, turned to the picturebook on an unprecedented scale."[4] After the Bolshevik Revolution in 1917, the ruling communist party faced the Herculean task of inculcating young people into Marxist beliefs. To do this, Russian educators turned to the informational genre, proliferating hundreds of cheaply made didactic books. The belief that providing party-line information could indoctrinate the young into the Communists' preexisting point of view parallels the Puritans' belief that religious tracts and hornbooks would indoctrinate children into Calvinist thinking.

Although not sharing Marxist beliefs, western authors and illustrators shared a faith in the power of informational literature, believing that an educated citizenry was the best way to support democracy. Following the Russians' lead, informational books in the West sought to teach children about the world. In the early 1900s there was a lot to explain because of the many inventions surrounding the industrial revolution.

The Swedish author Elsa Beskow published *Pelle's New Suit* in 1928, a model for those books that followed that teach us about cultures outside the United States. Advancements in photography made possible realistic glimpses into all aspects of life. Photographer Edward Steichen, in addition to his other accomplishments, contributed to the field of children's literature with the 1930 publication *The First Picture Book,* prepared by Mary Steichen Martin. Dorothy Waugh, an early nonfiction writer, published *Among the Leaves and Grasses* in 1931, illustrating it in the art deco style of the time. Author illustrators Maud and Miska Petersham began their long and prolific career with *The Story*

Book of Things We Use in 1933. Holling C. Holling, beginning in 1935, wrote children's books about geography, illustrated by Cornelius DeWitt, and Donald Culross Peattie published *A Child's Story of the World* in 1937, illustrated by Naomi Averill.

More photographic books followed: *They All Saw It* and *Big and Little* in 1937. During the 1940s, Lilo Hess, a photographer with a zoology background, provided expert information at a level children could easily understand. Also in the 1940s, Irma Webber continued developing the nonfiction genre.

The 1950s saw books by Millicent Selsam, such as *All About Eggs,* illustrated by Helen Ludwig. The inner world as well as the outer world became a subject for children with Herbert Zim's 1952 publication of *What's Inside of Me?* illustrated by Herschel Wartik. Other publications in the fifties include *Fast Is Not a Ladybug* by Miriam Schlein, illustrated by Leonard Kessler, and *Heavy Is a Hippopotamus* in 1954. Marc Simont began his career as an illustrator of children's nonfiction, and adults and children celebrated Edward Steichen's 1955 publication of *The Family of Man.*

In 1957, the Russians again spurred American educators and publishers to pay attention to informational books. The successful Sputnik launch affronted Americans' estimation of their military and scientific superiority. Responding to what was seen as a national crisis, Congress passed the National Defense Education Act in 1957 to infuse the schools with better academic instruction, especially in math and science. Publishing opportunities accompanied this new thrust.

During the 1960s, publishers began to see the possibility of more profit with series books, such as Crowell's *Let's-Read-and-Find-Out* series: *The Moon Seems to Change* by Franklyn M. Branley, illustrated by Helen Borten (1960); Judy Hawes's *Fireflies in the Night,* illustrated by Kazue Mizumura (1963); Judy Hawes's *Shrimps,* illustrated by Joseph Low (1966); Aliki's *My Visit to the Dinosaurs* (1969); followed by many others.

During the 1970s Tana Hoban's photographic books emerged. Close to forty years later, she still publishes high-quality children's informational books. During the twenty-first century, the market for informational books continues to expand (see Figure 8.2). There are a number of books today that blend narrative and expository writing—for example, Joanna Cole's *Magic School Bus Series* and *Math Curse.* These part-fantasy, part-informational books both teach and delight.

8.4 Categories of Informational Literature

Nonfiction has manifested itself in a variety of forms, often blending genres. The photographic book links with the essay to create the *photoessay.* Photography links with biography to create *photobiography,* giving both information and visual images to illuminate people and their times. *Blended-genre* or *mixed-genre* books combine narrative and expository writing. *Curricular* books inform some area of the curriculum—science, country studies, and so on.

In *biography* the author undertakes the task of writing about someone's life. If still living, the person is often interviewed. If deceased, biographers draw on diaries, letters, historical accounts, and, if still living, individuals who knew the person. *Hagiography*

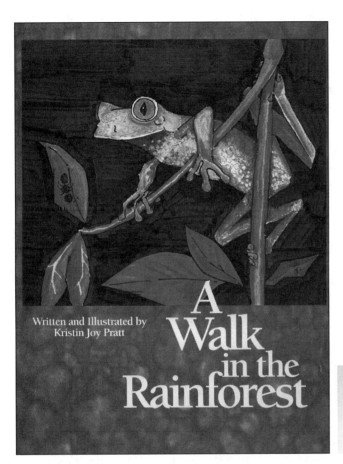

Written and Illustrated by
Kristin Joy Pratt

A
Walk
in the
Rainforest

Figure 8.2 Written when she was sixteen years old, Kristin Pratt's *A Walk
in the Rainforest* reflects care for the
natural world.

refers to biographies about the lives of the saints; biographers who seem to adore the person they are writing about omit mention of the person's faults. *Fictionalized biography* is
that category of biography in which the author fictionalizes dialogue and events, although
the story of the person's life is based on fact. Many biographies written for young people
are fictionalized, which has its hazards. There are a number of fictionalized series biographies—for example, Scholastic's *Dear America* series, which has examples of both
high- and low-quality writing. *Biography* is classified as *nonfiction* or *informational;* however, biographies are not ever purely factual. Each biography has its own slant because
authors pick and choose what they will put in and what they will leave out.

    Autobiography is written by an author depicting her own life and is usually chrono-
logical in scope. A *memoir,* also written by an author about her own life, spotlights a
specific time during her life, instead of trying to attain an accurate portrait of an entire
lifespan, as in an autobiography. The memoir also comments on the particular social,
political, and economic milieu.

    In this book, biography is discussed in Chapter 9 in relation to historical periods
and again in Chapter 10 in relation to careers and vocations. In Appendix C, you will find

general historical informational books in this chapter's section, and also in the interdisciplinary arrangement of the Chapter 9 bibliography in relation to specific periods of time.

Series books are especially prevalent in nonfiction publishing. Convenient for both publishers and librarians, series vary in quality from the mediocre and condescending to the aesthetically appealing and informative. Even within series, there is variation. However, questions of quality are not often considered. You can consult reviews in the journals and websites described in Chapter 3 to help you make these determinations. One fine example of a series that consistently contains high-quality books throughout is Leonard Everett Fisher's *Colonial Craftsmen,* first published in the mid 1960s, reprinted by Cavendish in 2000. Perusing this series can help you develop standards for judging others.

8.5 *Boys and Informational Literature*

As most librarians can tell you, boys have a preference for informational literature, which is supported by gender studies in children's literature.[5] This is not to say boys do not enjoy fantasy and other genres, yet there is concern that boys who are doing well in reading level off and, in some cases, decline in the amount they read as they move into the upper elementary grades. Part of the solution is for teachers to continue offering informational literature, including magazines and newspapers, which means choosing and sharing literature they may not enjoy themselves. As the National Education Association survey mentioned in Chapter 3.5 shows, the top 100 books teachers use are mostly fantasy.[6] Most elementary teachers are women who seem to prefer the fantasy genre. In the final chapter of their recent book *"Reading Don't Fix No Chevies": Literacy in the Lives of Young Men* based on extensive ethnographic research, Michael Smith and Jeffrey Wilhelm suggest that boys will read more if they are allowed to engage in inquiry learning, which means they can pose their own questions about topics that are important to them. Informational literature is often a source for discovering answers to important questions.[7]

To address better the needs and interests of boys, elementary teachers should be aware of high-quality informational books. Alex Law, a teacher of mostly bilingual children, chooses read-alouds that are nonfiction: "If it's important to read aloud stories and poetry, then it must be worthwhile to do the same with information books. . . . It opens up different possibilities."[8] When teachers read aloud and share informational books, it affirms boys' choices and preferences.

8.6 *Making Invisible Groups Visible*

As discussed in Chapter 3.6, Jaime Escalante's success, portrayed in the film *Stand and Deliver,* with students from the barrios of Los Angeles depended on his knowledge of their heritage. "Math is in your blood," he coaxed, detailing their ancestors' contributions to mathematics. Young people ask us who they are, and it is up to us to tell them. Seeing themselves in a long line of positive, strong, and courageous peoples provides life-transforming answers.

Currently Latino youth have more academic difficulties than any other ethnic group. They have the highest dropout rate of any ethnic group—about 28 percent.[9] To help improve Latino achievement, teachers can "incorporate Latino culture and traditions into the classroom when possible, particularly at the elementary level. Students should feel that their cultural background is welcomed and respected."[10] Waiting until middle school may be too late; the factors that lead students to drop out have their antecedents in the elementary school. Curricular invisibility negatively affects these children, who need to feel welcomed and respected.

Practicing teachers often do not have knowledge of ethnohistory—the development and contributions of cultures—because they were not taught it. Although textbooks from the 1950s and 1960s were better written, more complex, and had higher vocabulary levels than current textbooks, for the most part they left out the accomplishments of women and people of color. Textbooks written since the 1970s have been "dumbed down."[11] Today's teachers will have to become autodidacts—self-taught people who seek out knowledge about historically underrepresented groups.

In Appendix C you will find books from many categories of informational literature. In the Architecture section, note Bonnie Shemie's *Houses of Bark,* which explains the ingenious ways native people have created homes, or Margy Burns Knight's *Talking Walls* (see Figure 8.3), which includes international history and culture. In the Culinary Arts section, you can find books on food from around the world. How many of us know the

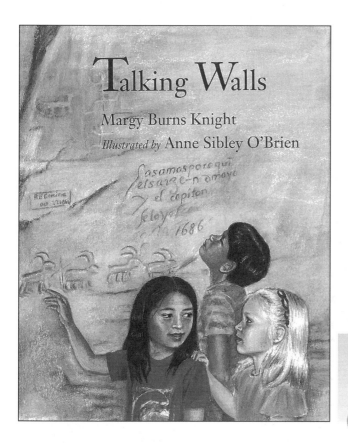

Figure 8.3 *Talking Walls* by Margy Burns Knight, illustrated by Anne Sibley O'Brien, takes readers on an architectural trip around the world.

contributions of the native peoples of the Americas, who developed more than 50 percent of the world's food supply? Then there is Norah Dooley's mouth-watering book, *Everybody Cooks Rice,* which tells the story of Carrie who, in her search through the neighborhood for her brother, tastes rice cooked by her neighbors from Barbados, Puerto Rico, Vietnam, India, China, Haiti (creole style), and Italy. As Pat Cummings says, we are "all multiculturalists when it comes to our stomachs."[12] It would be hard to imagine this country without all its ethnic restaurants.

The Ecology section in Appendix C chronicles worldwide efforts to save the environment, and the Fine Arts section includes international cultural expressions. *Linnea in Monet's Garden* by Christina Bjork, illustrated by Inga-Karin Eriksson, depicts a Swedish girl in the French artist's garden. The Math, Science, and Social Studies sections are as inclusive as possible, although more needs to be written, especially from an ethnohistorical perspective. Sheila Hamanaka and Ayano Ohmi's *In Search of the Spirit: The Living National Treasures of Japan* (see Figure 8.4), and Maywan Shen Krach's *D Is for Doufu* (see Figure 8.5), illustrated by Hongbin Zhang, set the standard for this kind of writing.

There are other examples of invisibility: How many know about Anna Julia Cooper? Born a slave, she taught mathematics and earned a Ph.D. in French at the University of Paris. What about the history of sports in pre-Columbian America? Indigenous peoples played lacrosse in the Northeast and hockey in the South and Midwest.[13] Learning in the content areas, and learning the history of the various disciplines from multiple perspectives, can be an unending source of inspiration and challenge. Continual learning

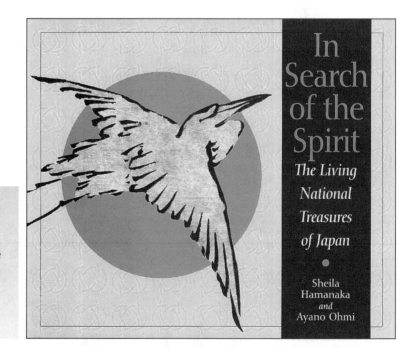

Figure 8.4 Sheila Hamanaka and Ayano Ohmi draw on their Japanese heritage to write and illustrate *In Search of the Spirit: The Living National Treasures of Japan.*

D is for Doufu

An Alphabet Book of Chinese Culture
Maywan Shen Krach • illustrated by Hongbin Zhang

Figure 8.5 *D is for Doufu: An Alphabet Book of Chinese Culture* by Maywan Shen Krach and illustrated by Hongbin Zhang is an important contribution to the informational genre.

in the content areas is part of the professionalization of elementary school teaching, and informational children's literature can be as enjoyable for inservice and preservice teachers as it is for children.

8.7 Criticism and Evaluation of Informational Literature

Since the 1950s, the information base has expanded exponentially and will continue to do so. Through Internet access, CD-ROM, daily newspapers, periodicals, and cable television, we have a superflux of information at our fingertips at all times. In the midst of all this plenty, however, we would do well to remember Russell Baker's philosophy of education: "The whole point of education," he says, "is to awaken innocent minds to a suspicion of information."[14] Even Alan Kay, whose genius shaped the Internet in its early days of development and whose enthusiasm for cyberspace has not waned, says, tongue-in-cheek, that one of the best metaphors for the Internet is "an ocean of spit a mile wide and an inch deep."[15]

To help children develop critical faculties, we must teach children how to ask these questions:

- Who wrote it? What is the source?
- Is it up-to-date?
- What is missing? Where is the gap, the lacuna? What is left out?
- What information is inaccurate? Unproved? A generalization?
- What is the point of view of the author? What is the author's background?
- Has the author used primary or secondary sources?
- How did the author write the book? Interviews? Travel? Direct observation?

A fallibilist philosophy of education is especially appropriate when evaluating information, both on the Internet and in books. Humans construct knowledge and because humans are fallible, the knowledge we create is fallible. "It can always be improved," says Henry Perkinson, an education historian and theorist of the critical approach. In his view, the role of teachers is to keep the critical dialogue going, so that their students can become critical learners:

> Instead of possessing shared bits and pieces of knowledge, people who are taught this way will have a common outlook toward all knowledge. They will recognize and accept human fallibility and thereby realize that all knowledge is conjectural—never final, never complete—but continually improvable, through criticism, through the uncovering and elimination of errors. They not only will be ready to hold all received and new knowledge open to criticism, but also will be prepared and able to participate in the critical conversation through which knowledge and culture grows and evolves.[16]

In addition to helping children learn to critique nonfiction, they can be helped to see the special features of informational books, usually marked by different typeface. Watching for cues from font, point size, bold, and italics can help them navigate the genre; not all books have to be read cover to cover. Walking them through these aspects scaffolds their learning:

- Table of contents
- Chapter titles
- Section headings
- Diagrams, charts, and maps
- Indexes
- Appendices

Students can also be helped to discriminate between photographs and illustrations. One of the best ways to develop discrimination between well-written and poorly written informational literature is to sample some of the best. Investigate some of the titles noted in this chapter or consult the Orbis Pictus Awards website list, then compare excellent books with others you find on library shelves.

8.8 Nurturing Individual Interests

As already discussed, elementary classroom teachers will encounter a variety of learning styles, interests, and abilities in the classes they teach. Some children simply do not need the time others do to master skills and concepts. Unfortunately, too many of these children mark time in schools; out of boredom, some of them become troublemakers.

What can teachers do? As described at the beginning of this chapter, you can organize well-equipped centers of interest, or learning stations, for children to explore, even in the upper elementary grades. One of the most important educational innovations is *curriculum compacting,* which allows children to "test out" of what they already know, giving them time to pursue what they love. This means that teachers must continually assess students' knowledge. If they already know nouns or direct objects or multiplication tables or fractions, and you are planning whole-class instruction on what they already know, allow those who have tested out to pursue investigating an area of interest.[17] *Curriculum Compacting: The Complete Guide to Modifying the Curriculum for High Ability Students* by Sally Reis et al., provides step-by-step procedures to help the classroom teacher, and ensures that students will not have gaps in their learning by providing templates for compactors.

According to E. Paul Torrance, one of the most important things teachers can do is to protect the passions, which means finding out what students love and helping them to pursue it.[18] The bibliography in Appendix C highlights many areas of human interest. Some of the books contain suitable activities for children, saving them from marking time while waiting for others. Informational books, such as Seymour Simon's *Earthquakes* (see Figure 8.6), stir children's interests. The people they read about are often themselves examples of those who learn to take responsibility for their time and talents. *In Search of the Spirit: The Living National Treasures of Japan* presents an array of people engaged in professions.

Csikszentmihalyi's study showed that for creative adults, domain knowledge is inexhaustible. All of his interviewees still possessed—even in their seventies and eighties—awe, fascination, and respect for the domains in which they work. However, Csikszentmihalyi writes, "Teachers rarely spend time trying to reveal the beauty and fun of doing math or science; students learn that these subjects are ruled by grim determinism instead of the freedom and adventure that the experts experience."[19] The range and quality of informational books available today can help teachers and their students approach disciplinary knowledge like experts.

Benjamin Bloom's study of gifted youths showed that their parents and teachers recognized their talents early, then provided encouragement and helped them work hard.[20] Csikszentmihalyi validates Bloom's study: "What *is* important is to recognize the interest when it shows itself, nurture it, and provide the opportunities for it to grow into a creative life."[21]

Figure 8.6 Seymour Simon's elegantly photographed series books, for example *Earthquakes,* help children discover answers to questions they have about the natural world.

8.9 Conclusion

Informational literature, because of its immense range, offers possibilities for growth for many children with unique interests. Gaining knowledge of this literature helps you attain an NCATE standard: Teachers "apply knowledge of the richness of contributions from diverse cultures to each content area studied by elementary students."[22]

Elliott Eisner says, "Each child in our schools should be given an opportunity to find a place in our educational sun. This means designing educational programs that enable children to play to their strengths, to pursue and exploit those meaning systems for which they have special aptitudes or interests."[23] Providing informational literature, and ways to respond to it, can invite that sunlight into classrooms.

Suggested Activities

1. Eleanor Duckworth's *The Having of Wonderful Ideas* suggests keeping a moon journal for a month. This exercise develops the powers of observation, and promotes skill in writing and thinking.

2. *Mr. Wizard's Supermarket Science* by Don Herbert, or *201 Awesome, Magical, Bizarre and Incredible Experiments* by Janice Van Cleaves, describe simple experiments easily

and, usually, cheaply, carried out in the elementary classrooms. Begin putting some of these together. See the bibliography of recommended books in Appendix C for other examples.

3. Using plasticene, create fossils or other artifacts.

4. Experiment with the crafts found in the Crafts section of the bibliography, or the arts in the Fine Arts section.

5. Using a scale of one, reconstruct the buildings found in the books in the Architecture section.

6. Prepare a dish from the Culinary Arts section.

7. After reading a book from the Ecology section, write an advocacy letter. Or write a feature news article on an environmental issue.

for further reading

Association for Supervision and Curriculum Development. 2000. "Differentiating Instruction: Finding Manageable Ways to Meet Individual Needs." *Curriculum Update,* (Winter). Association for Supervision and Curriculum Development.

Bamford, Rosemary A., and Janice V. Kristo. 2000. *Checking Out Nonfiction K–8: Good Choices for Best Learning.* Norwood, MA: Christopher Gordon.

Donovan, Carol A., and Laura B. Smoking. 2002. "Considering Genre, Content, and Visual Features in the Selection of Trade Books for Science Instruction." *The Reading Teacher, 55.6:* 502–520.

Duckworth, Eleanor. 1996. *"The Having of Wonderful Ideas" & Other Essays on Teaching & Learning.* New York: Teachers College Press.

Kobrin, Beverly. 1995. *Eyeopeners II: Children's Books to Answer Children's Questions about the World Around Them.* New York: Scholastic.

Moyer, Patricia S. 2000. "Communicating Mathematically: Children's Literature as a Natural Connection." *The Reading Teacher, 54.3:* 246–255.

Murphy, Stuart J. 2000. "Children's Books about Math: Trade Books That Teach." *The New Advocate, 13.4:* 365–374.

Whitin, David J., and Sandra White. 1995. *It's the Story That Counts: More Children's Books for Mathematical Learning, K–6.* Portsmouth, NH: Heinemann.

Young, Julie E. 2001. "Why Are We Reading a Book During Math Time? How Mathematics and Literature Relate." *The Dragon Lode, 19.2:* 13–18.

Magazines

National Geographic World:
www.nationalgeographic.com/kids

Odyssey: Adventures in Science, Cobblestone Publishing Co., 30 Grove St., Suite C, Peterborough, NH 03458
http://odysseymagazine.com

Ranger Rick, National Wildlife Federation, 8825 Leesburg Pike, Vienna, VA 22184

Zoobooks:
www.zoobooks.com

websites

Evaluating new books:
www.appraisal.new.edu

Science literacy:
www.ericse.rog

awards

American Library Association/Robert F. Sibert Informational Book Award:

>www.ala.org/alsc/sibert.html

American Nature Study Society:

>http://hometown.aol.com/anssonline/ myhomepage/index.html

Eva L. Gordon Award:

>www.urich.edu/~pstohrhu/literature/ gordon.html

The Giverny Award of Best Science Books:

>www.15degreelab.com/award.html

National Council for the Social Studies, Carter G. Woodson Award and Outstanding Merit Book Award Recipients:

>www.soemadison.wisc.edu/ccbc/woodson.html

National Council for Social Studies/Children's Book Council Notable Social Studies Trade Books for Young People is published annually in the May/June issue of *Social Education.*

National Council for Teachers of English Orbis Pictus Award:

>www.ncte.org/elem/pictus/

National Science Teachers Association/Children's Book Council Outstanding Science Trade Books for Children is published annually in the March issue of *Science and Children.*

notes

1. Mihaly Csikszentmihalyi, *Creativity: Flow and the Psychology of Discovery and Invention* (New York: HarperCollins, 1996), p. 125.
2. Harry K. Wong and Rosemary T. Wong, *The First Days of School: How to Be an Effective Teacher* (Mountain View, CA: Harry K. Wong Publications, 1998), p. 170.
3. Louise Rosenblatt, "The Literary Transaction: Evocation and Response." In: *Journeying: Children Responding to Literature,* Kathleen E. Holland, Rachael A. Hungerford, and Shirley B. Ernst, eds. (Portsmouth, NH: Heinemann, 1993), p. 9.
4. Barbara Bader, *American Picturebooks from Noah's Ark to the Beast Within* (New York: Macmillan, 1976), p. 88.
5. Myra Barrs, "Introduction: Reading the Difference." In: *Reading the Difference: Gender and Reading in Elementary Classrooms,* Myra Barrs and Sue Pidgeon, eds. (York, ME: Stenhouse, 1993), p. 10.
6. "NEA Spotlights 100 Books to Grow On," *Reading Today: The Bimonthly Newspaper of the International Reading Association* (April/May 1999): 10.
7. Michael W. Smith and Jeffrey D. Wilhelm, *"Reading Don't Fix No Chevies": Literacy in the Lives of Young Men* (Portsmouth, NH: Heinemann, 2002), p. 188.
8. Quoted in Sue Ellis, "Changing the Pattern." In: *Reading the Difference: Gender and Reading in Elementary Classrooms,* Myra Barrs and Sue Pidgeon, eds. (York, ME: Stenhouse, 1993), p. 121.
9. The University of Rochester 1997 McNair Education Abstracts. Available at www.nces.ed.gov/pubs2003/ 2003008.pdf
10. Laurel Shaper Walters, "Latino Achievement Reexamined," *Harvard Education Letter XIV.5* (September/ October 1998): 4–6.
11. Sally M. Reis, Deborah E. Burns, and Joseph M. Renzulli, *Curriculum Compacting: The Complete Guide to Modifying the Curriculum for High Ability Students* (Mansfield Center, CT: Creative Learning Press, 1992), p. 6.
12. Pat Cummings, *Multicultural Matters: Writing for ALL Readers.* Paper presented at the Children's Literature and Reading, Special Interest Group 3, International

Reading Association 45th Annual Convention, "Reading the New World," Indianapolis, IN, 2 May 2000.

13. Joseph Bruchac, *Roots of Survival* (Golden, CO: Fulcrum, 1996), p. 38.

14. Quoted in Gary Gumpert, *Talking Tombstones and Other Tales of the Media Age* (New York: Oxford University Press, 1987), p. 144.

15. Alan Kay, *Is the Best Way to Predict the Future to Invent It? Or to Prevent It?* Paper presented at "The Computer in Education: Seeking the Human Essentials," Teachers College, Columbia University, New York, NY; 5 December 1997.

16. Henry J. Perkinson, *Teachers without Goals Students without Purposes* (New York: McGraw-Hill, 1993), pp. 14, 76–77.

17. Reis et al., *Curriculum Compacting,* pp. 26–164.

18. E. Paul Torrance, "The Nature of Creativity as Manifest in Its Testing." In: *The Nature of Creativity: Contemporary Psychological Perspectives,* Robert J. Sternberg, ed. (New York: Cambridge University Press, 1998), p. 69.

19. Csikszentmihalyi, *Creativity,* p. 342.

20. Benjamin Bloom, *Developing Talent in Young People* (New York: Ballantine, 1985), pp. 508–509.

21. Csikszentmihalyi, *Creativity,* p. 182.

22. National Council for Accreditation of Teacher Education, *Program Standards for Elementary Teacher Preparation,* supporting explanation, 3b.

23. Elliot W. Eisner, *The Kind of Schools We Need: Personal Essays* (Portsmouth, NH: Heinemann, 1998), p. 18.

chapter 9

Integrated Historical Literature
The Human Dimension

The colonel was surprised to see the tears well up in Spotted Tail's eyes; he did not know that an Indian could weep.[1]

— DEE BROWN

9.1 Encountering Literature

Materials Needed

Several core sets of books all have read.

Prior to this session, prepare to participate in a literature circle by reading a work of historical fiction or a biography. The following books are suggested:

- Pam Muñoz Ryan's *Esperanza Rising*
- Eleanor Coerr's *Sadako and the Thousand Paper Cranes*
- Michael Dorris's *Morning Girl*
- Louise Erdrich's *The Birchbark House*
- Esther Hautzig's *The Endless Steppe*
- Bette Bao Lord's *In the Year of the Boar and Jackie Robinson*
- Mildred Taylor's *Roll of Thunder, Hear My Cry*
- Laurence Yep's *Dragon's Gate*
- Deborah Ellis's *The Breadwinner*
- Sterling North's *Rascal*
- Christopher Paul Curtis's *The Watsons Go to Birmingham—1963*

Choose the book group you want to join. Although there is no set number for the group size, about six to a group works well. Nancie Atwell suggests that book discussions take place like the ones that occur around your dining room table when you talk with friends and family about a book that excites you.[2] To set the mood, bring in a tablecloth (an old sheet will do) and a candle for each group. Light the candles, dim the lights, and let conversations begin. If groups are floundering on what to talk about, which rarely happens at the college level, look again at the prompts in Chapter 1.6 on reader response. Allow for about thirty minutes of class time.

About Literature Circles Literature circles offer the opportunity for students to work in small groups discussing books of their choice. We know that students must have some choice about what they read, and that they must have opportunities to discuss what they read with each other and with their teachers.[3] Based on reader response, or reception theory, readers construct meaning in a transaction in which their unique past experiences, memories, and personalities come into play. Wolfgang Iser, a reception theorist, writes, "[W]hat *is* said only appears to take on significance as a reference to what is not said; it is the implications and not the statements that give shape and weight to the meaning. . . . Whenever the reader bridges the gaps, communication begins." Literature circles, then, allow students to discuss with each other the unique way they have imaginatively filled the spaces between words. The act of conversing challenges, affirms, and extends aesthetic reading. Louise Rosenblatt suggests that if teachers find it necessary to guide their students' attention, questions should be "sufficiently open to enable the young readers to select concrete details or parts of the text that had struck them most forcibly. The point is to foster expressions of response that keep the experiential, qualitative elements in mind. Did anything especially interest? annoy? puzzle? frighten? please? seem familiar? seem weird?"[5] Sharing individual responses implies multiple interpretations. Instead of one correct response, readers can see that literature has multiple meanings. To create the trust necessary to evoke personal responses, Rosenblatt recommends, "An atmosphere of informal, friendly exchange should be created. The student should feel free to reveal emotions and to make judgments. . . . Frank expression of boredom or even vigorous rejection is a more valid starting point for learning than are docile attempts to feel 'what the teacher wants.'" She does, however, caution that teachers should help students see that "some interpretations are more defensible than others."[6]

A problem with literature circles is that they can sometimes lapse into free associations that float away from the book. Language arts expert Lucy Calkins says, "For me . . . red lights flash when there is no book in the book talk." To keep students centered on the text, Calkins suggests the following statements and questions:

- Show me what you mean.
- What makes you say that?
- What were you reading when you thought of that?
- Will you find one part of the book that makes you say that?
- Can you find a specific passage as an example for what you are saying?
- Can we look at the book together and see what it says?

Teachers can also disagree with students, citing the page number of supporting passages.[7] Both thoughts and feelings should be welcomed; to focus only on intellectual questions risks losing those students whose intellectual interest is piqued by their feelings. Latino educators tell us that affective questions—questions that center on feelings—are as important as cognitive questions.[8] Teachers can be active listeners who summarize and guide children's exploration of literature.

Students can independently conduct literature circles much in the way they participate in cooperative learning. A structured approach, suggested by Harvey Daniels, is to assign a discussion director, passage master, connector, illustrator, and so on.[9] It is most effective for students to create their own guidelines. Lisa Cross Stanzi's second graders decided to

- Keep the conversation going
- Stay on task
- Include all group members in the discussion
- Take turns

- Not to interrupt each other
- Respond to questions and ideas brought up by other members
- Be polite[10]

This open-ended exploration contrasts with the view of teachers as dispensers of knowledge who have all the right answers to students' questions. Helping children learn to ask questions is far more educative; it's the question askers who have led the advancement in all endeavors. See the For Further Reading section of this chapter for more information on literature circles.

9.2 Definitions

Most textbooks on children's literature have a chapter on historical fiction, which is the dominant genre for this chapter. However, also integrated into the bibliography for this chapter in Appendix C are the informational genres already discussed in Chapter 8.4, and the biographical genre in Chapter 10.

As discussed in Chapter 2.2, **historical fiction** is realistic fiction that pictures life in previous eras written by contemporary authors who, while using their imaginations, draw on the scholarly resources of documents, diaries, letters, and recorded history. These they shape into engaging stories by integrating characters from the past in settings that are often beyond the experience of modern readers. (See Figure 9.1.)

Constantine Georgiou, professor of children's literature at New York University, distinguishes between modern authors who write historical fiction and authors from the past who wrote realistic fiction in the period in which they lived. This he calls **historical realism.** When Louisa May Alcott wrote *Little Women* in 1868, it was considered contemporary. Now, however, the book gives us a glimpse into the mid nineteenth century while still holding our interest because of its enduring themes. If the book is more than seventy-five years old—an arbitrary dividing line—it can usually be defined as *historical realism.*

9.3 Integrating Historical Literature

As discussed in the preface, there are several reasons for integrating several genres with historical topics. Doing so helps preservice teachers pass national exit exams, which often elicit interdisciplinary approaches. If you explore the sets of texts, grouped chronologically and topically in Appendix C, you will be able to call to mind when studying the Civil Rights movement such books as

- *Leon's Story,* an autobiography by Leon Walter Tillage, a working-class African American whose story begins in the Depression, leading up to his involvement in civil rights
- *Rosa Parks: My Story,* an autobiography of the renowned woman who challenged Jim Crow laws in the South

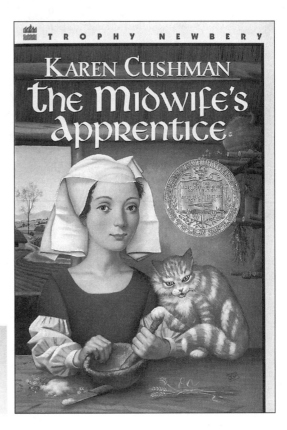

Figure 9.1 The Newbery Award-winning book, *The Midwife's Apprentice* by Karen Cushman, in addition to telling an engaging story, provides information about life in the Middle Ages.

- *Dare to Dream: Coretta Scott King and the Civil Rights Movement* by Angela Shelf Medearis, a biography of the wife of Martin Luther King; she was (and still is) a leader in her own right
- *The Watsons Go to Birmingham—1963* by Christopher Paul Curtis, a work of historical fiction that portrays both the humor and the injustice one northern family experiences during a trip to the South
- *Brown vs. Board of Education (1954): School Desegregation* by Mark Dudley, an informational book on the most important Supreme Court ruling in the twentieth century

Or, when studying the American West in the late nineteenth century, you might share

- An autobiography: *Chief Joseph's Own Story* from the Council for Indian Education
- A biography: *Indian Chiefs* by Russell Freedman
- A historical novel: *Dragon's Gate* by Laurence Yep
- An informational book: *Navajo Long Walk* by Joseph Bruchac

Figure 9.2 Ji-li Jiang's 1998 publication of *Red Scarf Girl: A Memoir of the Cultural Revolution* gives western readers insight into the Cultural Revolution in China during the 1960s and 1970s.

You will find many similar groupings in Appendix C. By approaching historical topics in this way, you provide for the varying interests and abilities of children (see Figure 9.2). Boys frequently choose nonfiction (informational books, biographies, and autobiographies). Girls frequently choose fiction.

Anecdotally, my daughter's consistent C grade in social studies throughout her elementary years zoomed to an A grade the semester her teacher used *Across Five Aprils* by Irene Hunt to teach the Civil War. When the teacher went back to the student-as-an-empty-bucket method of read-the-chapter-answer-the-questions-at-the-end-of-the-chapter, my daughter's grade went back to a C. For her to care about the Civil War, she had to connect with real human beings. She had to *feel* the internal conflicts, which Hunt brilliantly depicts in a family nearly torn apart by the war. Two brothers choose to fight for the North; another brother, although he despises slavery, chooses to fight for the South, in part because he sees the hypocrisy of the North, which had its own brand of slavery in factories. In addition to learning factual knowledge about the Civil War, readers of *Across Five Aprils* vicariously experience the heart-rending pain that surrounded the war.

When the progressive philosopher John Dewey was asked to comment on the relationship between mind and emotions, he answered: "Knowledge is a small cup of water floating on a sea of emotion."[11] Dewey intuitively sensed the intricate connection between the two, which seems to have been verified in psychology and other disciplines in the last several decades.

Too often, history seems to the young an endless litany of names, dates, and wars. The inclusion of literature in the study of history changes this, transforming students' experiences by touching their hearts and minds, and illuminating historical topics and periods in a way no other venue can. Real people with real feelings made hard choices, and we stand on their shoulders. Reading vibrant and moving stories can make children *want* to investigate wider frames of knowledge, renewing interest and motivation. Interdisciplinary learning is key to making sense of facts and fragmentation. In her book *The Dreamkeepers: Successful Teachers of African American Children*, Gloria Ladson–Billings describes how one teacher's use of *Charlie Pippin* and *Sadako and the Thousand Paper Cranes* brought about almost miraculous results with a sixth-grade class.[12]

Although all literature has a place in the existentialist vision of evoking passion, integrity, and choice, historical literature can particularly provoke and nurture a philosophy of life. For existentialist educators, the most important role of the teacher is to awaken students' awareness of personal agency. Historical literature allows us to see individuals, often in difficult situations, exercise their freedom to choose. By the projects they undertake, what they say yes to, and what they say no to, they change the course of their lives and times. When reading these historical stories, children find clues to who they are, where they come from, and who they want to become.

Philosopher and teacher educator Maxine Greene speaks of Nathaniel Hawthorne who said, "'The world owes all its onward impulses to men ill at ease.'"[13] When studying historical literature we meet men and women who achieved what they did by starting at a place of discomfort. Being uncomfortable often led to making a difference in their lives and times.

9.4 History and Timeline of Realistic Fiction

In the following timeline, the antecedents of the contemporary survival, mystery, animal, adventure, and domestic stories are noted; these will be looked at again in Chapter 11 on contemporary realism. *Ivanhoe*, published in 1816 by Sir Walter Scott, is generally considered the first example of historical fiction. I include earlier titles because of their significance to children. Also noted throughout the timeline are the childhood favorites of extraordinary childhood readers.

1719	*The Life and Strange Surprizing Adventures of Robinson Crusoe, of York, Mariner* by Daniel Defoe. This publication marked the beginning of the *survival* story, enjoyed by both children and adults. It was the only book the influential Romantic education philosopher Rousseau would allow his imaginary Emile to read.

1812   *Swiss Family Robinson* by Johann Wyss, both an *adventure* and a survival story

1823   *The Pioneers* (1823), *The Last of the Mohicans* (1826), *The Pathfinder* (1840), and *The Deerslayer* (1841) by James Fennimore Cooper. Although he wrote for adults, children read these books, which were translated into most European languages. If used, treatment of American Indians must be discussed.

1838   *Oliver Twist* by Charles Dickens. As a child, Norman Rockwell sketched characters from Dickens while his father read aloud.[14]

1847   *Jane Eyre*, a *romantic* novel by Charlotte Brontë. Although written for adults, generations of children have cherished it too. Brontë cited the influence of Sir Walter Scott, in books such as *Ivanhoe*, on her writing.

1851–1852   *Uncle Tom's Cabin* by Harriet Beecher Stowe. A primary abolitionist work, it has been translated into dozens of languages. Esther Hautzig read it before she was ten, and Sid Fleischman clearly remembers his mother reading it to him during his early years.[15] Objections to stereotypes in the book should be pointed out to readers.

1861   *Great Expectations* by Charles Dickens. Some of my students have reported that Dickens's books were their favorite childhood read-alouds.

1865   *Hans Brinker, or The Silver Skates* by Mary Mapes Dodge. This book reflected the didactic moralism prevalent at that time. The book also tends toward *melodrama,* a literary term that denotes extremes in characterization and an attempt at manipulating the emotions of readers.

1868   The *Ragged Dick* series by Horatio Alger, Jr. This series was one of many that had a rags-to-riches theme, reflecting a belief in a meritocracy: Anyone who works hard enough, and earns the attention of the wealthy, can rise to the top—a philosophy that guided educational practice and curriculum (for example, the *McGuffey* textbooks) in the United States during the late 1800s and early 1900s. Their overly simplistic and optimistic tone, which treated poverty in too reductive a manner, was eventually recanted by Andrew Carnegie, who realized this country was no longer the land of opportunity for everyone as it had once seemed to be.

    Little Women (1868), *Little Men* (1871), *Eight Cousins* (1875), *Rose in Bloom* (1876), and *Jo's Boys* (1886) by Louisa May Alcott. Alcott's books are examples of *domestic realism,* which pictures the drama and humor of family life. bell hooks [*sic*], an African American author and English professor, remembers reading all of Alcott: "I find remnants of myself in Jo, the serious sister, the one who is punished. I am a little less alone in the world."[16]

1876   *The Adventures of Tom Sawyer* (1876), *The Prince and the Pauper* (1881), *The Adventures of Huckleberry Finn* (1884), and *A Connecticut Yankee in King Arthur's Court* (1889) by Mark Twain. Twain wrote for an audience of adults and children, although Louisa May Alcott questioned his appropriateness for children. The stereotypical treatment of Injun Joe and Jim should be discussed.

1880   *Heidi* by Johanna Spyri. This book was translated into English in 1884.

1883   *Treasure Island* (1883) and *Kidnapped* (1887) by Robert Louis Stevenson. These books, originally written for his stepson, were *boys' stories,* full of swashbuckling adventure. Hearing the words *treasure island* still gives British illustrator-writer Michael Foreman as much of a thrill now as they did when he was a child.[17] Edmund Hilary, the first European to climb Mount Everest, as a child constantly read adventures like these to escape an abusive home life.[18]

1886   *Little Lord Fauntleroy* and *Sara Crewe* (1888) by Frances Hodgson Burnett, later expanded and titled *A Little Princess* and *The Secret Garden* (1911)

1895   *The Red Badge of Courage* by Stephen Crane

1903   *Call of the Wild* (1903) and *White Fang* (1906) by Jack London, in the subcategory of *animal realism*

          Rebecca of Sunnybrook Farm by Kate Douglas Wiggin

1908   *Anne of Greene Gables* by L. M. Montgomery. Continued as a series, these books took place on Prince Edward Island.

1912   *Pollyanna* by Eleanor Porter

1919   *Lad: A Dog* by Alfred Terhune. Joseph Bruchac discovered and enjoyed these books by age seven.[19]

1923   *The Dark Frigate* by Charles Boardman Hawes

1926   *Smoky: A Cow Horse* by Will James

          The Trumpeter of Krakow by Eric P. Kelly

1932   *Little House in the Big Woods* series by Laura Ingalls Wilder, which described her childhood in the 1870s. She began writing these books at age sixty-seven and, despite her editor's pleading, put down her pen eleven years later. Wilder did not have the benefit of hearing the diverse voices of our more multiculturally aware society, and so, unintentionally, some of the books in the series are insensitive to American Indians and should be discussed.

9.5 Historical Realism: Classics of Children's Literature

As indicated by the timeline, people from all over the globe and from all walks of life continue to treasure old books. Some of the books in the timeline reflect, perhaps unconsciously, the -isms of the time in which they were written. Beverly Tatum, a professor of psychology and dean of Mount Holyoke College, loved Gertrude Chandler Warner's *The Boxcar Children* and its sequels during her childhood. However, when introducing these books to her own children, she took the opportunity to discuss the book's sexism—the girls are the ones who do all the cooking and cleaning. Having made explicit the book's overtones, her son was then able to spot sexism in other books as well.[20]

What makes a book a classic? As discussed in Chapter 4.2 books that resonate with each succeeding generation are those that address universal questions, concerns, hopes, and dreams. The author's inventiveness and unique perspective bridge the worlds of former and contemporary times. Although the language may seem archaic, today's children should have the opportunity to read, and hear read, these classic books.

When Charlotte Brontë left the isolated moors of Haworth, England, to study in Belgium, she believed all she needed to be a great artist was her passion, intensity, thoughts, and feelings. "To write," she asked, "is anything else needed beside genius, converging with some sentiment, affection or passion?" Her beloved mentor, Monsieur Heger, responded, "Genius without study, without art, without the knowledge of what has been done, is strength without the lever . . . it is the soul that sings within and cannot express its interior song save in a rough and raucous voice."[21] Under his tutelage, Brontë further explored her literary heritage and then went on to become one of the greatest novelists of all time. Creativity and growth—regardless of the domain—depends, as Monsieur Heger intuitively knew and cognitive psychology has since affirmed (see Chapter 1.8), on knowledge of what has already been created within cultures. Engagement with classical literature promotes intertextuality—texts written in response to other texts.

Filipino Carlos Bulosan marks the beginning of his intellectual life during childhood when his brother, Macario, shared *Robinson Crusoe*. Macario told him, "You must remember the good example of Robinson Crusoe. Someday you may be left alone somewhere in the world and you will have to depend on your own ingenuity." Years later, after both had experienced a cruelty and hostility they did not expect as immigrants to the United States, Macario nevertheless enlisted to fight for the country that had so disappointed him. Reminiscent of Crusoe, he said, " 'The world is an island. We are cast upon the sea of life hoping to land somewhere in the world. But there is only one island and it is the heart.' "[22] Carlos took these words for the title of his autobiography.

N. Scott Momaday, whose love of his father's Kiowa stories was mentioned in Chapter 7, learned English literature from his mother: "My mother's love of books, and of English literature in particular, is intense, and naturally she wanted me to share in it. I have seen Grendel's shadow on the walls of Canyon de Chelly, and once, having led the sun around Hoskinini Mesa, I saw Copperfield at Olijeto Trading Post."[23] Momaday's artistic talent was nurtured by the different heritages—Kiowa and European—he received from both his mother and his father.

In her autobiography *The Endless Steppe* (see Figure 9.3), Esther Hautzig recounts her experience during the deportation of Polish Jews to Siberia in 1941. In a poorly equipped Siberian school that she was allowed to attend after amnesty was granted (her family and others could not return to Poland until after the war was over), Hautzig recalls, even with its emphasis on Marxism and its omission of any mention of Tsar Nicholas, her joy of learning. As a ten-year-old, in fifth grade, she read Tolstoi, Dumas, Balzac, Dickens, and other great writers. Dickens, of course, to the Soviet teacher,

Figure 9.3 Esther Hautzig's *The Endless Steppe* is an inspiring story of a young girl and her family's triumph in the face of great suffering during World War II.

showed that capitalism didn't work.[24] In addition to the school, Hautzig found in the forsaken reaches of Siberia an astoundingly wonderful library that became, despite its small size, a place where she forgot the cold, a place where she forgot her confinement. There she read, along with Russian writers, Pasternak, who translated Shakespeare, Mark Twain, and Jack London. She has never forgotten the privilege it is to read.[25]

Hautzig also reread and reread these books; classics invite rereading, readers gaining more insight each time they read. Their presence in the classroom fosters differentiated curriculum. Michael Clay Thompson, an advocate for using the classics with all children, tells of a conversation with Harry Passow, a professor of education from Teachers College, Columbia University. After Thompson had given a lecture on the classics, Passow asked how he would differentiate for gifted students. Thompson paused; he sensed something was coming. Passow continued, "Isn't that the beauty of the classics? They are *self*-differentiating. They are so deep that each person is able to read them at his own depth and get something out of them."[26] High-ability readers, especially, need the challenge of "substantive texts," as Joyce Van Tassel–Baska points out.[27]

Multiculturalism has taught us that great literature has emerged from global perspectives, as well as from western civilization. Thompson comments,

> Classics develop human values. If anything really explains why books become classics, it is simply because they are books that matter. There is always something in the story, some loyalty or bravery or curiosity, that matters. The humanity of the classics, including the inherent global perspective of world literature, is a beautiful and critically necessary counterpoint to the culture of violence and brutality that plagues our streets and our entertainment media.[28]

The delight and privilege of reading classic works of art should be emphasized in the literature-based classroom, and included in read-alouds.

Many classic books have been made into film; both book and film can be shared, compared, and enjoyed. Joy Boyum, a New York University professor of English education, although noting that we tend to evaluate film by the book rather than the other way around, notes that film making of books boosts reading.[29] Reading the book before seeing the film has the advantage of allowing readers first to create their own images and then compare these images with the interpretive creation of a film director. The 1994 Columbia Pictures production of *Little Women* sparked interest in the book, causing sales of the book to increase. Several film versions of *Jane Eyre* have inspired children to read the book. Reading William Armstrong's *Sounder,* then viewing the film in which Cicely Tyson starred, provokes dynamic conversations: Why did the filmmakers choose to alter Armstrong's original story?

Classics are considered again in Chapter 12, on fantasy. In Appendix C, you will find books that have two publishing dates—for example, *Spyri,* Johanna. 1955 [1880]. *Heidi.* New York: Dutton. The brackets indicate the year in which the book was first published. When you see two dates, especially those that span several decades, you know you are considering literature that several generations have cherished.

9.6 Criticism and Evaluation of Historical Literature

The problem with works of historical realism has been the treatment of women and people of color. The books are products of their times, negative as well as positive. Typically, women and people of color are either left out or treated as less than human in both literature and textbooks. The challenge for today's teaching force is to unlearn and relearn so that women and ethnic groups are better and more truthfully represented. Gary Howard says, "Whites can also contribute to the healing of dominance by demanding honesty in the teaching and construction of history. It is not the sole responsibility of marginalized groups to insist that their stories be accurately represented in the school curriculum. Honesty and fair representation ought to be a concern for all of us. . . ."[30]

One way to look at the issue is through the lens of colonial and postcolonial literature. Under imperialism, the goal of some western countries for centuries was to colonize other countries, largely for economic purposes, assimilating them into the conquering country's culture. From the time of their arrival, European Americans displayed an ethnocentric attitude toward people of color, expecting them to disappear in the melting pot, which meant leaving behind their heritage. For a long time, European Americans narrated through books and textbooks the nation's history. In postcolonial literature, previously silenced people of color tell their own stories, giving voice and visibility to writers who, several decades ago, had neither. When reading and learning about our nation's past, the honesty and integrity of postcolonial literature can help us see more clearly where we have been and where we need to go.

At what age do we introduce books about social injustice? Debbie Reese, a Nambé Indian, does not think it suitable to share deeply disturbing books with young children because they are likely to internalize and blame themselves. Instead, books for young children "should focus on providing information about contemporary Native children, presenting the traditional Native aspects of their lives, as well as the daily activities typical of other children in the United States (riding bikes, . . .)."[31] Similarly Marguerite Wright, an African American psychologist, is in no rush to acquaint young children with historical injustices. She offers this advice:

> [D]evelopmentally, young children are not equipped to cope with the knowledge of pervasive racial discrimination. Children who are prematurely sensitized to the existence of racial bigotry have difficulty processing such information, much less coping with it. I believe that instead of telling their children how tough life will be for them, truly caring parents and other adults should shield them from this information for as long as possible. Don't we try to protect our children from other information we think they are too immature to handle?[32]

Beginning in the upper elementary grades, however, teachers can introduce books that give diverse perspectives on history. For too long, this side of the story has not been told. Not to tell it harms both the white child as well as other ethnic groups. Historian James Loewen says, "The message that Eurocentric history sends to non-European American students is: your ancestors have not done much of importance. It is easy for European Americans and non-European Americans to take a step further and conclude that non-European Americans are not important today."[33] A sense of overprivilege and overvaluing of one's self is as damaging for white children as underprivilege and undervaluing one's self is for children of color.

Ignorance sometimes gets recycled in books and textbooks—for example, the idea that at the time of European arrival, North America was mostly an uninhabited continent. Precontact (before contact with Europeans) estimates are that there were as many as 100 million people.[34] The idea that the land in America was a vast wilderness is also wrong. Many Native people cultivated land; indeed, their agricultural developments continue to benefit the world's food supply. Joseph Bruchac offers this perspective, "The early pioneer heroes . . . people such as Daniel Boone, were, in fact, real estate speculators. When you look at the American landscape as a mother, as a home to be cherished, as do Native people, then the history of the 'settlement of America' is an unmitigated tragedy."[35]

The idea that indigenous peoples were brutal savages is also wrong. In fact, the Europeans displayed a brutality and savagery that appalled American Indians, sometimes propelling them to commit mass suicide.[36] Christopher Columbus's arrival signaled the beginning of a short and forceful genocide of the Taino and Arawak Indians—short because it took a mere twenty to thirty years to wipe them out almost completely.[37]

Yet, in literature, it is the American Indian who is most often presented as savage. Imagine you are a Native child in an elementary school listening to the teacher read aloud the passage in Laura Ingalls Wilder's *Little House on the Prairie* that describes Laura's fearful response to nude, barbarous, and smelly Indians.[38] Listen to Doris Seale, who is of Cree, Santee, and white lineage, as she recollects her feelings when she heard passages like these as a schoolgirl:

> Many years stand between the nowaday me and the round little girl with braids who, when this sort of thing came up in the classroom, used to sit, with dry mouth and pounding heart, head down, *praying* that nobody would look at her. But the feeling is the same. The heart begins to pound, the mouth goes dry. Only now, the emotion is not sick shame, but rage.[39]

In fact, the Europeans were the aggressors, taking land where they wanted and, because they had the guns, forcing Indians into submission. As for smell, Europeans have practiced hygiene for little more than a century; Squanto tried to convince the Pilgrim arrivals that they would be healthier if they took baths.[40]

Our more recent multicultural awareness does not guarantee sensitivity. Like Laura Ingalls Wilder, who wrote historical realism, Elizabeth George Speare, who writes historical fiction, is undoubtedly a fine writer. However, her *The Sign of the Beaver* reinforces the idea of the disappearing Indian. There are many alternatives to this old chestnut in classrooms: Louise Erdrich's 1999 publication of *The Birchbark House* and Bruchac's 1998 publication of *The Arrow over the Door,* based on a true story between Abenaki and Quaker boys. These postcolonial voices, among others, should be heard. When there is a choice between a cultural outsider and a cultural insider, try to give more curricular space to cultural insiders—they have not had the space they deserve.

Negative examples of biographies include Ingri and Edgar Parin D'Aulaire's *George Washington* and *Pocahontas*. These books, write Beverly Slapin and Doris Seale, "contain some of the most blatantly racist writing in modern children's literature." Jean Fritz's *The Double Life of Pocahontas*, they say, does little to challenge inaccurate perceptions. This aspect of our history "is treated with neither sensitivity nor insight."[41] Also of concern are an entire series of biographies from Troll Associates:

- Jane Fleischer's *Pontiac: Chief of the Ottawas, Sitting Bull: Warrior of the Sioux,* and *Tecumseh: Shawnee War Chief*

- Kate Jassem's *Chief Joseph: Leader of Destiny, Pochahontas: Girl of Jamestown, Sacajawea: Wilderness Guide,* and *Squanto: The Pilgrim Adventure*

- Joanne Oppenheim's *Black Hawk: Frontier Warrior, Osceola: Seminole Warrior,* and *Sequoia: Cherokee Hero*

Slapin and Seale assert that these "books feed directly into the myths of superiority and infallibility of white American institutions, myths that are force-fed to children in school.

They are not recommended."[42] In fact, in some cases, whites found the quality of life among American Indians better than that in European cultures. Bruchac writes,

> May Jemison, a white woman who was taken captive by the Seneca in the eighteenth century, refused to return to white society and lived out her life as an Indian by choice. Her observation of Native women's lives was that 'their task is probably not harder than white women, and their cares are certainly not half as numerous or so great.'[43]

Colonial works continue to be published. Ann Rinaldi's *My Heart Is on the Ground: The Diary of Nannie Little Rose, A Sioux Girl,* published in 1999 by Scholastic in its highly successful Dear America series, was met with outrage. In an extremely critical review of the book, nine coauthors lambast its author and its prestigious publisher, who has endorsed and marketed the book to millions of girls, describing the book's inauthenticity, inaccuracy, and lack of respect.[44] The book sanitizes the atrocities that were committed at Carlisle, a government-run school founded in 1879 in Pennsylvania that stayed open until the 1930s. The nine coauthors suggest better books on the Indian Boarding School experience—for example, the autobiography *My Name Is Seepeetza* by Shirley Sterling.

In historical literature, Asians have experienced invisibility in numerous ways. During the gold rush in the mid nineteenth century, many Chinese worked on the transcontinental railroad. Laurence Yep's fictional works have helped us better understand Chinese American sufferings and contributions (see Figure 9.4). During World War II, the government ordered the internment of 120,000 Japanese in concentration camps. Tragically, some of the imprisoned men had fought for this country during World War I. Books by Yoshiko Uchida and Jeanne Wakatsuki illuminate this period.

Bette Bao Lord's *In the Year of the Boar and Jackie Robinson* (see Figure 9.5) pictures the lives of Chinese immigrants to the United States after World War II. The novel is at times poignant, at times hilarious—for example, when the character Shirley chimes in the with the rest of the class during the recitation of the Pledge of Allegiance: "I pledge a lesson to the frog of the United States of America, and to the wee puppet for witches' hands. One Asian, in the vestibule, with little tea and just rice for all."[45]

The colonization of Puerto Rico and the annexation of huge parts of the Mexican population in the Southwest are historical events of which teachers often do not have knowledge. Latino writers have tended to focus more on the genres of folklore, poetry, and contemporary realism; therefore, there is a real need for more Latino postcolonial literature in the genre of historical fiction. The sixteenth century colonization by the Spaniards of Central and South America, and what is currently the southwestern United States, the annexation of Texas, and the Mexican War are all possible topics for future writers.

African American postcolonial literature has its antecedents in the slave narratives that appeared mostly during the late nineteenth and early twentieth centuries, sometimes recorded by white listeners. Rooted in slave narratives, Arna Bontemps published *Great Slave Narratives* in 1969, Julius Lester published *To Be a Slave* in 1968, and Belinda Hermence published *Slavery Time: When I Was Chillun* in 1997. This literature, an art form indigenous to the United States and created by former slaves, is a counterpoint to fictional works, which presented colonial perspectives, repressing the widespread brutality of slavery.

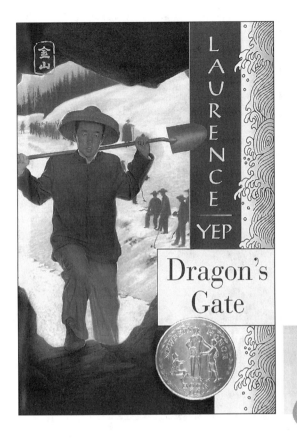

Figure 9.4 In *Dragon's Gate,* a Newbery Honor book, Laurence Yep gives voice to thousands of Chinese immigrants during the nineteenth century.

The contribution of the enslaved Africans to literature must be acknowledged and explored. However, African Americans must not, says Jane Skelton, appear only as "slaves and victims."[46] How many children know of the great intellectual W. E. B. DuBois? His writings are as pertinent today as they were a century ago. As a child, Maya Angelou loved reading DuBois. How many know Rosa Parks was *not* tired, as some biographies portray her, when she refused to give up her seat on the Montgomery bus to a white person? It was a deliberate act of resistance, for which she knew she would suffer. Violet J. Harris, a professor of children's literature, is "convinced that the literacy achievement of African-American children would improve if they could see themselves and their experiences, history, and culture reflected in the books they read."[47]

Gifted African American writers have successfully undertaken the task of writing the stories that, until recent decades, have mostly gone untold. Mildred Taylor's 1977 Newbery Award-winning novel, *Roll of Thunder, Hear My Cry,* set a standard of achievement other writers have emulated. Cultural insiders like Patricia and Frederick McKissack, Virginia Hamilton, Walter Dean Myers, and others have inspired people of all races through their writings that describe African Americans' struggle for education, resistance to Jim Crow, and loyalty and devotion to family and community. They have also

Figure 9.5 Because of its humor, its depiction of multiethnic relationships, and its glimpse into life after World War II, Bette Bao Lord's *In the Year of the Boar and Jackie Robinson* is a rewarding read-aloud.

documented the many, many ways African Americans have contributed to the well-being of all in this country, through inventions, the arts, and, ultimately, in times of war, through the gift of life.

As the twenty-first century unfolds, it is more important than ever that all children see these diverse perspectives. Henry Louis Gates says, "We need to reform our entire notion of core curricula to account for the comparable eloquence of the African, the Asian, the Latin American and the Middle Eastern traditions, to prepare our students for their roles in the twenty-first century as citizens of a world culture, educated through a truly human notion of the humanities" (see Figure 9.6).[48] Look at the journals and websites in Chapter 3 and at the end of this chapter for sources for this kind of literature.

9.7 Conclusion

Although historical literature will continue to expand to include postcolonial voices, there are currently many books available that were not available to previous generations. These books can be interactively shared, through literature circles and through the arts,

Figure 9.6 *Journey to Jo'burg: A South African Story* by Beverly Naidoo and illustrated by Eric Velasquez shows two children's first encounters with racism as they search for their mother after their sister becomes seriously ill. Their strong sense of family, while not shielding them from pain, helps them cope.

to help history come alive for today's children, helping you attain the NCATE standard, "Candidates help elementary students learn the power of multiple perspectives to understand complex issues."[49]

Suggested Activities

1. The ensemble of the arts—literature, the visual arts, music, dance, film, and theater— can illuminate history. For example, when studying the Civil War, the visual arts of the mid nineteenth century can be viewed, even on the Internet. Music, such as *John Brown's Body* and the *Battle Hymn of the Republic,* can be shared, as can the spirituals of enslaved Africans.[50] Increase your awareness of the music, art, and dance of this period.

2. Improvise a scene based on history or a current event.

3. After reading *Sadako and the Thousand Cranes,* work with origami.

4. Create tableaux of various historical moments.

5. Write an editorial on a historical or current event.

6. After reading diaries referenced in Appendix C, write a diary entry from the point of view of a character. Or, rewrite a chapter from historical fiction in diary form.

7. Oral interpretation is the encounter in the next chapter. After you have experienced it there, consider the following selections from historical literature for oral interpretation performance:

- *My Name Is Seepeetza* by Shirley Sterling, pp. 123–126
- *The Birchbark House* by Louise Erdrich, pp. 210–215, beginning with "One day, while Omakayas . . . " to the end of the chapter
- *Lincoln: A Photobiography* by Russell Freedman, "A Lincoln Sampler," pp. 133–137
- *The Endless Steppe: Growing Up in Siberia* by Esther Hautzig, pp. 41–42, beginning with "The flatness of the land was awesome" and ending with "I had neglected to pray to God to save us from a gypsum mine in Siberia. . . ." Then, perform pp. 203–205, beginning with "I was halfway home when I saw the first signs of danger" and ending with "Standing in the middle of the road, a few yards from our hut, endangering her own life, knowing that I was out there someplace, she had turned herself into a human beam, homing me as surely as if I were a plane being homed in on an electric beam. *Sh'mah Israel. . . .*"

for further reading

History

Child, Brenda J. 1998. *Boarding School Seasons: American Indian Families, 1900–1940.* Lincoln: University of Nebraska Press. (Ojibwa author)

Graham, Maryemma. 1998. "Introduction: When Teaching Matters." In: *Teaching African American Literature: Theory and Practice.* Maryemma Graham, Sharon Pineault–Burke, and Marianna White Davis, eds. New York: Routledge.

Hurst, Carol Otis, and Rebecca Otis. 1993. *In Times Past: Using Children's Literature to Teach United States History.* New York: Macmillan/McGraw-Hill.

Kraus, Joanna Halpert. 1985. "Dramatizing History." In: *Children and Drama.* Nellie McCaslin, ed. 2nd ed. New York: Longman.

Kronish, Miriam, and Jeryl Abelmann. 1989. *Focus on Fine Arts: Elementary.* Washington, DC: National Education Association. (Chapter 4 has a unit on the Civil War.)

Loewen, James W. 1995. *Lies My Teacher Told Me: Everything Your American History Textbook Got Wrong.* New York: New Press.

O'Hara, Elizabeth. 2001. "Curtains Up on Reading." *Stage of the Art,* 12.2: 12–14. (underground railroad unit)

Philbin, Meg, and Jeanette S. Myers. 1991. "Classroom Drama: Discourse as Mode of Inquiry in Elementary School Social Studies." *The Social Studies,* Sept./Oct.: 179–182.

Skelton, Jane. 1998. "Multiple Voices, Multiple Identities: Teaching African American Literature." In: *Teaching African American Literature: Theory and Practice.* Maryemma Graham, Sharon Pineault–Burke, and Marianna White Davis, eds. New York: Routledge.

Reader Response and Literature Circles

Atwell, Nancie. 1987. *In the Middle: Writing, Reading, and Learning with Adolescents.* Portsmouth, NH: Heinemann.

Brabham, Edna Greene, and Susan Kidd Villaume. 2000. "Questions and Answers: Continuing Conversations about Literature Circles." *The Reading Teacher,* 54.3: 278–280.

Cullinan, Beatrice, ed. 1993. *Children's Voices: Talk in the Classroom.* Newark, DE: International Reading Association.

Galda, Lee, Shane Rayburn, and Lisa Cross Stanzi. 2000. *Looking Through the Faraway End: Creating a Literature-Based Reading Curriculum with Sec-*

ond Graders. Newark, DE: International Reading Association.

Hill, Bonnie, Nancy J. Johnson, and Katherine L. Schlick Noe, eds. 1995. *Literature Circles and Response.* Norwood, MA: Christopher Gordon. (Although a good book about literature circles, the recommendation of *Knots on a Counting Rope* [p. 50] and *Indian in the Cupboard* [p. 227] should be questioned. The latter and Scott O'Dell's *Sing Down the Moon* unfortunately represent one student's knowledge of American Indians.)

Karolides, Nicholas J., ed. 1997. *Reader Response in Elementary Classrooms: Quest and Discovery.* Mahwah, NJ: Lawrence Erlbaum.

Paratore, Jeanne R., and Rachel L. McCormack, eds. 1997. *Peer Talk in the Classroom: Learning from Research.* Newark, DE: International Reading Association. (Again, a good book on literature circles; however, the recommendation of *Knots on a Counting Rope* [p. 65] should be questioned.)

Rosenblatt, Louise. 1983 [1935]. *Literature as Exploration.* 4th ed. New York: The Modern Language Association.

Rosenblatt, Louise. 1978. *The Transactional Theory of the Literary Work.* Carbondale: Southern Illinois UP.

Routman, Regie. 1999. *Conversations: Strategies for Teaching, Learning, and Evaluating.* Portsmouth, NH: Heinemann. (See Chapter 5, Literature Conversations.)

Samway, Katharine Davies, and Gail Whang. 1996. *Literature Study Circles in a Multicultural Classroom.* York, ME: Stenhouse.

Short, Kathy G., and Kathryn Mitchell Pierce. 1998. *Talking about Books: Literature Discussion Groups in K–8 Classrooms.* Portsmouth, NH: Heinemann. (Yet another good book on literature discussion, excepting the recommendation of *The Indian in the Cupboard* [p. 4].)

History Magazines

Calliope: Exploring World History:
    www.newsearching.com/education_magazine/
    Calliope_Magazine.html

Cobblestone
    www.cobblestonepub.com

websites

Carol Hurst's Children's Literature Site,
    www.carolhurst.com/subjects/ushistory/
    colonial.html and www.carolhurst.com/
    subjects/ushistory/revolution.html

Discovery Enterprises, Ltd.:
    www.ushistorydocs.com This publisher excerpts primary sources in their publications, making primary sources accessible to students.

Traveling through American History with Juvenile Fiction Picture Books 3rd and 4th Grades,
    www.co.fairfax.va.us/library/reading/elem/
    pichistorychron.htm

awards

Scott O'Dell Award for Historical Fiction,
    www.ucalgary.ca/ ~ dkbrown/
    odell.html

National Council for the Social Studies, Carter 6. Woodson Award
    www.soemadison.wisc.edu/ccbc/woodson.htm

notes

1. Dee Brown, *Wounded Knee: An Indian History of the American West,* adapted for young readers by Amy Ehrlich from Dee Brown's *Bury My Heart at Wounded Knee* (New York: Holt, 1993 [1974]), p. 92.

2. Nancie Atwell, *In the Middle: New Understandings About Writing, Reading, and Learning,* 2nd ed. (Portsmouth, NH: Heinemann, 1998).

3. M. Susan Burns, Peg Griffin, and Catherine E. Snow, eds. *Starting Out Right: A Guide to Promoting Reading Success* (Washington, DC: Academy Press, 1999); and James R. Squire, "Language Arts." In: *Handbook of Research on Improving Student Achievement,* Gordon Cawelti, ed. (Arlington, VA: Educational Research Service, 1995), p. 73.

4. Wolfgang Iser, *The Act of Reading: A Theory of Aesthetic Response* (Baltimore: Johns Hopkins University Press, 1978), pp. 168–169.

5. Louise Rosenblatt, "The Literary Transaction: Evocation and Response." In: *Journeying: Children Responding to Literature,* Kathleen E. Holland, Rachael A. Hungerford, and Shirley B. Ernst, eds. (Portsmouth, NH: Heinemann, 1993), pp. 20–21.

6. Louise Rosenblatt, *Literature as Exploration,* 4th ed. (New York: Modern Language Association, 1983), pp. 70, 115.

7. Lucy Calkins, *The Art of Teaching Reading* (Portsmouth, NH: Heinemann, 2001), pp. 244–245.

8. María Echiburu Berzins and Alice E. López, "Starting Off Right: Planting Seeds for Biliteracy." In: *The Best for Our Children: Critical Perspectives on Literacy for Latino Students,* María de la Luz Reyes and John J. Halcón, eds. (New York: Teachers College Press, 2001), p. 85.

9. Harvey Daniels, *Literature Circles: Voice and Choice in the Student-Centered Classroom* (Portland, ME: Stenhouse, 1994).

10. Lee Galda, Shane Rayburn, and Lisa Cross Stanzi, *Looking Through the Faraway End: Creating a Literature-Based Reading Curriculum with Second Graders* (Newark, DE: International Reading Association, 2000), p. 19.

11. Quoted in Stephen Fishman and Lucille McCarthy, *John Dewey and the Challenge of Classroom Practice* (New York: Teachers College Press, 1998), p. 21,

12. Gloria Ladson-Billings, *The Dreamkeepers: Successful Teachers of African American Children* (San Francisco: Jossey-Bass, 1994), p. 110.

13. Maxine Greene, *Landscapes of Learning* (New York: Teachers College Press, 1978), p. 121.

14. Beverly Gherman, *Norman Rockwell: Storyteller With a Brush* (New York: Atheneum, 2000), p. 1.

15. Esther Hautzig, *The Endless Steppe* (New York: HarperCollins, 1968), p. 38; and Sid Fleischman, *The Abracadabra Kid: A Writer's Life* (New York: Greenwillow, 1996), p. 23.

16. bell hooks, *Bone Black: Memories of Girlhood* (New York: Henry Holt, 1996), p. 77.

17. Michael Foreman, *After the War Was Over* (New York: Arcade, 1995), p. 58.

18. Kathleen Krull, *Lives of the Athletes: Thrills, Spills (and What the Neighbors Thought)* (San Diego: Harcourt, 1997), p. 55. (illustrated by Kathryn Hewitt)

19. Joseph Bruchac, *Bowman's Store: A Journey to Myself* (New York: Dial Books, 1997), p. 136.

20. Beverly Daniels Tatum, *"Why Are All the Black Kids Sitting Together in the Cafeteria?" and Other Conversations about Race* (New York: Basic Books, 1999), p. 47.

21. Lyndall Gordon, *Charlotte Brontë: A Passionate Life* (New York: W. W. Norton, 1994), p. 100.

22. Carlos Bulosan, *America Is in the Heart: A Personal History* (Seattle: University of Washington Press, 1973), pp. 32, 323.

23. N. Scott Momaday, *The Names: A Memoir* (Tucson: The University of Arizona Press, 1976), p. 61.

24. Hautzig, *The Endless Steppe,* p. 104.

25. Hautzig, *The Endless Steppe,* pp. 179–180.

26. Michael Thompson, "Mentors on Paper: How Classics Develop Verbal Ability." In: *Developing Verbal Talent: Ideas and Strategies for Teachers of Elementary and Middle School Students,* Joyce Van Tassel-Baska, Dana T. Johnson, and Linda Neal Boyce, eds. (Needham Heights, MA: Allyn & Bacon 1996), p. 60.

27. Joyce Van Tassel-Baska, "Creating a New Language Arts Curriculum for High-Ability Learners." In: *Developing Verbal Talent: Ideas and Strategies for Teachers of Elementary and Middle School Students,* Joyce Van Tassel-Baska, Dana T. Johnson, and Linda Neal Boyce, eds. (Needham Heights, MA: Allyn & Bacon, 1996), p. 196.

28. Thompson, "Mentors on Paper: How Classics Develop Verbal Ability," p. 74.

29. Joy Boyum, *Double Exposure: Fiction into Film* (New York: New American Library, 1985), pp. 15–16.

30. Gary R. Howard, *We Can't Teach What We Don't Know: White Teachers, Multiracial Schools* (New York: Teachers College Press, 1999), p. 71.

31. Debbie Reese, "Native Americans in Children's Literature." In: *Using Multiethnic Literature in the K–8 Classroom,* Violet J. Harris, ed. (Norwood, MA: Christopher-Gordon, 1997), p. 164.

32. Marguerite A. Wright, *I'm Chocolate, You're Vanilla: Raising Healthy Black and Biracial Children in a Race-Conscious World* (San Francisco: Jossey-Bass, 1998), p. 7.

33. James W. Loewen, *Lies My Teacher Told Me: Everything Your American History Textbook Got Wrong* (New York: New Press, 1995), p. 302.

34. Thom Hartmann, *The Last Hours of Ancient Sunlight: Waking Up to Personal and Global Transformation* (New York: Harmony Books, 1999), p. 194.

35. Joseph Bruchac, *Roots of Survival* (Golden, CO: Fulcrum, 1996), p. 21.

36. Hartmann, *The Last Hours of Ancient Sunlight,* p. 41.

37. Doris Seale, "1492–1992 From an American Perspective." In: *The Multicolored Mirror: Cultural Substance in Literature for Children and Young Adults,* Merri V. Lindgren, ed. (Fort Atkinson, WI: 1991), p. 104.

38. Laura Ingalls Wilder, *Little House on the Prairie* (New York: Harper, 1971), p. 137.

39. Doris Seale, "Let Us Put Our Minds Together and See What Life We Will Make for Our Children." In: *Through Indian Eyes: The Native Experience in Books for Children,* Beverly Slapin and Doris Seale, eds. (Philadelphia, PA: New Society Publishers, 1992), p. 9.

40. For this and other stories, see Loewen, *Lies My Teacher Told Me.*

41. Beverly Slapin and Doris Seale, *Through Indian Eyes: The Native Experience in Books for Children* (Philadelphia, PA: New Society Publishers, 1992), pp. 156–157.

42. Slapin and Seale, *Through Indian Eyes,* pp. 228–229.

43. Bruchac, *Roots of Survival,* p. 40.

44. Marlene Atleo, Naomi Caldwell, Barbara Landis, Jean Mendoza, Beverly Slapin, and Cynthia Smith, "*My Heart Is on the Ground* and the Indian Boarding School Experience," *MultiCultural Review* 8.3 (1999): 41–46.

45. Bette Bao Lord, *In the Year of the Boar and Jackie Robinson* (New York: Harper, 1984), p. 86.

46. Jane Skelton, "Multiple Voices, Multiple Identities: Teaching African American Literature." In: *Teaching African American Literature,* Maryemma Graham, Sharon Pineault–Burke, and Marianna White Davis, eds. (New York: Routledge, 1998), p. 56.

47. Violet J. Harris, ed., *Teaching Multicultural Literature in Grades K–8* (Norwood, MA: Christopher-Gordon, 1993), p. xvi.

48. Henry Louis Gates, Jr., *Loose Canons: Notes on the Culture Wars* (New York; Oxford University Press, 1992), p. 113.

49. National Council for Accreditation of Teacher Education, *Program Standards for Elementary Teacher Preparation,* Supporting Explanation, 2i.

50. See Miriam Kronish and Jeryl Abelmann, *Focus on Fine Arts: Elementary* (Washington, DC: National Education Association Publication, 1989), pp. 39–45, for an excellent integrated unit on the Civil War.

chapter 10

Life's Vocations and Callings
Biography, Autobiography, and Memoir

*V*ocation . . . is the place where your deep gladness
and the world's deep hunger meet.[1]

—FREDERICK BUECHNER

10.1 Encountering Literature
through oral interpretation

Materials Needed

If you so choose, bring selections like *Boy*, which I have included here.

Like choral reading, readers theater, and story theater, oral interpretation is a recreation of a literary work. The difference is that, instead of the ensemble work explored in previous chapters, oral interpretation is solo. The goal of oral interpretation is both the truthful revelation of self and of the literary work in the present moment. Of lesser importance are the conventions; however, attention can be given to nonverbal and verbal expression. Nonverbal considerations include, as experienced in the storytelling workshop (7.1) and based on the work of Kristin Linklater (1.8), picturing a long spine, your skull floating like a balloon, and hanging loose like a puppet with strings attached to the top of the head and the sternum. Remember that the spine is the support of breath, and breath is the source of sound. With this image firmly grounded, oral interpreters are freer to explore the conventions of

- Vocal variety—pitch, volume, rate, pause
- Projection
- Vocal quality and resonance
- Articulation
- Mood
- Characterization
- Style

Although oral interpretation is not acting, it may use gesture and movement. As artists, interpreters make choices about eye contact, and other verbal and nonverbal choices. Oral interpretation is used in this chapter as a way to learn more about beloved children's authors.

Double spacing allows for frequent eye contact, or otherwise seeing beyond the printed page. Large point size also allows for familiarity and greater range of interpretation. Consider placing the literary work inside a folder.

note to leader: I have provided one selection in the following pages. Either select some of your favorite passages from a biography, or have students select theirs so that there is variety when and if you decide to spotlight performances, either in small groups or large.

In preparation for an oral interpretation workshop, do the following:

- Silently read the entire selection.
- If a passage is divided between multiple interpreters, read your selection silently several times.

- When the direction is given, find a place at the parameters of the room, apart from others.

- Face the wall and read your selection quietly to the wall. Then, whisper your selection to the wall. Then, exploring the full range of the human voice, read your selection to the wall.

- When the leader gives the signal, rejoin your group, each person taking her turn orally interpreting the entire selections.

"Chocolates"

An Excerpt from *Boy: Tales of Childhood* by Roald Dahl (pp. 147–149)

In this passage, Roald Dahl recalls attending boarding school in the United Kingdom living near the Cadbury factory. The following experience later contributed to his book *Charlie and the Chocolate Factory.*

INTERPRETER A: Every now and again, a plain grey cardboard box was dished out to each boy in our House, and this, believe it or not, was a present from the great chocolate manufacturers, Cadbury. Inside the box there were twelve bars of chocolate, all of different shapes, all with different fillings and all with numbers from one to twelve stamped on the chocolate underneath. Eleven of these bars were new inventions from the factory. The twelfth was the 'control' bar, one that we all knew well, usually a Cadbury's Coffee Cream bar. Also in the box was a sheet of paper with the numbers one to twelve on it as well as two blank columns, one for giving marks to each chocolate from nought to ten, and the other for comments.

INTERPRETER B: All we were required to do in return for this splendid gift was to taste very carefully each bar of chocolate, give it marks and make an intelligent comment on why we liked it or disliked it.

It was a clever stunt. Cadbury's were using some of the greatest chocolate-bar experts in the world to test out their new inventions. We were of a sensible age, between thirteen and eighteen, and we knew intimately every chocolate bar in existence, from the Milk Flake to the Lemon Marshmallow. Quite obviously our opinions on anything new would be valuable. All of us entered into this game with great gusto, sitting in our studies and nibbling each bar with the air of connoisseurs, giving our marks and making our comments. 'Too subtle for the common palate,' was one note I remember writing down.

INTERPRETER C: For me, the importance of all this was that I began to realize that the large chocolate companies actually did possess inventing rooms and they took their inventing very seriously. I used to picture a long white room like a laboratory with pots of chocolate and fudge and all sorts of other delicious fillings bubbling away on the stoves, while men and women in white coats moved between the bubbling pots, tasting and mixing and concocting their wonderful new inventions. I used to imagine myself working in one of these labs and suddenly I would come up with something so absolutely unbearably delicious that I would grab it in my hand and go rushing out of the lab and along the corridor and right into the office of the great Mr. Cadbury himself. 'I've got it, sir!' I would shout, putting the chocolate in front of him. 'It's fantastic! It's fabulous! It's marvelous! It's irresistible!'

INTERPRETER D: Slowly, the great man would pick up my newly invented chocolate and he would take a small bite. He would roll it round his mouth. Then all at once, he would leap up from his chair, crying, 'You've got it! You've done it! It's a miracle!' He would slap me on the back and shout, 'We'll sell it by the millions! We'll sweep the world with this one! How on earth did you do it? Your salary is doubled!'

It was lovely, dreaming those dreams, and I have no doubt at all that, thirty-five years later, when I was looking for a plot for my second book for children, I remembered those little cardboard boxes and the newly-invented chocolates inside them, and I began to write a book called *Charlie and the Chocolate Factory*.

Permission to reproduce from *Encountering Children's Literature: An Arts Approach* by Jane M. Gangi.

10.2 History of Biography and Autobiography

In this chapter, biographies, memoirs, and autobiographies that focus on vocation and career choice are profiled (see Figure 10.1). In the previous chapter, we looked at biography to illuminate history. Of course, there is overlap between the two chapters. Depending

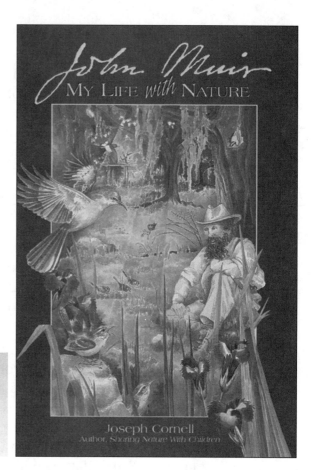

Figure 10.1 *John Muir: My Life with Nature* by Joseph Cornell is an award-winning account of the naturalist's life. Lyrical excerpts from Muir's personal diary make this a worthwhile read-aloud.

on your purposes, you can draw on books in Appendix C for both chapters to cluster around interdisciplinary themes and topics.

One of the first known works of biography appeared during the first century—Plutarch's *Parallel Lives of the Noble Greeks and Romans.* Two centuries later, St. Augustine wrote the first known autobiographical work, *Confessions.* However, biography as a significant literary genre did not blossom until the eighteenth century, perhaps as a result of the growing sense of an inner life. Benjamin Franklin, whose encyclopedic knowledge and unwavering curiosity shaped his genius, wrote his acclaimed autobiography after he retired in 1787, when he was well into his eighties. James Boswell's famous *Life of Samuel Johnson* appeared between 1790 and 1794. In 1831, Mary Prince wrote the first autobiography by a slave, *The History of Mary Prince, A West Indian Slave, Related by Herself.* As mentioned in Chapter 9, slave narratives are an important contribution both to history and to literature.

Biographies and autobiographies in children's literature did not become a distinct category until the twentieth century. Significant early works included Cornelia Miegs's Newbery Award-winning *Invincible Louisa* in 1933, a biography of Louisa May Alcott. Robert Lawson blended fantasy and nonfiction to write *Ben and Me* in 1939, about Benjamin Franklin. The world-renowned *Diary of a Young Girl* by Anne Frank, published in 1952, both poignantly depicted her entrapment in the evil of Nazism in World War II and validated the feelings of young readers who often feel confusions similar to Anne's. The play by Frances Goodrich and Albert Hackett is included in the recommended plays for Chapter 6 in Appendix C. Russell Freedman's *Lincoln: A Photobiography* won the Newbery in 1987. Although written for children, this book, as with most of Freedman's work, is loved and enjoyed as much by adults as it is by children.

10.3 Authors and Illustrators of Children's Literature

Although the bibliography in Appendix C attempts to provide a picture of people in all walks of life, the most extensive listings are of authors and illustrators of children's literature (see Figure 10.2). Many of these authors and illustrators are suitable for author studies, or illustrator studies, or author-illustrator studies. Like adults, once children find an author or illustrator they like, they want to continue reading and viewing the work of that

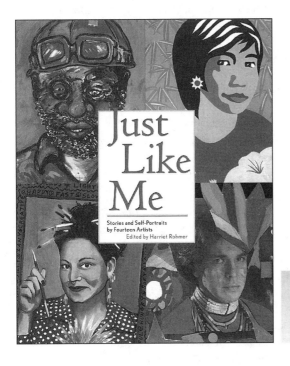

Figure 10.2 *Just Like Me,* edited by Harriet Rohmer, profiles contemporary authors and illustrators of colors.

special person, and learning about their lives when they were children. Many children's authors and illustrators have websites, which can be helpful in author and illustrator studies.

Through biography and autobiography, children can see people who have passions at a young age: Jan Brett, Arthur Rackham, and Mitsumasa Anno knew as children that they wanted to be artists, and spent hours and hours drawing. Eric Carle recalls how powerful simple walks through nature with his father were during his childhood. These examples can show persistence at work, and pose alternatives to television watching. The writers section in Appendix C also reveals that most writers were, in childhood, impassioned readers.

These various studies are a wonderful opportunity to introduce to children artists and writers of color. Brian Pinkney, Jerry Pinkney's son, writes,

> When I read *The Boy and the Ghost* I thought, 'That's me—that's me as a little boy.' And when I took the project and looked for a model, I looked for a little boy like me. The story is set in the South which interested me because I like projects that relate to my life, my heritage. I do research to find out more about myself, which is why I'm interested in Black projects.[2]

Both Pinkneys have given children of color many wonderful models in which to see themselves. Floyd Cooper consciously works with hope for the future. He says, "Illustrating children's books is a very exciting thing to do because it gives you the chance to have an impact on the way the world will be later. I believe that affection for other cultures leads to understanding, and I strive to create books that are a bridge between cultures."[3]

Often used in gifted programs—although certainly appropriate for regular classes—George Betts, a professor of gifted education at the University of Northern Colorado, requires students to spend several weeks investigating the life of a favorite notable person such as those in Figure 10.3. Having read biographies, and found other sources of information, students then, for a designated Night of the Notables, dress up as the person they have investigated. Parents are invited to attend, and in casual conversation seek to identify various accomplished people. They can ask about the Notables' major contributions, points of pride, difficult periods, easy periods, regrets, and anything else the Notables would like to tell about themselves. They can also ask about the Notables' world and times, and how they changed their society and their fields.[4]

10.4 *Value of Biography for Children*

Children need to have a vision of who they can become; biographies provide what Michael Clay Thompson calls "mentors on paper."[5] The development of a career image during the elementary school years may be of more importance than in middle or high school, when the opinion of the peer group tends to have more influence.

In the media, children see a preponderance of police, detectives, and criminals at work. These three professions comprise more than fifty percent of the careers represented on television.[6] There is a real need to counterbalance this flawed picture of American life. In his autobiography, Savion Glover (see Figure 10.4), whose genius at tap dancing is internationally acknowledged, shares his vision that, someday, tap would be as sought after as sports, that the audiences who view tap performances could fill a stadium.[7] Imagine a world in which the arts were as sought after on television as sports and criminal investigation.

Figure 10.3 *Lives of the Athletes: Thrills, Spills (and What the Neighbors Thought)* by Kathleen Krull and illustrated by Kathryn Hewitt offers biographical profiles intriguing to young people.

Figure 10.4 Savion Glover and Bruce Weber's *Savion: My Life in Tap* chronicles one young man's spectacular genius at the African American folk art of tap.

Biographies help us know better how to cope and manage. Stress is a factor in everyone's life; no one leads a trouble-free existence (see Figure 10.5). The human condition is fraught with conflict and crisis. How have others coped? How have they made their decisions? Biography helps us see, helps us enlarge our aspirations. Psychologists who have studied resilient children—those who somehow bloom despite the desert of their childhood lives—report that biographies have been one way some children have risen above their difficulties.[8]

As discussed in Chapter 8.5, gender studies show that boys prefer nonfiction. James Garbarino, who has spent his life studying violent boys, offers proactive guidelines: "We must help violent boys create the basis for new lives by exposing them to novels, biographies, and relationships with adults that provide good examples of positive meaningfulness in the face of loss and abandonment. We are in a struggle for the souls of these boys, and literacy is one of the important resources in this struggle."[9] Literature, and biographies in particular, can give children a future and hope. Then, says Garbarino, "Anchored in the future, these boys live in the present in a responsible way."[10]

10.5 Value of Biography for Future and Practicing Teachers

From a philosophical point of view, reflecting on the lives of people who have changed the world can contribute to our sense of empowerment. Existential educator Maxine Greene says,

> [W]e all believe that our efforts to understand the young and recover our own landscapes must be linked to notions of pedagogical praxis and that the pedagogies we de-

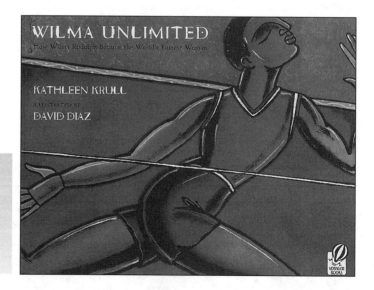

Figure 10.5 In *Wilma Unlimited: How Wilma Rudolph Became the World's Fastest Woman*, illustrated by David Diaz, Wilma Rudolph provides a powerful role model.

vise ought to provoke a heightened sense of agency in those we teach, empower them to pursue their freedom and, perhaps, transform to some degree their lived worlds.[11]

Envisioning a future creates the likelihood of valuing the present, learning to accept consequences, and persisting in the face of difficulties. These qualities are consistent with the existentialist project, referring to a personalized and intentional vision in which individuals construct themselves and their world.

Future and practicing teachers benefit from reading biographies because they themselves are entering a profession rife with conflict and difficult choices. Martin Haberman sketches out four examples that require teachers to know and be able to articulate their own values. What would teachers do in the event that they received a letter from a parent of a child who is a Jehovah's Witness requesting that, because celebrating birthdays is not part of their religion, they no longer celebrate birthdays in the elementary classroom? What would a teacher do if an adolescent killer was assigned by the court to his class and, in a private conversation, the adolescent responded to the teacher's question about why he had killed: "'Cause he needed killin', that's why.'" Haberman comments, "To certify people who are reluctant or incapable of acting in these situations is not preparing teachers for the reality of diverse schools."[12] By seeing people in choice-making situations, teachers can reflect on their own values and come closer to being able to articulate what they would do in the most difficult situations.

What is called for is deep reflection concerning one's personhood and commitments. Literature—and biography in particular—is especially significant in the education of the young. The conditions of choice making are revealed in its mosaic of the poetic, the aesthetic, the emotional, the spiritual, and the rational. Tolstoy was surely right when he said that science could not begin to address the most important questions that face us—what should we do and how should we live? Through biography, we see how others have answered these central questions.

10.6 Biography and Cultural Responsiveness

Biographies, by providing profiles of people of color (such as the biography featured in Figure 10.6), have the potential of reducing negative stereotypes, which damage both white children's perceptions of people of color, and children of color's perceptions of themselves. Stanford psychologist Claude Steele, among others, points out that the children of color who are most motivated to achieve are most debilitated by the negative stereotypes held against them by others.[13]

Too often, children of color, the working class, and the rural poor do not see themselves going to college and becoming professionals. In Sonia Nieto's case study, Rich Miller, an African American adolescent, says, "'We feel that after high school, that's it for us; we don't have to go on with it.'"[14] In the same case study, Manuel Gomes, a Cape Verdean, points to a solution: "I think [teachers] could help students, try to influence them, that they can do whatever they want to do, that they can be whatever they want to be, that they got opportunities out there. . . . Most schools don't encourage kids to be

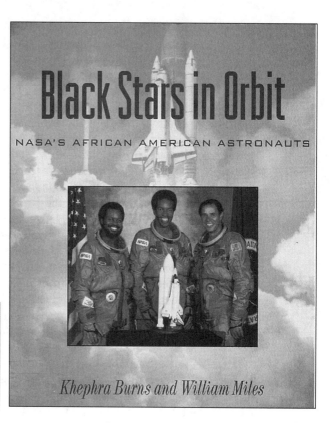

Figure 10.6 *Black Stars in Orbit: NASA's African American Astronauts* by Kephra Burns and William Miles opens up possibilities for young people.

all they can be."[15] The extraordinarily gifted illustrator and writer John Steptoe wrote, "[B]lack people are told they're not talented. We're not supposed to read or produce art; we're supposed to play a little basketball."[16] Commenting on a culture of oppositional identity that seems to appear in adolescence, Beverly Daniels Tatum writes, "If young people are exposed to African American academic achievement in their early years, they won't have to define school achievement as something for Whites only. They will know that there is a long history of Black intellectual achievement."[17] Exposure to numerous biographies in the elementary years can lay the foundation for creating a culture in which students of color aspire to high achievement because they know it is their heritage.

Waiting for middle and secondary school may be too late. Of the more than one million prisoners in this country, eighty percent are high school dropouts.[18] Giving children a strong sense of the possible in their elementary years can help them withstand the difficulties of adolescence, a time when they may downplay their capabilities to fit in. Geneva Gay synthesizes research from various ethnic groups: "[S]ome students with high academic potential deliberately sabotage or camouflage their intellectual abilities to avoid being alienated from their ethnic friends who are not as adept in school."[19] In her biography of Walter Dean Myers, the children's and young adult author, Rudine Sims Bishop asks the question: How did he succeed when other young Black men with his background were incarcerated? Myers's answer: His parents and teachers engaged him with literature, which gave him a vision of what is possible. This vision inspired in him a willingness to persist.[20]

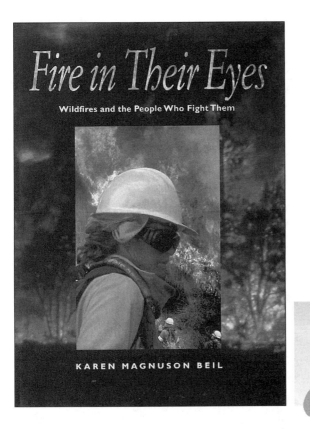

Fire in Their Eyes

Wildfires and the People Who Fight Them

KAREN MAGNUSON BEIL

Figure 10.7 The firefighting profession is fascinating to young readers. See, for example, *Fire in Their Eyes: Wildfires and the People Who Fight Them* by Karen Magnuson Beil.

Sharing biographies with children is yet another way to avoid low-level thinking skills. Linda Darling–Hammond recommends that, instead of worksheets and the memorization of discrete facts, "Fascinating ideas . . . could be explored through biographies, debates, papers, and models."[21]

10.7 Criticism and Evaluation

With the proliferation of biographical series books comes the need for evaluating literary quality. Although there are some good biographies in series, many are churned out quickly—an assemblage of facts and dates. A well-crafted biography is not only carefully researched, but is also an imaginative, engaging story that evokes a strong sense of character and setting for example, *Fire in Their Eyes* (see Figure 10.7). Photographs and primary documents are placed in the text with graceful design.

Susanna Reich's *Clara Schumann: Piano Virtuoso* is one such biography. Reich spent several years writing the book, in comparison with writers who publish four or five biographies a year in series books. Try reading Reich's book, along with biographies by Russell Freedman. Then, read a series book, and make your own comparisons; you'll recognize the qualitative difference between biographies by Reich and Freedman and other, lesser works.

y is considered nonfiction, there is no such thing as a purely
/ring their own perspectives and biases to whatever they write,
.ts of their subject's life, whitewashing or omitting other aspects.
.1's literature is to sanitize or play down what was actually said or
the surrender speeches of Indian chiefs during the nineteenth cen-
es given in Chapter 9.6 on criticism and evaluation are applicable to
, chapter as well.

ision

.gh beneficial to all children, biographies are especially important for boys and
.ren of color, helping you attain the NCATE standard, "Candidates understand how
.mentary students differ in their development and approaches to learning, and create
.1structional opportunities that are adapted to diverse students."[22] Use them in literature circles, read them aloud, and let children read them silently.

Suggested Activities

1. Using the example of *Boy* by Roald Dahl, select and rehearse material from other biographies and autobiographies for oral interpretation.

2. In your readings, note authors and/or illustrators you would be interested in pursuing
   in an illustrator and/or author study.

3. Try David and Myra Sadker's exercise: In three minutes, by yourself, jot down ten famous American women who are not entertainers or sports figures. Compare your answers with the rest of the class.

4. After researching a favorite author, write a short biography or profile of that author.

5. Try writing your own memoir.

for further reading

Harkins, Margaret A. 2001. "Literature Extension Activities: Connecting with Careers in Primary Grade
Classrooms," *The Dragon Lode*, 19.2: 26–32.

———. 2001. "Using Literature to Establish Career
Concepts in Early Childhood." *The Reading
Teacher*, 55.1: 29–32.

Hopkins, Lee Bennett. 1995. *Pauses: Autobiographical
Reflections of 101 Creators of Children's Books.*
New York: HarperCollins.

Pendergast, Sara, ed. 1999. *St. James Guide to Children's Writers.* 5th ed. Chicago: St. James Press.

Rockman, Connie C., ed. 2000. *Eighth Book of Junior
Authors and Illustrators.* New York: H. W. Wilson.

Rollock, Barbara. 1992. *Black Authors and Illustrators
of Children's Books.* 2nd ed. New York: Garland.

Silvey, Anita, ed. 1995. *Children's Books and Their
Creators.* Boston: Houghton Mifflin.

w e b s i t e s

Many authors and illustrators have websites. Simply type in their names and surf the Web.

Get Nosey with Aunt Rosie, How To Conduct an Oral History Interview:
    www.genealogy.com/70_tipsoral.html?Welcome = 1035842278

a w a r d s

See the Awards section in Chapter 8.

n o t e s

1. Frederick Buechner, *Wishful Thinking: A Seeker's ABC,* Rev. ed. (San Francisco: HarperSanFrancisco, 1993), p. 119.
2. Quoted in Julie Cummins, *Children's Book Illustration and Design* (New York: Library of Applied Design, PBC International, 1992), p. 148.
3. Donna Rand, Toni Trent Parker, and Sheila Foster, *Black Books Galore! Guide to Great African American Children's Books* (New York: Wiley, 1999), p. 34.
4. George T. Betts and Jolene K. Kercher, *Autonomous Learner Model: Optimizing Ability.* (Greeley, CO: Autonomous Learning Publications Specialists, 1999), pp. 87–89.
5. Michael Clay Thompson, "Mentors on Paper: How Classics Develop Verbal Ability." In: *Developing Verbal Talent: Ideas and Strategies for Teachers of Elementary and Middle School Students,* Joyce Van Tassel–Baska, Dana T. Johnson, and Linda Neal Boyce, eds. (Boston: Allyn & Bacon, 1996), pp. 56–74.
6. George Gerbner, *Television as a Shaper of Cultural Values: "Telling All the Stories,"* Paper presented at Media, Children and Culture Conference, Quinnipiac University, Hamden, CT, 21 October 2000.
7. Savion Glover and Bruce Weber, *My Life in Tap* (New York: Morrow, 2000), p. 78.
8. Steven J. Wolin and Sybil Wolin, *The Resilient Self: How Survivors of Troubled Families Rise Above Adversity* (New York: Villard Books, 1993), p. 157.
9. James Garbarino, *Lost Boys: Why Our Sons Turn Violent and How We Can Save Them* (New York: Simon and Schuster, 1999), p. 227.
10. Garbarino, *Lost Boys,* p. 152.
11. Maxine Greene, *Releasing the Imagination* (San Francisco: Jossey-Bass, 1995), p. 48.
12. Nancy L. Zimpher, "Right-Sizing Teacher Education: The Policy Imperative. In: " *Teachers for the New Millennium: Aligning Teacher Development, National Goals, and High Standards for All Students,* Leonard Kaplan and Roy A. Edelfelt, eds. (Thousand Oaks, CA: Corwin Press, 1996), pp. 110–131.
13. Claude Steele, "A Threat in the Air: How Stereotypes Shape Intellectual Identity and Performance," *American Psychologist, 52.6* (1997): 613–629.
14. Sonia Nieto, *Affirming Diversity: The Sociopolitical Context of Multicultural Education,* 3rd ed. (New York: Longman, 2000), p. 67.
15. Nieto, *Affirming Diversity,* p. 211.
16. Roni Natov and Geraldine De Luca, "An Interview with John Steptoe," *The Lion and the Unicorn, 11* (1987): 125.
17. Beverly Daniels Tatum, *"Why Are All the Black Kids Sitting Together in the Cafeteria?" and Other Conversations about Race* (New York: Basic Books, 1999), pp. 64–65.
18. Michael Fullan, *Change Forces: Probing the Depths of Educational Reform* (London: Falmer, 1993), p. 42.
19. Geneva Gay, *Culturally Responsive Teaching: Theory, Research, and Practice* (New York: Teachers College Press), p. 19.
20. Rudine Sims Bishop, *Presenting Walter Dean Myers* (Boston: Twayne, 1991), p. 17.
21. Linda Darling–Hammond, *The Right to Learn: A Blueprint for Creating Schools That Work* (San Francisco: Jossey-Bass, 1997), p. 55.
22. National Council for Accreditation of Teacher Education, *Program Standards for Elementary Teacher Preparation,* Supporting Explanation, 3b.

Contemporary Realism
Through the Eyes of Others

*C*ould a greater miracle take place than for us to look
through each other's eyes for an instant?[1]

— HENRY DAVID THOREAU

11.1 *Encountering Literature*
through role-playing

Materials Needed

A set of books that all read part of. Participants should not know the ending.

Prior to this session, read part of a mutually agreed-on book, for example Kazumi Yumoto's *The Friends,* winner of the Boston Globe-Horn Book Award, to page 43, then close the book. In groups of four, assign roles and improvise possible outcomes of what happens next. Then, share with each other the endings you improvised. After that, compare and contrast your endings with Yumoto's. Discuss the differences between Yumoto's version and yours.

A Culturally Responsive Pedagogy E. Paul Torrance, creativity researcher and university professor, has long encouraged the use of creative positives with young people, especially those who are disenchanted in the public schools. He defines creative positives as "[r]esponsiveness to the kinesthetic; ability to improvise with commonplace materials and objects; articulateness in role playing, sociodrama and storytelling; and enjoyment of and ability in creative movement, dance, dramatics and related fields."[2] Role-playing invites interaction and shows students that they can change outcomes by their choices. When working with elementary school children who role-play, Elaine Aoki recommends, "The students should read aloud only part of the chapter, from the beginning to where the problematic situation is introduced. Then the students should be guided in the role-playing activity by first defining the problem, delineating alternatives, exploring the alternatives through dramatization, and finally making a decision as to what was the best alternative."[3] Role-playing is yet another arts-based, learner-centered approach that holds appeal for diverse children.

11.2 *The Contemporary Realism Genre*

Unlike the happily ever-after endings of most folklore, contemporary realism presents life as it sometimes is: The good do not always win, and evil sometimes goes unpunished. Realistic fiction can address children's feelings of isolation. Because of their immaturity and vulnerability, children often feel that they are the only ones to undergo their trials. In realistic fiction, authors reach out to children in comforting ways, telling them that they are not alone, they are not the only ones to experience difficulties.

As discussed in Chapter 9.5, categories of historical realism provided the antecedents for contemporary realism. For example, the *survival story,* popular in books by Gary Paulsen and Jean Craighead George, first materialized in *Robinson Crusoe.* In addition to survival, adventure, and domestic stories, realism also includes *mysteries.* Edward Stratmeyer, then his daughter, Harriet S. Adams, wrote Nancy Drew mysteries beginning in the 1930s. Gertrude Chandler Warner's *The Boxcar Children* series, published in the 1940s, continue in popularity. Although Louis Sachar's *Holes* straddles a number of themes and topics, it also has elements of mystery.

The animal realism that began in the nineteenth century continued into the twentieth, and is still a category of realism greatly enjoyed by many children. Eric Knight's *Lassie Come-Home* was published in 1941, and *My Friend Flicka* by Mary O'Hara was published in 1942. In her autobiographical novel, Shirley Sterling tells that *The Black Stallion* was one of her favorite books as an elementary school-age child in an Indian Boarding School in the 1950s.[4]

When does contemporary realistic fiction become historical fiction? The boundaries are fluid and there is no one right answer. In Appendix C, I have placed a realistic book by Deborah Ellis published in 2000, *The Breadwinner,* about life under the Taliban in Afghanistan in the 1990s in historical literature because it deals with political and religious oppression, which seemed to follow other books in that chapter, such as Beverly Naidoo's *Journey to Jo'burg* on apartheid in South Africa, and civil rights in this country. On the other hand, I have placed *The Incredible Journey* by Sheila Burnford, which was first published in 1961, in this chapter's bibliography under Animal Realism. You will find other such cross-overs. By scanning for brackets in the bibliography for this chapter in Appendix C, you may see books published even as early as the 1930s. Although these books seem to have more to do with a particular topic or theme, they also provide insight into life in earlier times. *Where the Red Fern Grows* by Wilson Rawls is under Animal Realism in Appendix C; I could also have placed it in the Great Depression under Historical Literature.

Most contemporary fiction explores more than one theme. Katherine Paterson's *The Bridge to Terabithia* has the themes of friendship, death, and imaginative worlds, as does *Walk Two Moons* by Sharon Creech; however, because of space constraints, they are both placed along with other texts under Death. Similarly, E. L. Konigsburg's *The View from Saturday* could fit with friendship, school, divorce, death, and extended family. As you read some of these books, make notes about the themes and topics with which they connect; the best books, clearly, have multiple themes and complexity. Of special note is Maria Botelho's suggestion that exploring the theme of the immigrant experience is a way to make literacy meaningful, especially to children of color.[5]

11.3 Multicultural Contemporary Realistic Fiction

It is important for students to see people of color in realistic settings. When we rely only on folklore to learn about ethnic groups, children are left with little grasp of people of color who live modern lives. For example, many American Indians do not dress in regalia and do not live on reservations. Joseph Bruchac's *Eagle Song* profiles the life of a modern American Indian family. Danny, a young Mohawk, moves to Brooklyn with his father where he becomes the brunt of other children's jokes about stereotypes of American Indians. To help curb Danny's difficulties in finding new friends, his father, Richard Bigtree, comes to his fourth grade class. He tells how peace came to the Iroquois nations through Aionwahta (Hiawatha), symbolized by the four intertwined roots of the pine tree with an eagle at the top. As a metaphor, Mr. Bigtree holds up five arrows—hard to break when united together. He then explains that Benjamin Franklin knew of the Iroquois League, which then influenced the development of the U.S. Constitution.[6] Mr. Bigtree's classroom visit makes Danny's path to new friends easier, while providing an important historical perspective.

11.4 *The New Realism*

Prior to the 1960s, books for children rarely touched on subject matter considered the province of adults. However, a new genre materialized—literature for the young adult, or adolescent literature.

With the establishment of young adult fiction, more serious themes began to filter down to children's literature. In the 1960s and 1970s, an international movement in children's literature called *new realism* emerged, probably as a result of a growing openness in society. Instead of glossing over life's inevitable difficulties, troubles were looked at squarely. Judy Blume, Norma Klein, and others tackled problems that were long considered taboo when writing for children—racism, divorce (see Figure 11.1), sexuality, child abuse (see Figure 11.2), violence, death, substance abuse, and dysfunctional families. Children who knew their families did not look like *Leave It to Beaver* on television

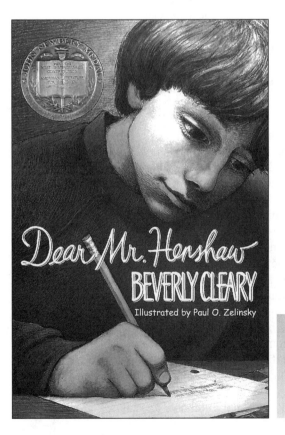

Figure 11.1 Paul Zelinsky's realistic pen-and-ink drawings capture the sensitivity of Beverly Cleary's Newbery Medal book, *Dear Mr. Henshaw,* about a boy from a single-parent home who develops a relationship with a writer.

Figure 11.2 Betsy Byars's *The Pinballs* tells a story of lonely foster children who find friendship—and family—in each other.

embraced these books that addressed the issues about which they were most concerned. The pathbreaking author S. E. Hinton, in her book *The Outsiders,* recognized both urban adolescents and the temptations of leading a life in a gang. Published almost forty years ago, Hinton's book remains in the hands of young people, sometimes propelling those who are otherwise uninterested in reading to read.

Now that these books are more common, and have become increasingly unsparing in their treatment of life, questions are raised about the literary quality: Have we risked children's interest by offering them the provocative without literary quality? Has the portrayal of realistic situations become sensationalized or inappropriate for children?

The discussion that follows is more speculative than definitive; cultural analyses are hard to verify in empirical ways. Throughout this book, we have considered the development of children's literature in connection with communications revolutions, highlighting changes in the conception of children as cultures moved from orality to print-based to electronic to digital communication environments. Since 1450, writers and publishers have offered children didacticism, moralism, romanticism, amusement, and entertainment. Since the electronic revolution, and especially since television in the 1950s, children have had access to more and more information, making practically invisible the line between adult content and what is suitable for children.[7]

Has the new realism gone too far in diminishing the lines between what is considered adult fare and what is appropriate for children? Are the flaws and defects of the older generation dwelt on to such a degree that children learn to distrust adults? These are controversial issues in the field of children's literature, and even the experts do not agree. Anne MacLeod, a children's literature professor at the University of Maryland, writes,

> Finally, when the awful weight of negativism is measured and the failures, disappointments, and betrayals in contemporary children's books are tallied together, [an] observation is hard to avoid: the literature is fundamentally antichild. Something in the eagerness of the authors to acquaint children with all the terrors of the contemporary world, in their unwillingness to offer any perspective or corrective to puerile emotions, something in the joylessness of the fiction as a whole, goes beyond the requirements of an unflinching realism designed, as its apologists claim, to prepare children for the real world. From an obscure level, and surely without conscious intention by the authors, much of current fiction communicates an adult hostility toward children and, ultimately, toward the very concept of childhood.[8]

On the other side of the question, Eliza Dresang, author of *Radical Change: Books for Youth in a Digital Age,* says,

> All adults are concerned for the welfare of children; the disagreement comes from differing opinions about what is safe for youth to know and experience, and what is important for them to know and experience. The focus on limiting rather than expanding options sometimes siphons energy from the effort to help children understand subjects and topics they are bound to encounter in any case, no matter what adults do or say. It deflects adult expertise away from the challenge of presenting material, including difficult material, to young people in a way that will be respectful rather than fearful of their intellectual needs and interests.[9]

Although it is true that most children will soon enough know the underside of life, is this reason enough to introduce it to them at a young age? Does this kind of approach make it easier for adults to abdicate responsibility for learning about children's developmental levels and, more specifically, about what the children they know can and cannot handle?

Ronald Kessler reports that serious depression occurs in about twenty-five percent of young people today—a twenty-three percent increase since the 1960s.[10] Whether through literature or other forms of media, perhaps one of the reasons for serious mental health problems is that we have failed to communicate to the younger generation that growing up is worth the effort it takes; the world, life, and the living of it, despite its difficulties, is ultimately rewarding. As I have pointed out, electronic media are biased toward the styles of realism and naturalism—the bleakest and least hopeful of artistic styles. By favoring naturalism and realism, and freely showing children the ugliest scenarios, do we deny them a sense of security and hopefulness that we ourselves may have found through our own childhood reading years ago, when less bleak materials were available?

Dresang continues,

> Are bleakness and chaos necessary in portraying complexity of character? The answer is No. It is not bleakness that matters most in current literature for youth, but rather depth and uniqueness. Authors can and do find numerous other ways to explore complexity of character. Bleakness is simply "more allowable" in the digital age. The bottom line is that the digital world brings the "real world" into young people's lives.[11]

Who decides what the real world is? The authors of bleak material? The inhabitants of cyberspace? Does the real world mean an overabundance of bleakness in classroom and library collections? Most children will encounter adversity; do they need bleak novels?

Dresang refers to James Garbarino's work with resilient children.[12] Since the 1960s, social scientists have described the phenomenon of these children—first labeled invulnerable, then called stress resilient (because no child is invulnerable)—who, despite all odds, seem to survive. Yet, this percentage of children is small, and as Garbarino has notes, the greater the number of stressors in a child's life, the less the likelihood of resilience.[13] Those who would allow children bleakness to bring them the real world might better heed Garbarino's plea that adults in today's world protect children from dehumanizing images.[14] Through the realism and naturalism of television and film, and through the Internet, children will see countless dehumanizing images; do they need more in their literature? Although exactness about Internet usage is hard to come by, there are estimates that the pornographic sites are used more frequently than all others.

My rationale for placing poetry, drama, folklore, and informational books before realistic fiction in this textbook is to expand the range of genres in which future and practicing teachers have expertise. All of us already get heavy doses of realism from our communication environment. Realistic books should be no more plentiful than drama or poetry or folklore or fantasy or informational literature.

In the last paragraph of her book, Dresang says,

> Those who want to protect children rather than inform them must look once more at the world of *The Giver.* The Giver experienced the pain and joy of knowing, and he passed it on to Jonas, who understood the gift. Many will agree with Jerusha Burnett, aged eleven, who said, "Of course Jonas and Gabe survive. Not many people in that society could. But they could. They had the information. You need information to survive."[15]

Is it *information* we need to survive? Or is it humor and hope and wisdom? In contrast with Jerusha Burnett, here is another middle-grade child's view:

> I like Clancy [a realistic writer] a lot, but he has a really negative view of the world. When I read a couple of his books, it wears me out. I need to read a fantasy as a relief from being dragged down by all the problems he sees in the world. I guess I just don't see the world as being that bad. Some authors just concentrate on the bad stuff and they don't give a complete picture and that can really get you down.[16]

The bleak literature of realism and naturalism has its place, although in my view a smaller one than it is currently accorded. Teachers can be aware of the realistic literature, which deals with brutalizing and traumatic situations children face. Then, they can use their discretion in recommending books to children, or to parents who ask them for help.

Ultimately, we have to ask ourselves, What is the purpose of childhood? Louise Rosenblatt says, "If a child has been given a feeling of being wanted and loved, if he has been able to feel that he is an accepted member of the family and social group, he will tend to develop the kind of inner security that will enable him to meet constructively much of the external insecurity and struggle of later life."[17] Heavy doses of overly bleak realistic literature can threaten children's inner security, rendering adulthood *more* difficult—not less—once children grow up.

Books written before the new realism of the 1960s and 1970s should not be allowed to slip into obscurity. The new realism graphically depicts the most extreme slices of life. However, earlier books like *Jane Eyre* or *Oliver Twist* also let children know there is misery in the world and that if they suffer acutely and chronically, they are not alone. Yet, these classics do so without the kinds of descriptions that destroy hope.

11.5 *Bleakness in Multicultural Books*

Bleakness in literature stands to hurt children of color more than any other group. To show the underside of life graphically can perpetuate negative stereotyping. Latino, African American, and American Indian groups are damaged by an overemphasis on the pathologies in the culture of poverty. When dysfunctional families become the norm in literature about people of color, children are deprived of seeing the very strengths and coping abilities that members of their ethnic group have.

Camille Yarborough's *The Shimmershine Queens* is an example of a balanced portrayal of a poor African American family. There are bleak aspects: The father leaves the three children in the care of their poverty-stricken mother, and Angie, the protagonist—deeply hurt by her father's departure—becomes involved in a violent fight at school, and she shoplifts. However, the novel also provides hope and a way out. Early in the book, Angie has a conversation with her old Great Cousin Seatta, who tells her the history of slavery, and its negative effect on its victims: "You see, Angie, we grown-ups ain't been telling you children what you need to know so da world makes sense to ya. . . . Dat's why our children runnin' around crazy as bedbugs. 'Cause they don't know our story. . . . a people's story is the anchor dat keeps um from driftin, it's the compass to show the way to go and it's a sail dat holds the power dat takes um forward."[18] At a pivotal moment later in the story when Angie has to make a difficult choice, it is Cousin Seatta's words that guide her: "'I'm not gonna let Mr. Fear set up housekeeping in me,' she thought."[19] By the end of the story, Angie has found a way to deal with her troubles—by celebrating the love she shares with her family and friends, and by developing the dramatic abilities she has. *The Shimmershine Queens* is an example of a realistic novel that does not deny hope to its readers and is an example of the good that comes from learning about and taking pride in one's own history.

11.6 *Censorship*

Censorship of children's books has existed throughout its history. The Puritans sanctioned only didactic materials, and during the Enlightenment, because they believed they could shape the way children turned out like ink on blank paper, adults fervently shared moral tales with children. During the Romantic period, when folklorists earnestly sought out the oral tales in their regions, they, perhaps unconsciously, sometimes left out tales in which women were heroic, courageous, risk takers. Such tales did not fit their preconceived notions of passive, sacrificial womanhood. Later, parents and educators suppressed folklore because of its violence.

Today, the questions surrounding censorship in the field of children's literature are: Do we protect children or do we grant them intellectual freedom in all matters? The American Library Association (ALA) has historically taken a strong stand on the side of intellectual freedom, basing their policy on the first amendment to the U.S. Constitution: "Congress shall make no law . . . abridging the freedom of speech, or of the press. . . ." Librarians seek to create and maintain public collections that represent all voices.

In September 2002, Tom Minnery, Vice President of Public Policy for Focus on the Family, attacked the ALA for its failure to protect children from pornographers and pedophiles.[20] To challenge the appropriateness of material for children, to Minnery, is not the same thing as censorship. Besides, he asks, if censorship is such a threat in this country, why do so many libraries have noticeable racks labeled "Banned Books," inviting communities to read? When is a parent exercising her responsibility as a parent, and when is this same person branded a censor who would take away citizens' first amendment rights?

Teachers may meet some seemingly irrational parents in their careers; however, most parents genuinely care about their children's education and, when they raise questions, it is best to respect their views. Parents' right to raise their children to the best of their abilities is a right worth defending. Raising questions is not the same thing as censoring; even Louisa May Alcott questioned whether Mark Twain's books were appropriate for children. Whether we agree with her or not, Alcott—and others—has the right to raise the question.

Because children's literature has sometimes offended its very supporters—parents who willingly go to libraries to borrow books and go to bookstores to buy books for their children—Nicholas Tucker has argued that the publishing industry should do what the film industry has done: Offer ratings for books with potentially disturbing material. Without such ratings, Tucker fears the children's book industry risks alienating adult allies. Trusting parents sometimes arrive home with a newly purchased book to find they are appalled at the contents of what they thought was children's literature.[21]

In a pluralistic society like ours, it is difficult to create a universal code of decency that all those who participate in the public schools will accept. Sylvia Iskander, formerly the president of the Children's Literature Association, says, "When Thomas Jefferson and other founding fathers wrote the Bill of Rights, they did not envision the problems of censorship on a world wide basis."[22] Little did the founding fathers guess that the media of communication would radically change, from their print-based culture to our image-based digital culture in which Internet availability means sex traders and hate groups have at least as much visibility as any other group that has a website.

Teachers, when building classroom libraries, may screen out some books they deem inappropriate for the classroom. Some would call this screening censorship and, therefore, wrong; others might call it protecting children from dehumanizing material and, therefore, right. Recall the discussion in Chapter 9.6: Debbie Reese, a Nambé Indian, does not think children should be introduced to deeply disturbing material at a young age. Marguerite Wright, an African American psychologist, believes children cope better if the adults in their lives protect them from viciousness in literature, especially during their early years. Participants in the ongoing debate surrounding censorship should take notice of the perspectives of Reese, Wright, and other educators of color.

The National Council of Teachers of English (NCTE) has "initiated a front-end process" that demonstrates that educators have chosen materials "responsibly and reflectively."[23] Suggested criteria that professionals use include connecting books and other print media to the curriculum goals, and connecting reading materials to the abilities and interests of students. The NCTE also makes available sample rationales for using books that have been challenged—for example, *The Bridge to Terabithia* by Katherine Paterson. In your early years of teaching, find out how other professionals in your school have handled censorship and concerns over book choices.

11.7 Conclusion

Teachers should not shy away from realistic books; they can offer solutions and comfort children who feel isolated in their circumstances such as *Walk Two Moons* (see Figure 11.3), and they can spur social action. Explore, on your own, the websites on censorship in this chapter, both for and against. Doing so will help you attain the NCATE standard, "Candidates are aware of and reflect on their practice in light of research on teaching resources available for professional learning. . . ."[24]

However, it may be that fantasy plays at least as large a role in helping some children face, and solve, their problems. Marcia Baghban writes, "Reality-based stories may give readers their own reality back to them, but the stories are too close to what is real. The characters are too often victims. They must wait for adults to save them. Such contexts unnerve readers of any age with their dreariness and despair. In fantasy, readers are empowered and assured that they can overcome obstacles."[25] It is to the fantasy genre that we now turn.

Suggested Activities

1. Read Joseph Bruchac's *Eagle Song*, then design oral interpretation and/or readers theater selections from it. Role-play the opening scene where Tyrone and Brad tease Danny for being Indian. Improvise a different outcome.

2. Readers theater: Yahaya Bello recommends *Climbing Clouds: Stories and Poems from the Bahamas* by Telcine Turner. Or see Cynthia Leitich Smith's website for a readers theater interpretation of her short story, "Don't Forget the Pants," from her book *Indian Shoes* (www.cynthialeitichsmith.com/dontforgetthepantsqp.htm).

Figure 11.3 *Walk Two Moons,* the 1995 Newbery Medal winner by Sharon Creech, depicts one girl's outer and inner journey as she comes to deal with her mother's death, with the help of her family and friends.

3. Improvise using pantomime and/or dialogue to recreate or extend a scene from a book or chapter.

4. Interviews: In pairs, one person becomes a journalist who interviews her partner, who becomes a character from a book (and answers the questions in character).

for further reading

Foerstel, Herbert. 1994. *Banned in the U.S.A.: A Reference Guide to Book Censorship in Schools and Public Libraries.* Westport, CT: Greenwood.

Lehr, Susan, ed. 1995. *Battling Dragons: Issues and Controversy in Children's Literature.* Portsmouth, NH: Heinemann.

National Council of Teachers of English. 1997. *English Journal,* 86.2. Published by the author. (censorship focus)

Paterson, Katherine. 2001. *The Invisible Child: On Reading and Writing Books for Children.* New York: Dutton.

Reichman, Henry. 2001. *Censorship and Selections: Issues and Answers for Schools.* 3rd ed. Chicago: American Library Association.

Rudman, Masha Kabakow. 1995. *Children's Literature: An Issues Approach.* 3rd ed. New York: Longman.

Scales, Pat R. 2001. *Teaching Banned Books: 12 Guides for Young Readers.* Chicago: American Library Association.

websites on censorship

The American Library Association Library Bill of Rights:
www.ala.org/work/freedom/lbr.html

Kay Vandergrift's Censorship, the Internet, Intellectual Freedom, and Youth:
www.scils.rutgers.edu/ ~ kvander/censorship.html

The Most Frequently Banned Books in the 1990s:
www-2.cs.cmu.edu/People/spok/most-banned.html

National Council of Teachers of English Anti-Censorship Home:
www.ncte.ogr/postitions/common.html and www.reading.org/~about/whoweare/specreps.htm

awards

Edgar Allen Poe Awards of the Mystery Writers of America:
www.ucalgary.ca/ ~ dkbrown/edgar97.html

The Newbery Medal and Honor Books have many works of realistic fiction:
www.ucalgary.ca/ ~ dkbrown/newb_hon.html

notes

1. Henry David Thoreau, *Walden* (New York: Bramhall House, 1951), p. 24.
2. Laurel E. Henegar, "Nurturing Creative Promise in Gifted Disadvantaged Youth," *Journal of Creative Behavior, 18.2* (1984): 111.
3. Elaine Aoki, "Turning the Page: Asian Pacific American Children's Literature." In: *Teaching Multicultural Literature in Grades K–8,* Violet J. Harris, ed. (Norwood, MA: Christopher-Gordon, 1993), p. 128.
4. Shirley Sterling, *My Name Is Seepeetza* (Toronto: Douglas & McIntyre, 1992), p. 22.
5. Sonia Nieto, *The Light in Their Eyes: Creating Multicultural Learning Communities* (New York: Teachers College Press, 1999), p. 111.
6. Joseph Bruchac, *Eagle Song* (New York: Dial, 1997), pp. 45–46. (illustrated by Dan Andreasen)
7. Joshua Meyrowitz, *No Sense of Place: The Impact of Electronic Media on Social Behavior* (New York: Oxford University Press, 1985), pp. 226–267.
8. Anne Scott MacLeod, *American Childhood: Essays on Children's Literature of the Nineteenth and Twentieth Centuries* (Athens, GA: University of Georgia Press, 1994), p. 209.
9. Eliza Dresang, *Radical Change: Books for Youth in a Digital Age* (New York: H. W. Wilson, 1999), p. 56.
10. Quoted in James Garbarino, *Lost Boys: Why Our Sons Turn Violent and How We Can Save Them* (New York: Simon and Schuster, 1999), p. 41.
11. Dresang, *Radical Change,* p. 217.
12. Dresang, *Radical Change,* p. 208.
13. James Garbarino, *Claiming Boys and Girls in a Socially Toxic Society,* Paper presented at the Bridgeport Child Advocacy Coalition and Casey Family Services Breakfast Conference, Bridgeport, CT, 28 April 1999.
14. Quoted in D. W. Miller, "Trying to Save the Lost Boys," *The Chronicle of Higher Education XLV.39* (4 June 1999): A12.
15. Dresang, *Radical Change,* p. 268.

16. Quoted in Jeffrey D. Wilhelm, *"You Gotta BE the Book": Teaching Engaged and Reflective Reading with Adolescents* (New York: Teachers College Press and National Council of Teachers of English, 1997), p. 80.

17. Louise Rosenblatt, *Literature as Exploration* (New York: MLA, 1983 [1935]), p. 171.

18. Camille Yarbrough, *The Shimmershine Queens* (New York: Knopf, 1989), pp. 20–21.

19. Yarbrough, *The Shimmershine Queens*, p. 112.

20. www.family.org/welcome/press/a0022343.cfm

21. Nicholas Tucker, *How Far Can We Go? Exploring Boundaries of What Can and Still Cannot Be Written About in Children's Literature*, Paper presented at the Children's Literature Association and the International Research Society for Children's Literature, "Children's Literature and the *Fin de Siècle*," Calgary, Canada, 7 July 1999.

22. Sylvia Iskander, "Presidential Address for ChLA, Calgary, 1999: Reading Challenges and Internet Censorship in the New Millennium," *Children's Literature Association Quarterly*, 24.4 (1999–2000): 175.

23. www.ncte.org/positions/materials.shtml

24. National Council for Accreditation of Teacher Education, *Program Standards for Elementary Teacher Preparation*, 5b.

25. Marcia Baghban, "Beyond Teachers as Researchers: Teachers as Advocates," *The Dragon Lode*, 19.2 (2001): 4.

Fantasy and Science Fiction
What If?

[*I*]n reading great literature I become a thousand men and yet remain myself. Like the night sky in the Greek poem, I see with myriad eyes, but it is still I who see. Here, as in worship, in love, in moral action, and in knowing, I transcend myself; and am never more myself than when I do.[1]

—C. S. LEWIS

229

12.1 *Encountering Literature*
through metaphor

Materials Needed

A fantasy or science fiction novel—or novels—that all have read

In small or large groups, ask one person to leave the room. While that person is gone, the group chooses one character (animal, human, or otherwise) from the book, then allows the person who has left to come back. This person must try to guess the character by asking metaphorical questions: "[Name of someone in the group], if this character were a musical instrument, what musical instrument would he [or she or it] be?" Members of the group respond only when called on by the person guessing. Other metaphors: If this person were a color (do not take skin color literally)? A car? A food? A time of day? A season of the year? A song? A famous person? A dog? And so on until the one asking the questions can guess. Then, another person from the group leaves the room while the group selects another character.

For example, in *Tuck Everlasting* by Natalie Babbitt, if Winnie were a musical instrument, what would it be? Answers will vary from person to person: A flute, a viola, and so on. If Tuck were a musical instrument? A cello or oboe. Mae? Jesse? Miles? The man in the yellow suit? Winnie's mother?

I have used this encounter with children as young as seven years with great success. After metaphorically exploring one book, they usually want to try others. Some groups then want to create metaphors for themselves and other members of the group. There's risk involved once it becomes personal; children may have to be told they can't use the exercise to insult others. When done positively, creating metaphors for group members can build the self-esteem of all.

12.2 The Fantasy and Science Fiction Genres

Fantastical literature, written by a single author, contrasts with the fantastical stories from the oral tradition, conceived by the community of authors. Fantasy and science fiction are more sophisticated, complex, and longer than the folk and fairy tales. However, these original works of literature could not have been written without the heritage of folklore. J. R. R. Tolkien drew heavily from Norse mythology in his creation of the *Ring* trilogy. Lloyd Alexander played with elements from the Welsh epic *Mabinogion* in his *Chronicles of Prydain*. C. S. Lewis mingled strands from myths, legends, and folk and fairy tales in his *The Chronicles of Narnia*.

In contrast to realistic fiction, when possible happenings occur, fantasy considers the impossible, although the action becomes probable within the context of an impossible world. In times past and present, animals talk in the *Redwall* series by Brian Jacques, humans have legs like goats in *The Lion, the Witch, and the Wardrobe* by C. S. Lewis, and princesses are as light as balloons and can be played with by the servants as in *The Light Princess* by George MacDonald. The imaginative worlds of fantasy allow these phenomena to occur, evoking the humorous, the whimsical, and the enchanting.

Science fiction speculates about possible future happenings and is sometimes predictive. Many of the nineteenth century speculations of the first science fiction writer, Jules Verne, materialized in the twentieth century. After trying his hand without success at historical fiction, Verne, who loved science as passionately as he loved writing, conceived the idea of literature that explored the future. As technology dominates more and more of our lives, science fiction attains greater importance in holding up a mirror to our society and in prodding us to reflect on our decisions.

Of all the genres, perhaps it is science fiction and fantasy that probe the deepest questions and mysteries of our lives:

- Although we may sometimes wish our lives would never end and we could live forever, what if we did live forever, in this life? *Tuck Everlasting* by Natalie Babbitt
- Although we may sometimes wish we could lead pain-free lives, what would a society with no pain look like? *The Giver* by Lois Lowry
- Most of us wish we had more power over our own lives. But what if we did have more power, and fell into the trap of focusing on it obsessively? What happens when that obsession turns to malice? *The Hobbit* by J. R. R. Tolkien
- What does love look like fleshed out in day-to-day existence? *The Chronicles of Narnia* by C. S. Lewis
- How can we both throw off and live with constraints? *Pippi Longstocking* by Astrid Lindgren
- What is of most worth? Is what we see all there is to know? How do we become the people we want to be? How can others know us the way we know ourselves? *The Wind in the Willows* by Kenneth Grahame

Most of these books are characterized by humor and fun while provoking more serious thought.

12.3 Fantasy and Science Fiction Timeline

1678	John Bunyan's *Pilgrim's Progress*. Children and adults read this allegorical adult book about Pilgrim's journey to heaven.
1726	Jonathan Swift's satire *Travels into Several Remote Nations of the World* (*Gulliver's Travels*). Zora Neale Hurston and Milton Meltzer both loved this book as children.[2]

1828	The beginning of Hans Christian Andersen's writing career
	A Christmas Carol by Charles Dickens. Beverly Cleary's mother read this to her before the age of five. Just the words *Scrooge* and *Marley*, she recalls, were "mysterious and filled with foreboding."[3]
1863	Charles Kingsley's *The Water Babies*
1865	*Alice's Adventures in Wonderland* (see Figure 12.1) by Lewis Carroll (Charles Lutwidge Dodgson), illustrated by Sir John Tenniel
1869	*Twenty-Thousand Leagues Under the Sea* by Jules Verne
1871	*At the Back of the North Wind* by George MacDonald. Beverly Cleary also loved George MacDonald as a child.
	Through the Looking Glass and What Alice Found There by Lewis Carroll
1872	*The Princess and the Goblin* by George MacDonald

The award-winning edition designed and illustrated by Barry Moser — "A dream unto itself" (Village Voice)

Lewis Carroll's

Alice

Alice's Adventures in Wonderland

Figure 12.1 *Alice's Adventures in Wonderland* by Lewis Carroll is one of the early works of fantasy, now a classic. Barry Moser's woodcuts capture the excitement, humor, and whimsy of the work.

1880	*Le avventure di Pinnochio* by Carlo Collodi, pseudonym of Carlo Lorenzini
1891	First English translation of Collodi's *Pinnochio.* Nicholasa Mohr recollects the most exciting day in her seven-year-old life was when she first visited a library and chose *Pinnochio,* a book she read again and again.[4]
1894	*The Jungle Book* by Rudyard Kipling. This book became the basis of the Boy Scouts and was followed by *Just So Stories* (1902). Kipling's highly stylized writing is based on fables and folk tales he learned in India.
1900	*The Wonderful World of Oz* by Frank L. Baum
1902	*Five Children and It* by E. Nesbit
1906	*Peter Pan* by J. M. Barrie. Treatment of American Indians must be discussed.
1906–1907	*The Wonderful Adventure of Nils* by Selma Lagerlöf
	The Wind in the Willows by Kenneth Grahame. Michael Clay Thompson believes that any child who can learn how to say and understand the meaning of *Sanfranciscofortyniner* or *teenagemutantninjaturtle* can handle such words as *replete, affable, portentous, fractious, despond, subterfuge, dejected, dolorous, countenance, languor, obtuse, vouchsafe, amiable, immure, lurid, sanguine, avidity, paroxysm, allude, wistful, asperity, copse, sinuous*—all words from *The Wind in the Willows.*[5]
1922	*Velveteen Rabbit* by Margery Williams
1926	Felix Salten's *Bambi* published in English
1923	*When We Were Very Young* by A. A. Milne, illustrated by Ernest Shephard; followed by *Winnie-the-Pooh* (1926) and *The House at Pooh Corner* (1928)
1929	*Emil and the Detectives* by Erich Kästner
1934	*Mary Poppins* by P. L. Travers
1937	*The Hobbit* by J. R. R. Tolkien
1938	*Mr. Popper's Penguins* by Richard and Florence Atwater
1943	*The Little Prince* by Antoine De Saint-Exupéry (see Figure 12.2)
1944	*Rabbit Hill* by Robert Lawson
1947	*The Twenty-One Balloons* by William Pène du Bois
	Finn Family Moomintroll by Tove Jansson
1949	*Red Planet* by Robert Heinlein
1950	*Pippi Longstocking* by Astrid Lindgren
	The Lion, the Witch and the Wardrobe by C. S. Lewis, followed by six more books in *The Chronicles of Narnia.* J. K. Rowling, author of the *Harry Potter* books, reports her willingness to reread these books even now.[6]
	I, Robot by Isaac Asimov

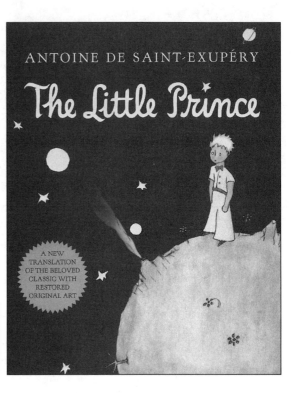

Figure 12.2 *The Little Prince* by Antoine de Saint-Exupéry probes what is most meaningful with humor and insight.

1951	*Charlotte's Web* by E. B. White, the most read-aloud book in the world. E. D. Hirsch argues that, although the book is a significant one, children should not have to hear it read aloud year after year.[7]
	Miss Pickerell Goes to Mars by Ellen MacGregor
1954	*The Wonderful Flight to the Mushroom Planet* by Eleanor Cameron
	The Lord of the Rings by J. R. R. Tolkien
1962	*A Wrinkle in Time* by Madeleine L'Engle

12.4 *Fantasy and Today's Children*

The phenomenal success of the *Harry Potter* series rocked the publishing world, and became some of the best-selling books of all time. What is it that makes children younger than ten years old breeze through 734-page books? Savvy marketing may be part of the answer, but not all. J. K. Rowling, the author, thinks Harry's vulnerability is part of his appeal; most people empathize with children like Harry, who have to take on adult responsibilities too soon.[8] Rowling's United States editor, Arthur Levine, explains he thought readers would connect with Harry: Underestimated and undervalued in his family—a feeling most us have, at least at times—he eventually gains recognition for surprising (nonathletic) abilities.[9]

A fifth-grade teacher in Waterbury, Connecticut, Lori Ercoli attributes the success of *Harry Potter* to a reason that only the rising generation can truly know: They live in a high-stakes testing environment that none of us (who are now the adults) lived in when we were children. Lori says, "Unlike children of my generation, today's children are constantly assaulted with statistics showing they don't meet the norm or standard. They identify with Harry—underestimated. They want to disprove statistics as Harry disproves his family. When he 'soars,' they soar vicariously" (personal communication). Children today are tested more than any preceding generation—the result of a misplaced faith in what multiple-choice, standardized testing can tell us about what students know, and a misplaced faith in the science of a numerical score.

Despite its popularity, the suitability of the *Harry Potter* books is sometimes questioned. Readers especially object to the occult content. This is too literal an interpretation. As has been discussed, well-meaning parents, teachers, and librarians, who feared the violence in the tales would damage young hearts and minds, have long censored folklore—the antecedent to the fantasy genre. But fantasy, like folklore, is metaphorical, symbolizing our deepest feelings, questions, and fears. Images of children flying on broomsticks playing quidditch breaks the confines of our ordered, routine existences. Such writing, instead of inspiring interest in the occult, may turn our attention to the most paramount of questions. During the Middle Ages and with the blessing of the church, the Feast of Fools allowed the least powerful subdeacons to reverse roles with the more powerful bishops. During the festivities, the now-powerful subdeacons ridiculed the bishops, sang off-key, used shoes for censers, wore grotesque masks, and otherwise creatively and playfully disrupted the liturgy. This permissible disorder revealed the limits of imposed order and, ultimately, may be divine laughter. Like the subdeacons of the Feast of Fools, Harry and his friends disrupt muggle order; in doing so, they may help us ask what is most important.

Nevertheless, I encourage my students to exercise caution, especially during their early years. During your first few years of teaching, you have to be careful, particularly with the selections you choose to read aloud. If you have concerns about the suitability of a book, you should talk to colleagues and supervisors. Local control means that *Harry Potter* may be acceptable in one district and not in another; each school, each district has its own culture. And, whether we agree with them or not, parents' wishes should be respected.

Exceptional Abilities

While appealing to all levels of readers, the genres of fantasy and science fiction often provide a glimpse into the life of the extraordinarily gifted child—and children from all ethnicities can be extraordinarily gifted. Robert Lake (Medicine Grizzly Bear) describes his son who possesses uncommon knowledge of Indian life and culture: "My son, Wind-Wolf, is not an empty glass coming into your class to be filled. He is a full basket coming into a different environment and society with something special to share."[10] In science fiction and fantasy, characters like Charles in Madeline L'Engle's *A Wrinkle in*

Time and Grace Chetwin's Mylanfyndra in *Child of the Air* possess uncanny abilities. Chetwin identifies the theme of her book:

> Ostensibly, it is about children who are born with the gift to rise and ride the winds. Really, it is about the terrors of being gifted, gifted in ways not yet recognized by one's culture; gifted in ways that bring nothing but trouble. The dreamers, the ones whose ears are tuned to music of the spheres are different, and being different is a curse.[11]

Books like these can help unusually gifted children better understand themselves. Exceptionally gifted students do not always accept or like themselves for the unique human beings they are.

12.5 *Criticism and Evaluation*

The Nobel prize-winning author and literary critic Toni Morrison examines how writers use people of color, especially those of African descent, in literature. Blackness in literature connotes for white readers a range of emotions and abstractions—evil, benevolence to the point of self-abnegation, taboo, and strangeness, are a few common associations.[12] Historically, people of color, in general, become a foil for white writers and for the imaginations of white readers.

Exceptions to Morrison's observations on the role of people of color in literature are C. S. Lewis's *The Lion, the Witch and the Wardrobe* and George MacDonald's *The Light Princess.* In the former, the witch is white (but still a woman), and in the latter the evil snake is also white. Children's attention can be drawn to the use of color in fantasy, science fiction, and other literary works.

The Indian in the Cupboard and *Return of the Indian* by Lynne Reid Banks, although bestsellers and popular movies, are highly controversial. Colonial works of literature, they lack both cultural specificity and authenticity. Little Bear is supposedly an Iroquois, yet is dressed as a Plains Indian and speaks pidgeon English. Calling this style of speech "early jawbreaker," Beverly Slapin and Doris Seale remark, "Nobody in the history of the world ever spoke this way." In *Return of the Indian,* Indians are pictured as brutal and mindlessly cruel; again, Slapin and Seale relate, "Not any amount of fine writing excuses such abuse of the child audience."[13] Donnarae MacCann says,

> Little Bear . . . grunts and snarls his way through the story, attacking the child, Omri, with a hunting knife, and later attacking a traditional enemy, a three-inch cowboy. At every turn of the plot, Little Bear is either violent or childishly petulant until he finally tramples upon his ceremonial headdress as a sign of remorse. The historical culpability of the cowboy and others who invaded Amerind territory is ignored. Native Americans are seen as the primary perpetrators of havoc, even as they defend their own borders. . . . Although Banks is writing fantasy, she is misrepresenting the Algonquin of the past as a means of amusing the white child today.[14]

The line of thinking Morrison takes up in *Playing in the Dark* could be used to examine the American Indian in the imagination of white readers: What purpose does it serve for white audiences to have images of savagery?

Several writers, including writers of color, have noted that there is not a large opus of works by authors of color in the fantasy genre.[15] Vicky Smith writes, "Even a fairly casual reader . . . would have to be color-blind not to notice that the worlds of fantasy are largely peopled by Caucasians or their non-human counterparts (Bilbo Baggins may not be human, but he clearly springs from a white English cultural matrix)."[16] People of color in the fantasy genre may be in the same phase people of color in children's literature were in 30 years ago—a child of color, like Ezra Jack Keats's Peter, was interchangeable with a white child.

Perhaps, because of the need to give voice to those who were long silenced and invisible, ethnic authors have devoted most of their writing time to realistic portrayals of history and contemporary life. However, this is beginning to change. Joseph Bruchac's recently published *The Skeleton Man* is an example of a literary work of fantasy, rooted in Algonquin folklore (as fantasy by white authors is often rooted in European folklore), while taking place in the present (computer technology is integrated into the plot). Also, as we have already seen in Chapter 4 on picture books, there are writers of color writing picture storybook fantasy, like *Chato's Kitchen* by Gary Soto. Walter Mosley predicts that science fiction by African Americans will explode in the next few years. It is a genre in which possibilities beyond the status quo can be imagined. Visualizing alternatives is ultimately empowering to the reader.[17]

12.6 *Categories of Fantasy*

One day my eleven-year-old, who discovered Brian Jacques's *Redwall* series in fifth grade, said, "Listen to this, Mom," then read a passage from *Outcast of Redwall:*

> The young hare turned his tearstained face up to Sunflash. "Why do creatures have to have wars and kill one another? Why can't everybeast live in peace and be contented? I was just thinkin' before you came, Sire, Fordpetal won't ever see another summer day or laugh an' smile again. Why?"
>
> Sunflash led Bradberry slowly away from the vault. "Why? It's a question I've often asked myself, Bradders, particularly when the life of a young one is wasted. Over quite a few seasons now I've found myself wanting to be only a farmer and grow things, but there are evil ones in the lands. One day when all the evil is gone, maybe then we'll be able to find peace and watch things grow. Until then it is up to the good ones, like yourself, to fight against evil. Fordpetal was doing just that today. War is a terrible thing, but until something arrives to stop the fighting, we must endure it and battle harder to make sure that good wins."[18]

When my son finished reading he asked, "Isn't that a great passage? Do you want to use it for your book?" It is indeed a great passage for it makes explicit one of the hardest questions of our lives, young or old: Why is there suffering? It also encapsulates the themes of *high fantasy.* These books usually have a theme of the quest: an unassuming character who sets out to overcome evil and make right. J. R. R. Tolkien, C. S. Lewis, Ursula Le Guin, Susan Cooper, Robin McKinley, and others who write in this category of fantasy create alternate worlds, complete with their own cartographies, histories, cultures, and so on

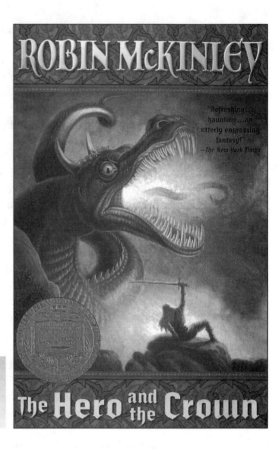

"Refreshing... haunting... an utterly engrossing fantasy!"
—*The New York Times*

ROBIN McKINLEY

The Hero and the Crown

Figure 12.3 In Robin McKinley's high fantasy, *The Hero and the Crown,* a strong female protagonist sets out on a quest.

(see Figure 12.3). Their *progressive plots* must be read in order when reading aloud; each chapter depends on the previous to make sense. In case you are wondering where to begin in Brian Jacques's *Redwall Series,* eleven-year-old Peter Gangi recommends the following top choices: *The Pearls of Lutra, Mariel of Redwall, The Long Patrol, Marlfox, Mattimeo, Mossflower,* and *Bellmaker.*

In addition to high fantasy, there are also *time slips* and *magical worlds, animal* fantasy, *remarkable characters,* and *tiny worlds. The Phantom Tollbooth* by Norton Juster, *Tom's Midnight Garden* by Phillipa Pearce, *A Wrinkle in Time* by Madeline L'Engle, and much of science fiction, occurs beyond the confines of chronological time. Animal fantasy includes Kenneth Grahame's *The Wind in Willows* and A. A. Milne's *The House at Pooh Corner,* illustrated by Ernest H. Shepard in pen-and-ink illustrations. These two books have *episodic plots* and can be read out of order. Other animal fantasies are Robert Lawson's *Rabbit Hill* and, of course, E. B. White's *Charlotte's Web, Stuart Little,* and *The Trumpet of the Swan. Remarkable characters* include such lovable protagonists as Pippi in Astrid Lindgren's *Pippi Longstocking.*

Invented, tiny worlds are found in *The Dolls' House* by Rumer Godden, *Gulliver's Travels* by Jonathan Swift, *The Little Prince* by Antoine St. Exupéry, and *The Borrowers*

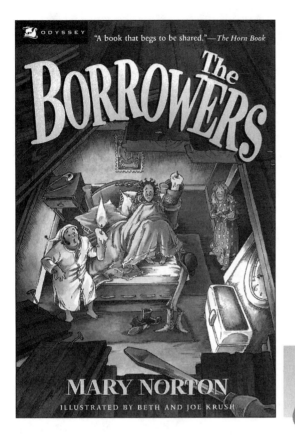

Figure 12.4 Tiny worlds are explored in *The Borrowers* by Mary Norton and illustrated by Beth and Joe Krush.

by Mary Norton (see Figure 12.4). These little worlds contain big ideas. The fox explains friendship—or taming—to the Little Prince, who is looking for friends:

"What does *tamed* mean?"

"It's something that's been too often neglected. It means, 'to create ties' . . ."

"'To create ties'?"

"That's right," the fox said. "For me, you're only a little boy just like a hundred thousand other little boys. And I have no need of you. And you have no need of me, either. For you I'm only a fox like a hundred thousand other foxes. But if you tame me, we'll need each other. You'll be the only boy in the world for me. I'll be the only fox in the world for you. . . ."

"My life is monotonous. I hunt chickens; people hunt me. All chickens are just alike, and all men are just alike. So I'm rather bored. But if you tame me, my life will be filled with sunshine. I'll know the sound of footsteps that will be different from all the rest. Other footsteps send me back underground. Yours will call me out of my burrow like music. And then, look! You see the wheat fields over there? I don't eat bread. For me wheat is of no use whatever. Wheat fields say nothing to me. Which is sad. But you have hair the color of gold. So it will be wonderful once you've tamed me! The wheat, which is golden, will remind me of you. And I'll love the sound of the wind in the wheat. . . ."[19]

This passage makes explicit the inherent richness of experience—whether in life or in reading—that successively intertwines and overlays, simultaneously calling up and calling forth, showing life's greatest rewards.

12.7 Conclusion

Fantasy and science fiction are the consummate genres for the meeting of imagination and word. Fantasy and science fiction challenge all our constraints: time, size, age, and all the laws of the physical world. In doing so, they lead us to imagine a better, more humane world.

Suggested Activities

1. Create a brochure for a science fiction or fantasy world—for example, Norton Juster's *The Phantom Tollbooth.*

2. Create a map of a land from a high fantasy, a time adventure, an animal fantasy, or a tiny world.

3. Using plasticene, create a mobile of characters from a favorite fantasy book.

4. Invite a trained Junior Great Books leader to conduct a discussion of *Tuck Everlasting* by Natalie Babbitt. The literature circles described in Chapter 9 are one way to discuss literature; the Junior Great Books method of shared inquiry is another. For information about Great Books in your area contact the foundation.[20] The rules of the discussion are the following:
   • The leader may only ask questions, not answer them. The questions discussed must reflect genuine doubt; your own curiosity is your best guide.
   • All participants must have read the story.
   • Stay focused on the selection; it is not necessary to refer to other literature.
   • Stay focused on thinking for yourself, rather than introducing the opinions of others.

   The goal is not consensus, but that you know why you think as you do. There are no right answers, only answers that can be supported by your reading of the text. Suggested questions:
   • Why did Winnie pour water over the toad when she knew the Tuck's secret? Why does she think it safe for the toad, but not use it herself?
   • Why does Jesse, after warning Winnie against the water, ask her to drink it on her seventeenth birthday? Why doesn't he market the water himself?
   • Why does not being able to die keep the Tucks from belonging?

   As briefly discussed in Chapter 3.7, creating spaces within the curriculum for children to ask questions is firmly supported in reading research as an essential reading strategy.

for further reading

Attebery, Brian. 1980. *The Fantasy Tradition in American Literature: From Irving to LeGuin.* Bloomington, IN: Indiana University Press.

Cooper, Susan. 1996. *Dreams and Wishes: Essays on Writing for Children.* New York: McElderry.

Egoff, Shelia A. 1988. *Worlds Within: Children's Fantasy from the Middle Ages to Today.* Chicago: American Library Association.

Lehr, Susan, ed. 1995. *Battling Dragons: Issues and Controversy in Children's Literature.* Portsmouth, NH: Heinemann.

Lynn, Ruth Nadelman. 1995. *Fantasy Literature for Children and Young Adults: An Annotated Bibliography.* 4th ed. New York: Bowker.

Smith, Vicky. 2000. "Are There Seats at the Round Table? An Examination of Black Characters in Heroic Fantasy." *The New Advocate,* 13.4: 333–345.

Stewart, Loretta T. 1997. "Readers Theatre and the Writing Workshop: Using Children's Literature to Prompt Student Writing." *The Reading Teacher,* 51.2: 174–175. (on *Charlotte's Web*)

websites

See those websites in Chapter 11 on censorship.

Science Fiction and Fantasy for Children
www.libnt1.lib.voguelph.ca/SFBib/

awards

Mythopoeic Awards:
www.mythsoc.org/awards.html

The Nebula Awards for Science Fiction:
www.literature-awards.com/nebula_science_fiction_awards.htm

These two awards are inclusive of both children's, young adult, and adult literature.

notes

1. C. S. Lewis, *An Experiment in Criticism* (Cambridge: Cambridge University Press, 1961), p. 141.

2. Zora Neale Hurston, *Dust Tracks on a Road* (New York: HarperPerennial, 1995 [1942]), p. 39; and Milton Meltzer, *Starting from Home: A Writer's Beginnings* (New York: Viking, 1988), p. 33.

3. Beverly Cleary, *A Girl from Yamhill: A Memoir* (New York: Morrow, 1995), p. 29.

4. Nicholasa Mohr, *Growing Up Inside the Sanctuary of My Imagination* (Englewood Cliffs, NJ: Julian Messner, 1994), p. 61.

5. Michael Thompson, "Mentors on Paper: How Classics Develop Verbal Ability." In: *Developing Verbal Talent: Ideas and Strategies for Teachers of Elementary and Middle School Students,* Joyce Van Tassel-Baska, Dana T. Johnson, and Linda Neal Boyce, eds. (Needham Heights, MA: Allyn & Bacon, 1996), pp. 63–64.

6. Quoted in Marc Shapiro, *J. K. Rowling: The Wizard Behind Harry Potter* (St. Martin's Griffin, 2000), p. 25.

7. E. D. Hirsch, *The Schools We Need and Why We Don't Have Them* (New York: Doubleday, 1996), p. 29.

8. Quoted in Shapiro, *J. K. Rowling,* p. 8.

9. Quoted in Shapiro, *J. K. Rowling,* p. 9.

10. Robert Lake (Medicine Grizzlybear), "An Indian Father's Plea," *Teacher Magazine, September* (1990): 53.

11. Grace Chetwin, "Creating Ethical Heroes Who Know How to Win: Or Muddling Through." In *Battling Dragons: Issues and Controversy in Children's Literature,* Susan S. Lehr, ed. (Portsmouth, NH: Heinemann, 1995), p. 187.

12. Toni Morrison, *Playing in the Dark* (New York: Random House, 1992), pp. v–xiii, 57, 87.

13. Beverly Slapin and Doris Seale, *Through Indian Eyes: The Native Experience in Books for Children* (Philadelphia, PA: New Society Publishers, 1992), pp. 120–121.

14. Donnarae MacCann, "Native Americans in Books for the Young." In: *Teaching Multicultural Literature in Grades K–8,* Violet J. Harris, ed. (Norwood, MA: Christopher-Gordon, 1993), p. 145. See also John Stott, *Native Americans in Children's Literature* (Phoenix, AZ: Oryx, 1995), pp. 15–18.

15. Julia Candace Corliss, *Crossing Borders with Literature of Diversity* (Norwood, MA: Christopher-Gordon, 1998), p. 9.

16. Vicki Smith, "Are There Seats at the Round Table? An Examination of Black Characters in Heroic Fantasy," *The New Advocate, 13.4* (2000): 333.

17. Walter Mosley, "Black to the Future," *New York Times Magazine (1 November 1998)*: 33–34.

18. Brian Jacques, *The Outcast of Redwall* (New York: Philomel, 1996), p. 263.

19. Antoine de Saint-Exupéry, *The Little Prince.* Richard Howard, trans. (San Diego: Harcourt, 2000 [1943]), pp. 59–60. Compare this translation with Katherine Woods's 1943 translation (San Diego: Harcourt, 1943), pp. 66–67.

20. Available at www.greatbooks.org. See the newsletter, *News from Great Books,* for reports on rising reading scores.

chapter 13

Celebrations and Commemorations:
Understanding Our World

*Y*ou cannot understand the culture of America if you don't understand the role religion has played. . . . Teaching about religion is not about promoting religion in general, or promoting any particular religion. It's about promoting understanding.[1]

—MARTHA BALL

13.1 Encountering Literature
through story dramatization

Materials Needed

In the Month of Kislev, retold by Nina Jaffe, or some other suitable story for story dramatization.[2] Such stories should be short and contain more action than narration, with a strong plot and interesting characters.

note to leader: First read the story to the class, then select and plan the order of the scenes. Story dramatization can encompass an entire story or focus on select scenes, depending on available time. Briefly discuss the characters, perhaps listing them on the board. Next, ask for volunteers. An option is to have different groups that are responsible for different scenes, allowing for double casting.

Characters

Mendel, the peddler

Rivkah, his wife

Their daughters:

    Leah

    Gittell

    Devorah

Feival, the rich man

Feival's wife

    Child 1

    Child 2

    Child 3

Beggar

Cook

Rabbi Yonah

The presentation of scenes might occur in this order:

Scene 1: Mendel either pantomimes or improvises, peddling his wares (pantomime pots, pans, trinkets, and so on).

Scene 2: Feival and the Beggar either pantomime and/or improvise a scene in which Feival refuses to help the Beggar.

Scene 3: Synagogue

Scene 4: Window: The children either pantomime and/or improvise smelling the latkes.

Scene 5: Home: Rivkah and Mendel create dialogue that reflects on their children's contentment.

Scene 6: Cook and window

Scene 7: With Rabbi Yonah

Props are not necessary. A minimalist style evokes more imagination than a realistic style. If used at all, a dreidel and a small bag that contains pennies can make the sound of gelt.

After the story dramatization, use the evaluation questions in Chapter 6.9. When dramatizing stories with children, you may need to say, "I choose those who are sitting quietly," because most children are so eager to participate that you may find yourself accosted.

Richard Colwell's synthesis of research led him to conclude, "Creating a story to be acted out by themselves and others can improve students' language arts skills, self-concept, peer relationships, and creativity."[3] See Chapter 6, the section entitled For Further Reading, for similar research.

13.2 Celebrations: Literature from Religious Traditions and Cultural Commemorations

Celebrations, rituals, worship, and festivals have historically been part of world cultures, focusing the community's attention on common values, traditions, and expression of care for others. Art, music, drama, dance, storytelling, and literature emanate from these events. Since time immemorial the arts have been forms of the deepest kinds of spiritual expression in all religions, often engendering a sense of awe and mystery.

These times apart from day-to-day routines have sometimes served to slow down the pace of life. In our hectic, fast-paced lives, it is hard to imagine the role holidays once had in our ancestors' lives. Phillipe Aries writes, "In the society of old, work did not take up so much time during the day and did not have so much importance in the public mind: It did not have the existential value which we have given it . . . games and amusements extended far beyond the furtive moments we allow them: they formed one of the principal means employed by a society to draw its collective bonds closer, to feel united."[4] *Homo Ludens: A Study of the Play-Element in Culture* shows that, for all its difficulties, medieval Europe was brimful of play.[5] Color and pageantry characterized much of the calendar year. Before the technology of the clock, people ate when they were hungry and slept when they were sleepy. At the time of St. Francis of Assisi, there were 150 religious holidays in the church year.

As a society, we have moved far from this conception of life. Media critic Neil Post-man observes that our communication environment, because of its instantaneous and fragmented messages, makes it harder for us to keep alive our awareness of those tran-scendent narratives that have traditionally given meaning to our lives.[6] Thom Hartmann links the loss of ritual with the tragic rise of suicides in the United States, which has dou-bled during the last thirty years. Rituals, Hartmann says, "are, in many ways, an impor-tant part of the glue which binds together a culture, society, family, or relationship."[7] The anthropologist Victor W. Turner suggests that rituals both maintain social order and make change possible. Social dramas provide an appropriate release of tensions, but they can transform. Ritual allows a time of separation or apartness from the routine of life, in which new insights can be recognized and incorporated. Turner describes liminality as the transitional state during which a group dynamically evolves, moving from the sta-tus quo.[8]

James Garbarino, codirector of Cornell University's Family Life Development Cen-ter and author of *Lost Boys: Why Our Sons Turn Violent and How We Can Save Them*, spent several years interviewing imprisoned juvenile killers to gain insight into why ado-lescent boys turn violent. He says, "If parents, schools and the clergy shield youngsters from dehumanizing images, stimulate their sense of empathy, encourage their ties to 'a non-punitive religious institution,' and learn to read the warning signs of warped moral development," then violence can be prevented.[9] Coming from the field of social sci-ences, which has long avoided anything it could not directly observe and measure such as spiritual life, Garbarino's recommendations that adults encourage spirituality are close to revolutionary. He continues, "When it is grounded in spirituality and love, reli-gion infuses life with purpose by connecting the ups and downs of everyday life to some-thing permanent and beyond the reach of day-to-day experiences."[10]

Douglas Sloan, a professor at Teachers College, Columbia University, develops the concept of insight–imagination. Although embracing the arts, insight–imagination goes beyond to recognize an implicate order. Sloan relates the diminishment of spiritual life to a rise in radical fundamentalism. Sloan wrote these prophetic words twenty years ago: "Our refusal to recognize Mystery, and the ensuing atrophy of the capacity to do so, has made the modern world particularly susceptible to the claims of irrational belief."[11] To share religious literature, even in classrooms, could help us to understand and respect one another, and the mystery of the universe. Such respect might lessen the hate.

13.3 *Culturally Responsive Teaching*

A great portion of the world's literature comes from religious beliefs. To avoid these con-tributions is a mistake and, ultimately, narrows rather than broadens children's knowl-edge and understanding of the world. Multicultural educators Donna Gollnick and Philip Chinn write,

> As part of the curriculum, students should learn that the United States (and indeed the world) is rich in religious diversity. Educators portray their respect for religious differ-

ences by their interactions with students from different religious backgrounds. Understanding the importance of religion to many students and their families is an advantage in developing effective teaching strategies for individual students. Instructional activities can build on students' religious experiences to help them learn concepts. This technique helps students recognize that their religious identity is valued in the classroom and encourages them to respect the religious diversity that exists.[12]

Since September 11, 2001, when terrorists hijacked four planes in an attack on the United States that cruelly destroyed the lives of innocent victims, this country has had to look closely at religious beliefs. Requests for information about Islam have mushroomed, and world leaders have repeatedly asked that we discern the difference between fanatical murderers and peace-loving Muslims. Sharing literature from world religions can help children begin to understand differences in religious beliefs—and the commonalities.

September 11 has awakened in many a sense of spiritual need. Written in response to the disaster, Northland Press published in the fall of 2001 *Children's Prayers for America: Young People of Many Faiths Share Their Hopes for Our Nation* (see Figure 13.1).[13] Northland usually runs about 7,500 copies for a first printing; this book sold 50,000 copies before it came off the press.

Figure 13.1 The publication of *Children's Prayers for America: Young People of Many Faiths Share Their Hopes for Our Nation* met a heartfelt need after the September 11, 2001, attack on the United States.

13.4 *Religious Literature in Schools*

Although today's teachers must follow guidelines set out in their districts by their local boards of education—local control of local schools is one of our most prized freedoms—in most public schools, bringing religious texts into the curriculum is not unlawful. It becomes unlawful only when teachers try to proselytize, or the reverse, denigrate the beliefs or nonbeliefs of others. As Martha Ball, a teacher in Utah who brings the study of religions into her elementary classroom, makes clear in the epigraph, we cannot understand this country if we do not include religion. Because religion plays a significant role in history and society, study about religion is essential to understanding both the nation and the world. Omission of facts about religion can give students the false impression that the religious life of humankind is insignificant or unimportant. Failure to understand even the basic symbols, practices, and concepts of the various religions makes much of history, literature, art, and contemporary life unintelligible.[14]

The First Amendment Center, articulating the consensus of twenty-four national organizations, offers these guidelines:

> Public schools may not inculcate nor inhibit religion. They must be places where religion and religious convictions are treated with fairness and respect. Public schools uphold the First Amendment when they protect the religious liberty rights of students of all faiths or none. Schools demonstrate fairness when they ensure that the curriculum includes study *about* religion, where appropriate, as an important part of a complete education.[15]

Including religious literature is important if we wish our children to participate intelligently in the global arena of the twenty-first century. Presently, there are approximately

- One billion Muslims
- Two billion Christians
- 900 million Hindus
- Between 300 to 600 million Buddhists
- Between 150 to 300 million Daoists
- 20 million Sikhs
- About 100 million Confucianists
- 12.8 million Jews
- Three million Shintoists
- Five million Jains

Compare the numbers of people who are believers in the world's *major* religions with 240 million atheists and 924 million agnostics. Clearly our children are more likely to meet religious rather than nonreligious people throughout their lives. We do not serve the next generation well if we do not acknowledge religion and the literature that is the expression of different beliefs.

13.5 Historical Sources of Religious Literature and Timeline

c. 2000 BCE	Abraham, one of the patriarchs and founders of Judaism, also honored by Muslims and Christians
c. 1400 BCE	Zarathustra, founder of Zoroastrianism (Parsi)
660 BCE	Jimmu Tenno, believed to be the great-grandson of the Shinto sun goddess, becomes the first emperor of Japan. It is almost impossible to understand World War II without understanding Shintoism.
563 BCE	Birth of the Buddhist leader, Siddhartha Gautama
551 BCE	Kong Fuzi (Confucius) born in China, founder of Confucianism
c. 500 BCE	Vardhamana Mahavira, founder of Jainism
500 BCE	Laozi writes down the ancient tenets of Daoism
300 BCE	*Daodejing* (The Dao and Its Power), 81 short poems, appears
c. 29 BCE	Jesus, founder of Christianity
c. 50 CE	Ban Zhao, Chinese Confucian female historian
570 CE	Muhammad, founder of Islam, born in Makkah (Mecca)
600 CE	*Glorious Qur'an* (recitations of Muhammad) inscribed on the media of leather, stones, and camel bones
622 CE	Muhammad leads his followers to Medina (City of the Prophet)
1469 CE	Birth of Nanak, founder of Sikhism
1708 CE	Tenth Sikh Guru designates *Guru Granth Sahib,* the longest book of rhymed poetry in the world, as the definitive Sikh teacher

One unifying factor is that these religious teachers were storytellers, whose stories were handed down orally from one generation to the next until writing made it possible to capture their wisdom and sayings in print. In addition to the stories, pithy proverbial sayings reflect a communication environment based in orality.

Risking oversimplification, the following summarizes the basic orientations of the world's major religions. Review the books in Appendix C for more information.

Buddhism rests in the Four Noble Truths that guide the way to end suffering and attain *nirvana,* oneness with the universe. This requires moral understanding, effort, concentration, and meditation. The result of Buddhist influences is quite different from mainstream beliefs and values. Elaine Aoki explains the implications for teachers: "Traditional Japanese culture, deeply rooted in Buddhism, emphasizes the importance of having no desire. It denies aggressiveness, and usually does not encourage goal-oriented behavior."[16] See Figure 13.2 for an example of Buddhist literature.

Islam, the world's second largest religion, is grounded in Five Pillars: a declared belief in God and that Mohammed is his prophet, daily participation in prayers, fasting, charity, and, for those who physically can, the Hajj—the pilgrimage to Mecca.[17] The

Figure 13.2 *One Hand Clapping: Zen Stories for All Ages,* introduced by Rafe Martin and illustrated by Junko Morimoto, presents Buddhist tales and sayings in a simple, inviting manner.

Qur'an is written in Arabic, which partially explains the strong adherence to Islam in the Middle East. Following the September 11 attacks, it must be noted that the *Qu'ran* forbids aggression, although among the different sects—for example, Shia, Kharijites, Sunna, and Wahabi—interpretations differ.

Judaism is a monotheistic religion, and although Jews are dispersed throughout the world, they are held together by the Hebrew Bible, from which the ten commandments are the most well known of 613 others. The Torah is the Jewish law, given to Moses by God. Stories, found in the Midrash and Talmud, are used for the purposes of teaching and discussion, illuminating the Torah and the commandments. Stories are also considered as active a force as prayer, and can be a mystical experience (see Figure 13.3).

Christianity, also a monotheistic religion, holds the belief that Jesus is the divine Son of God who died on the cross for the salvation of the world. Christians share the Old and New Testaments of the Bible, which include the parables—or stories—of Jesus. Children's author Mem Fox, a daughter of missionaries, reflects on the influence of the Bible on her writing:

All my childhood I was exposed to the music of the Bible. The sound of the oft-repeated word in all the church services I attended affected me forever, as a speaker and as a writer. The sonorousness, the position of the words, the number of words per phrase,

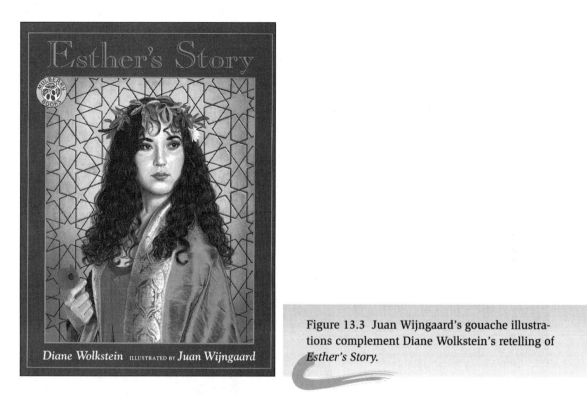

Figure 13.3 Juan Wijngaard's gouache illustrations complement Diane Wolkstein's retelling of *Esther's Story.*

the rhythms of those phrases, and the placement of the pauses have been collected in a storehouse from which I draw constantly. . . .[18]

Confucianism may be a religion, or may better qualify as a philosophy. The ordained state religion of China for almost 2,000 years, until 1911, the abiding ethic in Confucianism is respect for and devotion to family elders, loyalty, chastity, and faithfulness to friends. Many Confucians also hold other religious beliefs.

Hinduism, the world's oldest religion emanating from India, holds that Brahma is the omnipotent, omniscient spirit and ruler of the universe, along with many other Hindu gods. Union with Brahma is the spiritual goal and the religious books guide that goal, the *Vedas* being one of the oldest written books. The *Bhagavad-Gita* is translated into the Song of the Lord, and the *Ramayana* is a series of stories about the god Vishnu, who appeared in human form as man. Carvings illustrating the *Jatakas,* Indian fables, appeared early in history.

Shintoism was the religion of Japan from about the eighth century BCE until 1945, bestowing divine origin on the imperial family. The *Bushido,* code of Samurai, includes loyalty, gratitude, courage, justice, truthfulness, politeness, reserve, and honor.

Jainism, also from India, emphasizes nonviolence, inflicting no harm on any living creature—a way of life that influenced Gandhi, who in turn influenced Martin Luther King, Jr. Asceticism and detachment lead to freedom from karma into a state of bliss.

Sikhism blends elements of Hinduism and Islam. Beginning in Punjabi, India, Guru Nanak and his nine successive gurus provided spiritual leadership until in 1708, when the tenth and definitive guru made his appearance. Sikhs make the Khalsa covenant, which includes not cutting their hair.

To make generalizations about more than 400 tribal *American Indians* is a difficult task. For many of the indigenous people, the arts are very much a part of spiritual life. Storytelling itself has religious value. A graduate student of anthropology once asked Mesquakie Tom Youngman if he could record his stories. Youngman refused: "'I use my stories to pray. To me, they are sacred.'"[19] Among the Hopi, the Kachina dolls are used to teach Hopi beliefs.

In addition to the arts, most American Indian groups are deeply protective and appreciative of the earth (see Figure 13.4). The Apache Swift Eagle tells how the young in

Figure 13.4 Giving thanks did not start with Thanksgiving for American Indians; it has been part of their spiritual life for centuries. Chief Jake Swamp (Mohawk) shares traditional prayers in *Giving Thanks: A Native American Good Morning Message.* Erwin Printup Jr.'s (Cayuga/Tuscarora) seriagraphs express thanksgiving.

his nation were taught "to pass through the way a fish swims through the river, leaving little changed by their passing. Only a ripple in the water."[20] This concern for future generations sometimes doesn't seem apparent at the highest levels of decision making. Joseph Bruchac explains how the future of the earth influences the decisions indigenous people make today, "We are now in the seventh generation of Native people since the coming of the Europeans five centuries ago. That period of five centuries, hard as it has been for Native people, is not seen by Indians as a long time. It is still commonly said by the Iroquois and other Native people that we must make our decisions, not just with tomorrow's result in mind, but thinking of how it will affect seven generations to come."[21]

Stories and storytelling continually make us aware of our responsibilities to our children and our children's children. Bruchac says, "More now than ever before, we need the gift of stories which instruct and delight, explain and sustain. Such stories lead us . . . to an understanding of who we are and what our place is in the natural world. They help us find respect for ourselves and respect for the earth. They lead us toward understanding the sacred nature of the greatest story of all, that story which is told by the rising sun each dawn, the story of the gift of life."[22]

The chiefs of the nineteenth century often addressed this theme in their final speeches. To them, the earth itself was sacred. A Nez Percé, Old Chief Joseph told his son, the young and more famous Chief Joseph, as he lay dying: "You must stop your ears whenever you are asked to sign a treaty selling your home. A few more years and the white men will be all around you. They have their eyes on this land. My son, never forget my dying words. This country holds your father's body. Never sell the bones of your father and your mother."[23] Chief Seathl tried to explain a concept unknown to European immigrants to America: "To us the ashes of our ancestors are sacred and their resting place is hallowed ground."[24] In his final speech, he said,

> If I decide to accept, I will make one condition. The white man must treat the beasts of this land as his brothers. What is man without beasts? If all of the beasts were gone, men would die from great loneliness of the spirit, for whatever happens to the beasts also happens to man.
>
> One thing we know which the white man may one day discover: Our God is the same God. You may think that you own Him as you wish to own our land. But you cannot. He is the God of men. And His compassion is equal for the red man and the white. This earth is precious to Him, And to harm the earth is to heap contempt on its Creator. The whites, too, shall pass—perhaps sooner than other tribes. Continue to contaminate your bed and you will one night suffocate in your own waste. When the buffaloes are all slaughtered, the wild horses all tamed, the sacred corner of the forest heavy with the scent of men, and the view of the ripe hills blotted by talking wives, where is the thicket? Where is the eagle? And what is it to say goodbye to the shift and the hunt? The end of living and the beginning of dying.[25]

Gluskabe and the Four Wishes tells the story of four men who are granted their wishes. For three of the men, lust for power, materialistic greed, and the wish for eternal life are their undoing. For the fourth man, who is able to look into himself and cares only to help his people, peace ensues. Bruchac believes that, despite the many unique

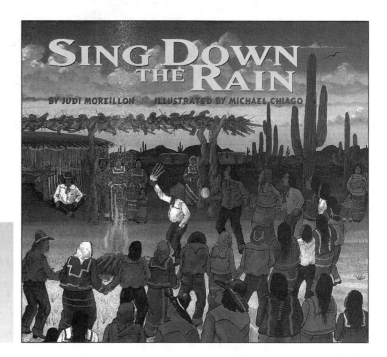

Figure 13.5 *Sing Down the Rain* by Judi Moreillon, illustrated by Michael Chiago (Tohono O'odham), is a poem about the Tohono O'odham Saguaro Wine Ceremony.

cultural variations among the native people, this is the spiritual essence of what binds them together, an essence from which we could all learn (see Figure 13.5).[26]

13.6 Historical and Cultural Commemorations

In addition to the world's religious literature, there is also literature about historical, cultural, and secular celebratory events. Some of these celebrations are particularly important to historically underrepresented groups. For example, a holiday of special significance to Mexican and Mexican Americans is *Cinco de Mayo* (May fifth), which celebrates the 1862 battle between the French and the overwhelmingly outnumbered Mexican army. As a result of the defeat, Napoleon sent in 30,000 troops and won—briefly. Benito Juárez and his followers finally defeated the French in 1867, when Mexico became an independent nation.

Other holidays are Earth Day in April; see Judy Allen's *Anthology for the Earth.* For Mother's Day, see Pat Mora's *Love to Mamá* or *Hazel's Amazing Mother* by Rosemary Wells. For Father's Day, see Javaka Steptoe's *In Daddy's Arms I Am Tall.* For Juneteenth, see Muriel Miller Branch's *Juneteenth: Freedom Day* or Valerie Wesley's *Freedom's Gifts;* these stories commemorate the enslaved Africans of Texas, who were not informed of the 1863 Emancipation Proclamation until 1865.

Diverse perspectives must be shared when using literature about Thanksgiving and Columbus Day—celebrated by those of European descent, mourned by those of American Indian descent. Read several accounts from the bibliographies.

13.7 Universal Celebrations

No matter the religion, human beings almost universally share common celebrations centered around birth, marriage, birthdays, coming of age, harvest, seasons, death, and ancestors. Although New Year's falls on different dates depending on the culture, many cultures do celebrate the advent of a new year, a new beginning (see Figure 13.6). *Dumpling Soup* by Jama Kim Rattigan, illustrated by Lillian Hsu–Flanders, takes place in Hawaii and tells the story from the point of view of a child, Marisa, about her family's celebration of New Year's Eve. Her relatives are Korean, Japanese, Chinese, Hawaiian, and white—a multiethnic fest.

Figure 13.6 Karen Chinn's *Sam and the Lucky Money,* illustrated in watercolors by Cornelius Van Wright and Ying-Hwa Hu, shows one boy's decision on how to spend his money while celebrating the Chinese New Year.

13.8 Conclusion

Hopefully, by placing this chapter at the end of the book instead of the beginning, you know that multicultural literature is not brought out just at holiday time, but rather *every* month of the school year. In bringing literature and the arts into the understanding of the world's religious literature, and different culture's historical events, children have multiple ways to understand and grow in this increasingly complex world.

Suggested Activities

1. In your readings, note other stories with action and strong plots, like *In the Month of Kislev,* for story dramatization.
2. Prepare food from a religious or historically significant story—for example, latkes and applesauce. See *Latkes and Applesauce: A Hannukah Story* by Fran Manushkin.

for further reading

Bruchac, Joseph. 1996. *Roots of Survival.* Golden, CO: Fulcrum.

First Amendment Center. 1999. *A Teacher's Guide to Religion in the Public Schools.* Nashville, TN: First Amendment Center.

websites

Bibliography of Children's Buddhist Literature:
http://pobox.upenn.edu/ ~ davidtoc.html

Council on Islamic Education (CIE):
www.cie.org

Freedom Forum First Amendment Center:
www.fac.org

Hinduism:
www.hindunet.orgindia.indiagov.or/culture/religion/hinduism.htm

Information and stories about Islam and Muslims:
http://npin.org/library/2002/n00651.html

Jainism:
www.cs.colostate.edu

awards

Catholic Library Association Regina Medal:
www.cathla.org/regina.html

notes

1. Bonnie Gardner, "Discussing All That's Holy," *NEA Today,* 16.4 (1997), p. 21.
2. To learn more about story dramatization, see Nellie McCaslin's *Creative Drama for the Classroom and Be-*

yond, 7th ed. (New York: Longman, 2000) and Winifred Ward's *Stories to Dramatize* (Louisville, KY: Press Plays Anchorage, 1981 [1952]).

3. Richard Colwell, "The Arts." In: *Handbook of Research on Improving Student Achievement,* Gordon Cawelti, ed. (Arlington, VA: Educational Research Service, 1995), p. 29.

4. Phillipe Aries, *Centuries of Childhood: A Social History of Family Life,* Robert Baldick, trans. (New York: Vintage, 1962), pp. 72–73.

5. Johan Huizinga, *Homo Ludens: A Study of the Play-Element in Culture* (Boston: Beacon Press, 1950), p. 179.

6. Neil Postman, *Technopoly: The Surrender of Culture to Technology* (New York: Knopf, 1992), p. 172.

7. Thom Hartmann, *The Last Hours of Ancient Sunlight: Waking Up to Personal and Global Transformation* (New York: Harmony, 1998), p. 297.

8. Victor W. Turner, *The Ritual Process* (Harmondsworth, Middlesex: Penguin, 1974).

9. Quoted in D. W. Miller, "Trying to Save the Lost Boys," *The Chronicle of Higher Education XLV.39* (4 June 1999): A12.

10. James Garbarino, *Lost Boys: Why Our Sons Turn Violent and How We Can Save Them* (New York: Simon & Schuster, 1999), p. 155.

11. Douglas Sloan, *Insight-Imagination: The Emancipation of Thought and the Modern World* (Westport, CT: Greenwood, 1983), p. 80.

12. Donna M. Gollnick and Philip C. Chinn, *Multicultural Education in a Pluralistic Society,* 4th ed. (New York: Merrill, 1994), p. 214.

13. Karlynn Keyes Lee, *Children's Prayers for America: Young People of Many Faiths Share Their Hopes for Our Nation* (Flagstaff, AZ: Northland, 2001).

14. Council on Islamic Education and the First Amendment Center, *Executive Summary: Teaching About Religion in National and State Social Studies Standards* (Nashville, TN: Author, 2000).

15. First Amendment Center, "A Teacher's Guide to Religion in the Public Schools," (Nashville, TN: First Amendment Center, 1999).

16. Elaine Aoki, "Turning the Page: Asian Pacific American Children's Literature." In: *Teaching Multicultural Literature in Grades K–8,* Violet J. Harris, ed. (Norwood, MA: Christopher-Gordon, 1993), p. 119.

17. Inea Bushnaq, *Arab Folk-Tales* (New York: Pantheon), preface.

18. Mem Fox, *Dear Mem Fox, I Have Read All Your Books Even the Pathetic Ones* (San Diego: Harcourt, Publishers, 1990), p. 31.

19. Joseph Bruchac, "Storytelling and the Sacred: On the Uses of Native American Stories." In: *Through Indian Eyes: The Native Experience in Books for Children,* Beverly Slapin and Doris Seale, eds. (Philadelphia, PA: New Society Publishers, 1992), p. 94.

20. Joseph Bruchac, *Roots of Survival* (Golden, CO: Fulcrum, 1996), p. 9.

21. Bruchac, *Roots of Survival,* p. 17.

22. Bruchac, *Roots of Survival,* p. 81.

23. Vine Deloria, Jr., *God Is Red* (New York: Grosset & Dunlap, 1973), p. 175.

24. Deloria, *God Is Red,* p. 176.

25. Quoted in Sloan, *Insight-Imagination,* p. 74.

26. Joseph Bruchac, *Gluskabe and the Four Wishes* (New York: Dutton, 1995).

Standards and Assessment

To Teacher Educators, Teachers, and Teacher Candidates

The field of teacher education is undergoing profound change. To prepare future and practicing teachers better, teacher preparation programs are focusing on performance-based learning, linked to national standards that have been articulated through the consensus of professional organizations. One of the motivating forces behind this change in teacher education is to prepare the kind of teachers better who can help all children learn in an increasingly diverse society.

The role of the teacher in this new framework differs from the role of the teacher in the factory model, in which teachers disseminate information then audit students by keeping a record of who succeeds and who fails, often using tests and other traditional forms of assessment. In contrast, when the focus is on performance-based learning, teachers help learners discover and develop their unique capabilities. Learners have multiple opportunities to develop foundational skills, knowledge, and competencies within a high-quality program. The latter approach requires more active and engaged learning than most teachers and teacher candidates experienced during their K–12 schooling.

It is not realistic to expect new teachers to give children learning opportunities they did not experience themselves. The encounters throughout the text are designed to help candidates grow in what they know and are able to do and, simultaneously, to model for candidates the many pedagogical strategies and processes available to them. Candidates can then draw on this research-based knowledge, which can improve the learning of children in the K–6 schools.

We know that elementary-age children learn best when actively engaged in learning. The same is true in higher education: "Learning that lasts," writes Marcia Mentkowski, "is integrative; experiential; self-aware and self reflective, self assessed and self-regarding; developmental and individual, transitional and transformative; active and interactive, independent and collaborative; situated and transferable; deep and expansive, purposeful and responsible."[1] Ongoing assessment is essential to this process.

The performance tasks that follow reflect the National Council for Accreditation of Teacher Education (NCATE) Program Standards for Elementary Teacher Preparation. They also reflect the International Reading Association and National Council of Teachers of English (IRA/NCTE) standards for the English Language Arts for children.

In connection with the standards, I ask candidates to do the following:

- Keep a log.
- Write and share one book review on a novel or chapter book of choice.
- Respond in writing to the elements, style, and media of art for one picture book of choice (ungraded—pass or redo).

- Participate in class by

    Reading aloud one picture book to a small group (ungraded)

    Learning to tell one brief story (ungraded)

    Bringing a favorite, high-quality book to class each week for the genre studied

    Experiencing the creative process in response to literature (ungraded)

    Creating a challenging enrichment activity in response to informational literature

    Bringing quality books for English Language Learners (ELL) during one session

The range of tasks and the use of multiple assessments allow candidates to build on their individual strengths and interests while meeting professional expectations. Some of these tasks are quite simple and do not require a lot of time.

Assessment, in its most positive sense, is as if teachers and students sit down together to review what went well and what could go better, which brings about competence.[2] To renew or attain accreditation, candidates in teacher preparation programs must demonstrate evidence of learning. I have piloted performance assessments for several years and have continuously improved them based on the feedback I have received from students, who anonymously answered surveys, and from four experts: Dr. Maggie Sneed, Elementary Coordinator at Alverno College; Dr. Catherine Oleksiw, formerly a Title II consultant for the Connecticut State Department of Education; and Dr. Jeff Cain, Director of Writing Across the Curriculum, and art professor Jack DeGraffenreid, both of Sacred Heart University. I thank them for their help.

Standards Addressed in Encountering Children's Literature: An Arts Approach

The following standards are addressed through much of this book. *Italics* indicate where the standard receives the most attention.

NATIONAL COUNCIL FOR ACCREDITATION OF TEACHER EDUCATION:

NCATE Program Standards

Introduction: "Teachers need access to the growing knowledge that exists about how to teach these learners [whose first language is not English] effectively." (*Chapter 5 on poetry and Appendix C, which lists many bilingual books*)

2a: "Candidates know, understand and use the central concepts, tools of inquiry, and structures of content for students across the K–6 grades and can create meaningful learning experiences that develop students' competence in subject matter and skills for various developmental levels." (*Chapter 2 on genre and Suggested Activities throughout*)

2b: "Candidates demonstrate a high level of competence in use of the English language arts and they know, understand, and use concepts from reading, language and child development, to teach reading, writing, speaking, viewing, listening, and thinking skills and to help students successfully apply their developing skills to many different situations, materials and ideas." (*The encounters in Chapters 1–13*)

2b, Supporting Explanation: "They are also familiar with, able to use, and recommend to students many reading materials based on different topics, themes, and a variety of situations and consisting of different types . . . " (*Chapter 3 and Appendix C*)

2e: "Candidates know, understand, and use the major concepts and modes of inquiry from the social studies—the integrated study of history, geography, the social sciences, and other related areas—to promote elementary students' abilities to make informed decisions as citizens of a culturally diverse democratic society and interdependent world." (*Chapters 7, 9, and 13, and Appendix C*)

2f: "Candidates know, understand, and use—as appropriate to their own knowledge and skills—the content, functions, and achievements of dance, music, theatre, and the visual arts as primary media for self-expression, communication, inquiry, and insight among students." (*Dance, Chapter 7 encounter; music, Chapter 7 encounter; For Further Reading in Chapter 7, and Appendix C, which includes many musical books; theater, Chapter 6 especially; and the visual arts, Chapter 4 especially*)

2i: "Connections across the curriculum—Candidates know, understand, and use the connections among concepts, procedures, and applications from content areas to motivate elementary students, build understanding, and encourage the application of knowledge, skills, tools, and ideas to real world issues." (*Chapter 6 on drama and Appendix C*)

2i, Supporting Explanation: "Candidates help elementary students learn the power of multiple perspectives to understand complex issues." (*Chapter 13 on celebrations and commemorations*)

3b: "Adaptation to diverse students—Candidates understand how elementary students differ in their development and approaches to learning, and create instructional opportunities that are adapted to diverse students." (*Chapters 3 and 9 on historical literature especially, and the encounters*)

3b, Supporting Explanation, "They are able to apply knowledge of the richness of contributions from diverse cultures to each content area studied by elementary students." (*Chapter 8 on informational literature*)

3c: "Candidates understand and use a variety of teaching strategies that encourage elementary students' development of critical thinking, problem solving, and performance skills." (*Chapter 7*)

3d: "Active engagement in learning—Candidates use their knowledge and understanding of individual and group motivation and behavior among students at the K–6 level to foster active engagement in learning, self motivation, and positive social interaction and to create supportive learning environments." (*Chapter 1*)

5b: "Candidates are aware of and reflect on their practice in light of research on teaching and resources available for professional learning . . . " (*Chapter 11*)

INTERNATIONAL READING ASSOCIATION AND NATIONAL COUNCIL OF TEACHERS OF ENGLISH (IRA/NCTE):

These standards are for K–12 students. Teacher candidates are best prepared for helping their students learn by acquiring the knowledge and developing the skills and competencies in their teacher preparation programs.

Standard 1: "Students read a wide range of print and nonprint texts to build an understanding of texts, of themselves, and of the cultures of the United States and the world; to acquire new information; to respond to the needs and demands of society and the workplace; and for personal fulfillment. Among these texts are fiction and nonfiction, classic and contemporary works."

Standard 2: "Students read a wide range of literature from many periods and many genres to build an understanding of the many dimensions (e.g., philosophical, ethical, aesthetic) of human experience."

Standard 3: "Students apply a wide range of strategies to comprehend, interpret, evaluate, and appreciate texts."

Standard 4: "Students adjust their use of spoken, written, and visual language (e.g., conventions, style, vocabulary) to communicate effectively with a variety of audiences and for different purposes.

Standard 5: "Students employ a wide range of strategies as they write and use different writing process elements appropriately to communicate with different audiences for a variety of purposes.

Standard 6: "Students apply knowledge of language structure, language conventions (e.g., spelling and punctuation), media techniques, figurative language, and genre to create, critique, and discuss print and nonprint texts."

Standard 7: "Students conduct research on issues and interests by generating ideas and questions, and by posing problems.

Standard 8: "Students use a variety of technological and information resources (e.g., libraries, databases, computer networks, video) to gather and synthesize information and to create and communicate knowledge."

Standard 9: "Students develop an understanding of and respect for diversity in language use, patterns, and dialects across cultures, ethnic groups, geographic regions, and social roles."

Standard 10: "Students whose first language is not English make use of their first language to develop competency in the English language arts and to develop understanding of content across the curriculum."

Standard 11: "Students participate as knowledgeable, reflective, creative, and critical members of a variety of literacy communities."

Standard 12: "Students use spoken, written, and visual language to accomplish their own purposes (e.g., for learning, enjoyment, persuasion, and the exchange of information)."

Assessments

LOG: PERFORMANCE AND ASSESSMENT

Description of Performance Task

Beginning the first week of class, keep a log. Read widely, investigating all genres, with an awareness of fair representation of male and female characters, and diverse cultures and ethnicities. Multicultural literature should be included in *all* genres. For *some* entries, not all—sometimes the best response to a good book is silence—describe ways you could use the book in an elementary classroom. When possible, make interdisciplinary connections: How could you use the book in connection with math, science, social studies, art, music, drama, or writing? What themes does the book touch on?

How many books should be included in your log? The answer depends on the nature of *your* particular exploration. Hold the standard high: *Immerse yourself in children's literature the way you hope your personal physician has immersed (and—hopefully—continues to immerse) herself in medical literature.* You'll have more fun than your doctor, and will raise the standards of the teaching profession in the process.

The goal is not that you meet a quota, but that you have actively sought to encounter all kinds of high-quality literature. If you are

- A lower grade elementary teacher (grades K–2), focus on picture books but don't forget the chapter books. Some kindergartners and first graders come to school already reading at high levels.
- An upper grade elementary teacher (grades 5–6), aim for fifteen to twenty novels and novellas, including some picture and illustrated books
- Teachers of grades 3 and 4, aim for a middle ground

In 1970, when I was an undergraduate taking a class like this, I was asked to read 100 books, which is still a fairly common assignment in children's literature classes. Doing it turned out to be much more enjoyable than it sounded. You will not be marked down if you don't read 100 books—a smaller number of high-quality chapter books may be the way you want to go. Put forth genuine effort and read every day. If you are consistent during the course of the semester, you'll find you've read more than you thought you could. We tell second graders to read thirty minutes a night: Try it and see what happens. Every semester I have at least one student who reads more than 200 books (the record is 224). A good pace would be a minimum of five books a week: $5 \times 12 = 60$ (or, ten children's books a week during a six-week summer course).

Keep in mind that we are looking at mostly picture books and collections the first half of the semester, and chapter books the second half of the semester. You may want to read about ten picture books a week during the first half of the semester (or several good collections of poetry, drama, or folklore) and several chapter books a week during the last half of the semester.

Write summaries and/or responses (or, a combination of summaries and responses—this is *your choice*) to the literature you read in your own words, using quotation marks where appropriate. Summaries and/or responses for picture books should be one to two paragraphs. If you are an upper grade teacher and choose to read the fifteen or so chapter books, make your log entries more in depth (three to five paragraphs per book). See Chapter 1.6 for reader response prompts.

The format of the log can be index cards, a three-ring binder, a word processor spreadsheet—whatever manner you think will be helpful to you in your teaching career and is compatible with your own organizational style (I have examples). Decide on format and organization as soon as possible. The organization should be clear; consider a table of contents. *Please, no sheet protectors.*

There is much self-selection in this assignment and you can "abandon" books you start. Personalize your log: Read lots of books by Joseph Bruchac or Katherine Paterson or Gary Soto or Faith Ringgold or Karen Hesse or Nicholasa Mohr or John Steptoe or Laurence Yep or Virginia Hamilton or—your choice. Or, read lots of World War II or Civil War or medieval literature. Or, read in depth in a specific genre: history, biography, fantasy. *Follow your interests and make the log your own.*

LOG CRITERIA

Name _____   Due _____

Please hand in the following form with your log, the second-to-last class of the semester. Points rate each component; you can rate yourselves numerically if you want—hopefully, I'll agree. If I don't agree, I'll tell you why.

> L1 _____ 10 pts.   *Performance Criteria for Reflective Practice. NCATE Program Standard 5b.*

On a separate sheet of paper—typing preferred—reflect on *your* journey into children's literature. How has your learning changed over the course of the semester? How do you plan to continue developing your knowledge of children's literature after the course is over?

This *self-reflection* is the first thing I read before looking at your log. It helps me to see what makes your log unique—an expression of who you are and what you enjoy.

L2 ____ 10 pts.	*Performance Criteria for Genre. NCATE Program Standard 2a, NCATE Program Standard 2b, and IRA/NCTE Standard 2.*

Rate your knowledge of genre by assigning a check or check-plus to each genre and subgenre:

___ Picture storybooks
___ Concept books
___ Wordless books
___ Poetry
___ Drama
___ Folklore:
___ Fables
___ Folktales
___ Fairy tales
___ Myths
___ Legends
___ Tall Tales
___ Epics
___ Literary fairy tales
___ Fractured fairy tales

___ Informational literature
___ Historical fiction novels and novellas
___ Biography
___ Contemporary realism
___ Fantasy
___ Books about celebrations and commemorations
___ Historical realism

Of the above, choose one that you have rated high and one you have rated low. Reflect on why this occurred (accessibility, personal favorites, and so on).

Your comments:

L3 ____ 10 pts.	*Performance Criteria for Multicultural Literature. NCATE Program Standard 2i, Supporting Explanation, 3b, Supporting Explanation, NCATE Unit Standard 4, and IRA/NCTE Standard 1.*

Were you able to find high-quality multicultural literature in all genres? Where did you find the most? The least? Review the Criticism and Evaluation sections in this book, especially in Chapter 3.7.

Your comments:

L4 ____ 5 pts.	*Performance Criteria for Nonstereotypical Roles for Boys and Girls. IRA/NCTE Standard 1 and NCATE Standard 3e.*

Have you included boys and girls in nonstereotypical roles (i.e., girls who take risks and have adventures and boys who are nurturing and caring)?

Your comments:

> L5 _____ 5 pts.   *Performance Criteria for High-Quality, Noncommercialized Books.*
> *NCATE Program Standard 2b.*

When creating a classroom collection, teachers have the opportunity to introduce children to books they may not see outside of school. Does your log reflect high-quality, noncommercialized books?

Your comments:

> L6 _____ 30 pts.   *Performance Criteria for Required Books. IRA/NCTE Standard 1.*

Have you included your response (two to three paragraphs for each book) to the six required chapter books? Where can I find them in your log? (You can use Post-Its.)

Your comments:

> L7 _____ 10 pts.   *Performance Criteria for One Self-Selected Classic. NCATE Standard*
> *2a and IRA/NCTE Standard 1.*

Choose one classic from historical realism or biography or fantasy. See the history of genre/time-line sections of Chapters 9, 10, and 12 for suggestions.

Your comments:

> L8 _____ 10 pts.   *Performance Criteria for Books on Music and Dance. NCATE*
> *Program Standard 2f.*

Choose one book on music and one on dance. Find suggestions for these in the section on Fine Arts in Appendix C. Where can I find these books in your log? (You can use Post-Its.)

Your comments:

> L9 _____10 pts.   *Performance Criteria for Websites. NCATE Program Standard 3e and*
> *IRA/NCTE Standard 8.*

Visit multicultural award-winning sites and read a minimum of two award-winning multicultural books. What books did you choose?

Your comments:

Also, visit two other sites of your choice; see the websites at the end of each chapter in this book for suggestions. Where can I find your response to these sites in your log? (You can use Post-Its.)

Your comments:

CRITERIA FOR CLASS PARTICIPATION (CP)

Name _____   Due _____

Please hand in a copy of this form on the last day of class. Much of what follows does not take much time and is not graded, but it does increase participation, which makes for a livelier class. These simple tasks allow you to try out skills and abilities in a low-risk setting.

> CP1 _____ 10 pts.   *Performance Criteria for Effective Communication. NCATE Standard 2b and IRA/NCTE Standards 1 and 2.*

Automatic 10 points for trying. Read aloud a picture book to a small group. The book should be no more than about five minutes; time yourself before presenting. Look at Chapter 1.8 for tips on how to approach performing, and Chapter 2.1 for things to think about when reading aloud.

Your comments:

> CP2 _____ 20 pts.   *Performance Criteria for Developing Your Capabilities. NCATE Program Standard 2f and 3d.*

Automatic 20 points for trying. Sometime during the semester, *you* experience the creative process in response to literature. Outside of class time, *do yourself* what elementary teachers often ask students to do: Write a letter to an author (send it or not, as you wish) or to one of the main characters, design a book jacket, write your own children's book, experiment with computer graphics, and so on. See Chapter 1.6 and the Suggested Activities in each chapter for more ideas. Or, having experienced them in class, you may want to design your own encounter.

If you choose to write something, please bring it to the second-to-last class so I have time to read it. If you choose the visual arts or plastic arts or crafts, bring them in for the last class; we'll have an exhibition. *Creating is a form of play. This experience should be fun.* Please avoid duplicated, predrawn art forms.

Your comments: (Include a brief description of your product.)

> CP3 _____ 20 pts.   *Performance Criteria for Genre, and Selecting and Evaluating Literature. NCATE Program Standard 2a and IRA/NCTE Standards 1 and 2.*

Bring one (ONE, 1, I, uno, un) of your very favorite books for the assigned genre/category to each class session. We will create a class bibliography each week. The rationale for sharing your favorite book is this:

a. It's an ongoing way of assessing your understanding of genre, selection, and evaluation, demonstrating that you have read and understood the chapters in the book. For example, if you bring Richard Scarry's *Busy, Busy World* to recommend to your classmates for our session on the picture storybook, you probably haven't read Chapters 3 and 4. If you bring Maurice Sendak's *Where the Wild Things Are* to the session on fables and folk tales, you don't yet understand genre.

b. More important, this weekly activity helps us develop a learning community within our class. Learning about each other's favorites helps you choose books for your log and ensures that this class involves not only you and me, but also you, me, and each other. You are on your way to becoming professionals who practice collegiality, helping each other develop expertise in children's literature.

Although I know it is sometimes hard to choose, please bring *just one book.* There are time constraints, and this way our class bibliography will hopefully reflect the very best children's literature available. A former student wrote, "[S]haring a different book every session . . . was the most enjoyable part of the class; the students were not lectured to—instead everyone participated" (personal communication).

Your comments:

CP4 _____ 20 pts.   *Performance Criteria for Interdisciplinary Connections. NCATE Program Standard 2i.*

In response to the informational book, bring in an activity you have constructed that could be used as enrichment. Make it durable so it lasts for years of teaching. For example, *Math Wizardry* suggests numerous ideas teachers can easily construct that would challenge mathematically advanced children. Avoid worksheets, word searches, and busy work.

Bring your construction to the session on informational literature and bring the informational book you used. Additionally, try to bring other texts (no more than three) from any genre that connects with your one informational book. For example, in response to *Math Wizardry,* you could bring sunflowers, pinecones, and other natural phenomena that demonstrate Fibonacci's Rule—a pattern found in nature. In connection with *Math Wizardry* you could also bring Jon Scieszka and Lane Smith's *Math Curse;* Mrs. Fibonacci is the math teacher in this fanciful book. You could also bring Demi's *One Grain of Rice,* a folktale from India.

Your comments: (Include a description of what you constructed.)

CP5 _____ 20 pts.   *Storytelling. Ungraded, automatic 20 pts. IRA/NCTE Standard 3 and NCATE Program Standards 2b, 3b, and 3d.*

See the Storytelling Guide that will be distributed at the time of the storytelling workshop.

Your comments:

CP6 _____ 10 pts.   *Performance Criteria for Books for English Language Learners. Introduction to NCATE Program Standards, and IRA/NCTE Standard 10.*

Bring in a high-quality book for ELLs. See Chapter 3 for selection and evaluation criteria.

Your comments:

CP7 _____ 10 pts.   *Performance Criteria for Class Discussions. NCATE Program*
Standard 2a and IRA/NCTE Standard 3.

Participate in class discussions of text, articles, literature circles, and shared inquiry.

Your comments:

Permission granted to reproduce from *Encountering Children's Literature: An Arts Approach* by Jane M. Gangi.

STORYTELLING GUIDE

Hand in this form when you tell your story. Due over Sessions 6 through 11; you choose your own sign-up date—no more than four to five stories per session.

Name _____

Story_____

What is the source of the story? _____   Time: _____

Description:

Participate in an hour-long storytelling workshop. This will help you develop confidence and artistry in interpreting your story (I promise!). To participate in this workshop, you must have already selected a story the week before the workshop and signed up for it so that we do not have duplicates. Read it over several times. Do not memorize. Storytelling is more about visualization and internalization than memorization. I will supply stories especially good for telling two weeks before the workshop, or you can choose your own. Choose a story from the oral tradition (ballad, sea chanty, fable, folk tale, fairy tale, myth, legend, tall tale—398.2 in the Dewey Decimal System). Consider telling a tale from your own ethnic heritage. If you play a musical instrument, consider using it. And, consider using nesting dolls or sand or cut paper, or other objects.

Your story should be **no less than two to three minutes and *not more than* five to seven minutes. Please, please, please time yourselves before choosing and presenting** (previous students have tended to talk longer than seven minutes without knowing it, and there are time constraints). If your story is particularly short (like a fable or rhyme), tell two short ones.

Nonverbal: As practiced in the storytelling workshop, the best *posture* is to hang loose, like a puppet, imagining invisible strings attached to the top of your head and sternum. Picture a long spine with your skull floating like a balloon. This allows your spine to give maximum to support your breath, which is the source of sound. Crossing your legs or slumping cuts off your breath, which limits your sound.[3]

Teacher comments:

If you use *gesture*—it is perfectly appropriate to tell a story without using gesture (see Tooze, Bryant, and Reed in Chapter 7.1)—let it flow freely in connection with the story. Hesitations to take and fill space can inhibit impulse, and sometimes gesture can be aimless and unconnected to the story.

Teacher comments:

If you use *eye contact,* try to connect with most everyone. In some cultures, it is customary for story-tellers and listeners to keep their eyes closed during the storytelling event.

Teacher comments:

If you use *movement*—it is perfectly appropriate to sit quietly on a stool or chair—let it flow freely, connected with the story. Sometimes tellers can wander aimlessly or restrict their use of space.

Teacher comments:

Verbal: With the breath support described in the nonverbal section, you can experiment with **vocal variety.**

Pitch denotes using the full range of the human voice, from very high to very low.

Volume, gradation in sound from very soft to extremely loud, can intensify the dramatic aspects of your story. *Rate,* from quick to slow, can heighten listeners' interest. *Sound and silence* can become part of your story; silence frames your words.

Teacher comments:

Vocal quality is attained when you fully support your voice with breath and spine. Without this support, there can be tension in your voice. Breathe deeply through your mouth to sustain quality through to the end of sentences.

Story:

Artistic choices contribute to the development of your own storytelling *style.* Make choices with which you are comfortable and that are congruent with your personality.

Make the *characters* in your story vivid and memorable.

If applicable, develop the *plot* with a clear beginning, middle, and end. The logical, linear sequence valued in western aesthetics is not universal to all cultures.

Teacher comments:

Permission granted to reproduce from *Encountering Children's Literature: An Arts Approach* by Jane M. Gangi.

BOOK REVIEW GUIDE

Depending on the genre you choose, your book review is due during the session on historical literature (Chapter 9), biography (Chapter 10), contemporary realism (Chapter 11), or fantasy and science fiction (Chapter 12). Sign up for your book review so that we do not have duplicates.

NCATE Program Standard 2a.

Write a two-page single-space book review of a novel, novella, or chapter book. Include a short summary of the book and your reflections on some of the following: characters, plot, theme, setting, point of view, tone, favorite quotes, and an indication of how the book could be used in the classroom. Also include complete bibliographical information. Photocopy for the class—preferably double sided. This assignment is due on the same date of the category you have chosen—for example, *The Wind and the Willows* during the session on fantasy; *Chevrolet Saturdays* during the session on contemporary realism; *The Arrow over the Door* during the session on historical fiction. Biography spans two sessions—historical literature and "Life's Experiences and Life's Callings." If you choose biography, you decide whether your biography does more to illuminate a historical era or to illuminate a career or calling, then sign up for that date.

When you are preparing the book review, imagine yourself as a textbook writer and consider what is of most value for your classmates. On the day you hand out your copies to your classmates, give a brief "book talk." Briefly,

- Give a summary of the book
- Tell why you chose the book and why you like it
- Share a short favorite quote

Optionally,

- Share how your book connects with other books we've read or heard about
- Tell about one of the characters you especially connected with

Hopefully, you'll inspire your classmates to want to read the book you've chosen for themselves.

When orally presenting your book, keep in mind Nancie Atwell's metaphor of her dining room table: Discussing these books should be as comfortable as the discussions held around your dining room table about books or movies. As future teachers who will be called on to talk in front of groups for the rest of your life, keep the following in mind:

- Do not read your notes or outline. Instead, talk conversationally, looking mostly at your classmates, looking down to refer to your notes occasionally.
- Aim for fluency, avoiding "ums" and "uhs" and "you knows" and "you know what I means" and "like." Dr. Bunny Calabrese offers this: Silence is the frame that enhances the picture (the frame does not have to be cluttered with "ums," "uhs," etc.).
- Credibility requires that we speak both from our background and in standard English: "mutter's sneakuhs" and "mother's sneakers." Only *you* can change it. Prior to student teaching, you could ask a partner to monitor disfluencies.
- Based on Kristin Linklater's *Freeing the Natural Voice,* the best posture is to imagine puppeteer's strings attached to the top of your skull and your sternum. This is the best way to support your spine, which supports your breath, which supports your voice (sound). Take a deep breath before beginning long sentences; this will carry you through *and* calm your nerves.

Permission granted to reproduce from *Encountering Children's Literature: An Arts Approach* by Jane M. Gangi.

GUIDE FOR RESPONDING TO THE VISUAL ARTS

(Prepared with the assistance of art professor Jack DeGraffenreid)

Hand in this form with your paper. Due on Session 7 _____

Name _____   Book _____

> NCATE Program Standard 2f.

PERFORMANCE TASK: Choose one picture book that appeals to you from any genre. In no more than two double-space pages, write four paragraphs. In the first paragraph, describe why you chose the book and why it appeals to you; I will not evaluate this because it is your personal response.

In the subsequent three paragraphs, discuss the elements, style, and media of art. In addition to the following questions, see Chapter 4.5 for definitions of the elements, styles, and media of art. Use the table in Chapter 4 to help you look at the visual art aspects of children's literature, and review the questions in the text in Chapter 4.1.

You will receive either a "pass" or a "redo."

The following questions are suggestions. You do not have to answer every one in your paper.

Elements of Art

How does line create and support shape?

How are light and dark used?

Does line create a physical sensibility (space and movement)?

How does line help construct images? In what kind of perspective?

Do the values, or colors, help contribute to a strong sense of emphasis?

Style of Art

Does the artist's choice of style serve as a unifying construct?

Is the style of art distinct? Does it resemble or is it influenced by any of those discussed in Chapter 4.5?

Is the style representational or nonrepresentational?

Can you see the elements of style: Rhythm? Repetition? Scale? Shape (positive and negative)? Proportion? Emphasis?

Media of Art

Describe the media of art. Is it dry (graphite, charcoal, etc.) or wet (ink, watercolor, etc.)?

Permission granted to reproduce from *Encountering Children's Literature: An Arts Approach* by Jane M. Gangi.

Notes

1. Marcia Mentkowski et al., *Learning That Lasts: Integrating Learning, Development, and Performance in College and Beyond* (San Francisco: Jossey-Bass, 2000), p. 224. See also Susan Sellman Obler, Julie Stark, and Linda Umdenstock, "Classroom Assessment." In: *Making a Difference: Outcomes of a Decade of Assessment in Higher Education,* Trudy W. Banta et al., eds. (San Francisco: Jossey-Bass, 1993), p. 216.
2. Georgine Loacker, Lucy Cromwell, and Kathleen O'Brien, "Assessment in Higher Education: To Serve the Learner." In: *Assessment in American Higher Education: Issues and Contexts,* Clifford Adelman, ed. (Washington, DC: Office of Educational Research and Improvement, U.S. Department of Education, 1986).
3. Kristin Linklater, *Freeing the Natural Voice* (New York: Drama Book Publishers, 1976).

More Professional Literature and Resources

Books

American Library Association. 1999. *The Newbery and Caldecott Awards: A Guide to the Medal and Honor Books.* Chicago, IL: American Library Association.

Ammon, Bette D., and Gale W. Sherman. 2000. *Handbook for the Newbery Medal and Honor Books, 1990–1999.* Fort Atkinson, WI: Alleyside Press/Highsmith.

———. 1991. *Handbook for the Newbery Medal and Honor Books, 1980–1989.* Hagerstown, MD: Alleyside Press.

Butler, Francelia, Anne Devereaux Jordan, and Richard Rotert. 1987. *The Wide World All Around: An Anthology of Children's Literature.* New York: Longman.

Cameron, Eleanor. 1993. *The Seed and the Vision: On the Writing and Appreciation of Children's Books.* New York: Dutton.

Chambers, Aidan. 1983. *Introducing Books to Children.* 2nd ed. Boston: The Horn Book.

Gillespie, John T., and Corinne J. Naden. 2001. *The Newbery Companion: Booktalk and Related Materials for Newbery Medal and Honor Books.* Englewood, CO: Libraries Unlimited.

Huck, Charlotte, Susan Hepler, Janet Hickman, and Barbara K. Kiefer. 2001. *Children's Literature in the Elementary School.* 7th ed. Dubuque, IA: McGraw-Hill.

Hurst, Carol Otis, with Margaret Sullivan Ahearn, Leslie Jacquelin Clark, Lynn Otis Palmer, and James Neill Yvon. 1991. *Long Ago and Far Away . . . : An Encyclopedia for Successfully Using Literature with Intermediate Readers.* Allen, TX: DLM.

Jenkins, Carol Brennan. 1999. *The Allure of Authors: Author Studies in the Elementary Classroom.* Portsmouth, NH: Heinemann.

Konigsburg, E. L. 1995. *Talk Talk: A Children's Book Author Speaks to Grown-Ups.* New York: Atheneum.

Levene, Donna B. 1993. *Music through Children's Literature: Theme and Variations.* Englewood, CO: Teacher Ideas Press.

Lukens, Rebecca. 2003. *A Critical Handbook of Children's Literature.* 7th ed. Boston: Allyn & Bacon.

Lurie, Alison. 1990. *Don't Tell the Grown-Ups: The Subversive Power of Children's Literature.* Boston: Little, Brown.

McClure, Amy A., and Janice V. Kristo, eds. 1996. *Books That Invite Talk, Wonder, and Play.* Urbana, IL: National Council of Teachers of English.

McGillis, Roderick. 1996. *The Nimble Reader: Literary Theory and Children's Literature.* New York: Twayne.

Nodelman, Perry, and Mavis Reimer. 2003. *The Pleasures of Children's Literature.* 3rd ed. Boston: Allyn & Bacon.

Norton, Donna E., Saundra E. Norton, and Amy McClure. 2003. *Through the Eyes of the Child: An Introduction to Children's Literature.* 6th ed. Upper Saddle River, NJ: Merrill/Prentice Hall.

Rahn, Suzanne. 1995. *Rediscoveries in Children's Literature.* New York: Garland.

Rothlein, Liz, and Anita Meyer Meinbach. 1996. *Legacies: Using Children's Literature in the Classroom.* New York: HarperCollins.

Rudman, Masha Kabakow. 1995. *Children's Literature: An Issues Approach.* 3rd ed. New York: Longman.

Short, Kathy G., ed. 1995. *Research and Professional Resources in Children's Literature: Piecing a Patchwork Quilt.* Newark, DE: International Reading Association.

Sutherland, Zena, and May Hill Arbuthnot. 1997. *Children and Books.* 9th ed. New York: HarperCollins.

Taylor, Denny, and Dorothy Strickland. 1986. *Family Storybook Reading.* Portsmouth, NH: Heinemann.

Temple, Charles, Miriam Martinez, Junko Yokota, and Alice Naylor. 1998. *Children's Books in Children's Hands.* Boston: Allyn & Bacon.

Thompson, Michael Clay. 1995. *Classics in the Classroom.* 2nd ed. Unionville, NY: Royal Fireworks.

Reading and Language Arts

Harvey, Stephanie, and Anne Goudvis. 2000. *Strategies That Work: Teaching Comprehension to Enhance Understanding.* Portland, ME: Stenhouse.

Hindley, Joanne. 1996. *In the Company of Children.* Stemmer, ME: Stenhouse.

Krashen, Stephen. 1993. *The Power of Reading: Insights from Research.* Englewood, CO: Libraries Unlimited, Inc.

Miller, Debbie. 2002. *Reading with Meaning: Teaching Comprehension in the Primary Grades.* Portland, ME: Stenhouse.

Moffett, James, and Betty Jane Wagner. 1992. *Student-Centered Language Arts, K–12.* Portsmouth, NH: Heinemann.

Routman, Regie. 2003. *Reading Essentials: The Specifics You Need to Teach Reading Well.* Portsmouth, NH: Heinemann.

———. 2000. *Conversations: Strategies for Teaching, Learning, and Evaluating.* Portsmouth, NH: Heinemann.

———. 1991. *Invitations: Changing as Teachers and Learners.* Portsmouth, NH: Heinemann.

Taylor, Denny, and Catherine Dorsey–Gaines. 1988. *Growing Up Literate.* Portsmouth, NH: Heinemann.

Yopp, Ruth Helen, and Hallie Kay Yopp. 1992. *Literature-Based Reading Activities.* Boston: Allyn & Bacon.

Journals

See the end of Chapter 3 for more.

Book Links
Bulletin of the Center for Children's Books
Children's Literature Association Quarterly (has a cultural pluralism column)
Children's Literature in Education
The Dragon Lode
The Five Owls
The Horn Book
Kirkus Reviews
The Lion and the Unicorn
The New Advocate
The Reading Teacher
School Library Journal
TALL (Teaching and Learning Literature)
The Washington Post Book Review

Online Journals and Resources

Carol Hurst's Children's Literature Site:
   www.carolhurst.com/

ERIC Clearinghouse on Reading, English, and Communication:
   www.indiana.edu/ ~ eric_rec/comatt/childlit.html

University of Calgary:
   www.acs.ucalgary.ca/ ~ dkbrown/index.html

Vandergrift's Children's Literature Page:
   www.scils.rutgers.edu/ ~ kvander/

Children's Magazines

Chickdadee
Owl Communications Group
Contactkids, www.contactkids.org
Cricket, www.cricketmag.com
Guideposts for Kids, www.gp4k.com
Highlights for Children, www.Highlights.com
Ladybug
Owl, www.owlkids.com
3–2–1 Contact

More Awards

Children's Book Council:
A comprehensive online database on awards is available at:
   www.awardsandprizes.cbcbooks.org/

Children's Literature Awards, A–Z:
   www.literature-awards.com/childrens_literature.htm

Individual states also have their own awards—for example, the Sasquatch Children's Book Award for the state of Washington and the Nutmeg Book Award for the state of Connecticut. On the Internet, type in the name of the state you want, followed by "children's book award."

Children's Literature Bibliographies: A Dessert Menu

Through the various encounters and suggested activities in this book, you can experience children's literature in a variety of ways during class time. Outside of class time, you can continue your experience with children's literature through reading. The full bibliographies are too large to include in this book, thus a full version of this appendix is posted at: http://faculty.sacredheart.edu/gangij. You can do word searches and you can download the sections that are interesting to you. Over a dozen children's literature experts helped develop these bibliographies: Connie Rockman, Julie Cummins, Laurie Brooks, Gayle Sergel, Barbara Reed, Joseph Bruchac, Jackie Norcel, Terry Neu, Karen Romano Young, Gabriella Kaye, Lyn Miller-Lachmann, Susanna Reich, and Mary Jackson Scroggins. Former students and friends helped, too: Madhavi Doshi, Constance Bond, Toby Elberger, and Alice Hutchinson. The consultants are introduced on the website in the section to which they contributed.

What follows is a dessert menu—*my* dessert menu, informed by the consultants. If you, or anyone else, were writing this book, you'd have different "desserts." The structure of the bibliographies frames the possibilities in literature for you as a reader and you as a teacher. I think you'll find, as I have, that much of what follows is literature that appeals to all ages. The asterick (*) means either the author or the illustrator is of color and, often, is a cultural insider. The plus sign (+) means that the book is both in English and another language.

Classics: Picture Storybooks That Have Lasted (Before 1960)

Burton, Virginia Lee. 1939. *Mike Mulligan and His Steam Shovel.* Boston: Houghton.

Daugherty, James. 1938. *Andy and the Lion.* New York: Viking.

Gág, Wanda. 1928. *Millions of Cats.* New York: Coward.

Johnson, Crockett. 1955. *Harold and the Purple Crayon.* New York: HarperCollins.

McCloskey, Robert. 1941. *Make Way for Ducklings.* New York: Viking.

Seuss, Dr. 1938. *The 500 Hats of Bartholomew Cubbins.* New York: Vanguard.

Shaw, Charles G. 1988 [1947]. *It Looked Like Spilt Milk.* New York: Harper.

Picture Storybooks: Biography and Autobiography

NOTE: The following books can connect with both historical literature (Chapter 9) and with biographies grouped by career (Chapter 10).

*Bruchac, Joseph. 2000. *Crazy Horse's Vision.* Illustrated by S. D. Nelson. New York: Lee & Low.

*Cha, Dia. 1996. *Dia's Story Cloth: The Hmong People's Journey of Freedom.* Stitched by Chue and Nhia Thao Cha. New York: Lee & Low and Denver Museum of Natural History.

*+Garza, Carmen. 1996. *In My Family/En mi familia.* As told to Harriet Rohmer. David Schecter, ed. San Francisco: Children's Book Press.

*Hopkinson, Deborah. 1999. *A Band of Angels: A Story Inspired by the Jubilee Singers.* Illustrated by Raúl Colón. New York: Atheneum.

*Lawrence, Jacob. 1993 [1968]. *Harriet and the Promised Land.* New York: Simon and Schuster.

*Mora, Pat. 2002. *A Library for Juana: The World of Sor Juana Ines.* Illustrated by Beatriz Vidal. New York: Knopf.

*———. 1997. *Tomás and the Library Lady.* Illustrated by Raul Colón. New York: Knopf.

*Pinkney, Andrea Davis. 1998. *Duke Ellington: The Piano Prince and His Orchestra.* Illustrated by Brian Pinkney. New York: Hyperion.

*Rockwell, Anne. 2000. *Only Passing Through: The Story of Sojourner Truth.* Illustrated by R. Gregory Christie. New York: Knopf.

*Ryan, Pam Muñoz. 2002. *When Marian Sang: The True Recital of Marian Anderson.* Illustrated by Brian Selznick. New York: Scholastic.

*Schroeder, Alan. 1996. *Satchmo's Blues.* Illustrated by Floyd Cooper. New York: Doubleday.

*Tallchief, Maria, with Rosemary Wells. 1999. *Tallchief: America's Prima Ballerina.* Illustrated by Gary Kelley. New York: Viking.

Picture Storybooks: Contemporary Realism

Aliki. 1998. *Miranthe's Story One: Painted Words* and *Miranthe's Story Two: Spoken Memories.* New York: Greenwillow.

*Anderson, Laurie Halse. 1996. *Ndito Runs.* Illustrated by Anita van der Merwe. New York: Holt. (Kenya)

Bunting, Eve. 1990. *The Wall.* Illustrated by Ronald Himler. New York: Clarion.

*Córdova, Amy. 1997. *Abuelita's Heart.* New York: Simon and Schuster.

English, Karen. 1999. *Nadia's Hands.* Illustrated by Jonathan Weiner. Honesdale, PA: Boyds Mills. (Pakistani American)

Garland, Sherry. 1993. *The Lotus Seed.* Illustrated by Tatsuo Kiuchi. San Diego: Harcourt. (Vietnamese)

*Gray, Libba Moore. 1995. *My Mama Had a Dancing Heart.* Illustrated by Raúl Colón. New York: Orchard.

*Khan, Rukhsana. 1998. *The Roses in My Carpets.* Illustrated by Ronald Himler. New York: Holiday. (Afghanistan)

LaMarche, Jim. 2000. *Raft.* New York: HarperCollins.

Lessac, Frané. 1984. *My Little Island.* New York: HarperCollins. (Caribbean)

Matze, Claire Sidhom. 1999. *The Stars in My Geddoh's Sky.* Morton Grove, IL: Whitman. (Middle East)

*⁺Pérez, Amada Irma. 2000. *My Very Own Room/Mi propio cuartito.* Illustrated by Maya Christina Gonzalez. San Francisco: Children's Book Press.

*Pinkney, Brian. 1994. *Max Found Two Sticks.* New York: Simon and Schuster.

Polacco, Patricia. 1998. *Thank You, Mr. Falker.* New York: Philomel. (reading difficulty)

Seymour, Tres. 1993. *Hunting the White Cow.* Illustrated by Wendy Anderson Halperin. New York: Orchard. (Appalachia)

*Smith, Cynthia Leitich. 2000. *Jingle Dancer.* Illustrated by Cornelius Van Wright and Ying-Hwa Hu. New York: Morrow.

*Steptoe, John. 1969. *Stevie.* New York: HarperCollins.

*Zolotow, Charlotte. 1972. *William's Doll.* Illustrated by William Pène du Bois. New York: HarperCollins.

Picture Storybooks: Fantasy

Barrett, Judi. 1978. *Cloudy with a Chance of Meatballs.* Illustrated by Ron Barrett. New York: Atheneum.

*Blood, Charles, and Martin Link. 1976. *The Goat in the Rug.* Illustrated by Nancy Winslow Parker. New York: Macmillan.

Cherry, Lynne. 1990. *The Great Kapok Tree.* San Diego: Harcourt.

Cronin, Doreen. 2000. *Click, Clack, Moo: Cows That Type.* Illustrated by Betsy Lewin. New York: Simon and Schuster.

*Dawavendewa, Gerald. 2001. *The Butterfly Dance.* Washington, DC: National Museum of the American Indian/Abbeville.

Fox, Mem. 1994. *Tough Boris.* Illustrated by Kathryn Brown. San Diego: Harcourt.

Hayes, Geoffrey. 1976. *Bear by Himself.* New York: Harper.

*Hoberman, Mary Ann. 2001. *It's Simple, Said Simon.* Illustrated by Meilo So. New York: Knopf. (movement)

Lester, Helen. 1988. *Tacky the Penguin.* Illustrated by Lynn Munsinger. Boston: Houghton.

Ryan, Cheli. 1971. *Hildilid's Night.* Illustrated by Arnold Lobel. New York: Macmillan.

Sendak, Maurice. 1963. *Where the Wild Things Are.* New York: Harper.

Seuss, Dr. 1973. *Did I Ever Tell You How Lucky You Are?* New York: Random House.

Swope, Sam. 1989. *The Araboolies of Liberty Street.* Illustrated by Barry Root. New York: Clarkson Potter. (tolerance theme)

Van Allsburg, Chris. 1982. *Ben's Dream.* Boston: Houghton.

Wells, Rosemary. 1997, 1998. *The McDuff Stories.* Illustrated by Susan Jeffers. New York: Hyperion.

Picture Storybooks: Historical Fiction

NOTE: These picture books can connect with the historical eras found in the bibliography for Chapter 9.

Bartone, Elisa. 1993. *Peppe the Lamplighter.* Illustrated by Ted Lewin. New York: Scholastic.

*Carling, Amelia Lau. 1998. *Mama and Papa Have a Store.* New York: Dial. (Chinese family in Guatemala, 1940s)

*Chocolate, Debbi. 1998. *The Piano Man.* Illustrated by Eric Velasquez. New York: Walker.

Cooney, Barbara. 1982. *Miss Rumphius.* New York: Viking.

*English, Karen. 1996. *Neeny Coming, Neeny Going.* Illustrated by Synthia Saint James. Mahwah, NJ: BridgeWater. (Dasufuskie Island, South Carolina, 1950s)

*Howard, Elizabeth Fitzgerald. 2000. *Virgie Goes to School with Us Boys.* Illustrated by E. B. Lewis. New York: Simon and Schuster.

Lorbiecki, Marybeth. 1998. *Sister Anne's Hands.* Illustrated by K. Wendy Popp. New York: Dial.

*McKissack, Patricia. 2001. *Goin' Someplace Special.* Illustrated by Jerry Pinkney. New York: Atheneum. (Jim Crow, 1950s)

McLerran, Alice. 1991. *Roxaboxen.* Illustrated by Barbara Cooney. New York: Lothrop. (Arizona)

*Mitchell, Margaree King. 1993. *Uncle Jed's Barber Shop.* Illustrated by James Ransome. New York: Simon and Schuster.

*Pace, Lorenzo. 2001. *Jalani and the Lock.* New York: PowerKids.

*Ringgold, Faith. 1991. *Tar Beach.* New York: Crown.

Schroeder, Alan. 1995. *Carolina Shout!* Illustrated by Bernie Fuchs. New York: Dial.

*Williams, Sherley Anne. 1998. *Working Cotton.* Illustrated by Carole Byard. San Diego: Harcourt.

*Woodson, Jacqueline. 2001. *The Other Side.* Illustrated by E. B. Lewis. New York: Putnam's.

Picture Storybooks: Wordless

*Anno, Mitsumasa. 1978. *Anno's Italy.* New York: Collins.

Bang, Molly. 1980. *The Grey Lady and the Strawberry Snatcher.* New York: Four Winds.

Banyai, Istvan. 1995. *Zoom.* New York: Viking.

Briggs, Raymond. 1978. *The Snowman.* New York: Random House.

Weitzman, Jacqueline Preiss, and Robin Preiss Glasser. 1998. *You Can't Take a Balloon into the Metropolitan Museum.* New York: Dial.

Wiesner, David. 1991. *Tuesday.* New York: Clarion.

Multiple Concepts

Carle, Eric. 1969. *The Very Hungry Caterpillar.* New York: Philomel.

Freymann, Saxton, and Joost Elffers. 1999. *How Are You Peeling? Foods with Moods.* New York: Scholastic.

Jonas, Ann. 1983. *Round Trip.* New York: Greenwillow.

Concept Picture Books: Alphabet

Agard, John. 1989. *Calypso Alphabet.* Illustrated by Jennifer Bent. New York: Holt. (Caribbean)

Azarian, Mary. 1981. *A Farmer's Alphabet.* Boston: Godine.

*Cline-Ransome, Lesa. 2001. *Quilt Alphabet.* Illustrated by James Ransome. New York: Holiday.

Crane, Walter. 1981 [1874]. *An Alphabet of Old Friends and The Absurd ABC.* New York: Metropolitan Museum of Art and Thames and Hudson.

Crosbie, Michael J. 2000. *Arches to Zigzags: An Architecture ABC.* Photography by Steve and Kit Rosenthal. New York: Abrams.

*de Cumptich, Roberto de Vicq. 2000. *Bembo's Zoo: An Animal ABC Book.* New York: Holt.

Fisher, Leonard Everett. 1991. *The ABC Exhibit.* New York: Macmillan.

Johnson, Stephen T. 1995. *Alphabet City.* New York: Viking.

Mendoza, George. 1970. *The Marcel Marceau Alphabet Book.* New York: Doubleday.

Micklethwait, Lucy, sel. 1992. *I Spy! An Alphabet in Art.* New York: Greenwillow.

Provensen, Alice, and Martin Provensen. 1978. *A Peaceable Kingdom: The Shaker Abecedarius.* New York: Viking.

Schmiderer, Dorothy. 1971. *The Alphabeast Book: An Abecedarium.* New York: Holt.

Van Allsburg, Chris. 1987. *The Z Was Zapped.* Boston: Houghton.

Concept Picture Books: Colors

Carle, Eric. 1998. *Hello Red Fox.* New York: Simon and Schuster.

*Chocolate, Debbi. 1996. *Kente Colors.* Illustrated by John Ward. New York: Walker.

Priceman, Marjorie. 2001. *It's Me, Marva!: A Story about Color and Optical Illusions.* New York: Knopf.

*Thong, Roseanne. 2001. *Red Is a Dragon: A Book of Colors.* Illustrated by Grace Lin. San Francisco: Chronicle.

Walsh, Ellen Stoll. 1988. *Mouse Paint.* San Diego: Harcourt.

Concept Picture Books: Counting

*Crews, Donald. 1968. *Ten Black Dots.* New York: Morrow.

*Feelings, Muriel. 1971. *Moja Means One: Swahili Counting Book.* Illustrated by Tom Feelings. New York: Dial.

Geisert, Arthur. 1992. *Pigs from One to Ten.* Boston: Houghton.

Johnson, Stephen T. 1998. *City by Numbers.* New York: Viking.

MacDonald, Suse, and Bill Oaks. 1988. *Numblers.* New York: Dial.

*+Mora, Pat. 1996. *Uno, dos, tres: One, Two, Three.* Illustrated by Barbara Lavallee. New York: Clarion.

Rankin, Laura. 1998. *The Handmade Counting Book.* New York: Dial.

Concept Picture Books: Manners

Buehner, Caralyn. 1995. *It's a Spoon, Not a Shovel.* Illustrated by Mark Buehner. New York: Dial.

Concept Picture Books: Months

Arnold, Tedd. 1990. *Mother Goose's Words of Wit and Wisdom: A Book of Months.* New York: Dial.

Provensen, Alice, and Martin Provensen. 1984. *The Year at Maple Hill Farm.* New York: Atheneum.

Updike, John. 1999. *A Child's Calendar.* Illustrated by Trina Schart Hyman. New York: Holiday.

Concept Picture Books: Opposites

+Emberley, Rebecca. 2000. *My Opposites/Mis opuestos.* Boston: Little, Brown.

Hoban, Tana. 1997. *Exactly the Opposite.* New York: Mulberry.

Concept Picture Books: Shapes

Burns, Marilyn. 1994. *The Greedy Triangle.* Illustrated by Gordon Silveria. New York: Scholastic.

Hoban, Tana. 2000. *Cubes, Cones, Cylinders and Spheres.* New York: Greenwillow.

*+Rosa-Mendoza, Gladys. 2000. *Colors and Shapes/Los colores y las figuras.* Illustrated by Michele Noiset. Wheaton, IL: Me-mi Publishing.

Concept Picture Books: Transportation

*Crews, Donald. 1986. *Flying.* New York: Greenwillow.

*———. 1980. *Truck.* New York: Greenwillow.

*————. 1978. *Freight Train.* New York: Greenwillow.

Dotlich, Rebecca Kai. 2000. *Away We Go!* New York: HarperCollins.

Picture Storybooks: Reprints of Old/Rare Stories

Bonn, Franz. 1975 [1878]. *The Children's Theatre.* New York: Viking. (toy book)

Nister, Ernest. 1985. *Moving Pictures.* New York: Philomel. (toy book)

Bibliography for Chapter 5
Poetry: The Music of Language

Collections and Anthologies

* + Alarcón, Francisco X. 1999. *Angels Ride Bikes and Other Fall Poems/Los ángeles andan en bicicleta y otros poemas de otoño.* Illustrated by Maya Christina Gonzalez. San Francisco: Children's Book Press. (sequels)

*Begay, Shonto. 1995. *Navajo Visions and Voices across the Mesa.* New York: Scholastic.

*Berry, James. 1991. *When I Dance.* Illustrated by Karen Barbour. San Diego: Harcourt.

*Brooks, Gwendolyn. 1956. *Bronzeville Boys and Girls.* Illustrated by Ronni Solbert. New York: Harper.

*Bruchac, Joseph, and Jonathan London. 1992. *Thirteen Moons on Turtle's Back: A Native American Year of Moons.* Illustrated by Thomas Locker. New York: Philomel.

Cole, Joanna, and Stephanie Calmenson. 1993. *Six Sick Sheep: 101 Tongue Twisters.* Illustrated by Alan Tiegreen. New York: Scholastic.

Cullinan, Berenice E. 1995. *A Jar of Tiny Stars: NCTE Award-Winning Poets.* Honesdale, PA: Wordsong.

* + Delacre, Lulu, sel. 1989. *Arroz con leche: Popular Songs and Rhymes from Latin America.* New York: Scholastic.

de Regniers, Beatrice Schenck, Eva Moore, Mary Michaels White, and Jan Carr, sels. 1988. *Sing a Song of Popcorn: Every Child's Book of Poems.* Illustrated by nine Caldecott Medal-winning artists. New York: Scholastic.

Dickinson, Emily. 1978. *I'm Nobody! Who Are You? Poems of Emily Dickinson for Young People.* Owings Mills, MD: Stemmer.

*Dunbar, Paul. 1999. *Jump Back Honey: The Poems of Paul Laurence Dunbar.* Illustrated by Ashley Bryan, Carole Byard, Jan Spivey Gilchrist, Brian Pinkney, Jerry Pinkney and Faith Ringgold. New York: Hyperion.

Dunning, Stephen, Edward Lueders, and Hugh Smith. 1967. *Reflections on a Gift of Watermelon Pickle . . . and Other Modern Verse.* New York: Lothrop.

Fleischman, Paul. 1988. *Joyful Noise: Poems for Two Voices.* Illustrated by Eric Beddows. New York: HarperCollins.

Florian, Douglas. 1994. *Bing Bang Boing.* San Diego: Harcourt.

*Giovanni, Nikki. 1993 [1973]. *ego-tripping and other poems for young people.* Illustrated by George Ford. New York: Lawrence Hill.

*Hallworth, Grace. 1996. *Down by the River: Afro-Caribbean Rhymes, Games, and Songs for Children.* Illustrated by Caroline Binch. New York: Scholastic. (Trinidad)

* + Herrera, Juan Felipe. 1998. *Laughing out Loud, I Fly: Poems in English and Spanish.* Illustrated by Karen Barbour. New York: HarperCollins.

*Ho, Minfong, trans. 1996. *Maples in the Mist: Children's Poems from the Tang Dynasty.* Illustrated by Jean and Mou-sien Tseng. New York: Lothrop.

Hoberman, Mary Ann, sel. 1994. *My Song Is Beautiful: Poems and Pictures in Many Voices.* Boston: Little, Brown.

*Hughes, Langston. 1994 [1932]. *The Dream Keeper and Other Poems.* Illustrated by Brian Pinkney. New York: Knopf.

Janeczko, Paul B., sel. 2001. *A Poke in the I: A Collection of Concrete Poems.* Illustrated by Chris Raschka. Cambridge, MA: Candlewick.

Koch, Kenneth, and Kate Farrell. 1985. *Talking to the Sun.* New York: The Metropolitan Museum of Art/Holt.

Larrick, Nancy, ed. 1985 [1968]. *Piping Down the Valleys Wild.* Illustrated by Ellen Raskin. New York: Delacorte.

Mavor, Salley, sel. 1997. *You and Me: Poems of Friendship.* Illustrated by Salley Mavor. New York: Orchard.

McCord, David. 1971. *Take Sky: More Rhymes of the Never Was and Always Is.* New York: Dell.

Milne, A. A. 1961 [1924]. *When We Were Very Young.* Illustrated by Ernest Shepard. New York: Dutton.

Morrison, Lillian, comp. 1992. *At the Crack of the Bat: Baseball Poems.* Illustrated by Steve Cieslawski. New York: Hyperion.

*Nye, Naomi Shihab. 1998. *The Space between Our Footsteps: Poems and Paintings from the Middle East.* New York: Simon and Schuster. (Israeli and Palestinian contributions)

* + Orozco, José-Luis. 1997. *Diez deditos/Ten Little Fingers and Other Play Rhymes and Action Songs from Latin America.* Illustrated by Elisa Kleven. New York: Dutton. (available on CD and cassette)

Panzer, Nora, ed. 1994. *Celebrate America in Poetry and Art.* Paintings, sculpture, drawings, photographs, and other works of art from the National Museum of American Art, Smithsonian. New York: Hyperion.

Richards, Laura E. 1955 [1902]. *Tirra Lirra: Rhymes Old and New.* Illustrated by Marguerite Davis. Boston: Little, Brown.

*Rochelle, Belinda, sel. 2001. *Words with Wings: A Treasury of African-American Poetry.* New York: HarperCollins.

Rossetti, Christina. 1968 [1872]. *Sing-Song: A Nursery Rhyme Book.* Illustrated by Arthur Hughes. New York: Dover.

Schertle, Alice. 1994. *How Now, Brown Cow?* Illustrated by Amanda Schaffer. San Diego: Harcourt.

Smith, Jessie Wilcox. 1913. *The Little Mother Goose.* New York: Dodd.

*Steptoe, Javaka. 1997. *In Daddy's Arms I Am Tall: African Americans Celebrating Fathers*. New York: Lee & Low.

Stevenson, Robert Louis. 1905. *A Child's Garden of Verses*. Illustrated by Jessie Wilcox Smith. New York: Scribner.

Wilbur, Richard. 2000. *The Pig in the Spigot*. Illustrated by J. Otto Seibold. San Diego: Harcourt.

*Wong, Janet S. 1994. *Good Luck Gold and Other Poems*. New York: Macmillan.

Worth, Valerie. 1994. *All the Small Poems and Fourteen More*. Illustrated by Natalie Babbitt. New York: Farrar.

Single Editions

Adoff, Arnold. 1973. *Black Is Brown Is Tan*. Illustrated by Emily Arnold McCully. New York: HarperCollins.

Appelt, Kathi. 1995. *Bayou Lullaby*. Illustrated by Neil Waldman. New York: Morrow.

*Barnwell, Ysaye M. 1998. *No Mirrors in My Nana's House*. Illustrated by Synthia Saint James. San Diego: Harcourt.

Conover, Chris. 1986. *Froggie Went A-Courting*. New York: Farrar.

———. 1976. *Six Little Ducks*. New York: Crowell.

Frost, Robert. 1978. *Stopping by Woods on a Snowy Evening*. Illustrated by Susan Jeffers. New York: Dutton.

Gerber, Carole. 1997. *Hush! A Gaelic Lullaby*. Illustrated by Marty Husted. Danvers, MA: Whispering Coyote Press.

*Giovanni, Nikki. 1994. *Knoxville, Tennessee*. New York: Scholastic.

*Grimes, Nikki. 1994. *Meet Danitra Brown*. Illustrated by Floyd Cooper. New York: Lothrop.

*Ho, Minfong. 1996. *Hush! A Thai Lullaby*. Illustrated by Holly Meade. New York: Orchard.

Jeffers, Susan. 1973. *Three Jovial Huntsmen*. New York: Bradbury.

Moss, Lloyd. 1995. *Zin! Zin! Zin! A Violin*. Illustrated by Marjorie Priceman. New York: Simon and Schuster. (introduces both musical instruments and counting)

*Nikola-Lisa, W. 1994. *Bein' with You This Way*. Illustrated by Michael Bryant. New York: Lee & Low.

Paxton, Tom. 1996. *The Marvelous Toy*. Illustrated by Elizabeth Sayles. New York: Metropolitan Teaching and Learning Co.

Serfozo, Mary. 1990. *Rain Talk*. Illustrated by Keiko Narahashi. New York: Macmillan.

Strauss, Barbara, and Helen Friedland. 1987. *See You Later Alligator*. . . . Illustrated by Tershia d'Elgin. Los Angeles: Price/Stern/ Sloan.

Thayer, Ernest Lawrence. 2000. *Casey at the Bat: A Ballad of the Republic Sung in the Year 1888*. Illustrated by Christopher Bing. Brooklyn, NY: Handprint.

*Thomas, Joyce Carol. 1993. *Brown Honey in Broomwheat Tea*. Illustrated by Floyd Cooper. New York: HarperCollins.

Vozar, David. 1998. *Rapunzel: A Happenin' Rap*. Illustrated by Betsy Lewin. New York: Doubleday.

———. 1993. *Yo, Hungry Wolf! A Nursery Rap*. Illustrated by Betsy Lewin. New York: Doubleday.

Poetry by Children

*Adedjouma, Davida, ed. 1996. *The Palm of My Heart: Poetry by African American Children*. Illustrated by Gregory Christie. New York: Lee & Low.

Koch, Kenneth. 1973. *Rose, Where Did You Get That Red? Teaching Great Poetry to Children*. New York: Random House.

*National Museum of the American Indian, Smithsonian Institution. 1999. *When the Rain Sings: Poems by Young Native Americans*. New York: Simon and Schuster.

*Sneve, Virginia Driving Hawk, sel. 1989. *Dancing Teepees: Poems of American Indian Youth*. Illustrated by Stephen Gammell. New York: Holiday.

*Volavkova, Hana, ed. 1993. *I Never Saw Another Butterfly: Children's Drawings and Poems from Terezín Concentration Camps*. New York: McGraw-Hill.

Bibliography for Chapter 6 Drama: The Art of the Present

Asher, Sandra Fenichel. 1993. *A Woman Called Truth: A Play in 2 Acts Celebrating the Life of Sojourner Truth*. Woodstock, IL: Dramatic Publishing.

———. 1992. *The Wise Men of Chelm*. Woodstock, IL: Dramatic Publishing.

Barchers, Suzanne I. 1993. *Readers Theatre for Beginning Readers*. Englewood, CO: Teachers Ideas Press.

Behm, Tom. 1990. *The Tarheel: From Stories Collected by Richard Chase*. Louisville, KY: Anchorage Press Plays.

Brooks, Laurie. 2001. *Devon's Hurt*. Woodstock, IL: Dramatic Publishing.

———. 1994. *Selkie*. Louisville, KY: Anchorage Press Plays.

*Bruchac, Joseph. 2000. *Pushing up the Sky: Seven Native American Plays for Children*. Illustrated by Teresa Flavin. New York: Dial.

*Bush, Max. 2001. *Ezigbo the Spirit Child*. An Igbo story as told by Adaora Nzelibe Schmiedl. Louisville, KY: Anchorage Press Plays.

Charlip, Remy, and Burton Supree. 2001. *Mother Mother I Feel Sick Send for the Doctor Quick Quick Quick*. Illustrated by Remy Charlip. Berkeley, CA: Tricycle Press. (shadow puppetry)

Gibson, William. 1960. *The Miracle Worker*. New York: Samuel French.

Harris, Aurand. 1980. *The Arkansaw Bear*. Louisville, KY: Anchorage Press Plays.

———. 1977. *Six Plays for Children*. Coleman Jennings, ed. Louisville, KY: Anchorage Press Plays.

*Hines, Kim. 1999. *Home on the Mornin' Train*. Woodstock, IL: Dramatic Publishing. (1839, 1939)

*Jennings, Caleen Sinette. 2000. *Free Like Br'er Rabbit.* Woodstock, IL: Dramatic Publishing.

Jennings, Lola H., and Coleman A., Jennings. 1989. *Braille: The Early Life of Louis Braille.* Woodstock, IL: Dramatic Publishing. (1812)

Pugh, Shirley. 1972. *In One Basket.* Louisville, KY: Anchorage Press Plays. (sources not included, but a valuable collection)

Swortzell, Lowell, ed. 1997. *Theatre for Young Audiences: Around the World in 21 Plays.* New York: Applause.

*Vigil, Angel. 1996. *¡Teatro! Hispanic Plays for Young People.* Englewood, CO: Teachers Ideas Press.

Zeder, Susan. 1976. *Step on a Crack.* Louisville, KY: Anchorage Press Plays.

Bibliography for Chapter 7
Folklore: A Global Legacy
Fables from around the World (retold, collected, adapted)

NOTE: See Buddhism in the bibliography for Chapter 13 for more Jataka stories.

Single Edition

Brett, Jan. 1994. *Town Mouse, Country Mouse.* New York: Putnam's.

*Shah, Idries. 2000. *The Clever Boy and the Terrible, Dangerous Animal.* Illustrated by Rose Mary Santiago. Boston: Hoopoe. (Sufi tale)

Ward, Helen. 1998. *The Hare and the Tortoise.* Brookfield, CT: Millbrook.

Wood, A. J. 1995. *The Lion and the Mouse.* Illustrated by Ian Andrew. Brookfield, CT: Millbrook.

Collection

Bader, Barbara, ed. 1991. *Aesop & Company.* Illustrated by Arthur Geisert. Boston: Houghton.

Demi. 1987. *A Chinese Zoo: Fables and Proverbs.* San Diego: Harcourt.

*Kherdian, David. 1992. *Feathers and Tails: Animal Fables from around the World.* Illustrated by Nonny Hogrogian. New York: Philomel.

*Montejo, Victor. 1991. *The Bird Who Cleans the World and Other Mayan Fables.* Wallace Kaufman, trans. East Haven, CT: Curbstone.

*Pinkney, Jerry. 2000. *Aesop's Fables.* New York: SeaStar.

Modern Literary Fables

Lobel, Arnold. 1980. *Fables.* New York: Harper.

Scieszka, Jon. 1998. *Squids Will Be Squids: Fresh Morals, Beastly Fables.* Illustrated by Lane Smith. New York: Scholastic.

Around the World through Folk and Fairy Tales (retold, collected, adapted)
General

Barchers, Suzanne I. 1990. *Wise Women: Folk and Fairy Tales from around the World.* Illustrated by Leann Mullineaux. Englewood, CO: Libraries Unlimited.

Clarkson, Atelia, and Gilbert B. Cross. *World Folktales: A Scribner Resource Collection.* New York: Scribner's.

Hamilton, Martha, and Mitch Weiss. 2000. *Noodlehead Stories: World Tales Kids Can Read & Tell.* Illustrated by Arain Elsammak. Little Rock, AK: August House.

Hearne, Betsy. 1993. *Beauties and Beasts.* Illustrated by Joanne Caroselli. Phoenix, AZ: Oryx.

Lipke, Barbara. 1996. *Figures, Facts, and Fables: Telling Tales in Science and Math.* Portsmouth, NH: Heinemann.

Livo, Norma, ed. 1988. *Joining In: An Anthology of Audience Participation Stories & How to Tell Them.* Teresa Miller, comp. Cambridge, MA: Yellow Moon.

MacDonald, Margaret Read. 1994. *Celebrate the World: Twenty Tellable Folktales for Multicultural Festivals.* Illustrated by Roxane Murphy Smith. Bronx, NY: Wilson.

———. 1986. *Twenty Tellable Tales: Audience Participation Folktales for the Beginning Storyteller.* Illustrations by Roxane Murphy. Bronx, NY: Wilson.

National Association for the Preservation and Perpetuation of Storytelling. 1991. *Best-Loved Stories Told at the National Storytelling Festival.* Jonesborough, TN: National Storytelling Press.

Pellowski, Anne. 1987. *The Family Storytelling Handbook.* New York: Macmillan.

———. 1984. *The Story Vine: A Source Book of Unusual and Easy-to-Read Stories from around the World.* New York: Macmillan.

Phelps, Ethel Johnston. 1981. *The Maid of the North: Feminist Folk Tales from around the World.* Illustrated by Lloyd Bloom. New York: Holt.

———. 1978. *Tatterhood and Other Tales.* Illustrated by Pamela Baldwin Ford. Old Westbury, NY: The Feminist Press.

Tchana, Katrin. 2000. *The Serpent Slayer and Other Stories of Strong Women.* Illustrated by Trina Schart Hyman. Boston: Little, Brown.

Yolen, Jane. 2000. *Not One Damsel in Distress: World Folktales for Strong Girls.* Illustrated by Susan Guevara. San Diego: Harcourt.

———. 1986. *Favorite Folktales from around the World.* New York: Pantheon.

Jewish Tales (retold, collected, adapted)

NOTE: See also Judaism in the bibliography for Chapter 13.

Forest, Heather. 1996. *A Big Quiet House: A Yiddish Folktale from Eastern Europe.* Illustrated by Susan Greenstein. Little Rock, AK: August House.

Jaffe, Nina. 1998. *The Way Meat Loves Salt: A Cinderella Tale from the Jewish Tradition.* Illustrated by Louise August. New York: Holt.

Schram, Peninnah, ed. 1995. *Chosen Tales: Stories Told by Jewish Storytellers.* Northville, NJ: Jason Aronson.

Weinreich, Beatrice Silverman. 1988. *Yiddish Folktales.* Leonard Wolf, trans. New York: Pantheon in cooperation with Yivo Institute of Jewish Research.

Africa (retold, collected, adapted)

Algeria

*Schwartz, Howard, and Barbara Rush. 1992. *The Sabbath Lion: A Jewish Folktale from Algeria.* Illustrated by Stephen Fieser. New York: HarperCollins.

Ashanti People

*Mollel, Tololwa. 1997. *Ananse's Feast: An Ashanti Tale.* Illustrated by Andrew Glass. New York: Clarion.

Benin

*Mama, Raouf. 1998. *Why Goats Smell Bad and Other Stories from Benin.* Illustrated by Imna Arroyo. North Haven, CT: Linnet.

Cameroon

*Mollel, Tololwa. 1993. *The King and the Tortoise.* Illustrated by Kathy Blankley. New York: Clarion.

Congo (formerly Zaire)

Aardema, Verna. 1991. *Traveling to Tondo: A Tale of the Nkundo of Zaire.* Illustrated by Will Hillenbrand. New York: Knopf.

Egypt

Bower, Tamara. 2000. *The Shipwrecked Sailor: An Egyptian Tale with Hieroglyphs.* New York: Atheneum.

Manniche, Lisa. 1981. *The Prince Who Knew His Fate.* New York: Metropolitan Museum of Art/Philomel.

Ethiopia

Kurtz, Jane. 1997. *Trouble.* Illustrated by Durga Bernhard. San Diego: Harcourt.

*———. 1994. *Fire on the Mountain.* Illustrated by E. B. Lewis. New York: Simon and Schuster.

*———. 1995. *Pulling the Lion's Tale.* Illustrated by Floyd Cooper. New York: Simon and Schuster.

*Price, Leontyne. 1990. *Aïda.* Illustrated by Leo and Diane Dillon. San Diego: Harcourt. (also Egypt)

Ghana

*Medearis, Angela Shelf. 1995. *Too Much Talk.* Illustrated by Stefano Vitale. Cambridge, MA: Candlewick.

Kenya

Aardema, Verna. 1996. *Bringing the Rain to Kapiti Plain: A Nandi Tale.* Illustrated by Beatriz Vidal. Boston: Houghton.

Liberia

*Paye, Won-Ldy, and Margaret H. Lippert. 2002. *Head, Body, Legs: A Story from Liberia.* New York: Holt.

Malawi

*Sierra, Judy. 1997. *The Mean Hyena: A Folktale from Malawi.* Illustrated by Michael Bryant. New York: Lodestar.

Mali

*Diakité, Baba Wagué. 1999. *The Hatseller and the Monkeys: A West African Folktale.* New York: Scholastic.

Masai People (East Africa)

Aardema, Verna. 1977. *Who's in Rabbit's House?* Illustrated by Leo and Diane Dillon. New York: Dial.

*Mollel, Tololwa. 1990. *The Orphan Boy: A Maasai Story.* Illustrated by Paul Morin. New York: Clarion.

Nigeria

*Echewa, T. Obinkaram. 1999. *The Magic Tree: A Folktale from Nigeria.* Illustrated by E. B. Lewis. New York: Morrow.

*Medearis, Angela Shelf. 1994. *The Singing Man.* Illustrated by Terea Shaffer. New York: Holiday.

*Mollel, Tololwa. 1994. *The Flying Tortoise: An Igbo Tale.* Illustrated by Barbara Spurll. New York: Clarion.

*Olaleye, Isaac O. 2000. *In the Rainfield: Who Is the Greatest?* Illustrated by Ann Grifalconi. New York: Blue Sky.

*Onyefulu, Obi. 1994. *Chinye: A West African Folk Tale.* Illustrated by Evie Safarewicz. New York: Viking. (Igbo people)

Senegal

* + Diop, Birago. 1981. *Mother Crocodile/Maman-Caïman.* Illustrated by John Steptoe. Rosa Guy, trans., adap. New York: Delacorte.

Sierra Leone

MacDonald, Margaret Read. 2001. *Mabela the Clever.* Illustrated by Tim Coffey. Morton Grove, IL: Whitman.

South Africa

*Aardema, Verna. 1973. *Behind the Back of the Mountain: Black Folktales from Southern Africa.* Illustrated by Leo and Diane Dillon. New York: Dial.

Swahili People (East Africa)

*Chocolate, Debbi. 1994. *Imani in the Belly.* Illustrated by Alexis Boies. Mahwah, NJ: BridgeWater.

Tanzania

*Mollel, Tololwa. 2000. *Subira, Subira.* Illustrated by Linda Saport. New York: Clarion.
*———. 1999. *Song Bird.* Illustrated by Rosanne Litzinger. New York: Clarion.
*———. 1998. *Shadow Dance.* Illustrated by Donna Perrone. New York: Clarion.

Tonga People

Aardema, Verna. 1997. *This for That: A Tonga Tale.* Illustrated by Victoria Chess. New York: Dial.

Uganda (Ik People)

*Serwadda, William Moses. 1974. *Songs and Stories from Uganda.* Illustrated by Leo and Diane Dillon. New York: Crowell. (music included)

West Africa (Adjoumba, Igalwa, M'pongwe, and Fang People)

*Diakité, Baba Wagué. 1997. *The Hunterman and the Crocodile.* New York: Scholastic.

Zambia

*Lester, Julius. 1994. *The Man Who Knew Too Much: A Moral Tale from the Baila of Zambia.* Illustrated by Leonard Jenkins. New York: Clarion.

Zanzibar

Aardema, Verna. 1985. *Bimwili and the Zimwi.* Illustrated by Susan Meddaugh. New York: Dial.

Zimbabwe

*Steptoe, John. 1987. *Mufaro's Beautiful Daughters.* New York: Lothrop.

Arctic (retold, collected, adapted)

NOTE: See Subarctic North American Indians.

*Bierhorst, John. 1997. *The Dancing Fox: Arctic Folktales.* Illustrated by Mary K. Okheena. New York: Morrow.

Asia (retold, collected, adapted) (I. Central and Asian Pacific; II. Southeast Asia)

General

Martin, Rafe. 1984. *The Hungry Tigress and Other Traditional Asian Tales.* Illustrated by Richard Wehrman. Boulder, CO: Shambhala.

I. CENTRAL AND ASIAN PACIFIC

China

*Chang, Margaret, and Raymond Chang. 1994. *The Cricket Warrior: A Chinese Tale.* Illustrated by Warwick Hutton. New York: McElderry.
*Chen, Kerstin. 2000. *Lord of the Cranes.* Illustrated by Jian Jiang Chen. J. Alison James, trans. New York: North-South.
*Greene, Ellin. 1996. *Ling-Li and the Phoenix Fairy: A Chinese Folktale.* Illustrated by Zong-Zhou Wang. New York: Clarion.
*Louie, Ai-Ling. 1982. *Yeh-Shen: A Cinderella Story from China.* Illustrated by Ed Young. New York: Philomel.
*Tseng, Grace. 1999. *White Tiger, Blue Serpent.* Illustrated by Jean and Mou-Sien Tseng. New York: Lothrop.
*Wolkstein, Dianne. 1996 [1979]. *White Wave: A Chinese Tale.* Illustrated by Ed Young. San Diego: Harcourt.
*Yep, Laurence. 1997. *The Dragon Prince: A Chinese Beauty and the Beast Tale.* Illustrated by Kam Mak. New York: HarperCollins.
*Young, Ed. 1998. *The Lost Horse: A Chinese Folktale.* San Diego: Harcourt.

India

Demi. 1997. *One Grain of Rice: A Mathematical Folktale.* New York: Scholastic.
*Jaffrey, Madhur. 1985. *Seasons of Splendor: Tales, Myths and Legends of India.* Illustrated by Michael Foreman. New York: Atheneum.
Kajpust, Melissa. 1997. *The Peacock's Pride.* Illustrated by Joanne Kelly. New York: Hyperion.
*Krishnaswami, Uma. 1999. *Shower of Gold: Girls and Women in the Stories of India.* Illustrated by Maniam Selven. North Haven, CT: Linnet.
*Ram, Govinder. 1987. *Rama and Sita.* New York: Peter Bedrick.

Japan

*Compton, Patricia A. 1991. *The Terrible EEK.* Illustrated by Sheila Hamanaka. New York: Simon and Schuster.
*Hamanaka, Sheila. 1993. *Screen of Frogs: An Old Tale Retold.* New York: Orchard.
*Uchida, Yoshiko. 1994. *The Wise Old Woman.* Illustrated by Martin Springett. New York: McElderry.
*Williams, Carol Ann. 1995. *Tsubu the Little Snail.* Illustrated by Tatsuro Kiuchi. New York: Simon and Schuster.

Kazakhstan

Masey, Mary Lou. 1968. *Stories of the Steppes: Kazakh Folktales.* Illustrated by Helen Basilevsky. New York: David McKay.

Korea: North and South

*Choi, Yangsook. 1997. *The Sun Girl and the Moon Boy: A Korean Folktale.* New York: Knopf.

*Curry, Lindy Soon. 1999. *A Tiger by the Tail and Other Stories from the Heart of Korea*. Englewood, CO: Libraries Unlimited.

*Han, Oki S., and Stephanie Haboush Plunkett. 1996. *Kongi and Potgi: A Cinderella Story from Korea*. Illustrated by Oki S. Han. New York: Dial.

* ⁺Han, Suzanne Crowder. 1995. *The Rabbit's Escape*. Illustrated by Yumi Heo. New York: Holt.

*Heo, Yumi. 1996. *The Green Frogs: A Korean Folktale*. Boston: Houghton.

*Kwon, Holly H. 1993. *The Moles and the Mireuk*. Illustrated by Woodleigh Hubbard. Boston: Houghton.

Malaysia

*Day, Noreha Yussof. 1996. *Kancil and the Crocodiles*. Illustrated by Britta Teckentrup. New York: Simon and Schuster.

Mongolia

*Yep, Lawrence. 1997. *The Khan's Daughter: A Mongolian Folktale*. Illustrated by Jean and Mou-sien Tseng. New York: Scholastic.

Nepal

*Shrestha, Kavita Ram, and Sarah Lamstein. 1997. *From the Mango Tree and Other Folktales from Nepal*. Englewood, CO: Libraries Unlimited.

Pakistan

Shepard, Aaron. 1995. *The Gifts of Wali Dâd: A Tale of India and Pakistan*. Illustrated by Daniel San Souci. New York: Atheneum.

Siberia

Bernhard, Emery. 1994. *The Girl Who Wanted to Hunt: A Siberian Tale*. Illustrated by Durga Bernhard. New York: Holiday.

Tibet

Berger, Barbara Helen. 2002. *All the Way to Lhasa*. New York: Philomel.

Demi. 1999. *The Donkey and the Rock*. New York: Holt.

II. SOUTHEAST ASIA

Cambodia

*Coburn, Jewell Reinhart, with Tzexa Cherta Lee. 1996. *Jouanah: A Hmong Cinderella*. Illustrated by Anne Sibley O'Brien. Fremont, CA: Shen's Books.

*Ho, Minfong, and Saphan Ros. 1997. *Brother Rabbit: A Cambodian Tale*. Illustrated by Jennifer Hewitson. New York: Lothrop.

*————. 1995. *The Two Brothers*. Illustrated by Jean and Mou-sien Tseng. New York: Lothrop.

Indonesia

Sierra, Judy. 2000. *The Gift of the Crocodile*. Illustrated by Reynold Ruffins. New York: Simon and Schuster.

Laos

*Livo, Norma J., and Dia Cha. 1991. *Folk Stories of the Hmong: Peoples of Laos, Thailand, and Vietnam*. Englewood, CO: Libraries Unlimited.

*Xiong, Blia. 1989. *Nine-in-One Grr! Grr! A Folktale from the Hmong People of Laos*. Illustrated by Nancy Hom. Cathy Spagnoli, adap. San Francisco: Children's Book Press.

Philippines

*Aruego, José, and Ariane Dewey. 1972. *A Crocodile's Tale: A Philippine Folk Story*. New York: Scribner's.

Singapore

*Chek, Chia Hearn. 1975. *The Redhill: A Singapore Folktale*. Illustrated by Kwan Shan Mei. Singapore: Federal-Alpha.

Thailand

* ⁺MacDonald, Margaret Read. 1998. *The Girl Who Wore Too Much: A Folktale from Thailand*. Thai text by Supaporn Vathanaprida. Illustrated by Yvonne Lebrun Davis. Little Rock, AK: August House.

*Vathanaprida, Supaporn. 1994. *Thai Tales: Folktales of Thailand*. Illustrated by Boonsong Rohitasuke. Margaret Read MacDonald, ed. Englewood, CO: Libraries Unlimited.

Vietnam

*Lee, Jeanne M. 1985. *Toad Is the Uncle of Heaven*. New York: Holt.

*Vuong, Lynette Dyer. 1982. *The Brocaded Slipper and Other Vietnamese Tales*. Illustrated by Vo-Dinh Mai. Reading, MA: Addison-Wesley.

*Vuong, Lynette Dyer, and Manabu Saito. 1993. *The Golden Carp and Other Tales from Vietnam*. New York: Lothrop.

Caribbean Basin (retold, collected, adapted)

Includes the Bahamas, Caribbean Basin Islands, Greater Antilles; Cuba, Hispaniola (Haiti and the Dominican Republic); Jamaica and Puerto Rico, Trinidad

*Alvarez, Julia. 2000. *The Secret Footprints*. Illustrated by Fabian Negrin. New York: Knopf.

*Ada, Alma Flor. 1993. *The Rooster Who Went to His Uncle's Wedding: A Latin American Folktale*. Illustrated by Kathleen Kuchera. New York: Putnam's.

*Belpré, Pura. 1978. *The Rainbow-Colored Horse*. Illustrated by Antonio Martorell. New York: Warne.

*+González, Lucía M. 1994. *The Bossy Gallito/El gallo de bodas: A Traditional Cuban Folktale.* Illustrated by Lulu Delacre. New York: Scholastic.

*Joseph, Lynn. 1991. *A Wave in Her Pocket: Stories from Trinidad.* Illustrated by Brian Pinkney. New York: Clarion.

*Mohr, Nicholasa. 1995. *The Song of El Coquí and Other Tales of Puerto Rico.* Illustrated by Antonio Martorell. New York: Viking.

*Moreton, Daniel. 1997. *La Cucaracha Martina: A Caribbean Folktale.* Apple, Mac/Adobe Illustrator. New York: Turtle Books.

*San Souci, Robert D. 1998. *Cendrillon: A Caribbean Cinderella.* Illustrated by Brian Pinkney. New York: Simon and Schuster. (Martinique)

Wolkstein, Dianne. 1978. *The Magic Orange Tree and Other Haitian Folktales.* New York: Knopf.

Central America (retold, collected, adapted)

NOTE: See also the Caribbean and South America for Latino tales.

El Salvador

*+Argueta, Manlio. 1990. *Magic Dogs of the Volcanoes/Los perros mágicos de los volcanoes.* Illustrated by Elly Simmons. San Francisco: Children's Book Press.

Guatemala

*Mora, Pat. 1995. *The Race of Toad and Deer.* Illustrated by Maya Itzna Brooks. New York: Orchard.

Inca (Quechua) Civilization

Kurtz, Jane. 1996. *Miro in the Kingdom of the Sun.* Woodcuts by David Frampton. Boston: Houghton.

Mayan Civilization

Bierhorst, John, ed. 1986. *The Monkey's Haircut and Other Stories Told by the Maya.* Illustrated by Robert Andrew Parker. New York: Morrow.

+Ehlert, Lois. 1997. *Cuckoo/Cucu.* Gloria de Aragón Andújar, trans. San Diego: Harcourt.

Nicaragua

+de Sauza, James. 1989. *Brother Anansi and the Cattle Ranch/El hermano Anansi y el rancho de Ganado.* Illustrated by Stephen Von Mason. Harriet Rohmer, adap. San Francisco: Children's Book Press.

+Rohmer, Harriet. 1989. *Uncle Nacho's Hat/El sombrero del tío Nacho.* Illustrated by Veg Reisberg. Spanish version by Rosalma Zubizarreta. San Francisco: Children's Book Press.

Europe (retold, collected, adapted) (I. Eastern Europe; II. Western Europe)

I. EASTERN EUROPE

General

Philip, Neil. 1991. *Fairy Tales of Eastern Europe.* Illustrated by Larry Wilkes. New York: Clarion.

Czech Republic

Wisniewski, David. 1996. *Golem.* New York: Clarion.

Estonia

Kreutzwald, Friedrich Reinhold, Juhan Kunder, and August Jakobson. 1993. *The Orphan's Hand-Mill.* Tallinn, Estonia: Perioodika.

Hungary

Greene, Ellin. 2000. *The Little Golden Lamb.* Illustrated by Rosanne Litzinger. New York: Clarion.

Latvia

Langton, Jane. 1985. *The Hedgehog Boy: A Latvian Folktale.* Illustrated by Ilse Plume. New York: Harper.

Lithuania

Zheleznova, Irina. 1974. *Tales of the Amber Sea: Fairy Tales of the Peoples of Estonia, Latvia and Lithuania.* Moscow: Progress Publishers.

Macedonia

Cvetanovska, Danica, Irma Rosenfeld, and William Rosenfeld. 1988. *The Moon in the Well and Other Macedonian Folk Tales.* Greenfield Center, NY: Greenfield Review Press.

Poland

Pellowski, Anne. 1980. *The Nine Crying Dolls.* Illustrated by Charles Mikolaycak. New York: Philomel.

Romania

Olson, Arielle. 1992. *Noah's Cats and the Devil's Fire.* Illustrated by Barry Moser. New York: Orchard.

Russia

Afanasyev, A. N. 1980. *Russian Folk Tales.* Illustrated by Ivan Bilibin. Robert Chandler, trans. New York: Random House.

Bell, Anthea. 1984. *Swan Lake.* Illustrated by Chihiro Iwasaki. Saxonville, MA: Picture Book Studio.

Fonteyn, Margot. 1989. *Swan Lake.* Illustrated by Trina Schart Hyman. San Diego: Harcourt.

Lurie, Alison. 1999. *The Black Geese: A Baba Yaga Story from Russia.* Illustrated by Jessica Souhami. New York: DK.

Onassis, Jacqueline, ed. 1978. *The Firebird and Other Russian Fairy Tales.* Illustrated by Boris Zvorykin. New York: Viking.

Ransome, Arthur. 1968. *The Fool of the World and the Flying Ship.* Illustrated by Uri Shulevitz. New York: Farrar.

Winthrop, Elizabeth. 1997. *The Little Humpbacked Horse: A Russian Tale.* Illustrated by Alexander Koshkin. New York: Clarion.

Serbia

Scott, Sally. 1987. *The Three Wonderful Beggars.* New York: Greenwillow.

Ukraine

Kimmel, Eric. 1996. *One Eye, Two Eyes, Three Eyes: A Hutzul Tale.* Illustrated by Dirk Zimmer. New York: Holiday.

II. WESTERN EUROPE

Austria

See Germany and Austria.

France

Craft, K. Y. 2000. *Cinderella.* New York: SeaStar.

DeFelice, Cynthia, and Mary De Marsh. 1995. *Three Perfect Peaches: A French Folktale Retold by the Wild Washerwomen Storytellers.* Illustrated by Irene Trivas. New York: Orchard.

Willard, Nancy. 1992. *Beauty and the Beast.* Wood engravings by Barry Moser. San Diego: Harcourt.

Germany and Austria

Babbitt, Natalie. 1998. *Ouch!* Illustrated by Fred Marcellino. New York: HarperCollins.

Dugina, Olga, and Andrej Dugin. 1999. *The Brave Little Tailor.* New York: Abrams.

Duntze, Dorothée. 1998. *The Six Swans.* Anthea Bell, trans. New York: North-South.

Grimm, Wilhelm, and Jacob Grimm. 1944. *The Complete Grimm's Fairy Tales.* New York: Pantheon.

Jarrell, Randall. 1980. *The Fisherman and His Wife.* Illustrated by Margot Zemach. New York: Farrar.

Palecek, Josef. 1988. *The Bremen Town Musicians.* Saxonville, MA: Picture Book Studio.

Sanderson, Ruth. 1990. *The Twelve Dancing Princesses.* Boston: Little, Brown.

Zelinsky, Paul O. 1997. *Rapunzel.* New York: Dutton.

———. 1986. *Rumpelstiltskin.* New York: Dutton.

Zwerger, Lisbeth. 1983. *Little Red Cap.* Elizabeth D. Crawford, trans. Saxonville, MA: Picture Book Studio.

Greece

Manna, Anthony L., and Christodoula Mitakidou. 1997. *Mr. Semolina-Semolinus: A Greek Folktale.* New York: Atheneum.

Iceland

Kötlum, Jóhannes úr. 1993. *The Fisherman's Boy and the Seal.* Illustrated by Ragnheiôur Gestsdóttir. Prentmidjan, Iceland: Mál og menning.

Ireland

Behan, Brendan. 1997 [1962]. *The King of Ireland's Son.* Illustrated by P. J. Lynch. New York: Orchard.

Byrd, Robert. 1999. *Finn MacCoul and His Fearless Wife: A Giant of a Tale from Ireland.* New York: Dutton.

Daly, Jude. 2000. *Fair, Brown & Trembling: An Irish Cinderella Story.* New York: Farrar.

Doyle, Malachy. 2000. *Tales from Old Ireland.* Illustrated by Niamh Sharkey. New York: Barefoot.

Hague, Michael. 2001. *Kate Culhane: A Ghost Story.* New York: SeaStar.

Italy

Calvino, Italo. 1956. *Italian Folktales.* George Martin, trans. San Diego: Harcourt.

Kimmel, Eric. 1996. *Count Silvernose: A Story from Italy.* Illustrated by Omar Rayyan. New York: Holiday.

Sanderson, Ruth. 1995. *Papa Gatto: An Italian Fairy Tale.* Boston: Little, Brown.

Stanley, Diane. 1995. *Petrosinella: A Neapolitan Rapunzel.* New York: Dial.

Vittorini, Domenico. 1995 [1958]. *The Thread of Life: Twelve Old Italian Tales.* Illustrated by Mary Grand-Pré. New York: Crown.

Netherlands

Miller, Olive Beaupré. 1926. *Tales Told in Holland.* Illustrated by Maud and Miska Petersham. Chicago: The Book House for Children.

Portugal

Lowe, Patricia Tracy. 1970. *The Little Horse of Seven Colors.* Illustrated and translated by Anne Marie Jauss. New York: World.

Scandinavia: Denmark, Finland, Norway, Sweden, and the Laplanders

Asbjørnsen, Peter Christian, and Jorgen E. Moe. 1991. *East O' the Sun and West O' the Moon.* Illustrated by P. J. Lynch. Cambridge, MA: Candlewick.

French, Vivian. 1995. *Why the Sea Is Salt.* Illustrated by Patrice Aggs. Cambridge, MA: Candlewick.

Lunge-Larsen, Lise. 1999. *The Troll with No Heart in His Body and Other Tales of Trolls from Norway.* Illustrated by Betsy Bowen. Boston: Houghton.

MacDonald, Margaret Read. 2001. *Fat Cat: A Danish Folktale.* Illustrated by Julie Paschkis. Little Rock, AK: August House.

Spain

*Ada, Alma Flor. 1999. *The Three Golden Oranges.* Illustrated by Reg Cartwright. New York: Simon and Schuster.

*Araujo, Frank P. 1993. *Nekane, The Lamiña and the Bear: A Tale of the Basque Pyrenees.* Illustrated by Xiao Jun Li. Windsor, CA: Rayve.

Vernon, Adele. 1987. *The Riddle.* Illustrated by Robert Rayevsky and Vladimir Radunsky. New York: Dodd. (Catalan tale; there is no source, but this is exceptionally well-done)

Switzerland

Brett, Jan. 1999. *The Gingerbread Boy.* New York: Putnam's.

Stone, Marti. 1992. *The Singing Fir Tree: A Swiss Folktale.* Illustrated by Barry Root. New York: Putnam's.

United Kingdom: England, Scotland, Wales

Beneduce, Ann Keay. 1999. *Jack and the Beanstalk.* Illustrated by Gennady Spirin. New York: Philomel.

Climo, Shirley. 1999. *Magic Mischief: Tales from Cornwall.* Illustrated by Anthony Bacon Venti. New York: Clarion.

Cooney, Barbara. 1958. *Chanticleer and the Fox.* New York: Harper. (based on Chaucer's *Canterbury Tales*)

Huck, Charlotte. 2001. *The Black Bull of Norroway: A Scottish Tale.* Illustrated by Anita Lobel. New York: Greenwillow.

Lang, Andrew, ed. 1965 [1892]. *The Green Fairy Book.* Illustrated by H. J. Ford. New York: Dover. (series)

MacDonald, Margaret Read. 1995. *The Old Woman Who Lived in a Vinegar Bottle: A British Fairy Tale.* Illustrated by Nancy Dunaway Fowlkes. Little Rock, AK: August House.

Wahl, Jan. 1999. *Little Johnny Buttermilk: After an Old English Folktale.* Illustrated by Jennifer Mazzucco. Little Rock, AK: August House.

Middle East (retold, collected, adapted)

Includes Armenia, Azerbaijan, Bahrain, Cyprus, Georgia, Iran, Iraq, Israel, Jordan, Kuwait, Lebanon, Oman, Palestine, Qatar, Saudi Arabia, Syria, Turkey, United Arab Emirates, and Yemen.

General

*Bushnaq, Inea, trans. 1986. *Arab Folktales.* New York: Pantheon.

Hickox, Rebecca. 1998. *The Golden Sandal: A Middle Eastern Cinderella Story.* Illustrated by Will Hillenbrand. New York: Holiday.

*Kherdian, David. 1997. *The Rose's Smile: Farizad of the Arabian Nights.* Illustrated by Stefano Vitale. New York: Holt.

Zeman, Ludmila. 1999. *Sindbad: From the Tales of the Thousand and One Nights.* Toronto: Tundra.

Armenia

*Kherdian, David. 1998. *The Golden Bracelet.* Illustrated by Nonny Hogrogian. New York: Holiday.

*———. 1971. *One Fine Day.* New York: Macmillan.

San Souci, Robert. 1998. *A Weave of Words.* Illustrated by Raúl Colón. New York: Orchard.

Iran (formerly known as Persia)

Balouch, Kristen. 2000. *The King and the Three Thieves: A Persian Tale.* New York: Viking.

Shepard, Aaron. 1999. *Forty Fortunes: A Tale of Iran.* Illustrated by Alisher Dianov. New York: Clarion.

Iraq

Hort, Lenny. 1989. *The Tale of Caliph Stork.* Illustrated by Friso Henstra. New York: Dial.

Shepard, Aaron. 1995. *The Enchanted Storks.* Illustrated by Alisher Dianov. New York: Clarion.

Jordan

*Odeh, Hikmat Ben. 1995. *Classic Fairy Tales from Ancient Palestine and Jordan.* Illustrated by Wided Ayal. Irbid, Jordan: Kanan Press.

Palestine

*Bahous, Sally. 1993. *Sitti and the Cats: A Tale of Friendship.* Illustrated by Nancy Malick. Niwot, CO: Odyssey/Roberts Rinehart.

Turkey

Hikmet, Murat. 1959. *One Day the Hodja.* Ankara, Turkey: Tarhan.

Walker, Barbara K. 1988. *A Treasury of Turkish Folktales for Children.* North Haven, CT: Linnet.

Yemen

*Gold, Sharlya, and Mishael Maswari Caspi. 1990. *The Answered Prayer and Other Yemenite Folktales.* Illustrated by Marjory Wunsch. Philadelphia: Jewish Publication Society.

North America (retold, collected, adapted)

General

Zeitlin, Steven J. Baker, Amy J. Kotkin, and Holly Cutting Baker. 1982. *A Celebration of American Family Folklore: Tales and Traditions from the Smithsonian Collection.* Cambridge, MA: Yellow Moon.

African American

Bang, Molly Garrett. 1976. *Wiley and the Hairy Man.* New York: Macmillan.

*Goss, Linda, and Marian E. Barnes, eds. 1989. *Talk That Talk: An Anthology of African American Storytelling.* New York: Simon and Schuster.

*Hamilton, Virginia. 1995. *Her Stories: African American Folktales, Fairy Tales, and True Tales.* Illustrated by Leo and Diane Dillon. New York: Blue Sky.

*———. 1985. *The People Could Fly: American Black Folktales.* Illustrated by Leo and Diane Dillon. New York: Knopf.

*Lester, Julius. 1987. *The Tales of Uncle Remus: The Adventures of Brer Rabbit.* Illustrated by Jerry Pinkney. New York: Dial. (sequels)

*McKissack, Patricia. 1988. *Mirandy and Brother Wind.* Illustrated by Jerry Pinkney. New York: Knopf.

*———. 1986. *Flossie and the Fox.* Illustrated by Rachel Isadora. New York: Dial.

*San Souci, Robert D. 1992. *Sukey and the Mermaid.* Illustrated by Brian Pinkney. New York: Four Winds. (South Carolina coast)

*———. 1989. *The Talking Eggs: A Folktale from the American South.* Illustrated by Jerry Pinkney. New York: Dial.

Wahl, Jan. 1998. *The Singing Geese.* Illustrated by Sterling Brown. New York: Lodestar. (music included)

American Indian: California, Eastern Woodlands, Great Basin, Native Alaskan, Northwest Coast, Plains, Plateau, Southeast, Southwest, and Subarctic

General

*Bruchac, Joseph. 1993. *Flying with the Eagle, Racing the Great Bear: Stories from Native North America.* Illustrated by Murv Jacob. Mahwah, NJ: BridgeWater.

*Bruchac, Joseph, and Gayle Ross. 1994. *The Girl Who Married the Moon: Tales from Native North America.* Illustrated by S. S. Burrus. Mahwah, NJ: BridgeWater.

*Caduto, Michael, and Joseph Bruchac. 1991. *Keepers of the Animals: Native American Stories and Wildlife Activities for Children.* Illustrated by John Kahionhes Fadden and Melody Lightfeather. Golden, CO: Fulcrum. (sequels)

California North American Indians

Karuk

*London, Jonathan, with Lanny Pinola. 1993. *Fire Race: A Karuk Coyote Tale about How Fire Came to the People.* Illustrated by Sylvia Long. San Francisco: Chronicle.

Rumsien Ohlone

*Yamane, Linda. 1998. *The Snake That Lived in the Santa Cruz Mountains and Other Ohlone Stories.* Berkeley, CA: Oyate.

Yahi

Hinton, Leanne. 1992. *Ishi's Tale of Lizard.* New York: Farrar.

Eastern Woodlands North American Indians

Abenaki

*Bruchac, Joseph. 1988. *The Faithful Hunter: Abenaki Stories.* Illustrated by Kahionhes. Greenfield Center, NY: Greenfield Review Press.

Delaware (Lenni Lenape)

Van Laan, Nancy. 1989. *Rainbow Crow: A Lenape Tale.* Illustrated by Beatriz Vidal. New York: Knopf.

Iroquois (Haudenosaunee): Cayuga, Mohawk (Akwesasne), Oneida, Onondaga, Seneca, Tuscarora Nations

*Bruchac, Joseph. 1995. *The Boy Who Lived with the Bears and Other Iroquois Stories.* Illustrated by Murv Jacob. New York: HarperCollins.

*———. 1985. *Iroquois Stories: Heroes and Heroines, Monsters and Magic.* Illustrated by Daniel Burgevin. Trumansburg, NY: Crossing Press.

*Bruchac, Joseph, and Jesse Bruchac. 2001. *How the Chipmunk Got His Stripes: A Tale of Bragging and Teasing.* Illustrated by Jose Aruego and Ariane Dewey. New York: Dial.

*Ha-yen-doh-nees (Leo Cooper). 1995. *Seneca Indian Stories.* Illustrated by Beth Ann Clark. Greenfield Center, NY: Greenfield Review Press.

Micmac

*Runningwolf, Michael B., and Patricia Clark Smith. 2000. *On the Trail of Elder Brother: Glous'gap Stories of the Micmac Indians.* Illustrated by Michael B. Running Wolf. New York: Persea.

Mohican

*Fawcett, Melissa Jane, and Joseph Bruchac. 1997. *Makiawisug: The Gift of the Little People.* Illustrated by David Wagner. Uncasville, CT: Little People Publications.

Ojibwa (Anishinabe or Chippewa)

*Johnston, Basil H. 1995. *The Bear-Walker and Other Stories.* Illustrated by David A. Johnson. Toronto: Royal Ontario Museum.

*Spooner, Michael, and Lolita Taylor. 1996. *Old Meshikee and the Little Crabs.* Illustrated by John Hart. New York: Holt.

Potawatomi

*DeMontaño, Marty Kreipe. 1998. *Coyote in Love with a Star.* Illustrated by Tom Coffin. Washington, DC: National Museum of the American Indian/Abbeville.

Wabanaki: Malecite, Micmac, Passamaquoddy, Penobscot, Western Abenaki

*Bruchac, Joseph. 1995. *Gluskabe and the Four Wishes.* Illustrated by Christine Nyburg Shrader. New York: Dutton.

Wampanoag

*Manítonquat (Medicine Story). 1994. *The Children of the Morning Light: Wampanoag Tales.* Illustrated by Mary F. Arquette. New York: Macmillan.

Great Basin North American Indians

Modoc

Simms, Laura. 1997. *The Bone Man: A Native American Modoc Tale.* Illustrated by Michael McCurdy. New York: Hyperion.

Paiute

Pope, Mary L. 1981. *Let Me Tell You a Story: Adapted Paiute Tales.* Yerington, NV: Yerington Paiute Tribe.

Shoshoni

Stevens, Janet. 1996. *Old Bag of Bones: A Coyote Tale.* New York: Holiday.

Ute

Stevens, Janet. 1993. *Coyote Steals the Blanket: A Ute Tale.* New York: Holiday.

Native Alaskans: Aleuts, Iñupiat, Yu'pik

Gallop, Louise. 1993. *Owl's Secret.* Illustrated by Shannon Cartwright. Homer, AK: Paws IV. (There is no source)

Northwest Coast North American Indians

Coast Salish (includes Songhees)

*Kwulasulwut/Ellen White. 1995 [1981]. *Kwulasulwut: Stories from the Coast Salish.* Illustrated by David Neel. Penticton, B.C.: Theytus.

Inuit

Martin, Rafe. 1997. *The Eagle's Gift.* Illustrated by Tatsuro Kiuchi. New York: Putnam's.

Norman, Howard. 1997. *The Girl Who Dreamed Only of Geese and Other Tales of the Far North.* Illustrated by Leo and Diane Dillon. San Diego: Harcourt.

Kootenai

*Kootenai Culture Committee. 2000. *Owl's Eyes & Seeking a Spirit.* Pablo, MT: Salish Kootenai College Press.

Kwakiutl

*Normandin, Christine, ed. 1997. *Echoes of the Elders: The Stories and Paintings of Chief Lelooska.* New York: DK. (CD enclosed; Chief Lelooska reads five stories)

Makah

Morgan, Pierr. 1995. *Supper for Crow: A Northwest Coast Indian Tale.* New York: Crown.

Nootka (Tse-Shaht)

Clutesi, George. 1994 [1967]. *Son of Raven Son of Deer.* Port Alberni, B.C.: Clutesi Agencies Limited.

Tlingit

*Williams, Maria. 2001. *How Raven Stole the Sun.* Illustrated by Felix Vigil. Washington, D.C.: National Museum of the American Indian/Abbeville.

Plains North American Indians

Apache: Chiracahua, Jicarilla, Kiowa, Lipan, Mescalaro, and Western

*Lacapa, Michael. 1992. *Antelope Woman: An Apache Folktale.* Flagstaff, AZ: Northland.

*———. 1990. *The Flute Player: An Apache Folktale.* Flagstaff, AZ: Northland.

Crow

*Joe Medicine Crow. 1998. *Brave Wolf and the Thunderbird.* Illustrated by Linda R. Martin. Washington, D.C.: National Museum of the American Indian/Abbeville.

Otoe

*Walters, Anna Lee. 1993. *The Two-Legged Creature.* Illustrated by Carol Bowles. Flagstaff, AZ: Northland.

Plains Nations: Arapaho, Cheyenne, Dakota, and Lakota

Goble, Paul. 1984. *Buffalo Woman.* New York: Bradbury.

Lakota: Dakota, Oglala Brulé, Minniconjou, Sans Arc, Blackfoot Lakota, Two Kettle, and Hunkpapa
*Yellow Robe, Rosebud. 1979. *Tonweya and the Eagles and Other Lakota Indian Tales.* Illustrated by Jerry Pinkney. New York: Dial.

Plateau North American Indians

Okanagan
Okanagan Tribal Council. 1991. *How Names Were Given.* Illustrated by Barbara Marchand. Penticton, B.C.: Theytus.

Salish
*Salish Culture Committee. 1999. *Coyote Stories of the Montana Salish Indians.* Helena, MT: Montana Historical Society Press.

Southeast North American Indians

Cherokee
*Bruchac, Joseph, and Gayle Ross. 1995. *The Story of the Milky Way: A Cherokee Tale.* Illustrated by Virginia Stroud. New York: Dial.
*Ross, Gayle. 1995. *How Turtle's Back Was Cracked: A Traditional Cherokee Tale.* Illustrated by Murv Jacob. New York: Dial.
*———. 1994. *How Rabbit Tricked Otter, and Other Cherokee Trickster Stories.* Illustrated by Murv Jacob. New York: HarperCollins.

Chickasaw
*Ata, Te. 1989. *Baby Rattlesnake.* Illustrated by Veg Reisberg. Lynn Moroney, adap. San Francisco: Children's Book Press.

Muskogee (Creek)
*Bruchac, Joseph. 1994. *The Great Ball Game: A Muskogee Story.* Illustrated by Susan L. Roth. New York: Dial.

Southwest North American Indians

Acoma
*Rushmore, Helen, with Wolf Robe Hunt. 1963. *The Dancing Horses of Acoma and Other Acoma Indian Stories.* Illustrated by Wolf Robe Hunt. Cleveland: World.

Hopi
*Lomatuway'ma, Michael. 1996. *The Magic Hummingbird: A Hopi Folktale.* Illustrated by Michael Lacapa. Ekkehart Malotki, coll., trans. Walnut, CA: Kiva.
* + Sekaquaptewa, Eugene. 1994. *Coyote and the Winnowing Birds: A Traditional Hopi Tale.* Illustrated by Hopi Children. Emory Sekquaptewa and Barbara Pepper, ed. and trans. Santa Fe, NM: Clear Light.

Navajo (Diné)
*Begay, Shonto. 1992. *Ma'ii and Cousin Horned Toad: A Traditional Navajo Story.* New York: Scholastic.
*Browne, Vee. 1997. *Monster Birds.* Illustrated by Baje Whitethorne. Flagstaff, AZ: Northland.
*Duncan, Lois. 1996. *The Magic of Spider Woman.* Illustrated by Shonto Begay. New York: Scholastic.

Pueblo: Cochiti, Isleta, Jemez, Laguna, Nambé, Picuris, Pojoaque, San Felipe, San Ildefonso, San Juan, Sandia, Santa Anna, Santa Clara, Santo Domingo, Taos, Tesuque, Tewa, and Zia
Hausman, Gerald. 1993. *The Story of Blue Elk.* Illustrated by Kristina Rodanas. New York: Clarion.
Taylor, Harriet Peck. 1995. *Coyote and the Laughing Butterflies.* New York: Macmillan.

Zuni
*Pollock, Penny. 1996. *The Turkey Girl: A Zuni Cinderella Story.* Illustrated by Ed Young. Boston: Little, Brown.

Subarctic North American Indians

Athabaskan
*Wallis, Velma. 1993. *Two Old Women.* Illustrated by Jim Grant. Fairbanks, AK: Epicenter.

Cree
* + Ahenakew, Freda. 1999. *Wisahkecahk Flies to the Moon.* Illustrated by Sherry Farrell Racette. Winnipeg, Manitoba: Pemmican.

Appalachian
Chase, Richard. 1948. *Grandfather Tales: American-English Folk Tales.* Boston: Houghton.
Compton, Joanne. 1995. *Sody Sallyratus.* Illustrated by Kenn Compton. New York: Holiday.
*Reneaux, J. J. 2001. *How Animals Saved the People: Animal Tales from the South.* Illustrated by James Ransome. New York: HarperCollins.
Schroeder, Alan. 1997. *Smoky Mountain Rose: An Appalachian Cinderella.* Illustrated by Brad Sneed. New York: Dial.

Canada
NOTE: See American Indians for Canadian First People.
Carlson, Natalie Savage. 1952. *The Talking Cat and Other Stories of French Canada.* Illustrated by Roger Duvoisin. New York: Harper. (There is no source, but this is an early collection)

Chinese American
*Yep, Laurence. 1989. *The Rainbow People.* Illustrated by David Wiesner. New York: HarperCollins.

Hawaiian Islands

*Rattigan, Jama Kim. 1996. *The Woman in the Moon: A Story from Hawai'i*. Illustrated by Carla Golembe. Boston: Little, Brown.

Hispanic Southwest

* *+ Hayes, Joe. 2000. *Little Gold Star/Estrella de oro*. Illustrated by Gloria Osuna Perez and Lucia Angela Perez. El Paso, TX: Cinco Puntos.
* *+ Vigil, Angel. 1994. *The Corn Woman/La mujer del maíz: Cuentos y leyendas del sudoeste Hispano*. Englewood, CO: Libraries Unlimited.

Mexico: Aztec, Mazahua, Oaxaca, and Tolteca People

Aardema, Verna. 1991. *Borreguita and the Coyote: A Tale from Ayutla, Mexico*. Illustrated by Petra Mathers. New York: Knopf.

Coburn, Jewell. 2000. *Domítíla: A Cinderella Tale from the Mexican Tradition*. Illustrated by Connie McLennan. Fremont, CA: Shen's Books.

* *+ de Mariscal, Blanca López. 1995. *The Harvest Birds/Los pájaros de la cosecha*. Illustrated by Enrique Flores. San Francisco: Children's Book Press.

*Madrigal, Antonio Hernández. 1997. *The Eagle and the Rainbow*. Illustrated by Tomie dePaola. Golden, CO: Fulcrum.

*Marcos, Subcomandante. 1996. *The Story of Colors: A Folktale from the Jungles of Chiapis*. Illustrated by Domitila Domínguez. Anne Bar Din, trans. El Paso, TX: Cinco Puntos.

Oceania (retold, collected, adapted)

Includes Fiji, Gilbert Islands, Guam, Mariana Islands, Marshall Islands, New Caledonia, Solomon Islands, Society Islands, Samoa, Vanuatu, Melanesia, Micronesia, and Papua New Guinea

Australia
Aborigines of Australia

*Oodgeroo. 1993. *Dreamtime: Aboriginal Stories*. Illustrated by Bronwyn Bancroft. New York: Lothrop.

Roth, Susan L. 1996. *The Biggest Frog in Australia*. New York: Simon and Schuster.

*Roughsey, Dick. 1975. *The Rainbow Serpent*. Sydney, Australia: Collins.

*Trezise, Percy, and Dick Roughsey. 1982. *Turramulli the Giant Quinkin*. Milwaukee: Gareth Stevens.

Bali

Sierra, Judy. 1999. *The Dancing Pig*. Illustrated by Jesse Sweetwater. San Diego: Harcourt.

Caroline Islands

*Wolfson, Margaret. 1999. *Turtle Songs: A Tale for Mothers and Daughters*. Illustrated by Karla Sachi. Hillsboro, OR: Beyond Words.

New Zealand (Maori)

*Te Kanawa, Kiri. 1989. *Land of the Long White Cloud: Maori Myths, Tales and Legends*. Illustrated by Michael Foreman. New York: Arcade.

Polynesia

Tune, Suelyn Ching. 1988. *How Maui Slowed the Sun*. Illustrated by Robin Yoko Burningham. Honolulu, HI: University of Hawaii Press.

South America (retold, collected, adapted)

NOTE: See also the Caribbean and Central America for Latino tales.

General

*Brusca, María Cristina, and Tona Wilson. 1995. *Pedro Fools the Gringo and Other Tales of a Latin American Trickster*. Illustrated by María Cristina Brusca. New York: Holt.

*Delacre, Lulu. 1996. *Golden Tales: Myths, Legends and Folktales from Latin America*. New York: Scholastic.

*González, Lucía. 1997. *Señor Cat's Romance and Other Favorite Stories from Latin America*. Illustrated by Lulu Delacre. New York: Scholastic.

Argentina

*Brusca, María, and Tona Wilson. 1992. *The Blacksmith and the Devils*. Illustrated by María Cristina Brusca. New York: Holt.

Brazil

DeSpain, Pleasant. 1998. *The Dancing Turtle: A Folktale from Brazil*. Illustrated by David Boston. Little Rock, AK: August House.

Gerson, Mary-Joan. 1994. *How Night Came from the Sea: A Story from Brazil*. Illustrated by Carla Golembe. Boston: Little, Brown.

Chile

Pitcher, Caroline. 2000. *Mariana and the Merchild*. Illustrated by Jackie Morris. Grand Rapids, MI: Eerdmans.

Ecuador

Vidal, Graciela. 1994. *The Search for the Magic Lake: A Folktale from Ecuador*. Illustrated by Donna Perrone. New York: Scholastic.

Peru

[+]Ehlert, Lois. 1992. *Moon Rope: A Peruvian Folktale/Un lazo a la luna*. Amy Prince, trans. San Diego: Harcourt.

Hickox, Rebecca. 1997. *Zorro and Quwi: Tales of a Trickster Guinea Pig*. Illustrated by Kim Howard. New York: Delacorte.

Suriname

Lichtveld, Noni. 1993. *I Lost My Arrow in the Kankan Tree*. New York: Lothrop.

MODERN LITERARY FOLK AND FAIRY TALES: SINGLE AUTHOR

Andersen, Hans Christian. 1974. *The Complete Fairy Tales and Stories*. Erik Christian Haugaard, trans. New York: Doubleday.
———. 1999. *The Little Match Girl*. Illustrated by Jerry Pinkney. New York: Penguin.
———. 1967. *The Little Mermaid*. Illustrated by Chihiro Iwasaki. Anthea Bell, adap. Saxonville, MA: Picture Book Studio.
———. 1979. *The Snow Queen*. Retold by Amy Ehrlich. Illustrated by Susan Jeffers. New York: Dial.
Clément, Claude. 1986. *The Painter and the Wild Swans*. Robert Levine, trans. Illustrated by Frédéric Clément. New York: Dial.
dePaola, Tomie. 1975. *Strega Nona*. New York: Simon and Schuster.
Kipling, Rudyard. 1996 [1902]. *Just So Stories*. Illustrated by Barry Moser. New York: Morrow.
Prokofiev, Sergei. 2000. *Peter and the Wolf: From the Symphony by Sergei Prokofiev*. Illustrated by Vladimir Vagin. New York: Scholastic.
Ward, Helen. 1997. *The King of the Birds*. Brookfield, CT: Millbrook.
Wilde, Oscar. 1994 [1888-1891]. *The Fairy Tales of Oscar Wilde*. Illustrated by Isabelle Brent. New York: Viking.

FRACTURED FAIRY TALES

Calmenson, Stephanie. 1989. *The Principal's New Clothes*. Illustrated by Denise Brunkus. New York: Scholastic.
*Rosales, Melodye. 1999. *Leola and the Honeybears: An African American Retelling of Goldilocks and the Three Bears*. New York: Scholastic.
Scieszka, John. 1992. *The Stinky Cheese Man and Other Fairly Stupid Tales*. Illustrated by Lane Smith. New York: Viking.
———. 1989. *The True Story of the Three Little Pigs! By A. Wolf*. Illustrated by Lane Smith. New York: Viking.

Epics

Babylon

Zeman, Ludmilla. 1992. *Gilgamesh the King*. Montreal: Tundra.

France

Sherwood, Merriam, trans. 1966 [1938]. *The Song of Roland*. Illustrated by Edith Emerson. New York: David McKay.

India

Souhami, Jessica. 1997. *Rama and the Demon King: An Ancient Tale of India*. New York: DK.

Ireland

Sutcliff, Rosemary. 1967. *Finn Mac Cool*. New York: Dutton.

Lenape People/Delaware

*Bruchac, Joseph. 1989. "The Walum Olum." In *Return of the Sun: Native American Tales from the Northeast Woodlands*. Illustrated by Gary Carpenter. Trumansburg, NY: Crossing Press.

Scandinavia

Synge, Ursula. 1978. *Land of Heroes: A Retelling of the Kalevala*. New York: Atheneum. (Finland)

Spain

Goldston, Robert. 1963. *The Legend of the Cid*. Illustrated by Stephanie. Indianapolis: Bobbs-Merrill.

United Kingdom

Thomas, Gwyn. 1984. *Tales from the Mabinogion*. Illustrated by Margaret Jones. Woodstock, NY: Overlook.
Sutcliff, Rosemary. 1961. *Beowulf*. Illustrated by Charles Keeping. New York: Dutton.

Legends

*[+]Anzaldúa, Gloria. 1995. *Prietita and the Ghost Woman/Prietita y la llorona*. Illustrated by Maya Christina Gonzalez. San Francisco: Children's Book Press. (Mexico)
*Bruchac, Joseph. 1993. *The First Strawberries: A Cherokee Story*. Illustrated by Anna Vojtech. New York: Dial.
*Eagle Walking Turtle. 1997. *Full Moon Stories: Thirteen Native American Legends*. New York: Hyperion.
Early, Margaret. 1991. *William Tell*. New York: Abrams.
Freedman, Florence B. 1985. *Brothers: A Hebrew Legend*. Illustrated by Robert Andrew Parker. New York: Harper.
*Harrell, Beatrice Orcutt. 1995. *How Thunder and Lightning Came to Be: A Choctaw Legend*. Illustrated by Susan L. Roth. New York: Dial.
Hodges, Margaret. 1984. *Saint George and the Dragon*. Illustrated by Trina Schart Hyman. Boston: Little, Brown. (England)

*Lee, Jeanne. 1983. *Legend of the Li River: An Ancient Chinese Tale*. New York: Holt.

Locker, Thomas. 1988. *Washington Irving's Rip Van Winkle*. New York: Dial. (United States)

Luenn, Nancy. 1997. *The Miser on the Mountain: A Nisqually Legend of Mount Ranier*. Illustrated by Pierr Morgan. Seattle, WA: Sasquatch.

Lurie, Alison. 1979. *The Heavenly Zoo: Legends and Tales of the Stars*. Illustrated by Monika Beisner. New York: Farrar.

*Otsuka, Yuzo. 1981 [1967]. *Suho and the White Horse: A Legend of Mongolia*. Illustrated by Suekichi Akaba. New York: Viking.

Sabuda, Robert. 1995. *Arthur and the Sword*. New York: Atheneum. (England)

Shepard, Aaron. 1998. *The Crystal Heart: A Vietnamese Legend*. Illustrated by Joseph Daniel Fiedler. New York: Atheneum. (readers theater and music)

*Velarde, Pablita. 1989. *Old Father Storyteller*. Santa Fe, NM: Clear Light.

*Vuong, Lynette Dyer. 1993. *Sky Legends of Vietnam*. Illustrated by Vo-Dinh Mai. New York: HarperCollins.

Myths

Burleigh, Robert. 2002. *Pandora*. Illustrated by Raul Colón. San Diego: Harcourt. (Greece)

Colum, Padraic. 1984 [1920]. *The Children of Odin: The Book of Northern Myths*. Illustrated by Willy Pogany. New York: Macmillan.

Craft, M. Charlotte. 1999. *King Midas and the Golden Touch*. Illustrated by K. Y. Craft. New York: Morrow. (Greece)

Fisher, Leonard. 1990. *Jason and the Golden Fleece*. New York: Holiday. (Greece)

Geringer, Laura. 1995. *The Pomegranate Seeds*. Illustrated by Leonid Gore. Boston: Houghton. (Greece)

*Hamilton, Virginia. 1988. *In the Beginning: Creation Stories from around the World*. Illustrated by Barry Moser. San Diego: Harcourt.

*Jaffe, Nina. 1996. *The Golden Flower: A Taino Myth from Puerto Rico*. Illustrated by Enrique O. Sánchez. New York: Simon and Schuster.

*Love, Hallie N. 1999. *Watákame's Journey: The Story of the Great Flood and the New World: A Huichol Indian Tale*. Illustrated by Huichol artists. Santa Fe, NM: Clear Light.

Mark, Jan. 1999. *The Midas Touch*. Illustrated by Juan Wijngaard. Cambridge, MA: Candlewick. (Greece)

Mayo, Margaret. 1996. *Mythical Birds & Beasts from Many Lands*. Illustrated by Janet Ray. New York: Dutton.

McCaughrean, Geraldine. 1999. *Roman Myths*. Illustrated by Emma Chichester Clark. New York: McElderry.

*Montejo, Victor. 1999. *Popol Vuh: A Sacred Book of the Maya*. David Unger, trans. Illustrated by Luis Garay. Toronto: Douglas & McIntyre.

Rackham, Arthur. 1979 [1911]. *Rackham's Color Illustrations for Wagner's "Ring."* New York: Dover. (Germanic)

*+Rohmer, Harriet, and Mary Anchondo. 1988. *How We Came to the Fifth World/Cómo vinimos al quinto mundo: A Creation Story from Ancient Mexico*. Illustrated by Graciela Carrillo. San Francisco: Children's Book Press.

*Taylor, C. J. 1993. *How We Saw the World: Nine Native Stories of the Way Things Began*. Toronto: Tundra.

Waldherr, Kris. 1995. *The Book of Goddesses*. Hillsboro, OR: Beyond Words.

Tall Tales

Johnson, Paul Brett. 1999. *Old Drye Frye: A Deliciously Funny Tall Tale*. New York: Scholastic. (Southeastern United States)

Kellogg, Steven. 1995. *Sally Ann Thunder Ann Whirlwind Crockett*. New York: Morrow.

*Lester, Julius. 1994. *John Henry*. Illustrated by Jerry Pinkney. New York: Dial.

MODERN LITERARY TALL TALES

Isaacs, Anne. 1994. *Swamp Angel*. Illustrated by Paul Zelinsky. New York: Dutton.

*McKissack, Patricia. 1991. *A Million Fish . . . More or Less*. Illustrated by Dena Schutzer. New York: Knopf.

*Medearis, Angela Shelf. 1996. *Tailypo: A Newfangled Tall Tale*. Illustrated by Sterling Brown. New York: Holiday.

Wood, Audrey. 1996. *The Bunyans*. New York: Scholastic.

Bibliography for Chapter 8 Informational Books: Finding the Aesthetic

Archeology

Avi-Yonah, Michael. 1993. *Dig This! How Archaeologists Uncover Our Past*. Brooklyn, NY: Runestone.

Duke, Kate. 1997. *Archaeologists Dig for Clues*. New York: HarperCollins.

Sloan, Christopher. 2002. *Bury the Dead: Tombs, Corpses, Mummies, Skeletons, and Rituals*. Washington, DC: National Geographic.

Architecture

NOTE: See Architects in the bibliography for Chapter 10.

Ceserani, Gian, and Piero Ventura. 1983. *Grand Constructions*. New York: Putnam's.

Knight, Margy Burns. 1992. *Talking Walls*. Illustrated by Anne Sibley O'Brien. Gardiner, ME: Tilbury House.

Macaulay, David. 1973. *Cathedral: The Story of Its Construction*. Boston: Houghton.

Munro, Roxie. 1996. *The Inside-Outside Book of Libraries*. Text by Julie Cummins. New York: Dutton. (series)

Crafts

NOTE: See Folk Artists in the bibliography for Chapter 10.

Fisher, Leonard Everett. 2000 [1965]. *The Printers.* New York: Cavendish. (series: The Colonial Craftsmen)

Houston, James. 1998. *Fire into Ice: Adventures in Glass Making.* Toronto: Tundra.

Presilla, Maricel E., and Gloria Soto. 1996. *Life around the Lake: Embroideries by the Women of Lake Pátzcuaro.* New York: Holt. (Tarascan Indians of Mexico)

Culinary Arts

Dooley, Norah. 1991. *Everybody Cooks Rice.* Illustrated by Peter J. Thornton. Minneapolis, MN. Carolrhoda.

Morris, Ann. 1993. *Bread, Bread, Bread.* Photographs by Ken Heyman. New York: Mulberry.

Pratt, Dianne. 1998. *Hey Kids! You're Cookin' Now! A Global Awareness Cooking Adventure.* Illustrated by Janet Winter. Sailsbury Cove, ME: Harvest Hill Press.

Yu, Ling. 2002. *Cooking the Chinese Way: Revised and Expanded to Include New Low-Fat and Vegetarian Recipes.* Minneapolis, MN: Lerner.

Zalben, Jane Breskin. 1996. *Beni's Family Cookbook for the Jewish Holidays.* New York: Holt.

Fine Arts

NOTE: See Actors and Entertainers; Choreographers and Dancers; Musicians; Visual Artists; and, Writers in the bibliography for Chapter 10.

General

Locker, Thomas. 1995. *Sky Tree: Seeing Science through Art.* New York: HarperCollins.

*+Nye, Naomi Shihab, ed. 1995. *The Tree Is Older Than You Are: A Bilingual Gathering of Poems & Stories with Paintings by Mexican Artists.* New York: Simon and Schuster.

Sullivan, Charles, ed. 1991. *Children of Promise: African-American Literature and Art for Young People.* New York: Abrams.

Calligraphy

*Lee, Huy Voun. 1998. *At the Beach.* New York: Holt.

*Young, Ed. 1997. *Voices of the Heart.* New York: Scholastic.

Dance

Barboza, Steven. 1992. *I Feel Like Dancing: A Year with Jacques d'Amboise and the National Dance Institute.* Photographs by Carolyn George d'Amboise. New York: Crown.

Bowes, Deborah. 1999. *The Ballet Book: The Young Performer's Guide to Classical Dance, The National Ballet School.* Photographs by Lydia Pawelak. Buffalo, NY: Firefly. (Canada)

Fonteyn, Margot. 1998. *Coppélia.* Illustrated by Steve Johnson and Lou Fancher. San Diego: Harcourt.

Jones, Bill T., and Susan Kuklin. 1998. *Dance.* New York: Hyperion.

Literature

*Curry, Barbara K., and James Michael Brodie. 1996. *Sweet Words So Brave: The Story of African American Literature.* Illustrated by Jerry Butler. Madison, WI: Zino.

Ross, Stewart. 1994. *Shakespeare and Macbeth: The Story Behind the Play.* Illustrated by Tony Karpinski. New York: Viking.

Music

Collier, James Lincoln. 1997. *Jazz: An American Saga.* New York: Holt.

Colón-Vilá, Lillian. 1998. *Salsa.* Illustrated by Roberta Collier-Morales. Houston, TX: Piñata.

*Igus, Toyomi. 1998. *I See the Rhythm.* Illustrated by Michele Wood. San Francisco: Children's Book Press.

Johnson, Anne E. 1999. *Jazz Tap: From Drums to American Feet.* New York: Rosen.

Kuskin, Karla. 1982. *The Philharmonic Gets Dressed.* New York: HarperCollins.

McMahon, Patricia. 2001. *Dancing Wheels.* Photographs by John Godt. Boston: Houghton. (dancers in wheelchairs)

Raschka, Chris. 1997. *Mysterious Thelonius.* New York: Orchard.

Puppetry

Baird, Bil. 1973. *The Art of the Puppet.* New York: Bonanza.

Keene, Donald. 1965. *Bunraku: The Art of the Japanese Puppet Theatre.* Tokyo: Kodansha.

Simmen, René. 1975. *The World of Puppets.* Photographs by Leonardo Bezzola. New York: Crowell.

Storytelling

NOTE: See bibliography for Chapter 7.

Pellowski, Anne. 1995. *The Storytelling Handbook: A Young People's Collection of Unusual Tales and Helpful Hints on How to Tell Them.* Illustrated by Martha Stoberock. New York: Simon and Schuster.

Theater

NOTE: See bibliography for Chapter 6.

*Haskins, James. 1982. *Black Theater in America.* Illustrated with photographs. New York: Crowell.

Visual Arts

Bang, Molly. 2000. *Picture This: How Pictures Work*. New York: SeaStar.

Belloli, Andrea. 1999. *Exploring World Art*. Los Angeles: The J. Paul Getty Museum.

Bjork, Christina. 1985. *Linnea in Monet's Garden*. Illustrated by Lena Anderson. New York: R & S.

Brust, Beth Wagner. 1994. *The Amazing Paper Cuttings of Hans Christian Andersen*. New York: Ticknor & Fields.

Emberley, Ed. 1979. *Ed Emberley's Big Green Drawing Book*. Boston: Little, Brown. (series)

*Ewing, Patrick. 1999. *In the Paint*. Illustrated by Linda L. Louis. New York: Abbeville.

*⁺Garza, Carmen Lomas. 1999. *Magic Windows/Ventanas mágicas*. San Francisco: Children's Book Press.

Hucko, Bruce. 1996. *A Rainbow at Night: The World in Words and Pictures by Navajo Children*. San Francisco: Chronicle.

Mayhew, James. 2000. *Katie and the Sunflowers*. New York: Orchard.

———. 1999. *Katie Meets the Impressionists*. New York: Orchard.

Rubin, Susan Goldman. 2001. *The Yellow House: Vincent Van Gogh and Paul Gaugin Side by Side*. Illustrated by Joseph A. Smith. New York: Art Institue of Chicago/Abrams.

Flags

*Ryan, Pam Muñoz. 1998. *The Flag We Love*. Illustrated by Ralph Masiello. Watertown, MA: Charlesbridge.

Smith, Nicole. 1998. *Flags of the World*. Rochester, Kent (UK): Grange Books.

Forensics

Jackson, Donna M. 1996. *The Bone Detectives: How Forensic Anthropologists Solve Crimes and Uncover Mysteries of the Dead*. Photographs by Charlie Fellenbaum. Boston: Little, Brown.

Games, Riddles, and Hobbies

Broner, Simon J. 1988. *American Children's Folklore: A Book of Rhymes, Games, Jokes, Stories, Secret Languages, Beliefs and Camp Legends*. Little Rock, AK: August House.

Burnie, Richard. 1999. *Monumental Mazes*. New York: Knopf.

Lankford, Mary D. 1992. *Hopscotch around the World*. Illustrated by Karen Milone. New York: Morrow.

Marzollo, Jean. 1996. *I Spy Spooky Night: A Book of Picture Riddles*. Photographs by Walter Wick. New York: Scholastic.

Munro, Roxie. 2001. *Mazescapes*. New York: SeaStar.

Geneology

Douglas, Ann. 1999. *The Family Tree Detective: Cracking the Case of Your Family's Story*. Illustrated by Stephen MacEachern. Toronto: Owl.

Inventions

NOTE: See Scientists and Inventors in the bibliography for Chapter 10.

Dash, Joan. 2000. *The Longitude Prize*. Illustrated by Dušn Petričič. New York: Farrar. (John Harrison, eighteenth century)

Duffy, Trent. 2000. *The Clock*. New York: Atheneum.

Krensky, Stephen. 1996. *Breaking into Print: Before and After the Invention of the Printing Press*. Illustrated by Bonnie Christensen. Boston: Little, Brown.

Language Arts

Agee, Jon. 1992. *Go Hang a Salami! I'm a Lasagna Hog! And Other Palindromes*. New York: Farrar. (series)

Burleigh, Robert. 1997. *Who Said That? Famous Americans Speak*. Illustrated by David Catrow. New York: Holt.

*⁺Gonzalez, Ralfka, and Ana Ruiz. 1995. *My First Book of Proverbs/Mi primer libro de dichos*. San Francisco: Children's Book Press.

Gwynne, Fred. 1989 [1970]. *The King Who Rained*. New York: Simon and Schuster. (idioms)

Heller, Ruth. 1990. *Behind the Mask: A Book about Prepositions*. New York: Putnam's. (series)

Wrixon, Fred B. 1998. *Codes, Ciphers and Other Cryptic and Clandestine Communications: 400 Ways to Send Secret Messages from Hieroglyphs to the Internet*. Rev. ed. New York: Black Dog.

Mathematics

NOTE: See Mathematicians in the bibliography for Chapter 10.

Burns, Marilyn. 1997. *Spaghetti and Meatballs for All!* Illustrated by Debbie Tilley. New York: Scholastic.

Kenda, Margaret, and Phyllis S. Williams. 1995. *Math Wizardry for Kids*. Hauppauge, NY: Barron's.

Ledwon, Peter. 2000. *Midnight Math: Twelve Terrific Math Games*. Illustrated by Marilyn Mets. New York: Holiday.

Leedy, Loreen. 1994. *Fraction Action*. New York: Holiday.

Murphy, Stuart J. 2002. *Racing Around*. Illustrated by Mike Reed. New York: HarperCollins.

Myller, Rolf. 1990 [1962]. *How Big Is a Foot?* New York: Dell.

Neuschwander, Cindy. 1999. *Sir Cumference and the Dragon of Pi*. Watertown, MA: Charlesbridge.

Schwartz, David M. 1998. *G Is for Googol: A Math Alphabet Book*. Illustrated for Marissa Moss. Berkeley, CA: Tricycle Press.

Scieszka, Jon and Lane Smith. 1995. *Math Curse*. New York: Viking.

Tang, Greg. 2001. *The Grapes of Math: Mind-Stretching Math Riddles*. Illustrated by Harry Briggs. New York: Scholastic.

Tompert, Ann. 1990. *Grandfather Tang's Story*. New York: Crown.

Science: Earth, Ecology, Life, Physical, and Space

NOTE: See Scientists and Inventors in the bibliography for Chapter 10.

Earth Science

George, Jean Craighead. 1995. *Everglades.* Illustrated by Wendell Minor. New York: HarperCollins.

George, Michael. 1992. *Deserts.* Mankato, MN: Creative Education. (series)

Hassler, David, and Lynn Gregor, eds. 1999. *A Place to Grow: Voices and Images of Urban Gardeners.* Photographs by Don Snyder. Cleveland, OH: Pilgrim.

Lauber, Patricia. 1990. *How We Learned the Earth Was Round.* Illustrated by Megan Lloyd. New York: Crowell.

Marshak, Suzanna. 1991. *I Am the Ocean.* Illustrated by James Endicott. Boston: Little, Brown.

Pfeffer, Wendy. 1997. *A Log's Life.* Illustrated by Robin Brickman. New York: Simon and Schuster.

Simon, Seymour. 1991. *Earthquakes.* New York: HarperCollins. (series)

Ecology

NOTE: See also works by Michael Caduto and Joseph Bruchac in Chapter 7 under American Indians/General, and see Naturalists, Ecologists, and Environmentalists in the bibliography for Chapter 10.

Bang, Molly. 1996. *Chattanooga Sludge.* San Diego: Harcourt.

Berger, Melvin. 1999. *Oil Spill!* Illustrated by Paul Mirocha. Boston: Houghton.

Carson, Rachel. 1956. *The Sense of Wonder.* Photographs by Charles Pratt. New York: Harper.

Cerullo, Mary M. 1996. *Coral Reef: A City That Never Sleeps.* Photographs by Jeffrey L. Rotman. New York: Dutton.

Cherry, Lynne. 1992. *A River Ran Wild: An Environmental History.* San Diego: Harcourt.

Cone, Molly. 1992. *Come Back, Salmon.* Photographs by Sidnee Wheelwright. San Francisco: Sierra Club.

Editions Gallimard. 1992. *The Rain Forest.* New York: Scholastic.

Goodall, Jane. 2001. *The Chimpanzees I Love: Saving Their World and Ours.* New York: Scholastic.

Holling, Holling C. 1998 [1941]. *Paddle-to-the-Sea.* Madison, WI: Turtleback.

Mazer, Anne. 2000. *The Salamander Room.* Boston: Houghton.

Pratt, Kristin Joy. 1992. *A Walk in the Rainforest.* Nevada City, CA: Dawn.

Sams, Carl R., and Jean Stoick. 2000. *Stranger in the Woods: A Photographic Fantasy.* Milford, MI: Carl Sams II Photography.

Vavra, Robert. 1990. *I Love Nature More.* New York: Morrow.

Life Science

*Astorga, Amalia, as told to Gary Paul Nauhan. 2001. *Efraín of the Sonoran Desert: A Lizard's Life among the Seri Indians.* Illustrated by Janet K. Miller. El Paso, TX: Cinco Puntos.

Brooks, Bruce. 1993. *Making Sense: Animal Perception and Communication.* New York: Farrar/Thirteen/WNET.

Burnett, Nancy, and Brad Matsen. 2002. *The Shape of Life.* Monterey, CA: Monterey Bay Aquarium Press/Sea Studios Foundation.

Cerullo, Mary M. 2001. *Sea Soup: Zooplankton.* Photographs by Bill Curtsinger. Gardiner, ME: Tilbury House/Gulf of Maine Aquarium.

George, Jean Craighead. 1994. *Animals Who Have Won Our Hearts.* Illustrated by Christine Herman Merrill. New York: HarperCollins.

Hawes, Judy. 1991 [1963]. *Fireflies in the Night.* Illustrated by Ellen Alexander. New York: Crowell.

Kramer, Stephen. 2001. *Hidden Worlds: Looking through a Scientist's Microscope.* Photographs by Dennis Kunkel. Boston: Houghton.

Munro, Margaret. 2000. *The Story of Life on Earth.* Illustrated by Karen Reczuch. Toronto: Douglas & McIntyre.

Snow, Alan. 1993. *How Dogs Really Work.* Boston: Little, Brown.

Taylor, Barbara. 1999. *Elephants.* Dr. Adrian Lister, cons. New York: Lorenz.

Zoehfeld, Kathleen Weidner. 2001. *Dinosaur Parents, Dinosaur Young: Uncovering the Mystery of Dinosaur Families.* New York: Clarion.

Physical Science

Ardley, Neil. 1992. *The Way It Works: Electricity.* New York: Macmillan.

Dalton, Stephen. 2001. *The Miracle of Flight.* Buffalo, NY: Firefly.

Herbert, Don. 1980. *Mr. Wizard's Supermarket Science.* New York: Random House.

Jennings, Terry. 1996. *101 Amazing Optical Illusions.* Illustrated by Alex Pang. New York: Sterling.

Kuklin, Susan. 1998. *Fireworks: The Science, the Art, and the Magic.* New York: Hyperion.

Wick, Walter. 1998. *Walter Wick's Optical Tricks.* New York: Scholastic.

———. 1997. *A Drop of Water: A Book of Science and Wonder.* New York: Scholastic.

Space

Cole, Joanna. 1990. *The Magic School Bus: Lost in the Solar System.* Illustrated by Bruce Degan. New York: Scholastic.

Fradin, Dennis. 1997. *The Planet Hunters: The Search for Other Worlds.* New York: Simon and Schuster.

Ride, Sally, with Susan Okie. 1986. *To Space & Back.* New York: Lothrop.

Simon, Seymour. 1988. *Galaxies.* New York: Morrow.

Siy, Alexandra. 2001. *Footprints on the Moon*. Watertown, MA: Charlesbridge.

Service

Lewis, Barbara A., and Pamela Espeland. 1995. *The Kid's Guide to Service Projects: Over 500 Service Ideas for Young People Who Want to Make a Difference*. Minneapolis, MN: Free Spirit.

Social Studies

Cultures, Geography and Travel, and History

NOTE: See Anthropologists and Historians in the bibliography for Chapter 10.

Cultures

*Ancona, George. 1997. *Mayeros: A Yucatec Maya Family*. New York: Lothrop.

Artley, Bob. 2001. *Once upon a Farm*. Gretna, LA: Pelican.

Ashabranner, Brent. 1986. *Children of the Maya: A Guatemalan Indian Odyssey*. Photographs by Paul Conklin. New York: Dodd.

Beeler, Selby B. 1998. *Throw Your Tooth on the Roof: Tooth Traditions from around the World*. Illustrated by G. Brian Karas. Boston: Houghton.

Beskow, Elsa. 2000 [1929]. *Pelle's New Suit*. Edinburgh, Scotland: Floris Books.

Buettner, Dan. 1997. *Africatrek: A Journey by Bicycle through Africa*. Minneapolis, MN: Lerner.

* +Ekoomiak, Normee. 1990. *Arctic Memories*. New York: Holt.

*Hamanaka, Shelia, and Ayano Ohmi. 1999. *In Search of the Spirit: The Living National Treasures of Japan*. Illustrated by Sheila Hamanaka. Calligraphy by Ayano Ohmi. New York: Morrow.

*Krach, Maywan Shen. 1997. *D Is for Doufu: An Alphabet Book of Chinese Culture*. Illustrated by Hongbin Zhang. Fremont, CA: Shen's Books.

Lauber, Patricia. 1999. *What You Never Knew about Fingers, Forks & Chopsticks*. Illustrated by John Manders. New York: Simon and Schuster.

*National Museum of the American Indian. 1997. *Stories of the People: Native American Voices*. Washington, DC: National Museum of the American Indian.

*Ortiz, Simon J. 1988 [1977]. *The People Shall Continue*. Illustrated by Sharol Graves. San Francisco: Children's Book Press.

Rylant, Cynthia. 1991. *Appalachia: The Voices of Sleeping Birds*. Illustrated by Barry Moser. San Diego: Harcourt.

Trimble, Stephen, ed. 1986. *Our Voices, Our Land*. Photographs by Stephen Trimble and Harvey Lloyd. Flagstaff, AZ: Northland.

Geography and Travel

Bjork, Christina. 2000. *Vendela in Venice*. Illustrated by Inga-Karin Eriksson. New York: R & S.

Keller, Laurie. 1998. *The Scrambled States of America*. New York: Holt.

Young, Karen Romano. 2002. *Small Worlds: A Book about Maps and Mapmakers*. New York: Scholastic.

History

NOTE: Histories specific to a particular chronological period of time are found in the Chapter 9 bibliography, Historical Literature/Informational.

*Bolden, Tonya. 2001. *Tell All the Children Our Story: Memories and Mementoes of Being Young and Black in America*. New York: Abrams.

*Bruchac, Joseph. 1997. *Lasting Echoes: An Oral History of Native American People*. Illustrated by Paul Morin. San Diego: Harcourt.

Murphy, Jim. 1998. *Gone A-Whaling: The Lure of the Sea and the Hunt for the Great Whales*. New York: Clarion.

*Myers, Walter Dean. 1991. *Now Is Your Time! The African-American Struggle for Freedom*. New York: HarperCollins.

Sports

NOTE: See Athletes in the bibliography for Chapter 10.

Macy, Sue. 1993. *A Whole New Ball Game: The Story of the All-American Girls Professional Baseball League*. New York: Holt.

Nemec, David. 1994. *Players of Cooperstown: Baseball's Hall of Fame*. Lincolnwood, IL: Publications International.

Ward, Geoffrey C., and Ken Burns with Jim O'Connor. 1994. *Shadow Ball: The History of the Negro Leagues*. New York: Knopf.

Technology

Baker, Christopher. 2000. *Virtual Reality: Experiencing Illusion*. Brookfield, CT: Millbrook.

Macaulay, David, with Neil Ardley. 1998. *The New Way Things Work: From Levers to Lasers, Cars to Computers—A Visual Guide to the World of Machines*. Boston: Houghton.

Platt, Richard. 1997. *Stephen Biesty's Incredible Everything*. Illustrated by Stephen Biesty. New York: DK.

Raatman, Lucia. 1999. *Safety on the Internet*. Mankato, MN: Bridgestone.

World Languages

The Editors of Passport Books. *Let's Learn Italian Picture Book*. Passport Books. Lincolnwood, IL: NTC. (series)

Rankin, Laura. 1996. *The Handmade Alphabet*. New York: Penguin. (American Sign Language)

Bibliography for Chapter 9
Integrated Historical Literature:
The Human Dimension

Prehistoric

Historical Fiction

Nolan, Dennis. 1989. *Wolf Child.* New York: Macmillan.

Informational

Arnold, Caroline. 1997. *Stone Age Farmers beside the Sea: Scotland's Prehistoric Village of Skara Brae.* Photographs by Arthur P. Arnold. New York: Clarion.

Ancient History

Biography

Stanley, Diane, and Peter Vennema. 1994. *Cleopatra.* Illustrated by Diane Stanley. New York: Morrow.

Historical Fiction

Fleischman, Paul. 1996. *Dateline: Troy.* Cambridge, MA: Candlewick.
McGraw, Eloise. 1986 [1961]. *The Golden Goblet.* New York: Viking.

Informational

Blacklock, Dyan. 2000. *Olympia: Warrior Athletes of Ancient Greece.* Illustrated by David Kennett. New York: Walker.
Fisher, Leonard Everett. 1986. *The Great Wall of China.* New York: Macmillan.
Greenblatt, Miriam. 2000. *Alexander the Great and Ancient Greece.* New York: Cavendish.
Macaulay, David. 1975. *Pyramid.* Boston: Houghton.
Reeves, Nicholas, and Nan Froman. 1992. *Into the Mummy's Tomb: The Real Life Discovery of Tutankhamun's Treasures.* New York: Scholastic.
Waldman, Neil. 1998. *Masada.* New York: Morrow.

The Middle Ages, 476–1450

Biography

*Burns, Kephra. 2001. *Mansa Musa: The Lion of Mali.* Illustrated by Leo and Diane Dillon. San Diego: Harcourt.
Roth, Susan L. 1990. *Marco Polo: His Notebook.* New York: Doubleday.
Stanley, Diane. 2002. *Saladin: Noble Prince of Islam.* New York: HarperCollins.
———. 1998. *Joan of Arc.* New York: Morrow.

Historical Fiction

Avi. 2002. *Crispin: The Cross of Lead.* New York: Hyperion.
Cushman, Karen. 1995. *The Midwife's Apprentice.* New York: HarperCollins. (Britain)
———. 1994. *Catherine Called Birdy.* New York: Clarion. (Britain)
deAngeli, Marguerite. 1949. *The Door in the Wall.* New York: Doubleday. (Britain)
Konigsburg, E. L. 1973. *A Proud Taste for Scarlet and Miniver.* New York: Atheneum. (Eleanor of Aquitaine)
*Park, Linda Sue. 2001. *A Single Shard.* New York: Clarion. (Korea)

Informational

Aliki. 1983. *A Medieval Feast.* New York: Crowell.
Clare, John D., ed. 1996. *Fourteenth-Century Towns.* San Diego: Harcourt.
Hunt, Jonathan. 1989. *Illuminations.* New York: Simon and Schuster.
Sancha, Sheila. 1982. *The Luttrell Village: Country Life in the Middle Ages.* New York: Crowell.
Wilson, Elizabeth B. 1994. *Bibles and Bestiaries: A Guide to Illuminated Manuscripts.* New York: Farrar/The Pierpont Morgan Library.

Exploration and Colonization, 1450–1600

Biography

Aronson, Marc. 2000. *Sir Walter Raleigh and the Quest for El Dorado.* New York: Clarion.
Stanley, Diane. 2000. *Michelangelo.* New York: HarperCollins.
———. 1996. *Leonardo daVinci.* New York: Morrow.
Stanley, Diane, and Peter Vennema. 1992. *Bard of Avon: The Story of William Shakespeare.* Illustrated by Diane Stanley. New York: Morrow.
Thomas, Jane Resh. 1998. *Behind the Mask: The Life of Queen Elizabeth I.* New York: Clarion.

Historical Fiction

*Dorris, Michael. 1992. *Morning Girl.* New York: Hyperion. (Taino Indians)
Konigsburg, E. L. 1978. *The Second Mrs. Giaconda.* New York: Macmillan. (Renaissance Italy, Leonardo da Vinci)
Stolz, Mary. 1990. *Bartholomew Fair.* Illustrated by Pamela Johnson. New York: Greenwillow.
Walsh, Jill Paton. 1983. *A Parcel of Patterns.* New York: Farrar. (plague in the 1600s)

Informational

Bigelow, Bill, and Bob Peterson. 1998. *Rethinking Columbus: The Next 500 Years.* Rev. ed. Milwaukee, WI: Rethinking Schools Ltd.

Kurlansky, Mark. 2001. *The Cod's Tale*. Illustrated by S. D. Schindler. New York: Putnam's.

1600–1776, Including the Colonial Period in the United States

NOTE: See Thanksgiving in the bibliography for Chapter 13.

Biography

Jacobs, Paul Samuel. 1997. *James Printer: A Novel of Rebellion*. New York: Scholastic. (Nipmuc)

Philpotts, Karl. 1990. *Nanny of the Maroons*. Illustrated by Wilfred Limonious. Brooklyn, NY: Handprint Publications. (Jamaica)

Historical Fiction

Bawden, Nina. 1966. *The Witch's Daughter*. Philadelphia: Lippincott.

*Bruchac, Joseph. 2002. *The Winter People*. New York: Dial. (French and Indian War, 1759)

Bulla, Clyde Robert. 1981. *A Lion to Guard Us*. New York: Crowell. (Bermuda and Virginia, 1609-1610)

Clapp, Patricia. 1982. *Witches' Children: A Story of Salem*. New York: Lothrop.

Hesse, Karen. 2000. *Stowaway*. Illustrated by Robert Andrew Parker. New York: Simon and Schuster. (explorer James Cook)

*Petry, Ann. 1964. *Tituba of Salem Village*. New York: Crowell. (Salem, 1692)

Speare, Elizabeth George. 1958. *The Witch of Blackbird Pond*. Boston: Houghton. (Connecticut, 1687)

Historical Realism

Defoe, Daniel. 1957 [1719]. *Robinson Crusoe*. Scribner's. (1632) (Survival Story)

Informational

*Hansen, Joyce, and Gary McGowan. 1998. *Breaking Ground, Breaking Silence: The Story of New York's African Burial Ground*. New York: Holt.

Waters, Kate. 1996. *Tapenum's Day: A Wampanoag Indian Boy in Pilgrim Times*. Photographs by Russ Kendall. New York: Scholastic.

War of Independence, 1776–1783

Biography

Bober, Natalie S. 1995. *Abigail Adams: Witness to a Revolution*. New York: Atheneum.

Fradin, Dennis. 2002. *The Signers: The Fifty-six Stories behind the Delaration of Independence*. Illustrated by Michael McCurdy. New York: Walker.

Giblin, James Cross. 2000. *The Amazing Life of Benjamin Franklin*. Illustrated by Michael Dooling. New York: Scholastic.

Harness, Cheryl. 2000. *George Washington*. Washington, D.C.: National Geographic.

Severance, John B. 1998. *Thomas Jefferson: Architect of Democracy*. New York: Clarion.

St. George, Judith. 2001. *John and Abigail Adams: An American Love Story*. New York: Holiday.

Historical Fiction

Avi. 1984. *The Fighting Ground*. Philadelphia: Lippincott. (Trenton, 1778)

*Bruchac, Joseph. 1998. *The Arrow over the Door*. Illustrated by James Watling. New York: Dial. (Abenaki and Quakers, based on historical incident)

Collier, James Lincoln, and Christopher Collier. 1974. *My Brother Sam Is Dead*. New York: Four Winds.

Forbes, Esther. 1998 [1943]. *Johnny Tremain*. Illustrated by Michael McCurdy. Boston: Houghton.

Gauch, Patricia Lee. 1974. *This Time, Tempe Wick?* Illustrated by Margot Tomes. New York: Coward.

Informational

Freedman, Russell. 2000. *Give Me Liberty! The Story of the Declaration of Independence*. New York: Holiday.

Ka-hon-hes. 1999. *Kaianerekowa Hotinonsionne/The Great Law of Peace of the Longhouse People*. Akwesasen, trans. Notes with the assistance of Ray Tehanetorens Fadden. Illustrated by John Kahiones Fadden. Berkeley, CA: Oyate. (influenced the Constitution)

Slavery and the Underground Railroad, 1619–1863

NOTE: See Christianity in the Chapter 13 bibliography for spirituals and slave songs. See also Chapter 5 on Poetry.

Autobiography

*Douglass, Frederick. 1994. *Escape from Slavery: The Boyhood of Frederick Douglass in His Own Words*. Edited and illustrated by Michael McCurdy. New York: Knopf.

Biography

deAngeli, Marguerite. 2000 [1940]. *Thee, Hannah!* 2nd ed. Scottdale, PA: Herald Press. (Philadelphia Quakers, 1850)

Fradin, Dennis Brindell. 2000. *Bound for the North Star: True Stories of Fugitive Slaves*. New York: Clarion.

*Hamilton, Virginia. 1993. *Many Thousand Gone: African-Americans from Slavery to Freedom*. Illustrated by Leo and Diane Dillon. New York: Scholastic.

*Hermence, Belinda. 1997. *Slavery Time: When I Was Chillun*. New York: Putnam's.

*McKissack, Patricia, and Frederick McKissack. *Sojourner Truth: Ain't I a Woman?* New York: Scholastic.

*Petry, Ann. 1983 [1955]. *Harriet Tubman: Conductor on the Underground Railroad*. New York: Harper.

*Rappaport, Doreen. 2002. *No More! Stories and Songs of Slave Resistance.* Illustrated by Shane W. Evans. Cambridge, MA: Candlewick.

*Walter, Mildred Pitts. 1996. *Second Daughter: The Story of a Slave Girl.* New York: Scholastic.

Historical Fiction

Armstrong, Jennifer. 1992. *Steal Away.* New York: Orchard. (1855, 1896)

Fleischman, Paul. 1991. *The Borning Room.* New York: HarperCollins. (Ohio Quakers, 1820)

*Hansen, Joyce. 1994. *The Captive.* New York: Scholastic.

*McGill, Alice. 2000. *Miles' Song.* Boston: Houghton.

*McKissack, Patricia C. 1997. *A Picture of Freedom: The Diary of Clotee, a Slave Girl.* New York: Scholastic.

Paulsen, Gary. 1993. *Nightjohn.* New York: Delacorte.

Informational

Bial, Raymond. 1997. *The Strength of These Arms: Life in the Slave Quarters.* Boston: Houghton.

———. 1995. *The Underground Railroad.* Boston: Houghton.

*Haskins, James, and Kathleen Benson. 1999. *Bound for America: The Forced Migration of Africans to the New World.* Illustrated by Floyd Cooper. New York: Lothrop.

*Lester, Julius. 1998. *From Slave Ship to Freedom Road.* Illustrated by Rod Brown. New York: Dial.

*Myers, Walter Dean. 1998. *Amistad: A Long Road to Freedom.* New York: Dutton.

1783–1861, Including American Indians and the European Settlers, Industrialization, and the Irish Potato Famine

Biography

Blumberg, Rhonda. 1985. *Commodore Perry in the Land of the Shogun.* New York: Lothrop. (Japan, 1853)

Klausner, Janet. 1993. *Sequoyah's Gift: A Portrait of the Cherokee Leader.* New York: HarperCollins.

Plain, Nancy. 1997. *The Man Who Painted Indians: George Catlin.* New York: Benchmark.

Historical Fiction

Anderson, Laurie Halse. 2000. *Fever, 1793.* New York: Simon and Schuster. (Philadelphia)

Avi. 1994. *The Barn.* New York: Orchard. (Oregon Territory, 1855)

Conlon-McKenna, Marita. 1990. *Under the Hawthorn Tree.* Illustrated by Donald Teskey. New York: Holiday. (Irish potato famine)

Cushman, Karen. 1996. *The Ballad of Lucy Whipple.* New York: Clarion. (California gold rush)

DeFelice, Cynthia. 1990. *Weasel.* New York: Atheneum. (government-Indian relations, Ohio, 1839)

*Erdrich, Louise. 1999. *The Birchbark House.* New York: Hyperion. (Great Lakes, 1847)

*Harrell, Beatrice O. 1999. *Longwalker's Journey: A Novel of the Choctaw Trail of Tears.* Illustrated by Tony Meers. New York: Dial.

Paterson, Katherine. 1996. *Jip: His Story.* New York: Dutton.

———. 1991. *Lyddie.* New York: Penguin. (Vermont, then Massachusetts mills, 1840s)

*Yep, Laurence. 1984. *The Serpent's Children.* New York: Harper. (Opium wars)

Historical Realism

Brontë, Charlotte. 1991 [1847]. *Jane Eyre.* New York: Knopf. (romantic novel)

Dickens, Charles. 2003 [1837]. *Oliver Twist.* London: Penguin.

Stevenson, Robert Louis. 1971 [1883]. *Treasure Island.* Illustrated by N.C. Wyeth. New York: Simon and Schuster. (boys' story)

Informational

Bartoletti, Susan Campbell. 2001. *Black Potatoes: The Story of the Great Irish Famine, 1845-1850.* Boston: Houghton.

Fitzpatrick, Marie Louise. 1998. *The Long March: The Choctaw's Gift to Irish Famine Relief.* Hillsboro, OR: Beyond Words.

Freedman, Russell. 1992. *An Indian Winter.* Illustrated by Karl Bodmer (in 1833-1834). New York: Holiday. (Mandans, Hidatsas)

Lyons, Mary E., ed. 2002. *Feed the Children First: Irish Memories of the Great Hunger.* New York: Simon and Schuster.

The Civil War, 1861–1865

Biography

Freedman, Russell. 1987. *Lincoln: A Photobiography.* New York: Clarion.

Meltzer, Milton, ed. 1993. *Lincoln, in His Own Words.* Illustrated by Stephen Alcorn. San Diego: Harcourt.

Sandburg, Carl. 1926. *Abe Lincoln Grows up.* Illustrated by James Daugherty. San Diego: Harcourt.

Historical Fiction

Beatty, Patricia. 1987. *Charley Skedaddle.* New York: Morrow. (Blue Ridge Mountains)

*Hansen, Joyce. 1986. *Which Way Freedom?* New York: Walker.

Hunt, Irene. 1964. *Across Five Aprils.* New York: Berkley.

Matas, Carol. 2001. *The War Within: A Novel of the Civil War.* New York: Simon and Schuster. (Jews in the Confederacy)

Perez, Norah A. 1984. *The Slopes of War.* Boston: Houghton.

Werstein, Irving. 1963. *Massacre at Sand Creek.* New York: Scribner's. (betrayal of the Cheyenne)

Wisler, G. Clifton. 1991. *Red Cap*. New York: Lodestar. (Andersonville prison)

Historical Realism

Alcott, Louisa May. 1968 [1868]. *Little Women*. Illustrations by Jessie Wilcox Smith. Boston: Little, Brown. (domestic realism)

Informational

Chang, Ina. 1991. *A Separate Battle: Women & the Civil War*. New York: Lodestar.

Cox, Clinton. 1991. *Undying Glory: The Story of the Massachusetts 54th Regiment*. New York: Scholastic. (African American Massachusetts 54th Regiment)

Hoobler, Dorothy, and Thomas Hoobler. 1977. *Photographing History: The Career of Mathew Brady*. Illustrated with Brady Photographs. New York: Putnam's.

1865–1900, Including the American West

Autobiography

*Chief Joseph. 1999 [1879]. *Chief Joseph's Own Story*. Billings, MT: Council for Indian Education.

*Waheenee. 1981 [1927]. *Waheenee: An Indian Girl's Story Told by Herself to Gilbert L. Wilson*. Lincoln: University of Nebraska Press.

Biography

Conrad, Pam. 1991. *Prairie Visions: The Life and Times of Solomon Butcher*. New York: HarperCollins. (photographer)

Fradin, Dennis Brindell, and Judith Bloom Fradin. 2000. *Ida B. Wells: Mother of the Civil Rights Movement*. New York: Clarion.

Giff, Patricia Reilly. 1987. *Laura Ingalls Wilder: Growing up in the Little House*. Illustrated by Eileen McKeating. New York: Viking.

*Hamilton, Virginia. 1972. *W. E. B. Du Bois: A Biography*. Illustrated with photographs. New York: Crowell.

Lawlor, Laurie. 1994. *Shadow Catcher: The Life and Work of Edward S. Curtis*. New York: Walker. (photographer)

Historical Fiction

Armstrong, Jennifer. 1997. *Mary Mehan Awake*. New York: Knopf. (deaf character featured)

*Hansen, Joyce. 1997. *I Thought My Soul Would Rise and Fly: The Diary of Patsy, a Freed Girl*. New York: Scholastic. (1865)

MacLachlan, Patricia. 1985. *Sarah, Plain and Tall*. New York: Harper.

Nixon, Joan. 1988-1989. *Orphan Train Quartet: A Family Apart; Caught in the Act; In the Face of Danger; A Place to Belong*. New York: Bantam.

O'Dell, Scott. 1960. *Island of the Blue Dolphins*. Boston: Houghton. (Ghalas-at Indians)

*Taylor, Mildred D. 2001. *The Land*. New York: Putnam's. (prequel to *Roll of Thunder, Hear My Cry*)

*Yep, Laurence. 1993. *Dragon's Gate*. New York: HarperCollins.

Historical Realism

Brink, Carol Ryrie. 1973 [1935]. *Caddie Woodlawn*. Illustrated by Kate Seredy. New York: Macmillan. (Wisconsin, 1864; treatment of American Indians needs to be discussed)

Spyri, Johanna. 1955 [1880]. *Heidi*. New York: Dutton. (Switzerland)

Wilder, Laura Ingalls. 1953 [1932]. *Little House in the Big Woods*. Illustrated by Garth Williams. New York: Harper & Row. (sequels, treatment of Indians must be discussed)

Informational

*Bruchac, Joseph. 2002. *Navajo Long Walk: The Tragic Story of a Proud People's Forced March from Their Homeland*. Illustrated by Shonto Begay. Washington, D.C.: National Geographic.

Cooper, Michael. 2001. *Slave Spirituals and the Jubilee Singers*. New York: Clarion.

Bartoletti, Susan Campbell. 1996. *Growing Up in Coal Country*. Boston: Houghton.

Brown, Dee. 1993 [1974]. *Wounded Knee: An Indian History of the American West*. Adapted for young readers by Amy Ehrlich from Dee Brown's *Bury My Heart at Wounded Knee*. New York: Holt.

Kurelek, William, and Margaret S. Engelhart. 1985. *They Sought a New World: The Story of European Immigration to North America*. Toronto: Tundra.

Murphy, Jim. 1995. *The Great Fire*. New York: Scholastic. (Chicago, 1871)

*Terry, Michael Bad Hand. 1999. *Daily Life in a Plains Indian Village, 1868*. New York: Clarion.

Turn of Century and Immigration

Biography

Bierman, Carol, with Barbara Hehner. 1998. *Journey to Ellis Island: How My Father Came to America*. Illustrated by Laurie McGaw. New York: Hyperion.

Landau, Elaine. 2001. *Heroine of the Titanic: The Real Unsinkable Molly Brown*. New York: Clarion.

Historical Fiction

DeFelice, Cynthia. 1994. *Lostman's River*. New York: Macmillan. (Florida Everglades, 1906)

Hesse, Karen. 1992. *Letters from Rifka*. New York: Holt.

Lasky, Kathryn. 1998. *Dreams in the Golden Country: The Diary of Zipporah Feldman, a Jewish Immigrant Girl*. New York: Scholastic.

*Namioka, Lensey. 1999. *Ties That Bind, Ties That Break.* New York: Delacorte.

*Yep, Laurence. 1975. *Dragonwings.* New York: Harper-Collins.

Historical Realism

Burnett, Frances Hodgson. 1962 [1911]. *The Secret Garden.* Illustrated by Tasha Tudor. Philadelphia: Lippincott.

Montgomery, L. M. 1987 [1908]. *Anne of Green Gables.* New York: Bantam. (sequels)

Yezierska, Anzia. 1999 [1925]. *Bread Givers.* New York: Persea.

Informational

Granfield, Linda. 2001. *97 Orchard Street, New York: Stories of Immigrant Life.* Photographs by Arlene Alda. Plattsburgh, NY: Tundra/Lower East Side Tenement Museum.

Armenian Persecution and the Holocaust, 1907–1924

Biography

*Bedoukian, Kerop. 1978. *Some of Us Survived: The Story of an Armenian Boy.* New York: Farrar.

*Kherdian, David. 1979. *The Road from Home: The Story of an Armenian Girl.* New York: Greenwillow.

Historical Fiction

*Bagdasarian, Adam. 2000. *Forgotten Fire.* New York: DK.

Russian Revolution, 1917

Biography

Brewster, Hugh. 1996. *Anastasia's Album.* New York: Hyperion.

Historical Fiction

Holman, Felice. 1983. *The Wild Children.* New York: Scribner's.

World War I, 1914–1918

Autobiography

North, Sterling. 1963. *Rascal.* Illustrated by John Schoenherr. New York: Penguin.

Historical Fiction

Rostkowksi, Margaret I. 1986. *After the Dancing Days.* New York: Harper.

Skurzynski, Gloria. 1992. *Goodbye Billy Radish.* New York: Bradbury.

Informational

Cooper, Michael L. 1997. *Hell Fighters: African American Soldiers in World War I.* New York: Lodestar.

1918–1929, Including the Harlem Renaissance and the Roaring Twenties

NOTE: In the bibliography for Chapter 10, which continues biography, see Writers and Visual Artists, and in the bibliography for Chapter 5, Poetry, see the Harlem Renaissance poets.

Historical Fiction

Collier, James Lincoln. 1994. *The Jazz Kid.* New York: Holt. (Chicago)

Hesse, Karen. 1995. *A Time of Angels.* New York: Hyperion.

Levine, Gail Carson. 1999. *Dave at Night.* New York: HarperCollins. (New York)

Informational

*Myers, Walter Dean. 1993. *The Great Migration: An American Story.* Illustrated by Jacob Lawrence. New York: HarperCollins/Museum of Modern Art/The Phillips Collection.

The Great Depression, 1929–1930s

NOTE: In the bibliography for Chapter 5, Poetry, see Cynthia Rylant's *Something Permanent,* and in the bibliography for Chapter 10 under Leaders and Humanitarians, see Russell Freedman's biographies of Franklin and Eleanor Roosevelt.

Autobiography

*Knockwood, Isabelle. 1992. *Out of the Depths: Experiences of the Mi'kmaw Children at the Indian Residential School at Shubenacadie, Nova Scotia.* Lockeport, N.S.: Roseway Publishing.

Kurelek, William. 1975. *A Prairie Boy's Summer.* Boston: Houghton. (Canada)

———. 1973. *A Prairie Boy's Winter.* Boston: Houghton.

*Rice, Dorothy Maire, and Lucille Mabel Walthall Payne. 1998. *The Seventeenth Child.* North Haven, CT: Linnet. (sharecropping)

*Wong, Jade Snow. 1989 [1945]. *Fifth Chinese Daughter.* Seattle: University of Washington.

Biography

*Govenar, Alan. 2001. *Osceola: Memories of a Sharecropper's Daughter.* Illustrated by Shane Evans. New York: Hyperion.

Historical Fiction

Armstrong, William. 1989 [1969]. *Sounder.* Illustrated by James Barkley. New York: Harper. (criticized for nameless characters and for pessimistic ending; see the film, *Sounder,* starring Cicely Tyson for changes in the story that are more acceptable to the African American community)

Burch, Robert. 1980. *Ida Early Comes over the Mountain.* New York: Viking. (Georgia)

*Curtis, Christopher Paul. 1999. *Bud, Not Buddy.* New York: Delacorte.

Dowell, Frances O'Roark. 2000. *Dovey Coe.* New York: Atheneum. (Appalachia)

Hesse, Karen. 1997. *Out of the Dust.* New York: Scholastic. (Oklahoma)

Peck, Richard. 1998. *A Long Way from Chicago.* New York: Dial.

*Ryan, Pam Muñoz. 2000. *Esperanza Rising.* New York: Scholastic.

*Taylor, Mildred. 1976. *Roll of Thunder, Hear My Cry.* New York: Dial.

*Uchida, Yoshiko. 1981. *A Jar of Dreams.* New York: Simon and Schuster.

Informational

O'Brien, Patrick. 2000. *The Hindenburg.* New York: Holt.

Stanley, Jerry. 1992. *Children of the Dust Bowl: The True Story of the School at Weedpatch Camp.* New York: Crown.

World War II, 1939–1945

NOTE: In the bibliography for Chapter 5, Poetry by Children, see Hana Volavkova's *I Never Saw Another Butterfly: Children's Drawings and Poems from Terezín Concentration Camps.*

Autobiography

Bitton-Jackson, Livia. 1999. *I Have Lived a Thousand Years: Growing up in the Holocaust.* New York: Simon and Schuster.

Cooper, Susan. 1989 [1970]. *Dawn of Fear.* New York: Aladdin. (England)

Fox, Anne L., and Eva Abraham-Podietz, eds. 1999. *Ten Thousand Children: True Stories Told by Children Who Escaped the Holocaust on the Kindertransport.* West Orange, NJ: Behrman House.

Frank, Anne. 1967 [1952]. *Anne Frank: Diary of a Young Girl.* New York: Doubleday. (Holland)

Friedman, Ina. 1990. *The Other Victims: First-Person Stories of Non-Jews Persecuted by the Nazis.* Boston: Houghton.

Hautzig, Esther. 1968. *The Endless Steppe.* New York: HarperCollins. (Poland/Siberia)

Nieuwsma, Milton J. 1998. *Kinderlager: An Oral History of Young Holocaust Survivors.* New York: Holiday. (Poland, Israel, United States)

Opdyke, Irene Gut, with Jennifer Armstrong. 1999. *In My Hands: Memories of a Holocaust Rescuer.* New York: Knopf.

*Uchida, Yoshiko. 1995 [1987]. *The Invisible Thread.* New York: Beech Tree.

*Wakatsuki, Jeanne Huston, and James D. Huston. 1973. *Farewell to Manzanar.* New York: Bantam. (Japanese internment)

Biography

Coerr, Eleanor. 1977. *Sadako and the Thousand Paper Cranes.* New York: Dell. (Japan)

Drucker, Malka, and Michael Halperin. 1993. *Jacob's Rescue: A Holocaust Story.* New York: Dell. (Poland)

Foreman, Michael. 1989. *War Boy: A Country Childhood.* New York: Arcade. (England)

Linnéa, Sharon. 1993. *Raoul Wallenberg: The Man Who Stopped Death.* Philadelphia: Jewish Publication Society. (Hungary)

Perl, Lila, and Marion Blumenthal Lazan. 1996. *Four Perfect Pebbles: A Holocaust Story.* New York: Greenwillow. (Germany, Holland, United States)

Rubin, Susan Goldman. 2000. *Fireflies in the Dark: The Story of Friedl Dicker-Brandeis and the Children of the Terazin.* New York: Holiday.

Historical Fiction

Anderson, Margaret. 1978. *Searching for Shona.* New York: Random House. (Canada)

Bawden, Nina. 1992 [1973]. *Carrie's War.* New York: HarperCollins. (Wales)

Bishop, Claire H. 1990 [1952]. *Twenty and Ten.* Illustrated by William Pène du Bois. New York: Scholastic. (France)

DeJong, Meindert. 1956. *The House of Sixty Fathers.* Illustrated by Maurice Sendak. New York: Harper. (China and Japan)

Giff, Patricia Reilly. 1997. *Lily's Crossing.* New York: Delacorte.

Greene, Bette. 1973. *The Summer of My German Soldier.* New York: Dial. (Arkansas)

Lowry, Lois. 1989. *Number the Stars.* Boston: Houghton. (Denmark)

McSwigan, Marie. 1986 [1942]. *Snow Treasure.* New York: Dutton. (Norway)

Salisbury, Graham. 1994. *Under the Blood-Red Sun.* New York: Delacorte. (Japanese internment)

Wunderli, Stephen. 1992. *The Blue between the Clouds.* New York: Holt.

*Yep, Laurence. 1995. *Hiroshima: A Novella.* New York: Scholastic. (Japan)

Yolen, Jane. 1990. *The Devil's Arithmetic.* New York: Viking.

Informational

Aaseng, Nathan. 1992. *Navajo Code Talkers.* New York: Walker.

Abells, Chana Byers. 1983. *The Children We Remember.* Photographs from the Archives of Yad Vashem, The Holocaust Martyrs' and Heroes' Remembrance Authority, Jerusalem, Israel. New York: Greenwillow.

Cooper, Michael L. 1998. *The Double V Campaign: African Americans and World War II.* New York: Lodestar.

Drucker, Olga Levy. 1992. *Kindertransport.* New York: Holt.

*Hamanaka, Sheila. 1990. *The Journey: Japanese Americans, Racism, and Renewal.* New York: Orchard. (internment)

Levine, Ellen. 2000. *Darkness over Denmark: The Danish Resistance and the Rescue of the Jews.* New York: Holiday.

Matas, Carol. 1998. *Greater Than Angels.* New York: Simon and Schuster.

*McKissack, Patricia. 1995. *Red-Tail Angels: The Story of the Tuskegee Airmen of World War II.* New York: Walker.

Rogasky, Barbara. 2002. *Smoke and Ashes: The Story of the Holocaust.* Rev. ed. New York: Holiday.

Post World War II

NOTE: See biographies of Jackie Robinson and Nicholasa Mohr in the bibliography for Chapter 10.

Autobiography

Foreman, Michael. 1995. *After the War Was Over.* New York: Arcade. (England)

*Ortiz Cofer, Judith. 1990. *Silent Dancing: A Partial Remembrance of a Puerto Rican Childhood.* Houston, TX: Arte Público.

*Sterling, Shirley. 1992. *My Name Is Seepeetza.* Toronto: Douglas & McIntyre. (Indian Boarding School experience)

*Uchida, Yoshiko. 1978. *Journey Home.* Illustrated by Charles Robinson. New York: McElderry. (United States internment of Japanese, after release)

Biography

Kossman, Nina. 1994. *Behind the Border.* New York: Lothrop. (USSR)

*Sansan, with Bette Bao Lord. 1964. *Eighth Moon: The True Story of a Young Girl's Life in Communist China.* New York: Harper.

Historical Fiction

Estes, Eleanor. 1974 [1944]. *The Hundred Dresses.* Illustrated by Louis Slobodkin. San Diego: Harcourt.

Holt, Kimberly. 2000. *My Louisiana Sky.* New York: Holt.

Lenski, Lois. 1995 [1945]. *Strawberry Girl.* New York: HarperCollins. (Florida)

*Lord, Bette Bao. 1984. *In the Year of the Boar and Jackie Robinson.* Illustrated by Marc Simont. New York: Harper. (China, Brooklyn, baseball, based on Lord's childhood)

Matas, Carol. 1996. *After the War.* New York: Simon and Schuster.

*Mohr, Nicholasa. 1986. *Nilda.* Houston, TX: Arte Público.

Wolff, Virginia Euwer. 1998. *Bat 6.* New York: Scholastic.

Informational

Epler, Doris. 1992. *The Berlin Wall: How It Rose and Why It Fell.* Brookfield, CT: Millbrook.

Greenfield, Howard. 2001. *After the Holocaust.* New York: Greenwillow.

Korean War

Autobiography

*Watkins, Yoko Kawashima. 1985. *So Far from the Bamboo Grove.* New York: Lothrop.

Historical Fiction

*Choi, Sook Nyul. 1991. *Year of Impossible Goodbyes.* Boston: Houghton.

Civil Rights

NOTE: See also in the bibliography for Chapter 6, Drama, Gloria Bond Clunie's *North Star* and in the bibliography for Chapter 10, Humanitarians, the biography of Marion Wright Edelman, and Leaders, the Kennedy brothers.

Autobiography

*Parks, Rosa, with Jim Haskins. 1992. *Rosa Parks: My Story.* New York: Dial.

*Tillage, Leon Walter. 1997. *Leon's Story.* Illustrated by Susan L. Roth. New York: Farrar. (begins in the Depression)

Biography

*Haskins, Jim. 1992. *I Have a Dream: The Life and Words of Martin Luther King, Jr.* Brookfield, CT: Millbrook.

*Medearis, Angela Shelf. 1994. *Dare to Dream: Coretta Scott King and the Civil Rights Movement.* New York: Putnam's.

*Myers, Walter Dean. 1993. *Malcolm X: By Any Means Necessary.* New York: Scholastic.

*Rochelle, Belinda. 1993. *Witnesses to Freedom: Young People Who Fought for Civil Rights.* New York: Lodestar.

Historical Fiction

*Curtis, Christopher Paul. 1995. *The Watsons Go to Birmingham–1963.* New York: Delacorte.

Informational

*King, Martin Luther, Jr. 1997. *I Have a Dream.* Illustrated by fifteen Coretta Scott King Award and Honor Book artists. New York: Scholastic. (King's landmark speech)

Levine, Ellen. 2000 [1993]. *Freedom's Children: Young Civil Rights Activists Tell Their Own Stories.* New York: Puffin.

Meltzer, Milton. 2001. *There Comes a Time: The Struggle for Civil Rights.* New York: Random House.
*Parks, Rosa, with Gregory J. Reed. 1996. *Dear Mrs. Parks: A Dialogue with Today's Youth.* New York: Lee & Low.

Women's Rights
NOTE: Women's rights began in the midnineteenth century with Seneca Falls.

Biography
Johnston, Johanna. 1973. *They Led the Way: 14 American Women.* New York: Scholastic.
Meltzer, Milton. 1985. *Betty Friedan: A Voice for Women's Rights.* Illustrated by Stephen Marchesi. New York: Viking Kestrel.

Cuban Immigration
Historical Fiction
Garcia, Pelayo. 1997. *From Amigos to Friends.* Houston, TX: Arte Público.

Chinese Cultural Revolution, 1966–1976
Autobiography
*Chen, Da. 2001. *China's Son: Growing Up in the Cultural Revolution.* New York: Delacorte.
*Jiang, Ji-li. 1998. *Red Scarf Girl: A Memoir of the Cultural Revolution.* New York: HarperCollins.

Informational
*Zhang, Song Nan. 1997. *Cowboy on the Steppes.* Toronto: Tundra.

American Indian Movement
Autobiography
*Mankiller, Wilma, and Michael Wallis. 2000. *Mankiller: A Chief and Her People.* New York: St. Martin's.

Chicano Movement
NOTE: See biography of César Chavez under Labor Leaders in the bibliography for Chapter 10.

Vietnam War, 1950s–1975
Autobiography
*Huynh, Quan Nhoung. 1999 [1982]. *The Land I Lost: Adventures of a Boy in Vietnam.* Illustrated by Vo-Dinh Mai. New York: HarperCollins.

Historical Fiction
*Boyd, Candy Dawson. 1987. *Charlie Pippin.* New York: Macmillan.

Clark, Ann Nolan. 1978. *To Stand Against the Wind.* New York: Viking.

Informational
Ashabranner, Brent, and Melissa Ashabranner. 1987. *Into a Strange Land: Unaccompanied Refugee Youth in America.* New York: Dodd.

Cambodian War
Historical Fiction
Baillie, Allan. 1985. *Little Brother.* New York: Viking.
Crew, Linda. 1991. *Children of the River.* New York: Doubleday. (Cambodia, Oregon)
*Ho, Minfong. 1991. *The Clay Marble.* New York: Farrar.

Informational
Graff, Nancy Price. 1993. *Where the River Runs: A Portrait of a Refugee Family.* Photographs by Richard Howard. Boston: Little, Brown.

South Africa, Apartheid
Biography
Hoobler, Dorothy, and Thomas Hoobler. 1987. *Nelson and Winnie Mandela.* New York: Watts.

Historical Fiction
Maartens, Maretha. 1989. *Paper Bird.* New York: Clarion.
Naidoo, Beverly. 1988. *Journey to Jo'burg: A South African Story.* New York: HarperCollins.

Informational
Blackshaw, Anne. 1998. *No More Strangers Now: Young Voices from a New South Africa.* Illustrated by Tim McKee. New York: DK.

Nigeria
Historical Fiction
Naidoo, Beverly. 2001. *The Other Side of Truth.* New York: HarperCollins.

Middle East
Biography
Holliday, Laurel, ed. 1998. *Children of Israel, Children of Palestine: Our Own True Stories.* New York: Pocket Books.

Historical Fiction
Laird, Elizabeth. 1992. *Kiss the Dust.* New York: Dutton. (Kurds)

Fall of the Iron Curtain

Historical Fiction

Mooney, Bel. 1997. *The Voices of Silence.* New York: Delacorte. (Romania)

War in Bosnia–Herzegovnia

Autobiography

Filipovic, Zlata. 1994. *Zlata's Diary: A Child's Life in Sarajevo.* New York: Scholastic.

O'Grady, Scott. 1997. *Basher-Five-Two: The True Story of F-16 Fighter Pilot Captain Scott O'Grady.* New York: Doubleday.

Informational

I Dream of Peace: Images of War by Children of Former Yugoslavia. 1994. Preface by Maurice Sendak. New York: HarperCollins.

El Salvador

Historical Fiction

Temple, Frances. 1993. *Grab Hands and Run.* New York: Orchard.

Colombia

Informational

Cameron, Sara. 2001. *Out of War: True Stories from the Front Lines of the Children's Movement for Peace in Colombia.* New York: Scholastic.

Haiti

Historical Fiction

Temple, Frances. 1990. *A Taste of Salt: A Story of Modern Haiti.* New York: Orchard.

Ethiopia

Historical Fiction

Kurtz, Jane. 2000. *The Storyteller's Beads.* New York: Scholastic.

Afghanistan

NOTE: See September 11 in the bibliography for Chapter 13.

Biography

Landau, Elaine. 2002. *Osama Bin Laden: A War against the West.* Millbrook, CT: Twenty-First Century Books.

Historical Fiction

Ellis, Deborah. 2000. *The Breadwinner.* Toronto: Douglas & McIntyre.

Bibliography for Chapter 10 Life's Vocations and Callings: Biography, Autobiography, and Memoir

Actors and Entertainers

NOTE: See Fine Arts in Chapter 8 bibliography.

Biography

Brooks, Philip. 1999. *Oprah Winfrey: A Voice for the People.* New York: Watts.

Brown, Gene. 1990. *Bette Davis: Film Star.* New York: Blackbirch Press.

*Hamilton, Virginia. 1975. *Paul Robeson: The Life and Times of a Free Black Man.* New York: Harper. (1898–1976)

Sonneborn, Liz. 1993. *Will Rogers: Cherokee Entertainer.* Philadelphia: Chelsea.

Stefoff, Rebecca. 1994. *Raul Julia.* Philadelphia: Chelsea.

Animators

Biography

Greene, Katherine, and Richard Greene. 1991. *The Man Behind the Magic: The Story of Walt Disney.* New York: Viking.

Anthropologists

NOTE: See Social Studies, Cultures in Chapter 8 bibliography.

Biography

*Batten, Mary. 2001. *Anthropologist: Scientist of the People.* Photographs by A. Magdalena Hurtado and Kim Hill. Boston: Houghton.

Lyons, Mary E. 1990. *Sorrow's Kitchen: The Life and Folklore of Zora Neale Hurston.* New York: Macmillan. (also a writer)

Architects

NOTE: See Architecture in Chapter 8 bibliography.

Biography

Greenberg, Jan, and Sandra Jordan. 2000. *Frank O. Gehry: Outside In.* New York: DK.

Malone, Mary. 1995. *Maya Lin: Architect and Artist.* Berkeley Heights, NJ: Enslow.

Astronauts

NOTE: See Science, Space in Chapter 8 bibliography.

Autobiography

*Jemison, Mae. 2001. *Finding Where the Wind Goes: Moments from My Life.* New York: Scholastic.

Biography

*Burns, Khephra, and William Miles. 1995. *Black Stars in Orbit: NASA's African American Astronauts.* San Diego: Harcourt.

*Haskins, James, and Kathleen Benson. 1984. *Space Challenger: The Story of Guion Bluford*. Minneapolis, MN: Carolrhoda.

Hurwitz, Jane. 1989. *Sally Ride: Shooting for the Stars*. New York: Fawcett.

Athletes and Coaches

NOTE: See Sports in Chapter 8 bibliography.

Autobiography

Baiul, Oskana, with Heather Alexander. 1997. *Oksana: My Own Story*. New York: Random House.

Boitano, Brian, and Suzanne Harper. 1997. *Boitano's Edge: Inside the Real World of Figure Skating*. New York: Simon and Schuster.

Cooper, Cynthia, with Russ Pate. 2000. *She Got Game: My Personal Odyssey*. New York: Warner.

Gordeeva, Ekaterina, with Antonina W. Bouis. 1998. *A Letter for Daria*. Boston: Little, Brown.

*Sifford, Charlie, with James Gullo. 1992. *"Just Let Me Play": The Story of Charlie Sifford, the First Black PGA Golfer*. Latham, NY: British American Publication.

Biography

Anderson, Joan. 2000. *Rookie: Tamika Whitmore's First Year in the WNBA*. Photographs by Michelle V. Agins. New York: Dutton.

Boyd, Aaron. 1997. *Tiger Woods*. Greensboro, NC: Morgan Reynolds.

Browne, Lois. 1993. *Girls of Summer: The Real Story of the All-American Girls Professional Baseball League*. New York: HarperCollins.

Christopher, Matt. 2000. *In the Goal—with Briana Scurry*. Boston: Little, Brown.

Collins, David R. 1994. *Arthur Ashe: Against the Wind*. New York: Macmillan.

Fillon, Mike. 1999. *Young Superstars of Tennis: The Venus and Serena Williams Story*. Greensboro, NC: Avisson Press.

Freedman, Russell. 1999. *Babe Didrikson Zaharias: The Making of a Champion*. New York: Clarion.

Krull, Kathleen. 1997. *Lives of the Athletes: Thrills, Spills (and What the Neighbors Thought)*. Illustrated by Kathyrn Hewitt. San Diego: Harcourt.

Lipsyte, Robert. 1994. *Joe Louis: A Champ for All America*. New York: HarperCollins.

———. 1993. *Jim Thorpe: 20th-Century Jock*. New York: HarperCollins.

Macy, Sue. 1996. *Winning Ways: A Photohistory of American Women in Sports*. New York: Holt.

*McKissack, Patricia, and Frederick McKissack. 1998. *Black Diamond: The Story of the Negro Baseball Leagues*. New York: Scholastic.

*McMane, Fred. 1984. *Michael Jordan: Superstar*. Chicago: Children's Press.

*Myers, Walter Dean. 2001. *The Greatest: Muhammad Ali*. New York: Scholastic.

Patrick, Jean L. S. 2000. *The Girl Who Struck Out Babe Ruth*. Illustrated by Jeni Reeves. Minneapolis, MN: Carolrhoda. (Jackie Mitchell)

Rappaport, Doreen. 2000. *Dirt on Their Skirts: The Story of Young Women Who Won the World Championship*. New York: Dial.

Walker, Paul Robert. 1986. *Pride of Puerto Rico: The Life of Roberto Clemente*. San Diego: Harcourt.

Weidhorn, Manfred. 1993. *Jackie Robinson*. New York: Atheneum.

Winter, Jonah. 2001. *Béisbol!: Latino Baseball Pioneers and Legends*. New York: Lee & Low.

Aviators

Autobiography

Van Meter, Vicki, with Dan Gutman. 1995. *Taking Flight: My Story*. New York: Viking.

Biography

Freedman, Russell. 1991. *The Wright Brothers: How They Invented the Airplane*. With original photographs by Wilbur and Orville Wright. New York: Scholastic.

Giblin, James Cross. 1997. *Charles A. Lindbergh: A Human Hero*. New York: Clarion.

*Grimes, Nikki. 2002. *Talkin' about Bessie: The Story of Aviator Elizabeth Coleman*. Illustrated by E. B. Lewis. New York: Orchard.

*Johnson, Dolores. 1997. *Bessie Coleman: She Dared to Fly*. New York: Benchmark.

Provensen, Alice, and Martin Provensen. 1983. *The Glorious Flight: Across the Channel with Louis Bleriot*. New York: Penguin.

Szabo, Corrine. 1997. *Sky Pioneer: A Photobiography of Amelia Earhart*. Washington, D.C.: National Geographic.

Choreographers and Dancers

NOTE: See Fine Arts, Dance in Chapter 8 bibliography.

Biography

Arnold, Sandra Martin. 1993. *Alicia Alonso: First Lady of the Ballet*. New York: Walker.

Freedman, Russell. 2000. *Martha Graham: A Dancer's Life*. New York: Clarion.

*Glover, Savion, and Bruce Weber. 2000. *Savion: My Life in Tap*. New York: Morrow.

Kuklin, Susan. 2001. *Reaching for Dreams: A Ballet from Rehearsal to Opening Night*. Lincoln, NB: iUniverse.com.

Maybarduk, Linda. 1999. *The Dancer Who Flew: A Memoir of Rudolf Nureyev*. Toronto: Tundra.

Pavlova, Anna. 2001. *I Dreamed I Was a Ballerina*. Illustrated with art by Edgar Degas. New York: Metropolitan Museum of Art/Atheneum.

Entrepreneurs

Biography

*Bundles, A'Lelia. 1991. *Madam C. J. Walker: Entrepreneur*. Philadelphia: Chelsea.

Halperin, Wendy Anderson. 1998. *Once Upon a Company . . . A True Story*. New York: Orchard.

Explorers
NOTE: See biographies and informational sections throughout the bibliography for Chapter 9, especially 1450–1600.

Biography
Armstrong, Jennifer. 1998. *Shipwreck at the Bottom of the World: The Extraordinary True Story of Shackleton and the Endurance.* New York: Crown.

Cobrun, Broughton. 2000. *Triumph on Everest: A Photobiography of Sir Edmund Hilary.* Washington, DC: National Geographic.

Facklam, Margery. 1997. *Tracking Dinosaurs in the Gobi.* New York: Holt.

Loewen, Nancy, and Ann Bancroft. 2001. *Four to the Pole! The American Women's Expedition to Antarctica, 1992–93.* North Haven, CT: Linnet.

Salkeld, Audrey. 2000. *Mystery on Everest: A Photobiography of George Mallory.* Washington, DC: National Geographic.

Firefighters
Biography
Beil, Karen Magnuson. 1999. *Fire in Their Eyes: Wildfires and the People Who Fight Them.* San Diego: Harcourt.

Folk Artists
NOTE: See Crafts in Chapter 8 bibliography.

Biography
Lyons, Mary. 1993. *Stitching Stars: The Story Quilts of Harriet Powers.* New York: Atheneum.

Senungetuk, Vivian. 1998. *Wise Words of Paul Tiulana: An Inupiat Alaskan's Life.* New York: Watts.

Historians
NOTE: See Social Studies, History in Chapter 8 bibliography.

Biography
*Haskins, Jim. 2000. *Carter G. Woodson: The Man Who Put "Black" in American History.* Illustrated by Melanie Reim. Brookfield, CT: Millbrook.

Humanitarians
Autobiography
Keller, Helen. 1988. *The Story of My Life.* New York: Bantam.

Biography
*Coleman, Evelyn. 1998. *The Riches of Oseola McCarty.* Illustrated by Daniel Mintner. Morton Grove, IL: Whitman.

Freedman, Russell. 1993. *Eleanor Roosevelt: A Life of Discovery.* New York: Clarion.

Journalists
Biography
Colman, Penny. 2002. *Where the Action Was: Women War Correspondents in World War II.* New York: Crown.

Finkelstein, Norman H. 1997. *With Heroic Truth: The Life of Edward R. Murrow.* New York: Clarion.

Judges and Lawyers
Biography
*Haskins, James. 1992. *Thurgood Marshall: A Life for Justice.* New York: Holt.

Hewett, Joan. 1991. *Public Defender: Lawyer for the People.* Photographs by Richard Hewett. New York: Lodestar. (Janice Fukai)

Laborers and Labor Leaders
Biography
Holmes, Burnham. 1994. *César Chavez: Farm Worker Activist.* Austin, TX: Steck-Vaughn.

Kuklin, Susan. 1998. *Iqbal Masih and the Crusaders Against Child Slavery.* New York: Holt.

*McKissack, Patricia, and Frederick McKissack. 1989. *A Long Hard Journey: The Story of the Pullman Porter.* New York: Walker.

Leaders
NOTE: See, especially, the Civil Rights Movement and Women's Rights in the bibliography for Chapter 9, and, in the bibliography for Chapter 13, biographies of religious leaders (Hinduism, Confucianism, etc.).

Biography
*Bernier-Grand, Carmen T. 1995. *Poet and Politician of Puerto Rico: Don Luis Muñoz.* New York: Orchard.

Giff, Patricia Reilly. 1986. *Mother Teresa: Sister to the Poor.* Illustrated by Ted Lewin. New York: Viking Kestrel.

Harrison, Barbara, and Daniel Terris. 1992. *A Twilight Struggle: The Life of John Fitzgerald Kennedy.* New York: Lothrop.

*Haskins, James. 1977. *Barbara Jordan.* New York: Dial.

Hewett, Joan. 2001. *Getting Elected: The Diary of a Campaign.* Photos by Richard Hewett. Boston: Houghton. (Gloria Molina)

*Mohr, Nicholasa. 1993. *All for the Better: A Story of El Barrio.* Illustrated by Rudy Gutierrez. Austin, TX: Steck-Vaughn. (Evalina Antonetty)

*Pinkney, Andrea Davis. 2000. *Let It Shine! Stories of Black Women Freedom Fighters.* Illustrated by Stephen Alcorn. San Diego: Harcourt.

Preusch, Deb, Tom Barry, and Beth Wood. 1981. *Red Ribbons for Emma.* Stanford, CA: New Seed Press. (Navajo Emma Yazzie and the power companies)

Severance, John B. 1997. *Gandhi: Great Soul.* New York: Clarion.

Siegel, Beatrice. 1988. *Corazon Aquino and the Phillipines.* New York: Lodestar.

Magicians

Biography

Lalicki, Tom. 2000. *Spellbinder: The Life of Harry Houdini.* New York: Holiday.

Mathematicians

NOTE: See Mathematics in the bibliography for Chapter 8.

Biography

Bendick, Jeanne. 2001. *Archimedes and the Door of Science.* Warsaw, ND: Bethleham.

Blue, Rose, and Corinne J. Nadeen. 2001. *Benjamin Banneker: Mathematician and Stargazer.* Brookfield, CT: Millbrook.

Stonaker, Frances. 1977. *Famous Mathematicians.* Philadelphia: Lippincott.

Medical Professionals

Autobiography

*Carson, Ben, with Cecil Murphey and Nathan Aaseng. 1992. *Ben Carson.* Grand Rapids, MI: Zondervan.

Biography

Clapp, Patricia. 1974. *Dr. Elizabeth, The Story of the First Woman Doctor.* New York: Lothrop.

Ferris, Jeri. 1991. *Native American Doctor: The Story of Susan LaFlesche Picotte.* Minneapolis, MN: Carolrhoda.

Ptacek, Greg. 1994. *Champion for Children's Health: A Story about Dr. S. Josephine Baker.* Illustrated by Lydia M. Anderson. Minneapolis, MN: Carolrhoda. (1873–1945)

Wells, Rosemary. 1998. *Mary on Horseback: Three Mountain Stories.* Illustrated by Peter McCarthy. New York: Dial. (Mary Breckenridge, Frontier Nursing Service, World War I, 1881–1965)

Musicians

NOTE: See Fine Arts, Music in the bibliography for Chapter 8.

Biography

Anderson, M. T. 2001. *Handel, Who Knew What He Liked.* Illustrated by Kevin Hawkes. Cambridge, MA: Candlewick.

Beirne, Barbara. 1993. *A Pianist's Debut: Preparing for the Concert Stage.* Boston: Houghton. (11-year-old Leah Yoon)

Hurwitz, Johanna. 1993. *Leonard Bernstein: A Passion for Music.* Illustrated by Sonia O. Lisker. Philadelphia: Jewish Publication Society.

Krull, Kathleen. 1993. *Lives of the Musicians: Good Times, Bad Times (And What the Neighbors Thought).* Illustrated by Kathryn Hewitt. San Diego: Harcourt.

*Lester, Julius. 2001. *The Blues Singers: Ten Who Rocked the World.* Illustrated by Lisa Cohen. New York: Hyperion.

*Monceaux, Morgan. 1994. *Jazz: My Music, My People.* New York: Knopf.

Reich, Susanna. 1999. *Clara Schumann: Piano Virtuoso.* New York: Clarion.

Younger, Barbara. 1998. *Purple Mountain Majesties: The Story of Katherine Lee Bates and America the Beautiful.* Illustrated by Stacey Schuett. New York: Dutton.

Naturalists, Ecologists, and Environmentalists

NOTE: See Science, Ecology in the bibliography for Chapter 8.

Autobiography

Audubon, John James. 1993. *Capturing Nature: The Writings and Art of John James Audubon.* Peter and Connie Roop, eds. Illustrated by Rick Farley. New York: Walker.

Biography

Bang, Molly. 2000. *Nobody Particular: One Woman's Fight to Save the Bays.* New York: Holt.

Cornell, Joseph. 2000. *John Muir: My Life with Nature.* Illustrated by Elizabeth Ann Kelly and Christopher Canyon. Nevada City, CA: Dawn.

Hildebrandt, Ziporah. 2001. *Marina Silva: Defending Rain Forest Communities in Brazil.* New York: Feminist Press of CUNY.

Kastner, Joseph. 1992. *John James Audubon.* New York: Abrams.

Ring, Elizabeth. 1992. *Rachel Carson: Caring for the Earth.* Brookfield, CT: Millbrook.

Photographers

Biography

Freedman, Russell. 1994. *Kids at Work: Lewis Hine and the Crusade against Child Labor.* New York: Clarion.

Partridge, Elizabeth. 1998. *Restless Spirit: The Life and Work of Dorothea Lange.* New York: Viking.

Rubin, Susan Goldman. 1999. *Margaret Bourke-White: Her Pictures Were Her Life.* New York: Abrams.

Producers

Biography

*Haskins, James. 1997. *Spike Lee: By Any Means Necessary.* New York: Walker.

Rubin, Susan Goldman. 2001. *Steven Spielberg.* New York: Abrams.

Psychologists

Biography

Reef, Catherine. 2001. *Sigmund Freud: Pioneer of the Mind.* New York: Clarion.

Resilient Individuals

NOTE: See the website on disabilities at the end of Chapter 3.

Autobiography

*Greenfield, Eloise, and Alesia Revis. 1981. *Alesia.* Illustrated by George Ford. Photographs by Sandra Turner Bond. New York: Philomel.

Kehret, Peg. 1996. *Small Steps: The Year I Got Polio.* Morton Grove, IL: Whitman.

Biography

Krementz, Jill. 1991. *How It Feels to Be Adopted.* New York: Knopf. (series)

Scientists and Inventors

NOTE: See Inventions and Science in the bibliography for Chapter 8.

Autobiography

Goodall, Jane. 1988. *My Life with the Chimpanzees.* New York: Simon and Schuster.

Biography

Bausum, Ann. 2000. *Dragon Bones and Dinosaur Eggs: A Photobiography of Roy Chapman Andrews.* Washington, D.C.: National Geographic.

Beshore, George. 2000. *Science in Early Islamic Culture.* New York: Watts.

Gherman, Beverly. 1994. *The Mysterious Rays of Dr. Röntgen.* Illustrated by Stephen Marchesi. New York: Atheneum.

Hager, Tom. 1998. *Linus Pauling and the Chemistry of Life.* New York: Oxford University Press.

Kendall, Martha E. 1994. *Steve Wozniak: Inventor of the Apple Computer.* New York: Walker.

Kittredge, Mary. 1991. *Barbara McClintock.* Philadelphia: Chelsea.

Krull, Kathleen. 1999. *They Saw the Future: Oracles, Psychics, Scientists, Great Thinkers, and Pretty Good Guessers.* New York: Simon and Schuster.

MacLachlan, James. 1997. *Galileo Galilei: First Physicist.* New York: Oxford University Press.

Matthews, Tom L. 1999. *Always Inventing: A Photobiography of Alexander Graham Bell.* Washington, D.C.: National Geographic.

———. 1998. *Light Shining through the Mist: A Photobiography of Dian Fossey.* Washington, D.C.: National Geographic.

Nelson, Marilyn. 2001. *Carver, a Life in Poems.* Asheville, NC: Front Street. (some mature sections)

Pasachoff, Naomi. 1996. *Marie Curie and the Science of Radioactivity.* New York: Oxford University Press.

Severance, John B. 1999. *Einstein: Visionary Scientist.* New York: Clarion.

St. John, Jetty. 1996. *Native American Scientists: Fred Begay, Wilfred F. Detclaw, Frank C. Dukepoo, Clifton Poodry, Jerrel Yakel.* Mankato, MN: Capstone Press.

Teachers

Biography

Freedman, Russell. 1997. *Out of Darkness: The Story of Louis Braille.* Illustrated by Kate Kiesler. New York: Clarion.

Marshall, Catherine. 1967. *Christy.* New York: Avon.

Meltzer, Milton. 1987. *Mary McLeod Bethune: Voice of Black Hope.* Illustrated by Stephen Marchesi. New York: Viking.

O'Connor, Barbara. 1993. *Mammolina: A Story about Maria Montessori.* Illustrations by Sara Campitelli. Minneapolis, MN: Carolrhoda.

Veterinarians

Autobiography

Herriot, James. 1973. *All Things Bright and Beautiful.* New York: St. Martin's. (series)

Visual and Plastic Artists

NOTE: See Fine Arts, Visual Art in the bibliography for Chapter 8. Also, some biographies of visual artists are found in Chapter 9, Historical Literature; for example, Michelangelo can be found in the 1450–1600 time frame. While series vary in quality, Abram's *First Impression* series is a good source for biographies of visual artists, as is Rizzoli's *A Weekend with the Artist* series.

Autobiography

* +Garza, Carmen Lomas. 1991. *A Piece of My Heart/ Pedacito de mi corazón: The Art of Carmen Lomas Garza.* Austin, TX: The New Press, in association with the Laguna Gloria Art Museum.

*Nickens, Bessie. 1994. *Walking the Log: Memories of a Southern Childhood.* New York: Rizzoli.

O'Kelley, Mattie Lou. 1983. *From the Hills of Georgia: An Autobiography in Paintings.* Boston: Little, Brown.

*Zhang, Song Nan. 1993. *A Little Tiger in the Chinese Night.* Toronto: Tundra.

Biography

Bie, Cecil de. 1998. *Vincent van Gogh.* Illustrated by Martijn Leene. Netherlands: Van Gogh Museum.

*Cummings, Pat, comp. and ed. 1992. *Talking with Artists, vols. 1, 2, & 3.* New York: Simon and Schuster.

Duggleby, John. 1998. *Story Painter: The Life of Jacob Lawrence.* San Francisco: Chronicle.

Elleman, Barbara. 1999. *Tomie dePaola.* New York: Putnam's.

Fritz, Jean. 2001. *Leonardo's Horse.* Illustrated by Hudson Talbot. New York: Putnam's.

Lyons, Mary E. 1998. *Talking with Tebé: Clementine Hunter, Memory Artist.* Boston: Houghton.

Marcus, Leonard S. 1998. *A Caldecott Celebration: Six Artists and Their Paths to the Caldecott Medal.* New York: Walker.

Reeves, Howard W. 1999. *Wings of an Artist: Children's Book Illustrators Talk about Their Art.* Introduction by Julie Cummins. Activity Guide by Barbara Kiefer. New York: Abrams.

Rohmer, Harriet, ed. 1997. *Just Like Me: Stories and Self-Portraits by Fourteen Artists.* San Francisco: Children's Book Press.

Zhensun, Zheng, and Alice Low. 1991. *A Young Painter: The Life and Paintings of Wang Yani—China's Extraordinary Young Artist.* Photographs by Zheng Zhesun. New York: Scholastic.

Writers

NOTE: Some biographies of writers are found in the bibliography for Chapter 9, Historical Literature. For example, Shakespeare can be found in the 1450–1600 time frame.

Autobiography

*Ada, Alma Flor. 1998. *Under the Royal Palms: A Childhood in Cuba.* New York: Atheneum.

Asher, Sandy, ed. 1999. *With All My Heart, With All My Mind: Thirteen Stories about Growing up Jewish.* New York: Simon and Schuster.

Bauer, Marion Dane. 1995. *A Writer's Story: From Life to Fiction.* New York: Clarion.

Cleary, Beverly. 1995. *My Own Two Feet: A Memoir.* New York: Morrow.

———. 1988. *A Girl from Yamhill.* New York: Morrow.

Dahl, Roald. 1984. *Boy: Tales of Childhood.* New York: Farrar.

George, Jean Craighead. 1996. *The Tarantula in My Purse and 172 Other Wild Pets.* New York: HarperCollins.

*Greenfield, Eloise with Lessie Jones Little. 1979. *Childtimes: A Three-Generation Memoir.* Illustrated by Jerry Pinkney. New York: Crowell.

Lowry, Lois. 1998. *Looking Back: A Book of Memories.* Boston: Houghton.

*Mohr, Nicholasa. 1994. *Growing Up Inside the Sanctuary of My Imagination.* Englewood Cliffs, NJ: Messner.

Rylant, Cynthia. 1989. *But I'll Be Back Again: An Album.* New York: Orchard.

Biography

Bober, Natalie S. 1991. *A Restless Spirit: The Story of Robert Frost.* New York: Holt.

Ehrlich, Amy. 1999. *When I Was Your Age: Original Stories about Growing Up.* Cambridge, MA: Candlewick.

Engel, Dean, and Florence B. Freedman. 1995. *Ezra Jack Keats: A Biography with Illustrations.* New York: Silver Moon Press.

Janeczko, Paul, sel. 1990. *The Place My Words Are Looking For: What Poets Say about and through Their Work.* New York: Bradbury.

Krull, Kathleen. 1994. *Lives of the Writers, Comedies, Tragedies, (and What the Neighbors Thought).* Illustrated by Kathryn Hewitt. San Diego: Harcourt.

*McKissack, Patricia C., and Frederick L. McKissack. 1998. *Young, Black, and Determined: A Biography of Lorraine Hansberry.* New York: Holiday.

Meigs, Cornelia. 1969 [1933]. *Invincible Louisa: The Story of the Author of Little Women.* Boston: Little, Brown.

*Ringgold, Faith, Linda Freeman, and Nancy Roucher. 1996. *Talking to Faith Ringgold.* New York: Crown.

Rylant, Cynthia. 1996. *Margaret, Frank and Andy: Three Writers' Stories.* San Diego: Harcourt.

Teeters, Peggy. 1992. *Jules Verne: The Man Who Invented Tomorrow.* New York: Walker.

*Walker, Alice. 2002 [1974]. *Langston Hughes: American Poet.* Illustrated by Catherine Deeter. New York: HarperCollins.

*Wilkinson, Brenda. 2000. *African American Women Writers.* New York: Wiley.

General

*Brafford, C. J., and Laine Thom. 1992. *Dancing Colors: Paths of Native American Women.* New York: Clarion.

*Hansen, Joyce. 1998. *Women of Hope: African Americans Who Made a Difference.* New York: Scholastic.

Welden, Amelie. 1999. *Girls Who Rocked the World: Heroines from Sacajawea to Sheryl Swoopes.* New York: Scholastic.

Bibliography for Chapter 11
Contemporary Realism:
Through the Eyes of Others

Abuse

Coman, Carolyn. 1995. *What Jamie Saw.* New York: Penguin.

Cormier, Robert. 1992. *Tunes for Bears to Dance to.* New York: Delacorte.

de Vries, Anke. 1996. *Bruises.* Stacey Knecht, trans. Asheville, NC: Front Street.

*Evans, Mari. 1999. *Dear Corinne, Tell Somebody Love, Annie: A Book about Secrets.* Orange, NJ: Just Us.

Animal Realism

Burnford, Sheila. 1996 [1961]. *The Incredible Journey: A Tale of Three Animals.* Illustrated by Carl Burger. New York: Dell.

Di Camillo, Kate. 2000. *Because of Winn-Dixie.* Cambridge, MA: Candlewick.

Gipson, Fred. 2001 [1956]. *Old Yeller.* New York: Harper-Perennial.

Henry, Marguerite. 2000 [1947]. *Misty of Chincoteague.* New York: Simon and Schuster. (series)

London, Jack. 2000 [1906]. *White Fang.* New York: Atheneum.

———. 1983 [1903]. *The Call of the Wild.* Illustrated by Barry Moser. New York: Penguin.

Naylor, Phyllis. 1991. *Shiloh.* New York: Atheneum.

Rawls, Wilson. 1961. *Where the Red Fern Grows: The Story of Two Dogs and a Boy.* New York: Dell.

Savage, Deborah. 1994. *To Race a Dream.* New York: HarperCollins.

Terhune, Albert Payson. 1919. *Lad, a Dog.* New York: Dutton.

Coming of Age

*Bruchac, Joseph. 1997. *Eagle Song.* Illustrated by Dan Andreasen. New York: Dial.

Burch, Robert. 1966. *Queenie Peavy.* Illustrated by Jerry Lazare. New York: Viking.

*Hamilton, Virginia. 1974. *M. C. Higgins, the Great.* New York: Macmillan.

Hunt, Irene. 1987 [1966]. *Up a Road Slowly.* New York: Berkley.

*Nye, Naomi Shihab. 1997. *Habibi.* New York: Simon and Schuster.

Rylant, Cynthia. 1986. *A Fine White Dust.* New York: Atheneum.

*Smith, Cynthia Leitich. 2001. *Rain Is Not My Indian Name.* New York: HarperCollins.

Spinelli, Jerry. 1990. *Maniac Magee.* Boston: Little, Brown.

Staples, Suzanne Fisher. 1989. *Shabanu: Daughter of the Wind.* New York: Knopf. (Cholistan Desert, Pakistan; mature themes)

Voigt, Cynthia. 1982. *Dicey's Song.* New York: Atheneum.

Death

Bauer, Marion. 1986. *On My Honor.* New York: Clarion.

Creech, Sharon. 1994. *Walk Two Moons.* New York: HarperCollins.

Freeman, Suzanne. 1996. *The Cuckoo's Child.* New York: Greenwillow. (Beirut to Tennessee)

*Mathis, Sharon Bell. 1975. *The Hundred Penny Box.* Illustrated by Leo and Diane Dillon. New York: Viking.

Paterson, Katherine. 1987. *Bridge to Terabithia.* Illustrated by Donna Diamond. New York: HarperCollins.

Paulsen, Gary. 1995. *The Rifle.* San Diego: Harcourt.

Rylant, Cynthia. 1992. *Missing May.* New York: Orchard.

Smith, Doris Buchanan. 1973. *A Taste of Blackberries.* Illustrated by Charles Robinson. New York: Crowell.

*Strete, Craig Kee. 1979. *When Grandfather Journeys into Winter.* Illustrated by Hal Frenck. New York: Greenwillow.

White, Ruth. 1996. *Belle Prater's Boy.* New York: Farrar. (Appalachia, suicide)

*Yumoto, Kazumi. 1996. *The Friends.* New York: Farrar. (Japan)

Disabilities

NOTE: See Chapter 3, http://www.kidsource.com/NICHCY/literature.html

Bang, Molly. 2001. *Tiger's Fall.* New York: Holt.

Butts, Nancy. 1996. *Cheshire Moon.* Asheville, NC: Front Street. (death and hearing impairment)

Byars, Betsy. 1981. *Summer of the Swans.* Illustrated by Ted Coconis. New York: Viking. (mental retardation)

Fraustino, Lisa Rowe. 1995. *Ash: A Novel.* New York: Orchard. (mental illness)

Gantos, Jack. 2000. *Joey Pigza Loses Control.* New York: Farrar. (ADHD)

Killilea, Marie. 1999 [1952]. *Karen.* Cutchogue, NY: Buccaneer. (cerebral palsy)

Konigsburg, E. L. 1970. *(George).* New York: Atheneum. (mental illness)

Lisle, Janet. 1989. *Afternoon of the Elves.* New York: Orchard. (mental illness)

Riskind, Mary. 1981. *Apple Is My Sign.* Boston: Houghton. (hearing impairment)

Slepian, Jan. 1980. *The Alfred Summer.* New York: Macmillan. (cerebral palsy)

Southall, Ian. 1968. *Let the Balloon Go.* Illustrated by John Weiman. New York: St. Martin's. (cerebral palsy)

Taylor, Theodore. 1991. *Tuck Triumphant.* New York: Doubleday. (hearing impaired)

Teague, Sam. 1987. *The King of Hearts' Heart.* Boston: Little, Brown. (Special Olympics)

Voight, Cynthia. 1987. *Izzy, Willy-Nilly.* New York: Ballantine. (amputation)

Divorce

Blume, Judy. 2001. *It's Not the End of the World.* Rev. ed. New York: Atheneum.

*Boyd, Candy Dawson. 1993. *Chevrolet Saturdays.* New York: Macmillan.

Cleary, Beverly. 1983. *Dear Mr. Henshaw.* Illustrated by Paul Zelinsky. New York: Morrow.

Danziger, Paula. 1998. *Amber Brown Is Feeling Blue.* Illustrated by Tony Ross. New York: Putnam's. (series)

Fine, Anne. 1996. *Step by Wicked Step.* Boston: Little, Brown.

Kästner, Erich. 1949. *Lisa and Lottie.* Illustrated by Victoria de Larrea. New York: Knopf.

Extended Families

*Alvarez, Julia. 2001. *How Tía Lola Came to Visit Stay.* New York: Knopf.

Bawden, Nina. 1989. *The Outside Child.* New York: Lothrop.

Byars, Betsy. 1993 [1972]. *The House of Wings.* Illustrated by Daniel Schwartz. Boston: Houghton.

Klein, Norma. 1974. *Mom, the Wolf Man and Me.* New York: Avon.

MacLachlan, Patricia. 1980. *Arthur for the Very First Time*. New York: HarperCollins.

Wilson, Jacqueline. 1998. *Double Act*. New York: Delacorte.

Family Life

Cameron, Eleanor. 1982. *That Julia Redfern*. New York: Dutton. (series)

*Choi, Sook Nyul. 1997. *The Best Older Sister*. Illustrated by Cornelius Van Wright and Yung-Hwa Hu. New York: Delacorte.

Cleary, Beverly. 2000 [1950]. *Henry Huggins*. Illustrated by Louis Darling. New York: HarperTrophy. (series)

Enright, Elizabeth. 2002 [1942]. *The Four Story Mistake*. New York: Holt. (series)

Fenner, Carol. 1995. *Yolanda's Genius*. New York: Simon and Schuster.

Hurwitz, Johanna. 2001 [1976]. *Busybody Nora*. Illustrated by Lillian Hoban. New York: HarperCollins.

Lowry, Lois. 1979. *Anastasia Krupnik*. Boston: Houghton. (series)

MacLachlan, Patricia. 1980. *Arthur, for the Very First Time*. Illustrated by Lloyd Bloom. New York: HarperCollins.

Tate, Eleanora E. 1992. *Front Porch Stories at the One Room School*. Illustrated by Eric Velasquez. New York: Bantam.

Foster Care and Adoption

Byars, Betsy. 1977. *The Pinballs*. New York: Harper.

MacLachlan, Patricia. 1993. *Baby*. New York: Delacorte.

Montgomery, Lucy M. 1990. *Akin to Anne: Tales of Other Orphans*. Rea Wilmshurst, ed. New York: Bantam.

*Myers, Walter Dean. 1982. *Won't Know Till I Get There*. New York: Viking.

Paterson, Katherine. 1978. *The Great Gilly Hopkins*. New York: Harper.

Friendship

Byars, Betsy. 1992. *Bingo Brown's Guide to Romance*. New York: Viking. (series)

Greene, Constance. 1982. *Al(exandra) the Great*. New York: Viking. (series)

Hurwitz, Johanna. 1981. *Aldo Ice Cream*. Illustrated by John Wallner. New York: Morrow. (series)

Konigsburg, E. L. 1996. *The View from Saturday*. New York: Atheneum.

*Myers, Walter Dean. 1988. *Scorpions*. New York: HarperCollins.

*Namioka, Lensey. 1992. *Yang the Youngest and His Terrible Ear*. Illustrated by Kees de Kiefte. Boston: Little, Brown.

Sharmat, Marjorie Weinman. 1973. *Getting Something on Maggie Marmelstein*. Illustrated by Ben Schecter. New York: HarperCollins. (series)

Stolz, Mary. 1985 [1963]. *The Bully of Barkham Street*. Illustrated by Leonard Shortall. New York: HarperCollins. (series)

Growing Up: Physical Maturity

Blume, Judy. 1970. *Are You There God? It's Me, Margaret*. New York: Bradbury.

Danziger, Paula. 1974. *The Cat Ate My Gymsuit*. New York: Delacorte.

Donovan, John. 1969. *I'll Get There, It Better Be Worth the Trip*. New York: HarperCollins.

Humor

Blume, Judy. 1972. *Tales of a Fourth Grade Nothing*. Illustrated by Roy Doty. New York: Dutton.

Cleary, Beverly. NOTE: See Family Life section for *Ramona* and *Henry Huggins* series.

McKay, Hilary. 1992. *The Exiles*. New York: McElderry.

Robinson, Barbara. 1972. *The Best Christmas Pageant Ever*. New York: Harper.

Rockwell, Thomas. 1973. *How to Eat Fried Worms*. Illustrated by Emily McCully. New York: Watts.

Mysteries

Andrews, Jean. 1990. *The Secret in the Dorm Attic*. Washington, D.C.: Kendall Green. (hearing impaired)

Avi. 1989. *The Man Who Was Poe*. New York: Orchard.

Bawden, Nina. 1991 [1966]. *The Witch's Daughter*. New York: Clarion.

Bellairs, John. 1993 [1973]. *The House with a Clock in Its Walls*. Illustrated by Edward Gorey. New York: Puffin.

*Draper, Sharon M. 1994. *Ziggy and the Black Dinosaurs*. Illustrated by James Ransome. Orange, NJ: Just Us. (series)

Fitzhugh, Louise. 1990 [1964]. *Harriet the Spy*. New York: HarperCollins.

Fleischman, Paul. 1999 [1982]. *Graven Images*. Illustrated by John Jude Palencar. New York: HarperCollins.

George, Jean Craighead. 1991 [1972]. *Who Really Killed Cock Robin? An Ecological Mystery*. New York: HarperTrophy.

Godden, Rumer. 1978. *The Rocking Horse Secret*. New York: Viking.

*Hamilton, Virginia. 1968. *The House of Dies Drear*. Illustrated by Eros Keith. New York: Macmillan.

Mahy, Margaret. 1992. *Underrunners*. New York: Viking.

Raskin, Ellen. 1978. *The Westing Game: A Puzzle Mystery*. New York: Dutton.

Sachar, Louis. 1998. *Holes*. New York: Farrar.

School

Cleary, Beverly. 2000 [1975]. *Ramona the Brave*. New York: Scholastic.

Clements, Andrew. 1996. *Frindle*. New York: Simon and Schuster.

Creech, Sharon. 1998. *Bloomability*. New York: HarperCollins.

MacKay, Claire. 1984. *The Minerva Program*. Toronto: Lorimer.

*Myers, Walter Dean. 1994. *Darnell Rock Reporting*. New York: Delacorte.

Nelson, Vaunda Micheaux. 1993. *Mayfield Crossing*. Illustrated by Leonard Jenkins. New York: Putnam's.

Sachar, Louis. 1987. *There's a Boy in the Girl's Bathoom*. New York: Knopf.

*Yarbrough, Camille. 1989. *The Shimmershine Queens*. New York: Putnam's.

Sports

Brooks, Bruce. 1984. *The Moves Make the Man*. New York: Harper. (multiethnic)

Christopher, Matt. 1994. *The Winning Stroke*. Illustrated by Karin Lidbeck. Boston: Little, Brown.

Dygard, Thomas. 1989. *Forward Pass*. New York: Morrow.

Miller, Mary Jane. 1994. *Going the Distance*. New York: Viking.

*Myers, Walter Dean. 1988. *Me, Mop, and the Moondance Kid*. New York: Delacorte.

Peck, Robert Newton. 1990. *Soup's Hoop*. Illustrated by Charles Robinson. New York: Delacorte.

Slote, Alfred. 1971. *Jake*. Philadelphia: Lippincott.

Smith, Robert Kimmel. 1989. *Bobby Baseball*. Illustrated by Alan Tiegreen. New York: Delacorte.

*Soto, Gary. 1991. *Taking Sides*. San Diego: Harcourt.

Survival and Adventure

Farmer, Nancy. 1996. *A Girl Named Disaster*. New York: Orchard. (Mozambique, Zimbabwe)

George, Jean Craighead. 1972. *Julie of the Wolves*. Illustrated by John Schoenherr. New York: HarperCollins.

——. 1959. *My Side of the Mountain*. New York: Dutton.

Konigsburg, E. L. 1967. *From the Mixed-up Files of Mrs. Basil E. Frankweiler*. New York: Atheneum.

Paulsen, Gary. 1987. *Hatchet*. New York: Penguin.

Roth, Arthur. 1976. *The Iceberg Hermit*. New York: Scholastic.

Skurzynski, Gloria. 1982. *Lost in the Devil's Desert*. Illustrated by Joseph Scrofani. New York: Lothrop.

Urban Childhood

Fleischman, Paul. 1997. *Seedfolks*. Illustrated by Judy Pedersen. New York: HarperCollins.

*Myers, Walter Dean. 1990. *The Mouse Rap*. New York: HarperCollins.

*——. 1979. *The Young Landlords*. New York: Viking.

*Woodson, Jacqueline. 2000. *Miracle's Boys*. New York: Putnam's.

Short Stories

*De Anda, Diane. 1997. *The Ice Dove and Other Stories*. Houston, TX: Arte Público.

*Mohr, Nicholasa. 1975. *El Bronx Remembered: A Novella and Stories*. New York: Harper.

*Monture, Joel. 1996. *Cloudwalker: Contemporary Native American Stories*. Illustrated by Carson Waterman. Golden, CO: Fulcrum.

*Myers, Walter Dean. 2000. *145th Street: Short Stories*. New York: Delacorte.

*Ortiz Cofer, Judith. 1995. *An Island Like You: Stories of the Barrio*. New York: Orchard.

*Smith, Cynthia Leitich. 2002. *Indian Shoes*. New York: HarperCollins.

*Soto, Gary. 1990. *Baseball in April and Other Stories*. San Diego: Harcourt.

Bibliography for Chapter 12 Fantasy and Science Fiction: What If?

Animal Fantasy

Adams, Richard. 1972. *Watership Down*. New York: Macmillan.

Atwater, Richard, and Florence Atwater. 1938. *Mr. Popper's Penguins*. Illustrated by Robert Lawson. Boston: Little, Brown.

Cleary, Beverly. 1965. *The Mouse and the Motorcycle*. Illustrated by Louis Darling. New York: Morrow. (series)

Grahame, Kenneth. 1940 [1908]. *The Wind in the Willows*. Illustrated by E. H. Shepard. New York: Scribner's.

Howe, James, and Deborah Howe. 1979. *Bunnicula*. New York: Scholastic. (series)

Lawson, Robert. 1988 [1939]. *Ben and Me*. Boston: Little, Brown.

——. 1944. *Rabbit Hill*. New York: Viking.

Milne, A. A. 1991 [1928]. *The House at Pooh Corner*. Illustrated by Ernest H. Shepard. New York: Dutton.

——. 1991 [1926]. *Winnie-the-Pooh*. Illustrated by Ernest H. Shepard. New York: Dutton.

O'Brien, Robert C. 1972. *Mrs. Frisby and the Rats of NIMH*. Illustrated by Zena Bernstein. New York: Atheneum.

Selden, George. 1960. *The Cricket in Times Square*. Illustrated by Garth Williams. New York: Farrar. (series)

White, E. B. 1952. *Charlotte's Web*. Illustrated by Garth Williams. New York: Harper.

Williams, Margery. 1983 [1922]. *The Velveteen Rabbit*. Illustrated by Allen Atkinson. New York: Knopf.

High Fantasy

Alexander, Lloyd. 1999 [1964–1968]. The "Chronicles of Prydain" series. New York: Holt.

Cooper, Susan. 1965–1977. "The Dark Is Rising" series. New York: Atheneum.

Jacques, Brian. 1986–2003. The "Redwall" series. New York: Philomel.

Le Guin, Ursula. 1968–1990. The "Earthsea" series. New York: Atheneum.

Lewis, C. S. 1994 [1950–1956]. The "Chronicles of Narnia" series. New York: HarperCollins.

McKinley, Robin. 1984. *The Hero and the Crown.* New York: Greenwillow.

Pierce, Tamora. 1983–1988. "Song of the Lioness" quartet. New York: Random House.

Pullman, Philip. 1996–2000. "His Dark Materials" trilogy. New York: Knopf.

Tolkien, J. R. R. 2001 [1937]. *The Hobbit.* Boston: Houghton.

———. 1965. "Lord of the Rings" trilogy. Boston: Houghton.

*Yep, Laurence. 1982–1992. "Dragon of the Lost Sea" series. New York: HarperCollins.

Remarkable Characters

*Bruchac, Joseph. 2001. *Skeleton Man.* New York: HarperCollins.

Cooper, Susan. 1993. *The Boggart.* New York: McElderry.

Lindgren, Astrid. 1950. *Pippi Longstocking.* Florence Lamborn, trans. Illustrated by Louis S. Glanzman. New York: Viking. (series)

Time Slips and Magical Worlds

Babbitt, Natalie. 1975. *Tuck Everlasting.* New York: Farrar.

Baum, Frank. 1996 [1900]. *The Wonderful Wizard of Oz.* Illustrated by Lisbeth Zwerger. New York: North-South.

Billingsley, Franny. 1999. *The Folk Keeper.* New York: Atheneum.

Boston, L. M. 2002 [1955]. *The Children of Green Knowe.* Illustrated by Peter Boston. San Diego: Harcourt.

Cameron, Eleanor. 1973. *The Court of the Stone Children.* New York: Dutton.

Carroll, Lewis. 2001 [1866]. *Alice's Adventures in Wonderland.* Illustrated by De Loss McGraw. New York: HarperCollins.

Clarke, Pauline. 2000 [1963]. *The Return of the Twelves.* Pleasantville, NY: Akadine Press. (based on the Brontës)

Collodi, Carlo. 1988 [1891]. *The Adventures of Pinocchio.* Illustrated by Roberto Innocenti. New York: Knopf.

Dahl, Roald. 2001 [1964]. *Charlie and the Chocolate Factory.* Illustrated by Quentin Blake. Rev. ed. New York: Knopf.

———. 1961. *James and the Giant Peach.* Illustrated by Nancy Burkert. New York: Knopf.

Hunter, Mollie. 1975. *A Stranger Came Ashore.* New York: Harper.

Ibbotson, Eva. 1998. *The Secret of Platform 13.* Illustrated by Sue Porter. New York: Dutton.

Jones, Diana Wynne. 1986. *Howl's Moving Castle.* New York: Greenwillow.

Kingsley, Charles. 1997 [1863]. *The Water Babies.* Illustrated by Jessie Wilcox Smith. New York: Morrow.

Levine, Gail Carson. 1997. *Ella Enchanted.* New York: HarperCollins.

MacDonald, George. 2001 [1871]. *At the Back of the North Wind.* Illustrated by Arthur Hughes. London: Everymans.

Mahy, Margaret. 1997. *The Five Sisters.* Illustrated by Patricia MacCarthy. New York: Viking.

Napoli, Donna Jo. 1993. *The Magic Circle.* New York: Dutton.

Pearce, Phillipa. 1992 [1958]. *Tom's Midnight Garden.* Illustrated by Susan Einzig. New York: HarperTrophy.

Rowling, J. K. 1997–2000. The "Harry Potter" series. New York: Scholastic.

Saint-Exupéry, Antoine de. 1943. *The Little Prince.* Katherine Woods, trans. San Diego: Harcourt.

Walsh, Jill Paton. 1978. *A Chance Child.* New York: Farrar.

Waugh, Sylvia. 1994. *The Mennyms.* New York: Greenwillow.

Tiny Worlds

Godden, Rumer. 1947. *The Dolls' House.* Illustrated by Tasha Tudor. New York: Viking.

Norton, Mary. 1952. *The Borrowers.* Illustrated by Beth and Joe Krush. San Diego: Harcourt. (series)

Swift, Jonathan. 1960 [1727]. *Travels into Several Remote Nations of the World* or, *Gulliver's Travels.* New York: New American Library.

Science Fiction

Asimov, Isaac. 1950. *I, Robot.* New York: Doubleday.

Bawden, Nina. 1998. *Off the Road.* New York: Clarion.

Cameron, Eleanor. 1954. *The Wonderful Flight to the Mushroom Planet.* Illustrated by Robert Henneberger. Boston: Little, Brown. (series)

Card, Orson Scott. 2002 [1985]. *Ender's Game.* New York: Starscape.

Christopher, John. 1967–1988. "The Tripods" series. New York: Macmillan.

Dickinson, Peter. 1986. "The Changes Trilogy" series. New York: Delacorte.

Engdahl, Sylvia. 2001 [1970]. *Enchantress from the Stars.* New York: Walker.

Heinlein, Robert. 1991 [1949]. *Red Planet.* New York: Ballantine.

Jones, Diana Wynne. 1988. *Dogsbody.* New York: Greenwillow.

L'Engle, Madeleine. 1962–1986. "The Time Quartet." New York: Farrar.

Lowry, Lois. 1993. *The Giver.* Boston: Houghton.

MacGregor, Ellen. 1951. *Miss Pickerell Goes to Mars.* Illustrated by Paul Galdone. New York: McGraw-Hill.

Norton, Andre. 2001 [1958]. *Time Traders.* Riverdale, NY: Baen Books.

———. 2001. *Time Traders II.* Riverdale, NY: Baen Books.

Verne, Jules. 2001 [1869]. *20,000 Leagues under the Sea.* London: HarperCollins World.

Walsh, Jill Paton. 1982. *The Green Book.* New York: Farrar.

Bibliography for Chapter 13 Celebrations and Commemorations: Understanding Our World

Birthdays

De Groat, Diane. 1999. *Happy Birthday to You, You Belong in a Zoo.* New York: Morrow.

*Howard, Elizabeth Fitzgerald. 2001. *Lulu's Birthday.* Illustrated by Pat Cummings. New York: Greenwillow.

Lansky, Bruce, and friends. 1998. *Happy Birthday to Me! Kids Pick the Funniest Birthday Poems.* Illustrated by Jack Lindstrom. Minnetonka, MN: Meadowbrook.

*Mora, Pat. 1992. *A Birthday Basket for Tía.* Illustrated by Cecily Lang. New York: Macmillan.

*Soto, Gary. 2000. *Chato and the Party Animals.* Illustrated by Susan Guevara. New York: Putnam's.

Lunar Calendar

NOTE: For other festivals based on the lunar calendar, see *Buddhism, Hinduism,* and *Islam* at the end of this section.

Chinese New Year

*Chinn, Karen. 1995. *Sam and the Lucky Money.* Illustrated by Cornelius Van Wright & Ying-Hwa Hu. New York: Lee & Low.

+Demi. 1997. *Happy Chinese New Year/Kung-His Fa-Ts'ai!* New York: Crown.

*Wong, Janet S. 2000. *This Next New Year.* Illustrated by Yangsook Choi. New York: Farrar.

*Zhang, Song Nan, and Hao Yu Zhang. 2000. *A Time of Dragons.* Illustrated by Song Nan Zhang. Toronto: Tundra.

Ramadan (Ninth month), and Eid-ul-Fitr Festival That Ends Ramadan

Ghazi, Suhaib Hamid. 1996. *Ramadan.* Illustrated by Omar Rayyan. New York: Holiday.

Hoyt-Goldsmith, Diane. 2001. *Celebrating Ramadan.* Photographs by Lawrence Migdale. New York: Holiday.

Matthews, Mary. 1996. *Magid Fasts for Ramadan.* Illustrated by E. B. Lewis. New York: Clarion.

GREGORIAN CALENDAR

January

New Year's

*Delacre, Lulu. 2000. *Salsa Stories.* Linocuts by Lulu Delacre. New York: Scholastic.

*Rattigan, Jama Kim. 1993. *Dumpling Soup.* Illustrated by Lillian Hsu-Flanders. Boston: Little, Brown.

Three Kings' Day, Puerto Rican, Christian

Zapatar, Beatriz Mc Connie. 1993. *Three Kings' Day.* Morristown, NJ: Modern Curriculum Press.

Martin Luther King Day

NOTE: See biography, Civil Rights, in the bibliography for Chapter 9.

*Rappaport, Doreen. 2001. *Martin's Big Words: The Life of Dr. Martin Luther King, Jr.* Illustrated by Bryan Collier. New York: Hyperion.

*Ringgold, Faith. 1996. *My Dream of Martin Luther King.* New York: Crown.

February

Black History Month

NOTE: See in the bibliography for Chapter 9, Underground Slavery, Civil War, and Civil Rights, and in the bibliography for Chapter 10, Leaders.

Groundhog Day, February 2

Freeman, Don. 2000. *Gregory's Shadow.* New York: Viking.

Abraham Lincoln's Birthday, February 12

NOTE: See Civil War, Biography, in the bibliography for Chapter 9 and Biography Picture Books in the bibliography for Chapter 4.

George Washington's Birthday, February 22

NOTE: See War of Independence, Biography, in the bibliography for Chapter 9.

Giblin, James Cross. 1992. *George Washington: A Picture Book Biography.* Illustrated by Michael Dooling. New York: Scholastic.

Valentine's Day, February 14

Sabuda, Robert. 1992. *Saint Valentine.* New York: Atheneum.

Tudor, Tasha, sel. and ed. 2000. *All for Love.* New York: Simon and Schuster.

Purim, February or March, Jewish

Cohen, Barbara. 1984. *Here Come the Purim Players.* Illustrated by Shoshana Mekibel. New York: UAHC Press.

Wolkstein, Dianne. 1996. *Esther's Story.* Illustrated by Juan Wijngaard. New York: Morrow.

Shrove Tuesday, Mardi Gras, Christian

Hoyt-Goldsmith, Dianne. 1995. *Mardi Gras: A Cajun Country Celebration.* Photographs by Lawrence Migdale. New York: Holiday.

*Shaik, Fatima. 1999. *On Mardi Gras Day.* Illustrated by Floyd Cooper. New York: Dial.

Carnaval
*⁺Delacre, Lulu. 1993. *Vejigante/Masquerader.* New York: Scholastic.
*Dorros, Arthur. 1991. *Tonight Is Carnaval.* Illustrated with *arpilleras* sewn by the Club de Madres Virgen del Carmen of Lima, Peru. New York: Dutton.

March

St. Patrick's Day
Hodges, Margaret. 1993. *Saint Patrick and the Peddlar.* Illustrated by Paul Brett Johnson. New York: Orchard.
Tompert, Ann. 1998. *Saint Patrick.* Illustrated by Michael Garland. Honesdale, PA: Boyds Mills.

April

April Fools' Day
Kelley, Emily. 1983. *April Fools' Day.* Illustrated by C. A. Nobens. Minneapolis, MN: Carolrhoda.

Arbor Day
Alexander, Sue. 2001. *Behold the Trees.* Illustrated by Leonid Gore. New York: Scholastic.

Passover (Pesach); Late March or Early April, Jewish
Goldin, Barbara Diamond. 1997. *The Passover Journey: A Seder Companion.* Illustrated by Neil Waldman. New York: Penguin.
Manushkin, Fran. 1995. *The Matzah That Papa Brought Home.* Illustrated by Ned Bittinger. New York: Scholastic.

Good Friday and Easter, Late March or Early April, Christian and Secular
Fisher, Aileen. 1997 [1968]. *The Story of Easter.* Illustrated by Stefano Vitale. New York: HarperCollins.
Heyward, Du Bose. 1939. *The Country Bunny and the Little Gold Shoes.* Illustrated by Marjorie Flack. Boston: Houghton.
Joyce, William. 1992. *Bently and Egg.* New York: Scholastic.
Kimmel, Eric. 1999. *The Birds' Gift.* Illustrated by Katya Krenina. New York: Holiday.

Earth Day, April 22
NOTE: See the Ecology section under Science in the bibliography for Chapter 8.
Allen, Judy, ed. 1997. *Anthology for the Earth.* Various illustrators. Cambridge, MA: Candlewick.
Paladino, Catherine. 1993. *Land, Sea, and Sky: Poems to Celebrate the Earth.* Boston: Joy Street Books.
Roop, Connie, and Peter Roop. 2001. *Let's Celebrate Earth Day.* Brookfield, CT: Millbrook.

May

Children's Day, Korea and Japan, May 5–6
MacMillan, Dianne. 1997. *Japanese Children's Day and the Obon Festival.* Berkeley Heights, NJ: Enslow.
McCoy, Karen Kawamoto. 1998. *Bon Odori Dancer.* Illustrated by Carolina Yao. Chicago, IL: Polychrome.

Cinco de Mayo, Mexico, May 5
*⁺Ada, Alma Flor. 1993. *The Empty Piñata/La piñata vacia.* Illustrated by Vivi Escrivá. Rosalma Zubizarreta, trans. Compton, CA: Santillana.
*Soto, Gary. 1998. *Big Bushy Mustache.* Illustrated by Joe Cepeda. New York: Knopf.

Mother's Day
*Fisher, Aileen. 1967. *My Mother and I.* Illustrated by Kazue Mizumura. New York: Crowell.
*Mora, Pat, ed. 2001. *Love to Mamá: A Tribute to Mothers.* Illustrated by Paula S. Barragán. New York: Lee & Low.
Wells, Rosemary. 1989. *Hazel's Amazing Mother.* New York: Penguin.

Memorial Day
Philip, Neil, ed. 1998. *War and the Pity of War.* Illustrated by Michael McCurdy. New York: Clarion.
Sorensen, Linda. 1994. *Memorial Day: Holidays.* Vero Beach, FL: Rourke.

June

Flag Day, June 14
Spier, Peter. 1973. *The Star-Spangled Banner.* New York: Dell.

Juneteenth, Emancipation in Texas, 1865
*Branch, Muriel Miller. 1998. *Juneteenth: Freedom Day.* Photographs by Willis Branch. New York: Dutton.
*Wesley, Valerie. 1997. *Freedom's Gifts: A Juneteenth Story.* Illustrated by Sharon Wilson. New York: Simon and Schuster.

Father's Day
Collins, Judy. 1968/1989. *My Father.* Illustrated by Jane Dyer. Boston: Little, Brown. (music included)
In Daddy's Arms I Am Tall: African Americans Celebrating Fathers. 1997. Illustrated by Javaka Steptoe. New York: Lee & Low.
*Lauture, Denizé. 1992. *Father and Son.* Illustrated by Jonathan Green. New York: Philomel.
Lindbergh, Reeve. 1995. *Grandfather's Lovesong.* Illustrated by Rachel Isadora. New York: Penguin.

July

Independence Day

Bertrand, Diane Gonzales. 2001. *Uncle Chente's Picnic.* Illustrations by Pauline Rodriguez Howard. Houston, TX: Piñata.

Key, Francis Scott. 1973. *The Star-Spangled Banner.* Illustrated by Peter Spier. New York: Doubleday.

Thomas, Jane Resh. 1997. *Celebration!* Illustrated by Raúl Colón. New York: Hyperion.

Bastille Day, France; July 14

Harris, Nathaniel. 1986. *The Fall of the Bastille.* London: Dryad Press Limited.

September

Labor Day

Scott, Geoffrey. 1982. *Labor Day.* Illustrated by Cherie R. Wyman. Minneapolis, MN: Carolrhoda.

September 11, 2001

Goodman, Robin F., and Andrea Henderson Fahnestock. 2002. *The Day Our World Changed: Children's Art of 9/11.* New York: New York University Child Study Center/Museum of the City of New York/Abrams.

Lee, Karlynn Keyes. 2001. *Children's Prayers for America: Young People of Many Faiths Share Their Hopes for Our Nation.* Flagstaff, AZ: Northland.

The New York Times. 2002. *A Nation Challenged: A Visual History of 9/11 and Its Aftermath.* New York: Calloway.

Rosh Hashanah, Jewish New Year

Fishman, Cathy Goldberg. 1997. *On Rosh Hashanah and Yom Kippur.* Illustrated by Melanie W. Hall. New York: Atheneum.

Goldin, Barbara Diamond. 1990. *The World's Birthday: A Rosh Hashanah Story.* Illustrated by Jeanette Winter. San Diego: Harcourt.

Kimmel, Eric. 1991. *Days of Awe: Stories of Rosh Hashanah and Yom Kippur.* Illustrated by Erika Weihs. New York: Viking.

Yom Kippur, Jewish

Cohen, Barbara. 1981. *Yossel's Prayer: A Yom Kippur Story.* Illustrated by Michael J. Deraney. New York: Mulberry.

October

Harvest

Jackson, Ellen. 2000. *The Autumn Equinox: Celebrating the Harvest.* Brookfield, CT: Millbrook.

Pennington, Daniel. 1994. *ITSE SELU: Cherokee Harvest Festival.* Illustrated by Don Stewart. Watertown, MA: Charlesbridge.

Columbus Day

NOTE: See in the bibliography for Chapter 9, 1450–1600.

Divali Festival of Lights; October through November—Hindu and Sikh

MacMillan, Dianne M. 1997. *Diwali: Hindu Festival of Lights.* Berkeley Heights, NJ: Enslow.

Halloween

NOTE: See in the bibliography for Chapter 7, Folklore, for more scary stories.

Hubbell, Patricia. 1998. *Boo! Halloween Poems and Limericks.* Illustrated by Jeff Spackman. New York: Cavendish.

Justice, Jennifer. 1992. *The Ghost & I: Scary Stories for Participatory Telling.* Photographs by Susan Wilson. Cambridge, MA: Yellow Moon.

*Nikola-Lisa, W. *Shake Dem Halloween Bones.* Illustrated by Mike Reed. Boston: Houghton.

Olson, Arielle North, and Howard Schwartz, retellers. 1999. *Ask the Bones: Scary Stories from around the World.* Illustrated by David Linn. New York: Viking.

Preston, Tim. 2001. *Pumpkin Moon.* Illustrated by Simon Bartram. New York: HarperCollins.

*Smalls, Irene. 1996. *Jenny Reen and the Jack Muh Lantern.* Illustrated by Keinyo White. New York: Atheneum.

Van Rynbach, Iris. 1995. *Five Little Pumpkins.* Honesdale, PA: Boyds Mills.

November

Days of the Dead/Los días de muertos, Mexican American; November 1 and 2

*Ancona, George. 1993. *Pablo Remembers: The Fiesta Day of the Dead.* New York: Lothrop.

Hoyt-Goldsmith, Diane. 1994. *Day of the Dead: A Mexican-American Celebration.* New York: Holiday.

+Luenn, Nancy. 1998. *A Gift for Abuelita: Celebrating the Day of the Dead/Un regalo para Abuelita: En celebración de Día de los Muertos.* Illustrated by Robert Chapman. Flagstaff, AZ: Northland.

Veterans Day, United States; November 11

Ansary, Mir Tamim. 1999. *Veterans Day.* Des Plaines, IL: Heinemann Library.

Sorensen, Linda. 1994. *Veterans Day: Holidays.* Vero Beach, FL: Rourke.

Thanksgiving

Bauer, Caroline Feller. 1994. *Thanksgiving Stories and Poems.* Illustrated by Nadine Bernard Westcott. New York: HarperCollins.

*Bruchac, Joseph. 2000. *Squanto's Journey: The Story of the First Thanksgiving.* Illustrated by Greg Shed. San Diego: Harcourt.

Cohen, Barbara. 1998 [1983]. *Molly's Pilgrim*. Illustrated by Daniel M. Duffy. New York: Lothrop.

*Grace, Catherine O'Neill, and Margaret M. Bruchac. 2001. *1621: A New Look at Thanksgiving*. Washington, D.C.: National Geographic.

Koller, Jackie French. 1999. *Nickommoh! A Thanksgiving Celebration*. Illustrated by Marcia Sewall. New York: Atheneum.

December

Hanukkah, Jewish

Cohn, Janice. 1995. *The Christmas Menorahs: How a Town Fought Hate*. Illustrated by Bill Farnsworth. Morton Grove, IL: Whitman.

Jaffe, Nina. 1992. *In the Month of Kislev: A Story of Hanukkah*. Illustrated by Louise August. New York: Penguin.

Kimmel, Eric. 1989. *Hershel and the Hanukkah Goblins*. Illustrated by Trina Schart Hyman. New York: Holiday.

Levine, Arthur A. 1991. *All the Lights in the Night*. Illustrated by James Ransome. New York: Morrow.

Schram, Peninnah. 2000. *The Chanukah Blessing*. Illustrated by Jeffrey Allon. New York: UAHC Press.

The Inns/Las posadas; December 15–24

Hoyt-Goldsmith, Diane. 1999. *Las Posadas: An Hispanic Christmas Celebration*. Photographs by Lawrence Migdale. New York: Holiday.

Christmas December 25—Christian and Secular

*Anaya, Rudolfo. 1995. *The Farolitos of Christmas: A New Mexico Christmas Story*. Illustrated by Richard C. Sandoval. New York: Hyperion.

Bunting, Eve. 1996. *Going Home*. Illustrated by David Diaz. New York: HarperCollins.

Collington, Peter. 1990. *On Christmas Eve*. New York: Knopf.

Dickens, Charles. 1991. *A Christmas Carol*. Illustrated by Lisbeth Zwerger. New York: Simon and Schuster.

*Hughes, Langston. 1998. *Carol of the Brown King: Nativity Poems by Langston Hughes*. Illustrated by Ashley Bryan. New York: Atheneum.

Kurelek, William. 2000 [1976]. *A Northern Nativity: Christmas Dreams of a Prairie Boy*. Toronto: Tundra.

*Kusugak, Michael Arvaarluk. 1990. *Baseball Bats for Christmas*. Illustrated by Vladyana Krykorka. Toronto: Annick.

Laird, Elizabeth. 1987. *The Road to Bethlehem: An Ethiopian Nativity*. New York: Holt.

*Langstaff, John, sel. and ed. 1987. *What a Morning! The Christmas Story in Black Spirituals*. Illustrated by Ashley Bryan. Arrangements by John Andrew Ross. New York: Macmillan.

*McKissack, Patricia, and Frederick McKissack. 1994. *Christmas in the Big House, Christmas in the Quar-ters*. Illustrated by John Thompson. New York: Scholastic.

*Momaday, N. Scott. 1994. *Circle of Wonder: A Native American Christmas Story*. Santa Fe, NM: Clear Light.

Moore, Clement C. 1998. *The Night Before Christmas*. Illustrated by Jan Brett. New York: Putnam's.

Robinson, Barbara. 1972. *The Best Christmas Pageant Ever*. New York: Harper.

*Soto, Gary. 1993. *Too Many Tamales*. Illustrated by Ed Martinez. New York: Putnam's.

Thomas, Dylan. 1995 [1954]. *A Child's Christmas in Wales*. Illustrated by Fritz Eichenberg. New York: New Directions.

Van Allsburg, Chris. 1985. *The Polar Express*. Boston: Houghton.

Kwanzaa, African, African American

*Goss, Linda, and Clay Goss. 1995. *It's Kwanzaa Time!* Illustrated by Ashley Bryan, Carole Byard, Floyd Cooper, Leo and Diane Dillon, Jan Spivey Gilchrist, Johnathan Green and Jerry Pinkney. New York: Putnam's.

*Medearis, Angela Shelf. 2000. *Seven Spools of Thread*. Illustrated by Daniel Minter. Morton Grove, IL: Whitman.

*Pinkney, Andrea Davis. 1993. *Seven Candles for Kwanzaa*. Illustrated by Brian Pinkney. New York: Penguin.

*Saint James, Synthia. 1994. *The Gifts of Kwanzaa*. Morton Grove, IL: Whitman.

New Year's Eve

Ziefert, Harriet. 1999. *First Night*. Illustrated by S. D. Schindler. New York: Putnam's.

Celebrations and Religious Traditions around the World

General

Bauer, Caroline Feller. 1995. *Celebrations: Read-Aloud Holiday and Theme Book Programs*. Illustrated by Lynn Gates Bredeson. Bronx, NY: Wilson.

Chorao, Kay, col. 1995. *The Book of Giving: Poems of Thanks, Praise and Celebrations*. New York: Dutton.

Forest, Heather. 1996. *Wisdom Tales from around the World: Fifty Gems of Story and Wisdom from Such Diverse Traditions as Sufi, Zen, Taoist, Christian, Jewish, Buddhist, African and Native American*. Little Rock, AK: August House.

Osborne, Mary Pope. 1996. *One World, Many Religions: The Ways We Worship*. New York: Knopf.

Yen, Ho Siow. 1998. *Festivals of the World: South Korea*. Milwaukee: Gareth Stevens.

Yolen, Jane. 1996. *O Jerusalem*. Illustrated by John Thompson. New York: Blue Sky.

American Indian

NOTE: To most American Indians, stories are sacred; see bibliographies for Chapter 7.

*Braine, Susan. 1995. *Drumbeat Heartbeat: A Celebration of Powwow.* Minneapolis, MN: Lerner.

*Left Hand Bull, Jacqueline, and Suzanne Haldane. 1999. *Lakota Hoop Dancer.* Photographs by Suzanne Haldane. New York: Dutton.

*Regguinti, Gordon. 1992. *The Sacred Harvest: Ojibway Wild Rice Gathering.* Photographs by Dale Kakkak. Minneapolis, MN: Lerner.

*Swamp, Chief Jake (Tekaronianeken). 1995. *Giving Thanks: A Native American Good Morning Message.* Illustrated by Erwin Printup, Jr. New York: Lee & Low.

*Van Camp, Richard. 1997. *A Man Called Raven.* Illustrated by George Littlechild. San Francisco: Children's Book Press.

*Whetung, James. 1996. *The Vision Seeker.* Illustrated by Paul Morin. New York: Stoddart.

Buddhism

NOTE: See in the bibliography for Chapter 7 Fables for more Jataka tales.

Demi. 1998. *The Dalai Lama: A Biography of the Tibetan Spiritual and Political Leader.* New York: Holt.

———. 1997. *Buddha Stories.* New York: Holt.

*Lee, Jeanne M. 1999. *I Once Was a Monkey: Stories Buddha Told.* New York: Farrar.

*Martin, Rafe, and Manuela Soares. 1995. *One Hand Clapping: Zen Stories for All Ages.* Illustrated by Junko Morimoto. New York: Rizzoli.

Christianity

Armstrong, Carole. 1995. *Lives and Legends of the Saints with Paintings from Great Art Museums of the World.* New York: Simon and Schuster.

Beckett, Sr. Wendy. 1995. *A Child's Book of Prayer in Art.* New York: DK.

*Bryan, Ashley. 1991. *All Night, All Day: A Child's First Book of African-American Spirituals.* Music arrangements by David Manning Thomas. New York: Atheneum. (sequels)

*Graham, Lorenz. 2000 [1946]. *How God Fix Jonah.* Illustrated by Ashley Bryan. Honesdale, PA: Boyds Mills.

*Grimes, Nikki. 1996. *Come Sunday.* Illustrated by Michael Bryant. Grand Rapids, MI: Eerdmans.

Hunt, Angela Elwell. 1989. *The Tale of Three Trees: A Traditional Folktale.* Illustrated by Tim Jonke. Colorado Springs, CO: Lion Publishing.

*Johnson, James Weldon. 2000. *Lift Every Voice and Sing: A Pictorial Tribute to the Negro National Anthem.* New York: Hyperion.

Ladwig, Tim. 2000. *The Lord's Prayer.* Grand Rapids, MI: Eerdmans.

L'Engle, Madeleine. 1990. *The Glorious Impossible.* Illustrated with frescoes from the Scrovegni Chapel by Giotto. New York: Simon and Schuster.

Yolen, Jane. 1998. *Raising Yoder's Barn.* Illustrated by Bernie Fuchs. Boston: Little, Brown.

Confucianism

Freedman, Russell. 2002. *Confucius: The Golden Rule.* Illustrated by Frédéric Clément. New York: Scholastic.

Hoobler, Thomas. 1993. *Confucianism: World Religions.* New York: Facts on File.

Daoism

Hartz, Paula R. 1993. *Taoism: World Religions.* New York: Facts on File.

Hinduism

NOTE: See also the fables section and tales from India in the bibliography for Chapter 7 for more Jataka tales. See also the epics in the bibliography for Chapter 7.

Godden, Rumer. 1996. *Premlata and the Festival of Lights.* Illustrated by Ian Andrew. New York: Greenwillow.

Jendresen, Erik, and Joshua M. Greene. 1998. *Hanuman: Based on Valmiki's Ramayana.* Berkeley: Tricycle Press.

*Johari, Harish, with Sapna Johari. 2002. *Little Krishna.* Illustrated by Pieter Weltevrede with Suresh Johari. Rochester, VT: Bearclub Books.

*Kadodwala, Dilip. 1995. *Hinduism.* New York: Thomson Learning.

Islam

NOTE: See also tales from the Middle East, Pakistan, and Indonesia in the bibliography for Chapter 7.

Gordon, Matthew S. 1991. *Islam: World Religions.* New York: Facts on File.

*Khan, Rukhsana. 1999. *Muslim Child: Understanding Islam through Stories and Poems.* Illustrated by Patty Gallinger. Morton Grove, IL: Whitman.

*Knight, Khadijah. 1997. *Islam.* Des Plaines, IL: Heinemann Library.

Penney, Sue. 2001. *Islam.* Des Plaines, IL: Heinemann Library.

Wormser, Richard. 1994. *American Islam: Growing up Muslim in America.* New York: Walker.

Jainism

NOTE: See also the fables section and tales from India in the bibliography for Chapter 7 for more Jataka tales.

*Jain, Duli Chandra. 1990. *Studies in Jainism.* Flushing, NY: Jain Study Circle.

Judaism

NOTE: See also Jewish Tales in the bibliography for Chapter 7.

Berger, Gilda. 1998. *Celebrate! Stories of the Jewish Holidays*. Illustrated by Peter Catalanotto. New York: Scholastic.

Cone, Molly. 2000. *The Story of Shabbat*. Illustrated by Emily Lisker. New York: HarperCollins.

Jaffe, Nina. 1993. *The Uninvited Guest and Other Jewish Holiday Tales*. Illustrated by Elivia Savadier. New York: Scholastic.

Schur, Maxine Rose. 1994. *Day of Delight: A Jewish Sabbath in Ethiopia*. Illustrated by Brian Pinkney. New York: Dial.

Schwartz, Howard. 1996. *Next Year in Jerusalem: 3000 Years of Jewish Stories*. Illustrated by Neil Waldman. New York: Penguin.

Judaism and Christianity:

Hebrew Bible or Old Testament

Armstrong, Carole, 1998. *Women of the Bible with Paintings from Great Art Museums of the World*. New York: Simon and Schuster.

Bach, Alice, and J. Cheryl Exum. 1991. *Miriam's Well: Stories about Women in the Bible*. New York: Delacorte.

*Dillon, Leo, and Diane Dillon. 1998. *To Everything There Is a Season: Verses from Ecclesiastes*. New York: Blue Sky.

*McKissack, Patricia, and Frederick McKissack. 1998. *Let My People Go: Bible Stories Told by a Freeman of Color*. Illustrated by James Ransome. New York: Atheneum.

Renberg, Dalia Hardof. 1994. *King Solomon and the Bee*. Illustrated by Ruth Heller. New York: HarperCollins.

Spier, Peter. 1977. *Noah's Ark*. New York: Doubleday.

Shintoism

Nomura, Noriko S. 1996. *I Am Shinto*. New York: PowerKids.

Sikhism

Aggarwal, Manj, Harjeet Singh Lal, and Chris Fairclough. 1985. *I am a Sikh*. New York: Watts.

Penney, Sue. 2001. *Sikhism*. Des Plaines, IL: Heinemann Library.

Multicultural and International Authors and Illustrators

Note: All of these authors and illustrators can be found in the full Appendix C, Children's Literature Bibliographies posted at http://faculty.sacredheart.edu/gangij/. Many of them appear in Appendix C in this book.

Africa

Arusha Maasi
 Tololwa M. Mollel

Beninese/American
 Raouf Mama

Botswanan
 Barolong Seboni

Ghanaian
 Meshack Asare

Kikuyu
 Peter Kagathi Gitema

Mali
 Baba Wagué Diakité

Nigerian/Nigerian American
 T. Obinkaram Echewa
 Isaac O. Olaleye
 Ifeoma Onyefulu
 Obi Onyefulu
 Adaora Nzelibe Schmiedel

Senegalese
 Birago Diop

South African
 Jude Daly
 Niki Daly
 Dianne Stewart

Ugandan
 William Moses Serwadda
 Anita van der Merwe

Arctic

Canadian Yuit
 Mary K. Okheena

Canadian Inuit
 Michael Arvaarluk Kusugak
 Normee Ekoomiak

West Baffin Island
 Kiakshuk
 Pudlo

Asia
I. Central and Asian Pacific/ Central and Asian Pacific American

Afghanistan
 Idries Shah

Chinese/Chinese American
 Amelia Lau Carling (Guatemalan)
 Raymond Chang
 Cheng-Khee Chee
 Da Chen
 Debby Chen
 Jian Jiang Chen
 Ju-Hong Chen
 Linda Fang
 Nancy Hom
 Lily Toy Hong
 Lillian Hsu-Flanders
 Ji-li Jiang
 Xiao Jun

Milly Lee
Grace Lin
Betty Bao Lord
Ai-Ling Louie
Wehnai Ma
Kam Mak
Kwan Shan Mei
Li Ming
Yang Ming-Yi
Lensey Namioka
Sansan
Meilo So
Amy Tan
Keizaburō Tejima
Jeffrey Dao-Sheng Tung
Zong-Zhou Wang
Jade Snow Wong
Janet S. Wong (Korean)
Dana Ying-Hui Wu
Paul Yee (Canadian)
Laurence Yep
Yin
Ed Young
Youngsheng Xuan
Hongbin Zhang

Indian/Indian American
Uma Krishnaswami
Jaffrey Madhur
Govinder Ram
Paramasivam Samanna
Maniam Selven
Rabindranath Tagore

Japanese/Japanese American
Suekichi Akaba
Noriyuki Ando
Mitsumasa Anno
Tomie Arai
Sheila Hamanaka
Seishi Horio
Toyomi Igus
Yoko Imoto
Chihiro Iwasaki
Steven Izuki
Shiro Kasamatsu
Tatsuro Kiuchi
Tatsuharu Kodama
Ken Kuroi
Michio Mado
Toshi Maruki
Kazue Mizumura
Ken Mochizuki

Junko Morimoto
Ayano Ohmi
Manabu Saito
Allen Say
Aki Sogabe
Kazuko G. Stone
Mari Takabayashi
Ronald Takaki (Chinese)
Yoshiko Uchida
Jeanne Huston Wakatsuki
Yoko Kawashima Watkins
Taro Yashima
Kazumi Yumoto

Korean/Korean American
Sook Nyul Choi
Yangsook Choi
Lindy Soon Curry
Oki S. Han
Suzanne Crowder Han
Yumi Heo
Holly H. Kwon
Dom Lee
Min Paek
Frances Park
Ginger Park
Linda Sue Park
Chris K. Soentpiet

Malayasian
Noreha Yussof Day

Nepalese
Kavita Ram Shrestha

Taiwanese/Taiwanese American
Ying-Hwa Hu
Maywan Shen Krach
Grace Tseng
Jean and Mou-Sien Tseng

Asia: II. Southeast Asia/ Southeast Asian Americans

Cambodian/Cambodian American
Huy Voun Lee

Hmong/Hmong American
Chue and Nhia Thao Cha
Dia Cha
Tzexa Cherta Lee

Laotian/Laotian American
Blia Xiong

Myanmar (Burma)/American
Minfong Ho (raised in Thailand)

Filipino/Filipino American
Carl Angel
Francisco Arcellana
José Aruego

Thai/Thai American
Boonsong Rohitasuke
Supaporn Vathanaprida

Vietnamese/Vietnamese American
Quan Nhoung Huynh
Jeanne M. Lee
Vo-Dinh Mai

Caribbean

Bahamanian
Amos Ferguson

Barbados
Irving Burgie

Cuban/Cuban American
Alma Flor Ada
Lucía M. González
Daniel Moreton

Dominican Republic
Julia Alvarez

Grenada
Richardo Keens-Douglas

Haitian/Haitian American
Denizé Lauture
Pierre Marcelin
Phillipe Thoby–Marcelin
François Turenne des Prés

Jamaican/Jamaican American
James Berry
Tony Chen
Regina Hanson
Velma Pollard
Dorminster Wilson

Puerto Rican/Puerto Rican American
Pura Belpré
Carmen T. Bernier-Grand
Judith Ortiz Cofer
Nicholasa Mohr
Marisa Montes
Felix Pitre
Ernesto Ramos
Eric Velasquez

Trinidadian/Trinidadian American
Faustin Charles

Lynn Joseph
Vashanti Rahaman

Eastern Europe

Czech Republic
Vít Horejš
Kvetaë Pacovská
Josef Palecek
Peter Sís
Anna Vojtech

East German
Friedrich Recknagel

Hungarian/American
Istvan Banyai
Emöke de Papp Severo
Laszlo Kubinyi
Maud and Miska Petersham

Latvian
Nicolas Sidjakov

Polish/Polish American
Tomek Bogacki
Anita Lobel
Janina Porazinska
Uri Shulevitz
Isaac Bashevis Singer

Romanian
Mihai I. Spariosu

Russian/Russian American
A. N. Afanasyev
Katya Arnold
Dmemma Bider
Alisher Dianov
Olga Dugina
Susan Gaber
Mirra Ginsburg
Nikolai Gogol
Leonid Gore
Julia Gukova
Alexander Koshkin
Rafe Martin
Patricia Polacco (Irish)
Vladimir Radunsky
Robert Rayevsky
by Feodor Rojankovsky
Symeon Shimin
Esphyr Slobodkina
Gennady Spirin
Vladimir Vagin

Balery Vasiliew
Boris Zvorykin

Ukrainian/Ukranian American
Eric Kimmel
Katya Krenina

(Former) Yugoslavian
Manya Stojic

Western Europe

Austrian
Ludwig Bemelmans
Annegert Fuchshuber
Monika Laimgruber
Lisbeth Zwerger

Belgian
Jo Roets

British
Richard Adams
Janet and Allan Ahlberg
Brian Alderson
Anthea Bell
Charles W. Bennett
Stephen Biesty
Caroline Binch
Quentin Blake
Raymond Briggs
L. Leslie Brooke
Robert Browning
John Burningham
Susan Cooper
Lucy Cousins
Helen Craig
Walter Crane
Kevin Crossley-Holland
Roald Dahl
Michael Foreman
Alan Garner
Rumer Godden
Kenneth Grahame
James Herriot
Mary Hoffman
Ted Hughes
Deirdre Hyde (and Costa Rica)
Eva Ibbotson
Joseph Jacobs
Brian Jacques
John Matthews
James Mayhew
Margaret Mayo
Geraldine McCaughrean

A. A. Milne
Michael Morpurgo
Steve Parker
Phillipa Pearce
Beatrix Potter
Arthur Rackham
J. K. Rowling
Jessica Souhami
Alan Snow
Mary Stewart
J. R. R. Tolkien
Helen Ward
Sylvia Waugh
Brian Wildsmith

French
Claude Clément
Frédéric Clément
Andrej Dugin
Dorothée Duntze
Gilles Eduar
Jo Hoestlandt
Johanna King
Anaïs Vaugelad

German
Hans Magnus Enzensberger
Georg Hallensteben (lives in France)
Britta Teckentrup
Udo Weiglet
Hans Wilhelm
Dirk Zimmer

Greek/Greek American
Anthony L. Manna
Georgios A. Megas
Christodoula Mitakidou
Eugene Trivias

Dutch
Meindert DeJong

Iceland
Ragnheiôur Gestsdóttir
Jóhannes úr Kötlum

Irish/Irish American
Brendan Behan
Marita Conlon-McKenna
Tomie dePaola
Malachy Doyle
Marie Heaney
P. J. Lynch
Niamh Sharkey
James Stephens

Jonathan Swift
Oscar Wilde

Italian/Italian American
  Italo Calvino
  Sara Campitelli
  Gian Ceserani
  Carlo Collodi
  Tomie dePaola
  Giovanni Manni
  Beni Montresor
  Anita Riggio
  Piero Ventura
  Stefano Vitale
  Domenico Vittorini

Scandinavian: Danish, Finnish, Norwegian, Swedish, and the Laplanders
  Linda Allen
  Peter Christian Asbjørnsen (Norwegian)
  John Bauer (Swedish)
  Christina Bjork (Swedish)
  Betsy Bowen (Norwegian)
  Inga-Karin Erikkson (Swedish)
  Tove Jansson (Norwegian)
  Selma Lagerlöf (Swedish)
  Lise Lunge–Larsen (Norwegian)
  Jorgen E. Moe (Norwegian)
  Tord Nygren (Swedish)
  Bjørn Sortland (Norwegian)
  Tre Tryckare (Swedish)

Scottish
  Sheila Burnford
  Andrew Lang
  George MacDonald
  Robert Louis Stevenson

Spanish
  Frank P. Araujo (Basque)
  Garcia Lorca
  Ana Ruiz

Swiss
  Karl Bodmer
  Roger Duvoisin
  Rosmarie Hausherr
  Marcus Pfister
  Johanna Spyri

Welsh
  William Morris
  Dylan Thomas
  Gwyn Thomas
  Ellen Pugh

Jewish Authors and Illustrators
  Arnold Adoff
  Sandra Fenichel Asher
  Carol Bierman
  Heather Forest
  Adèle Geras
  Susan Greenstein
  Amy Hest
  Joanna Hurwitz
  Nina Jaffe
  Eric A. Kimmel
  Joanna Kraus
  Kathryn Lasky
  Carol Matas
  Harriet Rohmer
  Steve Sanfield
  Peninnah Schram
  Elly Simmons
  Phyllis Shalant
  Emily Sper
  Jane Breskin Zalben
  Steve Zeitlin

Middle East

Arab American
  Naomi Shihab Nye

Armenian/Armenian American
  Adam Bagdasarian
  Kerop Bedoukian
  Nonny Hogrogian
  David Kherdian
  Armen Kojoyian
  Virginia Tashjian

Israeli
  Naomi Adler
  Giora Carmi
  Uri Orlev

Pakistani
  Rukhsana Khan

Palestinian
  Sally Bahous

Yemeni
  Mishael Maswari Caspi

North America

African American
  Maya Angelou
  Camera Ashe

Ysaye M. Barnwell
Jean-Michel Basquiat
Gwendolyn Battle-Lavert
Harry Belafonte
Nneka Bennett
Rudine Sims Bishop
Tonya Bolden
Arna Bontemps
Candy Dawson Boyd
Muriel Miller Branch
Gwendolyn Brooks
Marjorie Wheeler Brown
Ashley Bryan
Michael Bryant
A'Lelia Bundles
Kephra Burns
Adjoa Burrowes
Jerry Butler
Carole Byard
Ben Carson
Dorothy Carter
Alice Childress
Debbi Chocolate
R. Gregory Christie
Lucille Clifton
Lesa Cline-Ransome
Gloria Bond Clunie
Evelyn Coleman
Bryan Collier
Anna J. Cooper
Floyd Cooper
Donald Crews
Pat Cummings
Christopher Paul Curtis
Ossie Davis
Leo Dillon
Frederick Douglass
Sharon Draper
Paul Laurence Dunbar
Veronica Freeman Ellis
Mari Evans
Shane W. Evans
Gwen Everett
Patrick Ewing
Muriel Feelings
Tom Feelings
Valerie Flournoy
George Ford
Jan Spivey Gilchrist
Nikki Giovanni

Savion Glover
Linda Goss
Lorenz Graham
Eloise Greenfield
Nikki Grimes
Rosa Guy
Virginia Hamilton
Joyce Hansen
James Haskins
Belinda Hermence
Carolivia Herron
Kim Hines
Varnette P. Honeywood
Deborah Hopkinson
Elizabeth Fitzgerald Howard
Cheryl Willis Hudson
Wade Hudson
Langston Hughes
Leslie Jean-Bart
Mae Jemison
Caleen Sinette Jennings
Angela Johnson
Dolores Johnson
James Weldon Johnson
William H. Johnson
Brenda Joysmith
Jacob Lawrence
Julius Lester
E. B. Lewis
Cedric Lucas
Sharon Bell Mathis
Cheryl Warren Mattox
Alice McGill
Frederick McKissack
Patricia McKissack
Fred McMane
Anglea Shelf Medearis
Tony Medina
Phil Mendez
William Miles
Morgan Monceaux
Emily Moore
Jeanne Moutonoussamy-Ashe
Margaret Musgrove
Christopher Myers
Walter Dean Myers
Kadir Nelson
Marilyn Nelson
Bessie Nickens
Lorenzo Pace

Rosa Parks
Denise Patrick
Ann Petry
Andrea Davis Pinkney
Brian Pinkney
Jerry Pinkney
Myles C. Pinkney
Leontyne Price
James Ransome
Faith Ringgold
Aminah Brenda Lynn Robinson
Belinda Rochelle
Synthia Saint James
Charlie Sifford
Irene Smalls
Will Smith
Javaka Steptoe
John Steptoe
Natasha Anastasia Tarpley
Clifton L. Taulbert
Mildred Taylor
Joyce Carol Thomas
Velma Maia Thomas
Leon Walter Tillage
Stephen Von Mason
Alice Walker
Mildred Pitts Walter
Carol Boston Weatherford
Valerie Wesley
Brenda Wilkinson
Michele Wood
Jacqueline Woodson
Camille Yarbrough

American Indians (includes Canadians)
Te Ata (Chickasaw)
Freda Ahenakew (Plains Cree)
Amos Bad Heart Bull (Lakota)
Robert Annesley (Cherokee)
Jeanette Armstrong (Okanagan)
Shonto Begay (Navajo)
D. L. Birchfield (Choctaw)
Charles Blood (Penobscot)
William Sauts Netamuxwe Bock (Lenape)
Linda Boyden (Cherokee/French Canadian)
Susan Braine (Assiniboine)
Linda Skinner Brewer (Choctaw)
Ignatia Broker (Ojibway)
Vee Browne (Navajo)
James Bruchac (Abenaki/Slovack)

Jesse Bruchac (Abenaki/Slovack)
Joseph Bruchac (Abenaki/Slovack)
Margaret M. Bruchac (Abenaki/Slovack)
Jaqueline Left Hand Bull (Lakota)
S. S. Burrus (Cherokee)
Jeffrey Chapman (Ojibwa)
Tom Charging Eagle (Lakota)
Joyce Simmons Cheeka (Squaxin)
Michael Chiago (Tohono O'odham)
Chief Joseph (Nez Percé)
Beth Ann Clark (Seneca)
Bill Cohen (Okanagan)
Charlie Craigan (Sechelt)
Beatrice Culleton (Métis)
Gerald Dawavendewa (Hopi/Cherokee)
Robert DesJarlait (Anishinabe)
Sandra De Coteau Orie (Oneida)
Marty Kreipe DeMontaño (Prairie Band
    Potawatomi)
Kim Doner (Cherokee)
Michael Dorris (Modoc)
Eagle Walking Turtle (Arapaho)
Charles Eastman (Santee Dakota)
Anthony Chee Emerson (Navajo)
Louise Erdrich (Turtle Mountain Chippewa)
David Kanietakeron Fadden (Mohawk)
John Kahionhes Fadden (Mohawk)
Melissa Jayne Fawcett (Mohegan)
GaWaNi Pony Boy (Tsa-la-gi)
Jonas George (Chippewa)
Benjamin Harjo (Seminole/Cherokee)
Ha-yen-doh-nees (Leo Cooper, Seneca)
Joe Medicine Crow (Crow)
Joy Harjo (Muscogee-Creek)
Beatrice Orcutt Harrell (Choctaw)
Edna Henry (We-cha-pi-tu-wen, Blue Star Woman,
    Nipmuc/Cherokee)
Donna Joe (Sechelt)
Basil Johnston (Canadian Anishinabe)
Betty Mae Jumper (Seminole)
Moses Jumper (Seminole)
Fred Kabotie (Hopi)
Dale Kakkak (Menominee)
John Kauffman (Nez Percé and German)
Geri Keams (Navajo)
Lenore Keeshig-Tobias (Ojibway)
Polly Keeshig-Tobias (Ojibway-Delaware)
Isabelle Knockwood (Mi'kmaw)
Kwulasulwut (Ellen White, Coast Salish)
Guy LaBree (Seminole)

Kathleen Lacapa (Irish/English/Mohawk)
Michael Lacapa (Apache/Hopi/Tewa)
Philomine Lakota (Lakota)
Chief Lelooska (Kwakiutl)
Melody Lightfeather (Pima)
George Littlechild (Plains Cree)
Michael Lomatuway'ma (Hopi)
Judith Lowry (Mountain Maidu/Hamawi Pit
    River/Australian)
Murv Jacob (Kentucky-Cherokee)
Manítonquat, Medicine Story (Wampanoag)
Linda R. Martin (Navajo)
N. Scott Momaday (Kiowa)
Joel Monture (Mohawk)
David Neel (Kwagiulth First Nation)
S. D. Nelson (Lakota)
Redwing T. Nez (Navajo)
Simon J. Ortiz (Acoma Pueblo)
Simon Otto (Ojibwa/Odawa)
Daniel Pennington (Cherokee descendant)
Russell M. Peters (Mashpee/Wampanoag)
Lanny Pinola (Pomo/Miwok)
Erwin Printup (Cayuga/Tuscarora)
Penny Pollock (Wyandotte/European)
Sherry Farrell Racette (Timiskaming)
Myrelene Ranville (Canadian Anishinabe)
Gordon Regguinti (Ojibway/Leech Lake Band)
Marcie R. Rendon (White Earth Anishinabe)
Monty Roessel (Navajo)
Gayle Ross (Cherokee)
Michael B. Runningwolf (Micmac)
Chiori Santiago (Native American/Italian/Japanese)
Cheryl Savageau (Abenaki/French Canadian)
Eugene and Emory Sekaquaptewa (Hopi)
Duke Sine (San Carlos/Yavapai Apache)
Beverly R. Singer (Santa Clara Pueblo)
Cynthia Leitich Smith (Muscogee)
Virginia Driving Hawk Sneve (Lakota)
Ken Syrette (Anishinaubae)
Shirley Sterling (Niakapmux)
Craig Kee Strete (Cherokee)
Virginia Stroud (Cherokee-Creek)
Chief Jake Swamp/Tekaronianeken (Mohawk)
Rina Swentzell (Santa Clara Pueblo)
Herschel Talashoema (Hopi)
Maria Tallchief (Osage)
Luci Tapahonso (Navajo)
C. J. Taylor (Mohawk)
Lolita Taylor (Ojibwe/Fon-du-Lac band)
Michael Bad Hand Terry (Seminole)
Simon Tookome (Inuit)

Andrew Tsihnahjinnie (Navajo)
Richard Van Camp (Dogrib)
Pablita Velarde
Felix Vigil (Apache/Jemez Pueblo)
Jan Bordeau Waboose (Nishinawbe Ojibwe)
Velma Wallis (Athabascan)
Waheenee (Hidatsa)
Carson Waterman (Seneca)
James Whetung (Anishinaabe)
Baje Whitethorne (Navajo)
Maria Williams (Tlingit)
Wolf Robe Hunt (Acoma)
Linda Yamane (Rumsien Ohlone)
Rosebud Yellow Robe (Lakota)
Zitkala-Sa (Yankton-Nakota)

Appalachian
Joanne Compton
Kenn Compton
Donald Davis
Ray Hicks
Cynthia Rylant

Canadian
Jan Andrews
Ann Blades
Rhian Brynjolson
Normand Cousineau
Stefan Czernecki
Blair Drawson
Deborah Ellis
Peter Eyvindson
Nan Froman
Priscilla Galloway
Phoebe Gilman
Joy Kogawa (Japanese)
William Kurelek
Michèle Lemieux
Jean Little
Tony Meers
Paul Morin
Julian Mulock
Margaret Munro
Andrew Plewes
Raffi
Shizuye Takashima (Japanese)
W. D. Valgardson
Leo Yerxa
Ludmila Zeman (Czech)
Hao Yu Zhang (Chinese)
Song Nan Zhang (Chinese)

Hawaiian Islanders
  Jama Kim Rattigan
  Karla Sachi

Mexican/Mexican American
  Francisco X. Alarcón
  Rudolfo Anaya
  George Ancona (Mayan)
  Gloria Anzaldúa
  Alberto Blanco
  Fabricio Vanden Broeck
  Graciela Carrillo
  Sandra Cisneros
  Amy Córdova (and Native American)
  Lucha Corpi
  Felipe Dávalos
  Blanca López de Mariscal
  María Isabel Delgado
  Domitila Domínguez (Mazatecan)
  Carlos Encinas
  Gaspar Enriquez
  Enrique Flores
  Daniel Galvez
  Stephanie Garcia
  Carmen Lomas Garza
  Elizabeth Gómez
  Maya Christina Gonzalez
  Ralfka Gonzalez
  Susan Guevara
  Juan Felipe Herrera
  Francisco Jiménez
  Antonio Hernádez Madrigal
  Subcomandante Marcos (Zapatista)
  Alejandro Cruz Martinez (Zapotec)
  Leovigildo Martinez
  Francisco X. Mora
  Pat Mora
  Rodolfo Morales
  Ed Martinez
  José-Luis Orozco
  Amada Irma Pérez
  Gloria Osuna Perez
  Lucia Angela Perez
  Luis J. Rodriguez
  Pam Muñoz Ryan
  Enrique O. Sánchez
  Simón Silva
  Gary Soto
  Angel Vigil

Oceania

Australia
  Graeme Base
  Margaret Early
  Max Fatchen
  Gordon Fitchett
  Mem Fox
  Patricia Mullins
  Oodgeroo (Aborigine)
  Dick Roughsey (Aborigine)
  Ian Southall
  Ilse van Garderen
  Julie Vivas

New Zealand
  Kiri Te Kanawa (Maori)
  Margaret Mahy

Central and South America

Argentinian
  María Cristina Brusca
  Lulu Delacre (Puerto Rican)
  Fabian Negrin
  Beatriz Vidal

Brazilian
  Roberto de Vicq de Cumptich
  Juan Wijngaard (Dutch)

Colombian
  Nelly Palacia Jaramillo
  Leyla Torres

Ecuadorian
  Paula S. Barragán

El Salvadorian
  Jorge Argueta
  Manlio Argueta

Guatemalan
  Omar S. Casteñada
  Victor Montejo (Mayan)

Guyanese
  Jan Carew

Nicaraguan
  Octavio Chow
  Luis Garay
  Morris Vidaure

Venezuela
  A. Magdalena Hurtado (French)

Name Index

Subject Index

From Working Girl
to Working Mother

From Working Girl

to Working Mother

The Female Labor Force in the United States, 1820–1980

LYNN Y. WEINER

The University of North Carolina

Chapel Hill and London

29280

First printing, January 1985
Second printing, May 1986

Library of Congress Cataloging in Publication Data

Weiner, Lynn Y., 1951–
    From working girl to working mother.

    Bibliography: p.
    Includes index.
    1. Women—Employment—United States   History.
I. Title.
HD6095.W39   1984   331.4'0973   84-7276
ISBN 0-8078-1612-4
ISBN 0-8078-4159-5 (pbk.)

Portions of Chapter 3 first appeared in somewhat different form in the
author's articles: "Sisters of the Road: Women Transients and Tramps,"
published in *Walking to Work: Tramps in America, 1790–1935*, edited by
Eric Monkkonen, by permission of the University of Nebraska Press.
Copyright 1984 by the University of Nebraska Press; and " 'Our Sisters'
Keepers': The Minneapolis Woman's Christian Association and Housing
for Working Women," originally published in *Minnesota History* 46:
189–200 (Spring 1979), copyright by the Minnesota Historical Society
and used with permission.

For Tom, Andrew, and Jeffrey

Contents

Tables

Tables

Figure

Acknowledgments

I take great pleasure in acknowledging the help I have received during the writing of this book.

Sam Bass Warner and Roslyn Feldberg encouraged this study in its earliest forms. Richard Bushman, David Hall, Aileen Kraditor, and Cecelia Tichi were among those at Boston University who taught me how to think about American history and culture. Kathryn Kish Sklar sparked my initial interest in history when I was an undergraduate at the University of Michigan; she has remained a mentor and a friend ever since.

I am also grateful to Northwestern University, where the History Department's Associate Program provided me with an affiliation and with access to an excellent library. The American Historical Association generously awarded me a Beveridge Grant during the final stages of research and writing.

The manuscript was greatly improved because of suggestions and criticisms offered by Thomas Dublin, Alice Kessler-Harris, Eric Schneider, Kathryn Kish Sklar, Winifred Wandersee, and Sharon Weiner. For their useful comments on portions of the book presented at conferences, I thank Estelle Freedman, Brian Gratton, Barbara Hobson, and Ruth Rosen. An early version of the manuscript benefited from discussions with Mary Ann Garnett, Heather Huyck, Linda Lounsbury, Susan Smith, and Meryl Weinreb.

Many librarians and archivists have been most helpful, especially David Klaassen of the Social Welfare History Archives, Mary Ann Bamberger of the Special Collections library at the University of Illinois at Chicago, Archie Motley of the Chicago Historical Society, Dallas R. Lindgren of the Minnesota Historical Society, and the staff of the Schlesinger Library at Radcliffe College.

For granting permission to use their unpublished records, I am indebted to the Child Welfare League of America, the Minneapolis Woman's Christian Association, the Travelers' Aid Association of America, and the Women's Educational and Industrial Union.

I also wish to express my appreciation to the editors at the University of North Carolina Press: to Iris Tillman Hill, for seeing the manuscript through several revisions, and to Sandra Eisdorfer, for her critical eye and excellent suggestions during the editing process.

Finally, my family has always encouraged my efforts, and I would like to

thank them, too. My mother, Audrey Allen Weiner, always believed in the potential of her children. My extended family—my father Charles, and Inge Weiner, Sharon Weiner, Tom Hospelhorn, Stuart Weiner, Maria Treccapelli, Alan Weiner, and Robert and Virginia Moher—have remained supportive during the long years of education and writing. My greatest debt is to my husband, Tom Moher. He has been involved in this project from the beginning; his confidence in me, his astute criticism of the manuscript at every stage, and his skill at juggling the demands of work and fatherhood have contributed immeasurably to the completion of this book.

From Working Girl
to Working Mother

Introduction

The volatile debate in the 1980s over the social consequences of working mothers is firmly rooted in a historical controversy over the employment of women. Where the absence of men from the labor force has long been considered an anomaly, the presence of women in the labor force has continually inspired controversy, investigation, and reform.[1] The dramatic expansion of the female labor force in modern times has revolutionized the nature of work and family life in the United States.

This book looks at the general history of the working woman in the United States through 1980. The study emphasizes two levels of analysis—the material basis of changing social and economic behavior and the concomitant ideological debate over appropriate female roles, which has in turn affected social reform and public policy.

The female sector of the labor force has more than tripled in the last century, growing from 14 percent in 1870 to 42 percent in 1980. These gains reflect the increasing propensity of women to work. Where just one in seven women worked for wages in 1870, by 1980 one in two women were gainfully employed (see table 1). Moreover, in the course of the last century, the identity of the woman worker has changed. The married woman and the mother have replaced the young single woman as the largest subgroups within the female labor force. This revolution in the female labor force has attracted the attention of historians in recent years. For the most part, however, scholars have studied the history of working women for relatively limited time spans or localities, or for specific occupational, marital, ethnic, or racial groups.[2] There have yet been few attempts to take a long-term historical perspective on the employment of American women.

The long view shows that the expansion of the female labor force occurred in two distinct phases. The first phase was the era of the "working girl."[3] During this period, from the mid-nineteenth century until the early decades of the twentieth century, the single, and often self-supporting, young woman worker became a visible member of the urban labor force. The second phase was the era of the working mother. In this period, from the early twentieth century until the present day, married women and mothers came to the forefront of the female labor force and also dominated the accompanying debate over women and work.

Table 1

Number[a] and Proportion of Working Women
in the U.S. Labor Force, 1870–1980

Year	Total Labor Force	Working Women	Percent of All Women Who Work	Women as Percent of Labor Force
1870	12,160	1,717	15	14
1880	16,274	2,354	16	14
1890	21,814	3,597	19	16
1900	27,323	4,834	21	18
1910	35,749	7,011	24	20
1920	41,017	8,278	24	20
1930	48,163	10,546	25	22
1940	52,711	12,951	27	25
1950	59,223	16,443	30	28
1960	69,234	22,222	36	32
1970	82,048	30,547	41	37
1980	106,066	44,741	51	42

Sources: U.S. Bureau of the Census, *Comparative Statistics for the U.S., 1870–1940*, p. 92, table xv; U.S. Bureau of the Census, *Nineteenth Census of the U.S.*, vol. 1, pt. 1, p. 372, table 78; U.S. Bureau of the Census, *1980 Census of Population*, p. 25, table p. 3.

[a]In thousands.

These two phases of labor force expansion were characterized by factors of class and race. Although poor, black, and immigrant women had long labored in the marketplace for subsistence wages, they had excited little public controversy because they had not been considered subject to middle-class expectations of domesticity. It was when "respectable" groups of women—that is, women who were white, native-born, and nondestitute—entered the labor force that public attention was first drawn to the changing work patterns of women.[4]

The controversy caused by the movement of these women into the labor force led to cycles of reaction and reform based on the desire to reestablish women within the framework of middle-class domestic values. This public response to working women has shaped social policy on issues including wages, housing, job opportunities, and child care. The examination of these policies helps us to understand the origins of such varied reform movements as

the Young Women's Christian Associations and the relief programs for dependent mothers and their children.

The first phase of the expansion of the female labor force—the era of the working girl—was marked by the accelerating work rate of young single women. Unfortunately the growth of this trend before 1890 can only be inferred, as the Census Bureau did not categorize women workers by marital status until that decade. By then, however, the population of women who worked included an increased proportion of native-born women, many of them migrants from farms. In 1890, over two-thirds of women workers were single, while married women constituted the smallest marital group within the female labor force (see table 2). The typical woman worker at the turn of the century was unmarried, young, and a domestic servant. Moreover, one out of three urban workers were self-supporting and living away from home.

Society first discovered in the late nineteenth century that these women were working alongside the poor, black, and immigrant women who had always worked for wages without inspiring public comment. The labor of "respectable" women brought them one step away from their prescribed place at home, where middle-class expectations would decree a life of domesticity. Even more removed were the rural women who migrated to the cities to find work. Public opinion maintained that these working girls, adrift from any domestic influence, endangered their physical and moral health and the health of future generations. Popular literature and the records of reform institutions reflect a heated discussion at this time replete with rhetoric about the purity and morality of the working girl. The young single woman worker, in short, was seen as "unfitting" herself for her future role as wife and mother.

The result of this debate over the working girl was an amorphous reform movement that attempted both to extend domestic influences to young working women through such institutions as supervised boarding homes and clubs for working girls and also to protect female health and morality through the regulation of wages and hours of work. By ameliorating the worst conditions facing women entering the work force, these reforms to some degree sanctioned social change. At the same time, however, reform measures characterized by class and gender concerns attempted to bring young women under a form of social control by channeling them into models of housing and work that reinforced domestic values.[5]

In the twentieth century, married women began to enter the labor force. The proportion of wives who work has grown ninefold since 1890, and the proportion of mothers who work has at least doubled. Since statistics for working mothers do not exist on a national level before 1940, however, the latter figure is probably understated (see table 2).

Table 2

Percentage of Women in the U.S. Labor Force, by Family Status, 1890–1980

	1890	1900	1910	1920	1930	1940	1950	1960	1970	1980[c]
				All U.S. Women						
Single	32	34	32	41[b]	28	28	17	16	18	21
Wid.-Div.	11	11	11	—[b]	12	13	15	15	16	19
Married	57	55	57	59	60	59	68	69	65	60
				Total Female Labor Force						
Single	68	67	61	77[b]	54	49	32	23	22	25
Wid.-Div.	18	18	15	—[b]	17	15	16	6	14	15
Married	14	15	24	23	29	36	52	61	63	60
Mothers[a]	—	—	—	—	—	11	26	27	38	40
				Female Labor Force Participation Rate						
Single	41	41	48	44[b]	46	48	51	44	53	62
Wid. Div.	30	33	35	—[b]	34	32	36	13	46	41
Married	5	6	11	9	12	17	25	32	41	51
Mothers[a]	—	—	—	—	—	28	33	37	43	56

Sources: U.S. Bureau of the Census, *Women at Work*, p. 14, table VII, p. 15, table VIII; U.S. Department of Labor, Women's Bureau, *Employed Mothers and Child Care*, p. 9, table 3; U.S. Department of Labor, Bureau of Labor Statistics, *Working Women: A Databook*, p. 19, table 18; U.S. Department of Labor, Bureau of Labor Statistics, *Marital and Family Statistics of Workers*, p. 5, table 3; U.S. Department of Labor, Bureau of Labor Statistics, *Marital and Family Patterns*, p. 1, table 1, p. 2, table 2, p. 25, table C-1.

[a]Mothers of children under age 18.
[b]Single women counted with widows and divorced women.
[c]Figures for March 1980.

By 1980, the typical woman worker was married, a mother, and a clerical worker.[6] By 1980, too, married women comprised nearly two-thirds of all women workers, fully reversing the trend of a century earlier. This reversal is illustrated in figure 1, in which the declining proportions of single women in the female labor force are contrasted with the rising proportions of married women workers. The steady growth in the numbers of married women workers has been to a large degree a growth in the numbers of middle-income wives in the labor force, particularly after 1940. More recent developments include a startling rise in the proportions of working mothers with very young children.

Figure 1
Composition of Female Labor Force by Marital Status, 1890–1980

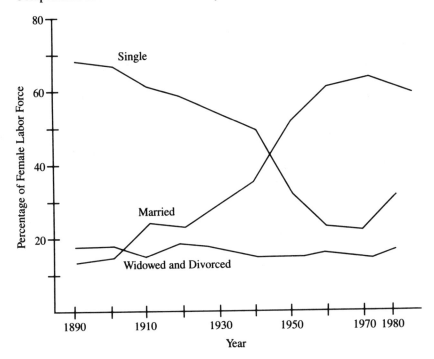

Source: See table 2.

In the course of a century, the working mother has moved from the periphery of the American labor force into the mainstream.

These material changes in the labor force contributed to the changing ideas about women and work that were widely shared by middle-class Americans. As white middle-income married women moved into the labor force in the twentieth century, motherhood, rather than future motherhood, became the subject of concern. As a result, single women workers were no longer considered "controversial" members of the labor force. In the era of the working mother, reformers used psychological rather than moral arguments in the debate over woman's enlarging sphere, reflecting changes in the cultural milieu. "Delinquency" and "neurosis" replaced "purity" and "sin" in the rhetoric about women who worked. The social response to the working mother also reinforced domestic values, but it served to confirm rather than mitigate the controversial status of employed women, particularly if they had children. Because reforms like day care and mothers' pensions were originally meant

only for destitute or widowed women, the "respectable" working mother confronted a society that remained unresponsive to her needs for quality child care and for more flexible working conditions. Unlike reforms targeted for the working girl, reforms for the working mother were not shaped in response to rising numbers in the labor force. Rather, social responses to mothers at work emerged in an earlier time as a charitable measure meant to alleviate the consequences of poverty for children.

The shift in the subject of the debate from single to married women reflected both new labor force conditions and changes in the ideology of domesticity. Whereas all "respectable" women had been considered bound by the domestic ideology in the nineteenth century, single working women and working wives in the twentieth century gradually lost their controversial status. For these twentieth-century women, employment practices that were at one time considered suspect were absorbed into the mainstream of acceptable behavior. Their participation in the work force was no longer collectively defined as a transgression of the domestic ideology, as that ideology was narrowed to include only mothers of young children.

The extent to which the domestic ideology will be further modified by the growing population of working mothers remains to be seen. For working mothers, possible solutions to the problem of child care—such as equal parenting responsibilities of both father and mother—strike deep at the heart of the concept of separate male and female spheres. Hence the traditional association of biological difference (reproduction) with social behavior (child care) makes the working mother the gravest threat yet to the standard definitions of family life. Moreover, as more and more mothers of very young children join the labor force, the debate over women's work has become sharply focused on the issue of day care for those children.

This book considers the interaction of work, family, and cultural patterns in the long history of the working woman in America. The historical evidence examined includes both demographic and documentary materials. While government census and survey data are limited by the questions originally asked and by errors in the survey process, they provide the best perspective on national trends and patterns of labor force participation.[7] The writings of government investigators, clergymen, journalists, and working women provide insight into how different segments of the public have responded to the changing female labor force. I have often used specific cases from various cities to illustrate general trends.

The first part of the study examines the development of the era of the working girl. Chapters 1 through 3 look at the growth of the population of self-supporting women in nineteenth-century cities, the "social problem" of purity

and future motherhood that emerged after the Civil War, and subsequent social and legislative reforms that were meant to close the gap between behavior and ideology. The second half of the book—chapters 4 through 6—provides a parallel discussion of the era of the working mother. In both cases, changing behavior in the work force fueled a controversy over the employment of women, which itself resulted from the cultural lag between new patterns of labor force behavior and traditional ideas of domesticity.[8] The ideology of domesticity itself has been transformed over time, in a dialectic with changing social and material conditions.

Part One

The Era of the Working Girl, 1820–1920

Chapter 1
"Women Adrift": The Growth of an Urban Class

T he era of the working girl unfolded in the nineteenth century. By the years after the Civil War, the typical woman worker was young and single. In addition, hundreds of thousands of working women had migrated to cities from American small towns and farms or had immigrated from Europe. By the 1870s, women who worked and lived apart from traditional networks of home and family formed a growing urban class; reformers singled them out with labels such as "homeless women," "women adrift," and "working girls."

By the turn of the century, these self-supporting women were a third of the urban female labor force, and they were also at the heart of a widespread public controversy over the morality of women's work. Yet in modern times young single working women have as a group become socially and historically invisible. The widening of "woman's sphere" in the twentieth century has been accompanied by the acceptance of employment and housing practices that were at one time considered to be a threat to social order.

This chapter examines the history of that generation of single women which first challenged conventional social roles by their entrance into the urban labor force. Immigrant and black women have always worked. But when native-born white women increased their propensity to work, producing in effect a new labor supply, the question of woman's proper place gathered strength in the public debate.

The chapter will first look at the antecedents of the era of the working girl. In particular, this era was shaped by the collapse of paternalistic employment structures in the nineteenth century, particularly the decline in domestic service and factory housing customs which imposed a supervised domestic environment upon working women before the Civil War. This care was thought necessary to insure the respectability of women who worked temporarily before marriage. Ironically, as these customs faded, the supply of young single women who were living on their own increased. The discussion will conclude with a description of the female labor force that had developed by 1900.

Antebellum Women Workers: Maids and Mill Girls

Since colonial times, the urban female labor force included self-supporting women—those who had to work to survive, prostitutes, vagabonds, and widows. By the antebellum era, urban growth and population pressures pushed and pulled thousands of single women to the cities, as young women abandoned the New England countryside to seek work in the burgeoning mill towns and in Boston.[1] But the geographical movement of rural single women did not become a national phenomenon until after the Civil War, when the development of steam railroads and the acceleration of urban and industrial growth launched the journeys of tens of thousands of migrants. At that time, too, the rapid increase in immigration added thousands of foreign-born women to the numbers of female workers living on their own in large cities.

Prior to this time, self-supporting women had not been visible as a social group. Women workers in large cities such as Boston, Philadelphia, or New York were generally considered to be beyond the pale of middle-class respectability; they were usually destitute, black, or immigrant.[2] In smaller communities, however, paternalistic structures allowed thousands of white rural women to migrate, work temporarily, and retain the status conferred by the domestic ideology. In small towns and villages, young women lived as servants with their employers, or they resided in the pseudo-families of supervised boardinghouses. In both cases, they were surrounded by domestic influences and family constraints.

These living arrangements stemmed in part from the colonial axiom that all individuals be attached to those microcosms of social order—well-governed families. In the mid-seventeenth century, for example, the single young person could not legally "be for himself" in Plymouth or Massachusetts Bay, but instead had to reside within an established family unit.[3] This stricture loosened for young men in the nineteenth century. Single men boarded not only with families, but increasingly in commercial boardinghouses and hotels.[4] The expectation for women, however, remained stringent. Woman's respectability rested on her ties to family life. If she could not live within the province of her parents' governance, she was expected to reside within a substitute family environment that insured a modicum of supervision and protection during the years before she married and established her own home.

To some degree, domestic service provided this supervision. Domestic service was the leading occupation for women in the United States through the 1940s, and until the 1920s servants commonly accepted partial payment for their labor in the form of room and board with their employers. A brief

overview of the history of domestic service illustrates how the status of the servant evolved.

MAIDS

During the colonial period, female servants were indentured or "redemptioned" whites, or enslaved blacks. White female servants were usually European immigrants who paid sponsors for their passage across the Atlantic with a term of labor that generally ranged from four to five years. Wages were low; at the time of release a servant could expect some food, clothing, and a pittance of money. These early servants were considered to be inferior to their employers; they were stigmatized as a lower social class.[5]

In the early national and antebellum periods, however, the status of domestic service improved to some degree in the northern United States. Particularly in New England, patriarchy fused with democracy to remove the social stigma of domestic work. Antebellum servants were often women born into the same community as their employers. They commonly "attended the same church, sat at the same fireside, ate at the same table, had the same associates; they were often married from the homes and buried in the family lots of their employers."[6] These young women were treated as surrogate daughters "helping" within their employers' households; they were not merely servants laboring for contracted wages.

Significantly, wage-work for single women was at this time socially approved because of the popular belief that workers avoided the sin of idleness and learned "habits of industry."[7] This sanction of women's work evolved because women were needed to meet labor demand. At the same time, social approval rested on the maintenance of moral order and the continuance of quasi-parental supervision.

With the influx of Irish and German immigrants to the United States in the 1840s and 1850s, however, domestic service lost status. Native-born women feared they would lose social position if they competed with immigrant labor. Foreign-born women entered households not as surrogate daughters but as servants of inferior social rank. For these young immigrants, domestic boarding became the female equivalent of the male practice of "boarding out" with strangers before marriage. These women were continuing a long-standing European tradition in which a servant's household membership and the implied protection of her employer sanctioned her departure from home.[8] In Buffalo, New York, for example, newly arrived Irish and German women had by the mid-nineteenth century established a pattern of working for a few years

before marriage as live-in servants with the resident native-born families of the city.[9] As domestic service became a major job channel for immigrants, it no longer served as acceptable employment for native-born women between the stages of childhood and marriage.

MILL GIRLS

Factory work developed similarly to domestic service. A system that at one time provided paternalistic safeguards for female respectability declined as immigrants replaced native-born workers in the 1850s and 1860s. The American factory age began at the end of the eighteenth century, when New England "manufactories" hired rural women and children to doff, weave, and spin on factory premises rather than at home. Because labor was scarce, unmarried women had been used to provide an extensive and cheap labor supply for the nascent textile industry.[10]

Many New England factories promoted the Waltham, or boardinghouse, system. Women applying for factory work were required to sign a "regulation paper" promising regular church attendance, strict moral behavior, and residence in a corporation boardinghouse. Men also signed a regulation paper, but for them corporation boarding was not a requirement. Corporation lodgings provided a substitute family environment for young women that effectively transferred parental authority from the farm to the factory.[11]

This moral authority was meant not only to protect the virtue of young women but also to insure factory productivity by maintaining a class of "industrious, sober, orderly, and moral" operatives. Without such a class of workers, the Lowell clergyman Henry Miles suggested in 1846, "profits would be absorbed by cases of irregularity, carelessness, and neglect; while the existence of any great moral exposure in Lowell would cut off the supply of help from the virtuous homesteads of the country." Miles concluded that "public morals and private interests . . . are here seen to be linked together in an indissoluble connection. Accordingly, the sagacity of self-interest, as well as more disinterested considerations, has led to the adoption of a strict system of moral police."[12]

Factory lodgings established to protect the workers were supervised by matrons who were frequently the widowed mothers of operatives and who were often called "mother" by the young residents. Inmates were expected to obey a plethora of rules and regulations, including a strict curfew. Labor historian Norman Ware described the "moral policing" of the Waltham system. "The operatives were told when, where, how, and for how much they must work," he wrote, "when and where they were to eat and sleep. They were ordered to

attend church, for which they had to pay pew rent. They were discharged for immoral conduct, for bad language, for disrespect, for attending dancing classes, or for any other cause that the agents or overseers thought sufficient."[13] Discharge was a powerful threat; in Lowell, a blacklisting code guaranteed that a worker dismissed from one mill would not be hired by another.[14]

At the same time, factory boardinghouses attempted to provide the amenities of the country homes left behind by the young migrants. Harriet Hanson Robinson, one of the early "factory girls," nostalgically recalled in her autobiography the pianos, libraries, and carpeted parlors of her factory lodgings, and maintained that the operatives' surroundings were as pure and refined as their own homes.[15] The cultural activities and domestic duties carried on in the boardinghouses—reading, sewing, letter writing—secured a domestic atmosphere of gentility meant to protect both the reputations of the workers and the morality and social order of the factory villages.

This moral strategy succeeded in maintaining the respectability of the Lowell operatives. In 1844, William Scoresby, a British clergyman, visited Lowell and later reported that, among the operatives, "there was not the slightest appearance of boldness or vulgarity; on the contrary, a very becoming propriety and respectability of manner."[16] In the 1860s, the respectability of the Lowell mill girls was still legend. Asa Mercer, an imaginative Washington bachelor, traveled to Lowell to recruit women to migrate to Seattle, a city where marriageable women were scarce. He recruited more than a hundred mill workers, who became popularly known in Seattle as "Mercer girls."[17]

With increasing European immigration and with growing wage and hour demands on the part of the workers, factory employment gradually lost status, paralleling the process that occurred in domestic service. Immigrants were willing to work longer hours for lower wages, the factories filled with foreign-born instead of native-born women, and women mill workers as a group lost the ideological sanctions they had gained in antebellum years.[18]

The era of the "factory girl" was gone by the end of the 1860s. By the 1880s, operative resentment of boardinghouse regulations and the decrease in native-born women seeking jobs in factories led to the abandonment of the Waltham system. The immigrant women who ran the looms and doffed the bobbins did not transgress the class lines crossed by native-born farm women a generation earlier.

By the time of the Civil War, two traditional patriarchal systems that had provided protection and "respectability" for young women who left their families to work were decaying. Domestic work and factory labor no longer offered a mantle of rectitude through the extension of middle-class domestic

values. These occupations became provinces of the immigrant, black, and poor women who were already excluded from the pedestal of "pure woman-hood." Rural native-born women were displaced from their approved foothold in the labor force as maids or mill girls, and they were instead expected to remain home as "ladies." Female idleness became a status symbol rather than a disgrace as the domestic ideology was used to heighten distinctions between classes of women.[19]

Still, hundreds of thousands of women who were included in the domestic "place" nevertheless continued to sidestep their prescribed role. As historian Thomas Dublin has pointed out, textile mill workers had often worked not only because of compelling economic need, but sometimes for economic and social independence from their families. These workers worked to build up their dowries, to buy clothing, or to save for an education. And some, like Sally Rice, of Somerset, Vermont, worked for personal satisfaction alone. Sally Rice left home in 1838 and worked as a farm laborer and mill hand. She wrote her parents the next year, "I have but one life to live and I want to enjoy myself as well as I can while I live."[20]

Even after the time that domestic service and mill work lost "respectability," women continued to work for wages outside the home, and a growing proportion of them continued to migrate within and between cities seeking housing and employment. The ideology of domesticity never reflected real experience for this segment of the female population.

The Growth of the Female Labor Force, 1865–1900

Although comparative data are not available, it seems that the tendency of young women to work and live away from their homes increased in the postbellum era. In 1889, the United States Department of Labor surveyed 22 cities and found that an estimated 14 percent of the working women studied were living "adrift" from their families. That same year, labor statistician Carroll Wright observed in his report, "The Working Girls of Boston," that while the number of women who were boarders and lodgers was "much less than is generally supposed," still about a third of all working women, *excluding* domestic servants, were living away from home. If servants were included, of course, that proportion would be even higher. In 1891, the United States Department of Labor issued a bulletin on boarding homes and clubs for working women, commenting on the "large working population of women without local homes in great cities."[21]

LABOR SUPPLY

Why did the numbers of wage-earning women, and of self-supporting women in particular, seem to increase so dramatically in postbellum years? A combination of factors may explain the occurrence. Nativity, age, and marital patterns produced a relatively large supply of young single women who for cultural and economic reasons were more prone to seek work outside their homes than were women in previous times. Concomitantly, opportunities on farms were shrinking for women, as labor demand in large cities expanded. Middle-class urban families increasingly sought servants, and factories, mills, and offices demanded female rather than male labor.[22]

There are, unfortunately, few reliable accounts of the self-supporting woman in this era. Some self-supporting women chose not to identify themselves to investigators, believing, one investigator suggested, "that it is more aristocratic, or fashionable, or something else, to state that they live at home, when as a matter of fact, they do not."[23] The richest source on the subject is the Census Bureau's compilation of Twelfth Census manuscript returns, published in 1907 as *Statistics of Women at Work*. This lengthy volume presents information on the nativity, marital status, occupation, and living arrangements for adult women workers in twenty-seven cities and in Brooklyn.[24] An analysis of this information provides a picture of women workers for one year—1900—a year at the height of the era of the working girl.

The majority of women workers at the end of the nineteenth century were young, single, and living at home with their parents. But the practice of young women living on their own had become common in cities by the turn of the century. Of 1,232,000 women workers reported in cities, some 434,000 of them—over a third—lived apart from their parents. In the cities surveyed, boarders and lodgers comprised from 18 to 49 percent of all women workers and from 11 to 34 percent of workers excluding domestic servants (see table 3).

The cities surveyed by the Census Bureau included all those with populations over 150,000 in 1900 except for San Francisco, which was omitted because of the disorder caused by the great earthquake in 1906. Four smaller cities—Paterson, Fall River, Lowell, and Atlanta—were surveyed as well. In general, the relative proportions of self-supporting women in a city were determined by a mix of local conditions and not by any one factor such as size, location, composition of population, or degree of industrialization.[25]

It is evident from the census data that urban women were more likely to work for wages than were women in the United States as a whole. In 1900, 28

Table 3

Percentage of Boarders and Lodgers among Women Workers
for Selected Cities, 1900

Cities	All Boarders	Boarders Excluding Servants[a]	Cities	All Boarders	Boarders Excluding Servants[a]
St. Paul	49	34	Cleveland	32	16
Minneapolis	48	31	Brooklyn	32	13
Boston	44	28	Providence	32	19
New York[b]	41	20	Rochester	31	20
Pittsburgh	40	18	Baltimore	30	16
Kansas City	39	25	Milwaukee	30	14
Philadelphia	38	22	Louisville	27	14
Lowell	37	32	Newark	27	12
Detroit	37	21	Cincinnati	26	12
Washington	36	23	Jersey City	24	11
Chicago	36	21	New Orleans	23	13
Buffalo	35	17	Paterson	21	13
St. Louis	34	16	Atlanta	20	13
Indianapolis	32	19	Fall River	18	14

Sources: U.S. Bureau of the Census, *Statistics of Women at Work*, pp. 218–305, table 28, p. 29, table XX.

[a]"Servant" includes servants, housekeepers and stewardesses, and waitresses.
[b]Includes Manhattan and Bronx boroughs only.

percent of the urban female population worked, compared with 21 percent in the continental United States. Immigrants and the daughters of immigrants were more likely to live and work in the city than were their native-born counterparts.[26]

It is at first surprising to see, in table 3, that Minneapolis and St. Paul ranked highest in the relative numbers of women who boarded away from home and so were presumably self-supporting. Most studies of working women concentrated on the larger cities of the East Coast. The disproportionately higher migrant female population of urban Minnesota can be explained, however, by immigration and migration patterns in the upper Midwest. In 1900, fully four out of five self-supporting women in Minneapolis and St. Paul were immigrants or daughters of immigrants. Immigrants to the upper Midwest arriving before 1890 tended to settle in rural rather than urban districts. Minneapolis

and St. Paul therefore attracted the restless daughters of settlers from a large geographic area including Minnesota, Wisconsin, the Dakotas, and Iowa.[27]

But the situation in these hinterland cities was the exception, not the rule. In the more dense urban centers of the East, immigrants settled in cities from the start, and their working daughters were more likely to live at home than with employers or in boardinghouses. In the seaport cities of Boston, New York, and Philadelphia, the majority of women who lived away from home were immigrants and native-born women of native parentage—the latter being migrants from the countryside.[28] Nationally, immigrant women constituted almost half of the female boarding population. Within each racial and nativity group, however, the propensity to live away from home varied. Almost half of all immigrant working women were boarders and lodgers, over 40 percent of black working women were boarders, and over a third of those women born to native-born parents boarded.

But domestic servants skewed this data toward the immigrant population. When servants are excluded, native-born women of native parentage become the first ranked group of boarders and lodgers. The importance of native-born white migrant women will be discussed in chapter 2 as a factor in the growing concern with women who lived apart from traditional family life.

The relative proportions of women workers and boarders by nativity and race reflect larger trends in social history. Immigration to the United States from Europe increased in spurts through the 1800s, peaking in the first decade of the twentieth century, when over eight million aliens entered the country. These immigrants were largely young and single. Through the 1800s, over two-thirds were under the age of 39, and from 1911 to 1920, over 60 percent were single.[29]

Immigrants were also predominantly male. The ratio of men to women was about 3 to 2 from 1820 to 1860 and nearly 5 to 2 from 1900 to 1910. But these sex ratios varied by nationality. Among some immigrant groups were thousands of single women seeking work. Between 1870 and 1890, for example, almost 20 percent of Danish and 30 percent of Swedish immigrants were unmarried women.[30]

How did these women journey to the United States? Many traveled with their families to large cities, others came alone and were met at the stations by relatives and friends, and the rest arrived on their own at American ports without having made arrangements for work or housing. Studies of immigrant women in Boston and Minneapolis found that most initially lodged with relatives or friends before finding work as servants, or in hotels and restaurants where they would also receive room and board.[31]

Internal migration patterns especially favored the development of a class of women boarders and lodgers. At the turn of the century, most Americans still lived on farms or in small villages and towns. But there was little opportunity for employment for women in these rural districts. The inheritance of farms usually went to sons rather than to daughters, and activities were limited for women remaining at home. The 1865 diary of a 19-year-old Wisconsin farm woman portrays a round of life bounded by household and agricultural tasks, school teaching, and loneliness. After a week of teaching, sewing, cleaning, and boiling sugar sap, Sarah Beaulieu wrote, "I think I am getting very much like the old maid that sat down on Monday morning and cried because Saturday did not come twice a week."[32] In a similar vein, the fictional farm girl Rose Dutcher, in Hamlin Garland's *Rose of Dutcher's Coolly* (1895) argued that in an "age of cities" to live in the country was "to be a cow, a tadpole!" On the farm, she complained that "you could arise at five o'clock to cook breakfast and wash dishes, and get dinner, and sweep and mend, and get supper, and so on, till you rotted, like a post stuck in the mud."[33] This farm girl's solution, too, was to go to the big city. Toward the end of the century, agricultural technology further lessened both the opportunity and the need for female labor on farms, contributing even more to the attractiveness of the city for young rural women.

In small towns, opportunities for young women were also limited. Edith H., a 20-year-old from Mankato, Minnesota, wrote the Minnesota Bureau of Labor for help in her search for work. "I want something to do," she pleaded. "There isn't anything to do here because it is a small place and I was tole [*sic*] to go to the cities but to write to you people first as I am a stranger there." Although the state labor bureau had a policy discouraging the migration of young women to the large cities, it is likely that Edith H. joined the stream of eager travelers to Minneapolis and St. Paul.[34]

In general, young single women migrated at a greater rate and at an earlier age than men to seek work in the cities, resulting in both the increase in the female labor supply and the feminization of some urban populations. The movement of migrants to the cities was, unlike that of immigrants, disproportionately female. The migration of women peaked at about the age of 18, while most young men did not leave their homes until they were in their early twenties.[35]

These migration and immigration processes contributed to the relative youth of the urban female working population. Working women in large cities were likely to be younger than working women in smaller cities and country districts. This was most evident in women who were from 18 to 24 years old. Almost half of the women in this age group who lived in cities of at least

50,000 worked in 1900, compared with about a quarter of the same-aged women in rural areas.[36]

A consequence of the younger age of urban women workers was the increased likelihood that they would be unmarried and thus more likely to live away from home. Three out of four white women workers, and four out of five white women boarders and lodgers, were single in 1900. Native-born daughters of immigrants were most likely to be single in both the working and boarding populations. Married women were slowly increasing their tendency to work, especially if they were black, and female heads of household who worked, we will see, were also a growing group. But single women continued to dominate the female labor force at the turn of the century.[37] Patterns of age, marriage, and fertility had important consequences for the female labor supply. The large numbers of unmarried women in the late nineteenth century diminished in ensuing decades, as the female population both aged and married at a faster rate.

There was a relatively large population of young single women in the late 1800s. Since then, there have been lesser proportions of single women in the young- and middle-age groups as the age of first marriages has fallen. But prior to 1900 the majority of women remained single until the age of 25, reflecting both a rising age of first marriage and decreasing marriage rates. More than half of all women from 20 to 24 years of age were single in birth cohorts up to 1884, and a decline in the proportion of single women in that age group prevailed thereafter until 1934 when less than a third of the women between 20 and 24 years old were single (table 4). Women born before 1885—the core of the female labor supply through the early twentieth century—were therefore more likely to remain single for a longer period of time than were women born in succeeding years.

The age of first marriage moved downward from 1890 to 1955. In 1890, the median age of first marriage for women was 22 years; by 1955, the median age was 20.2 years. The decline in the marriage rate was accompanied by a decline in the fertility rate, which dropped from about 55 per 1,000 in 1820 to 20 per 1,000 in 1955. As a result, the population gradually aged. From 1880 to 1950, the proportions of persons under the age of 24 declined.[38]

Demographic factors alone cannot explain why women began to work in this period. The composition of the female labor force reflects cultural and economic transformations as well as demographic trends. As the sociologist Valerie Kincade Oppenheimer points out, analysis of population distribution alone cannot account for changes in female labor force behavior. Rather, explanations for the shifting propensity of some groups of women to work must be sought as well.[39]

Table 4
Percentage of Single Women, by Age, in Birth Cohorts,
1865–1874 to 1925–1934

	Cohort Groups						
Age	1865–1874	1875–1884	1885–1894	1895–1904	1905–1914	1915–1924	1925–1934
15–19	90.3	88.6	87.9	87.0	86.8	88.1	82.9
20–24	51.8	51.5	48.3	45.6	46.0	47.2	32.3
25–29	27.5	24.9	23.0	21.7	22.8	13.3	—
30–34	16.6	16.1	14.9	13.2	14.7	9.3	—
35–44	11.4	11.4	10.0	10.4	8.3	—	—
45–54	9.6	9.1	8.7	7.8	—	—	—
55–64	8.9	9.0	7.9	—	—	—	—
65+	9.3	8.9	—	—	—	—	—

Source: Adapted from Taeuber and Taeuber, *Changing Population of the United States*, p. 153, table 47.

Cultural and attitudinal changes were important factors in the work habits of single women in postbellum years. Traditionally, unmarried women were expected to live within the homes of relatives. Two exceptions, we have seen, were domestic servants and factory operatives who lived in supervised housing provided by employers. Events in the postbellum period—especially urbanization and industrialization—stimulated new work and family processes that led to a life-cycle stage of autonomy for women who were in between the stages of adolescence and an expected adulthood of marriage and motherhood. Moreover, a trend toward higher education combined with widening work opportunities to create among women "a feeling of independence and self-reliance."[40] By the end of the nineteenth century, a period of female economic autonomy— that is, of female self-support—became more common than it had been in previous times.

Urban young women who lived at home with their parents, even those of middle-income groups, did not necessarily remain idle or take in home work, such as sewing, as they might have done in an earlier era. Rather, they increasingly sought employment in shops, offices, and mills. Rural and immigrant women went a step further, leaving their parents' homes to live in the cities among strangers. For all of these women, of course, paid employment was expected to be a temporary activity engaged in only before marriage.[41]

Young women were now working for a variety of reasons. For many young native-born white women a desire for new experiences, independence, personal satisfaction, and excitement impelled them to leave the sanctuary of home. Bessie Van Vorst, in the 1903 study *The Woman Who Toils*, reported that a statement pronounced repeatedly by young factory operatives who had migrated to a New York mill town was: "I don't have to work; my father gives me all the money I need, but not all the money I *want*. I like to be independent and spend my money as I please."[42] Other women echoed this sentiment. In 1908, working women submitted autobiographical essays to *Harper's Bazaar* on the topic "The Girl Who Comes to the City." Among the motivations for employment cited in these firsthand accounts were boredom at home and the "unendurable" life in the country.[43]

Even more women, like most men, worked for economic reasons. Young women worked not only for considerations of independence but also because of changing family-income needs. As middle-class standards of consumption rose, a daughter's salary could make the difference between family subsistence and family comfort. A more compelling reason for seeking work, however, was the need to provide self-support. A large proportion of women workers had no alternative but to work in order to survive. Many of the testimonies in the *Harper's Bazaar* series recounted tales of women who worked because they were orphaned, had to support brothers and sisters, or experienced "family misfortunes" of some kind.[44]

During this period, however, women's wages were inadequate for more than "pin money"—supplemental household income. Women provided a supply of cheap labor for expanding business and industry. Their wages were abysmally low, especially with respect to men in comparable positions. Throughout the nineteenth century, for example, female factory operatives were paid on the average half of what male operatives earned.[45]

In the late 1880s, the urban woman worker was paid an average of $5.68 weekly; when the "lost time" of illness and layoff was taken into account, this sum fell to $5.24. Yet the average cost of living for a self-supporting woman was estimated at $5.51 a week—for housing, food, clothing, the support of dependents, and other expenses. A close look at the data supplied in the 1889 United States Department of Labor report, "Working Women in Large Cities," brings these figures to life. There was, for instance, a bag maker in Philadelphia who earned $4.49 and spent $4.17 a week, a Boston bustle maker who earned $5.19 and spent $4.71 a week, and a Chicago saleswoman who earned $8.42 and spent $7.92 a week. Many women, such as the New York seamstress who earned $4.42 and spent $5.12 weekly, listed "other sources" beyond their salaries as income; these sources probably included sums from their

families back home, savings, or, as reformers most feared, money from male friends.[46]

Employers commonly justified their low payrolls by arguing that women worked only for extra luxuries. As late as 1904, an employer reported to the Minnesota Department of Labor that "girls are frivolous, dishonest, and inefficient" and that they worked only for "the excitement, the 'opportunity for ogling customers,' and display of cheap finery."[47] Many employers preferred hiring young women who lived at home with their parents, although some businesses, like hotels and restaurants, paid workers in part with room and board.

Surveys of working women in postbellum decades repeatedly found that many women who worked did so out of necessity. State labor bureau investigations in Kansas, Missouri, and New Jersey in the 1890s found that from 26 to 68 percent of the women studied supported dependents. In 1888, the United States Bureau of Labor found that over half of those surveyed, including women who lived at home with their parents, contributed to family finances.[48] These studies often stressed that boarders and lodgers were responsible for dependents back home as well as for their own self-support.

Like the other investigators, the Bureau of the Census affirmed that many working women labored because of financial need rather than for pin money. In 1907, the Census Bureau noted that, for most women, "it is the necessity of supporting themselves wholly or in part, and perhaps contributing to the support of those dependent upon them, that is usually the impelling motive" for their employment.[49] Of the women surveyed in 1900, over a third were self-supporting and living away from home. Of the remaining two-thirds, 12 percent were "heads of families" supporting dependents as well as themselves. Another 26 percent lived with their fathers, suggesting that the remaining women workers may have supported widowed mothers, destitute siblings, or, rarely, husbands and young children.[50]

These findings were reinforced by the Women's Bureau of the United States Department of Labor in the 1920s. The Women's Bureau analyzed the contributions of women wage earners to family support in 1922 and 1923. Almost all of the women studied who lived at home aided their families, the Women's Bureau found. Of those who lived away from home, nearly half "apparently had sharply defined responsibilities for personal or family support." The Women's Bureau noted that these tasks were accomplished on salaries barely adequate for self-support.[51] Economic need, it is clear, remained a compelling factor in the labor force behavior of many women in this era. But at the same time, the anxious efforts of some investigators to prove that women worked because they had to, rather than because they chose to, to some degree

obscured the more complex motivations of women seeking paid employment outside the home.

LABOR DEMAND

Labor demand was as important as demographic, cultural, and economic factors in shaping the supply of labor for the female work force. Women workers were sought by a growing urban middle class desiring household help and by factories, shops, mills, and offices. Traditional female occupations, such as teaching and nursing, were also widening as population growth, mandatory education, and the professionalization of medicine occurred.[52]

The sex segregation of the labor force functioned to insure that labor demand would continue to be sex-specific. That is, as long as certain occupations were labeled "women's work," there would be a continuous need for women workers.[53] Sex segregation also minimized the cultural disjuncture between the need for labor and the cultural expectations of a woman's domestic role. The most common paid occupations for women—domestic service, sewing, nursing, and teaching—were among the occupations traditionally linked to female tasks of household maintenance and nurturing. Moreover, sex segregation guaranteed a supply of cheap labor. The lower status of women's work combined with the domestic ideology to keep female employment subordinate to the primary task of domesticity. This idea that women's work was secondary to family life in turn kept wages down and women unorganized, since so many women workers viewed their wage-earning activities as temporary.[54]

The Bureau of the Census reported with some surprise that women engaged in 294 of 303 recorded occupations in 1900. The only jobs that were exclusively male were those of soldiers, sailors, marines, firemen, streetcar drivers, telegraph and telephone linemen, apprentices to roofers and slaters, and helpers to steam boilermakers and brass workers.[55] But this list is deceiving. An examination of table 5 indicates that most women workers clustered in traditional sex-segregated jobs.

The occupations most often reported by women workers in the cities surveyed in 1900 were domestic service, sewing trades, clerical work, teaching, laundry work, nursing, sales, and textile manufactures. Factors of class, nativity, and race influenced which women entered which occupations. Native-born white women dominated clerical, teaching, and sales work in 1900. Foreign-born women constituted the majority of domestic servants and cotton factory operatives, while black women were half of all laundry workers.

At least 15 percent of the workers in each category were boarders and

Table 5
Percentage of Women Workers in Selected Occupations, by Native Origin and Race, in Selected U.S. Cities, 1900

Occupations[a]	Native White, Native Parents	Native White, Foreign Parents	Foreign-Born White	Black
Domestic service	12	19	47	21
Sewing work	23	41	32	4
Clerical work	41	48	11	—[b]
Teaching	44	42	11	3
Laundry work	7	15	27	51
Nursing and midwifery	32	22	37	9
Sales	30	54	16	—[b]
Cotton mill work	15	26	60	—[b]

Source: U.S. Bureau of the Census, *Statistics of Women at Work*, pp. 198–207, table 26.

[a]Domestic servants include stewardesses and housekeepers, waitresses, and domestic servants; sewing workers include dressmakers, milliners, seamstresses, and tailoresses; clerical workers include bookkeepers and accountants, clerks and copyists, and stenographers and typewriters (typists); teachers include teachers and college professors as well as musicians and teachers of music.
[b]Less than 1 percent.

lodgers, although some jobs were more likely to attract women living on their own than were others. Domestic service, nursing, teaching, and factory work were occupations where at least one in five workers boarded away from home. Other occupations, especially low-paying jobs such as telephone operating and store cashiering, were more likely to be filled by young women still living with their parents.

In general, women workers were most likely to be domestic servants; servants comprised more than a fourth of the urban female labor force in 1900. Almost 276,000 women worked as maids, cooks, waitresses, and kitchen help in private homes, hotels, boardinghouses, restaurants, and businesses. Nearly 80 percent of them received room and board as partial compensation for their labor. For this reason, domestic service was at that time an occupation requiring a population of transient women who were able to leave their parents' homes to live among strangers.

Domestic work was an especially important occupation for Scandinavians.

More than half of all female Swedish immigrant workers, 47 percent of the Norwegians, and 44 percent of the Danish immigrants labored as servants.[56] As David Katzman has noted, domestic service introduced rural and immigrant women to a more urban and modern environment. Indeed, for the unskilled foreign-born woman, domestic work was a major channel into the American culture, one in which she could learn the language and the mores of the middle class through daily contact with its family life.[57]

Sewing workers were the second most populous group of workers. Dressmakers, milliners, seamstresses, and tailors comprised a fifth of the female labor force. Immigrants or the daughters of immigrants made up more than two-thirds of the women in these trades. Additionally, almost two-thirds of the operatives in cotton-textile mills were foreign-born.

Clerical work was the third most important job category for urban women workers in 1900, representing 9 percent of the female labor force. These women—almost entirely native-born and white—labored in city offices as bookkeepers, accountants, clerks, copyists, stenographers, and "typewriters." Stenographers and typists evidenced the greatest increase of all women workers between 1890 and 1900, when the numbers of women in these occupations jumped 305 percent—from 21,000 to 86,000. The feminization of office work was unusually rapid. In 1870, 97.5 percent of the clerical labor force was male. In 1888, the New York City Young Women's Christian Association opened the first typing class for women, and female clerical education soon proliferated. By 1900, women comprised more than a third of the clerical labor force; by 1920, more than half.[58]

Like clerical work, the expansion of sales work opened job opportunities for native-born white women. Sales work for women developed at the same time as clerical work. In 1870, "sales women" were too few to be counted separately in the census records. By 1900, they numbered over 65,000 in the surveyed cities and over 142,000 nationally.[59]

By the 1890s, discussion of suitable work for women often included clerical and sales occupations along with medicine, law, "architecture and decorating," and journalism. These jobs, some argued, would not cause a woman to "lose caste" if she had to earn a living. One advice-book writer contended in 1893 that shorthand writing and typing were skills "well suited to the finer nature and more delicate organization of womankind. . . . The prejudice against employing young ladies in office-work is rapidly dying out."[60] The fast growth of white-collar work as a female sector of the labor force greatly broadened earning opportunities for native-born white women. Expanding labor force needs interacted with cultural expectations to force the widening of the definition of respectable behavior for young women.

The widening of "woman's sphere" in the years after the Civil War engendered deep tensions in American society. By the end of the nineteenth century, the working girl had become symbolic of the movement of women away from traditional domestic pursuits. Investigations into the subject of women and work often focused on the subgroup of self-supporting women who were native-born and white. A coalescence of interest in moral reform, wages, and living conditions sparked the development of a new social problem characterized by race and class concerns as material changes led to ideological debate. All women workers were to some degree controversial, but those living away from home who, because of their class status, were also visibly separated from their "proper place" seemed to pose an especially grave threat to social order.

Chapter 2
The Discovery of "Future Motherhood"

I n the postbellum era new work and migration patterns fueled a widespread controversy about the working woman's effect on morality and traditional family life. As working conditions began to impinge on the lives of "respectable" women, the middle class could no longer ignore the disjuncture between its domestic ideology and the behavior of women who worked for wages. In the lively debate that followed, discussion focused on the impact of industrialism on the single woman worker's moral and physical potential for future motherhood.

This phase of the debate over women and work reflected the concerns of the social gospel and progressive movements. Public discovery of the young working woman mirrored collective anxieties about changing gender roles, moral purity, the displacement of rural tradition by urban culture, and the fate of future generations. The young women who migrated to the cities to work came to symbolize the threat to middle-class ideals of family life posed by economic and social trends of the nineteenth century.

Antecedents of the Debate

The postbellum debate over the employment of women echoed even earlier concerns about women's place in society. In 1836, British author Harriet Martineau observed that American women practiced eight occupations in the workplace: teaching, needlework, keeping boarders, mill work, shoe binding, typesetting, bookbinding, and domestic service. But as early as 1820, women were working in at least seventy-five different kinds of manufacturing occupations.[1] Like their later counterparts, antebellum writers could not reach a consensus on the question of female employment. In the late eighteenth century, there were efforts to sanction the wage-work of women, but by the mid-nineteenth century the rise of the domestic ideology and the worsening of industrial conditions removed that sanction in most occupations, at least for "respectable" women.

Because most of the women who worked in the antebellum era were immigrant, black, or impoverished, the concern with their exploitation never became a widespread social issue, and women workers as a group remained largely invisible to the public. Only the exceptional New England mill workers received much attention, but their status was secured by the paternalism of the textile manufacturers, which undercut any overt threat of independence on the part of the workers. Of the early positions on the issue of women and work, only one—an argument for a separate female domestic sphere—gained much popularity.

One of the early positions on the question of female employment in the United States maintained that women should work for both economic and moral reasons: they were needed in the labor force, and idleness was sinful. Household manufactures, of course, had long permitted women to be economically productive without leaving the protection of the family. But at the end of the eighteenth century the textile industry spawned factories where spinning and weaving were done on shop premises rather than in the worker's home. In 1791, Secretary of the Treasury Alexander Hamilton, in his *Report on Manufactures*, encouraged women to work in the burgeoning factories. Women could then supplement family income, and those who might otherwise be dependent upon the community for support would be "rendered more useful."[2]

Calvinist moralists and manufacturers alike argued that supervised female factory operatives were a boon to the nation's economic order. The factory system, besmirched by the European experience of "dark satanic mills," would be cleansed when transferred to American villages and staffed with bucolic American girls. Female factory operatives would avoid the fate of those unemployed women who were "doomed to idleness and its inseparable attendants, vice and guilt."[3] The women workers at Lowell, Lawrence, and other New England textile towns could work and still retain social status.

At the same time, a few writers countered the proposal that women *could* work with the more radical idea that women *should* work. The feminist themes of Mary Wollstonecraft's *A Vindication of the Rights of Women*, published in England in 1792, were echoed in the United States by Charles Brockden Brown, in *Alcuin: A Dialogue* (1798), and by "Constantia"—Judith Sargent Stevens Murray—a Massachusetts merchant's daughter who penned similar essays in the 1790s.[4] But these proponents of feminism were far ahead of their time and did not reflect popular sentiment.

By the 1820s and 1830s a more conservative viewpoint on the issue of women and work was gaining strength. The middle-class prescription of domesticity maintained that women should not work for wages but should con-

centrate instead on creating a domestic paradise for husband and children. Even single young women should be preparing themselves for their future domestic role. Male and female social behavior was seen as distinct and immutably tied to the biology of reproduction. Motherhood and the preparation for motherhood were taken to be the foremost concerns of women.

Historians agree that the domestic realm was becoming a distinctly female sphere in the United States in the antebellum era. An older tradition of male dominance within the family eroded as the self-contained household economy of the colonial era disintegrated under pressures of industrialism and urbanization. The patriarchal father no longer governed child rearing and household management with a stern hand. Women gained a new measure of power, although it was sharply limited, as child rearing and domestic economy became their preserve alone. Female education, religion, and manners turned toward the enhancement of the domestic role, as the one-wage-earner family, headed by the father, took root.[5]

As "woman's sphere" became exclusively domestic, adherence to the socially prescribed role became tightly tied to the health of the social order. Families had long been seen as the cornerstone of society. For the clergy, the mother's duty was to raise pious children; for the patriot, it was to raise loyal citizens. As historian Nancy Cott observes, the confluence of religious and secular influences set up a "cultural halo ringing the significance of home and family" for the well-being of society.[6] Female role behavior became imbued with powerful connotations for the future of the nation.

Within this domestic vision the role of the mother became sanctified. Although motherhood had not been an idealized state through the early eighteenth century, "the rise of the moral mother" accompanied the rise of the domestic ideology.[7] The biological processes of motherhood and the social processes of child rearing became symbolic of the possibilities and the limitations of the female role. In this symbolism the separation of childbearing from child rearing was branded immoral, justifying the sexual division of labor and its underpinnings of patriarchy.[8] By the mid-nineteenth century, writers commonly praised the special ability of women to nurture children. Horace Bushnell, Lydia Maria Child, and the authors of the proliferating advice books agreed with the sentiment expressed by Catharine Beecher about "mother" in 1846: "Oh sacred and beautiful name . . . a *whole nation* will have received its character and destiny from her hands."[9]

This domestic ideology placed women firmly within a role that was expected to transcend class boundaries and that reflected the belief that gender roles stemmed from biological differences between men and women. Whereas men were expected to be acquisitive and aggressive, women were thought to

represent virtues of self-sacrifice, piety, purity, and nurture. The home came to represent a counterweight to the harshness of modernization, a salve for the husband and father bruised by the daily work encounter. "Woman's sphere" was to be a domestic spiritual oasis within the desert of industrial materialistic culture.

This ideology prescribed expected behavior for white native-born women— they were ultimately to be full-time mothers. Other women, however, continued to work for wages away from farm and home in dusty workrooms and in grimy factories. Although they were a minority of women, their concentration in large cities brought some limited attention to their plight. To some critics, the danger in female employment sprang from the potential for exploitation rather than from concern over role transgression. By the 1820s, urban expansion had created a market for ready-made clothing in the cities, and thousands of women on the East Coast hand-sewed garments for low wages under miserable working conditions.[10] These conditions gave rise to a recognition of the need for work opportunities for women while condemning the culture of industrialism and the exploitative conditions that prevailed. An 1845 report in the *New York Tribune* said of women workers that "their frames are bent by incessant and stooping toil, their health destroyed by want of rest and proper exercise, and their minds as effectively stunted, brutalized, and destroyed over their monotonous tasks as if they were doomed to count the bricks in a prison wall—for what is life to them but a fearful and endless imprisonment, with all its horrors and privations?"[11]

Some reformers argued for the improvement of working conditions for these women wage earners through the expansion of particularly female spheres of work in a sex-segregated labor force. Catharine Beecher, for example, suggested in 1846 that the problem of the female factory worker's ruining her health and the problem of the educated woman without an outlet for her talents could be solved alike by the development of teaching as a woman's profession. This, she wrote, "will prove the true remedy for all those *wrongs of women* which her mistaken champions are seeking to cure by drawing her into professions and pursuits which belong to the other sex."[12]

Publisher and social critic Mathew Carey also proposed that "female" jobs be provided for those women who must earn a living. He was particularly concerned with the plight of urban seamstresses. In his "Appeal to the Wealthy of the Land, Ladies as Well as Gentlemen," published in 1835, Carey offered nine solutions to the problem of exploitative working conditions for women. His recommendations included the expansion of job opportunities, increased job training, and the opening to women of those "low employments" that were monopolized by men.[13]

One of his solutions was for the separation of employment spheres for men and women. Men, Carey suggested, should perform industrial and heavy agricultural labor, while women should take over all domestic, sewing, and sales work—the last still a male occupation in the antebellum years. Carey argued that women were "admirably calculated" for work in retail stores. The *New York Sun*, in 1845, proposed similarly that dry goods store owners hire women exclusively, "dismiss their men to manly occupations, and save for society a thousand women from want and temptation."[14]

The idea that work roles should reflect qualities of gender was reiterated in 1869 by Virginia Penny in her book *Think and Act*. Penny insisted that "a strong, healthy man behind the counter of a fancy store, in a millinery establishment, on his knees fitting ladies' shoes, at hotels laying the plates and napkins of a dinner table, is as much out of place, as a woman chopping wood, carrying in coal, or sweeping the streets."[15] These arguments for distinct employment spheres for men and women extended job opportunities to women who had to work. At the same time, however, a sex-segregated labor market protected many male occupations from encroachment by women and preserved gender roles. Catharine Beecher's proposal for the feminization of the teaching profession, for example, stemmed from a belief that the education of children was a natural function of women.[16]

Some working-class commentators linked the ideology of domesticity to criticisms of exploitative working conditions. In 1845, "Julianna," a writer for the Lowell Female Labor Reform Association, argued that factory life deprived women of domestic attributes. The workers, "instead of being qualified to rear a family . . . have need to be instructed in the *very first* principles of living well and thinking right," she wrote. If the factory system continued, she added, "what . . . will be the mental and intellectual character of the future generations of New England?" The association advocated the establishment of a ten-hour workday in order to prevent damage "to the constitutions of future generations" through injury to women who would one day be mothers.[17]

Women protested their situation elsewhere as well. Needlewomen organized in New York, Philadelphia, and Boston in the 1840s to appeal to the public for higher wages. In 1846 in New York City, seamstresses complained of producing shirts at four cents apiece "while agents of debauchery circulated among them with offers of ease and plenty."[18]

Some working-class men resented the presence of women in industry. The National Trades Union, at their 1836 convention, termed female labor "the most disgraceful escutcheon on the character of American freemen" and noted that women's work "should be only of a domestic nature." Factory work, the unionists insisted, injured both the health and the morals needed for the

"culture and bearing of healthy children." They also foreshadowed later criticisms of the use of women to cut wages, contending that women competed for jobs with men and that the female factory operative who worked for low wages was therefore "tying a stone around the neck of her natural protector, Man."[19]

The Discovery of the Working Girl

By the 1860s, changing demographic patterns combined with the effects of industrialism and urbanization to produce a growing class of women workers—"respectable" single self-supporting women. The widening distance between the domestic ideology and women's behavior was bridged by the labeling of self-supporting women as a problematic group—a process that crystallized public unease over larger social changes in work and family life. Because white native-born women who worked most clearly violated norms of sex-role behavior, they captured public attention, bringing attention also to the larger population of women workers, of which they were but a part. The voices of the middle class—journalists, charity workers, reformers, clergymen, and jurists—combined to shape a rhetoric that stressed the dangers of and to women who lived apart from their proper place.

The postbellum phase of the debate over female employment evolved in three stages: the discovery and labeling of self-supporting women; fact-finding and hence legitimization of the problem; and social policy decisions based on a public consensus about the requisites of future motherhood. A fourth stage, the implementation of reform, will be discussed in chapter 3.[20]

The initial discovery of the new problem of the working girl occurred as morality and the economic situation of working women were linked in large cities to the problem of social order. The woman living on her own, it was feared, was prone to behave in an immoral fashion. Women who worked and lived away from home became known as "homeless women" and "women adrift." These terms applied not only to the female boarder and lodger but also to the destitute women of the slums who were literally without shelter and who slept in police stations, public parks, and alleys.[21] The double meaning of these labels buttressed the idea that the woman living outside of traditional family life was on the cutting edge of disrepute. Without the anchor of domesticity, she was adrift in a sea of ambiguous identity.

There was no parallel terminology for "respectable" young men living apart from their families. The "homeless man" was invariably the tramp, the hobo, and the skid-row denizen; the term "self-supporting man" has always seemed redundant. What was controversial for women—living apart from the family

while earning a living—was expected for young men. Male boarders and lodgers acquired status through their occupation, wealth, or education.[22] For women, however, traditional identification as daughter, wife, or mother shaped their rank within society in conjunction with class, occupation, and racial status.

The discovery and labeling of "women adrift" first occurred in largely impressionistic newspaper exposés published in the mid-nineteenth century. These articles emphasized the economic exigencies of the self-supporting woman. New York newspapers through the 1860s maintained that tens of thousands of women workers were "in a constant fight with starvation and pauperism." In 1868, a Boston newspaper found 20,000 women toiling for "starvation rates." Urban newspapers across the nation published similar articles through the 1880s. One commentator noted that these stories "arrested the attention of the thinking class to woman's needs as it has never been arrested before."[23]

The heightened concern with working women stressed the physical misery, potential pauperism, and moral danger believed attendant to female employment. Perhaps the best known of the journalistic exposés on working women was Helen Campbell's *Prisoners of Poverty*, originally published as a series in the Sunday edition of the *New York Tribune* in the late 1880s. *Tribune* readers became acquainted with shop girls, domestic servants, and garment workers of New York City, and with women such as Rose Haggarty, a seamstress supporting dependent siblings, who was forced into prostitution by economic need.[24]

This genre of reporting proliferated throughout the country. In Minneapolis, for instance, readers learned of the plight of laundresses, hotel workers, printers, and other women workers in a series of articles by Eva McDonald Valesh, published from 1888 until 1891 in the *St. Paul Globe*. Stories entitled "Song of the Shirt," "Working in the Wet," and "In Cap and Apron" presented readers with colorful portraits of working women, while raising questions about morality, wages, and working conditions.[25]

This publicity about urban work conditions contributed to a public demand for fact-finding agencies. Massachusetts established the first state labor-statistics bureau in 1869; by 1887, twenty-two states had organized similar institutions. In 1885, the Department of Labor was founded in Washington to provide a similar service on the federal level.[26]

The fact-finding efforts of these bureaus confirmed the newly labeled deviance of single self-supporting women. The Massachusetts bureau published the earliest study of urban working women in 1870, corroborating press accounts of low wages, long hours, and the "miserable state of living that was the lot of wage-earning women in the manufacturing towns of Massachusetts."

New York, Maine, California, Iowa, New Jersey, and Minnesota were among the states that followed in the next decade with separate chapters on working women in their annual reports. "No class of wage-earners is more deserving yet receives less attention from reformers, philanthropists, and lawmakers," a typical report from Wisconsin began in 1884, "than the girls and women of cities who are compelled to support themselves, and frequently dependent relatives also, by their daily labor."[27]

Attention to working women continued apace. In 1889, the United States Department of Labor published *Working Women in Large Cities*—a 613-page survey of over 17,000 women employed in twenty-two cities. In 1895, the New York State Assembly appointed a committee to investigate the "condition of female labor" in New York City. They held thirty-six public meetings, heard 258 witnesses, and concluded that "from this terrible and unprecedented condition of affairs arises untold misery, immorality, and crime." In 1907, the United States Senate began a nineteen-volume study of employed women and children. And in 1911, the Debaters' Handbook series, which popularized opposing viewpoints on such issues as capital punishment and the income tax, added a volume of articles on the employment of women, further reflecting the controversial nature of women's work.[28]

As rural and middle-class young women entered the labor force, another genre of reporting emerged. These were the "firsthand" reports of investigators examining the experience of women's work at the turn of the century. Though limited by a middle-class and often patronizing perspective, these accounts remain a valuable source about the lives of working women. "First-person" investigations such as Bessie and Marie Van Vorst's *The Woman Who Toils* (1903) and Cornelia Parker's *Working with the Working Woman* (1922) were typical of the reports written by middle-class women posing as workers; Bessie Van Vorst cast off her "Parisian clothes" to don "coarse woolen garments" and a "shabby felt sailor hat" to transform herself into a "working girl of the ordinary type."[29] Other firsthand chronicles were written by "respectable" women who had to work, such as Dorothy Richardson, in *The Long Day* (1905); the anonymous author of *Four Years in the Underbrush: Adventures of a Working Woman in New York* (1921); and the young women submitting essays to *Harper's Bazaar* for the 1908 series, "The Girl Who Comes to the City."[30]

This wealth of literature reflected a new urgency about the controversial status of the working woman. Most commentators agreed that acquired characteristics—such as debilitation resulting from overwork—could be transmitted through heredity to children, and hence the work life of young women,

though temporary, could permanently damage their future lives as mothers.[31] They differed, however, in proposals for change. Conservatives argued that women could and should return to their proper sphere at home, reflecting assumptions rooted in the domestic ideology of the mid-nineteenth century. Radicals on this issue, like earlier feminists, encouraged women to participate in any kind of work they desired and proposed that women not be barred from traditionally male occupations. Progressives took a middle view. They accepted the fact that women were working, but proposed that domestic influences and protections be extended into the work and living environments of self-supporting women. The social structure rather than the behavior of workers would be transformed. Like earlier activists, progressives sought a way to mesh the realities of women's work with ideological prescriptions about future motherhood.

The conservative viewpoint held that the working woman transgressed her proper place in society. Advocates of domesticity viewed gender roles as inflexible and upheld the idea of patriarchy, particularly the economic dominance of men. The conservatives focused their arguments on the status of white native-born women. These commentators, blind to the realities of economic need for so many women, contended that since working women had voluntarily left home, they could just as easily return.

The subject of interest for many conservatives was the young farm girl whose innocence and purity were contrasted to the depravity of urban life. The "ideal farm girl," a *Farm Journal* writer suggested in 1903, should accept her future as a mother in a quiet country home. For the girl who rebelled against her lot, moral disaster was inevitable:

> The farm girl is all right until she gets herself worked into the notion that she is capable of something higher than helping her folks at home—that there is a "career" for her that will lead on to wealth and distinction, and she must leave the paternal roof and go in pursuit of the good things she feels sure are laid up for her somewhere. When she feels herself pretty well assured that she is of better stuff than her mother, and that she will marry no "hayseed" for a husband and settle down for life to domestic drudgery as she did, there is trouble brewing for her that will sooner or later overwhelm her.[32]

The picture painted here of domestic drudgery could not be attractive to many high-spirited young women, but the alternative was presented in even less desirable terms. If farm life were hard and dreary—and articles and readers' letters in the rural women's magazines attested to lives of isolation, loneliness,

and adversity—life in the city was presented as no less than the road to ruin.[33] The problems of nonwage work in a rural home did not inspire public debate; the consequences of the rejection of that life did.

These opponents of women's work claimed that employment was for many women a frivolous choice motivated by a shallow desire for excitement. One writer with this point of view was Bessie Van Vorst, who posed as a factory hand in Pittsburgh and in Perry, a New York mill town, in 1903. Van Vorst stated that the native-born woman "works for luxury until the day when a proper husband presents himself." She added that "the American woman is restless, dissatisfied. . . . For natural obligations are substituted the fictitious duties of clubs, meetings, committees, organizations, professions, a thousand unwomanly occupations." She proposed that those women who worked for any reason but dire necessity should leave the labor force, where they only competed with their impoverished self-supporting sisters. If a woman desired to earn extra money, Van Vorst concluded, she should work in such industrial arts as lace-making, goldsmithing, or bookbinding, tasks "more consistent" with her destiny as a woman.[34]

Instead of absorbing lessons in cooking, budgeting, and child care, critics charged, women who worked learned ultimately useless tasks, developed a taste for extravagance, and, perhaps worst of all, nurtured a dissatisfaction with mundane domestic life. Women, one writer claimed, were becoming "mentally and morally unfit" for the traditional female role within the family.[35]

This growing unfitness for motherhood, some believed, was related to the failure of education for women. Opposition to higher education for women in this era came from critics who contended that schooling in anything but domesticity encouraged an "incoherent rebellion" against wifehood and motherhood and fomented invalidism and physical disability. The psychologist G. Stanley Hall, in his study *Adolescence*, published in 1904, presented a typical argument against "excessive intellectualism" in young women. "Just as a man must fight the battles of competition, and be ready to lay down his life for his country," Hall stated, "so woman needs a heroism of her own to face the pain, danger, and work of bearing and rearing children, and whatever lowers the tone of her body, nerves, or *morale* so that she seeks to escape this function, merits the same kind of opprobrium which society metes out to the exempts who can not or who will not fight to save their country in time of need."[36] Hall, along with others, argued against training women for careers that were "disfunctional" for their roles as future mothers.[37]

The belief that women were innately limited by biological constraints was common. Dorothy Richardson, author of *The Long Day*, suggested in an essay published in 1906 that the reproductive potential of women brought special

dangers to their efforts to expand their sphere of activities. Women, she argued, could not develop the "equal industrial abilities" of men because "as potential mothers they are functionally limited mentally and physically."[38]

This perspective was taken also by the social critic Henry Finck, who suggested in a widely circulated 1901 essay, "Employments Unsuitable for Women," that the woman who chose to work "coarsened" herself and lessened her chances for successful marriage and motherhood. He criticized women who left home to work, claiming that "girls should be taught that, except under the stress of poverty, it is selfish as well as suicidal on their part to go out and work." He wrote, "Men still prefer, and always will prefer, the home girl to any other kind. They want a girl who has not marred her beauty and ruined her health by needless work, or rubbed off the peach bloom of innocence by exposure to a rough world."[39] For women who did have to work, Finck recommended only those jobs which insured that women "remain womanly":

> Having once discovered the charm of the eternal womanly, man will never allow it to be taken away again, to please a lot of half-women who are clamoring for what they illogically call their "rights." Men will find a way of making these misguided persons understand that it is as unseemly for them to be—as many of them are now—butchers, hunters, carpenters, barbers, stump speakers, iron and steel workers, miners, etc., as it would for them to try to take the places of our soldiers, sailors, firemen, mail carriers, and policemen. All employments which make women bold, fierce, muscular, brawny in body or mind will be more and more rigidly tabooed as unwomanly.[40]

Finck concluded that employments which did not threaten female purity and "womanliness" should be accessible to them, but he cautioned, "Let this be regarded, not as a special privilege and an indication of social progress, but as a necessary evil, to be cured in as many cases as possible by marriage or some other way of bringing the workers back to their deserted homes."[41]

Like the conservatives, feminists were for the most part concerned with the situation of middle-class women; unlike the proponents of domesticity, however, they sought expanded rather than constricted work opportunities. In lyceum lectures and in publications, feminists promoted the idea that women should be able to choose employment instead of marriage as their primary role. In 1865, Mary Abigail Dodge argued that "respectable" women should be able to work without the danger of losing their class status. "Let a poor girl go to work, and it is nothing at all," she wrote. "She is obligated to do it, and society does not so much as turn a look upon her; but let a girl go out from her brown-stone five-story house, from the care and attendance of servants, to

work for three or five hours a day . . . and immediately there is a commotion."[42] Dodge asserted that women should consider the independence of work preferable to the dependence of an unhappy marriage. Women, she maintained, need not accept "the debasement of [themselves] which an indifferent marriage necessitates. It is better to be not wholly well placed than to be wholly ill placed."[43]

Kate Gordon, of Mount Holyoke College, responded directly to Hall's attack on higher education for women. She suggested in 1905 that Hall's characterization of women was of "a very apotheosis of the vegetable" and that the domestic sphere for women that was so strongly advocated by Hall was but "one of a large number of possible occupations for women."[44]

In response to Henry Finck's essay on occupations unsuitable for women, suffragist Ida Husted Harper insisted that women had the right to work when and if they pleased. Not all women, she pointed out, had the opportunity to "stay at home and take care of their peach-bloom."[45] The active encouragement of widening work opportunities for women was on the radical edge of postbellum thought. More common was the idea that some women were going to work, for better or for worse, and that reformers should improve the conditions that surrounded working women bereft of domestic influences.

Conservatives sought to recapture a past in which women did not work for wages outside of the home, and feminists looked to a future of equality. But progressives acknowledged present realities about women who worked, and they interpreted the controversy of women's employment as one of exploitation rather than one of role transgression. At the same time, progressives argued that society should be adjusted to provide economic and moral security for working women who were still fundamentally domestic beings.

Progressive reformers were influenced in their approach to the problem of the working woman by their attempt to rebut conservative accusations that women worked for supplemental income alone. Investigators produced survey after survey that attempted to demonstrate that even the women at home were often wholly or partly dependent upon their own wages for self-support.[46] Moreover, progressive reformers believed, if the economic situation of the working woman who lived at home was precarious, what of the woman who lived on her own, and who had to purchase rent, food, and other necessities of life on her all-too-meager salary? The remedy, they argued, was the melioration of harsh working conditions.

The progressive viewpoint reflected a changing cultural climate of reform. The laissez-faire view of William Graham Sumner and others, which supported the doctrine of the "survival of the fittest," had been increasingly countered by advocates of social change in the latter part of the nineteenth

century. The maxims of the social gospel and progressive movements maintained that social conditions were not fixed but were malleable and that the greater good was the active shaping and reshaping of society to advance ideals of social harmony and justice.[47]

The social gospel was a creed of "applied Christianity" preached by Protestant clergymen such as Washington Gladden and Walter Rauschenbusch in the late nineteenth and early twentieth centuries. The gospel held that sin and salvation were social concerns, particularly in the cities beset by the effects of rapid growth and industrialism. "Our cities are the battle ground of Christian civilization," Washington Gladden contended. "They are destined to become, more and more, the arena upon which our greatest conflicts for liberty and order and morality are to be waged."[48] These conflicts included the fight against such "sins" as government corruption, the toleration of prostitution, and the exploitation of urban workers.

The social gospel gained an enlarged forum in 1908, when the Federal Council of the Churches of America was founded in Philadelphia by thirty-three Protestant denominations. Among the declarations for social justice espoused by the council was the need to "safeguard the physical and moral health of the community" with the protective regulation of women's work conditions.[49] The social gospel provided a religious sanction and an evangelical rhetoric for the doctrines of the progressive reform movement. Henry May has demonstrated the links between the two movements in the widespread "social awakening" of late nineteenth- and early twentieth-century cities faced with the adjustment to industrialism, particularly in the challenge to the laissez-faire doctrine and the search for a better society through the gradual reform of American capitalism.[50]

The progressives were particularly preoccupied with children. As the historian Robert Wiebe has noted, to the progressive "the child was the carrier of tomorrow's hope. . . . Protect him, nurture him, and in his manhood he would create that bright new world of the progressives' vision."[51] Hence the interpretation that working women endangered their future motherhood magnified the progressive viewpoint while reinforcing traditional values about women's role in society. The protection of working women from physical and moral danger became even more tightly linked to the harmonizing of social order when the well-being of future generations was at stake.

In his "Prayers of the Social Awakening," the clergyman Walter Rauschenbusch encapsulated the viewpoint about working women:

O God, we pray Thee for our sisters who are leaving the ancient shelter of the home to earn their wage in the store and shop amid the press of

modern life. Grant them strength of body to bear the strain of unremitting toil, and may no present pressure unfit them for the holy duties of
home and motherhood which the future may lay upon them. Give them
grace to cherish under the new surroundings the old sweetness and
gentleness of womanhood, and in the rough mingling of life to keep the
purity of their hearts and lives untarnished. . . . If it must be so that our
women toil like men, help us still to reverence in them the mothers of the
future.[52]

Rauschenbusch here effectively summed up the progressive interpretation of
the working woman—that she endangered her future motherhood through the
vulnerability of her health and morality and that domestic values still prevailed. Rauschenbusch also believed that protections should be extended to the
woman outside the home that would extend the vision of "woman's place" into
the industrial environment.

A major theme of progressive reformers was that unregulated conditions of
employment imperiled the physical health of the young women who would one
day be mothers. In *Women and Industry*, Annie MacLean stated that harsh
working conditions "make for a weaker generation to replace the present
one."[53] The widely circulated Debaters' Handbook on the employment of
women opened with the statement that work risked a young woman's "future
usefulness" and asked, "Can society afford to maintain any system of industry
that involves the physical, mental, and moral neglect of children through the
employment of girls and women?"[54] Some reformers suggested that an especially dangerous aspect of industrialism was that young women who worked
were not preparing for their future roles as mothers. The lack of domestic
education was linked by the United States Senate investigators to infant mortality. In a 1912 study of Fall River, Massachusetts, the researchers found that
"the mother's ignorance of proper feeding, of proper care, and of the simplest
requirements of hygiene" was the major cause of infant death.[55]

Social-gospel advocates agreed that women workers were a special class
requiring protection because of their status as future mothers. Walter Rauschenbusch wrote in 1917 that "women . . . demand special attention because life
springs from their bodies. They alone can exercise the sacred function of
maternity, which is higher than the production of goods. Their capacity to bear
and rear sound children is the most important physical asset of the race."[56]
This argument reached its apex when the United States Supreme Court upheld
the constitutionality of a workday limited to ten hours for women laundry
workers in Oregon. In the landmark 1908 case *Muller* v. *Oregon*, Justice

David Brewer deemed that female dependence and physiology justified protective legislation. A working woman's long hours of standing on her feet, he wrote, "tends to injurious effects upon the body, and as healthy mothers are essential to vigorous offspring, the physical well-being of woman becomes an object of public interest and care in order to preserve the strength and vigor of the race."[57] As we will see in chapter 3, protective legislation became one of the remedies proposed for the problem of the self-supporting woman.

Work itself was seen as a demoralizing influence on young women workers. Some observers, such as Virginia Penny, argued that women gained sharpened wits and quickened perceptions because of their work experiences, and the United States Senate investigation countered accusations that the "new occupations" of women led them into immorality.[58] Carroll Wright, of the Massachusetts Bureau of Statistics of Labor, had similarly defended the virtue of the working girls of Boston in 1889. These young women, he argued, were "making an heroic, an honest, and a virtuous struggle to earn an honorable livelihood."[59]

But most commentators appeared to agree with the Wisconsin Vice Commission, which stated that working conditions contributed to immoral behavior. "In many stores and factories men and women of all degrees of morality and immorality mingle with promiscuous familiarity," the commission noted, adding that "it must also be stated that the requirement that women employees shall stand all day, and the active nature of the day's work cause a severe nervous strain, leading to fatigue and weakening of the will power by the time the day is ended."[60] A state factory inspector in Minnesota concurred, observing in 1912 that the "moral tone" of factories and laundries was low because of the familiarity of working men toward working women, "the prevailing practice of telling suggestive stories," unsanitary conditions, and a "spirit of discontent." She also suggested that the monotony of the work routine caused women to seek the "rest in excitement. . . . Imagine spending ten hours a day washing dishes in a restaurant . . . putting eyelets in shoes, or feeding towels in a mangle. . . . The machine is master, the operator is slave. . . . I remarked recently to a foreman that the girls must be tired. He said, 'No, they are so used to it, they are like the machine, they don't feel it.' "[61] The routinization of work, the inspector declared, deadened the sensibility of workers and increased their vulnerability toward immoral behavior.[62]

Whereas the criticism of industrialism in the antebellum era resulted in an isolated movement to ease women into "female" occupations, now reformers vigorously strove to adjust industrial society itself to meet standards of domesticity. Jane Addams argued that "as working women enter fresh fields of labor

. . . society must endeavor to protect them by an amelioration of the economic conditions which are now so unnecessarily harsh and dangerous to health and morals."[63] This amelioration would occur through a series of remedies by which reformers attempted to safeguard the "future motherhood" of the hundreds of thousands of young women who had abandoned their traditional place within the home.

Chapter 3
The Working Girl and
the Social Order

The ideological controversy over the status of the working girl in the late nineteenth century led to extensive reform efforts to protect her physical and moral health. From about 1865 to 1920, reformers attempted to "soften the harshest experiences" of working women through the provision of such ameliorative measures as Travelers' Aid services, boarding homes, and recreational programs, which would extend domestic values into the lives of those women considered to be most "adrift" from their proper place. From about 1890 to 1923, another reform was increasingly advocated—the protection of future motherhood through the improvement of conditions in the workplace itself.

In both cases there was a recognition of social change. Young women were joining the urban labor force in increasing numbers and would continue to do so. But there was also the assumption that the working life of the young girl was temporary and that marriage would pull her back into the domestic domain. As a result, reform measures were for the most part targeted for the young, inexperienced, but "respectable" woman worker, and other groups of women, such as older career women or black women, were largely ignored. At the same time, the health of the social order would be preserved. If the entrance of single women into the labor force promised great social change, the extension of these reform measures would help to control and regulate the effects of that change.

The effort to protect the working girl was an urban phenomenon. The city was viewed as hostile to the preservation of domestic values both because of the visibility of prostitution and because of behavior practices of urban women workers that were widely believed by the middle class to be immoral, such as the patronage of dance halls and saloons. The virtue of the young country girl was believed to be especially endangered by exposure to urban life. The story of Nelly Haynes, told in *The Household* magazine in 1892, was typical for its contrast of rural virtue with urban depravity; Nelly's beauty and ambition prod her to leave the dull country town of "Mantlewood" for the glitter of the big city. There her path leads, inevitably, to prostitution and squalid death.[1]

Prostitution in this era was more than a mere rhetorical symbol of role transgression. Prostitution was quasi-legal in most American cities from the 1870s through the 1910s. Reglementation—a system of controlling prostitutes through a monthly fine system and regulated red-light districts—kept prostitutes highly visible. St. Louis, Washington, Chicago, New Orleans, and Minneapolis were among the cities tolerating wide-open "vice zones" in the 1870s and 1880s.[2]

Young working women were seen as vulnerable to the lures of prostitution for two reasons—low pay and loneliness. It was commonly thought that prostitutes were recruited from the ranks of poorly paid working women, many of them turning to vice because of the higher standard of living they thought they could achieve. Whereas the average working woman at the turn of the century could earn from $4.00 to $6.00 weekly, the prostitute could earn from $50 to $400 in the same amount of time—if she were young and attractive.[3] Prostitutes themselves testified that low wages motivated their downfall. In 1888, a Minneapolis prostitute told a newspaper reporter, "I tried for three years to support life on the wages I was paid as a cashier in a big store. . . . I gave up the struggle at last. . . . They call me unworthy of any person's notice now, but I don't starve and freeze since I quit being respectable."[4]

Other women told of the need for love, acceptance, and social life as a reason for their turn to prostitution. The vulnerability of young women living outside of domestic influences was the subject of a series of articles in the 1910 *Ladies' Home Journal*. The anonymous author of "My Experiences in New York" described life for a young migrant, lonely and frightened, and warned that the unsupervised working girl could be easily led into temptation and immorality, at worst, or a dreary "unnatural" life as a single career woman, at best.[5]

Reformers feared that young women seeking entertainment and friendship might turn to the commercial manifestations of urban culture—dance halls, saloons, and amusement parks. These aspects of city life could be so dangerous, William Sanger suggested in 1858, that inducements should be provided "for young women to leave the city, thus removing them from its baneful influences to a part of the country where their own labor would give them the means of a comfortable subsistence and a virtuous life."[6]

Others feared that danger was even more overt. Fears of "white slavery" abounded in cities in this era, as reformers saw panderers ready to pounce on unwary country girls at every way station and on every street. Ernest Bell, a minister and leader of the Illinois Vigilance Association, warned mothers in 1910 that "the country girl is in greater danger from the 'white slavers' than the

city girl . . . because [she is] less sophisticated, more trusting and more open to the allurements of those who are waiting to prey upon [her]."[7]

But most reformers recognized that warnings alone would not prevent young women from seeking work in the city. They instead mounted a "purity crusade" in the postbellum era. Groups including the National Purity Congress, incorporated in 1895, and the vice commissions of dozens of cities proposed that red-light districts be outlawed and preventive moral measures be supported. They would thus suppress the immediate problem of prostitution while offering working women some alternatives to the dismal living conditions that, they believed, led inexorably to immorality.[8]

Reform of the Urban Environment

Efforts to protect women workers from the lures of the urban environment through ameliorative measures were dominated by middle-class charity workers. These philanthropists believed that they shared a common sisterhood with young women less fortunate than they. The statement of the Minneapolis Woman's Christian Association in 1886 was typical of this sentiment: "Dear Sisters, . . . The shops, factories, and stores are full of girls— many of them away from home and friends. They are our young sisters and we shall be held accountable by God for their safe-keeping. We *are* our sisters' keepers."[9] Although these reformers often declared that the shared status of gender was more important than the notion of class, their activities belied this concept. If class were obviated, it was because reformers assumed that working women shared, or could share, in their middle-class ideals.[10] The protection of working women was promoted through the extension of middle-class domestic values through such institutions as Travelers' Aid, boarding homes, and recreation clubs.

TRAVELERS' AID

One remedy for the problem of the working woman that took shape in the 1860s was the institution of Travelers' Aid—a movement that brought the geographic mobility of young women under the watchful guardianship of moral reformers. Travelers' Aid had begun in the United States in 1851, when the former mayor of St. Louis, Bryan Mullanphy, bequeathed over $300,000 for a "fund to furnish relief to all poor emigrants and travelers coming to St. Louis on their way, bona fide, to settle in the West."[11] By 1866, when the

Boston Young Women's Christian Association (YWCA) was founded to protect migrant women, the idea of Travelers' Aid had narrowed to mean protection for young women and the concomitant prevention of urban prostitution.

The Boston YWCA, in its first annual report in 1867, expressed the attitude that had been embraced by the Travelers' Aid movement for nearly half a century:

> It is well known that many young women come to the city from homes in the country where they have enjoyed the blessings of parental affection and care and guardianship. Their world circumstances necessitate their separation from loved ones and compel them to seek employment where there is a larger demand for it. They generally come inexperienced, unacquainted with the difficulties which are before them, obliged to seek their homes where snares are spread on every side, with no kind hand to lead, or wise and judicious acquaintance to advise. It was felt that some agency should be devised that would *meet young women on their arrival in the city*, conduct them to proper homes and counsel them.[12]

The first Travelers' Aid work of the YWCA was to advertise referral services for housing and employment in railway depots and in circulars sent to clergymen throughout the New England countryside. By 1875, YWCAs, state labor bureaus, and other groups had established similar services in Providence, Hartford, Cleveland, New York, and Minneapolis.

By the 1880s, reformers determined that young migrants needed more than an address posted on a depot wall. In 1885, the Brooklyn Society of Friends funded the nation's first full-time Travelers' Aid worker. She sat in the terminal of Grand Central Station, distributing cards and notices, and was soon advising hundreds of young migrants. By the 1890s, Travelers' Aid workers were common sights in the train and boat stations of most large cities.

The matrons, wearing brightly colored sashes and badges, attempted to protect young women by distributing religious tracts, providing addresses and train schedules, promoting supervised boardinghouses, and publicizing employment agencies run by benevolent groups. They counseled young runaways who had not yet "fallen" into disrepute, sent pregnant unmarried women to rescue missions, and occasionally advised penniless young women to return to their parents' homes in the country. Matrons monitored the depots from 6:30 in the morning until 10:00 at night in some cities, and most kept extra cots in their own lodgings for women in need of emergency housing. Chicago matrons in 1893 reported aiding over 4,500 persons, 17 of whom were young women rescued "directly from the hands of evil persons."[13]

Some Travelers' Aid organizations also provided more extensive transient lodgings for women. "Women's hotels" and transient homes were often located near train depots for the use of women traveling through the city. Unlike the boarding homes, the transient lodgings were open to a broader group of women, including older women with children and pregnant single women. The Travelers' Aid Home in Minneapolis, for example, was founded in 1909 to "provide a temporary home under healthful influences"; the home accepted lodgers for up to two weeks' residence for free, in some cases, or for from fifteen to fifty cents a night for those who could afford to pay.[14]

New York philanthropist Grace Hoadley Dodge, later the president of the national YWCA, spearheaded the drive to unify the diverse Travelers' Aid organizations into a single group at the turn of the century. She became the national spokesperson for Travelers' Aid work, attending international conferences of station workers and speaking widely on the importance of modern social work organization. The need for Travelers' Aid work was imperative, Dodge wrote in 1906, because "pure womanhood" alone no longer protected virtue. "[T]he changes in economic condition that have brought millions of girls from the shelter of the home into the dangerous independence of the factory, the shop, or the office," Dodge argued, "and the general relaxation of standards accompanying a growing cosmopolitanism, have worked together to make it unhappily true that a girl's innocence, instead of being her safeguard, may prove to be her worst enemy."[15] In 1905, Dodge promoted the founding of the New York Travelers' Aid Society, which united such diverse groups as the YWCA, the Council of Jewish Women, and the Female Auxiliary Bible Society.[16]

In 1912, the concept of Travelers' Aid reached the White House, when Illinois Vice Commission members visited President Woodrow Wilson to discuss the relationship of women's work to immorality. Illinois Senator Niels Juul advanced the idea that Travelers' Aid homes be government-sponsored: "The government takes care of a pound of tobacco. It follows the commodity from Kentucky or Virginia across the state line, and even counts the number of cigars made out of that pound of tobacco. If the national government can devote so much time to a pound of butterine, it can surely devote some time to the care of womanhood traveling from one state to another."[17] But the attempt to elevate Travelers' Aid work from voluntary local reform to state policy failed, and Travelers' Aid remained in the domain of women reformers and state labor board workers. In 1917, Dodge's efforts toward unification came to fruition, and the National Travelers' Aid Society was formed.[18]

From the 1860s through the 1920s, Travelers' Aid services centered on the perceived needs of young migrant women for moral protection in the city.

During the same era, reformers attempted to provide another service for the girl living on her own—the extension of a middle-class domestic environment through the subsidized and supervised boarding home.

BOARDING HOMES

Self-supporting women faced limited choices for housing in late nineteenth-century cities. One government report estimated in 1889 that over half of the women found alone in large cities lived with private families, 29 percent lived in boardinghouses, and 8 percent resided in lodging houses. Toward the end of the century, the practice of lodging with families and in small, family-like boardinghouses gave way to large commercial lodging houses, "housekeeping apartments," and a related café and restaurant culture.[19]

Women seeking housing were often barred from the "better class" of accommodations by low wages and social biases. Landladies often preferred male renters, as they believed women living alone would lessen the "respectability" of their lodgings. The prejudice against women living outside of families was noted by George Ellington in his book, *The Women of New York: Or, the Underworld of the Great City*, when he wrote in 1869 that the "lone woman" looking for a room in New York City was often assumed to be "not a good woman, but quite the contrary."[20] This point of view proved long-lived; as late as 1935 the arbiter of middle-class manners, Emily Post, maintained that "in the world of society no young girl may live alone," lest "Mrs. Grundy" set tongues to wagging.[21]

Reformers feared that the kind of housing available to poorly paid working women imperiled their health and morality. Too many working women, argued the United States Department of Labor in 1889, lived in "narrow crowded streets, where drinking shops, gambling houses, and brothels abound." In these districts, the Labor Department observed, were the "ordinary homes of the poorer paid among the working girls in large cities."[22] Cheap boarding and lodging houses lacked a parlor, investigators noted, and the woman alone could not be expected to entertain her male friends in her bedroom and remain respectable. The lack of a parlor became a keynote for reformers, who warned repeatedly that women might all too easily turn from their dingy, parlorless houses to frequent instead "the warmth and brightness of the dance houses and saloons, where they must of necessity meet undesirable and unsafe acquaintances."[23]

Studies of working and living conditions in cities emphasized the dangers of cheap lodgings. In 1869, Virginia Penny related the tale of two boardinghouses in New York City that were patronized by men who chose their

lodgings "for the influence they might obtain over the girls." Nearly forty
years later, Albert Wolf's 1906 study of lodging house culture in Boston
included two narratives of respectable women residing in lodging houses
who were distressed by their close proximity to gambling, prostitution, and
alcoholism.[24]

These housing conditions attracted the attention of purity reformers, who
proposed to extend "family influences" to self-supporting women in the form
of supervised boarding homes. Unlike homes for immigrant women that were
training grounds for domestic servants, or the antebellum rescue homes for
prostitutes, these boarding homes were intended for the "respectable" women
who were temporarily, and regrettably, on their own.[25]

The boarding home, proponents promised, would extend family influences
to women who worked by providing affordable lodgings, religious services,
and supervised leisure-time activities in a respectable location. The 1889
report of the United States Department of Labor contrasted the meager surroundings of cheap commercial boarding and lodging houses with the life
offered by supervised boarding homes:

> A quiet, respectable street; clean halls and stairways; a neat parlor, and
> usually a library or reading room . . . young men allowed to call almost
> every evening, and permission accorded the girls to remain out after 10
> o'clock under proper escort for special entertainments; religious services
> regular and earnest, but not obtrusive or compulsory; a matron ready
> with sympathy or suggestion . . . an air of refinement pervading the
> house and surrounding the inmates; no rough associations or immoral
> influences; such conditions make a veritable home where girl or woman
> may live in accordance with her individual nature, sheltered from in-
> trusion, self-supporting, self-respecting, useful, respected, and even
> beloved.[26]

The first boarding home that offered permanent residence to nondestitute
women was established by the Ladies Christian Union in New York City in
1856. The Young Woman's Home contained sewing, laundry, meeting and
dining rooms, two parlors, and sleeping rooms. Its interior was, according
to one reporter, a display of "neatness and taste."[27] By 1877, at least twenty
similar homes had been organized in cities including Boston, New York,
Cincinnati, and Denver. Most of these were founded by women's organizations like the YWCA, WCA, and such church groups as the Sisters of Mercy.
Some public-spirited individuals sponsored homes as well. In Chicago, Cyrus
McCormick, the founder of International Harvester, funded a large YWCA
residence. In New York City, department-store magnate Alexander Turney

Stewart founded the much-publicized, opulent, and short-lived Hotel for Working Women.[28]

By 1898, there were at least ninety boarding homes opened in forty-five cities. These homes could house over 4,500 women at one time; because many boarders and lodgers were temporary, large numbers of women passed through the homes yearly. In 1898, over 30,000 different women registered at the nation's boarding homes, and the United States Department of Labor reported that over 120,000 different women had patronized the homes since the first temporary supervised lodging for women was established in 1848.[29]

The boarding homes ranged from large to small, modest to splendid. At one end of the spectrum was the Chicago YWCA on Michigan Boulevard, a seven-story building containing some three hundred single and double bedrooms, a library, parlor, auditorium, gymnasium, laundry, bathrooms, dining rooms, and classrooms. Less ambitious but more typical were the small institutions like the Minneapolis Woman's Boarding Home, which housed 70 women, or the St. James Guild Boarding Home in Philadelphia, which accommodated 12 women.[30]

Most of the homes accepted both temporary and permanent boarders. In many cities, YWCAs and WCAs established separate homes for permanent boarders and transients; the latter were Travelers' Aid services often labeled as "branch homes" that followed less strict daily routines. In houses that accepted both kinds of residents, long-term boarders often resented the transients. In Boston, for example, the "permanent" boarders at the YWCA home preferred to live on the upper floors, for those on the lower floors were likely to return from work to "find a stranger asleep in the other bed, or an unfamiliar hat and coat over the chair."[31]

Typical conditions of admission to the boarding homes were that women be of "good character" and provide references—a stipulation also common in many commercial hotels in the nineteenth century. Admissions officers usually insisted that women earn wages of less than $5.00 a week, demonstrate a lack of "natural protection" in the city, be white, young (usually under the age of 30) and unmarried. Although most clubs were sponsored by Protestant women's groups, many accepted any "respectable" white applicants. Some homes were open exclusively to Catholics, Jews, various ethnic groups, and blacks. Although prices ranged from $1.00 to $7.00 weekly, most homes charged about $3.00.[32]

Most of the boarding homes were intended to meet the needs of rural migrants, women who were, according to the Chicago YWCA, "orphaned, so far as natural protections are concerned" but still "lofty in sentiment."[33] The Minneapolis Woman's Boarding Home officials welcomed "all honest women

but prefer to aid the young and inexperienced. The innocent, unsophisticated country girl comes all unprepared for a city life of trial and temptation. She comes fresh from green fields, and the liberty of home life, to work in [a] stuffy factory, or dusty office."[34] The Young Woman's Home in New York City reported a similar concern with a "respectable" class of women. Of their boarders in 1865, the Woman's Home officers reported, "Many of them are the daughters of clergymen and other distinguished gentlemen. . . . Of 29 inmates, in 1865, 18 were artists, one a copyist, three were teachers, eight dressmakers and seamstresses. . . . Many young ladies tarry here while completing their education."[35]

A study of forty-three homes in 1898 indicated that domestic workers—including servants, waitresses, and nurses lodging on their days off—comprised a quarter of the boarders; office workers and store cashiers were 13 percent; saleswomen were 11 percent; and sewing women were 11 percent. Students, missionaries, teachers, and others also boarded. Factory workers made up only 3 percent of the boarding population.[36] These figures, however, are deceptive. Of the homes reporting domestic servants—and only half of them reported any at all—two-thirds of the servants were found in only four homes—the St. Mary Home in Detroit, the French Evangelical Church Home in New York, the House of Mercy in Cincinnati, and the WCA home in Cleveland.[37]

Many of the homes barred domestic servants, laundry workers, black women, and factory operatives, reflecting their concern with the white native-born women dispossessed of their status by the need or desire to work. For the native-born women, the homes acted as a buffer between the urban environment and the domestic ideology. Although they worked for a living, they still lived "at home," and so their bodies, reputations, and status remained protected.[38]

This protection was insured by the matron, who, as the Providence, Rhode Island, YWCA officers noted, was intended as a substitute mother who "attends to all the details of house keeping and presides over the home as a mother does in her family."[39] The matron admitted applicants and saw that lodgers ate meals at the ringing of one bell and that they turned out the lights at the ringing of another—usually by 10:30 at night. Sunday and daily worship services were often mandatory. In some cases, members of the sponsoring organization regularly visited the homes to transmit "ennobling influences" so that the young boarders, in turn, could "become a power of good in their homes" when they eventually married.[40] In all of the homes, moral behavior and daily routine were strictly regulated, as the rules of the Buffalo, New York, WCA Home in 1898 typified:

1. Applications for board may be presented to the matron. . . . Satisfactory testimonials of character will be required. . . . No boarder will be allowed to remain whose conduct is not satisfactory. . . .

3. Rooms must be well aired every morning, and kept in all respects neat by the occupants. . . . The use of the bathroom will be carefully adjusted, occupants of each room being assigned its use on certain days and hours. . . .

6. Family worship is held daily, which all are required to attend. It is expected that no boarder will absent herself from these exercises without a reasonable excuse to the matron. . . .

7. All visitors must leave the house promptly at 10 p.m. . . . when it is expected that all boarders will retire to their respective rooms and perfect quiet will be secured. . . .

8. All visitors will be received in the parlors, and, under no circumstances taken into the other parts of the building without the knowledge and consent of the matron. Men callers will be received only on Tuesday and Thursday evenings.[41]

Although strict rules were upheld in the homes, amenities were also provided. A parlor—often with a piano—was made available to boarders and their guests. But the problem of the parlor was not as easily solvable as it seemed. Some surveys indicated that young women lived in boardinghouses with parlors but still preferred to entertain in their bedrooms, or in public places, for the communal parlor lacked privacy.[42] Recognizing that young women desired more privacy than was afforded in a common parlor, some homes, such as the Boston YWCA Franklin Square House, set up several small parlors that could be reserved and used privately. Homes also typically provided libraries of books and magazines, savings and loan programs, low-cost vacation or convalescent retreats, and emergency-loan funds for unemployed or sick lodgers.[43]

More than half of the homes surveyed by the Department of Labor in 1898 provided free meals and deferred rent to unemployed boarders. The Minneapolis Woman's Boarding Home, for one, provided free temporary housing for women actively seeking employment; in 1879, two women were allowed to stay and "pay what they could, as they found it impossible to pay their board even at the reduced rate."[44] For many women, had there been no such emergency service, their only alternative resource would have been lodging in the police station, or fending for themselves on the streets.[45]

The "safety-net" feature of the boarding home movement was illustrated by an investigation published in the *Chicago Chronicle* in 1887. "Miss Hayseed's

Adventures" recounted the experience of the reporter Elinor Raymond Maxwell, who garbed herself in old clothes and "a sailor hat of an ancient block" and then set off to discover what would happen if she landed in Chicago "without a cent in her purse and no friends to meet her." Maxwell found her way paved by friendly police officers and Travelers' Aid workers, who sent her to the local YWCA. There she was given a free room, meals, and an offer of work as a servant.[46]

Boarding home proponents also argued that structured leisure time would advance the cause of moral purity. The Minneapolis WCA, for example, cautioned in 1888 that "an ounce of prevention is worth a pound of cure, and were this work of guiding the leisure hours of young girls looked after, there would be less need of reformatories."[47] In many homes, young women read poetry in literary societies, studied typewriting, stenography, languages, dressmaking, and cooking, and formed enthusiastic athletic teams.[48]

Some women expressed gratitude to the homes for providing them with a substitute family. They contributed aphorisms, news articles, short stories, and gossip to publications sponsored by the organizations. Boarders of the Minneapolis WCA homes, for example, published a newsletter, aptly titled the *Annals of No Man's Land*, in the 1910s and 1920s. Much of the material in these publications emphasized the importance of friendships made between women who had arrived in the city as strangers, reflecting the importance to many women of the sociability of the homes. One poem, about the Pillsbury Home, expressed this common theme:

> P is for the port in distress
> I is for the incense of friendship
> L is for two lights in the fog,
> S is for the spirit of kinship
>
> .   .   .   .
>
> Little bachelor girl finally finds "home"
> Maybe it isn't so bad after all
> To go limping along alone.[49]

Some boarders also demonstrated their appreciation for the homes in their decisions to marry in the parlors of their residences.[50]

But other women harshly criticized the boarding homes. Labor Department investigator Mary Fergusson observed in 1898 that many working women disliked the supervised homes because of the "odor of charity," the discipline, and the institutionalism.[51] This view was reflected in Minneapolis, where young women petitioned the officers of the Woman's Boarding Home in 1885 to change the name of the home, "as the present name is obnoxious on many

accounts." Their petition was tabled, and two years later, some of the boarders took matters into their own hands and destroyed the nameplate on the building. In 1922, a similar opinion was registered by a New York clerical worker, who suggested, "Don't call whatever you build a 'Home for Women;' girls must feel self-respecting."[52]

Other women resented the rules and regulations. When Louise Bosworth, of the Boston Women's Educational and Industrial Union, surveyed Boston's women workers in 1911, she found that to many "the rules of an institution are shackles; the customs to which inmates must conform are fetters."[53] In 1883, journalist Helen Campbell told the tale of "Katy," a young New York City shop girl, who said, "I've a good mind to live at the 'home' only I should hate to be bossed 'round, and you can't get in very often either, it's so crowded."[54] Maimie Pinzer, a reformed Philadelphia prostitute, wrote that at the YWCA "the atmosphere in such a place would make me want to do something hideously wicked, just to see what it was like."[55] And a young worker, "Minnie," was reported by Clara Laughlin in *The Work-a-Day Girl* in 1913 as saying:

> Maybe you could stand it if they wouldn't always be tryin' to improve you. You come home at night dead tired after sellin' brass tacks or makin' paper boxes, and they set you up in the parlour an' have a missionary woman tell you how the Chinese girls bind their feet. It's awful—when what you're dyin' for is a chance to shake a leg. You have to get a permit to stay out after 10:30. And you gotta pray before you eat and pray before you sleep, an' give an account of everything you do. . . . You kin try one o' them places if you want to—I've had enough o' them.[56]

Still, the homes were crowded and received more requests for admission than they had places. In Manhattan in 1921, for example, fifty-eight organized homes reported long waiting lists for admission.[57] The discrepancy between the criticisms and the demand for places lies in part in the class differences among working women. Working-class women, particularly those who were servants or factory operatives, testified that boarding homes were oppressive and didactic; rural migrants and others of "respectable" origins saw instead a reflection of the homes they had left behind. This self-selection was buttressed by the policies of the homes, which accepted only office workers, students, or sales clerks. In 1890, Clare De Graffenried of the Department of Labor charged that selection policies meant that "the most deserving are barred out by the class distinctions which mark almost every stage of philanthropy."[58]

The partial subsidization of the homes by charity came under criticism as well. Despite the subsidies, many poorly paid workers still found the homes

too expensive and located too far from the factory districts. Others argued that the subsidized homes hurt the fight for higher wages. Critics maintained that employers justified low wages by pointing to the boarding homes, saying that they were not responsible for the dangers of low wages when cheap and safe housing was available. Some corporations that were notorious for the low wages paid to their women workers sponsored boarding homes. Fairfax Hall, for example, was a boarding home established by the Illinois Bell Telephone Company for its switchboard operators by the 1920s.[59]

The boarding-home movement provided housing for a limited number of women. It offered long-term shelter to several thousands of women who saw themselves as "respectable" and in need of the protection of a form of family life. It provided temporary lodgings to larger numbers of women from rural areas who needed help in adjusting to urban culture and who patronized the homes only until they earned enough money to live on their own, or found other women with whom to set up housekeeping apartments.[60] But the boarding-home movement did not meet the needs of many factory operatives, domestic servants, older wage-earning women, mothers, or black women. Nor did it address the housing needs of working women who desired a place to live without the constraints of a tightly regulated home operated by moralistic philanthropists.

Many women preferred another solution to the housing problem—cooperative housekeeping. Although some commentators suggested that cooperative housekeeping would allow women to live well and even "keep a girl to do the housework," working women who shared rooms testified to a less genteel life. Most women living together worked and divided costs and housekeeping tasks. A young woman who had migrated to New York in 1902, for example, wrote how upon arriving in the city she was advised that cooperation with other women was the alternative to becoming a part of the "submerged tenth." She rented a five-room apartment with four other women.[61]

While cooperative housekeeping kept costs down, still boarding for full-time workers sometimes proved difficult. One young woman complained to the Minnesota labor commissioner in 1888: "Four of us hired a large room. We cooked, sewed, washed and ironed for ourselves and managed to live. Our wages were $3.00 per week apiece, but our clothes were always so shabby that we didn't go to parties evenings or to church on Sunday. We were so tired after doing our work that we had no time to read or do anything but sleep."[62] By the end of the century, some women attempted to formalize these housekeeping arrangements by establishing boarding clubs. Unlike the boarding homes, which were hierarchical in structure, the clubs were cooperative and self-governing. The Eleanor Club of Chicago, for example, was founded in 1898 to

provide housing, recreation, and dining facilities to women able to pay a set rate. Another example of cooperative housing was a New York City boarding-house for some fifty residents that was established with a loan from the International Ladies' Garment Workers' Union; the tenants paid rates high enough to repay the loan and secure an independent status.[63]

These clubs offered members considerably more autonomy than was available in the supervised boarding homes. Maggie Toomey, the treasurer of Chicago's Jane Club, for example, said in 1892 that cooperative clubs differed from boarding homes "in as much as we have no rules and no matron to order us around. We do as we please—in most things. Here every girl has a say in the affairs of the club. . . . [I]f she cares to go out of an evening she does so, and lets herself in with a latch-key."[64]

Whether cooperative housekeeping was formal or informal, it was the housing of choice for growing numbers of women. A Minneapolis social worker explained this choice in 1917. "From my own point of view, and that of most of my friends," she stated, "a boarding house life, even the best of its kind, is a poor apology for living, and we all agree if we had the problem of home finding to face we would settle it by combining and taking an apartment."[65] In 1922, a survey of working women in Manhattan found that most women, given a choice, preferred the independence of living in housekeeping apartments. Although less than a fifth of the store, office, and factory workers surveyed lived in apartments, more than two-thirds listed the housekeeping apartment as their preferred housing arrangement.[66]

Recognizing that many young women could or would not live under the supervision of the philanthropic boarding home, and that the majority of young women workers lived at home with their families in any case, reformers also advocated another method for extending the influence of domesticity into the urban environment—recreation clubs, which would provide an alternative to commercial entertainments.

RECREATION CLUBS

The concern with the leisure-time activities of working women expressed by the proponents of boarding homes was also evidenced in the establishment of recreation clubs for women. Jane Addams was among those who criticized the culture of commercial recreation for its demoralization of women. "The whole apparatus for supplying pleasure is wretchedly inadequate and full of danger to whomsoever may approach it," she warned in 1909.[67] Five years later, Addams further admonished that "the modern city sees in these girls only two possibilities, both of them commercial: first, a chance to utilize, by day their

new and tender labor power . . . and then another chance in the evening to extract from them their petty wages by pandering to their love of pleasure."[68]

Reformers believed that the pleasures of the city appealed to the sensual instincts of workers exhausted by long days of labor. In 1912, the U.S. Senate investigation described the situation for the working woman: "The dance hall with a saloon connection is probably the most harmful, but it is by no means the only dangerous opportunity for recreation within her reach. The cheap theater with its highly miscolored pictures of life; the penny vaudeville, the moving picture show, the summer resort of one kind or another—in all she is liable to find abnormal excitement, dangerous companionship, and every incitement to begin the course which leads so many to harm."[69] Hull House reformer Louise DeKoven Bowen also warned of the dangers of commercial entertainment. The clientele, moral tone, and sexual mores of the dance hall, she argued, were but "feeders to the underworld." Other forms of urban pleasure, including excursion steamers, amusement parks, and theaters were pathways on "a road easily leading to destruction."[70] Some organizations were formed in the postbellum era to counter the attractions of these amusements by offering alternative programs of recreation. The YWCA was the best known and longest-lived of these, pioneering not only in Travelers' Aid and housing work but in recreational reform as well.

When the first YWCA in the United States was founded in Boston in 1866, it was meant to meet "the temporal, moral, and religious welfare of young women who are dependent on their own exertions for support." Early YWCAs were established by young "business women"—white-collar workers and students—or by philanthropists. By 1915, there were YWCAs in over two hundred cities, each attempting to build "Christian character" and extend domestic influences to young working women. Among the services offered by urban YWCAs were not only employment bureaus, boarding homes, and housing registers but also libraries, cafeterias, bicycle and rowing clubs, gymnasium and physical culture classes, vacation lodges, and recreation clubs. By 1889, the YWCA began "extension work" in factories, leading noon prayer meetings accompanied by a melodeon carried from factory to factory. Soon city associations were setting up recreation clubs for factory operatives. The YWCA in Dayton, Ohio, for example, organized the "Busy Girl's Half Hour" at the National Cash Register factory, offering talks on health, dress, and morality.[71]

The YWCAs were only the best known of a host of similar organizations concerned with providing recreational outlets for young women. There was also the Massachusetts League of Girls Clubs, founded in 1889 to provide recreational programs for women workers.[72] Nationally, the Association of Working Girls Societies was founded in 1881 when Grace Hoadley Dodge

began her efforts toward club work with an inauspicious meeting with a group of silk factory workers. The operatives disrupted the first meeting by overturning benches and jeering, one worker later saying, "You ladies do not know us; you do not know the temptations, the trials; you do not care for us. The girls in this factory feel so bitterly toward you all." But Dodge eventually succeeded in securing the cooperation of the workers to create the association. By 1890, there were seventy-five clubs representing over 2,000 women. Their goal was to "lighten the burdens of the working girl, to increase her efficiency, and to elevate her character" through classes, club work, and moral instruction.[73]

In addition to these groups, the National League of Women Workers was founded in 1897 and by 1914 consisted of one hundred clubs of 14,000 members. Working women met regularly in groups like the Friendly Associates, of Boston, or the Amethyst Club, of Pittsburgh, where they upheld ideals of "nonsectarianism, self-government, and self-support." Club members, most of them factory operatives, participated in activities designed to develop character, citizenship, loyalty, and efficiency. They could also take advantage of savings and loan programs, insurance plans, and industrial training opportunities.[74] Finally, there were the vacation clubs. Organizations such as the YWCA, churches, and boarding homes sponsored lodges or summer camps where young working women could find relatively inexpensive vacation accommodations.[75] Reformers intended these clubs not only to encourage efficient work habits but also to be morally elevating. And some clubs also stressed lessons on physical development, sex education, decorum, and such topics as "qualities of womanhood" and "social relationships."[76]

Many women reformers believed that activities like recreation clubs brought the "wealthier, more educated, better placed women" into relations with "the poorest and most friendless." The Department of Labor, in 1889, noted that in working girls' clubs "earnest, intelligent and cultivated women acknowledge the close bond of sisterhood with rough, ignorant girls, and by tact, patience and gentle influence develop the best that is in them."[77] Club proponents believed that their work would help to "obliterate class lines" by stressing the shared status of womanhood. Journalist and club leader Jane Croly, for instance, wrote in 1891 that club life protected and stimulated young women. The club member's mind "no longer dwells upon her little attempts at finery, or the small jealousies and complexities of daily life. She is in a measure removed from them, and rises superior to them," Croly maintained.[78] But some working women resented the patronizing attitude of reformers who denied class divisions while exemplifying them. Rose Phelps Stokes reported how the philanthropic clubwoman looked "from the working woman's viewpoint" in 1906: "Not long ago, in one of the principal settlement houses of

New York, a very fashionably dressed woman, a lorgnette dangling from her fingertips, opened the door of a working girls' club, uninvited, and, raising her lorgnette to her eyes, surveyed the group before her, and, as though desiring to compliment the girls, remarked in the hearing of all, 'What a very attractive looking lot of working girls these are!' This sort of thing is by no means rare."[79] Stokes suggested that working women disliked condescension but that they readily recognized "true friendliness" and good will.[80]

Some working women organized their own clubs for self-support. A New York woman who worked in a publisher's office at the turn of the century, for example, formed a club with her friends in order that they might help each other secure better jobs. In two years they had 80 members. "We learned comradeship and the moral support this gives," she wrote in *Harper's Bazaar*.[81] In large cities, working women also organized self-governing lunch clubs, where they cooperated in managing cafeterias, rest rooms, libraries, and parlors. In Chicago, for instance, the Noonday Rest Club enrolled some 700 members by 1896; the Oguntz Club in the same city reported 150 clerical and factory workers among its members.[82]

Club work, along with housing and Travelers' Aid efforts, was a patchwork response to deeper problems facing women workers in large cities. The response of women's benevolent groups to the conditions of work and wages in cities was to try to obviate what they saw as the moral danger resulting from low wages and the separation from home. By the 1910s, another response to the discovery of the working woman gained strength—the attempt to alter the worst abuses in the world of work itself.

Reform of Working Conditions

The conditions of work encountered by young women in this era were criticized on several counts. We have seen that some commentators argued that the familiarity of men and women workers in stores and factories led to immorality; in this era the low wages and long hours attendant to women's work also were linked to physical and moral debilitation. While some reformers argued that the solution to the problem of immorality was to remove women from the workplace and return them to a home environment as domestic servants, a more widespread effort attempted to improve the abysmal conditions of store and factory work by promoting minimum-wage and maximum-hour laws.

THE PROMOTION OF DOMESTIC SERVICE

Some reformers contended that domestic service was the "natural vocation" for women and that the removal of women from industry and into middle-class homes would insure their moral protection. Julia Ward Howe was among those supporting this idea. She wrote in 1891, "When I see, as I often do, our American girls deteriorating in health, and not unseldom in character, through the experience of the shop and the factory, I feel a deep regret at the thought of the refined and well-ordered homes in whose comforts and good influences they might so easily be sharers, their service being to the right-minded an occasion of respect and gratitude, not of supercilious patronage or fault-finding."[83] Howe was joined by state labor commissioners, some manufacturers, and such organizations as the Women's Educational and Industrial Union, organized in 1877, in the promotion of domestic service as a field well fit for female needs and abilities. Minnesota Labor Commissioner John O'Donnell, for one, stated in 1901 that "it is my belief that there is no better place for the female wage-earner to be employed than in our American homes, surrounded by an atmosphere of refinement."[84] A New York writer criticized society for stigmatizing domestic work, arguing that "in all our large cities thousands of girls employed in stores and factories could live far more comfortably and qualify themselves to be excellent housewives by accepting situations in private families."[85]

Some critics suggested upgrading domestic service to meet the status needs of young native-born workers and proposed that the women form unions, associations, clubs, take classes, and demand better treatment from employers. At Chicago's Hull House settlement, for example, the Bureau for Women's Labor hoped to organize women workers to raise the standards of domestic service, with the aim of "diverting young girls from the drudgery of the cash girls' bench and the mill, to the life of the home."[86] And some young women did find domestic service to be acceptable work. A number of them told Lucy Salmon, according to her 1901 study of household servants, that their occupation provided vacations, good wages, and, most important, domestic influences. "I like a quiet home in a good family better than work in a public place, like a shop," one woman stated. Another said, "When I came to ____ and saw the looks of the girls in the large stores and the familiarity of the young men, I preferred to go into a respectable family where I could have a home."[87]

But most native-born white women rejected these arguments. Young women in survey after survey cited as reasons for their distaste for domestic service the days of ten hours or longer, the lack of free evenings and privacy, isolation,

low wages, and maltreatment.[88] The advantages of domestic service paled next to the loss of status, lack of freedom, and monotonous work routine. A list of "daily duties" for servants, published in a 1904 handbook, had the servant rising at 6:00 A.M., preparing, serving, and cleaning up after meals, making beds, dusting and cleaning, and cheerfully answering the door.[89] "There is a very bitter feeling against housework among the shop girls," the Minnesota labor commissioner reported in 1888. In Wisconsin, 94 percent of the women surveyed by the state Labor Bureau in 1901 preferred factory to domestic work. In Boston, the Women's Educational and Industrial Union surveyed 564 factory operatives and shop girls to encourage a switch to domestic work, but only 26 women considered the change.[90]

Many women protested the low status of domestic work. "Girls who work in factories are more respected," a servant told the Minnesota labor commissioner. "I worked for one family who used me like a dog around the house. I will never do that kind of work again," stated another.[91] Lucy Salmon wrote of male factory operatives who would invite to their parties young self-supporting milliners, stenographers, and salesclerks but who drew the social line at servants.[92]

The low status of domestic work, established by the mid-nineteenth century, was reinforced in this era by efforts of some groups to channel immigrants into middle-class homes as servants. Mary Gove Smith, of the Boston Women's Educational and Industrial Union, argued that special homes for immigrant women could help train them for appropriate work as servants. "The girl who comes perhaps from the mud hut of some little Austria-Hungarian village sees in the model immigrant's home new possibilities," she wrote. "Cleanliness, order, system are about her, and she realizes vaguely or definitely, as her intelligence permits, that progression means the formation of new habits, of adaptation to new modes of life, of new ambitions."[93] Smith cited as an example the immigrant home in East Boston, which accommodated 35 to 40 women and promoted "the atmosphere of home." Thirty similar homes were established by the 1910s for Protestant, Jewish, and Catholic immigrants in New York City, Baltimore, and Philadelphia.[94]

The motive in promoting domestic work for immigrant women was not to preserve respectability as much as to prevent immorality and maintain a well-regulated class of servants. In 1904, women's groups in Boston, Philadelphia, and New York established the Inter-Municipal Committee on Household Research to study conditions of domestic service, publicize needed remedies, and endorse approved employment agencies.[95]

One member of the committee argued that employers needed to be protected from their servants, reporting that the demoralizing effects of "promiscuous

mingling" on ship, in lodging houses, and in intelligence offices (employment bureaus) could permit situations in which "the girl passes from these surroundings with their increment of dishonesty, promiscuousness, and vice directly into the presence of an American family. . . . [S]ince she . . . becomes a member of our households, it is a grave question as to how far the atmosphere of lax morality which she brings with her may extend."[96]

The committee believed intelligence offices were especially dangerous to the welfare of young immigrants. Two-thirds of all servants were hired from these agencies, and critics charged that the offices were corrupt institutions from which women were often sent to brothels or to households "about whom nothing is known." Between 1904 and 1909, fourteen agencies in New York City had their licenses revoked for sending women to "immoral places" and brothels. Reformers recommended licensing and inspection legislation to protect the unsophisticated immigrant woman from immoral practices and unsanitary conditions.[97]

There was concern, too, for young black women who migrated north to find work as domestic servants. Francis Kellor condemned the practice of southern employment agencies that sent agents into rural districts to recruit servants for northern households. "Men grotesquely dressed," she wrote, "carrying drums, . . . parade through the smaller towns, and cry the rare opportunities offered by the agency to any girls who wish to go North, shouting 'Fall into line! Free passage! No fees!' " Once north, Kellor stated, these young women were often sent to brothels or forced to work without wages because they had signed exploitative contracts, or they were "turned loose" upon the cities without work. Kellor and others recommended that the protections proposed for immigrant women, such as lodging houses and licensing of agencies, be enacted for these young black women as well.[98]

There had long been criticisms of domestic service as a breeding ground for prostitution. In the 1870s, the Boston Female Asylum reported that young women placed in homes as servants complained of sexual advances made by the husbands and sons of their employers' households.[99] Several surveys of urban prostitution in this period discovered that about a third or more of the women studied had first been domestic workers. In 1888, the Department of Labor found that of 3,866 prostitutes studied, a third had first been domestic workers—the largest single occupational group from which prostitutes came. In its 1911 report, "Relation between Occupation and Criminality of Women," the Department of Labor learned that the most frequent previous occupation of women prisoners and prostitutes was domestic service, and not factory work or saleswork as had been commonly hypothesized.[100] This link of vice to domes-

tic service helped to entrench its low status, and efforts to upgrade the reputation of domestic service as an occupation for native-born white women failed.

WORKING WOMEN'S ASSOCIATIONS

Others recognized that most women would not be talked into leaving the industrial labor force and attempted instead to improve conditions and safeguard motherhood by promoting the associationism of working women. Unions had long been a traditional method by which men had bettered their conditions of work. After 1860, women's trade unions, which had been only sporadically active since the 1820s, multiplied. Laundresses, cap makers, and shoe workers were among groups that united to improve conditions.[101]

A powerful public demonstration of the women's union movement occurred in 1903, when 35,000 women in twenty-six trades were organized in Chicago. That year, a labor-day parade included the performance by women marchers of the following song:

> Shall song and music be forgot
> When workers shall combine?
> With love united may they not
> Have power almost divine?
> Shall idle drones still live like queens
> On labor not their own?
> Shall women starve while thieves and rings
> Reap where they have not sown?[102]

But the participation of women in unions was limited by traditional attitudes; most women did not define themselves as workers but saw their employment as a temporary measure before marriage. Moreover, many employers blocked the formation of unions, and predominantly male unions were often hostile toward women workers. In 1905, a survey of union membership in fifteen occupations revealed that over 20 percent of the men but only 3 percent of the women in the surveyed trades were union members. Even during World War I, the peak period of union organization for men, less than 10 percent of women in manufacturing occupations belonged to unions. In 1924, a Women's Bureau study found that barely 140,000, or less than 5 percent, of women workers were union members.[103]

Although most women were not organized in trade unions in this period, some did participate in other kinds of groups that attempted to improve working conditions. Protection leagues, for example, were an early form

of women's labor activity. The Boston Women's Educational and Industrial Union was founded in 1877 to "aid, strengthen, and elevate women, by drawing them into a bond of unity." The union formed committees to protect women's legal rights and to redress complaints about salary disputes. In New York City, the Working Woman's Protective Union was founded in 1868, and by 1890 had collected, through court action, some $41,000 for 12,000 women "who would otherwise have been defrauded of their hard-earned wages." Similar organizations were founded in Philadelphia, Indianapolis, Chicago, and St. Louis.[104]

The Consumers' League, which was instrumental in research and lobbying for hour and wage legislation, was another important organization for women. The league originated with the New York City Working Women's Society, which was organized in 1886 by young garment workers and cash girls who first met to protest harsh working conditions. Their early activities included the support of strikes, advocacy of legislation to hire female factory inspectors, and the study of local working conditions. In 1890, an investigation of saleswomen resulted in the formation of a committee to publish a "white list" of stores that dealt "justly with their employees." The first list, which included only eight establishments, was publicized in an effort to convince consumers to patronize only approved stores, hence pressuring employers to raise the standards of employment. This committee became the New York Consumers' League in 1891. By 1900, there were sixty-four Consumers' Leagues in the United States and a national league that aimed to "abolish the sweatshop."[105]

By 1903, the Working Women's Society itself was absorbed into a second organization—the Women's Trade Union League. The league was a federation of women's unions and middle-class sympathizers which worked with the American Federation of Labor to assist women in the formation of unions. Like some of the earlier working-girls clubs, the league emphasized the importance of contacts between women of different classes in a ritualized social context. Although some garment, textile, laundry, and shoe workers did succeed in organizing, their success was still limited to relatively few women.[106] It was the achievement of protective legislation, promoted of course by the unions, which altered the environment for thousands of working women.

PROTECTIVE LEGISLATION

By the end of the nineteenth century, many of those concerned with the issues of women and work realized that unions would not be the remedy to improve working conditions for women, nor would strictly ameliorative measures succeed. Protective legislation, advocates argued, would safeguard future moth-

erhood not by the extension of domestic influences, but by the insurance of economic security and the protection of health. Laws mandating maximum hours of work and minimum wages were enacted by state governments in this period in an effort to protect the physical and moral health of working women.

Proponents of protective legislation defended their proposals on the basis of the needs of young self-supporting women who were then at the forefront of the debate over women and work. But at the same time, as laws were enacted to protect this group, the population of the female labor force was beginning to shift as older, married women began to increase their numbers in the labor force. Laws that were designed to protect young temporary workers were in fact often applied to older workers or to single career women who did not desire work restrictions. For these latter women, the legislation of hours and wages forged an especially tightly linked "chain of protection."[107]

Many voices were heard in the debate over labor legislation. Social reformers and politicians argued that women's employment should be regulated in order to preserve the health of future mothers, to counter oppressive conditions of long hours and low wages, and to set standards that could be applied to men as well as to women. Opponents included businessmen who saw legislation as interference with their constitutional right to make contracts with their employees, and those who maintained that restrictions would damage business opportunities. Some feminists, particularly those in the National Woman's Party (the sponsor of the first Equal Rights Amendment proposal in 1923) also opposed protective legislation contending that it implied inequality under the law. Legislation intended for young, inexperienced workers needing protection, the feminists argued, unduly restricted older women who were competing with men for jobs. Hence laws meant only for women would doom women to inferior status in the workplace. Trade unionists were divided between those who thought protective legislation would enhance union goals, others who sought to use legislation to keep women out of certain occupations, and still others who saw legislation as a threat to organizing efforts. Women workers, for the most part unorganized and unwilling to participate in state legislative commissions, were rarely heard.[108]

Arguments favoring protective legislation often rested on commonly held assumptions about differences in the physical capabilities and social responsibilities of men and women. Azel Ames, Jr., a physician and investigator for the Massachusetts Bureau of Labor Statistics, wrote in 1875 that "the normal, the God-appointed work of women . . . is that of the home and the mother, the rearer, the trainer, the blessing of man." Ames was an early advocate of laws regulating hours, wages, sanitary conditions, and the kinds of work women could do. "The highest moral and physical well-being of a race," he claimed,

"demands that there will be nothing in its conditions of life and labor that shall injure the richness and purity of the chief source whence its existence and its best influences come."[109] Nearly forty years later, this same argument was still being advanced in favor of protective legislation. In 1913, a Connecticut state commission concluded that the "physical well-being of woman is essential if we are to have a strong and vigorous race, and when through overstrain and exhaustion woman's vitality is lowered, her fitness for motherhood may be destroyed, and her children will pay the penalty with weakened or vitiated physical vigor. Therefore as a potential mother the state has a right to protect her."[110] Similarly, Marie Pfeiffer, a Pennsylvania silk worker, told a YWCA convention in 1920 that working conditions should be improved so "our next generation will be strong." "Weak women will mean a weak race," she argued, "unless we give them some help. The girls in industry today, I feel, are the mothers of the next generation."[111]

Many progressive-era reformers believed that women were weaker than men in energy, strength, and powers of "persistent attention" and that they were vulnerable to disease and to injuries of the "generative organs." Dozens of studies were marshaled in legal briefs and in state investigations to support the contention that unregulated industry rendered women unfit for mother-hood. Citing statistics of infant mortality, morbidity, and lowered birthrates, these studies attempted to determine the effects of unsanitary working conditions, low wages, and long hours on the lives of young women in their childbearing years.[112]

Hours

Among the earliest labor legislation in the United States were laws restricting the maximum hours of employment. By the 1890s, hours laws were often justified on the basis of the need to protect the physical health of future mothers. Hours legislation has a tangled history, beginning in the antebellum era as a drive for the improvement of factory conditions for male as well as female workers. As early as 1842, Lowell factory operatives had demanded a ten-hour day, and union agitation had led seven states to enact general hours statutes between 1847 and 1855. These early laws, however, were ineffective because they mandated only that workers not be "compelled" to work more than ten hours a day.[113]

By 1867, the ten-hour movement had narrowed to exclude men. This reflected the efforts of organized labor to improve conditions in textile factories, which employed large numbers of women and children. Labor's strategy was to facilitate acceptance of a general reduction in mill hours by shortening hours

for women. As one labor historian noted, unionists hoped "to fight the battle from behind women's petticoats."[114]

Massachusetts enacted the first effective ten-hour law for women who worked in manufacturing employments in 1874. In 1893, the Illinois legislature passed an eight-hour law for women, but the state supreme court struck down the law, ruling that it interfered with the employer's right to freedom of contract and that it also denied women equal protection under the law. This and other rulings rendered most hours laws ineffective, and women continued to work in some industries up to eighteen hours a day.[115]

Hours laws received new life in a 1908 Supreme Court ruling, *Muller* v. *Oregon*. The Court deemed that the effects of long hours on women's health justified legislation to limit the number of hours per day of work. Between 1909 and 1917, forty-one states wrote new or improved hours laws for women, often extending the scope of the law to cover both factories and mercantile establishments. The working day was limited to nine hours and the working week to fifty-four hours.[116]

The working night, as well as the working day, also became a subject of legislation. In the United States, night-work laws for women were passed in four states between 1890 and 1904. In 1906, fourteen European nations endorsed the Bern Convention, which prohibited the employment of women from ten at night until five in the morning. In Massachusetts, the law again was intended to improve textile-industry conditions, where unionists sought to counteract a growing trend to overtime evening work by barring night work for women, hence forcing the mills to close by six at night. Most state night-work laws, however, were blocked by court injunctions, and women continued to work late hours in industries such as laundries, telephone and telegraph offices, and factories.[117]

In 1913, the New York State Court of Appeals ruled in the case of *People* v. *Charles Schweinler Press* in favor of a state law barring night work for women, and by 1928 ten states had outlawed women's night employment in at least two industries. But there was wide variation in the state regulation of working hours. In Kansas, the law for some industries was extensive, mandating limits to the hours of employment, requiring minimum periods for rest and for meals, and barring night work. In other states, including Alabama, Florida, Georgia, and Iowa, there were no hours regulations at all.[118]

Hours laws were viewed by advocates as a panacea for a variety of social ills. In 1890, Clare De Graffenried of the Department of Labor declared: "Each reduction in the hours of work, from sixteen to fourteen, from fourteen to twelve, from twelve to ten, has occasioned immediate and enormous im-

provement in the condition of the laboring classes. Shorter hours tend not only to provide occupation for millions of unemployed, but they will stimulate production and widen our markets by multiplying wants; they will make education possible, and conduce to a higher social and moral development in the home."[119] Hours laws for men, in contrast, were justified by the need for workers to remain healthy to insure efficiency and public safety. By 1912, thirteen states restricted miners to eight-hour days, and drug clerks, railroad and streetcar workers, and federal employees were among other men who were subject to maximum-hour statutes in some states.[120]

For women, hours laws were often defended as necessary to protect future motherhood. In 1870, the Massachusetts Bureau of Statistics of Labor suggested that long hours of work made women "unfit for the reproduction of their kind." The Maryland Bureau of Industrial Statistics stated in 1896 that more than ten hours of work daily led to weary women "with no pleasant anticipations for the morrow." The bureau queried in its report, "What lives are these for future wives and mothers? Future generations will answer." In 1908, the Michigan Bureau of Labor contended that working long hours "injures the mothers of our citizens. . . . We shall begin to see that . . . for the injury to the women, the mothers, the homes, and the rising generation, there must be special laws for the conditions under which women work."[121]

The United States Supreme Court agreed with the concept that women had special needs for regulated working hours. In 1908, Louis Brandeis submitted to the Court a 113-page brief prepared by Josephine Goldmark in the case of *Muller v. Oregon*. The brief cited more than one hundred studies purporting to show that long work hours damaged women's health and imperiled industrial output. "Deterioration of any large portion of the community inevitably lowers the entire community physically, mentally, and morally," Brandeis and Goldmark noted. "When the health of women has been injured by long hours, not only is the working efficiency of the community impaired, but the deterioration is handed down to succeeding generations. . . . The overwork of future mothers thus directly attacks the welfare of the nation."[122]

The evidence submitted in the Brandeis brief did not prove a causal relationship between the employment of women in industry and sex-related dangers to health and morals. In fact, some proponents of labor legislation argued that the "procreative power" of men was also injured by night work.[123] But the Court's decision relied heavily on the arguments about the dangers of long work for future motherhood. Justice David Brewer wrote for the majority:

> The two sexes differ in structure of body, in the functions to be performed by each, in the amount of physical strength, in the capacity for

long-continued labor, particularly when done standing, the influence of vigorous health upon the future well-being of the race, the self-reliance which enables one to assert full rights, and the capacity to maintain the struggle for subsistence. This difference justifies a difference in legislation and upholds that which is designed to compensate for some of the burdens which rest upon her.[124]

In 1913, Brandeis and Goldmark prepared a similar argument for the New York Court of Appeals in defense of a law barring night work for women. They maintained that women night workers suffered from the same dangers as those who worked long hours by day, but that they endured additional burdens of increased exhaustion, deprivation of sunlight, the moral dangers of traveling on the streets after dark, difficulty in finding respectable boarding places where they could return at odd hours, and exposure to the increased vulgarity of men night workers. The Court found these arguments convincing, deeming that "the health of thousands of women working in factories should be protected and safeguarded from any drain which can reasonably be avoided. This not only for their own sakes, but as is and ought to be constantly and legitimately emphasized, for the sake of the children whom a great majority of them will be called on to bear and who will almost inevitably display in their deficiencies the unfortunate inheritance conferred upon them by physically broken down mothers."[125]

Some discussion of night work for women recognized that the problem of night work included the married woman who chose to work at night in order to meet family responsibilities during the day. But, in general, reformers focused on the subject of hours for single women, as the length and spacing of work hours remained correlated to the state's need for healthy future mothers. In 1928, Mary Hopkins of the Women's Bureau offered a typical defense of night-work laws: "It is the state's imperative concern to see that the vitality [working women] should pass on to their children is not prematurely sapped or endangered by night work."[126]

The Women's Bureau claimed that maximum-hour statutes benefited men as well as women. "Just as the polling place has become cleaner and more presentable since women have started using it," the bureau stated, "so has the factory in many instances shown the influence of the higher standards which are imposed where women work." The bureau also indicated that there were few cases of women encountering undue discrimination because of hours legislation and that more women had been hired to take the place of overtime workers.[127]

But some women workers disagreed. In Chicago, women ticket agents for

the elevated railroads protested in 1911 when their schedules were cut from twelve to ten hours a day because of a new law limiting the hours of women's employment. In New York, women printers won an exemption from a night-work statute in 1924, successfully arguing that they would otherwise be deprived of their livelihoods. In other cities and states there were cases of women being fired or shifted to less remunerative shifts because of hours laws.[128]

Wages

The minimum wage was the second link in the "chain of protection." State labor bureaus in the 1880s and 1890s had related the low wages of women workers to the prevalence of prostitution in cities. By the 1910s, the concern with the morality of self-supporting women led to public pressure for the regulation of women's wages. City and state vice commissions, labor bureaus, trade unions, and purity reformers joined in the advocacy of a "living wage" for women workers.

In 1910, the National Consumers' League initiated the promotion of minimum-wage laws, and other groups, including the Progressive party and the Women's Trade Union League, followed with similar demands for legislation. Massachusetts enacted the nation's first minimum-wage law in 1912, and eight states passed similar statutes the following year. By 1917, seventeen states had laws legislating women's wages. These laws set minimum weekly salaries for women workers by city, industry, age, and experience, establishing a separate wage scale for apprentice workers.[129]

Like hours legislation, minimum-wage laws were for the most part defended on the grounds of protection for future mothers. But where hours laws focused on the physical well-being of women, laws that regulated wages were seen as critical for the preservation of public morality at a time when low salaries forced many women to seek supplemental sources of income.

Fears of prostitution continued to keep the controversy over working women in the public eye. Robert Bremner has credited a popular novel, *The House of Bondage* (1910), with bringing increased attention to the link between low wages and immorality. In this novel, an innocent country girl is deceived into leaving rural Pennsylvania for New York City, where she is tricked into a life of prostitution in a brothel. Although she manages to escape, she returns to the prostitute's trade after failing to find employment at a wage sufficient for self-support.[130]

Fears about the morality of women were reflected in the state minimum-wage campaigns. In California, clubwomen adopted the following slogan: "Employed womanhood must be protected in order to foster the motherhood of

the race." Voters in that state agreed in a 1913 general election that the absence of subsistence wages "is the cause of ill health, lack of strength for a good motherhood, and frequently degeneracy and prostitution for the weakest."[131] In Chicago, the city Vice Commission reported in 1911 that "there is no doubt that many girls do live on even $6 and do it honestly, but we can affirm that they do not have nourishing food or comfortable shelter, or warm clothes, or any amusement, except perhaps free public dances, without outside help. . . . Is it any wonder that a tempted girl who receives only $6 a week working with her hands sells her body for $25 when she learns that there is a demand for it and men are willing to pay the price?"[132]

Manufacturers and employers countered that morals were not related to wages and that most of their young women workers were in any event not self-supporting. Julius Rosenwald, the president of Sears, Roebuck and Company, testified before the Illinois Vice Commission that "we make it a point not to hire any girl for less than $8.00 a week who does not live at home." Manufacturers claimed that a minimum wage would force them to replace inefficient women workers with more efficient men and that the law of supply and demand would be abrogated.[133] Some women trade unionists joined in the opposition to the minimum wage. In California, women labor activists charged that a minimum wage could too easily become a maximum wage, undermine union-scale rates, inhibit organization efforts, and bar women from certain occupations.[134]

States considering minimum-wage laws debated the economic needs of young self-supporting women as a guideline for the establishment of salaries deemed necessary for the "reasonable comforts and conditions of life." These wage levels were determined by legislatures, administrative commissions, and advisory boards that gathered survey data, examined payrolls, and suggested theoretical budgets to support suggested wage levels.

Estimated budgets varied widely. Of seven states that investigated cost-of-living data by 1915, suggested weekly budgets for women living on their own ranged from $7.30 in Kansas to $10.48 in Oregon.[135] Wage boards also varied on the proportion of income to be spent by women on various items but shared a concern with the minutia of the working woman's life. As one historian observed, boards "would come to sword points over a relatively minor matter; for example, whether a working girl was entitled to a new hat every year or car fare for Sundays as well as weekdays."[136]

The clothing budget arrived at by the Minnesota Minimum Wage Board demonstrates this extraordinary effort to mandate the working woman's economic life down to the last detail:

Item	Price
1 heavy waist	$ 1.50
4 heavy waists at $1.00	4.00
1 stocking cap	.50
1 pair cloth gloves	.25
1 pair mittens	.50
1 pair leather gloves	1.00
2 suits heavy underwear	2.00
4 suits summer underwear	2.00
2 summer dresses	7.00
1 skirt	4.00
4 pair shoes	13.00
1 pair rubbers	.50
2 working aprons	.50
1 winter coat . . .	9.00
1 suit . . .	9.50
1 heavy dress	8.00
1 slicker	3.00
1 Sunday dress	7.50
3 nightgowns at .75	2.25
2 hats at 3.00	6.00
2 corsets	4.00
4 corset covers	1.40
3 underskirts	2.40
1 and a half dozen handkerchiefs	.90
2 pair dress shields	.50
2 ties, ball string, . . . misc.	1.50
12 pair stockings	3.00
Margin for unforeseen necessities	4.30
Total annual expenditure	$100.00[137]

Wage boards also estimated weekly costs for food, rent, laundry, carfare, medical bills, church gifts, insurance, club dues, amusements, vacations, books, magazines, and newspapers.[138] Savings were not considered; the budgets assumed that women were entitled to a minimal standard of living, and nothing more.

But wages legislated in the states did not even meet the minimum cost of living, nor did they allow for support of dependents. The methods used to determine the "living wage" were criticized by some observers for unnecessary

stringency and inaccuracy. Elizabeth Brandeis, the author of several articles on labor law, noted that "these women, all of whom were self-supporting, necessarily had to live in some fashion on what they earned."[139] Some women continued to deny themselves food or clothing in order to make ends meet, a practice documented in several investigations from the 1880s through the 1910s.[140]

In 1920, a Minneapolis factory worker, Naomi M., wrote to the Minnesota Wage Commission that working women attending the public minimum-wage meetings had presented a most incorrect picture of their lives:

> I'll begin by saying that it is impossible for a girl to live in "comfort and in health" on eleven dollars per wk. as all the others who spoke at the meeting said. Of course there are many who are doing so, and no one took the trouble to tell you how they do it. . . . The majority of the girls who receive only $11 per week have a "friend" who will help them out, but there are girls who have high ideals of life and are trying to live up to them who will not accept such help. I am in this class, and I have lived on eleven dollars a week, but I had to go hungry most of the time. You see, if I ate all I wanted there would be nothing left for clothing, so when I would contemplate buying a new dress or hat or shoes, that meant that I would have to go on a diet for several weeks, and my daily menu was usually an apple for breakfast, a sandwich and cup of coffee for lunch and maybe another sandwich or a bowl of milk toast for supper. I was amused at all the girls who spoke Friday eve. They said they spent about a dollar a day for food. They were too proud to tell the honest truth, just how little they eat. Of course if they ate nourishing food such as they should eat it would cost them about $1.25 per day. But the girl who gets only $11.00 per week goes hungry to work every day.[141]

The writer concluded that a minimum wage should be $18.00 per week "in order to meet the needs of comfort and health." But the wage set in Minnesota that year ranged from $10.25 to $12.00 per week, Naomi M.'s recommendations notwithstanding.[142]

The Women's Bureau compared the state minimum wages to the cost of living indexes and found that in many cases legislated wages did not meet the "necessary cost of living." Adjustments in minimum-wage rates year by year rarely kept pace with inflation. In 1920, nine states had established minimum-wage rates that were from $2.00 to $7.00 lower than cost-of-living estimates.[143]

Some observers argued that the minimum-wage statutes, though flawed, were still a step in the right direction. Rose Schneiderman stated that while

minimum-wage rates did not "permit the full expression of life," still they helped to elevate wages to some degree.[144] Minimum-wage rates were most effective in raising salary levels for young, inexperienced women workers, particularly in states and in occupations where wages were traditionally low. In Oregon, for example, in the year following the enactment of a wage law, there was an upward trend in the salaries of inexperienced women workers under the age of 18, who were paid the newly established apprentice salaries.[145] But there was less visible benefit for older, more experienced workers, who reported static or even declining salaries.

Some working women complained that they were under new pressures to work harder because of the legislation of wages. One department store supervisor protested to investigators from the United States Bureau of Labor Statistics: "It's mighty fine for the young girls beginning now, but for us, who have worked our way up from the bottom to near the top, to have to see that the wherewithal is made to pay the younger girls a living wage is making us pay a heavy price for the benefit of the next generation."[146] There were other reports of women fired when they completed their stint as apprentices, when employers were ordered to increase their salaries, or when men were willing to work for less than the set rate for women. But it is difficult to discern the actual influence of the minimum wage on salaries, as other factors affected the economy during the 1910s. These factors included a rise in price levels, acceleration of industrial production, and a curtailment of immigration with a resulting labor shortage in some occupations, particularly during wartime.[147]

Minimum-wage laws for women were ultimately doomed by court rulings. The freedom-of-contract argument was invoked by the Supreme Court in *Adkins* v. *Children's Hospital* in 1923 to overturn the minimum wage in the District of Columbia. Justice George Sutherland argued for the majority that physical differences between the sexes, used to justify hours laws, did not apply to wages. As a result, minimum-wage laws were either overruled or fell into disuse in most states. It was not until the New Deal, when National Recovery Act codes and the Fair Labor Standards Act mandated government control of working conditions in occupations relating to interstate or foreign commerce, that labor legislation was revived.[148]

The Disappearance of the "Working Girl"

The eclipse of protective legislation was accompanied by a diminishing public interest in the status of self-supporting women. The ameliorative reforms discussed earlier lost ground during the 1920s. Travelers' Aid, for

example, began to turn in new directions. By the 1930s, Travelers' Aid had redefined its role to include men as well as women travelers, and it became widely involved in social welfare during the depression, as its governing principle shifted from "moral protection" to "social casework."[149] Boarding homes also changed, some closing because of lack of patronage, and others turning into residences without excessive rules, and certainly without the attempt to re-create a hierarchical family environment.[150]

Demographic changes had led to a lessened visibility of self-supporting women by the mid-1920s. Stricter immigration laws and urbanization, which led to a smaller rural population from which migrant women might come, stemmed to some degree the tide of in-migration, at least as reflected in statistics on the proportions of women boarders and lodgers in cities. Joseph Hill, of the U.S. Census Bureau, suggested in 1929 that the relatively lower numbers of self-supporting women in cities was connected to patterns of urban growth. Rapidly growing cities, like Atlanta, reported higher proportions of female boarders and lodgers than did cities experiencing a decline in the rate of population increase. Of eleven cities surveyed by the Census Bureau in 1920, ten reported decreases in the relative numbers of women boarders and lodgers since 1900. St. Paul, for example, found 44 percent fewer women living on their own in 1920 than in 1900. Hill suggested that this occurred as "city conditions were becoming more settled, and home or family life for working women was becoming more common or general, as a natural result of retardation in the growth of that city."[151]

But the apparent decrease in the relative proportions of self-supporting women living on their own must also be viewed in the context of other factors. First, the occupational patterns of women were changing. By 1920, fewer women were servants, and more were clerical and sales workers. The domestic servant was no longer as likely to be a single young woman as much as she was likely to be an older married or widowed woman doing "daywork" to support her family. Since so many young single servants of the earlier era had roomed with their employers, the decrease in their numbers necessarily affected the enumeration of women who lived away from their own homes.[152]

Second, attitudes toward single women workers had changed. The self-supporting woman, once considered controversial, was by the 1920s viewed as a normal figure in the labor force. Her work and life outside the home became more acceptable. The domestic ideology was no longer thought to include the unmarried daughter; her status was no longer imperiled by employment and lodging away from home. This change was acknowledged by a Toledo, Ohio, real estate agent, who remarked in 1926 that, while "he remembered the time when he would have considered it very questionable if detached women had

wanted to rent an apartment," he now thought that self-supporting women "are [as] desired as tenants as well as anyone else."[153] The first generation of women living on their own had provided a bridge between the older hegemony of domesticity and the modern, though still limited, diversity of roles for single women.

Finally the composition of the female labor force itself was changing. Young single women still continued to work. But at the same time, by the 1920s older married women had begun to enter the labor force in increasing numbers. As we shall see in chapter 4, the movement of married women into the labor force occurred as child labor declined. At least to some degree, mothers took the place of their children as contributors to family income.

The increase in the numbers of working wives and mothers led to a shift in the debate over women, work, and social order. At the 1923 Women's Industrial Conference, Commissioner of Labor James Davis argued, "We can do no greater service to humanity and the future of the Nation than to stir American public opinion that this evil shall vanish once and for all from American industrial life."[154] The evil was no longer the malevolent effect of industry on the young woman who would one day be a mother. What was now at issue was the growing labor force participation of the older woman who already had children at home.

Part Two

The Era of the Working Mother, 1920–1980

Chapter 4
The Transformation of
the Female Labor Force

During the twentieth century, the working wife moved from the periphery of the female labor force into the mainstream. In 1900, fewer than one in ten married women worked for wages. By 1980, married women comprised almost two-thirds of the female labor force, as one in two of all married women worked (see table 2). Scholars have suggested that demographic changes, including the decline in the relative proportion of single women in the population, a long-term drop in the fertility rate, and urbanization, have contributed to the dramatic rise in the number of married women who work.[1] But at least as important an influence on the rising work rate of wives have been changing social values about women, work, and family life that have interacted with changing factors of labor supply and demand.

As we have seen, the movement of single women into the urban labor force in the late nineteenth century was characterized by a growing visibility of the "working girl"—the white native-born woman worker. Similarly, the movement of married women into the job market was characterized by the entrance of white middle-income wives into the labor force. At the same time, the work behavior of mothers shifted. At the turn of the century, mothers who worked often did so while their children were very young. They left the labor force when their sons and daughters were old enough to join the ranks of child labor and thus contribute to family income. By the mid-twentieth century, mothers typically did not work while their children were young but entered the labor force at the time that their youngest child entered school. This pattern was eroding by the 1970s, when even mothers of preschool-aged children were joining the labor force at an accelerating pace.

This chapter charts the history of the working wife and mother through three periods in the twentieth century. From 1900 to 1940, middle-income white wives typically did not work outside the home. The female labor force was comprised mainly of single, widowed, and divorced women, and the wives who did work were for the most part poor and black. From 1940 to 1970, the married woman overtook the single woman as the largest group in the female

labor force, and the participation rate for white married women rapidly accelerated. In the era from 1970 to the present, mothers—particularly mothers of young children—have become the fastest-growing group of workers. In each period, changes in labor supply, labor demand, and social values have interacted to shape the composition of the female labor force.

The Working Wife from 1900 to 1940

Relatively few wives worked at the turn of the century. Sixty-seven percent of women workers in 1900 were single, and only 15 percent were married. Just 6 percent of the population of married women worked, in contrast to 41 percent of single women (table 2).

Working wives came from a different population than did single women. They were much more likely to be black or poor. At the turn of the century, black wives were eight times as likely to work as were their white counterparts. Only 3 percent of white native-born married women worked, compared with more than a fourth of black wives. This affected the overall composition of the female labor force. In 1900, when two-thirds of single women workers were native-born whites, nearly half of the married women workers were black.[2]

As a rule, wives who worked in this era were poor women who needed to help support their families. Whereas it had become commonplace for single young women to work even if their families could have supported them, most wives worked only because of severe economic need. The work of wives was considered "a final defense against destitution" rather than an expected activity.[3] Married women worked only when other family income was insufficient for survival.

In this period there was an inverse correlation between family income and the employment of wives. Married women worked when their husbands earned low wages, were ill, or were unemployed. Katherine Anthony's investigation of working mothers on the west side of New York City in 1914 found that the employment of married women dropped as family income rose. "The mother works when she must," Anthony reported, "and when necessity is less stringent she relaxes her efforts outside and gives more attention to her home."[4]

A 1918 Philadelphia study also found that most wives who worked did so only because of desperate family circumstances. Three-fifths of the families with working mothers interviewed by the Philadelphia Bureau of Municipal Research lived on incomes less than the minimum standards set by the bureau for a family consisting of a husband, wife, and three children under le-

gal working age. Of women with husbands who were employed, three out of four wives worked because their husbands' earnings were too low for family support.[5]

Some twenty years later, this inverse correlation between family income and the employment of wives still prevailed. A 1940 examination of families in seven cities showed that four to five times as many wives of low-income men worked as did wives of wealthier men. In general, the higher the husband's income, the lower the tendency of the wife to work.[6]

The relatively common practice of child labor, particularly at the turn of the century, also affected the work of married women. In 1900, nearly one out of five children aged from ten to fifteen years were employed.[7] The younger the age of children in working-class families at the turn of the century, the more likely the mother was to work outside the home. But as children reached the age of nine or ten, their mothers left the labor force, as both sons and daughters had better opportunities for earning higher wages.[8] Fourteen-year-old Fannie Harris, who worked for a necktie manufacturer, gave testimony before a committee of the New York legislature in 1895 that illustrates the process by which children replaced their mothers in the labor force:

Q. Have you got any older brothers and sisters?

A. I have an older sister.

Q. Does she work?

A. Yes, sir.

Q. Does your mamma work?

A. Now she ain't working because I'm working, but before, when I didn't work, she worked.

. . . .

Q. And if you don't go to work then your mamma will have to work?

A. Sure.[9]

As we shall see, the pattern of wives working when their children were too young to work, and then staying home when the children were old enough to find employment, was reversed by the mid-twentieth century. By then, mothers of young children withdrew from the labor force, reentering when their youngsters were old enough to attend school.

The social stigma attached to the working wife was a strong deterrent to women entering the work force. Until the 1940s, paid employment outside the home was considered to be respectable only for single women or for widows who took over the management of their family businesses. For the married woman, paid employment could bring social anathema; the working wife was often considered to be beyond the pale of middle-class respectability.

But there was in this era a foreshadowing of a new employment pattern for married women. A minority of wives worked not because of absolute economic need but because of relative economic need—the desire to better the standard of living for their families. In 1915, the United States Bureau of Labor reported that some women textile workers hoped to "raise the family scale of living" with their earnings.[10] The 1918 Philadelphia study of mothers in industry found that 18 percent of the working mothers surveyed listed as their reasons for employment "personal preference." Many of these mothers were planning to build up family savings or earn enough for a family vacation.[11] Also in 1918, of 590 mothers working in the meat-packing plants of the Chicago stockyards, over a fourth worked in order to help their families buy property, discharge debts, or educate their children.[12] In 1920, a Census Bureau study discovered that on occasion a woman would work "not strictly from necessity but rather from choice, for the sake of securing a better living for herself and her husband than his income alone could provide."[13]

Some of the immigrant women interviewed in a 1925 Women's Bureau study also cited a desire to improve their families' standard of living. Theresa M., for example, a Hungarian immigrant with an employed husband and three children, worked as a roller in a cigar factory. She worked not to fend off family starvation, but to make things "nice"; her earnings helped her family to build a cellar, install plumbing and electricity, and buy a washing machine.[14] From 1920 to 1940, historian Winifred Wandersee suggests, family values were becoming redefined under the pressures of a rising standard of living and new consumption patterns. Although most married women still resisted work for wages in this era, those who worked did so not only because of absolute need, but also because employment opportunity was favorable or because the material comfort of their families superseded traditional concepts of women's role. Those who worked for the last two reasons "represented a change in family values, aimed at satisfying new needs rather than avoiding a poverty-level existence," Wandersee states. "But these women were able to rationalize their activities outside the home within the existing framework of traditional family values by defining their work in terms of the economic needs of the family."[15] This redefinition of family roles, however, was still nascent in 1940. For most married women, the inverse relationship between their employment and the income of their husbands remained powerful. It was not until the 1950s and 1960s that attitudinal change caught up with the factors of labor supply and demand, as increasing numbers of wives worked for reasons other than family subsistence.

In general, in the period before 1940, married women were reluctant to seek employment outside the home, and with good reason. Their lack of training

and lack of commitment to full-time work, along with employer preference and the social values that led to a loss of status for working wives, relegated married women to the most menial and low-paying of jobs. As a result, married women and single women did different kinds of work. Although the majority of single women, we have seen, worked in domestic service at the turn of the century, still nearly 20 percent of them were employed in the white-collar occupations of clerical, sales, and telephone and telegraph work. In contrast, most married women workers were farm laborers, laundresses, domestics, or home pieceworkers; less than 2 percent of them was employed in occupations that could be defined as white-collar work. The kind of work performed predominantly by married women was the lowest status work; for example, married women were the majority of oyster canners and preservers— workers in a trade characterized by the government as one "in which . . . conditions were more unpleasant and the wage level lower than in any other industry studied."[16]

The occupations undertaken by wives in part reflected their need to work in occupations that would mesh with their need for time at home. Mothers in New York City in 1914 preferred jobs in neighborhood factories where conditions were worse than in other places but where they were closer to their homes. Wives often worked in jobs with short hours or night hours so that they might leave the care of their children to their husbands. Jobs that were not sought after by single women because of oppressive conditions or odd hours were taken up by married women who had little choice. A Philadelphia office cleaner reported of her choice of night work in 1918 that "single women want their evenings, but the married women can get along without a good time."[17]

Much of the work of married women was performed within their homes and was undercounted by the Census Bureau. As late as 1920, at least one-fourth to one-third of married women workers were home workers.[18] In rural areas, wives toiled on family farms or as sharecroppers; in cities, they produced piecework in the clothing, artificial flower, or cigar trades, took in laundry or dressmaking, or kept boarders. Thus they could tend their children while earning a wage and often put their children to work as well.[19]

Clothing pieceworkers, for example, often taught their children to help out at an early age. *New York Tribune* reporter Helen Campbell described how young children assisted their mothers with clothing production in the late 1880s. She wrote of a New York overall maker who said of her children, ages seven and five, "I couldn't do as well if it wasn't for Jinny and Mame there. Mame has learned to sew on buttons first-rate, and Jinny is doing almost as well. . . . We'll do better yet when Mame gets a bit older."[20] Elizabeth Butler stated in her 1907 study of Pittsburgh working women that in families living in

the "outwork" districts of the city, "as fast as children could hold a needle they were pressed into service" as button makers, thread pullers, and machine operators.[21]

Some women, impelled by economic need, worked a variety of low-paying jobs. The Bureau of Labor Statistics reported the story of a widowed mother who worked nine hours a day in a bookbindery. As janitor of the building where she lived she cleaned halls before she left for work in the morning; in the evening, after cooking and cleaning, she colored picture postcards at the rate of fifteen cents a hundred. "She said that she often went to bed too tired to sleep and felt more tired when she got up in the morning than when she went to bed," the bureau stated.[22]

But perhaps the most common means of income for married women in this period was cooking and cleaning for boarders and lodgers. In 1901, nearly one in four urban families investigated by the Bureau of Labor reported that boarders brought them an average of $250 yearly—a sum representing over a third of the average annual family income, which was estimated to be $749.50.[23] Half of the New York City families studied in a 1907 report took in one or more boarders. Most of the wives who took in boarders and lodgers did not consider this activity as an occupation but rather as part of routine house-keeping duties. The Census Bureau agreed; it considered boarding and lodging housekeeping to be a formal occupation only for those whose primary means of support was the care of five or more boarders.[24]

One factor retarding the entrance of wives into the labor force in this era was the value placed on work within the home. Working-class wives might keep boarders and make clothing for their children; middle-income wives placed a higher value on child care, leisure, and housework. For both groups, home work was preferable to work outside the home.[25]

Before 1940, most wives and mothers who worked for wages outside the home remained on the fringe of the female labor force. Their children and husbands had greater opportunities for employment, and when married women sought work it was in the occupations with the lowest status. Married women worked outside the home only when they had to. Women's Bureau investigator Caroline Manning reported that "trouble, if not tragedy, had cast its shadow" over most of the working wives in the 1920s.[26] But developments in the supply and demand for female labor had begun in this era which would accelerate after 1940, bringing into the labor force white middle-income wives who worked not because of trouble or tragedy but because of choice.

Forces for Change, 1940–1970

Although the number of married women who worked increased steadily through the twentieth century, the greatest gains were made after 1940. From 1940 to 1970, married women increased their work rate each decade by at least 28 percent. As a group, married women became the most important source of new workers in the United States. From 1951 to 1961, wives accounted for nearly half of the total growth of the American labor force.[27]

The change in the racial composition of the female married labor force was also dramatic. In 1890, only one in fifty white wives was employed; black wives were more than ten times as likely to work. But after 1940, the labor force rate of white married women accelerated. The decade from 1950 to 1960 saw the greatest growth for white wives, as their work rate jumped from 17 to 30 percent. By 1970, the differential in work rates between black and white wives had narrowed further (table 6).

The transformation of the female labor force has been attributed to a number of factors. Analysts have cited demographic changes as responsible for the rising work rate of married women. They have noted that women in 1970 were older, less likely to have children, more likely to be living in cities than in rural areas, and more likely to have college degrees than they were in 1900.[28]

These changes alone, however, could not account for the fast rise in the female labor force participation rates after 1940. For native-born white women, especially, the key factor in work behavior has not been changing family structures or urbanization but rather a rising propensity to work, which reflects a change in social values.[29] Work for wages outside the home came to

Table 6

Percentage of Married Women in the Labor Force, by Race, Selected Years, 1890–1980

	1890	1900	1920	1930	1940	1950	1960	1970
All women	5	6	9	12	17	25	32	40
White	2	3	7	10	14	17	30	39
Black	23	26	33	33	32	36	47	51

Sources: Brownlee, "Household Values," p. 200, table 1; Durand, *Labor Force in the U.S.*, pp. 216–17, table A-7; U.S. Bureau of the Census, *U.S. Census of Population, 1960*, pp. 501–6, table 196; U.S. Bureau of the Census, *Nineteenth Census of the U.S., 1970*, pp. 688–89, table 216.

be valued as highly as was nonwage work within the home and the status of domesticity. In short, changes in the nature of work and in the role of women explain why the labor force participation rate of married women was so much higher than what can be explained by demographic factors alone.

Population changes did in part affect the supply of women available as workers. The relatively high proportion of single women in the nineteenth century gradually diminished. In 1958, economist Gertrude Bancroft commented on the "almost complete disappearance of the spinster and the increasing proportion of married women in the population."[30] The proportion of single women fell from about a third of all women in 1890 to about a fifth in 1970. Yet, although the proportion of single women fell by 14 percent, their representation in the female labor force fell from 68 to 22 percent—a decline of over three times what could be expected on the basis of increasing marriage rates alone.[31]

Whereas women were more likely to be married in the mid-twentieth century, they were also likely to bear fewer children. The decrease in the birthrate, a result of birth control as well as of changing family ideologies, has been cited as a factor lessening the burden of housewifery and thus increasing the tendency of married women to work outside the home.[32] There has been a gradual decline in the fertility rate of American women since at least 1810.[33] And from 1920 to 1970, fertility rates fell from 117.9 births per thousand women to 87.9.

The relationship between declining fertility and the rising employment of wives, however, must be viewed with caution. Despite the "baby boom" of the 1950s and 1960s, the labor force participation rate of wives did not decline but instead continued to rise. From 1940 to 1960, when the fertility rate jumped from 72.9 to 118.0, the work participation rate of married women still rose by 88 percent.[34]

The overall drop in the fertility rate, combined with rising life expectancies, did lead to a gradual aging of the population. In 1890, the largest age group in the adult female population was the group from 16 to 24 years, and over half of all adult women was younger than 30 years old. Eighty years later, in 1970, the largest age group of women was in the population aged 35 to 44, and over half of all adult women was older than 35.[35]

This aging of the population was reflected in the female labor force. In 1900, the largest age group of women workers was from 16 to 20 years old, but in 1970, the largest group was aged from 35 to 44. Still, the aging of the population alone could not account for the changing female labor force composition. The work rate increased in every age group for married women from 1900 to 1970, most markedly for women between the ages of 20 and 24 and for

women over the age of 35. In every age group, married women increased their labor force participation at a much greater rate than did single, widowed, or divorced women.[36]

Another factor suggested as influential for the rising work rate of wives was the continued urbanization of the population that occurred in the twentieth century.[37] Historically, women in cities have been more likely to work for wages outside the home than have women in rural areas. In 1900, when 28 percent of women in large cities worked, only 18 percent of women in smaller cities and country districts were employed.[38] In 1950, apparently residence was still a factor in women's employment. Then, 22 percent of nonfarm white wives and 35 percent of nonfarm black wives worked for wages, compared with 13 percent of white wives and 18 percent of black wives who lived on farms.[39] But this determinant is complicated by the fact that farm wives, who often contributed to the work on their family farms, were viewed as unpaid family laborers and therefore were not counted by the Census Bureau as wage earners.[40]

The final demographic factor that seems to have altered the female labor force has been the growth in education for women, which has occurred since 1940. Before World War II, women earned about 20 percent of bachelor's and first professional degrees. By 1940, women received over 40 percent of those degrees, and by 1968, nearly one in five women had secured a college diploma.[41]

More and more educated and skilled women from higher-income families entered the work force. A study of the census returns of 1940 and 1950 showed that the inverse correlation between the rate of female employment and median male income in 1940 and earlier was reversed for white women by 1950. The more a woman was capable of earning, because of increased education, the more likely she was to work.[42] Still, many college-educated married women did not work in this period, so the factor of education by itself does not explain the growth rate of married women in the labor force.

Demographic changes may have contributed to the enormous influx of wives into the labor force in this era. But we must also consider other factors that led married women into the job market, particularly changes in the nature of work and in the role of women within the family.

Work outside the home had become less demanding in terms of time and relatively more profitable. The reduction in the weekly hours of work made employment more attractive to women who performed the dual jobs of wage earner and housewife.[43] The average hours of work in manufacturing occupations fell from an estimated fifty-nine a week in 1899 to forty in 1939, and a corresponding acceptance of the eight-hour day in white-collar work made

employment still more feasible for women with children.[44] Moreover, a rise in real wages over time may have encouraged more women to work outside the home. Economists have pointed out that as wages rise leisure time becomes more expensive. From 1890 to 1960, real income tripled, while the participation rates of married women in the work force increased sixfold.[45]

A related factor was the value of work performed at home and rendered by wives in services such as child care, food preparation, and household maintenance.[46] Some scholars have argued that the proliferation of laborsaving devices in the twentieth century eased the burden of housework and hence provided wives with more time for outside employment. The electricity-powered washing machine and refrigerator have been linked to a reduction in the time needed for household tasks.[47] But inventions related to the mechanization of housework, such as the vacuum cleaner and electric iron, were widely used before 1940, prior to the time when the work rate of married women accelerated.[48]

Moreover, the spread of laborsaving devices appeared as domestic servants disappeared from middle-class homes, and higher expectations for housekeeping may have added to rather than subtracted from the hours put into those tasks by middle-income women. The average household spent more time on laundry work in 1964 than in 1925, for example. Washing machines and electric driers eased the physical burden of clothes cleaning, but most families now had more clothes that were washed more often.[49]

The age and presence of children in the home also affected the propensity of women to work. As we have seen, in the first third of the twentieth century, mothers worked, if ever, when their children were young. As children became old enough to find jobs, their mothers dropped out of the labor force. By mid-century, this pattern had been reversed. In 1950, only 12 percent of women with young children worked outside the home (see table 7). By 1960, more than a third of the women with school-aged children were employed, a higher rate than married women with no children living at home. By 1970, nearly half of the women with children aged from six to seventeen worked. Clearly, the life-cycle pattern described for turn-of-the-century working women had changed. By mid-century, mothers of young children were not commonly employed but instead worked after their children had entered school.

The entrance of these mothers into the labor force occurred as their children were moving out of the labor force and into the schools. The proportions of children who worked for wages decreased in the years that mothers began to work. In 1870, 13.2 percent of all children from ten to fifteen years old were employed. By 1900, 18.2 percent of children in this age group worked; one out

Table 7

Percentage of Married Women in the Labor Force, by Presence and Age of Children, 1948–1970

	1948	1950	1960	1970
With no children under 18	28.4	30.3	34.7	42.2
With children aged 6–17 only	26.0	28.3	39.0	49.2
With children under 6	10.8	11.9	18.6	30.3

Source: U.S. Department of Labor, Bureau of Labor Statistics, *Handbook of Labor Statistics, 1978*, p. 64, table 14.

of four boys and one in ten girls reported wage-earning activities.[50] After the turn of the century, however, child labor diminished. By 1920, 11.3 percent, and by 1930, 4.7 percent of children in this age group worked.[51]

The decrease in child labor occurred in part because of a movement to abolish the employment of children. Reformers feared that children who worked were not being properly educated, and they pushed for laws to prohibit the work of children and to mandate compulsory schooling.[52] Thus the changing pattern of family economics saw the increasing employment rate of mothers at the same time as children were being moved out of the labor force.

Even as the presence of children in the home was becoming less of an influence on a mother's decision to work, so the dollar amount of her husband's paycheck was becoming less important. Economists predicted that the work rate of married women should decrease as their husbands' incomes rose.[53] As it turned out, a rapid rise in the labor force participation of middle-income wives in the 1950s and 1960s confounded this expectation.

Investigators examined the labor force participation of married women as a function of their husbands' incomes for 1950, 1959, and 1968. For 1950, there was a fairly linear negative correlation between the two variables, as the work rate of wives fell as their husbands' income rose. By 1959, and even more in 1968, this trend began to erode. By 1968, the work rate of married women was highest for those whose husbands' annual incomes were close to the then national average of about $6,500.[54]

These income studies reflect the increasing propensity of married women to work for reasons other than absolute economic need. Middle-income wives had begun to seek employment to achieve both personal satisfaction and to raise their family standards of living. Union women surveyed by the Women's Bureau as early as 1950 reported that they worked for objectives beyond family survival. The level of economic need had been enlarged to include

items that at one time were considered to be luxuries. These women worked to buy a house or car, pay bills, or educate their children. Two out of three women members of the Brotherhood of Railway and Steamship Clerks, for example, worked to make house payments. One out of four of the International Association of Machinists listed the education of their children as a work objective.[55] These women might argue that they worked to support their families, but the definition of what constituted family support had changed to reflect higher expectations of consumption needs.

Attitudinal factors about women's work outside the home had more influence on certain groups of women than on others. For women for whom work was not a role transgression, such as poor women, such factors as the age of their youngest child may have been more critical in their decision whether or not to work. But for middle-income women, the shift of values that increasingly permitted women to work without losing class status probably was one of the more important factors influencing their work decision.[56]

As the supply of women workers grew to include married women, the demand for female labor was rising. Historians differ on the nature of the pull of the labor market for wives. William Chafe has argued that World War II was a watershed for American women, prompting a "revolution" in the labor force by bringing the first large numbers of married women into the marketplace.[57] Other scholars suggest that the war did not initiate this process but instead temporarily speeded up the trend of increasing demand for female labor. Leila Rupp, for one, dismisses the importance of the war for the history of women's work, arguing that "the influx of women into the labor force during the war had nothing to do with . . . long-term changes, and had no permanent impact on the female labor force."[58] It seems clear that the long-term effects of occupational segregation that were established by the turn of the century influenced the growing demand for women workers. There were well-defined spheres of women's and men's work, as certain jobs, such as elementary school teaching and typing, were deemed women's occupations, and others, such as construction work and accounting, were designated for men.[59]

The years from 1900 to 1960 were characterized by the general decrease in the need for farm labor and a concomitant increase in the demand for white-collar workers. The demand for manual labor and service work has remained relatively constant over that period. The trend for men is quite clear. When men's efforts were no longer required on the farm, they turned to manual and service jobs and, to a lesser extent, to nonclerical white-collar work. At the same time, women, and particularly married women, were filling the growing demand for white-collar workers. It was office work, which had become women's work, for which demand was now the greatest. For married women,

farm, manual, and service work gave way to white-collar work by mid-century.

As labor demand opened up new opportunities for women, the gap that existed at 1900 between married and single women workers narrowed. Although single women were about twice as likely to hold white-collar jobs as were married women in 1900, by 1960 there was little difference in the occupational distribution of married women and women workers in general.[60]

The shift of wives to white-collar work especially favored the employment of white women. Black women found barriers to work opportunities in offices because of higher educational requirements and because of institutional racism. In 1960, when two in five white wives worked in clerical or sales occupations, only one in ten black married women was in the same category.[61]

Whereas the expansion of work opportunities for women was the more important factor in the overall demand for female labor, the short-term experiences of millions of married women during World War II were also significant. During the war, there were great gains in the female labor force. Over 6 million women, three-fourths of them married, took jobs for the first time between 1940 and 1945. These women increased the size of the female labor force by more than 50 percent.[62] This pattern differed from the experience of women during World War I, when only 5 percent of women war workers had joined the labor force for the first time.[63]

During World War II, women produced engines, guns, shells, and tanks in war plants and took 2 million new clerical jobs. The aircraft industry reflected the influx of new women workers. In April 1941, 143 women were employed in seven aircraft factories. By October 1943, these same factories had hired 65,000 women—an increase of over 450-fold.[64] By 1944, both married and single women were working in greater proportions than previously; single women had increased their labor force participation rate by 15 percent, and married women by 6 percent.

But layoffs and demotions reduced the female labor force after the war. By the end of 1945, one out of four women in industry had quit or been laid off. Between 1945 and 1946, more than 3 million women who had worked during the war had dropped out of the labor force.[65] Still, millions of women continued to work after the war, taking advantage of work opportunities that had been expanding for decades. For married white women, the most important gains came not from 1940 to 1950 but from 1950 to 1960, when they increased their work rate by 13 percent—the fastest rise per decade up to that time.

The forces of labor supply and demand were interactive. Shortages of single women combined with increased job opportunities to create a demand for married workers, and increased job opportunities in the female sector of the

labor force in turn attracted more of them into the job market as social values about the economic role of women began to change. The patterns of labor supply and labor demand that were established at mid-century had shaped a female labor force that by 1970 differed markedly from the female labor force of 1900.

The Working Wife and Mother in the 1970s

By 1976, 62 percent of the female labor force was married—the exact proportion of women workers who had been single in 1900. In the 1970s, trends favoring the work of married women continued.

The working wife was no longer likely to be black or poor. Racial differences in the work rates of married women continued to narrow; in 1978, 58 percent of black wives worked, but the rate for white wives had risen to 47 percent. Black women were also beginning to obtain relatively higher-status jobs; the proportion of black women who held clerical jobs nearly tripled between 1960 and 1976. By 1980, nearly half of all employed black women were white-collar workers.[66]

At the same time, the service sector of the economy—which included white-collar work—continued to grow. The ratio of service-to-goods producing jobs widened from 1.5 to 1 in 1950 to nearly 2.5 to 1 by 1976. By 1979, too, clerical workers had become the largest occupational group for women in the United States, overtaking manual and service jobs.[67]

The tie between a woman's employment and her husband's income, loosened in the postwar era, became undone in the 1970s. Between 1967 and 1974, the labor force participation rate of women whose husbands earned $2,000 to $6,000 rose by 11 percent, but the work rate of wives whose husbands earned over $30,000 a year jumped by 38 percent. A 1974 survey found that among women with children under the age of eighteen, employment rates for middle-income wives were the highest. Whereas participation rates continued to rise for women in all income categories, the overall rate for married women rose as their husbands' incomes rose to the annual salary level of $7,000 to $10,000, and dropped off thereafter for women whose husbands earned over $10,000 a year. In 1978, this trend continued, as the highest proportion of wives who worked—more than half of all married women—had husbands who earned from $10,000 to $20,000 a year.[68] Finally, the fertility rate continued to drop, falling from 87.9 in 1970 to 66.4 in 1979, at the same time as the female labor force participation rate increased by 10 percent.[69]

But the 1970s, while continuing the labor force trends of the postwar era,

also saw some new developments. First, there was a sharp increase in the numbers of female-headed households. The proportion of single-parent families, most of them headed by women, more than doubled since 1950, comprising 18.9 percent of all families by 1978. From 1970 to 1978 alone there was an increase of over 2.5 million single-parent families. This trend, a result of the rising divorce rate and the rise in the numbers of babies born to unmarried mothers—was important because female-headed families were so much poorer than two-parent families. Forty percent of single-parent families in 1978 lived on incomes below the poverty level—a status held by only 6 percent of families with two parents living at home.[70]

The other major change in the labor force involved the rapidly growing work rate of mothers of very young children. In 1950, only 12 percent of mothers of preschool-aged children worked. In 1969, fewer than one in four mothers of children under the age of three worked, and by 1979, this percentage had risen to over two in five.[71] In 1978, a new subgroup of working women was recognized by the Census Bureau for the first time. These were the mothers of infants under the age of one year. The Census Bureau found that in 1978, a startling 30 percent of mothers with infants under a year old worked, at least part-time, and 41 percent of mothers with children under the age of two were also employed.[72] The practice of mothers of young children staying at home and out of the labor force, evident in the 1950s, was apparently eroding. And although economic pressures were partly responsible, as they were in 1900, changing social values also played an important role.

Developments in the supply-and-demand factors in the female labor force in the twentieth century resulted in a changing identity for the woman worker. The single self-supporting woman had been replaced in the job market by the wife and mother. In turn, the working wife who had been black or poor at the turn of the century was by the 1970s more likely to be middle income and white. Because of her class status, the working wife and mother could no longer be treated strictly as a charity case or be ignored. The concern with the protection of the future motherhood of the single woman, which had been the cornerstone of the public debate over working women in the early twentieth century, now shifted to a concern with the protection of motherhood itself.

Chapter 5
The Discovery of
the Working Mother

The married woman who worked for wages had long been considered to be an aberration, a "social accident" of scant public significance.[1] Because she was usually poor or black, her status elicited little controversy. Reform efforts aimed at the child care or health needs of the working mother were in general secondary to the larger measures meant to protect the working girl. By the 1920s, however, the female labor force was beginning to be affected by the increasing work rates of white middle-income wives. The disjuncture between the domestic ideology and the employment patterns of women resulted in the discovery and labeling of a new social problem. The working mother replaced the working girl as a symbol of female role transgression and social change.

The development of the debate over the work of married women mirrored a narrowing of the domestic ideology. By the 1930s, daughters who worked for wages before marriage were no longer considered to be "adrift" from their proper place. But the domestic role prescription still held strong for married women and mothers. As Robert and Helen Lynd noted of public opinion in "Middletown"—Muncie, Indiana—during the 1930s, "there is more indulgent tolerance of a business-class girl's working between school and marriage, but when she marries, 'all that foolishness stops.' "[2]

Once married, a woman was expected to devote full time to home activities. These activities were increasingly less economic in scope, as home production of goods for family consumption and for industry was rapidly diminishing.[3] Rather, a new emphasis on a mother's role in meeting the emotional needs of her family was taking hold in American culture. "The chief concern over the family nowadays," a sociologist suggested in 1933, "is not how strong it may be as an economic organization but how well it performs services for the personalities of its members."[4] A mother's responsibility for the nurture of her husband and children gained new importance as her economic responsibilities, whether making overalls at home as piecework, sewing clothes, or baking bread for her family, lessened.

The work of married women in the period from 1920 to 1940 provoked

questions about the moral, economic, and psychological aspects of a woman's role as wife as well as mother. After 1940, these concerns narrowed still further; the work of wives without children and of mothers of children in school gradually came to be accepted. But the employment of mothers of young children captured public attention. This was the bottom line for the controversy over women and work. The consequences of a woman's employment outside the home on the physical and psychological health of her young children became the center of public debate.

Working Mothers before 1920

Before 1920, the concern with married women in the work force was subordinate to the concern with single women. When the labor of married women came to light, two themes were expressed that would shape the controversy throughout the twentieth century. Even after the composition of the female labor force shifted toward the working wife and mother after the mid-twentieth century, public opinion about these women was still mired in the outdated conceptions of the nineteenth century.

The first theme advanced in the nineteenth century was about the effect of the employment of mothers on the health and upbringing of their children. For the most part, this aspect of the debate focused on poor women; some critics feared that their work caused them to neglect their children and thus contributed to such social ills as delinquency and dependency. Moreover, the effect of long hours of toil on a mother's well-being and, in turn, on her progeny was seen as consequential for the future of the working class.

Carroll Wright said in his 1875 report of the Massachusetts Bureau of Labor Statistics that the work of married women in factories was an evil "sapping the life of our operative population, and must sooner or later be regulated, or, more probably, stopped."[5] The United States Industrial Commission, in 1902, maintained that married women debilitated by hard work would give birth to sickly children, thus weakening the "physical and moral strength of the new generation of working people."[6] The problem of the "mother who must earn" was, like the problem of the working girl, one of the effects of a woman's work on her children.

The second theme in the discussion of working wives in this era stemmed from the rare but highly visible employment of middle-class married women, who consciously sought work as an alternative to their domestic role. For these women, work was seen as a matter of choice rather than of necessity. By taking jobs, they were seen as deliberately transgressing their proper place.

The challenge posed by this role transgression was exemplified in the writings of Charlotte Perkins Gilman. In *Women and Economics*, published in 1898, and in *The Home*, published in 1903, Gilman argued that the financial independence brought by earning a paycheck was critical for the freedom of women, and she proposed that the employment of wives be encouraged by the establishment of communal kitchens and nurseries.[7] But Gilman's ideas were on the edge of contemporary thought. More common was the contention that the issue for middle-class women was not how to combine work and marriage but how to choose between them.

In an 1893 article in the *North American Review*, Mary Hawes Terhune argued that women faced a choice between "counting room and cradle." It was, she advised, not a matter of equal alternatives. For the woman who chose life in the counting room, Terhune warned, "native branches have been pruned to make room for the alien. If the result satisfy her, it is because she has unsexed herself. If longings for the shelter, the sacred joys and loves of wifehood and motherhood have survived through the unnatural process, she is an object of pity."[8] This point of view was also expressed in the popular women's magazines of the era. An article in the 1900 *Ladies' Home Journal*, for example, stressed the primacy of homemaking as the sphere of women. "An American Mother" instructed *Journal* readers that "if fate has denied to any woman a home, a husband, and a baby, let her take up art, or medicine, or blacksmithing. . . . But to claim that these are higher occupations than her own craft—the high calling of wife-hood and motherhood—is the most shallow and dangerous cant."[9]

While the employment of married women was not seen as a social problem on a large scale before 1920, still the themes evoked throughout the twentieth century were taking shape in the earlier period. The problem of role transgression for the woman who chose career over marriage, and the dangers to the children of the poor working wife, were ideas that converged after 1920 to create a second era in the debate over women and work—a debate that was now acutely concerned with the social consequences of the employment of married women.

Wives, Mothers, and Work, 1920–1940

During the 1920s, married women edged onto center stage in the rhetoric over working women. Progressive reformers had noted the plight of the poverty-stricken woman with children and intended to restore her to her home. In a contrary direction, articulate feminists brought attention to their

point of view, publishing in mass magazines and books. A spirited debate ensued, as the working wife of any class was seen by critics as a danger to long-hallowed ideals of family life, while feminists applauded the employment of women as a prerequisite for female independence.

The new controversy was reflected in a proliferation of newspaper and magazine articles, in surveys, in investigations, and in public-opinion polls. Whereas *Harper's Bazaar* in 1908 published a series of articles on self-supporting single women, *Harper's Magazine* in the mid-1920s devoted its pages to the discussion of working wives. And while a student-debate handbook in 1911 summarized the pros and cons of work for single women, a 1928 debate volume entitled *Jobs and Marriage?* questioned the results of employment for a married woman's health, her husband, her home, and her children.[10]

During the early period of the debate over working wives, the actual number of married women in the labor force was relatively small. We have seen that in 1920 only a fifth of the female labor force was married, and under a tenth of all wives worked. By 1940, 17 percent of wives worked, constituting just over a third of the female labor force.[11] Yet the emotional rhetoric of the debate over women's employment belied these statistics; the great majority of married women did not work, while the minority who did captured public attention. The employment of the married woman at this time touched a sensitive nerve in American culture. She was perceived by different factions as a symbol of the failure, or of the salvation, of the family and the social order.

There were two dominant viewpoints in the debate over working wives in this era. The first was the widely held conservative notion that the work of wives was dangerous for both moral and economic reasons. The married woman who left home to work was a "menace to the race" because she endangered the integrity of the family, the birthrate, the economic system—indeed, she threatened civilization itself. Proponents of this view contended that the ideal family should contain one wage earner—the husband. The wife should devote her time to caring for her children and spouse, and to maintaining the home. If a woman had to work because of financial need, her position was considered to be most unfortunate. If she chose to work for reasons other than survival, her decision was considered to be both selfish and immoral.

This perspective surfaced at the Women's Industrial Conference sponsored by the Department of Labor and the Women's Bureau in 1923. Labor Commissioner James Davis decried the employment of married women, stating that "we must see to it that we do not sacrifice motherhood upon the altar of greed for industrial production."[12] But a counter viewpoint was advanced by a minority group of feminists who argued that working wives were at the

vanguard of women's emancipation, for they established "the greater personal freedom and financial independence of women."[13] The feminist position represented a challenge to traditional family life: either the family as commonly conceived would disappear, or it would be transformed as people other than the mother would share in child care and household duties.

Ironically, there was little discussion in either camp about why most married women were really motivated to seek employment, which was to contribute to family income in order to attain a higher standard of living. The Lynds, in *Middletown in Transition*, saw this factor as most important in the changing perspective of wives who began to work. Middletown residents attached great weight to the idea that a married woman's place was at home, the Lynds reported: "At every point this value is buttressed against change. The thing that is changing it most is not changes from within its own coherently knit ideologies—not changes in awareness of woman's individual differences, capacities, and propensities, not changes in the conception as to what "home" means or what the role of a "wife" or "mother" is—but the pressure from without of a culturally stimulated rising psychological standard of living."[14]

It was not the relative standard of living that framed the debate between proponents and opponents of working wives and mothers. Rather, the controversy focused on questions of how employment affected a woman's health in the context of prescribed social roles. Although the economic class of the working mother shaped the tenor of different aspects of this debate, in the end it was sex rather than class that characterized the social dogma of the times. The question was, What effect would work have on the physical and mental health of married women? Conservatives, focusing on poor women, warned that the activities of housework and employment constituted a "double burden" for women, while feminists countered that employment enhanced both physical and mental health. Several investigators argued that a wife who both worked and tended her household was left in a "shocking state of exhaustion" by day's end.[15] When critics pointed to the problems of the working wife, they cited cases of poor women whose health was threatened by insufficient medical care and years of unremitting toil as factory operatives and domestic workers. The ill health of working mothers was noted in a Children's Bureau study of Chicago women in 1922. Typical passages reported constant fatigue: "Mother complained of being tired all the time"; "Mother well and strong but very tired. Got up at 5 A.M. and left for work at 6"; "Mother . . . wearing out."[16]

The complaint of the employed working-class mother was one of physical debilitation—a result of work under oppressive conditions. It appears that many of these women did not suffer as much as did their middle-class counter-

parts from another complaint—that of psychological tension caused by role ambiguity. Rather, working-class mothers endorsed the ideology of domesticity. The New York working mothers surveyed by Katherine Anthony in 1914 approved of values opposed to the employment of women and aspired to leaving the labor force. "Not to work is a mark of the middle-class married woman," Anthony found, "and the ambitious West Side family covets that mark."[17] Nearly fifty years later, in 1962, Mirra Komarovsky in her study, *Blue-Collar Marriage*, similarly found little evidence of status frustration among working-class homemakers.[18]

But middle-class women in the 1920s were beginning to display a psychological tension when they confronted the dilemma between work and marriage. This tension, often termed the "problem with American women," has been cited repeatedly throughout the century. In 1926, Helen Glenn Tyson, a social scientist, outlined the mental conflict endured by the professional woman with a family:

> . . . on the one hand, a keen interest in her professional work, a real need of income, the fear of mental stagnation, and the restlessness that comes from filling all her day with petty things; on the other hand, new demands in child-care that were unknown even a decade ago; a supply of domestic helpers that is fast diminishing both in quality and quantity; and, like a cloud over all her activities, her own emotional conflict that is rooted deep in her maternity. . . . The feeling that the world is organized to her disadvantage alone is not conducive to resignation.[19]

Women attempting to fulfill two roles were often confounded; those choosing one role over the other were often dissatisfied. Women were repeatedly told they could not have it both ways. In a 1936 advice manual, for example, girls were cautioned that the attempt to work while married "detracts materially from success in both the home and in the business world because of the added physical and mental strain."[20]

Feminists were not convinced by these arguments. They contended that it was full-time housewifery, and not employment, that imperiled women's health. Feminists cited studies that hypothesized that the repression of mental abilities led to neurasthenia, fatigue, depression, and other ailments. Employment was suggested as a health remedy; some proponents suggested that by working married women could become "alert, brisk, hopeful" people rather than frustrated, thwarted individuals.[21]

The role of women as marriage partners was also under fire in this era, as the effect of employment on issues of dependence and independence were questioned. Some argued that if a woman worked outside the home, she undercut

the status of her spouse. Others replied that working wives fulfilled important needs for self-expression and would as a result be better companions to their husbands.

Social scientist Ernest Groves maintained in 1926 that the average husband felt his place within the family to be endangered by a working wife. "In the past supremacy of the male in the family rested on his command of the family income and the prestige that has been his from being looked upon as the producer of the family funds," he wrote. "When the woman herself earns and her maintenance is not entirely at the mercy of her husband's will, diminishing masculine authority necessarily follows." This loss of authority, Groves added, was buttressed by a loss of social status, for public opinion opposed the work of wives and looked with suspicion on the competence of a husband whose wife earned a paycheck.[22]

Public opinion in 1929 tolerated the employment of only a few classes of married women, notably blacks, immigrants, women with grown children, and, occasionally, "women of rare talents." For the ordinary woman, housewifery was the expected pursuit, "the husband being sufficiently successful to assure a sufficient income to purchase all supplies and to accumulate some savings."[23] A survey of men in 1924 supported these findings; 65 percent of men in clerical, commercial, and professional occupations believed that married women should devote full time to family affairs. Another 31 percent believed that while it was acceptable for some wives to work, mothers of young children should stay at home.[24]

Working married women themselves were cognizant of the threat that their employment posed to their husbands. One woman wrote in the *Atlantic Monthly* in 1924 that the husband of a working wife was easily threatened. "He feels his crown as master of the household slipping," she noted. "He acquires an inferiority complex. . . . [I]t takes a steady hand to keep a marriage off the rocks at this period; . . . the husband wants to be the strong one in the family. . . . Really, he wants [his wife] to keep her place as the minor part of the family."[25] When a husband's self-esteem was threatened, critics warned, he might too easily lose his own drive for business success. A group of New York bankers declared that they would not hire married women. "A working wife," they stated, "often deadens ambition in a man. If he knows his wife is earning money just as he earns it, it encourages him to laziness. Her husband becomes a parasite without stamina or self-respect."[26] A social scientist, Anna Garlin Spencer, agreed with this opinion, stating that "the husband and the father is more easily tempted to shirk his family duties" when wives worked. She contended that in black families, where women were more likely to find

jobs than were men, "the man grows flabby in character and lazy in habit because it is easy for him thus to depend upon his wife."[27]

Feminists countered these arguments by promoting the work of wives as the basis of egalitarian marriages. One woman writer proclaimed in 1927 that the working wife was a "feminist—new style" rather than the traditional home-maker or the militantly unmarried, grim, "old-style" feminist. The new feminist was a "full-fledged" individual who both worked and shared an egalitarian marriage.[28] Another writer suggested that a benefit of her job was a new comradeship—a sort of partnership—with her husband. "A working wife has a better chance of being friends with her husband than the stay-at-home wife. . . . She is no longer a dependent," the writer maintained. "She is an equal partner. The chances for domestic happiness seem greater than in the old-fashioned marriage where a woman could be nothing but what her husband made her."[29] A third woman agreed in 1926, stating in *Survey Graphic* maga-zine that "it is practically impossible to create a satisfactory relationship when one person is entirely dependent on the other, and that other is forced to carry the sole economic responsibility for the lives of both as well as of the family." Independence, these women argued, both enhanced their lives and improved their marriages.[30] But the feminist viewpoint was not widely shared. To many Americans before 1940, a working wife was a sign of a flawed marriage.

Another issue in the debate over married women workers was the effect of work on a woman's role as a mother. Two fears fueled this discussion: the possibility that employed wives consciously limited the size of their families, and the question of the impact of their employment on the health and upbring-ing of the offspring they did have.

The specter of "race suicide" had been raised earlier in the century; some feared that native-white and college-educated women were choosing to have fewer children than were immigrants, blacks, and poor women, and that the result would be a disastrous fall in "quality" in the American population.[31] Theodore Roosevelt led the charge of these critics, condemning women who deliberately avoided childbearing as "criminal against the race." One cause of the avoidance of childbirth, commentators warned, was the employment of women outside the home. In his study of the American family, for example, Arthur Calhoun suggested that to a working wife "children are an embarrass-ment and interfere with a career, hence the tendency to avoid maternity."[32]

In 1926, Paul Popenoe, a eugenicist, linked working women to forces that were destroying the family. He urged that only middle-aged and handicapped women, and, possibly, "geniuses" be encouraged to work. Young girls should not be allowed to work lest they be taught to find "all good things of life

outside the scope of the home" and abandon marriage and motherhood. Young wives who had not yet had children should also be discouraged from employment, Popenoe maintained, for they might delay pregnancy, "and such postponement for more than a year is harmful, both mentally and physically."[33]

In fact, some studies found that college-educated women who were both married and working did have fewer children than did nonworking wives.[34] A 1927 study of Radcliffe graduates who were both married and employed showed that more than half of 243 women surveyed chose not to have any children. The average number of children for the group was 2.21 compared with from 3.35 to 4.32 for other college-educated mothers who did not work. The investigator concluded that these college-educated mothers who worked had fewer children than did other women of their class.[35]

Another contested issue was the impact of a woman's work on infant mortality and on the health of her children. Many people believed that women who worked before and after pregnancy damaged their health and so gave birth to fragile and sickly offspring. One Chamber of Commerce representative wrote in 1931 that married women in his city often chose to work in factories because of relatively higher wages. This was a cause, he suggested, "of the high infant mortality rate as the women work in the factories as long as possible prior to the birth of their children and return to the factory invariably within a month after the birth of a child and sometimes much sooner."[36]

The government conducted a number of studies examining the relationship of maternal employment to infant mortality in the 1910s. A Children's Bureau survey of Manchester, New Hampshire, in 1912 and 1913 revealed that the infant mortality rate—the number of infant deaths per thousand live births— rose when mothers worked during their pregnancy. The infant mortality rate for children of working mothers was 199.2 compared with 133.9 for unemployed mothers. Studies of Johnstown, Pennsylvania, and New Bedford, Massachusetts, found similar correlations.[37]

The Children's Bureau also argued that the employment of mothers after the birth of their children was linked to a higher death rate, and attributed this in part to the common practice of working mothers forgoing breast feeding in favor of nourishing their babies with infant formula or cow's milk. But the bureau cautioned that these correlations between employment and mortality did not necessarily imply causality. Equally important factors were the low wages of fathers and overcrowded, unsanitary housing conditions.[38] In these and other studies, the evidence mustered against the employment of mothers was drawn from studies of destitute and working-class women; the conditions of poverty that drove these women to the workplace were therefore the conditions under which their children died.

All classes of married women, however, were subject to questions about the child-rearing practices of employed women. The mother's role was changing. Whereas in the nineteenth century a mother's duty was to instill moral attributes of faith and "good character" into her progeny, now her duty was to shape the psychological well-being of her child.[39] In the progressive era there developed a new emphasis on efficiency and expertise in child rearing. An ideology of "educated motherhood" stressed the importance of scientific insight over maternal instinct in the nation's nurseries.[40] Child nurture became a topic of national import, as childhood development research centers and kindergartens proliferated, reflecting a recognition of the importance of the early years of life on later adult behavior.

The role of the mother in this era was to steer her children through the dangerous psychological shoals of infancy and childhood. Both proponents and opponents of the employment of married women acknowledged that childhood had become increasingly complex, with new needs for socialization and training. Anna Garlin Spencer's tally of a mother's duty held that a mother's role was to provide protection, care, shelter, and food for her offspring; to drill them in personal habits and in such skills as walking and talking; and to instill "preliminary training toward social order and social welfare."[41]

The standard text on child rearing in this era was John B. Watson's *Psychological Care of Infant and Child*, a behaviorist tract that advocated a rigorous regimen of activity for young children. Watson proposed strict schedules for care, discipline, and play: "Once a child's character has been spoiled by bad handling, which can be done in a few days, who can say that the damage is ever repaired?"[42] The mother, particularly if she worked, faced more demands on her time at home now than previously.

Those who discouraged wives from working believed that women could not possibly have time to both work and raise their children properly. The Children's Bureau contended that the children of working mothers suffered in various ways. These children, the bureau claimed, did less well in school than did their peers with mothers at home; these children had more behavior problems and sustained "the strain of the mother, the untidy homes, and the pressure of housework left to them to do."[43] Willystine Goodsell, a social scientist, noted that "a woman cannot be employed nine hours a day . . . and at the same time maintain a clean, well-ordered home and give intelligent care and oversight to her children."[44]

Although the conservative solution to the problem was for mothers to remain at home, feminists suggested that family structure should change to ease the burden of household responsibilities for women. And some, like

Goodsell, also suggested that a mother's absence from home could even be beneficial. Some psychologists in the 1920s warned against the formation of "mother-fixation" in children—a condition in which a mother, overly absorbed in the lives of her offspring, created spoiled children and made "the upbuilding in a child of an independent personality difficult, if not impossible."[45]

As the mother's role within the home had come to rest almost entirely on meeting the emotional needs of her family, her role had become double-edged. Her employment outside the home might result in the neglect of her children. On the other hand, by having an outside interest she might "relieve the child of the dangerous role of being the recipient of boundless love and anxiety."[46] As we shall see, this theme continued in the postwar period when the mother, whether working or not, was blamed for anything less than perfection in her children.

At issue also was not only a working wife's absence from the home but her presence in the marketplace. Feminists maintained that the lack of productive activity by housewives constituted a loss for society. In 1921, Elizabeth Kemper Adams, in a study for the Women's Educational and Industrial Union, reported a "deepening conviction" that "in order to bring up children to be intelligent citizens and workers, both parents alike must be intelligent citizens and workers themselves." A woman's obligation, she argued, was not only to her own children but also to the community at large.[47] In 1926, Willystine Goodsell asked, "Who can say that our tens of thousands of educated wives and mothers have nothing to offer by way of meeting . . . human needs; or that their work in managing a small household and rearing two or three children constitutes the full job of a lifetime, enlisting all their capabilities?"[48] No less a figure than Eleanor Roosevelt concurred. In 1933, Roosevelt argued that although a married woman's first duty was to her home, that did not "of necessity preclude her having another occupation" and contributing her talents to society. Full-time motherhood was enough for many women, she stated, but for others the sole role of "nurse and governess" was insufficient.[49]

But others were not convinced that the social benefits of the employment of married women outweighed the costs. Some argued that the work of wives took jobs from others who needed employment, including the by now acceptable self-supporting single women, and that since married women worked for "pin money," salaries were lowered.[50] Despite studies by the Women's Bureau, which earnestly attempted to disprove this thesis, business practice reflected the pin-money myth. Until 1917, no married women had been hired by the school board in Detroit. In 1921, the city of Highland Park, Michigan, discharged married women from city positions and barred the future hiring of single women, arguing that without the competition of cheap female labor,

men's wages would rise and permit the establishment of a "family wage" for the married man. In 1924, more than three-fourths of Minneapolis firms surveyed preferred to hire only single women as clerical workers. In 1928, a nationwide survey found that 60 percent of school boards did not hire married women as teachers.[51]

Public sentiment against the employment of married women sharpened during the economic depression of the 1930s. In 1930 and 1931, a National Education Association poll of 1,500 cities found that 77 percent of the school boards questioned did not employ wives as teachers, and half of the boards fired women who married while on the job. In 1930, the Massachusetts Commission on Unemployment Relief recommended that industrial and government organizations fire married women who lived with husbands who supported them, and replace these women with men or with single women. The New England Telephone Company, as a result, dismissed their married women workers. From 1932 to 1937, the federal government barred more than one member of a family from working in civil service positions—a policy that effectively functioned to keep married women off government payrolls.[52]

Public opinion during the 1930s favored these policies. In 1937, an American Institute of Public Opinion poll found that only 18 percent of those surveyed believed that a woman should work if she "has a husband capable of supporting her." A *Fortune Magazine* poll the previous year found only 15 percent believed wives should work full time outside the home; 35 percent stated that "woman's place is in the home"; 36 percent thought working women took jobs that otherwise could be filled by men; 21 percent maintained that nonworking mothers had healthier children and a happier home life; and 7 percent believed that the working wife brought down the standard of living because of the lower wages she received.[53]

Supporters of restrictive employment policies justified their position by arguing that they hoped to decrease the unemployment of single women and of men and to strengthen the traditional values of home life at the same time. In 1934, a businessman reported, "We do not employ any married women nor do we believe in it. Their place is in the home!"[54] The organization of Women in the Naval Reserve resolved that "every married woman who is holding a job, who has a husband earning enough to keep the family, should give up her job for six months or so that men can take jobs to support their families."[55]

Those who believed that wives should work, on the other hand, argued that married women contributed an essential proportion of family income and that discrimination against any one class of worker threatened ideals of democracy. In 1932, the National Association of Working Women was founded to combat the movement against the employment of married women. Discrimination,

they charged, was "only the beginning of an attempt to eliminate all women from the business and professional world" as well as a "sorry travesty upon freedom." In 1933, a proposal to eliminate all married women workers from the payroll of the Chesapeake and Ohio Railroad was dropped following protests from the National Business and Professional Women's Club.[56]

But during the depression, with its shortage of jobs, public opinion solidified against the employment of wives; most Americans firmly believed that the married woman should not work outside the home. This attitude persisted until 1940. A Women's Bureau investigation that year found that discrimination continued against married women in the work force of several large cities. In Los Angeles, banks and many business firms would not hire wives. In Kansas City, most oil and meat companies, as well as the public utilities, discriminated against married women. In Richmond, insurance offices, railroads, and wholesale establishments preferred hiring single women only, and one out of ten businesses surveyed summarily fired women if they married after they had been hired.[57]

The Working Mother during World War II

At the time that the United States entered World War II, the popular domestic ideology still prevailed over feminist proposals for social change. The Women's Bureau noted in 1941 that although the public recognized the need of paid work for widows and single women, it "still has to be convinced that married women have the right to work . . . and that they can work without harm being done to the home and to the working standards of men and women wage earners."[58] But the imperative need for labor caused by the military mobilization of the nation's men led the government to conduct a propaganda campaign aimed at convincing the public that wives could and should replace their husbands in factory and mill.[59] Yet even at the same time, this campaign appealed to those who valued women as preservers of the home, and although it eased the way for the employment of wives, it reinforced the ideology that mothers of young children should spurn employment.

Rosie the Riveter—the symbol of working women during the war years— appeared as a housewife in factory overalls in posters, magazine articles, and in such popular songs as "The Janes Who Make Planes," and "The Lady at Lockheed." She was expected to work for patriotic reasons and to support the war effort of the men in her life. She was just as strongly expected to gratefully trade in her factory goggles for an apron at war's end. The War Manpower Commission and the Office of War Information sold the idea of

work to married women by casting Rosie the Riveter as a housewife who worked temporarily in order to preserve domestic values. One government publication declared that women's primary instinct "has been, and still is, to cherish their greater interest in the protection of the home, the family, and the community."[60]

Many books and magazines emphasized the new sanction of work for married women. Some authors, such as the grandniece of Susan B. Anthony, continued the earlier theme that a woman could be productive outside the domestic sphere; Susan B. Anthony II argued that "the key to Victory in this war is the extraction of women—all women—from the relative unproductivity of the kitchen, and the enrolling of them in the high productivity of factory, office, and field."[61]

The propaganda campaign paid off, both in expanding the numbers of wives who kept factory assembly lines rolling and in changing the attitudes of the public. Whereas 82 percent of those surveyed in 1936 had disapproved of married women working, only six years later, in 1942, 60 percent of the respondents in a National Opinion Research Center poll believed that married women should work in war industries. Other wartime surveys also found the objection to working wives eased during the 1940s.[62]

But the new social sanction of the employment of married women was limited. Although wives without young children were urged to work, official policy, as articulated by the Manpower Commission, mandated that mothers of young children stay at home. "The first responsibility of women with young children," the commission stated in 1942, "in war as in peace, is to give suitable care in their own homes to their children."[63] The old arguments were advanced once again that there was no substitute for a mother at home.

During the war, these arguments centered on the problem of "latch-key" children—youngsters expected to fend for themselves after school until their mothers returned from work. The National Association of Day Nurseries, one of the organizations concerned with the latch-key child, stated in 1941 that maternal employment would result in unsupervised, underfed children ripe for the "breeding grounds [of] delinquency." The Children's Bureau agreed, contending in 1943 that working mothers were "a hazard to the security of the child in his family."[64]

Many women undoubtedly worked for patriotic reasons, but economic necessity still impelled other women to seek employment. A 1944 Women's Bureau survey found that 80 percent of the women working in war-related industries wanted to continue working after the war's end. Sixty-one percent of employed women surveyed by the American Institute of Public Opinion in 1945 planned to continue working after the war.[65] But appeals made to women

during the war foreshadowed the growth of the postwar "feminine mystique." "Because you are a wife as well as a working-woman you want something for the returning man as well as for yourself," the author of *So Your Husband's Gone to War!* reminded her readers in 1942. "And your most important job right now, you feel, is not necessarily entrenching your sex but keeping the home fires burning however you can."[66] The message was clear. The work of wives was a temporary necessity. When the soldiers came home, patriotism dictated that wives return their jobs to men and find in motherhood their major social role.

The Feminine Mystique, 1945–1960

In spite of this prescription, the employment rate of wives escalated dramatically in the years after the war. By 1950, we have seen, one in four married women worked. At the same time, the fertility rate was rising during the "baby boom" of the 1950s and 1960s. Hence the working wife was now more likely to be a working mother than previously. The rhetoric in the debate over women and work now occurred in a social context that had changed dramatically.

Proponents of the domestic ideology launched a virulent attack after the war, focusing on mothers who worked. In this foray, the battlefield was the nursery and the weapon psychological theory as sociologists and psychologists emphasized the relationship of a mother's employment to child neglect. The feminist voice was for the most part stilled, drowned out by the feminine mystique that grew to dominate popular opinion.[67] The working mother was roundly condemned for abandoning her place at home and for creating a nation of neurotic men and women.

A heightened emphasis on psychology after the war reflected the growth in the popularization of Freudian psychoanalytic theory in America.[68] Woman's transgression of her domestic role was viewed as a neurosis, a rejection of femininity. Earlier arguments that defended domesticity had been couched in the language of morality; now the language of psychology was put to work to defend the domestic prescription for women.

The popular dissemination of these psychological theories constituted what Betty Friedan has termed the "feminine mystique" of the postwar era. The mystique—a complex of popular attitudes about the feminine nature of women and the primacy of "nurturing maternal love"—was reflected in an outpouring of sentiment throughout American popular culture. As magazines, newspapers, books, and, later, television glorified the role of the housewife, the

feminist perspective of earlier times was all but forgotten. "As swiftly as in a dream," Friedan observed, "the image of the American woman as a changing, growing individual in a changing world was shattered. . . . Her limitless world shrunk to the cozy walls of home."[69]

The most strident articulation of this mystique was Ferdinand Lundberg's and Marynia Farnham's notorious 1947 book, *Modern Woman: The Lost Sex.* This antifeminist tome went through six printings in one year and reached a wide audience through extensive publicity in newspapers, magazines, and textbooks. The authors contended that women, dissatisfied with their domestic role, were transmitting their confusion to their children, thus disrupting social order. Women had been unduly swayed by feminist proposals for careers, feminism being "at its core a deep illness" that encouraged women to assume the male traits of aggression, dominance, independence, and power. The "masculinization" of women, the authors warned, represented "enormously dangerous consequences to the home, the children . . . dependent on it, and to the ability of the woman, as well as her husband, to obtain sexual gratification." And if this were not enough, for the children of mothers who had rejected or were ambivalent about their domestic duties, a sense of confusion and abandonment was inevitable.[70]

The ideal woman, the authors proposed, was a "fully maternal" woman who "accepted her femininity" and understood that the phrase "independent woman" was a contradiction in terms. The working wife thus failed in her psychologically appointed task. Lundberg and Farnham cautioned that the masculinized strivings of women careerists should be minimized so that a woman's "femininity" would be available for the satisfaction of herself, her husband, and her children.[71]

The idea that "anatomy was destiny" and that gender roles were biologically determined was repeatedly advanced by social scientists in this period. Eric Dingwall, a British anthropologist, criticized those who claimed otherwise. "To maintain, as Margaret Mead does, that when women 'can act by choice rather than by necessity' they will be content, is to engage in that favorite feminine pastime of crying for the moon," he argued. "Indeed, it is precisely to the minimization of the biological factor of female life that we can ascribe so much of the growing lack of satisfaction among the women of so many lands, and above all of the United States."[72] This "growing lack of satisfaction" was often cited as a result of feminist proposals that offered women a choice of roles at a time when social conditions did not support that choice. When women were unhappy and ambivalent about their lives within the home, the possible result, critics claimed, was the overprotection of their children.[73]

Feminists in the 1920s had suggested that women confined to the domestic

role might raise children with unhealthy "mother fixations." In the postwar period, charges of "momism" blamed women unhappy with their domestic duties for the neuroses of their children, particularly of their sons.[74] Dingwall maintained that American mothers were responsible for the demasculinization of their sons and for the creation of infantile "boys" rather than strong, independent men. The American mother, he commented, "is not at all anxious to see her sons exhibit too many of the male characteristics, which may remind her of her own deficiencies and thus tend to deflate her assertive personality."[75] Dingwall cited the findings of Dr. E. A. Strecker, a psychiatrist who consulted for the United States War Department. Strecker held that the large numbers of neurotic soldiers in the American army during the war stemmed from the behavior of mothers who had smothered their sons with too much love.[76] Lundberg and Farnham similarly censured mothers for being overaffectionate or domineering, claiming that these women played out tendencies of penis envy by thwarting the lives of their sons.[77]

At the same time, the working mother was presented as a source of disintegrating family life. In a well-known textbook on child development published in 1948, James Bossard placed his discussion of working mothers in a chapter entitled "Families under Stress." The social costs of a mother's decision to work, he claimed, included tired women and lonely, neglected, and unsupervised children. Other studies suggested that working mothers were more likely to have children who were delinquent because they were neglected and resentful, or because the children had fathers who were overly strict because of the mother's absence from home.[78]

Although the mother, and especially the working mother, was blamed on all sides for a variety of social ills, there was some recognition in this period that the antifeminist case was overstated. Some social scientists were beginning to question the imperative of biological determinism, finding that personality formation was shaped in part by the environment. Gender qualities were the result of social conditioning rather than of innate characteristics.[79] Mirra Komarovsky was one of those rejecting the thesis that a woman's discontent was the result of individual maladjustment. She argued instead that female role ambivalence resulted from the sharp conflicts caused by the differing expectations of education, career, and marriage.[80] Other researchers suggested that the question of the working mother was individual and dependent upon the needs of specific women and their children.[81] But the defense of the widening of "woman's sphere," and the relativistic view of qualities of gender, were overshadowed by the feminine mystique.

The mystique was reinforced by studies in the psychology of child development that stressed the importance of consistent mothering for infants

and young children. These studies condemned working mothers for causing trauma in children left without maternal care for even a short part of the day. John Bowlby, in 1950, presented a seminal study to the World Health Organization on the subject of deprivation of maternal care in children. His investigation of young inmates in such institutions as hospitals and orphanages led him to conclude that "deprivation of mother-love in early childhood can have a far-reaching effect on the mental health and personality development of human beings." Bowlby stated that young children required a continuous relationship with one person—a mother or mother-substitute—for both the child's and the mother's well-being. He wrote, "The provision of constant attention day and night, seven days a week and 365 in the year, is possible only for a woman who derives profound satisfaction from seeing her child grow from babyhood . . . to become an independent man or woman, and knows that it is her care which has made this possible."[82] Bowlby enlisted as examples of family failure those families that were "broken up and therefore not functioning" because of the full-time employment of the mother. When the child did not have the full care of a mother, he or she was thus considered a victim of "maternal deprivation."[83]

Bowlby's findings of the trauma caused by extreme maternal deprivation were generalized by other scholars to include children who experienced "partial maternal deprivation" when their mothers worked. Subsequent studies suggested that a phenomenon of "attachment" of an infant to its mother required continuous interaction of mother and child. The regular removal of a mother from the home for even part of the day, critics claimed, interfered with the attachment process and snapped important bonds between mother and child that were crucial for the formation of trust, stability, and cognitive development.[84]

These arguments rose to dominate the debate about women and work at a time when more married women than ever before were working outside the home. The working mother was now labeled a neurotic or, worse, a cause of neurosis in her children. Public opinion again reflected the feminine mystique and turned to support the concept of a one wage-earner family and the domestic ideology.

The Resurgence of Feminism, 1960–1980

After 1960, a new wave of feminism reopened the case for the working mother. In 1963, Betty Friedan reminded the American public of the feminist position with her best-selling book, *The Feminine Mystique*: "We can

no longer ignore that voice within women that says: 'I want something more than my husband, my children, and my home.'" Friedan insisted that employment was needed to insure fulfillment for women:

> Who knows what women can be when they are finally free to be themselves? . . . Who knows of the possibilities of love when men and women share not only children, home, and garden, not only the fulfillment of their biological roles, but the responsibilities and passions of the work that creates the human future and full human knowledge of who they are? It has barely begun, the search of women for themselves. But the time is at hand when the voices of the feminine mystique can no longer drown out the inner voice that is driving women on to become complete.[85]

Friedan's call for women's liberation from the ideology of domesticity was echoed in a surge of sentiment applauding the employment of women, whether married or single. The 1960s and 1970s saw the publication of hundreds of books in sociology, psychology, and other fields urging that women be given a full range of choices that included both marriage and career.[86]

Many scholars focused on the effect on family life of a wife's employment. A 1963 study, for example, found that when wives worked, husbands helped more with household tasks, and wives gained a stronger say in major economic decisions.[87] Social scientists also increasingly challenged concepts of masculinity and femininity, stating that social conditions, rather than innate sexual qualities, had the greater bearing on gender behavior.[88]

Several of the postwar studies proclaiming the damage done by a mother's employment were also questioned in this period. Bowlby's findings about the need for uninterrupted and exclusive mothering, for example, were challenged by scholars such as Margaret Mead, who suggested that "multiple mothering" was possible.[89] Others attacked the earlier studies on maternal deprivation for unsupported claims of causality. Lois Meek Stoltz, a psychologist, surveyed the literature on maternal employment and concluded that "one can say almost anything one desires about the children of employed mothers and support the statement by some research study."[90] The head of the Children's Bureau, Katherine Brownell Oettinger, similarly found that factors such as the temperament of mother and child, and the motivations for and conditions of a woman's work, were important considerations in the assessment of maternal employment. "Other things being equal," she stated, "we think few mothers with children under six, and fewer mothers with children under three, are able to carry a full-time job and also fill the needs of their children in these crucial and vulnerable early years. But other things are not always equal. Therefore

the qualifications and the need to discuss them."[91] The fourth edition of Bossard's textbook on child development came out in 1966, and in it the earlier stance against the working mother was eased. The working mother was no longer portrayed as a symptom of family stress but as a possible benefit to family life. If wives worked, they and their husbands might "both have a greater appreciation of each other's roles," the textbook stated. "The children see them as a unity of parents with roles that are tightly interlocked."[92]

The feminist ideology reverberated throughout American society, influencing changes in government policy. In 1964, the United States Congress added the word "sex" to Title VII of the Civil Rights Bill, prohibiting discrimination in employment on the basis of race, color, religion, and national origin. Organizations such as the National Organization for Women, founded in 1966, and the Women's Equity Action League, founded in 1969, strove to combat employment discrimination against women.[93]

Public opinion had begun to reflect to some degree the changing work practices of women. In 1936, only 18 percent of those surveyed in a Gallup poll agreed that married women should work, but forty years later, in 1976, 68 percent approved of working women, even of those who had husbands who could support them.[94] However, this shift in values was tempered by a countermovement. Opponents of feminism were as insistent in their views as were feminists in theirs in the 1970s. A best-selling book of 1974, *The Total Woman*, was a tract advocating once again that the fulfillment of a woman could only be found in the wholehearted embrace of the role of wife and mother.[95]

Moreover, the 1970s witnessed a new twist in the class argument against working married women. In 1978, a *Wall Street Journal* article suggested that the increased work rate of middle- and upper-income wives was in part responsible for the widening of the gap between rich and poor. The *Journal* cited economist Lester Thurow's statement that "if males who earn high incomes are married to women who could earn high incomes in a perfectly fair and liberated world, then women's liberation will make the distribution of income more unequal." Once again, the class issue of women and work surfaced, as the work of married women who had to earn a salary to help support their families was contrasted with the work of women who chose employment for personal as well as economic reasons.[96]

In general, however, the debate in the 1970s narrowed to the troubling problem of employment for mothers of very young children. Psychologist Selma Fraiberg, in *Every Child's Birthright*, contended in 1977 that children under the age of three required uninterrupted caretaking from one person, preferably the mother, because human development rested on the quality of

first attachments. The lack of adequate opportunities for day care, she implied, meant that most mothers of infants should not work outside the home. In 1978, Jerome Kagan, also a psychologist, countered that the early experience of childhood was not as important a factor in personality development as some persons believed; implicitly, then, a mother's duty to stay home during the infancy of her child was not as great an imperative.[97]

By the beginning of the 1980s, the changing social and economic behavior of women, and the changing ideological debate over female employment, had contributed to a widening of the idea of "woman's proper place." First single women, then wives, and then mothers of school-aged children were, in a sense, freed from social constraints against work outside the home. For each of these groups, wage labor was at one time controversial and debatable, but eventually employment became a socially acceptable—and even expected— act. But the mother of young children was left at the core of the debate over women and work. Whether her participation in the labor force would also become acceptable rather than problematic would depend on the success or failure of proposals for the care of her children.

Chapter 6
The Working Mother
and the Social Order

We have seen that the discovery of "respectable" single women workers in the late nineteenth century led to a heated debate over future motherhood, which in turn sparked a variety of reforms meant to extend domestic influences, improve the work environment, and control the impact of social change. At the same time, these reforms, by providing such services as housing, acknowledged de facto that the "place" of the single woman was now the labor force as well as the home, at least before marriage. The increased employment of married women in the twentieth century similarly provoked public controversy, this time about the nature of motherhood itself.

In contrast to the working-girl controversy, the working-mother controversy engendered by changing labor force demographics was not the primary motivator for social policy. Rather, policies enacted for the care of children of poor mothers before 1920 influenced later policies and reforms that arose because of the growing numbers of working mothers of all classes later in the twentieth century. As yet, society has remained ambivalent about the movement of mothers from home to work. The identification of day care as a class issue and the lack of quality day-care opportunities has combined with the retrenchment of the domestic ideology to insure that the working mother of young children still retains her controversial status.

The public consensus is that the full weight of child care should fall upon the shoulders of the mother alone, but it has been tempered by factors of class and race. That is, the exception to the rule that mothers not work outside the home has historically been the poor, unmarried, or widowed mother, whose employment has for the most part been seen as a preferable alternative to her economic dependency on the state. Hence a tension has developed in the philosophy of day care between the ideals of reluctant charity or social service.

Before discussing the public response to the working mother after 1920, then, we must first look back to those events during the "era of the working girl" which also concerned the working mother. In that time, child-care ser-

vices first became defined as a charitable response to the needs of widows with dependent children rather than as a social service for parents who worked.

The Widow and Her "Half-Orphans" before 1920: Forerunners of Modern Policy

In the nineteenth and early twentieth centuries, the only working mothers who attracted public attention were widows or the desperately poor. "Respectable" single women were at the forefront of the debate over women and work, but still the older employed mother was also a beneficiary of the reform impulse. In sharp contrast to the single woman worker, however, what is most notable about this group of workers is their constancy over time. That is, although the proportion of single women in the female labor force rose markedly during the era of the working girl, and although the proportion of married women and mothers in the labor force similarly rose during the era of the working mother, the proportions of widowed and divorced women in the female labor force has remained relatively constant. Of all workers in the female labor force in 1890, 18 percent were widows, while 14 percent were widows in 1970. Moreover, while widows, like all groups of women, increased their relative numbers in the female labor force during the last century, still this increase has been at a much lower rate than that of both married and single women.

It was not, then, an increase in numbers that sparked the concern to reform conditions for working mothers. Rather, the social and cultural conditions that contributed to the public concern for working girls also contributed, at least in part, to a concern with their older and poorer sisters. But whereas the reforms for the working girl diminished as her dominance in the female labor force declined, the reforms for the working mother were maintained, even as the identity of the working mother was changing. In short, policies shaped by the early twentieth century which meant to help the destitute widow were still being used by mid-century—a time when the working mother was no longer a poor and minor segment of the female labor force but was instead a member of the fastest-growing group in the American labor force as a whole.

In the nineteenth century, the common response to the plight of the working mother was public charity. Reforms for widows were engineered not only to meet the moral and physical needs of dependent children, but also to meet the perceived moral needs of the women themselves.

The children of working mothers in the early twentieth century were cared

for in a haphazard fashion at best. Most school-aged children received their primary care during the day from teachers; after school they looked after themselves, although occasionally working mothers sent their offspring to supervised programs at settlement houses, churches, and libraries. Generally, mothers believed that if children were old enough to dress themselves, make their own meals, and avoid being run over in the street, they were old enough to fend for themselves.

Despite the contention of middle-class reformers that even school-aged children required constant supervision for both physical and moral well-being, many working-class mothers believed otherwise. In 1918, for example, only 5 percent of the children of mothers who worked in the Chicago stockyards attended day nurseries; 40 percent received no care at all; and the rest were left to the "slight supervision" of night-working or disabled fathers, or neighbors. "The mothers of these children do not feel the need of a day nursery," the investigators concluded, "for as soon as a child can minister to his physical needs, he is considered fit to be left [alone]."[1]

Similarly, in Philadelphia in 1918, more than a third of the children aged from five to sixteen in the families of working mothers had no formal supervision after school. Infants and younger children were for the most part tended by relatives in their own homes, or watched over by neighbors. Some 82 percent of the young children of working mothers surveyed on the west side of New York City in 1914, and more than two-thirds of these children in Philadelphia in 1918, received this type of informal home day care.[2]

Occasionally a desperate mother would lock her children alone in the house as she left for work, sometimes asking a neighbor to "keep an eye" on them. These were the children whose condition most concerned reformers. Samuel Royce argued in 1877 that employment led the poor mother into such practices as "dosing the children with narcotic cordials . . . if not to shutting them up between cheerless walls, or converting them through this isolation . . . into semi-idiots."[3] In 1910, Jane Addams told the National Conference of Charities and Correction the story of a widowed scrubwoman, who locked three children in her tenement rooms as she left for work each day. When their constant wailing led to an eviction notice, Addams reported, the mother left the windows open, hoping the children would fall to their deaths.[4] Gwendolyn Hughes told the story of a Polish widow who left three children under the age of six locked up in her tenement home when she worked. The neighbor who sporadically checked up on the children could not prevent such tragedies as the scalding of the child who ignited a fire with coal oil.[5] Reformers, fearing for the safety of the children of working mothers, labeled these children "half-orphans" and considered them subject to public pity and public benevolence.

A common response to the plight of the widowed mother was the provision of limited "outdoor relief"—the donation of cords of wood, boxes of used clothing, and, occasionally, envelopes of money from philanthropists, churches, and city charity groups.[6] But the charity community agreed that too much help would demoralize the recipient and encourage the vice of pauperism. Oscar McCullogh, a minister, warned the 1888 gathering of charity workers that, at most, widows should receive loans, for "when the woman has tasted the bitter and poison bread of public relief, it is only the beginning of moral, physical, and intellectual death."[7]

CHILD REMOVAL

Removal of the child from the home was the most extreme remedy for the destitute mother, who faced no alternative but the starvation of her children. Many families relied on the help of kin, "putting out" their children with those relatives who were more able to care for them. Katherine Anthony reported that many women in her study of the west side of New York City claimed to have been raised by their aunts.[8] When family aid was unavailable, desperate mothers turned to the state.

In the early nineteenth century, destitute mothers sometimes committed their children to the local almshouse, where the children languished with a mix of other dependents, including the insane. Reformers argued that this proximity of innocent children to unstable adults would corrupt the children, and so they advocated the development of such specialized institutions as orphanages. By the latter part of the century, charity organizations or courts would commonly remand a dependent child to an orphanage, or pay the cost of support in a foster home.[9]

Many of the inmates in children's homes were "half-orphans"—the children of destitute, separated, divorced, or widowed parents. One charity worker reported as typical the case of Mary Morson, a stonecutter's widow, who supported seven children in New York City by scrubbing floors and doing piecework. When she failed to make ends meet in 1912, she turned four of her children over to the St. Rachel Orphan Asylum, and the city of New York paid $38.57 monthly for their upkeep.[10]

Thousands of "half-orphans" were cared for in this way through the early twentieth century. In Ohio, from 1867 to 1898, of 17,133 children resident in county children's homes, only six percent were orphans; the rest were the children of widowed, destitute, divorced, or otherwise incapacitated parents.[11] Nationally, in 1904, the Census Bureau found more than 3,000 children in orphan asylums, and another 50,000 in foster homes at state expense; many of

these were the children of widows.[12] In New York in 1913, nearly 1,000 children were committed to orphanages because their widowed mothers were ill; an additional 2,716 were committed—like the children of Mary Morson—because of the poverty of their families.[13]

The institutionalization of the children of the married woman worker was much rarer. Of the New York mothers surveyed in 1914, only 7 percent "put away" their offspring—half were sent to institutions and half to relatives. In Philadelphia in 1918, 4 percent of the children of working mothers surveyed were cared for away from home.[14] Most working-class mothers abhorred the possibility that their children might be separated from them. As Anthony noted, their attitude was shaped by fear and suspicion, for, she asked, "What were they working for, if not to keep the home together?"[15]

Most reformers, too, decried the institutionalization of children, arguing that separation of mother and child was unnatural, that their upkeep was expensive to the public, and that separation made children unfit for their later roles as workers. Anthony cited the problems that institutionalized children experienced in later years when they were returned home. "Fresh from an environment which has deprived him of even a normal sense of property," she stated, "often the institution child doesn't know how to handle money or count change—he is thrust into industry and wage earning. The little autocratic world he has left did not train him in responsibility, but now he must suddenly assume it."[16]

Because institutional life was so criticized, many dependent children were sent instead to foster homes. Charles Loring Brace marshaled the movement of city children to country homes in the late nineteenth century; children were also sent to foster parents in cities. But this solution too was inadequate; often the children were little more than indentured servants, and reformers bewailed the lack of screening of foster parents. The secretary of the Minnesota State Board of Charities observed the placement of children sent to rural Minnesota by the New York Children's Aid Society from 1883 to 1885. He reported:

> The children arrived at about half-past three p.m. and were taken directly from the train to the Court House, where a large crowd was gathered. Mr. Matthews set the children, one by one, before the company, and in his stentorian voice gave a brief account of each. Applicants for children were then admitted in order behind the railing and rapidly made their selection. Then, if the child gave assent, the bargain was concluded on the spot. . . . I know that the Committee consented to some assignments against their better judgement.[17]

The separation of children from their mothers became controversial in the nineteenth century. However, another remedy was suggested that would partially solve the problem for the family faced with the separation dilemma. The subsidized day nursery, it was observed, would provide a family environment for the children of working-class mothers at the same time that it allowed the mother to retain primary responsibility for the upbringing and financial support of her children. It would do no less than stand "for the preservation and maintenance of the home."[18]

THE DAY NURSERY

Day nurseries were based on the models of the French *crèche* of the 1840s and on the infant school of early nineteenth-century America. Both institutions were intended to permit mothers to work while their children were being taught middle-class values. The first day nurseries were established before the Civil War. In Boston, a day nursery was formed in 1828; in New York, a children's hospital opened a day nursery for the children of wet nurses and former patients in 1854. But the growth of the day-nursery movement was slow; by 1880, only six were recorded in the United States.[19]

The concept of the day nursery gradually caught on, mostly in the large cities of the East Coast. The Chicago World's Fair of 1893 further spurred the acceptance of the day nursery, as some 10,000 children of visitors to the fair were cared for in a model day-nursery exhibit.[20] By 1897, there were 175 nurseries reported to the Census Bureau; by 1912, the National Federation of Day Nurseries had records for some 500 institutions.[21]

Advocates of the day nursery acknowledged that widowed mothers would often have to work. These reformers sought to provide an alternative to the institutionalization of children who would otherwise have no supervision during the day. The philosophy of the philanthropic day nursery was set forth by Josephine Jewell Dodge. She was related to Grace Hoadley Dodge, who had spearheaded many of the reforms for the single woman worker. Josephine Dodge established the Jewell Day Nursery in New York City in 1888, organized the first conference on day nurseries in 1892, and formed the National Federation of Day Nurseries in 1898. She was the archetypical moral entrepreneur, who believed that her mission was to bring middle-class values to the working class. The day nursery, as Josephine Dodge saw it, would be an instrument of moral nurture as well as of charity.[22]

According to Dodge, the day nursery would protect mothers from the evils of total dependency, protect children from the evils of neglect, and save

society from unsupervised children who were a "serious menace to the state." It would provide an alternative to leaving the care of children in unsatisfactory hands, such as under the supervision of brothers and sisters, incapacitated fathers, or, worst of all, male lodgers whose "evil traits" might be "intensified by long periods of idleness." Dodge and her followers claimed the day nursery would be, in sum, a superior "second home" for children that would not only provide skillful care but would also save the state the costs of institutionalization. As Marjory Hall, of the National Federation of Day Nurseries, stated in about 1904, the advent of the day nursery meant that the cry "put away the children" was far less often heard.[23]

Early day nurseries were careful to screen their clients, preferring to serve the needs of destitute widows rather than married women. Most nurseries sent "friendly visitors" to investigate applicants to insure that home situations were of the most desperate kind. The proper case, one charity worker stated, was the child who was "necessarily homeless" during the day. "I say *necessarily* because I wish to exclude from my definition those cases where the mother works from a mere whim or the desire to have a little more in the way of dress or furniture or even money saved, or for any reason wishes to shirk the care of her children," she wrote. "This is to be condemned when it causes her to neglect her home duties. The mother's place is in the home, except in cases of absolute necessity."[24] Some nurseries required proof that the children had been born to married women. The nursery in Buffalo, New York, for example, claimed this was necessary because of the "sensitivity" of the mothers who patronized the nursery. Once a mother got past the friendly visitors, she was to pay a small fee, usually five cents a day, in order to "sustain . . . dignity and a sense of independence."[25]

Commonly the nurseries, set up in converted houses or brownstones, were open from seven in the morning until seven at night to children of all ages, including infants. Upon being dropped off at the nursery in the morning, the young children were usually bathed, fed, and dressed in clean clothes or nursery pinafores; older children arrived during lunch times or after school. Daily activities, supervised by a matron, included lessons in moral precepts, domestic training, religious instruction, singing, and play; a few of the more progressive nurseries taught "order and discipline" using the methods of the kindergarten pioneer Friedrich Froebel. In some nurseries, tickets were distributed for good behavior and punctuality, and redeemed for clothing.[26]

The child would be taught through these routines the virtues of cleanliness of body and spirit, according to day-nursery officials. In 1900, the National Federation of Day Nurseries stated, "If these children can be taught from

infancy to be physically and morally clean, to eat proper food in an approved manner, to adopt our customs and our language, they will become a power for good; otherwise, like many who have developed under less favorable influences, they will fill up our hospitals, our homes for dependents, and our penal institutions."[27] The lessons learned, however, were strongly flavored with a dollop of class expectations. The federation noted that training should make children "useful and desirable" from an economic standpoint, and it suggested that children be given lessons in sewing and domestic service to "equip them for their station in life."[28]

Mothers, too, were to benefit from the largesse of the day-nursery workers. Nursery advocates were careful to stress that their charity did not absolve the mother of her "divinely appointed responsibility"; some nurseries guarded the "homemaking habit" by requiring that mothers stay home one day a week besides Sunday. On the other hand, many nurseries provided employment services, finding women jobs as scrubwomen or laundresses.[29]

The day nursery often tried to influence the mother in even more overt ways. At the Buffalo Fitch Creche, a mother was allowed to visit the nursery and absorb some of its influence only after a matron's investigation determined she was "clean." Many nurseries offered mothers classes in child care, thrift, sewing, and nutrition, hoping to teach them to "come to know something of the little decencies of life . . . [but] above all else . . . to be self-supporting, self-reliant, and self-respecting."[30]

Moreover, by visiting the nurseries, mothers came under the goodly influence of the matron, a personage who aspired to represent "all that is motherly and good" to children and "wisdom and power" to mothers. The nurseries also encouraged temperance; the Buffalo nursery, for example, offered tea to mothers picking up their children at night, hoping to discourage stops at the "grog shop" on the way home.[31]

The day nurseries did not have a large influence on the lives of working women in this era. Anthony found that only 3 percent of the mothers in her study used the nurseries in 1914; Hughes found that only 12 percent of the working mothers in Philadelphia in 1918 patronized them. There simply were not enough nurseries to meet the demand. Of the 166 day nurseries recorded by the Census Bureau in 1904, 113 were located in only four states—Massachusetts, New Jersey, New York, and Pennsylvania. The nurseries were overcrowded and understaffed. At the Kensington Day Nursery in Philadelphia in 1891, for instance, up to fifty children at a time were tended by a matron, nurse, cook, and housemaid.[32]

Furthermore, some mothers may have chosen not to use the nurseries because of rigid rules and regulations, or because they disliked being labeled

as subjects for charity. Katherine Anthony reported a conflict between the mothers and the administrators of a New York nursery in 1914:

> The women regard the day nursery as a type of institution, and as such distrust it. It must be said that the attitude of the management too often shows the strain of autocracy with which we are prone to dilute our charity. At one nursery, the hotheaded Irish mothers were always getting their baby carriages mixed and then squabbling over them. Righteously indignant, the management finally forbade them to leave their go-carts at the nursery any longer. This severe ruling made it necessary for the mother either to carry a heavy child to the nursery in her arms or to let him walk too far on his unsteady legs, for it was impossible for her to return the go-cart to her home and get to work on time.[33]

Many mothers turned to a less formal kind of day care. Hughes noted in her Philadelphia study that many women took their children to neighbors and paid for their supervision. One widow, for instance, sent her two children to a neighbor and paid $3.00 weekly for their board. The neighbor claimed that this payment was inadequate for the price of food, but added, "We got to help each other."[34]

Less benevolent were the nurseries run by women for profit. The number of proprietary day nurseries is unknown, but charity workers often criticized the unhealthy conditions in which children were tended. According to historian Leslie Tentler, a Children's Bureau field-worker reported that in some nurseries in Cleveland in 1918, "one woman occupying four dark, poorly ventilated rooms was crowding into them thirty and forty children each day; another was caring for twelve children in equally bad surroundings; a third who had less than a tenth vision was caring for eight children whom she had the habit of shutting behind two locked doors on the second floor while she did her marketing. In all these places the food was sent by the mothers and was given cold."[35] Even in the charitable nurseries abuses were common. Critics cited unsanitary conditions, too few attendants for the number of children, and, occasionally, total lack of supervision.[36]

Other critics leveled further charges against day nurseries, claiming that their services encouraged married mothers, whose proper place was in the home, to work. Although widows were the desired group of clients, in practice other women also used nursery services. The New York Association of Day Nurseries found that nearly two-thirds of its clients were married women; only 17 percent were widows, and 20 percent were women whose husbands had deserted them.[37] For those dissatisfied with the remedies of the day nursery and the boarding out of children, another solution seemed more appropriate.

Instead of spending charitable and public funds on substitute care for children outside their homes, a growing number of charity workers endorsed the concept of "subsidized motherhood" through the meting out of mothers' pensions.

MOTHERS' PENSIONS

Charity workers had for some time argued that the goals of preserving the home were undercut when funds were paid to foster mothers, institutions, or day nurseries to care for children of mothers who worked because of destitution. They opposed the long-held view that a mother must work if no other family support was available. In 1888, one charity worker suggested that "benevolent individuals" take on the task of funding mothers to stay in their own homes; in 1910, the Jewish Charities of Chicago provided money to "board children" with their own mothers. Funding mothers to stay at home and care for their own children was increasingly proposed as a method to safeguard traditional family life.[38]

In 1909, President Theodore Roosevelt called the first Conference on the Care of Dependent Children, a gathering that resulted in the founding of the Children's Bureau of the Department of Labor and in the wholehearted advocacy of pensions for mothers. The National Congress of Mothers—later the National Congress of Parents and Teachers—took up the banner of subsidizing motherhood as an alternative to both the boarding out of children and the employment of mothers outside the home.[39] Missouri passed the first state pension law in 1911, providing cash assistance to qualified mothers in Jackson County, which included Kansas City. The idea spread rapidly. By 1915, twenty-three states adopted mothers' pension laws; by 1935, all but two states provided aid for dependent children.[40]

Most of the state pension laws specified that recipients be widowed or deserted women, or wives of men unable to work because of imprisonment or mental or physical disability. Children were considered to be dependent up to ages ranging from 14 to 18 and would under most state laws receive from $5.00 to $15.00 a month. In addition, most states had "suitable home" provisions; a mother was to be judged morally worthy before receiving state aid. In Kansas City, for example, the law stipulated that "the mother must, in the judgement of the juvenile court, be a proper person, morally, physically and mentally, for the bringing up of her children."[41] Pension officers could intervene in a family's private life to assure that a suitable home prevailed. Routine interviews with neighbors and relatives were meant to scout out such unacceptable behavior as the keeping of male boarders, sexual activity, or even

"laziness." Besides immoral behavior, illness—particularly tuberculosis—and undesirable housing were also grounds for pension disqualification.[42]

In New York, the Commission on Relief for Widowed Mothers advocated the following principles as guidelines for a state pension law:

1. The mother is the best guardian of her children.
2. Poverty is too big a problem for private philanthropy.
3. No woman, save in exceptional circumstances, can be both the home-maker and the bread-winner of her family.
4. Preventive work, to be successful, must concern itself with the child and the home.
5. Normal family life is the foundation of the state, and its conservation an inherent duty of government.

The commission found that the work available to poor women "inevitably breaks down the physical, mental and moral strength" of the family by causing a low standard of living and parental neglect, which led to the delinquency and backwardness of children. Because other remedies for the problem of the working mother were thought to be failures, the commission recommended the immediate enactment of state aid for the dependent children of widowed mothers.[43]

Mothers' pensions were to be a panacea for delinquency of children deprived of a mother's care. Merrit Pinckney, a judge for the Chicago juvenile court, argued in 1912 that overworked and underpaid mothers were at best poor guardians for their children. "Many of these unfortunate children who never had a decent chance," he contended, "grow up into a depraved manhood and womanhood and drift naturally into that great and ever increasing army of criminals who are a menace to society."[44] Another reformer argued that the "lack of a mother's hand" led children to roam the streets and fall into bad company.[45] More affirmatively, some progressive reformers saw the mothers' aid movement as a way to rear useful citizens for the future.[46]

But mothers, too, were to profit from the pension system. Women were believed to be imperiled if their relationship with their children was inadequate. A judge in 1912 described the "otherwise fit" mother who worked because of poverty and was forced to board her children away from home. She was, he said, heartbroken and alone, "her children widely separated, not only from her but from each other. . . . [W]eakened now, mentally and physically and morally, by the ruthless tearing of maternal heart-strings, where will her footsteps tend to lead . . . ? Will she survive the test and continue to lead an honest, upright life, or will she drift along the line of least resistance, ending in

the brothel or in the madhouse?"[47] A similar view was expressed by charity workers concerned with the fate of unmarried mothers. The Boston Society for Helping Destitute Mothers and Infants stated in 1912 that unwed mothers should receive a pension, for "one who retains the personal charge of her baby has a wholesome occupation for her mind and heart, and a constant incentive to an upright, industrious life."[48]

Still another argument suggested that pensions for mothers were justified on the grounds of social justice. William Hard, for one, suggested that mothers' pensions be seen not as charity but as payment for public service. Judge Ben Lindsey similarly noted that pensions for mothers were a right, like soldiers' pensions. He wrote, "As justice due mothers whose work in rearing their children is a work for the state as much as that of the soldier, . . . it is a recognition for the first time by society that the state is responsible in a measure for the plight of the mother, and acknowledges its responsibility by sharing the burden of her poverty that it created largely by the conditions that the state permits to exist."[49] And at the First International Congress of Working Women, held in 1919, delegates proposed the idea of "maternity aid" for women regardless of financial need, as well as the idea of maternity insurance, so that motherhood would be a "joy and not a burden."[50] Finally, some argued that pensions were financially more sound than public support of children in institutions.[51]

But opponents of mothers' pensions were equally vehement. Some argued that pensions would increase the desertion of fathers, or at least encourage working-class families to falsely claim that the father had deserted. Others argued that pensions would increase public expenditures and relieve families of "wholesome responsibilities for the assistance of unfortunate relatives." Some claimed, too, that if the state entered the business of social welfare, private charity would be doomed. Finally, some critics argued that mothers' pensions treated the symptom rather than the cause of impoverished widowhood by not remedying the preventable deaths of husbands in dangerous occupations or the low wages paid to women workers.[52]

The ideological underpinnings of the mothers' pension movement prescribed that a mother's place was in a home suitable for the rearing of proper citizens. But to what degree was the administration of the pension laws coincident with this prescription? In practice, the mothers' pension laws rarely achieved their goals of subsidizing motherhood. Rather, they promoted the employment of women in the marginal labor market outside the home. There were two reasons for the failure of the mothers' pension movement: pension laws excluded too many potential recipients, and, for those who did qualify, assistance was too limited to support the family without additional income.

Qualifications for pension eligibility varied from state to state. In general, by 1919, self-supporting mothers could apply for pensions if they had little in the way of savings, insurance, equity, or personal property. In nine states, only widows could qualify; in others, deserted wives and wives of prisoners, hospital patients, or disabled men were also eligible for assistance. In only three places—Hawaii, Michigan, and Nebraska—could unmarried mothers apply for relief.[53]

But additional standards were also enforced. In Philadelphia, up to two-thirds of the women who were financially entitled to pensions were rejected for other reasons. In Pennsylvania in general, mothers' aid applicants had to prove they had lived at least two years in the state. Other restrictions, in various states, included the disqualification of women whose children were adopted, who were pregnant at the time of their husband's death, and who had only one child.[54] Black women were implicitly ineligible because of their color. A 1931 Children's Bureau study of eighteen states found that 96 percent of mothers' pensions beneficiaries were white, even in districts where nearly half of the population was black.[55]

Even when a woman met the eligibility requirements, the process of application for relief was slow and discouraging. In Cook County, Illinois, a widow applying for a pension through the juvenile court faced a waiting period of from four to six months while a social worker scrutinized her financial and moral fitness. In New York, after the pension law passed in 1915, less than half of the 12,000 initial applicants had been processed by the end of the first year. In 1931, the Children's Bureau estimated that less than a third of those eligible for pensions nationally had received any assistance.[56]

Once a woman was accepted for a pension, her financial security was not assured. In most cases, mothers' pensions were inadequate. In 1919, pensions ranged from an $8 maximum monthly allowance per child in Iowa and Vermont to a $25 maximum monthly allowance per child in Nevada. Additional children in a family received smaller grants. Observers agreed that, in general, a pension alone would not support a family. In Pennsylvania, for example, investigators said of the maximum monthly grants of $20 for the first child and $10 for each additional child that between one-third and one-fourth of the families dependent upon state support could not survive on the income supplied by the pension.[57]

Yet despite the financial inadequacy of the pensions, most states did not permit welfare recipients to work, thus reflecting the prevailing ideology that a mother's place was in the home. Whereas some welfare workers continued to support the idea of part-time work for widows, all agreed that the employment of a mother should be secondary to the needs of her children. In eighteen

states, in 1919, a woman could not work "regularly" away from home and remain eligible for public funds; in other states, she could not work more than one to three days a week away from home. Some pension advocates further suggested that fit work for women would be domestic service, waitressing, and the care of women and children boarders.[58]

Despite these restrictions on employment, a high proportion of women who received mothers' pensions worked "regularly." Reliable statistics are difficult, if not impossible, to obtain, because many women who worked would not report employment to the officials who might then cut off their funding. But there is ample evidence that pension recipients worked. In Chicago, more than a fourth of the pensioned women worked full time by 1920, and Illinois was one of the states prohibiting "regular" work outside the home. In 1922, at least 20 percent of the mothers receiving assistance in Boston, and 40 percent of the pension recipients in New York, were employed.[59]

Some self-supporting women preferred employment to public relief. In Philadelphia, of 237 widows studied in 1921, only 38 had applied for pensions.[60] In 1910, Boston charity workers observed that a certain kind of widow felt that it was "unnatural, in her eyes and those of her neighbors, to earn nothing" even after pension laws were established.[61] In 1931, the Children's Bureau found that of some 7,000 women who had been disqualified from pension eligibility, only 44 percent had remarried. More often, women were declared ineligible because they preferred to work for a higher income for their families than the pensions allowed.[62]

Though limited by qualification restrictions and inadequate budgeting, mothers' pensions reshaped the welfare process in the United States. By 1921, the Census Bureau estimated that some 121,000 children in 45,000 families were at least partially supported by public funds and that thousands of these children might otherwise have been committed to institutions because of the poverty of their families.[63] Pensions, moreover, proved to be a less expensive means of welfare than were institutions. In 1922, the city of New York supported 27,000 children in their own homes for about half of the cost of institutional care.[64]

The spread of the mothers' pension movement affected other forms of aid for working women. Most important, it retarded the growth of the day-nursery movement. In Kansas City, for example, the United Jewish Charities abandoned their day nursery for a pension program by 1911.[65] Furthermore, as widows were widely believed to be taken care of by state aid, the day nurseries that survived were forced to redefine their admissions policies to favor the children of working mothers who were married.

Day-Care Policy and Practice, 1920–1960

As the 1920s began, public pensions for widows were seen by many as the solution to the problem of the working mother. The home was preserved; the mother had been reinstated in her proper place. But by this time, more married women had entered the labor force, including an articulate class of middle-income women. How did they care for their children?

Middle-income women who worked came up with their own solutions to the child-care dilemma. Those who could afford the cost hired servants to care for their sons and daughters during the day. A "wage-earning wife" told readers of the *Woman's Home Companion* in 1925, for example, that she relied on "Mrs. Maguire, our incredibly neat, competent, amiable cook-housekeeper" to solve her career-family problem.[66] A 1927 survey of women who had graduated from Radcliffe found that almost three out of four of those both married and working had hired household help.[67] The option of hiring servants, however, was becoming less feasible for working wives both because of the decreasing availability of domestic servants and because many more married women who worked could not so easily afford to hire household help.

There is evidence that some middle-class mothers had approached the philanthropic day nurseries for child-care services. The secretary of the National Federation of Day Nurseries reported "numerous requests for nursery care for the children of business and professional women who were able and willing to pay the full cost for such service."[68] But these women were turned down by most nurseries because of the belief that the day nursery was meant as a last resort for poor women rather than as a service for women who worked.

Middle-income women relied instead on the growing nursery school movement, on proprietary day care, and on relatives and neighbors. By this time, nursery schools did not promise mere custodial care for children but rather promoted the educational enrichment of their students. In 1929, one writer argued that nursery schools would "give the child an eminently safe and hygienic environment during his mother's working hours, and furnish him with the physical, mental and moral nourishment that he needs. . . . Perhaps it is not too much to say that such an institution can give the child better care, physically and psychologically, than most mothers, with their limited knowledge of the far-reaching sciences that contribute to the welfare of the child, could hope to give."[69] Nursery schools began to slowly increase in the 1920s, growing from a recorded 16 schools in 1923 to 108 by 1928. Some day nurseries evolved into nursery schools in order to meet the new expectations of clients; the Chicago Hull-House Day Nursery, for example, became the Mary Crane Nursery School in 1925.[70]

The philanthropic day nursery itself was changing in the 1920s. The impact of the widow's pension caused a shift in the day-nursery movement; if the widow was the expected client before 1920, now it was the employed married woman, especially if she was seen as coming from an "economically handicapped" family.[71] The professionalization of social work also had an effect, as new standards of nutrition, health, and education were proposed. What had once been a service for poor working mothers was becoming more of a social welfare agency for women defined as "problem cases." Nursery school teachers and social workers replaced matrons and nurses, with the result that infants were gradually excluded from day-nursery eligibility. Mothers of very young children, social workers deemed, should not work. Those who did were less visible than previously. The most destitute of mothers—widows—had been taken care of through the pension system, and so the mother who came to the day nursery was viewed as having another problem—a social-psychological problem subject to the expert remedies of the caseworker.

Many working married women defined their situation quite differently. They saw the interest of social workers in their lives not as helpful inquiry but as intrusion. A social worker at the Leila Day Nursery in New Haven, Connecticut, noted with some surprise the hostile attitude of families to the intrusion of social workers into their homes: "In most of the families the parents' attitude is that the Nursery is a community resource, such as the public school, and it is, therefore, for them to use as they wish. Families find it difficult to see the need of discussing financial, social and personal factors affecting their lives, as in their minds these facts are not related to nursery care."[72] Other observers noted the struggle that went on between parent and social worker over the admission of children to a nursery. One woman, for example, sputtered after an interview, "I guess I know my own business best. She can refuse my baby if she wants to. But telling me to stay at home is too much!"[73]

By the early 1930s, the day-nursery movement was marginal at best and suspect as a welfare agency for troubled families. In 1935, federal funds were appropriated for the first time for day care in the form of nursery schools for the children of poor mothers. The Works Project Administration provided money for rapid expansion, and by 1935, 1,900 WPA nurseries, as they were called, tended some 75,000 children. But these nurseries were not geared toward the needs of mothers who worked or toward the educational and psychological needs of children. Rather, their avowed function was to provide employment for teachers, nurses, nutritionists, cooks, janitors, and clerical workers. With the end of the New Deal, the WPA nurseries lost their federal funding and began to close.[74]

But this decline was temporary. During World War II, day nurseries once again revived, this time to free mothers for work in the wartime labor force. Although mothers of young children were not officially encouraged to work, still mothers as a group were the reserve of labor identified as necessary for the success of wartime production. The care of their children was therefore seen as a function of the government defense program. "Good care for the children of working mothers," the federal Office of Education argued, "means more planes and armaments for our fighting men, and victory *sooner*." The Office of Education suggested that public school hours be extended to provide day care for children of working mothers.[75] Others suggested the expansion of services in the day nursery. The National Association of Day Nurseries argued the need for stemming the tide of "latch-key children of war industry mothers": "This is the day nursery part in the Home Defense program—in order to see to it that as little damage as possible is done to family life and childhood by the present upheavals and to conserve human values for the period of reconstruction when the crisis is past."[76]

In 1941, Congress passed the Community Facilities Act, also known as the Lanham Act, to meet on a fifty-fifty basis the social service needs of communities affected by the war. In 1942, the Lanham Act was interpreted as being applicable to day-care centers. By July 1944, there were over 3,000 centers servicing 129,000 children. By 1945, nearly $50 million had been spent to support day-care facilities for more than 1.5 million children.[77]

Private industry, too, experimented with funding day-care centers during the war. The best-known of these was the Kaiser shipbuilding business in Oregon. The Kaiser firm established centers open to its workers twenty-four hours daily, providing not only child care for children as young as eighteen months, but also medical care, and hot meals that could be picked up along with the children and taken home.[78]

It is important to note that even at that time day care was limited. Most mothers relied on the old methods—using relatives, friends, and neighbors to watch their children. Federally funded day care remained insufficient—there were no services for the care of infants, for example, and the centers open to older children met less than 10 percent of the need.[79]

But some mothers did support the idea of government-funded care for their children—an idea that was threatened when the Lanham funds were cut off after the war. In 1945, the Child Care Center Parents' Association of New York organized to battle for the survival of the day-care centers as well as for free public nursery schools, free hot lunches in schools, and equal pay for equal work. Day care, they argued, was a right, not a charitable gift:

We working mothers have been holding down three full-time jobs, as mothers, housewives, and wage earners. 24 hours a day gives us barely enough time to get everything done. And yet we do it. . . . Superwomen? No! Just women who love their children and want to keep their families together. That's why we are going to take on a fourth full-time job! That of convincing our government . . . that investing in our children is not a philanthropic enterprise! It is a privilege! For when they invest in our children, they will reap the kind of profits that pay dividends in good, healthy, well-adjusted useful citizens![80]

When the state of New York discontinued its day-care program, these mothers picketed the residence of Governor Thomas Dewey, who promptly labeled them Communists.

But the day-care mothers persisted, fighting to shake off the welfare label and to get the recognition and approval of middle-class mothers. The Child Care Center Parents' Association recorded the struggle, for example, to get PTA meetings held at night, after work, rather than during the day.[81] This battle was aided by the Child Welfare League of America, which proposed that Congress consider a bill to fund locally administered day-care centers. "It is hardly American," the league argued, "to leave a mother, too often poorly paid for her work, to shift for her child without some minimum guarantee of community service and some subsidy for the child's care."[82]

Generally, however, the end of the war signaled the closing of hundreds of day-care centers; the official need for working mothers had ended. By 1946, only 1,504 centers for some 40,000 children were still in operation. Centers closed because of money problems and "changing needs." The Brightside Day Nursery, for example, which had opened in 1894 to serve the community on New York's Lower East Side, shut down in 1948.[83]

Ironically, as the day-care movement was once again in eclipse, the number of working mothers was in its greatest acceleration. In 1953, as we have seen, more than 2 million women with children under the age of six were working outside the home.[84] But the feminine mystique continued to define the problems of the working mother as individual and not social. Old attitudes persisted; one community-chest worker wrote in 1952 that children in day nurseries were "day-time orphans whose mothers must work to pay the rent and buy the groceries."[85]

Most children in this era continued to be cared for by relatives and neighbors. In 1958, a Children's Bureau study found that of children of mothers working full time, 80 percent of the children under the age of twelve were cared for at home, most by a father, grandparent, sibling, friend, or neighbor.

Eight percent of these children had no supervision at all. Only 2 percent of the children of working mothers were in day care or nursery school.[86] Hidden within these figures, of course, were proprietary day-care businesses—neighborhood women who took in children for a fee.

Some social workers pushed for the transformation of the day-care ideal. Gertrude Binder argued in 1953 that day care should adapt to the changing employment practices of mothers, "to promote the well being of an expanding circle of human beings rather than merely to mitigate the ill-being of the exceptionally unfortunate." Day care, she concluded, should shift from an emergency resource only for poor women to a community-based educational resource for children.[87]

1960 to 1980

Day care resurfaced as a vital social issue in the 1960s. In this period, the movement to define day care as a normal rather than as an exceptional service gained strength; increasing numbers of people saw day care not as a charity, or as a welfare function, but as a community service for normal families, similar to public education or public transportation.

But this trend was tempered by the resurgence of the link between publicly supported day care and the needs of dependent children. State-supported mothers' pensions had, by 1935, become Aid to Dependent Children, a federal program under the Social Security Act.[88] In 1962, as Aid and Services to Needy Families with Children, the pension movement had come full circle, as interest in the preservation of family life had given way to fears that "welfare mothers" were taking advantage of public support. As a result, a requirement for aid in many cases was that recipients had to work.[89] This in turn led to assumptions about day care. If poor mothers were expected to work, then provisions were needed for the care of their children. In 1967, Congress amended the Social Security Act to provide funds for day care, intending to meet the needs of mothers on public assistance. But the lack of adequate child care led to the failure of governmental efforts to get welfare mothers into the workplace.[90]

In 1970, the White House Conference on Children deemed day care the most serious problem confronting American families and urged the massive infusion of federal funds to meet the growing need. The Comprehensive Child Development Act of 1971 recommended that the government provide day care for all children. In Senate hearings, day-care advocates proposed that child care would not only free mothers to work but would also bring the children of

various races and classes together, facilitate community control of public services, and enhance health care. To some advocates, too, federally funded day care would also "invest in the development of the next generation and thereby . . . begin to break the terrible, dehumanizing cycle of poverty." Secretary of Health, Education, and Welfare Elliot Richardson told the Senate Committee on Finance:

> Many parents are unable to give their offspring the experiences necessary to achieve success in our fast-paced society. They themselves often lack experience and schooling and are ill-prepared to assure the full development their children need to compete in a highly technological world. . . . If we fail to invest in these children now . . . we are likely to find them on the welfare rolls as parents 15 years from now. In short, there is a great need for child care programs which contribute to the development of the child as well as provide a safe place for the child while the mother is working.[91]

Other day-care proponents, debating standards of care and priorities of clients, questioned whether middle-income families required services as desperately as did welfare mothers.[92] But the idea of federal funding for day care, particularly the national network of centers proposed in the child-development centers sponsored by the Senate, was defeated by the veto of President Richard Nixon, who maintained that government's involvement in child care should be kept "to an absolute minimum" and that "family-centered" rather than "communal" care should be supported.[93] With Nixon's veto, the idea of federally funded day care—begun as a response to the dependency of poor mothers—was again submerged. Once again, child care was to be sanctioned only in terms of the dependent mother and not because it was needed by working mothers of every class.

But some parents spoke out for continued subsidized day care. In New York City in 1972, for example, some 350 parents, children, and day-care workers took over a government office to oppose a state order limiting eligibility for government-financed day care.[94]

A related trend was the growth in programs for early education for children. From 1967 to 1979, there was a dramatic rise in the proportion of children aged three to five enrolled in preschool programs. Whereas 6.8 percent of all three-year-olds were registered for preschool in 1967, by 1979 25 percent of this group spent at least part of the day in educational activities. Of all children aged three to five, excluding five-year-olds enrolled in elementary school, 51 percent were reported to be in preschool in 1979. In part this trend was spurred by federal programs such as Head Start, which attempted to compensate for

the "cultural deprivation" of poor children, and in part by the growth of nursery and preschool programs for the middle class.[95]

By the mid-1970s, there were still far too few day-care centers to meet the needs of working mothers. In 1973, there were 700,000 day-care slots for the 6 million preschoolers whose mothers worked. Child-care programs were of diverse sponsorship, ranging from profit-making franchises, which critics labeled "Kentucky-Fried Children" centers for their emphasis on quantity care, and nonprofit centers run by church groups, welfare organizations, educational institutions, and other community associations. Some corporations, including Polaroid and the John Hancock Company, also sponsored day-care centers for the children of employees.[96] Most children, however, continued to be cared for at home. In 1974 and 1975, of children aged three to six with working mothers, 81 percent received primary care in their own homes, 13 percent in someone else's home, and only 2 percent in day-care centers.[97]

By the end of the decade, there appeared to be increased support for the idea of day care as a social service for average families. The Tax Reform Act of 1976 and the Revenue Act of 1978 established tax credits for parents who purchased day-care services for their children.[98] Social critics proposed a range of improvements in the child-care system, including more business-sponsored day care at the workplace, state-supported neighborhood child-care centers, increased foster-home care for infants, and the extension of school services for preschoolers. Reformers suggested that a diversity of day-care opportunities would allow parents to choose the best arrangements for their families and would also benefit business by reducing the absenteeism of mothers.[99]

Increased recognition was now also given to the adjustment of work hours to allow parents to work and yet tend their own children. Mothers had for decades attempted to adjust their work hours by working odd hours, part-time, or on split shifts. The Working Family Project, a study of lower-middle-income families in the Boston area, reported in 1975 that parents in one-third of the dual-income families surveyed worked staggered hours in order to meet child-care needs. Case studies illustrate this practice. The Project reported, for example, that "Mr. Henry works from 8 a.m. to 4 p.m., except for two evenings a week. . . . Mrs. Henry works a 4 p.m. to 11 p.m. shift. Because of their commuting time, there is an hour each day when they must use a child-care arrangement; also there is an occasional evening to be covered when Mr. Henry works overtime. To cover these hours, the Henrys exchange child care with one of their neighbors."[100] The practice of exchanging child care was also found in more formal baby-sitting cooperatives, where parents relied on friends and neighbors for a consistent sharing of child care.[101]

Reformers in the 1970s urged that part-time work be upgraded by securing benefits for part-time workers, by widening part-time opportunities, and by encouraging job-sharing programs. Still, part-time workers remained a surprisingly constant segment of the labor force, given the remarkable growth in the numbers of mothers of young children at work. From 1965 to 1980, the proportion of women workers employed part-time (less than thirty-five hours a week) remained steady, ranging from 19 to 21 percent of all working women over the age of twenty.

More recently, the idea of "flexitime" has been brought to public attention. Flexitime would allow workers to put in a full eight-hour day on a staggered schedule, such as from 6 A.M. to 2 P.M., or by squeezing a full work week into four long days. In 1973, an amendment to the Comprehensive Employment and Training Act targeted funds for research on flexitime arrangements; by the end of the decade many civil service and corporation offices provided this opportunity for their workers. By 1980, some 12 percent of all workers surveyed worked on flexible schedules; the largest proportions of flexitime workers were salespersons (26.5 percent), managers and administrators (20.2 percent) and federal workers (20.2 percent).[102]

By 1980, only about 27 percent of American families reflected the idealized image of the home, where the father worked while the mother did not.[103] But still working mothers were caught between the traditional definition of woman's sphere, the association of day care with welfare, and changing economic roles. Despite their rapidly growing numbers and despite more than a half century of public discussion, working mothers remain defined as a social problem. The continued failure of American society to reconcile the reality of women's work patterns with the ideology of domesticity has reinforced the identification of working mothers as an unresolved issue on the national agenda.

Conclusion

The historical debate about women, work, and social order continues in the 1980s. In the nineteenth century, the entrance of young single women into the labor force generated a controversy over the "working girl" that contributed to both meliorative reform and structural change in the workplace. By the turn of the century, young single women had become well established in the American labor force and were no longer thought of as problematic. But in the twentieth century, there was a startling transformation in the composition of the female labor force, as first wives and then mothers rapidly increased their numbers among the employed. Because social responses to twentieth-century working mothers remain mired in nineteenth-century concepts of domesticity and dependency, American society has not yet implemented policies necessary for the full and equitable integration of women into the economic structure.

The disjuncture between the work of mothers of young children and the domestic ideology remains powerful and may even deepen. The Bureau of Labor Statistics predicts that, by 1990, up to two-thirds of women aged 25 to 54 will be in the work force, as the demand for female labor continues to grow. Moreover, by 1990, mothers may be more likely to work full time continuously rather than part-time and intermittently.[1]

Two themes persist in the debate about working women. One is the problem of day care for very young children; the other is the question of structural change in the workplace.

If present trends continue, the expansion of the American labor force will mean the rising work participation of mothers of very young children. By March 1981, 8.2 million children under the age of six had working mothers. As of March 1982, nearly half of married women with preschool-aged children were employed and more than half of unmarried mothers with preschool children were also working.

Day care for children over the age of three seems to have become an accepted practice in the United States. But 45 percent of married women with children under the age of three were working by 1982 as well.[2] It is the care for these younger children that must be addressed by policymakers and parents. Most very young children of working mothers are cared for in family or home day-care situations, but there has been a movement to provide more institu-

tional day-care facilities for these infants. Yet child-care provisions remain underfunded and understudied. Recent scholarship suggests that, for children under the age of two, group day care outside the home *may* "put at risk" their future cognitive and emotional development. Although studies are preliminary, and in the main focused on lower-income children in proprietary day-care situations, for many young children it is clear that present day-care opportunities are often not in their best interests.[3]

In *The Erosion of Childhood*, Valerie Polakow Suransky presents case studies of different types of day care to illustrate the lack of child-centered arrangements for the children of working mothers. Suransky maintains that it is ironic that the movement for women's liberation may too often rely on the dialectical antithesis of the "containment of children"—that humanistic freedom for one group endorses the early and anti-humanistic institutionalization of the other. Suransky suggests that the "current call for free and universal daycare should not be viewed as a progressive or radical answer to the social needs of women in society entering the work force seeking equalization of opportunity; rather, the daycare phenomenon merely extends and exacerbates the corporate paradigm, thereby contributing to the *maintenance*, not the *transformation* of the social order."[4] For example, if day care has become too often an industry supporting such franchised centers as the Mary Moppets of the Southwest or the Universal Education Corporation of the East Coast, questions must surely be raised about how the growing *business* of child care affects the very nature of childhood. With an emphasis on profit rather than on human development, day care as it is available for many people to some degree abrogates the freedom and rights of children.[5]

Suransky has joined that group of Americans who urge alternative forms of day care for the children of working mothers. In particular, she calls for the deinstitutionalization of early childhood through a variety of measures. These measures range from a form of income redistribution—perhaps through a type of government subsidy like the mothers' pensions, which would allow parents to choose whether or not to work when their children were very young—to the spread of cooperative day-care centers. These latter cooperatives would be small and community-based, and they would rely on the support of society and employers to help parents take an active role in the daily lives of their young children. Other possible reforms might include more liberal policies for maternity and paternity leaves, especially during the first year of parenthood, increased tax benefits for parents, and expanded child-care facilities at the work site. Mothers are working, and will continue to work, and the availability of good quality, affordable day care has become an increasingly critical problem.

As Alison Clarke-Stewart has pointed out, day care is now a fact of life and no longer a debatable issue.[6]

What remains debatable is the structure of work in American society. As the entrance of young single women into the labor force in the nineteenth century contributed to a movement for legislation shortening the hours of work and setting a minimum wage, so the entrance of mothers into the labor force has spurred the still-nascent movement for flexible hours of work, job-sharing arrangements, and a more fluid approach to the boundaries of work and home. This new posture is reflected in the efforts of mothers to keep their babies with or near them in the workplace, and in the efforts of other parents who choose to work, via remote computer terminal or telephone, at least part of the time in their own homes.

It will be a combination of child care and work reforms that, in the end, will protect and benefit not only the rights of mothers and their children but all members of society. These changes will require a transformation of the domestic ideology. The current undervaluation of women's work, characterized by the two-tiered labor force with its sexual divisions of status and pay, must give way to economic and social equity. As long as the worlds of men and women are separated by differing prescriptions for family and economic roles, and as long as economic need is seen as a determinant in the acceptance or rejection of work for women, the employment of mothers outside the home will remain defined as a problem. Working mothers will continue to be condemned, explained, and justified until the right to work is recognized as being within the normal range of experience for women just as it is for men.

Notes

Abbreviations

CWLA Child Welfare League of America
JAMC Jane Addams Memorial Collection
TA   Travelers' Aid
WCA   Woman's Christian Association
WEIU Women's Educational and Industrial Union
YWCA Young Women's Christian Association

Introduction

1. See, for instance, Kreps, *Sex in the Marketplace*; Kessler-Harris, "Stratifying by Sex."
2. Examples of recent scholarship include Wandersee, *Women's Work*; Walsh, *Doctors Wanted*; Yans-McLaughlin, *Family and Community*. A more recent work that takes a broad view of the integration of women into wage labor is Kessler-Harris, *Out to Work*.
3. The phrase "working girl" will be used throughout to label those young—and not so young—women who were so designated by their contemporary culture. For a discussion of the regulation of female behavior by labeling, see Fox, " 'Nice Girl.' "
4. This interaction of ideology and reality is also considered in Kessler-Harris, "Women's Wage Work."
5. The analysis of the intent and function of reform movements and social policy has generated a debate among historians. For a summary of this controversy, see Grob, "Reflections on the History of Social Policy in America."
6. For an extensive discussion of the changing composition of the female labor force, see Oppenheimer, *Female Labor Force*.
7. Examples of problems with longitudinal comparisons of census data include differing instructions to enumerators about what constitutes work, and different times of the year during which enumeration took place. See Oppenheimer, *Female Labor Force*, pp. 2–6; Conk, "Accuracy, Efficiency, and Bias," pp. 65–72.
8. The attempt to make industrial life more "domestic," both for nineteenth-century self-supporting women and for twentieth-century working mothers, illustrates an interweaving of "family time" and "social time." Tamara Haraven has argued that the family life-cycle should be seen as dynamic rather than static; this would lead to an analysis of boarding and lodging, for example, as a function both of life-cycle and economic needs. See Haraven, "Family as Process."

Chapter 1

1. For a discussion of antebellum migrations of women, see Hobson, "Seduced and Abandoned."
2. Self-supporting women in Philadelphia in the 1820s are depicted in Carey, *Miscellaneous Essays*, pp. 267–71.

3. Demos, *A Little Commonwealth*, p. 78.
4. For a discussion of urban housing practices, see Wolfe, *Lodging House Problem*.
5. Salmon, *Domestic Service*, chap. 3.
6. Ibid., pp. 54–55.
7. Abbott, *Women in Industry*, p. 32.
8. Salmon, *Domestic Service*, pp. 71–73; Scott and Tilly, "Women's Work and the Family," pp. 52–53. Faye Dudden views this shift as a redefinition of household workers from "hired girls" or "help" to "domestics" or "servants." See Dudden, *Serving Women*, pp. 5–8.
9. Glasco, "Life Cycles and Household Structure," pp. 122–43.
10. Abbott, *Women in Industry*, chap. 3; Meserve, *Lowell*, chap. 6.
11. Meserve, *Lowell*, p. 61. See also Dublin, *Women at Work*.
12. Miles, *Lowell*, p. 128.
13. Ware, *Industrial Worker*, p. 107.
14. Meserve, *Lowell*, p 61.
15. Robinson, *Loom and Spindle*, pp. 80–91. See also Bushman, "*A Good Poor Man's Wife*."
16. Scoresby, *American Factories*, p. 16.
17. Engle, "Story of the Mercer Expeditions," pp. 225–37.
18. Abbott, *Women in Industry*, pp. 138–39; Lerner, "Lady and the Mill Girl," pp. 5–14.
19. Lerner, "Lady and the Mill Girl."
20. Dublin, *Women at Work*, pp. 35–40. A fascinating glimpse of the lives of these women through the perspective of their letters home is offered in Dublin's *Farm to Factory*.
21. U.S. Department of Labor, Commissioner of Labor, *Working Women in Large Cities*, p. 64; Wright, *Working Girls of Boston*; U.S. Department of Labor, *Boarding Homes and Clubs*, p. 142.
22. For a discussion of supply-and-demand factors in the shaping of the female labor force, see Oppenheimer, *Female Labor Force*, chap. 5.
23. Maclean, *Women Workers and Society*, pp. 88–89.
24. U.S. Bureau of the Census, *Women at Work*.
25. Ibid., p. 28. Louise Tilly cautions against the common assumption that industrialization alone might cause an increase in the employment of women. Her study of Milan, Italy, found no link between industrialization and the feminization of the work force. See Tilly, "Urban Growth," pp. 467–84.
26. For statistics on the distribution of women in the population and in the labor force at the turn of the century, see U.S. Bureau of the Census, *Women at Work*, pp. 132–33, table 2, p. 146, table 9.
27. Ibid., pp. 260–62, table 28, pp. 298–300.
28. In Boston, New York, and Philadelphia, native-born white women of foreign parentage were 14, 15, and 17 percent of women boarders respectively. In Minneapolis and St. Paul, they were 40 and 44 percent. See ibid., p. 224, table 28, pp. 266, 280–84.
29. Taeuber and Taeuber, *Changing Population*, p. 53, table 11, p. 68.
30. Ibid.; Hvidt, *Flight to America*, p. 92, table 9.1.
31. One study of immigrant women in Philadelphia found that two out of five crossed the ocean alone. U.S. Department of Labor, Women's Bureau, *Immigrant Woman and Her Job*. See also "Immigrant Women and Girls in Boston," 1907, typewritten, Women's Educational and Industrial Union Papers, Box 7; Kowaleska, "Conditions of Work for Immigrant Girls," pp. 51–59.
32. Sarah Beaulieu, "A Farm Girl's Diary," in *Women in the American Economy*, ed. Brownlee and Brownlee, p. 130.
33. Garland, *Rose of Dutcher's Coolly*, pp. 148–49.
34. Edith H. to Women's Department, Minnesota Bureau of Labor, 7 July 1909, Minnesota Labor and Industry Department Records, Employment Correspondence. The full names of cor-

respondents to the Bureau of Labor are not given in the text and notes in keeping with current privacy regulations.
35. This is by no means a universal law of migration. A review of the literature shows a diversity of sex-selectivity by time and place. It appears, however, that rural-urban migrants were more likely to be women, while urban-rural migrants were more likely to be men. One estimate made in the United States suggested that the rural-urban migration of women exceeded that of men by about 22 percent between 1920 and 1930. See Jansen, *Sociology of Migration*, pp. 18–19; Sorokin and Zimmerman, *Principles of Rural-Urban Sociology*, chap. 24; Zimmerman, "Migration to Towns and Cities," pp. 450–55; Williams, "Rural Youth Studies," pp. 166–78.
36. U.S. Bureau of the Census, *Women at Work*, p. 18, table XI.
37. Ibid., pp. 198–207, table 26.
38. Taeuber and Taeuber, *Changing Population*, pp. 15, 152–55, 249.
39. Oppenheimer, *Female Labor Force*, p. 27.
40. Calhoun, *Social History of the American Family*, 1:67–69; 3:107.
41. U.S. Bureau of the Census, *Women at Work*, pp. 9–11; Smuts, *Women and Work in America*, chap. 2.
42. Van Vorst and Van Vorst, *Woman Who Toils*, p. 82.
43. "Girl Who Comes to the City," July 1908, p. 694; December 1908, p. 1228.
44. Ibid., March 1908, p. 277; May 1908, p. 595; December 1908, p. 1226; Smuts, *Women and Work*, chap. 2.
45. Smuts, *Women and Work*, chap. 3. For a comparison of men's and women's wages, see U.S. Bureau of the Census, *Earnings of Factory Workers*, pp. 394–95.
46. U.S. Department of Labor, *Working Women in Large Cities*, p. 625, table XXXII, p. 532, table XXXI.
47. Minnesota Bureau of Labor, *Ninth Biennial Report of . . . 1903–04*, 1:129.
48. For a comprehensive survey of local and national studies of working women, see U.S. Department of Labor, Women's Bureau, *Women Workers and Their Dependents*, pt. 2.
49. U.S. Bureau of the Census, *Women at Work*, p. 10.
50. Ibid., p. 198, table 26.
51. U.S. Department of Labor, Women's Bureau, *Family Status of Breadwinning Women*; U.S. Department of Labor, Women's Bureau, *Share of Wage-Earning Women in Family Support*.
52. Brownlee and Brownlee, *Women in the American Economy*, pp. 20–23.
53. Oppenheimer, *Female Labor Force*, chap. 1.
54. See Kessler-Harris, "Stratifying by Sex."
55. U.S. Bureau of the Census, *Women at Work*, p. 31.
56. The next highest nativity group for urban servants was Hungarians (42 percent) followed by Austrians (36 percent), Irish (31 percent), and Germans (31 percent). In the country as a whole, however, only 28 percent of domestic servants were immigrants. Ibid., p. 41, table XXXIV, p. 47.
57. Katzman, *Seven Days a Week*, p. 268. See also Sutherland, *Americans and Their Servants*, and Dudden, *Serving Women*, for the history of domestic service in the United States.
58. Bliven, *Wonderful Writing Machine*; Davies, "Woman's Place Is at the Typewriter," pp. 1–28.
59. U.S. Department of Labor, Bureau of Labor Statistics, *Summary of Report on Condition of Woman and Child Wage-Earners*, p. 296. For a discussion of the emerging culture of sales work for women, see Benson, "Customers Ain't God," pp. 185–211.
60. Rayne, *What Can a Woman Do?*, p. 123. See also Candee, *How Women May Earn a Living*.

Chapter 2

1. U.S. Congress, Senate, *Report on Condition*, 9:17.
2. Hamilton, "Report on Manufactures," 1:87. Hamilton also thought that children could be usefully employed by manufacturing establishments. For a discussion of the promotion of female factory labor as an antidote to dependency, see Nash, "Failure of Female Factory Labor," pp. 165–88.
3. Marx, *Machine in the Garden*, p. 159; Abbott, *Women in Industry*, p. 57.
4. Benson, *Women in Eighteenth-Century America*, chap. 6.
5. Cott, *Bonds of Womanhood*; Sklar, *Catharine Beecher*, chap. 6; Kraditor, *Up from the Pedestal*, pp. 12–13.
6. Cott, *Bonds of Womanhood*, p. 199.
7. Bloch, "American Feminine Ideals in Transition," pp. 101–26.
8. Gordon, *Woman's Body, Woman's Right*, pp. 10–11.
9. Beecher, *Evils Suffered*, p. 11.
10. Brownlee and Brownlee, *Women in the American Economy*, p. 135.
11. *New York Daily Tribune*, 19 August 1845, quoted in U.S. Congress, *Report on Condition*, 9:22.
12. Beecher, *Evils Suffered*, p. 12.
13. Cited in U.S. Congress, Senate, *Report on Condition*, 9:131–33.
14. Ibid., pp. 234–35.
15. Penny, *Think and Act*, p. 25.
16. Beecher, *Evils Suffered*, p. 12.
17. Julianna, "Factory Life as It Is, By an Operative," in *America's Working Women*, ed. Baxandall, Gordon, and Reverby, p. 67.
18. *Voice of Industry*, 4 September 1846, cited in Ware, *Industrial Worker*, p. 53.
19. National Trades Union, "Report of the Committee on Female Labor," in *Documentary History of American Industrial Society*, ed. Commons et al., 6:281.
20. Adapted from Herbert Blumer, quoted in Douglas, *Defining America's Social Problems*, pp. 106–8.
21. See, for example, "Report of the Committee on Vagrancy," p. 244.
22. For a discussion of male social status, see Thernstrom, *Poverty and Progress*.
23. Rhine, "Women in Industry," pp. 287–88. For a discussion of the rise of feature journalism as a function of urban culture, see Hofstadter, *Age of Reform*, pp. 188–90.
24. Campbell, *Prisoners of Poverty*.
25. Eva McDonald Valesh, writing under the pen name "Eva Gay," published her articles in the Minneapolis Sunday edition of the *St. Paul Globe* from 26 March 1888 through 3 August 1891. Valesh was later an organizer for the American Federation of Labor. I am grateful to Rhoda Gilman, of the Minnesota Historical Society, for bringing the "Eva Gay" articles to my attention.
26. Rhine, "Women in Industry," pp. 302–3.
27. Wisconsin Bureau of Labor Statistics, *First Biennial Report of . . . 1883 and 1884*, p. 109.
28. *Report and Testimony*, 1:3–4; U.S. Department of Labor, *Working Women in Large Cities*; U.S. Department of Labor, Bureau of Labor Statistics, *Summary of Report*; Bullock, *Employment of Women*.
29. Van Vorst and Van Vorst, *Woman Who Toils*, p. 11; Parker, *Working with the Working Woman*.
30. Richardson, *The Long Day*; *Four Years in the Underbrush*; "Girl Who Comes to the City." The expression of similar themes in fiction can be found in such novels as Theodore Dreiser's *Sister Carrie* (1900) and Sinclair Lewis's *The Job* (1917).

31. For a discussion of this idea, see Smith-Rosenberg and Rosenberg, "Female Animal," p. 338.
32. Mary Sidney, "The Ideal Farm Girl," *Farm Journal*, March 1903, reprinted in *So Sweet to Labor*, ed. Juster, p. 65.
33. Juster, *So Sweet to Labor*, pp. 140–78.
34. Van Vorst and Van Vorst, *Woman Who Toils*, pp. 80–82; 160–62.
35. Flora McDonald Thompson, "Truth about Women in Industry," *North American Review*, May 1904, reprinted in Bullock, *Employment of Women*, p. 107.
36. Hall, *Adolescence*, 2:609; Calhoun, *History of the American Family*, 3:92–93.
37. Hall, *Adolescence*, 2:630. See also Hyde, *College Man and the College Woman*.
38. Richardson, "Difficulties and Dangers," pp. 624–26.
39. Henry T. Finck, "Employments Unsuitable for Women," *Independent*, 11 April 1901, portions reprinted in Bullock, *Employment of Women*, pp. 76–78, and in Minnesota Bureau of Labor, *Eighth Biennial Report of . . . 1901–02*, pp. 335–41.
40. Finck, in Bullock, *Employment of Women*, p. 77.
41. Ibid., p. 78.
42. Mary Abigail Dodge, *A New Atmosphere*, p. 27.
43. Ibid., pp. 31–32.
44. Gordon, "Wherein Should the Education of a Woman Differ," pp. 790–91.
45. Ida Husted Harper, "Women Ought to Work," *Independent*, 16 May 1901, reprinted in Bullock, *Employment of Women*, pp. 63–70.
46. A listing of some of the progressive-era studies of working women is presented in U.S. Department of Labor, Women's Bureau, *Women Workers and Their Dependents*, pt. 2.
47. May, *Protestant Churches and Industrial America*; Dorn, *Washington Gladden*.
48. Dorn, *Gladden*, p. 303.
49. Rauschenbusch, *Christianizing the Social Order*, pp. 14–15.
50. May, *Protestant Churches*, pp. 225–31.
51. Wiebe, *Search for Order*, p. 169.
52. Minnesota Bureau of Labor, *Twelfth Biennial Report of . . . 1909–10*, p. 625.
53. MacLean, *Women and Industry*, p. 103.
54. Bullock, *Employment of Women*, p. 4.
55. U.S. Congress, Senate, *Report on Condition*, 13:169.
56. Rauschenbusch, *Christianizing the Social Order*, p. 414.
57. Brandeis and Goldmark, *Women in Industry*, appendix.
58. Penny, *Think and Act*, p. 64; U.S. Congress, Senate, *Report on Condition*, 15:114.
59. Wright, *Working Girls*, p. 128.
60. The commission's report is summarized in Illinois General Assembly, Senate, *Report of the Senate Vice Committee*, p. 26. Hull House reformer Louise DeKoven Bowen found department store work to be especially dangerous. She argued that salesgirls not only worked "surrounded by . . . the luxuries which they all crave" but also exposed to a constant flow of strangers, some of them procurers or otherwise immoral. Bowen, *Department Store Girl*.
61. Klapp, "Relation of Social Vice to Industry," pp. 147–52.
62. Ibid. For the concurring opinion of working-class women that factory work meant low status, see Anthony, *Mothers Who Must Earn*, pp. 51–52.
63. Addams, *A New Conscience*, pp. 91–92.

Chapter 3

1. "Poor Nelly—A Life Sketch," *Household*, 1892, quoted in Juster, *So Sweet to Labor*, pp. 71–72.
2. Pivar, *Purity Crusade*.
3. Rosen and Davidson, eds., *Maimie Papers*, p. xxvii. This estimate may be too high. Prostitutes testifying before the Illinois Vice Commission earned relatively high wages, but paid a good proportion of this money to their madams. See Illinois General Assembly, Senate, *Report of the Senate Vice Committee*, pp. 153, 164, 211, and 215.
4. Valesh, *St. Paul Globe*, 2 September 1888, p. 1. For a discussion of prostitution and the culture of the working class, see Stansell, "Women of the Laboring Poor," chap. 5. Prostitution in the progressive era is examined in Rosen, *Lost Sisterhood*.
5. Anonymous, "My Experiences in New York."
6. Sanger, *History of Prostitution*. See also Ellington, *Women of New York*, p. 389.
7. Bell, *Fighting the Traffic*, p. 68.
8. Pivar, *Purity Crusade*; Wagner, "Virtue against Vice."
9. Minneapolis WCA, *1886 Report*, p. 13, Minneapolis WCA Papers.
10. For another perspective on the issue of reform and its relationship to class, see Berg, *Remembered Gate*.
11. "100-Year Travelers' Aid Calendar," n.d., typewritten, TA Records, Box 2. See also Bertha McCall, "Historical Résumé of Bryan Mullanphy Fund," 1949, typewritten, TA Records, Box 2.
12. Quoted in "Early History of Selected Travelers' Aid Societies and Events in the History of the National Travelers' Aid Association 1917–1918 with Exhibits Compiled by Bertha McCall," n.d., typewritten, p. 4, TA Records, Box 2.
13. "Early History," TA Records, Box 2. See also Weiner, "Our Sisters' Keepers," pp. 193–95, and Chicago YWCA, *1893 Report*, p. 31, Chicago YWCA Records, Box 3.
14. Minneapolis WCA, "Minutes of Meetings of the Travelers' Aid Committee, 1909–1915," typewritten notebook; Minneapolis WCA *1942 Report*, p. 19, Minneapolis WCA Papers.
15. "Early History," p. 41, TA Records, Box 2; Graham, *Grace H. Dodge*, pp. 221–26.
16. "Early History," p. 24, TA Records, Box 2; Baker, *Travelers' Aid Society in America*, p. 20.
17. Russell, *Girl's Fight for a Living*, p. 146.
18. "100-Year Calendar," p. 2, TA Records, Box 2.
19. U.S. Department of Labor, *Working Women in Large Cities*, p. 64; Wolfe, *Lodging House Problem*, pp. 44–50; U.S. Department of Labor, *Summary of Report*, p. 219.
20. Ellington, *Women of New York*, p. 640. See also Hendee, *Growth and Development*, p. 25; Valesh, "Search for Homes," *St. Paul Globe*, 5 August 1888, p. 1; Van Vorst and Van Vorst, *Woman Who Toils*, p. 30. In a novel published in 1863, the heroine, Madge, has a hard time finding respectable lodgings in a New England mill town. When she finally sets up a cottage for herself and a cousin, public opinion is stirred. According to the author, neighbors opine that "'tis very odd and strange for a young lady to commence housekeeping before she is married." Talcott, *Madge*, p. 358.
21. Post, *Etiquette*, p. 288.
22. U.S. Department of Labor, *Working Women in Large Cities*, p. 31.
23. Ibid., p. 32; U.S. Department of Labor, *Boarding Homes and Clubs*, p. 142; Dorothy Richardson, *Long Day*, pp. 287–88.
24. Penny, *Think and Act*, p. 215; Wolfe, *Lodging House Problem*, pp. 145–49. See also Chicago YWCA, *Report 1892–93*, p. 32.
25. The confusion of identity for these early boarding homes is reflected by the difficulties of the Minneapolis Woman's Boarding Home, which reported in 1874 that it had to overcome the "common notion" that it was a rescue home for prostitutes. See *Minneapolis Tribune*, 3

May 1874. This confusion was long-lived. In its 1910 survey of welfare institutions, the U.S. Census Bureau included working women's homes among its tally of homes for dependents, immigrants, prostitutes, the aged, and veterans. See U.S. Bureau of the Census, *Benevolent Institutions*, table III.

26. U.S. Department of Labor, *Working Women in Large Cities*, p. 32.
27. Richmond, *New York*, p. 468. The first temporary home for "respectable women" was the Philadelphia Temporary Home Association, founded in 1849. See U.S. Department of Labor, *Boarding Homes and Clubs*, p. 186.
28. U.S. Department of Labor, *Boarding Homes and Clubs*, pp. 186–88; Richmond, *New York*, pp.470–71; Gardner, "Hotel Is Not a Home."
29. Calculated from U.S. Department of Labor, *Boarding Homes and Clubs*, pp. 190–91, table III.
30. Ibid., p. 152; Tolman and Hemstreet, *Better New York*, p. 139.
31. Bosworth, "Living Wage," p. 29.
32. U.S. Department of Labor, *Boarding Homes and Clubs*, pp. 188–89, table II, pp. 190–91, table III; U.S. Department of Labor, *Working Women in Large Cities*, chap. 2; Gardner, "Hotel Is Not a Home," p. 3; Humphries, "Working Women," pp. 49–52.
33. Chicago YWCA, *1883 Report*, p. 10, Chicago YWCA Records.
34. Minneapolis WCA, *1898 Report*, p. 34, Minneapolis WCA Papers.
35. Richmond, *New York*, pp. 468–69.
36. U.S. Department of Labor, *Boarding Homes and Clubs*, p. 183.
37. Ibid., pp. 194–96, table V.
38. Ibid., pp. 144–45; Kellor, "Immigrant Woman," p. 406.
39. Providence YWCA, *1876 Report*, quoted in Hyman, "Young Women's Christian Association," p. 12; Minneapolis WCA, *1881 Report*, p. 22, Minneapolis WCA Papers.
40. Providence YWCA, *1893 Report*, quoted in Hyman, "Young Women's Christian Association," p. 12; U.S. Department of Labor, *Working Women in Large Cities*, chap. 2.
41. U.S. Department of Labor, *Boarding Homes and Clubs*, p. 156. In the Philadelphia Clinton Street Boarding House, additional restrictions included the exclusion of women from their bedrooms from 7 to 9 P.M., in order to "insure fresh, pure air for sleeping." Board of Commissioners of Public Charities of the Commonwealth of Pennsylvania, *Twenty-second Annual Report* (1892), p. 118.
42. Bosworth, "Living Wage," p. 28; Laughlin, *Work-a-Day Girl*, pp. 137–38.
43. Bosworth, "Living Wage," p. 28; U.S. Department of Labor, *Boarding Homes and Clubs*, pp. 90–91; U.S. Department of Labor, *Working Women in Large Cities*, chap. 2.
44. Minutes of the Woman's Boarding Home, 1879, handwritten, Minneapolis WCA Papers.
45. For a discussion of police station lodging for women who were not criminals, see Barney, "Care of the Criminal," pp. 368–69, and Devoll, "Results of Employment," p. 311.
46. "Miss Hayseed's Adventures," reprinted in Chicago YWCA, *1887–88 Report*, pp. 57–63, Chicago YWCA Papers.
47. Minneapolis WCA, *1888 Report*, p. 14, Minneapolis WCA Papers.
48. U.S. Department of Labor, *Boarding Homes and Clubs*, chap. 2.
49. "Limping Alone," *Annals of No Man's Land*, October 1924, p. 11, Minneapolis WCA Papers. See also Bosworth, "Living Wage," p. 30.
50. Providence YWCA, *1890 Report*, quoted in Hyman, "Young Women's Christian Association," p. 12.
51. U.S. Department of Labor, *Boarding Homes and Clubs*, pp. 146–47.
52. Minneapolis WCA, Minutes of the Woman's Boarding Home, 5 June 1888; May 1887, Minneapolis WCA Records; New York Bureau of Social Hygiene, *Housing Conditions*, p. 66.
53. Bosworth, "Living Wage," p. 30.
54. Campbell, *Problem of the Poor*, p. 225.

55. Rosen, *Maimie Papers*, p. 155.
56. Laughlin, *Work-a-Day Girl*, p. 132. See also Butler, *Women and the Trades*, p. 322.
57. New York Bureau of Social Hygiene, *Housing Conditions*, p. 7.
58. De Graffenried, "Needs of Self-Supporting Women," p. 8.
59. U.S. Department of Labor, *Boarding Homes and Clubs*, p. 145; *Four Years in the Under-brush*, p. 14; Spencer, "What Machine-Dominated Industry Means," p. 208; Nathan, "Women Who Work and Women Who Spend," pp. 648–50.
60. Bosworth, "Living Wage," p. 30; "Girl Who Comes to the City," February 1908, p. 71; December 1908, p. 1226; Donovan, *Saleslady*, p. 176.
61. "Girl Who Comes to the City," February 1908, p. 170; May 1908, p. 593.
62. Minnesota Bureau of Labor Statistics, *First Biennial Report of . . . 1887–88*, pp. 188–89. Another solution to the problem was for women to divide work and housekeeping tasks among themselves. In 1890, for example, five Irish flaxmill operatives rented an apartment and appointed one of their number to stay home and keep house for the group. See De Graffenried, "Needs of Self-Supporting Women," p. 6, and also Anna Steese Richardson, *Girl Who Earns Her Own Living*, pp. 278–81.
63. U.S. Department of Labor, *Boarding Homes and Clubs*, p. 170; McLean, "Eleanor Clubs," pp. 60–61; New York Bureau of Social Hygiene, *Housing Conditions*, pp. 65–76.
64. "The Jane Club," *Inter-Ocean* (July 1892), found in Hull House Scrapbook, 1:15, JAMC. The Jane Club, connected to Hull House, was named for Jane Addams.
65. Marguerite Wells, "Report of the Sub-Committee on Homes for Working Girls," 1917, type-written, p. 6, Minneapolis WCA Papers.
66. New York Bureau of Social Hygiene, *Housing Conditions*, p. 108. For further discussion of cooperative housekeeping in this period, see Hayden, *Grand Domestic Revolution*, pp. 167–70.
67. Addams, *Spirit of Youth*, p. 15.
68. Addams, *Plea for More Pay*, p. 5.
69. U.S. Congress, Senate, *Report on Condition*, 15:91–92.
70. Bowen, *Road to Destruction*. See also Erenberg, *Steppin' Out*, chap. 3, and Addams, "Why Girls Go Wrong."
71. For the history of the YWCA, see Simms, *Natural History*, and Wilson, *Fifty Years of Asso-ciation Work*. For a comparison of the efforts of the YWCA to protect young women with the parallel movement of the YMCA to protect young men, see Boyer, *Urban Masses and Moral Order*, pp. 112–20.
72. Massachusetts League of Girls Clubs, leaflet, n.d., Niles Papers, Box 1, folder 7.
73. Graham, *Grace H. Dodge*, pp. 67–68, 103–4; U.S. Department of Labor, *Working Women in Large Cities*, p. 39; National League of Women Workers and Association of Working Girl's Societies, *1890 Report; 1894 Report; 1897 Report; 1901 Report*.
74. National League of Women Workers, leaflet, n.d., Niles Papers, Box 1, folder 2; National League of Girls Clubs, *History of the National League*, pp. 5–36.
75. Grace Hoadley Dodge, "Sunny Spots for Working Girls," p. 8.
76. Ferris, *Girls Clubs*, pp. 155–58.
77. U.S. Department of Labor, *Working Women in Large Cities*, p. 39; Blackwell, "Responsibil-ity of Women," p. 79.
78. Croly, *Thrown on Her Own Resources*, p. 142.
79. Stokes, "Condition of Working Women," pp. 627–37.
80. Ibid., p. 628.
81. "Girl Who Comes to the City," February 1908, p. 172.
82. "The Working Girls Clubs of Chicago," March 1896, clipping, Hull House Scrapbook, 3:69–70, JAMC.

83. Julia Ward Howe, "A Symposium—Domestic Service," *Chatauquan*, February 1891, clipping, Howe Papers, scrapbook vol. 5, p. 6.
84. Minnesota Bureau of Labor, *Eighth Biennial Report of . . . 1901–02*, p. 304.
85. Quoted in Wisconsin Bureau of Labor Statistics, *First Biennial Report of . . . 1883 and 1884*, p. 112.
86. Salmon, *Domestic Service*, chaps. 10–15; Klink, "Housekeeper's Responsibility," pp. 372–81; "Household Labor," *Union Signal*, 4 February 1892, Hull House Scrapbook, 1:13, JAMC.
87. Salmon, *Domestic Service*, p. 133.
88. Ibid., chaps. 8–9; Minnesota Bureau of Labor Statistics, *First Biennial Report of . . . 1887–88*, pp. 149–53; Klink, "Put Yourself in Her Place," p. 16.
89. Herrick, *Expert Maid-Servant*, pp. 125–33. See also Katzman, *Seven Days a Week*, pp. 120–24.
90. Minnesota Bureau of Labor Statistics, *First Biennial Report of . . . 1887–88*, p. 149; Wisconsin Bureau of Labor and Industrial Statistics, *Tenth Biennial Report of . . . 1900–1901*, p. 677; Klink, "Put Yourself in Her Place," p. 16.
91. Minnesota Bureau of Labor Statistics, *First Biennial Report of . . . 1887–88*, pp. 149–51.
92. Salmon, *Domestic Service*, p. 153.
93. Mary Gove Smith, "Immigration as a Source of Supply for Domestic Workers," n.d., typewritten, p. 9, WEIU Papers, Box 7.
94. Ibid., p. 10; Wald, "Immigrant Young Girl," p. 264.
95. This committee was composed of representatives of the Boston Women's Educational and Industrial Union, the New York Association of Household Research, the Philadelphia Civic Club and Housekeeper's Alliance, the College Settlements Association, and the Association of Collegiate Alumnae. See *Bulletin of the Inter-Municipal Committee*, November 1904; Kellor, "Inter-Municipal Research Committee," pp. 193–200.
96. Burrington, "Immigrant in Household Employment," p. 6.
97. Wald, "Immigrant Young Girl," p. 263; Kellor, *Out of Work*, chap. 7; Kellor, "Rights of Patrons," pp. 6–7.
98. Kellor, "Southern Colored Girls," pp. 5–6.
99. Huggins, *Protestants against Poverty*, p. 88; Campbell, *Prisoners of Poverty*, p. 234.
100. Kneeland, *Commercialized Prostitution*, p. 212, table X; U.S. Department of Labor, *Working Women in Large Cities*, pp. 64–75, 625; U.S. Congress, Senate, *Report on Condition*, 15:114.
101. U.S. Congress, Senate, *Report on Condition*, 10:89–91.
102. Dorothy Richardson, "Trades-Unions in Petticoats," p. 489.
103. Raybeck, *History of American Labor*, p. 259; Chafe, *American Woman*, p. 68. For a discussion of the historically low level of unionization among clerical workers, see Feldberg, "Union Fever."
104. Agnes Donham, "History of the Women's Educational and Industrial Union," n.d., typewritten, p. 6, WEIU Papers, vol. 1; Rhine, "Women in Industry," pp. 291–92.
105. For the history of the Consumer's League, see Stewart, *Philanthropic Work*, chap. 16; Nathan, *Story of an Epoch-making Movement*.
106. U.S. Congress, Senate, *Report on Condition*, 10:157–59; U.S. Department of Labor, Women's Bureau, *Towards Better Working Conditions for Women*, pp. 3–5; Clark and Wyatt, *Making Both Ends Meet*, p. 187, n. 1. In 1919, the Women's Trade Union League convened the International Federation of Working Women, a group that met three times between 1919 and 1923 to promote the worldwide organization of women workers. See "International Federation of Working Women," pamphlet, ca. 1919, International Federation of Working Women Papers. For a discussion of the cross-class organization processes

of the Women's Trade Union League, see Moore, "Life and Labor."

107. For a recent examination of labor legislation history, see Baer, *Chains of Protection*.

108. Ibid.; Hutchinson, "Women's Wages," chap. 5. The Women's Bureau cautioned that protective legislation might exclude women from labor that was really less taxing than work at home, adding that "safe standards of work for women must come to be safe standards of work for men also if women are to have an equal chance in industry." U.S. Department of Labor, Women's Bureau, *Employment of Women*, p. 8.

109. Ames, *Sex in Industry*, pp. 151, 141–44.

110. Connecticut Special Commission to Investigate Conditions of Wage-Earning Women and Minors, *1913 Report*, quoted in Brandeis and Goldmark, *Case against Nightwork*, p. 223.

111. John Quincy Ames, *Cooperation*, p. 43.

112. Goldmark, *Fatigue and Efficiency*, pt. 2, pp. 1–26. This volume contains the material submitted in four briefs to the supreme courts of the United States, Illinois, and Ohio between 1908 and 1912 in defense of hours laws for women.

113. U.S. Congress, Senate, *Report on Condition*, 9:62–73; Elizabeth Brandeis, "Women's Hour Legislation," in *History of Labor*, ed. Commons et al., 3:461; Hutchinson, "Women's Wages," p. 147.

114. Brandeis, "Women's Hour Legislation," p. 462.

115. Baer, *Chains of Protection*, pp. 53–54.

116. Brandeis and Goldmark, *Women in Industry*; Brandeis, "Women's Hour Legislation," pp. 474–75.

117. Brandeis, "Women's Hour Legislation," p. 472; U.S. Department of Labor, Women's Bureau, *Employment of Women at Night*, p. 16.

118. U.S. Department of Labor, Women's Bureau, *State Laws Affecting Working Women*, pp. 5–9.

119. De Graffenried, "Needs of Self-Supporting Women," p. 1.

120. Raybeck, *History of American Labor*, p. 265; Brandeis, "Hours Laws for Men," in *History of Labor*, ed. Commons et al., 3:540–63.

121. These reports are cited in Goldmark, *Fatigue and Efficiency*, pt. 2, pp. 267–68.

122. Brandeis and Goldmark, *Women in Industry*, p. 47; Brandeis and Goldmark, *Case against Nightwork*, p. 209.

123. Baer, *Chains of Protection*, pp. 79–80.

124. *Muller v. Oregon*, p. 7, in Brandeis and Goldmark, *Women in Industry*, appendix.

125. Brandeis and Goldmark, *Case against Nightwork*, pp. 426–27.

126. Ibid., pp. 187–208; Baer, *Chains of Protection*, p. 84; U.S. Department of Labor, Women's Bureau, *Employment of Women at Night*, p. 57.

127. U.S. Department of Labor, Women's Bureau, *Effects of Legislation*, p. 15; U.S. Department of Labor, Women's Bureau, *Effects of Labor Legislation*, p. 105.

128. U.S. Department of Labor, Women's Bureau, *Summary: Effects of Labor Regulation*; Chafe, *American Woman*, pp. 124–25; Rothman, *Woman's Proper Place*, p. 163; *Chicago Tribune*, 3 August 1911, p. 1.

129. U.S. Department of Labor, Women's Bureau, *Development of Minimum Wage Laws*.

130. Kauffman, *House of Bondage*, cited in Bremner, *From the Depths*, p. 239.

131. U.S. Department of Labor, Women's Bureau, *History of Labor Legislation*, p. 130.

132. Russell, *Girl's Fight for a Living*, p. 29.

133. Illinois General Assembly, Senate, *Report of the Senate Vice Committee*, p. 178; Hutchinson, "Women's Wages," pp. 90–92; U.S. Department of Labor, Women's Bureau, *Development of Minimum-Wage Laws*, p. 75. Department store owners had long taken the stand that their saleswomen were not self-supporting. In 1895, a representative of Lord and Taylor's argued that they never hired self-supporting saleswomen because they could not afford to pay wages sufficient for women to live on. See *Report and Testimony*, p. 91.

134. U.S. Department of Labor, Women's Bureau, *History of Labor Legislation*, p. 130.
135. Elizabeth Brandeis, "Minimum Wage Legislation," in *History of Labor*, ed. Commons et al., 3:525; U.S. Department of Labor, Women's Bureau, *Development of Minimum-Wage Laws*, pp. 80–81, table 19.
136. Brandeis, "Minimum Wage Legislation," p. 526.
137. Minnesota Minimum Wage Commission, *First Biennial Report, 1913–1914*, p. 43.
138. Ibid., pp. 32–34, table IX.
139. Brandeis, "Minimum Wage Legislation," p. 525.
140. For example, see Clark and Wyatt, *Making Ends Meet*.
141. Naomi M. to chairman of Minnesota Minimum Wage Commission, 10 November 1920, Minnesota Labor and Industry Department Records, Minimum Wage Correspondence, Box 15.
142. Ibid.; Minnesota Minimum Wage Commission, *Report*; Brandeis, "Minimum Wage Legislation," p. 529.
143. U.S. Department of Labor, Women's Bureau, *Development of Minimum-Wage Laws*, pp. 880–81.
144. U.S. Department of Labor, Women's Bureau, *Proceedings of the Women's Industrial Conference*, p. 139.
145. Hutchinson, "Women's Wages," pp. 129–40.
146. Ibid., p. 136.
147. Ibid., p. 134; Brandeis, "Minimum Wage Legislation," p. 536; Chafe, *American Woman*, p. 125; U.S. Department of Labor, Women's Bureau, *Development of Minimum-Wage Laws*, p. 370.
148. U.S. Department of Labor, Women's Bureau, *Development of Minimum-Wage Laws*, pp. 323–25; Brandeis, "Minimum Wage Legislation," pp. 688–89; Chafe, *American Woman*, p. 81; Wandersee, *Women's Work*, p. 95.
149. "Early History," TA Records, Box 2.
150. See, for example, Hyman, "Young Women's Christian Association," p. 53.
151. U.S. Bureau of the Census, *Women in Gainful Occupations*, pp. 140–47.
152. Katzman, *Seven Days a Week*, pp. 87–91; Stigler, *Domestic Servants*. See also Sutherland, *Americans and Their Servants*, chap. 10.
153. Information Bureau on Women's Work, *Floating World*, p. 11.
154. U.S. Department of Labor, Women's Bureau, *Proceedings of the Women's Industrial Conference*, p. 4.

Chapter 4

1. See, for example, Bancroft, *American Labor Force*; Durand, *Labor Force in the U.S.*
2. U.S. Bureau of the Census, *Women at Work*, p. 15.
3. Tentler, *Wage-Earning Women*, p. 39; U.S. Department of Labor, *Summary of Report*, p. 18. A study of Italian women in New York from 1900 to 1950 observes that married Italian women viewed employment as a component of their strategy for family maintenance. See Cohen, "Workshop to Office," p. 198.
4. Anthony, *Mothers Who Must Earn*, pp. 128–29.
5. Hughes, *Mothers in Industry*, pp. 107–9.
6. Long, *Labor Force under Changing Income and Employment*, pp. 92–93.
7. U.S. Bureau of the Census, *Comparative Occupation Statistics*, p. 92, table XV.
8. Fraundorf, "Labor Force Participation," pp. 401–18.
9. *Report and Testimony*, 1:604.
10. U.S. Department of Labor, *Summary of Report*, pp. 106–7.

11. Hughes, *Mothers in Industry*, pp. 111–13.
12. Untitled MS (ca. 1918), McDowell Papers, Box 4.
13. U.S. Bureau of the Census, *Women in Gainful Occupations*, pp. 73–74.
14. U.S. Department of Labor, Women's Bureau, *Immigrant Woman and Her Job*, p. 17.
15. Wandersee, *Women's Work*, p. 3.
16. U.S. Department of Labor, *Summary of Report*, p. 410; U.S. Bureau of the Census, *Women at Work*, p. 170, table 21.
17. Anthony, *Mothers Who Must Earn*, p. 58; Tentler, *Wage-Earning Women*, p. 47; Hughes, *Mothers in Industry*, p. 143.
18. U.S. Bureau of the Census, *Women in Gainful Occupations*, pp. 80–81.
19. For a discussion of home work, see U.S. Department of Labor, Women's Bureau, *Homework in Bridgeport, Connecticut*, Bulletin 9.
20. Campbell, *Prisoners of Poverty*, p. 201.
21. Butler, *Women and the Trades*, pp. 136–37.
22. U.S. Congress, Senate, *Report on Condition*, 5:57.
23. U.S. Department of Labor, Commissioner of Labor, *Eighteenth Annual Report*, pp. 63, 260, 368.
24. Smuts, *Women and Work*, p. 14; U.S. Department of Labor, Women's Bureau, *Immigrant Woman and Her Job*, p. 62; U.S. Bureau of the Census, *Comparative Occupation Statistics*, p. 30.
25. Brownlee, "Household Values," pp. 199–209.
26. U.S. Department of Labor, Women's Bureau, *Immigrant Woman and Her Job*, p. 13.
27. Schiffman, "Marital and Family Characteristics," p. 13.
28. See, for instance, Ivan Nye and Lois Hoffman, "The Socio-Cultural Setting," in Nye and Hoffman, *Employed Mother in America*, chap. 1; Kreps, *Sex in the Marketplace*, p. 49; Bancroft, *American Labor Force*, pp. 28–29.
29. Oppenheimer, *Female Labor Force*, pp. 39–52; Sum, "Women in the Labor Force," p. 19.
30. Bancroft, *American Labor Force*, p. 29.
31. See table 2, above.
32. National Bureau of Economic Research, *Aspects of Labor Economics*, pp. 98–99. For a discussion of the history of birth control, see Gordon, *Woman's Body, Woman's Right*.
33. Wilson H. Grabill et al., "A Long View," in *American Family in Social-Historical Perspective*, ed. Gordon, pp. 374–76.
34. U.S. Department of Labor, Bureau of Labor Statistics, *Working Women: A Databook*, p. 26, table 26.
35. U.S. Bureau of the Census, *Nineteenth Census of the U.S., 1970*, vol. 1, pt. 1, pp. 688–89, table 216.
36. U.S. Bureau of the Census, *Historical Statistics*, pp. 13–25, table D; U.S. Bureau of the Census, *Nineteenth Census . . . , 1970*, vol. 1, pt. 1, p. 688, table 216; Oppenheimer, *Female Labor Force*, p. 11, table 1.4.
37. See U.S. Bureau of the Census, *Farm Population of the U.S.*, chap. 2.
38. U.S. Bureau of the Census, *Women at Work*, p. 17, table X.
39. Bancroft, *American Labor Force*, p. 54.
40. Sweet, *Women in the Labor Force*, pp. 199–200.
41. Kreps, *Sex in the Marketplace*, p. 49.
42. National Bureau of Economic Research, *Aspects of Labor Economics*, p. 101.
43. Ibid., p. 91.
44. Durand, *Labor Force in the U.S.*, p. 21.
45. Jacob Mincer, "Labor Force Participation," in National Bureau of Economic Research, *Aspects of Labor Economics*, pp. 63–64.
46. Ibid., p. 67.

47. See, for example, Nye and Hoffman, *Employed Mother*, p. 35.
48. Oppenheimer, *Female Labor Force*, pp. 30–35.
49. Cowen, "Case Study of Technological and Social Change," pp. 245–53; Vanek, "Time Spent in Housework," pp. 116–21.
50. U.S. Bureau of the Census, *Occupations of the Twelfth Census*, p. cxlvii.
51. U.S. Bureau of the Census, *Comparative Occupation Statistics*, p. 92, table XV.
52. For a discussion of the child-labor movement, see Trattner, *Crusade for the Children*; Clark, *Child Labor and the Social Conscience*.
53. For an economist's interpretation of why this did not happen, see Mincer, "Labor Force Participation," in National Bureau of Economic Research, *Aspects of Labor Economics*.
54. Schiffman, "Marital and Family Characteristics," p. 363; Kreps, *Sex in the Marketplace*, p. 23, table 2.2.
55. U.S. Department of Labor, Women's Bureau, *Women Workers and Their Dependents*, pp. 12, 40.
56. Dowsall, "Structural and Attitudinal Factors," pp. 121–30.
57. Chafe, *American Woman*, pp. 183–84.
58. Rupp, *Mobilizing Women for War*, p. 177.
59. Oppenheimer, *Female Labor Force*, chap. 3.
60. Bancroft, *American Labor Force*, p. 209, table D-2; Oppenheimer, *Female Labor Force*, p. 47, table 5.3.
61. U.S. Bureau of the Census, *U.S. Census of Population, 1960*, pp. 97–98, table 5.
62. Chafe, *American Woman*, pp. 135–45.
63. Ibid., p. 52.
64. Ibid., p. 141. See also Clive, "Women Workers in World War II," pp. 44–72.
65. Durand, *Labor Force in the U.S.*, p. 26.
66. U.S. Department of Labor, Employment Standards Administration, Women's Bureau, *Minority Women Workers*, p. 9, table 8, p. 6, table 5. See also U.S. Department of Labor, Bureau of Labor Statistics, *Perspectives on Working Women*, p. 102, table 100.
67. Bednarzik and Klein, "Labor Force Trends," p. 3; U.S. Department of Labor, Bureau of Labor Statistics, *Marital and Family Characteristics*, p. 49; U.S. Department of Labor, Bureau of Labor Statistics, *Perspectives*, p. 9, table 10.
68. U.S. Department of Labor, Employment Standards Administration, Women's Bureau, *1975 Handbook on Women Workers*, p. 23; David Ignatius, "Women at Work: The Rich Get Richer as Well-to-do Wives Enter the Labor Force," *Wall Street Journal*, 8 September 1978, p. 1; U.S. Department of Labor, Bureau of Labor Statistics, *Marital and Family Characteristics*, p. A-28, table G.
69. U.S. Department of Labor, Bureau of Labor Statistics, *Perspectives*, p. 26, table 25.
70. Waldman et al., "Working Mothers," pp. 45–48.
71. U.S. Department of Labor, Bureau of Labor Statistics, *Marital and Family Characteristics*, p. A-23, table F; U.S. Department of Labor, Bureau of Labor Statistics, *Perspectives*, p. 27, table 26; Grossman, "Children of Working Mothers," p. 32; Oppenheimer, "Demographic Influence," p. 185.
72. "Census Shows 30% of Mothers with Children under One Held Jobs in '78," *Minneapolis Tribune*, 14 November 1979, p. 8B; Waldman, "Working Mothers," p. 43.

Chapter 5

1. Helen Glenn Tyson, introduction to Hughes, *Mothers in Industry*, p. xiii.
2. Lynd and Lynd, *Middletown in Transition*, p. 182.
3. The decline of family production is evidenced by the increase in commercial food services.

From 1914 to 1925, the production of bakeries increased 60 percent; in the same period, there was growth in the canned goods, delicatessen, and restaurant industries. See LaFollette, *Married Women Homemakers*, p. 27; U.S. Department of Labor, Children's Bureau, *Children of Working Mothers in Philadelphia*; Ogburn, "Family and Its Functions," pp. 664–66.

4. Ogburn, "Family and Its Functions," p. 661.

5. Massachusetts Bureau of Statistics of Labor, *Sixth Annual Report (1875)*, cited in Baker, *Technology and Women's Work*, p. 84.

6. U.S. Industrial Commission, *Report*, vol. 19 (1902), cited in Goldmark, *Fatigue and Efficiency*, p. 285.

7. Gilman believed that children were better off in the hands of experts than in the care of their mothers. She wrote that "a newborn baby leads a far happier, healthier, more peaceful existence in the hands of the good trained nurse, than it does when those skilled hands are gone, and it is left on the trembling knees of the young, untrained mother." See Gilman, *Home*, p. 340; *Women and Economics*.

8. Terhune, "Counting Room," p. 340.

9. "American Woman in the Marketplace," p. 19. For a fuller discussion of the debate over marriage and career in this period, see Masteller, "Marriage or Career, 1880–1914."

10. See, for example, Bromley, "Feminist—New Style," pp. 552–60; Mativity, "Wife, the Home, and the Job," pp. 189–99; Hansel, "What about the Children?," pp. 220–27. See also Coyle, *Jobs and Marriage?*

11. See table 2, above.

12. U.S. Department of Labor, Women's Bureau, *Proceedings of the Women's Industrial Conference*, p. 5

13. Hughes, *Mothers in Industry*, p. 1.

14. Lynd and Lynd, *Middletown in Transition*, p. 181.

15. Goodsell, *Problems of the Family*, pp. 169–70. For an expression of the idea that women were handicapped in employment pursuits because of "maternal function and periodic illness," see Macy, "Equality of Woman with Man," pp. 705–10.

16. U.S. Department of Labor, Children's Bureau, *Children of Wage-Earning Mothers*, p. 49, quoted in Tentler, *Wage-earning Women*, p. 152.

17. Anthony, *Mothers Who Must Earn*, pp. 15–16.

18. Komarovsky, *Blue-Collar Marriage*.

19. Tyson, "Professional Woman's Baby," p. 192.

20. Van Duzer, *Everyday Living*, pp. 233–34.

21. Coyle, *Jobs and Marriage?*, pp. 53–55.

22. Groves, "Psychology of the Woman Who Works," pp. 94–96.

23. Peters, *Status of the Married Woman Teacher*, pp. 21–22.

24. Pruette, *Women and Leisure*.

25. Littell, "Meditations of a Wage-Earning Wife," pp. 732–33.

26. Coyle, *Jobs and Marriage?*, p. 83.

27. Spencer, *Women's Share in Social Culture*, pp. 165–66.

28. Bromley, "Feminist—New Style."

29. Littell, "Meditations of a Wage-Earning Wife," p. 734.

30. Hinkle, "Changing Marriage," p. 288.

31. For an overview of the "race-suicide" issue, see Gordon, *Woman's Body, Woman's Right*, chap. 7.

32. Calhoun, *Social History of the American Family*, 3:250–52.

33. Popenoe, *Conservation of the Family*, pp. 231–32.

34. Coyle, *Jobs and Marriage?*, pp. 40–41; LaFollette, *Married Women Homemakers*, pp. 54–56.

35. Anna Byrd Kennon, "College Wives Who Work," quoted in Coyle, *Jobs and Marriage?*, p. 40; Kennon, "Gainful Employment of Former Radcliffe Students Who Are Married," 1927, typewritten, WEIU Papers.
36. LaFollette, *Married Women Homemakers*, p. 14; Coyle, *Jobs and Marriage?*, pp. 52–53.
37. U.S. Department of Labor, Children's Bureau, *Infant Mortality*.
38. Ibid. See also Goodsell, *Problems of the Family*, pp. 157–65.
39. Wishy, *Child and the Republic*.
40. Rothman, *Woman's Proper Place*, chap. 3; Greenblatt, *Responsibility for Child Care*, pp. 41–44.
41. Spencer, *Family and Its Members*, chap. 11.
42. Watson, *Psychological Care of Infant and Child*, p. 3. One historian cautions that the expert's advice to mothers does not necessarily reflect common child-rearing practice. See Mechling, "Advice to Historians," pp. 44–63.
43. U.S. Department of Labor, Children's Bureau, *Children of Wage-Earning Mothers*, quoted in Coyle, *Jobs and Marriage?*, p. 50.
44. Goodsell, *Problems of the Family*, pp. 166–67.
45. Ibid., pp. 313, 426.
46. Groves, "Psychology of the Woman Who Works," p. 96.
47. Adams, *Women Professional Workers*, p. 32.
48. Goodsell, *Problems of the American Family*, p. 286.
49. Eleanor Roosevelt, *It's Up to the Women*, pp. 145–50.
50. Peters, *Status of the Teacher*, p. 6.
51. Ibid., p. 23; Hughes, *Mothers Who Must Earn*, pp. 15–16; Elmer, *A Study of Women*. A summary of arguments for and against the employment of married teachers is presented in Lewis, *Personnel Problems*, pp. 185–88.
52. Pruette, *Women Workers through the Depression*, p. 104; Peters, *Status of the Teacher*, p. 9.
53. Gallup, *Gallup Poll*, 1:39; Cantril, *Public Opinion*, p. 1044.
54. LaFollette, *Married Women Homemakers*, p. 15.
55. Peters, *Status of the Teacher*, pp. 10–11.
56. For a summary of these views during the 1930s, see ibid., pp. 11–12; Wandersee, *Women's Work*, chap. 4; and Chafe, *American Woman*, chap. 4.
57. U.S. Department of Labor, Women's Bureau, *Office Work and Office Workers in 1940*.
58. U.S. Department of Labor, Women's Bureau, *Women Workers in Their Family Environment*, p. 1.
59. Rupp, *Mobilizing Women for War*; Straub, "United States Government Policy," pp. 240–54.
60. Rupp, *Mobilizing Women for War*, p. 139; Straub, "United States Government Policy," pp. 241–42.
61. Susan B. Anthony, *Out of the Kitchen*, p. 5.
62. Cantril, *Public Opinion*, p. 1045.
63. Susan B. Anthony, *Out of the Kitchen*, p. 130.
64. Ibid., pp. 6–8; "A Statement from the National Association of Day Nurseries," 15 July 1941, typewritten, CWLA Records, Box 46, folder 8. The National Association of Day Nurseries, formed in 1938, merged with the CWLA in 1942.
65. U.S. Department of Labor, Women's Bureau, *Women Workers in Ten Production Areas*; Cantril, *Public Opinion*, p. 1047.
66. Gorham, *So Your Husband's Gone to War!*, p. 38.
67. One notable exception was the publication in the U.S. of Simone de Beauvoir's *The Second Sex*.
68. Harris, *Beyond Her Sphere*, chap. 6.
69. Friedan, *Feminine Mystique*, p. 38.
70. Friedan notes that *Modern Woman* was "paraphrased ad nauseam in the magazines and in

marriage courses, until most of its statements became a part of the conventional, accepted truth of our time." Ibid., p. 111. See also Lundberg and Farnham, *Modern Woman*, chaps. 7 and 12.

71. Lundberg and Farnham, *Modern Woman*, chap. 12.

72. Dingwall, *American Woman*, p. 273.

73. For a discussion of role confusion, see Craven, *American Family*, pp. 19–20.

74. The popularization of this idea came with the publication of Philip Wylie's *Generation of Vipers* in 1942.

75. Dingwall, *American Woman*, pp. 137–38.

76. Ibid., pp. 138–39.

77. Lundberg and Farnham, *Modern Woman*, chap. 12.

78. Bossard, *Sociology of Child Development*, pp. 380–83. For a review of the experimental literature on maternal employment, see Stoltz, "Effects of Maternal Employment," pp. 749–82.

79. See Schaffer, *Mothering*, pp. 95–100.

80. Komarovsky, *Women in the Modern World*.

81. Josselyn and Goldman, "Should Mothers Work?," pp. 74–87.

82. Bowlby, *Maternal Care*, pp. 15, 67. Bowlby was first published by the World Health Organization in 1951.

83. Ibid., pp. 73, 11.

84. For a critical discussion of Bowlby's theories, see Bowlby, *Maternal Care*, pt. 2; Ainsworth et al., *Deprivation of Maternal Care*; Galinsky and Hooks, *New Extended Family*, pp. 16–17.

85. Friedan, *Feminine Mystique*, pp. 27, 364.

86. For a summary of contemporary feminist writings, see Yates, *What Women Want*.

87. Robert O. Blood, Jr., "The Husband-Wife Relationship," in Hoffman and Nye, *Employed Mother in America*, chap. 20.

88. Callahan, *Working Mother*, p. 20; Benton, *American Male*, chap. 2.

89. Margaret Mead, "A Cultural Anthropologist's Approach to Maternal Deprivation," in Ainsworth et al., *Maternal Deprivation*, pp. 237–54.

90. Stoltz, "Evidence from Research," pp. 722–23.

91. Oettinger, "Maternal Employment," p. 135.

92. Bossard and Boll, *Sociology of Child Development*, p. 277.

93. Yates, *What Women Want*, pp. 3–13.

94. Gallup, *Gallup Poll*, 2:702.

95. Morgan, *Total Woman*.

96. Ignatius, "Women at Work," pp. 1, 18.

97. Fraiberg, *Every Child's Birthright*; Kagan, *Growth of the Child*.

Chapter 6

1. Untitled MS (ca. 1918), McDowell Papers, Box 4.

2. Anthony, *Mothers Who Must Earn*, pp. 151–52; Hughes, *Mothers in Industry*, pp. 194–98.

3. Quoted in Calhoun, *History of the American Family*, 3:73.

4. Addams, "Charity and Social Justice," p. 7.

5. Hughes, *Mothers in Industry*, p. 197.

6. See Bennett, *Woman's Work among the Lowly*.

7. McCullogh, "Poor Widows with Dependent Children," p. 419.

8. Anthony, *Mothers Who Must Earn*, p.154.

9. Thurston, *Dependent Child*; Huggins, *Protestants against Poverty*, pp. 83–94.

10. William Hard, "Motherless Children of Living Mothers," *Delineator* (January 1903), quoted in Bullock, *Mothers' Pensions*, pp. 108–14.
11. Ohio Board of State Charities, *Twenty-third Annual Report*, p. 17.
12. U.S. Bureau of the Census, *Benevolent Institutions* (1904).
13. Bullock, *Mothers' Pensions*, p. 33.
14. Anthony, *Mothers Who Must Earn*, p. 153; Hughes, *Mothers in Industry*, p. 193.
15. Anthony, *Mothers Who Must Earn*, p. 53.
16. Ibid., p. 153.
17. Thurston, *Dependent Child*, pp. 115–16. See also Schneider, "In the Web of Class," chap. 2.
18. Marjory Hall, "For What Does the Day Nursery Stand?," National Federation of Day Nurseries, leaflet no. 5 (ca. 1904), p. 3, Day Care Subject File.
19. "Development of Day Nurseries in Charity Work," n.d. but ca. 1900, typewritten, CWLA Records, Box 21, folder 9; "Origins of Day Nursery Work," 1940, typewritten, CWLA Records, Box 21, folder 9; Beer, *Working Mothers*, p. 35; Steinfels, *Who's Minding the Children?*, p. 36.
20. "The Association of the Day Nurseries of New York City," leaflet, n.d. but ca. 1908, p. 4, Day Care Subject File.
21. "Origins of Day Nursery Work," CWLA Records, Box 21, folder 9; Josephine J. Dodge, "Neighborhood Work," pp. 113–18; U.S. Department of Labor, Women's Bureau, *Employed Mothers*.
22. For a biography of Dodge, see James et al., eds., *Notable American Women*, 1:492–93.
23. "Development of Day Nurseries," p. 2, CWLA Records, Box 21, folder 9; Untitled MS, n.d. but ca. 1910, typewritten, CWLA Records, Box 21, folder 9; Mulry, "Care of Children," p. 170; Hall, "For What Does the Day Nursery Stand?," p. 14; Josephine J. Dodge, "Neighborhood Work," p. 113.
24. Burgess, "Day Nursery Work," p. 424.
25. Rosenau, "Schemes for Self-Help," pp. 179–80.
26. "Historical Sketch of the Day Nursery Movement," 1940, typewritten, pp. 3–7, CWLA Records, Box 21, folder 9; Steinfels, *Who's Minding the Children?*, p. 48; Greenblatt, *Responsibility for Child Care*, pp. 24–27; Burgess, "Day Nursery Work," pp. 426–27.
27. "Development of Day Nurseries," p. 12, CWLA Records, Box 21, folder 9.
28. "Historical Sketch," p. 3, CWLA Records, Box 21, folder 9.
29. Rosenau, "Schemes for Self-Help," p. 181; Higgins and Windom, "Helping Widows," p. 141.
30. Rosenau, "Day Nurseries," p. 337; "Development of Day Nurseries," p. 5.
31. Rosenau, "Day Nurseries," pp. 333–40; "Duties of a Matron," leaflet no. 7, n.d., p. 7, CWLA Records, Box 46, folder 13.
32. Anthony, *Mothers Who Must Earn*, p. 152; Hughes, *Mothers in Industry*, p. 194; U.S. Bureau of the Census, *Benevolent Institutions, 1904*, pp. 30–32; Board of Commissioners of Public Charities of the Commonwealth of Pennsylvania, *Twenty-second Annual Report*, pp. 136–38.
33. Anthony, *Mothers Who Must Earn*, p. 152.
34. Hughes, *Mothers in Industry*, p. 197.
35. Quoted in Tentler, *Wage-Earning Women*, p. 162.
36. Ibid.
37. Steinfels, *Who's Minding the Children?*, p. 52; E. H. Lewinski-Corwin, "Day Nurseries in New York City," in Association of Day Nurseries of New York City, *1924 Report*, CWLA Records, Box 21, folder 9.
38. Addams, "Charity and Social Justice," p. 7; Wolcott, "Discussion," p. 423.
39. C. C. Carstens, "Social Security through Aid for Dependent Children in their Own Homes,"

n.d., typewritten, Carstens Papers, Box 1.

40. U.S. Department of Labor, Children's Bureau, *Laws Relating to Mothers' Pensions.*
41. L. A. Halbert, "The Widows' Allowance Act in Kansas City," *Survey*, 28 February 1914, pp. 675–76, quoted in Bullock, *Mothers' Pensions*, p. 9.
42. U.S. Department of Labor, Children's Bureau, *Administration of Mothers' Aid*; U.S. Department of Labor, Children's Bureau, *Laws Relating to Mothers' Pensions*, pp. 12–16; Hall, *Mothers' Assistance in Philadelphia*, p. 2.
43. New York Commission on Relief for Widowed Mothers, *1914 Report*, quoted in Bullock, *Mothers' Pensions*, pp. 32–34.
44. Merrit W. Pinckney, "Public Pensions to Widows," *Child*, July 1912, quoted in Bullock, *Mothers' Pensions*, p. 150.
45. "The Needy Mother and the Neglected Child," *Outlook*, 7 June 1913, quoted in Bullock, *Mothers' Pensions*, p. 28; New York Conference of Charities and Correction, *Proceedings, 1912*, p. 77.
46. I would like to thank Blanche D. Coll for sharing with me her ideas about mothers' pensions and the progressives.
47. William Hard, "Motherless Children of Living Mothers," *Delineator*, January 1913, quoted in Bullock, *Mothers' Pensions*, p. 113.
48. Boston Society for Helping Destitute Mothers and Infants, *1912 Report*, Schlesinger Library, Radcliffe College, Cambridge, Mass.
49. Ben B. Lindsey, "The Mothers' Compensation Law of Colorado," *Survey*, 15 February 1913, quoted in Bullock, *Mothers' Pensions*, p. 23.
50. *Life and Labor*, December 1919, pp. 307–10; "Working Women and the World," leaflet, 1919, International Federation of Working Women Papers.
51. C. C. Carstens, "Recent Trends in Child Care," 21 June 1932, typewritten, Carstens Papers, Box 1.
52. Bullock, *Mothers' Pensions*, p. x; New York Conference of Charities and Correction, *Proceedings, 1912*, pp. 93–94; Bremner, *From the Depths*, pp. 222–23.
53. U.S. Department of Labor, *Laws Relating to Mothers' Pensions*, pp. 12–14.
54. Bogue, "Problems in Administration," p. 352; U.S. Department of Labor, *Laws Relating to Mothers' Pensions*, p. 14; Hall, *Mothers' Assistance in Philadelphia*, pp. 2–11.
55. U.S. Department of Labor, Children's Bureau, *Mothers' Aid 1931*, pp. 13–14.
56. Travis, "Origins of Mothers' Pensions," pp. 422–43; "Widows' Pension Legislation," p. v.; Lundberg, "Aid to Mothers," p. 101.
57. U.S. Department of Labor, *Laws Relating to Mothers' Pensions*, pp. 15–16; U.S. Department of Labor, *Administration of Mothers' Aid*, p. 43.
58. U.S. Department of Labor, *Laws Relating to Mothers' Pensions*, p. 15; "Widows' Pension Legislation," p. 73; Tyson, "The Fatherless Family," p. 86.
59. U.S. Department of Labor, *Children of Wage-Earning Mothers*, p. 81; U.S. Congress, Senate, *Proceedings of the Conference on the Care of Dependent Children*, p. 35; Bogue, "Problems in Administration," p. 354.
60. Helen Tyson, Foreword to Hughes, *Mothers in Industry*, p. xiv.
61. Richmond and Hall, *Study of Nine Hundred and Eighty-Five Widows*, p. 21.
62. Lundberg, "Aid to Mothers," p. 101.
63. U.S. Bureau of the Census, *Children under Institutional Care, 1923*, p. 14, table 1, p. 29, table 9; U.S. Congress, Senate, *Mothers' Aid in the District of Columbia*, p. 35.
64. U.S. Congress, Senate, *Mothers' Aid in the District of Columbia*, p. 34.
65. Halbert, "Widows' Allowance Act," quoted in Bullock, *Mothers' Pensions*, p. 8. See also Lewinski-Corwin, "Day Nurseries in New York City."
66. Anonymous, "We Both Had Jobs," *Woman's Home Companion*, August 1925, quoted in Coyle, *Jobs and Marriage?*, p. 34.

67. See Kennon, "Gainful Employment of Radcliffe Students."

68. Greenblatt, *Responsibility for Child Care*, p. 49.

69. Chambers, "Plea for Teachers," p. 574.

70. Greenblatt, *Responsibility for Child Care*, p. 53; Lois Hayden Meek, "Minimum Essentials for Nursery School Education," 1929, typescript, CWLA Records, Box 21, folder 9.

71. Greenblatt, *Responsibility for Child Care*, p. 48.

72. Steinfels, *Who's Minding the Children?*, p. 63.

73. Ibid., p. 64.

74. Ibid., p. 767; Marion S. Newcombe, "Nursery Education in New York City," n.d., typewritten, CWLA Records, Box 46, folder 14; U.S. Department of Labor, Women's Bureau, *Employed Mothers and Child Care*, p. 15.

75. U.S. Office of Education, "School Services," p. 6.

76. "A Statement from the National Association of Day Nurseries," 15 July 1941, typewritten, p. 3, CWLA Records, Box 46, folder 8.

77. Emma O. Lundberg, "A Community Program of Day Care for Children of Mothers Employed in Defense Areas," December 1941, typewritten, CWLA Records, Box 22, folder 1; Steinfels, *Who's Minding the Children?*, p. 67.

78. Susan B. Anthony II, *Out of the Kitchen*, p. 134; Goodlad et al., *Early Schooling*, pp. 6–7.

79. "Day Care of Children in Post-War United States," May 1945, typewritten, p. 2, CWLA Records, Box 22, folder 1; Rothman, *Woman's Proper Place*, p. 223.

80. Child Care Center Parents' Association of New York, *1948 Report*, p. 4, Child Care Center Parents' Association of New York Records, Box 1, folder 2.

81. Child Care Center Parents' Association of New York, untitled MS, n.d., Child Care Center Parents' Association of New York Records, Box 2, folder 11; Greenblatt, *Responsibility for Child Care*, p. 64.

82. "Day Care of Children in Post-War United States," CWLA Records, p. 4.

83. "History of Brightside Day Nursery," 1948, typewritten, p. 9, CWLA Records, Box 22, folder 1.

84. U.S. Department of Labor, Women's Bureau, *Employed Mothers and Child Care*.

85. Cited in Binder, "Affirmative Day Care," p. 24.

86. Steinfels, *Who's Minding the Children?*, p. 72.

87. Binder, "Affirmative Day Care," pp. 24–28.

88. For a general history of government aid to mothers, see Bell, *Aid to Dependent Children*.

89. Steinfels, *Who's Minding the Children?*, pp. 81–82; Greenblatt, *Responsibility for Child Care*, p. 134.

90. Greenblatt, *Responsibility for Child Care*, pp. 267–69; Bane et al., "Child-Care Arrangements," p. 52.

91. U.S. Congress, Senate, *Hearings . . . before the Committee on Finance*, p. 93.

92. For the details of this debate, see ibid.; Rothman, *Woman's Proper Place*, pp. 267–81. See also Clarke-Stewart, *Daycare*.

93. See U.S. Congress, Senate, *Veto Message*.

94. Michael T. Kaufman, "Day-Care Truce Ends Sit-In at Lindsay Center," *New York Times*, 20 January 1972, p. 41.

95. Steinfels, *Who's Minding the Children?*, p. 197; Levitan and Alderman, *Child Care*, p. 3; U.S. Bureau of the Census, *Statistical Abstract, . . . 1980*, p. 147, table 234; Bane, "Child-Care Arrangements," p. 52.

96. Featherstone, "Kentucky-Fried Children," pp. 12–16; Thomas J. Bray, "Mother's Helper," *Wall Street Journal*, 10 April 1970, p. 1.

97. U.S. Department of Labor, *Working Women*, p. 25, table 25.

98. Waldman, "Working Mothers in the 1970s," pp. 39–40; Grossman, "Children of Working Mothers," p. 32.

99. Levitan and Alderman, *Child Care*, pp. 110–11; Nona Glazer et al., "The Homemaker, the Family, and Employment," in *Women in the U.S. Labor Force*, ed. Cahn, pp. 155–69.

100. Bane, "Child-Care Arrangements," p. 51.

101. For a comparison with European day-care policies, see Alice H. Cook, "Working Women: European Experience and American Need," in *Women in the U.S. Labor Force*, ed. Cahn, pp. 271–306.

102. Carol S. Greenwald, "Part-Time Work," in *Women in the U.S. Labor Force*, ed. Cahn, pp. 182–94; Waldman, "Working Mothers in the 1970s," p. 40. See also U.S. Bureau of the Census, *Statistical Abstract, . . . 1981*, p. 384, table 642, p. 389, table 657.

103. Giraldo, *Public Policy*, p. 29.

Conclusion

1. U.S. Department of Labor, Bureau of Labor Statistics, *Working Women*, p. 15; Masnick and Bane, *Nation's Families*, chap. 3.

2. U.S. Department of Labor, Bureau of Labor Statistics, *Children of Working Mothers*, p. 1; Shreve, "Careers and the Lure of Motherhood," p. 39.

3. I am grateful to Patsy L. Chronis, director of the Circle Children's Center, University of Illinois at Chicago, and Brian Vaughn, Psychology Department, University of Illinois at Chicago, for sharing with me their ideas about current issues in child-care policy. For a recent discussion of the literature on maternal employment, see Shreve, "Careers and the Lure of Motherhood," pp. 48–50.

4. Suransky, *Erosion of Childhood*, p. 185.

5. Ibid.; Featherstone, "Kentucky-Fried Children," p. 15. For another point of view, see Clarke-Stewart, *Daycare*.

6. Clarke-Stewart, *Daycare*, p. 136; Suransky, *Erosion of Childhood*, pp. 200–203.

Bibliography

Manuscript Sources

Cambridge, Massachusetts
  Schlesinger Library, Radcliffe College
    Child Care Center Parents' Association of New York Records.
    Day Care Subject File.
    Julia Ward Howe Papers.
    International Federation of Working Women Papers.
    Marion H. Niles Papers.
    Women's Educational and Industrial Union Papers.
Chicago, Illinois
  Chicago Historical Society
    Mary McDowell Papers.
  The University Library, University of Illinois at Chicago
    Jane Addams Memorial Collection.
    Young Women's Christian Association of Metropolitan Chicago Records.
Minneapolis, Minnesota
  Minneapolis Woman's Christian Association
    Minneapolis Woman's Christian Association Papers.
  Social Welfare History Archives, University of Minnesota
    Christian Carl Carstens Papers.
    Child Welfare League of America Records.
    Travelers' Aid Association of America Records.
St. Paul, Minnesota
  Minnesota State Archives, Minnesota Historical Society
    Minnesota Labor and Industry Department Records.

Government Publications

U.S. Bureau of the Census. *Benevolent Institutions*. Washington, D.C.: GPO, 1904.
_____. *Benevolent Institutions*. Washington, D.C.: GPO, 1910.
_____. *Children under Institutional Care, 1923*. Washington, D.C.: GPO, 1927.
_____. *Comparative Occupation Statistics for the United States, 1870–1940*, by Alba M. Edwards. Washington, D.C.: GPO, 1943.
_____. *Earnings of Factory Workers, 1899 to 1927*, by Paul F. Brissenden. Washington, D.C.: GPO, 1929.
_____. *Farm Population of the United States*, by Leon E. Truesdell. Washington, D.C.: GPO, 1926.
_____. *Historical Statistics of the United States*. Washington, D.C.: GPO, 1960.
_____. *Nineteenth Census of the U.S., 1970: U.S. Summary*. Vol. 1. Washington, D.C.: GPO, 1971.
_____. *Occupations of the Twelfth Census*. Washington, D.C.: GPO, 1904.
_____. *Statistical Abstract of the United States, 1980*. 101 ed. Washington, D.C.: GPO, 1980.

————. *Statistical Abstract of the United States, 1981.* 102 ed. Washington, D.C.: GPO, 1981.

————. *Statistics of Women at Work.* Washington, D.C.: GPO, 1907.

————. *U.S. Census of Population, 1960: Subject Reports: Marital Status.* Final Report PC(2)-4E. Washington, D.C.: GPO, 1966.

————. *Women in Gainful Occupations, 1870–1920,* by Joseph Hill. Washington, D.C.: GPO, 1929.

U.S. Congress. Senate. *Hearings on S. 2003, before the Committee on Finance,* 92d Cong., 1st sess., 1971.

————. *Mothers' Aid in the District of Columbia: Hearings on S. 120 and S. 129.* 69th Cong., 1st sess., 1926.

————. *Proceedings of the Conference on the Care of Dependent Children.* 60th Cong., 2d sess., 1909. S. Doc. 721.

————. *Report on Condition of Woman and Child Wage-Earners in the United States.* Vol. 5: *Wage-Earning Women in Stores and Factories.* 61st Cong., 2d sess., 1910. S. Doc. 645.

————. *Report on Condition of Woman and Child Wage-Earners in the United States.* Vol. 9: *History of Women in Industry in the United States,* by Helen L. Sumner. 61st Cong., 2d sess., 1910. S. Doc. 645.

————. *Report on Condition of Woman and Child Wage-Earners in the United States.* Vol. 10: *History of Women in Trade Unions,* by John B. Andrews and W. D. P. Bliss. 61st Cong., 2d sess., 1910. S. Doc. 645.

————. *Report on Condition of Woman and Child Wage-Earners in the United States.* Vol. 13: *Infant Mortality and Its Relation to the Employment of Mothers.* 61st Cong., 2d sess., 1912. S. Doc. 645.

————. *Report on Condition of Woman and Child Wage-Earners in the United States.* Vol. 15: *Relation between Occupation and Criminality of Women,* by Mary Conyington. 61st Cong., 2d sess., 1912. S. Doc. 645.

————. *Veto Message—Economic Opportunity Amendments of 1971.* 120th Cong., 1st sess., 1971. S. Doc. 92-48.

U.S. Department of Labor. *Boarding Homes and Clubs for Working Women,* by Mary S. Fergusson. Department of Labor Bulletin no. 15. Washington, D.C.: GPO, 1898.

U.S. Department of Labor. Bureau of Labor Statistics. *Children of Working Mothers.* Bulletin 2158. Washington, D.C.: GPO, 1983.

————. *Children of Working Mothers, March 1977.* Special Labor Force Report no. 217. Washington, D.C.: GPO, 1977.

————. *Families and the Rise of Working Wives: An Overview.* Special Labor Force Report no. 189. Washington, D.C.: GPO, 1979.

————. *Handbook of Labor Statistics, 1978.* Bulletin 2000. Washington, D.C.: GPO, 1979.

————. *Marital and Family Characteristics of Workers, 1970–1978.* Special Labor Force Report no. 219. Washington, D.C.: GPO, 1979.

————. *Marital and Family Patterns of Workers: An Update.* Bulletin 2163. Washington, D.C.: GPO, 1983.

————. *Perspectives on Working Women: A Databook.* Bulletin 7080. Washington, D.C.: GPO, 1980.

————. *Summary of the Report on Condition of Woman and Child Wage-Earners in the United States.* Women in Industry Series no. 5. Bulletin of the Bureau of Labor Statistics no. 175. Washington, D.C.: GPO, 1916.

————. *Working Women: A Databook.* Bulletin 1977. Washington, D.C.: GPO, 1977.

U.S. Department of Labor. Children's Bureau. *Administration of Mothers' Aid in Ten Localities,* by Mary F. Bogue. Publication no. 184. Washington, D.C.: GPO, 1928.

————. *Children of Wage-Earning Mothers: A Study of a Selected Group in Chicago.* Publication no. 102. Washington, D.C.: GPO, 1922.

_____. *Children of Working Mothers in Philadelphia*, by Clara M. Beyer. Publication no. 204. Washington, D.C.: GPO, 1931.

_____. *Infant Mortality: Results of a Field Study in New Bedford, Mass.* Publication no. 68. Washington, D.C.: GPO, 1920.

_____. *Laws Relating to "Mothers' Pensions" in the United States, Denmark, and New Zealand.* Publication no. 7. Washington, D.C.: GPO, 1914.

_____. *Mothers' Aid 1931.* Publication no. 220. Washington, D.C.: GPO, 1933.

U.S. Department of Labor. Commissioner of Labor. *Eighteenth Annual Report: Cost of Living and Retail Prices of Food.* Washington, D.C.: GPO, 1904.

_____. *Fourth Annual Report: Working Women in Large Cities.* Washington, D.C.: GPO, 1889.

U.S. Department of Labor. Employment Standards Administration. *Minority Women Workers: A Statistical Overview.* Rev. ed. Washington, D.C.: GPO, 1977.

_____. *1975 Handbook on Women Workers.* Bulletin no. 297. Washington, D.C.: GPO, 1975.

U.S. Department of Labor. Women's Bureau. *The Development of Minimum-Wage Laws in the United States, 1912 to 1927.* Bulletin no. 61. Washington, D.C.: GPO, 1927.

_____. *The Effects of Labor Legislation on the Employment Opportunities for Women.* Bulletin no. 65. Washington, D.C.: GPO, 1928.

_____. *Employed Mothers and Child Care.* Bulletin no. 246. Washington, D.C.: GPO, 1953.

_____. *The Employment of Women at Night*, by Mary D. Hopkins. Bulletin no. 64. Washington, D.C.: GPO, 1928.

_____. *The Employment of Women in Hazardous Industries in the United States.* Bulletin no. 6. Washington, D.C.: GPO, 1920.

_____. *The Family Status of Breadwinning Women: A Study of Material in the Census Schedules of a Selected Locality.* Bulletin no. 23. Washington, D.C.: GPO, 1922.

_____. *History of Labor Legislation for Women in Three States*, by Clara M. Beyer, and *Chronological Development of Labor Legislation for Women in the United States*, by Florence Smith. Bulletin no. 66. Washington, D.C.: GPO, 1929.

_____. *Homework in Bridgeport, Connecticut.* Bulletin no. 9. Washington, D.C.: GPO, 1920.

_____. *The Immigrant Woman and Her Job*, by Caroline Manning. Bulletin no. 74. Washington, D.C.: GPO, 1930.

_____. *Office Work and Office Workers in 1940.* Bulletin no. 188. Washington, D.C.: GPO, 1942.

_____. *Proceedings of the Women's Industrial Conference.* Bulletin no. 33. Washington, D.C.: GPO, 1923.

_____. *The Share of Wage-Earning Women in Family Support.* Bulletin no. 30. Washington, D.C.: GPO, 1923.

_____. *Some Effects of Legislation Limiting Hours of Work for Women.* Bulletin no. 15. Washington, D.C.: GPO, 1921.

_____. *State Laws Affecting Working Women: Hours, Minimum Wage, Home Work.* Bulletin no. 63. Washington, D.C.: GPO, 1927.

_____. *Summary: The Effects of Labor Regulation on the Employment Opportunities of Women.* Bulletin no. 68. Washington, D.C.: GPO, 1928.

_____. *Towards Better Working Conditions for Women.* Bulletin no. 352. Washington, D.C.: GPO, 1953.

_____. *Women Workers and Their Dependents*, by Mary-Elizabeth Pidgeon. Bulletin no. 239. Washington, D.C.: GPO, 1951.

_____. *Women Workers in Ten Production Areas and Their Postwar Production Plans.* Bulletin no. 209. Washington, D.C.: GPO, 1946.

_____. *Women Workers in Their Family Environment.* Bulletin no. 183. Washington, D.C.: GPO, 1941.

U.S. Office of Education. *School Services for Children of Working Mothers*. School Children
and the War Leaflet no. 1. Washington, D.C.: GPO, 1943.

Books and Articles

Abbott, Edith. *Women in Industry: A Study in American Economic History*. New York: D. Appleton and Company, 1910.

Adams, Elizabeth Kemper. *Women Professional Workers: A Study Made for the Women's Educational and Industrial Union*. New York: Macmillan, 1921.

Addams, Jane. "Charity and Social Justice." *Proceedings of the National Conference of Charities and Correction, 37th Annual Meeting*. Fort Wayne, Ind.: Archer Publishing, 1910.

———. *A New Conscience and an Ancient Evil*. New York: Macmillan, 1912.

———. *A Plea for More Play, More Pay, and More Education for Our Factory Girls and Boys*. Chicago: Chicago Association of Commerce, [1914?].

———. *The Spirit of Youth and the City Streets*. New York: Macmillan, 1909.

———. "Why Girls Go Wrong." *Ladies' Home Journal*, September 1907, pp. 13–14.

Ainsworth, Mary D. *Deprivation of Maternal Care: A Reassessment of Its Effects*. New York: Schocken, 1966. Part 2 of *Maternal Care and Mental Health: A Report Prepared on Behalf of the World Health Organization as a Contribution to the United Nations Programme for the Welfare of Homeless Children*, by John Bowlby. 1951. Reprint. New York: Schocken, 1966.

"The American Woman in the Marketplace." *Ladies' Home Journal*, April 1900.

Ames, Azel, Jr. *Sex in Industry: A Plea for the Working-Girl*. Boston: James R. Osgood and Co., 1875.

Ames, John Quincy, comp. *Co-operation between the Young Women's and the Young Men's Christian Associations*. Chicago: Young Men's Christian Association College, 1929.

Anthony, Katherine. *Mothers Who Must Earn*. New York: Survey Associates, 1914.

Anthony, Susan Brownell, II. *Out of the Kitchen—Into the War*. New York: Stephan Daye, 1943.

Baer, Judith A. *The Chains of Protection: The Judicial Response to Women's Labor Legislation*. Contributions to Women's Studies no. 1. Westport, Conn.: Greenwood Press, 1978.

Baker, Elizabeth Faulkner. *Technology and Woman's Work*. New York: Columbia University Press, 1964.

Baker, Orin C. *Travelers' Aid Society in America: Protection from Danger and Prevention of Crime for Travelers, Especially Young Women, Girls, and Boys Travelling Alone*. New York: Funk and Wagnalls, 1917.

Bancroft, Gertrude. *The American Labor Force: Its Growth and Changing Composition*. New York: John Wiley and Sons, 1958.

Bane, Mary Jo, et al. "Child-Care Arrangements of Working Parents." *Monthly Labor Review* 102 (October 1979): 50–56.

Barney, Susan Hammond. "Care of the Criminal." In *Woman's Work in America*, edited by Annie Nathan Meyer, pp. 359–72. New York: Henry Holt, 1891.

Baxandall, Rosalyn; Gordon, Linda; and Reverby, Susan, eds. *America's Working Women: A Documentary History 1600 to the Present*. New York: Vintage Books, 1976.

Beauvoir, Simone de. *The Second Sex*. New York: Alfred A. Knopf, 1952.

Bednarzik, Robert W., and Klein, Deborah P. "Labor Force Trends: A Synthesis and Analysis." *Monthly Labor Review* 100 (October 1977): 3–11.

Beecher, Catharine E. *The Evils Suffered by American Women and Children: The Causes and the Remedy*. New York: Harper and Brothers, 1846.

Beer, Ethel S. *Working Mothers and the Day Nursery*. New York: Whiteside, Inc., and William Morrow and Co., 1957.

Bell, Ernest. *Fighting the Traffic in Young Girls, Or War on the White Slave Trade.* N.p.: 1910.

Bell, Winifred. *Aid to Dependent Children.* New York: Columbia University Press, 1965.

Bennett, Sarah R. I. *Woman's Work among the Lowly: Memorial Volume of the First Forty Years of the American Female Guardian Society and Home for the Friendless.* New York: American Female Guardian Society, 1877.

Benson, Mary Sumner. *Women in Eighteenth-Century America: A Study of Opinion and Social Usage.* Columbia University Studies in History, Economics and Public Law no. 405. New York: Columbia University Press, 1935.

Benson, Susan Porter. " 'The Customers Ain't God': The Work Culture of Department-Store Saleswomen, 1890–1940." In *Working-Class America: Essays on Labor, Community, and American Society,* edited by Michael H. Frisch and Daniel J. Walkowitz, pp. 185–211. Urbana, Ill.: University of Illinois Press, 1983.

Berg, Barbara J. *The Remembered Gate: Origins of American Feminism.* New York: Oxford University Press, 1978.

Binder, Gertrude. "Affirmative Day Care." *Social Work Journal* 34 (January 1953): 24–28.

Blackwell, Emily. "The Responsibility of Women in Regard to Questions Concerning Public Morality." In *The National Purity Congress,* edited by Aaron M. Powell. New York: American Purity Alliance, 1896.

Bliven, Bruce, Jr. *The Wonderful Writing Machine.* New York: Random House, 1954.

Bloch, Ruth H. "American Feminine Ideals in Transition: The Rise of the Moral Mother, 1785–1815." *Feminist Studies* 4 (June 1978): 101–26.

Board of Commissioners of Public Charities of the Commonwealth of Pennsylvania. *Twenty-second Annual Report.* Harrisburg, Pa.: Edwin K. Meyers, 1892.

Bogue, Mary. "Problems in the Administration of Mothers' Aid." *Proceedings of the National Conference of Charities and Correction, 45th Annual Meeting.* Chicago: Rogers and Hall, 1918.

Bossard, James H. S. *The Sociology of Child Development.* New York: Harper and Row, 1948.

―――――, and Boll, Eleanor Stokes. *The Sociology of Child Development.* 4th ed. New York: Harper and Row, 1966.

Bosworth, Louise Marion. "The Living Wage of Women Workers: A Study of Incomes and Expenditures of Four Hundred and Fifty Women Workers in the City of Boston." Supplement to the *Annals of the American Academy of Political and Social Science* 37 (May 1911): 1–90.

Bowen, Louise DeKoven. *The Department Store Girl: Based upon Interviews with 200 Girls.* Chicago: Juvenile Protective Association, 1911.

―――――. *The Road to Destruction Made Easy in Chicago.* Chicago: Hale-Crossley Printing, 1916.

Bowlby, John. *Maternal Care and Mental Health: A Report Prepared on Behalf of the World Health Organization as a Contribution to the United Nations Programme for the Welfare of Homeless Children.* Part 1. 1951. Reprint. New York: Schocken, 1966.

Boyer, Paul. *Urban Masses and Moral Order in America.* Cambridge, Mass.: Harvard University Press, 1975.

Brandeis, Louis D., and Goldmark, Josephine. *The Case against Nightwork for Women; The People of the State of New York, Respondent, against Charles Schweinler Press, A Corporation, Defendant-Appellant.* 1914. Rev. ed. New York: National Consumers' League, 1914.

―――――. *Women in Industry; Decision of the United States Supreme Court in Curt Muller vs. State of Oregon Upholding the Constitutionality of the Oregon Ten-Hour Law for Women, and Brief for the State of Oregon.* New York: National Consumers' League, [1908]. Reprint. New York: Arno Press, 1969.

Bremner, Robert. *From the Depths: The Discovery of Poverty in the United States.* New York: New York University Press, 1956.

Brenton, Myron. *The American Male.* Greenwich, Conn.: Fawcett Publications, 1966.

Bromley, Dorothy Dunbar. "Feminist—New Style." *Harper's Monthly Magazine*, October 1927, pp. 552–60.

Brownlee, W. Elliot. "Household Values, Women's Work, and Economic Growth, 1880–1930." *Journal of Economic History* 39 (March 1979): 199–209.

————, and Brownlee, Mary M., eds. *Women in the American Economy: A Documentary History, 1675 to 1929.* New Haven: Yale University Press, 1976.

Bullock, Edna, comp. *Selected Articles on the Employment of Women.* Debaters' Handbook Series. Minneapolis: H. W. Wilson, 1911.

————. *Selected Articles on Mothers' Pensions.* Debaters' Handbook Series. New York: H. W. Wilson, 1915.

Burgess, M. H. "Day Nursery Work." *Proceedings of the National Conference of Charities and Correction, 19th Annual Meeting.* Boston: Geo. H. Ellis, 1892.

Burrington, Venila S. "The Immigrant in Household Employment." *Bulletin of the Inter-Municipal Committee on Household Research, February 1905, pp. 5–8.*

Bushman, Claudia L. *"A Good Poor Man's Wife" : Being a Chronicle of Harriet Hanson Robinson and Her Family in Nineteenth-Century New England.* Hanover, N.H.: University Press of New England, 1981.

Butler, Elizabeth Beardsley. *Women and the Trades: Pittsburgh, 1907–1908.* Volume 1 of the Pittsburgh Survey, edited by Paul Underwood Kellogg. New York: Charities Publication Committee, 1909.

Cahn, Anne Foote, ed. *Women in the U.S. Labor Force.* New York: Praeger Publishers, 1979.

Calhoun, Arthur Wallace. *A Social History of the American Family from Colonial Times to the Present.* 3 vols. Cleveland: Arthur H. Clark, 1917–19.

Callahan, Sidney Cornelia. *The Working Mother.* New York: Macmillan, 1971.

Campbell, Helen. *Prisoners of Poverty: Women Wage-Workers, Their Trades and Their Lives.* Boston: Roberts Brothers, 1887.

————. *The Problem of the Poor: A Record of Quiet Work in Unquiet Places.* New York: Fords, Howard and Hulbert, 1882.

Candee, Helen Churchill. *How Women May Earn a Living.* New York: Macmillan, 1900.

Cantril, Hadley. *Public Opinion, 1935–1946.* Princeton, N.J.: Princeton University Press, 1951.

Carey, Matthew. *Miscellaneous Essays.* Philadelphia: Carey and Hart, 1830.

Chafe, William H. *The American Woman: Her Changing Social, Economic, and Political Roles, 1920–1970.* New York: Oxford University Press, 1972.

Chambers, M. M. "A Plea for Married Women Teachers." *School and Society* 30 (26 October 1919): 572–75.

Clark, Davis Wasgatt. *Child Labor and the Social Conscience.* New York: Abingdon Press, 1924.

Clark, Sue Ainslie, and Wyatt, Edith. *Making Both Ends Meet: The Income and Outlay of New York Working Girls.* New York: Macmillan, 1911.

Clarke-Stewart, Alison. *Daycare.* Cambridge, Mass.: Harvard University Press, 1982.

Clive, Alan. "Women Workers in World War II: Michigan as a Test Case." *Labor History* 20 (Winter 1979): 44–72.

Cohen, Miriam Judith. "From Workshop to Office: Italian Women and Family Strategies in New York City, 1900–1950." Ph.D. dissertation, University of Michigan, 1978.

Commons, John Roger, et al., eds. *A Documentary History of American Industrial Society.* Vol. 6. New York: Russell and Russell, 1958.

————. *History of Labor in the United States.* Vol. 3. New York: Macmillan, 1918–35.

Conk, Margo A. "Accuracy, Efficiency, and Bias: The Interpretation of Women's Work in the U.S. Census of Occupations, 1890–1940." *Historical Methods* 14 (Spring 1981): 65–72.

Cott, Nancy F. *The Bonds of Womanhood: "Woman's Sphere" in New England, 1780–1835.* New Haven: Yale University Press, 1977.

Cowan, Ruth Schwartz. "A Case Study of Technological and Social Change: The Washing Machine and the Working Wife." In *Clio's Consciousness Raised: New Perspectives on the History of Women*, edited by Mary S. Hartman and Lois W. Banner, pp. 245–53. New York: Harper and Row, Harper Colophon Books, 1974.

Coyle, Grace L. *Jobs and Marriage? Outlines for the Discussion of the Married Woman in Business*. New York: Woman's Press, 1928.

Craven, Ruth Shonle. *The American Family*. New York: Thomas Y. Crowell, 1956.

Croly, Jane C. *Thrown on Her Own Resources: Or, What Girls Can Do*. New York: Thomas Y. Crowell, 1891.

Davies, Margery. "Woman's Place Is at the Typewriter: The Feminization of the Clerical Labor Force." *Radical America* 8 (July–August 1974): 1–28.

De Graffenried, Clare. "The Needs of Self-Supporting Women." *Johns Hopkins University Studies in Historical and Political Science, Supplementary Notes No. 1* 10 (1890).

Demos, John. *A Little Commonwealth: Family Life in Plymouth Colony*. New York: Oxford University Press, 1970.

Devoll, Sarah W. "The Results of the Employment of a Police Matron in the City of Portland, Maine." *Proceedings of the National Conference of Charities and Correction, 8th Annual Meeting*. Boston: Geo. H. Ellis, 1881.

Dingwall, Eric John. *The American Woman*. New York: Rinehart and Co., 1957.

Dodge, Grace Hoadley. "Sunny Spots for Working Girls." *Ladies' Home Journal*, January 1892.

Dodge, Josephine Jewell. "Neighborhood Work and Day Nurseries." In *Proceedings of the National Conference of Charities and Correction, 39th Annual Meeting*. Fort Wayne, Ind.: Fort Wayne Printing Co., 1912.

Dodge, Mary Abigail [Gail Hamilton, pseud.]. *A New Atmosphere*. Boston: Ticknor and Fields, 1865.

Donovan, Frances R. *The Saleslady*. Chicago: University of Chicago Press, 1929.

Dorn, Jacob Henry. *Washington Gladden: Prophet of the Social Gospel*. Columbus, Ohio: Ohio State University Press, 1967.

Douglas, Jack D. *Defining America's Social Problems*. Englewood Cliffs, N.J.: Prentice-Hall, 1974.

Dowsall, Jean. "Structural and Attitudinal Factors Associated with Female Labor Force Participation." *Social Science Quarterly* 55 (June 1974): 121–30.

Dublin, Thomas. *Farm to Factory: Women's Letters, 1830–1860*. New York: Columbia University Press, 1981.

———. *Women at Work: The Transformation of Work and Community in Lowell, Massachusetts, 1826–1860*. New York: Columbia University Press, 1979.

Dudden, Faye E. *Serving Women: Household Service in Nineteenth-Century America*. Middletown, Conn.: Wesleyan University Press, 1983.

Durand, John D. *The Labor Force in the United States, 1890–1960*. New York: Social Science Research Council, 1948.

Ellington, George. *The Women of New York: Or, the Underworld of the Great City*. New York: New York Book Co., 1869.

Elmer, M. C. *A Study of Women in Clerical and Secretarial Work in Minneapolis, Minn*. Minneapolis: Woman's Occupational Bureau, 1925.

Engle, Flora A. P. "The Story of the Mercer Expeditions." *Washington Historical Quarterly* 6 (October 1915): 225–37.

Erenberg, Lewis A. *Steppin' Out: New York Nightlife and the Transformation of American Culture, 1890–1930*. Contributions in American Studies, no. 50. Westport, Conn.: Greenwood Press, 1981.

Featherstone, Joseph. "Kentucky-Fried Children." *New Republic*, 5 September 1970, pp. 12–16.

Feldberg, Roslyn L. "Union Fever: Organizing among Clerical Workers, 1900–1930." *Radical*

America 14 (May–June 1980): 53–67.

Ferris, Helen. *Girls Clubs, Their Organization and Management: A Manual for Workers.* New York: E. P. Dutton, 1918.

Four Years in the Underbrush: Adventures of a Working Woman in New York City. New York: Charles Scribner's Sons, 1921.

Fox, Greer Litton. " 'Nice Girl': Social Control of Women through a Value Construct." *Signs* 2 (Summer 1977): 805–17.

Fraiberg, Selma. *Every Child's Birthright: In Defense of Mothering.* New York: Basic Books, 1977.

Fraundorf, Martha Norby. "The Labor Force Participation of Turn-of-the-Century Married Women." *Journal of Economic History* 34 (June 1979): 401–18.

Friedan, Betty. *The Feminine Mystique.* New York: Dell Publishing Co., 1964.

Galinsky, Ellen, and Hooks, William H. *The New Extended Family: Day Care That Works.* Boston: Houghton Mifflin, 1972.

Gallup, George H. *The Gallup Poll: Public Opinion, 1935–1971.* 3 vols. New York: Random House, 1972.

Gardner, Deborah S. "A Hotel Is Not a Home: Architecture Too Splendid for the Working Women of New York." Paper presented at the Second Conference on the History of Women, St. Paul, Minn., October 1977.

Garland, Hamlin. *Rose of Dutcher's Coolly.* 1895, 1899. Reprint of 1899 ed. New York: AMS Press, 1969.

Gilman, Charlotte Perkins. *The Home.* New York: McClure, Phillips and Co., 1903.

———. *Women and Economics.* Boston: Small, Maynard and Co., 1898.

Giraldo, E. I. *Public Policy and the Family.* Lexington, Mass.: D. C. Heath and Co., Lexington Books, 1980.

"The Girl Who Comes to the City: A Symposium." *Harper's Bazaar,* January 1908–January 1909.

Glasco, Laurence A. "The Life Cycles and Household Structures of American Ethnic Groups: Irish, German, and Native-born Whites in Buffalo, New York, 1855." In *Family and Kin in Urban Communities, 1700–1930,* edited by Tamara K. Haraven, pp. 122–43. New York: New Viewpoints, 1977.

Goldmark, Josephine. *Fatigue and Efficiency: A Study in Industry.* New York: Charities Publication Committee, 1912.

Goodlad, John I.; Klein, Frances M.; and Novotney, Jerrold M. *Early Schooling in the United States.* New York: McGraw-Hill, 1973.

Goodsell, Willystine. *Problems of the Family.* New York: Century Co., 1928.

Gordon, Kate. "Wherein Should the Education of a Woman Differ from That of a Man." *School Review* 13 (1905): 789–94.

Gordon, Linda. *Woman's Body, Woman's Right: A Social History of Birth Control in America.* New York: Grossman Publishers, 1976.

Gordon, Michael, ed. *The American Family in Social-Historical Perspective.* New York: St. Martin's Press, 1973.

Gorham, Ethel. *So Your Husband's Gone to War!* New York: Doubleday, Doran and Co., 1942.

Graham, Abbie. *Grace H. Dodge: Merchant of Dreams.* New York: Women's Press, 1926.

Greenblatt, Bernard. *Responsibility for Child Care.* San Francisco: Jossey-Bass, 1977.

Greenwald, Maurine Weiner. *Women, War, and Work: The Impact of World War I on Women Workers in the United States.* Westport, Conn.: Greenwood Press, 1980.

Grob, Gerald N. "Reflections on the History of Social Policy in America." *Reviews in American History* 7 (September 1979): 293–306.

Grossman, Allyson Sherman. "Children of Working Mothers, March 1977." *Monthly Labor Review* 101 (January 1978): 30–33.

Groves, Ernest R. "The Psychology of the Woman Who Works." *Family* (May 1927): 92–97.

Hall, Elizabeth L. *Mothers' Assistance in Philadelphia: Actual and Potential Costs.* Hanover, N.H.: Sociological Press, 1933.

Hall, G. Stanley. *Adolescence.* 2 vols. New York: D. Appleton and Co., 1904.

Hamilton, Alexander. "Report on Manufactures." In *Reports of the Secretary of the Treasury of the United States,* vol. 1. Washington, D.C.: Duff, Green, 1828.

Hansel, Harriet. "What about the Children?" *Harper's Monthly Magazine,* January 1927, pp. 220–27.

Haraven, Tamara K. "The Family as Process: The Historical Study of the Family Cycle." *Journal of Social History* 7 (Spring 1974): 322–29.

Harris, Barbara J. *Beyond Her Sphere: Women and the Professions in American History.* Contributions in Women's Studies no. 4. Westport, Conn.: Greenwood Press, 1978.

Harris, Louis, and Associates. *The 1970 Virginia Slims American Women's Opinion Poll.* Vol. 1. N.p., n.d.

Hayden, Dolores. *The Grand Domestic Revolution: A History of Feminist Designs for American Homes, Neighborhoods, and Cities.* Cambridge, Mass.: MIT Press, 1982.

Hendee, Elizabeth Russell. *The Growth and Development of the Young Women's Christian Association.* New York: Women's Press, 1930.

Herrick, Christine Terhune. *The Expert Maid-Servant.* New York: Harper and Brothers, 1904.

Higgins, Alice L., and Windom, Florence. "Helping Widows to Bring Up Citizens." *Proceedings of the National Conference of Charities and Correction, 37th Annual Meeting.* Fort Wayne, Ind.: Archer Publishing, 1910.

Hinkle, Beatrice M. "Changing Marriage." *Survey Graphic,* December 1926.

Hobson, Barbara M. "Seduced and Abandoned—A Tale of the Wicked City: The Response to Prostitution in Boston, 1820–1850." Paper presented at the Fourth Berkshire Conference on the History of Women, Mt. Holyoke, Mass., August 1978.

Hofstadter, Richard. *The Age of Reform.* New York: Vintage Books, 1955.

Huggins, Nathan I. *Protestants against Poverty: Boston's Charities, 1820–1900.* Contributions in American History no. 9. Westport, Conn.: Greenwood Press, 1971.

Hughes, Gwendolyn Salisbury. *Mothers in Industry: Wage-Earning Mothers in Philadelphia.* New York: New Republic, 1925.

Humphries, Elizabeth Jeanne. "Working Women in Chicago Factories and Department Stores, 1870–95." Master's thesis, University of Chicago, 1943.

Hutchinson, Emilie Josephine. "Women's Wages: A Study of the Wages of Industrial Women and Measures Suggested to Increase Them." Ph.D. dissertation, Columbia University, 1919.

Hvidt, Kristian. *Flight to America: The Social Background of 300,000 Danish Emigrants.* New York: Academic Press, 1975.

Hyde, William Dewitt. *The College Man and the College Woman.* Boston: Houghton Mifflin, 1906.

Hyman, Colette A. "The Young Women's Christian Association and the Women's City Missionary Society: Models of Feminine Behavior, 1868–1920." Senior thesis, Brown University, 1979.

Illinois. General Assembly. Senate. *Report of the Senate Vice Committee Created under the Authority of the Senate of the Forty-Ninth General Assembly as a Continuation of the Committee Created under the Authority of the Senate of the Forty-Eighth General Assembly, State of Illinois.* Chicago, 1916.

Information Bureau on Women's Work. *The Floating World.* Toledo, Ohio: Information Bureau on Women's Work, 1927.

James, Edward T., et al., eds. *Notable American Women, 1607–1950: A Biographical Dictionary.* 3 vols. Cambridge, Mass.: Harvard University Press, 1971.

Jansen, C. J. *Readings in the Sociology of Migration.* Oxford: Pergamon Press, 1970.

Josselyn, Irene M., and Goldman, Ruth Schley. "Should Mothers Work?" *Social Service Review* (March 1949): 74–87.

Juster, Norton. *So Sweet to Labor: Rural Women in America, 1865–1895*. New York: Viking Press, 1979.

Kagan, Jerome. *The Growth of the Child: Reflections on Human Development*. New York: W. W. Norton, 1978.

Katzman, David. *Seven Days a Week: Domestic Service in Industrializing America*. New York: Oxford University Press, 1978.

Kauffman, Reginald Wright. *The House of Bondage*. New York: Grosset and Dunlap, 1910.

Kelley, Florence. *Modern Industry in Relation to the Family, Health, Education, Morality*. New York: Longmans, Green and Co., 1914.

Kellor, Francis A. "The Immigrant Woman." *Atlantic Monthly*, September 1907, pp. 401–7.

———. "The Inter-Municipal Research Committee." *Annals of the American Academy of Political and Social Science* 27 (March 1906): 193–200.

———. *Out of Work: A Study of Unemployment*. New York: Knickerbocker Press, 1915.

———. "The Rights of Patrons of Employment Agencies." *Bulletin of the Inter-Municipal Committee on Household Research*, December 1904.

———. "Southern Colored Girls in the North." *Bulletin of the Inter-Municipal Committee on Household Research*, May 1905, pp. 5–9.

Kessler-Harris, Alice. *Out to Work: A History of Wage-Earning Women in the United States*. New York: Oxford University Press, 1982.

———. "Stratifying by Sex: Understanding the History of Working Women." In *Labor Market Segmentation*, edited by Richard C. Edwards, Michael Reich, and David M. Gordon, pp. 217–55. Lexington, Mass.: D. C. Heath, 1975.

———. "Women's Wage Work as Myth and History." *Labor History* 19 (Spring 1978): 287–307.

Klapp, Louise. "Relation of Social Vice to Industry." *Proceedings of the Minnesota State Conference of Charities and Correction, 21st Annual Meeting*. Minneapolis: Minnesota State Board of Control, 1912.

Klink, Jane Seymour. "The Housekeeper's Responsibility." *Atlantic Monthly*, March 1905, pp. 372–81.

———. "Put Yourself in Her Place." *Atlantic Monthly*, February 1905, pp. 169–77.

Kneeland, George. *Commercialized Prostitution in New York City*. New York: Century Co., 1913.

Komarovsky, Mirra. *Blue-Collar Marriage*. 1962. Reprint. New York: Vintage Books, 1967.

———. *Women in the Modern World: Their Education and Their Dilemmas*. Boston: Little, Brown, 1953.

Kowalewska, Monica. "Conditions of Work for Immigrant Girls in Restaurants." *Proceedings of the Minnesota State Conference of Charities and Correction, 25th Annual Meeting*. St. Paul: Minnesota State Board of Control, 1917.

Kraditor, Aileen S., ed. *Up from the Pedestal: Selected Writings in the History of American Feminism*. 5th ed. New York: New York Times Book Co., Quadrangle Books, 1968.

Kreps, Juanita. *Sex in the Marketplace: American Women at Work*. Policy Studies in Employment and Welfare no. 11. Baltimore: Johns Hopkins University Press, 1971.

LaFollette, Cecile Tipton. *A Study of the Problems of 652 Gainfully Employed Married Women Homemakers*. Contributions to Education no. 619. New York: Columbia University Press, 1934.

Laughlin, Clara E. *The Work-a-Day Girl: A Study of Some Present-Day Conditions*. New York: Fleming H. Revell, 1913.

Lerner, Gerda. "The Lady and the Mill Girl: Changes in the Status of Women in the Age of Jackson." *Midcontinent American Studies Journal* 10 (Spring 1969): 5–14.

Levitan, Sar A., and Alderman, Karen Cleary. *Child Care and ABC's Too.* Baltimore: Johns Hopkins University Press, 1975.

Lewis, Ervin Eugene. *Personnel Problems of the Teaching Staff.* New York: Century Co., 1925.

Littell, Jane. "Meditations of a Wage-Earning Wife." *Atlantic Monthly,* December 1924, pp. 728–34.

Long, Clarence D. *The Labor Force under Changing Income and Employment.* Princeton, N.J.: Princeton University Press, 1958.

Lundberg, Emma O. "Aid to Mothers with Dependent Children." *Annals of the American Academy of Political and Social Science* 98 (November 1921): 97–104.

Lundberg, Ferdinand, and Farnham, Marynia. *Modern Woman: The Lost Sex.* New York: Harper and Brothers, 1947.

Lynd, Robert, and Lynd, Helen M. *Middletown in Transition.* New York: Harcourt, Brace and Co., 1937.

McCullogh, Oscar. "Poor Widows with Dependent Children." *Proceedings of the National Conference of Charities and Correction, 15th Annual Meeting.* Boston: Geo. H. Ellis, 1888.

MacLean, Annie Marion. "The Eleanor Clubs of Chicago." *Survey,* 11 April 1914, pp. 60–61.

————. *Women Workers and Society.* Chicago: A. C. McClurg, 1916.

Macy, John. "Equality of Woman with Man: A Myth." *Harper's Monthly Magazine,* November 1926, pp. 705–10.

Marx, Leo. *The Machine in the Garden: Technology and the Pastoral Ideal in America.* New York: Oxford University Press, 1964.

Masnick, George, and Bane, Mary Jo. *The Nation's Families: 1960–1990.* Boston: Auburn House Publishing, 1980.

Masteller, Jean Carwile. "Marriage or Career, 1880–1914: A Dilemma for American Women Writers and Their Culture." Ph.D. dissertation, University of Minnesota, 1978.

Mativity, Nancy Barr. "The Wife, the Home, and the Job." *Harper's Monthly Magazine,* July 1926, pp. 189–99.

May, Henry F. *Protestant Churches and Industrial America.* New York: Harper and Brothers, 1949.

Mechling, Jay. "Advice to Historians on Advice to Mothers." *Journal of Social History* 9 (Fall 1975): 44–63.

Meserve, H. C. *Lowell—An Industrial Dream Come True.* Boston: National Association of Cotton Manufacturers, 1923.

Meyer, Annie Nathan, ed. *Women's Work in America.* New York: Henry Holt, 1891.

Miles, Henry Adolphus. *Lowell, As It Was, and As It Is.* Lowell, Mass.: Nathaniel L. Dayton, Merrill, and Heywood, 1846.

Minnesota Bureau of Labor. *Eighth Biennial Report of the Bureau of Labor of the State of Minnesota, 1901–02.* N.p.: Great Western Printing, 1902.

————. *Ninth Biennial Report of the Bureau of Labor of the State of Minnesota, 1903–04.* 2 vols. N.p.: Great Western Printing, 1904.

————. *Twelfth Biennial Report of the Bureau of Labor, Industries and Commerce of the State of Minnesota, 1909–10.* N.p.: Great Western Printing, 1910.

Minnesota Bureau of Labor Statistics. *First Biennial Report of the Bureau of Labor Statistics of the State of Minnesota, 1887–88.* N.p.: Thos. A. Clark, 1888.

Minnesota Minimum Wage Commission. *First Biennial Report, 1913–1914.* St. Paul, Minn., 1914.

Moore, Elizabeth Payne. "Life and Labor: Margaret Dreier Robins and the Women's Trade Union League." Ph.D. dissertation, University of Illinois at Chicago, 1981.

Morgan, Marabel. *The Total Woman.* Old Tappan, N.J.: Fleming H. Revell, 1973.

Mulry, J. M. "The Care of Destitute and Neglected Children." *Proceedings of the National Conference of Charities and Correction, 26th Annual Meeting.* Boston: Geo. H. Ellis, 1900.

"My Experiences in New York: The True Story of a Girl's Long Struggle." *Ladies' Home Journal*, March 1910–December 1910.

Nash, Gary B. "The Failure of Female Factory Labor in Colonial Boston." *Labor History* 20 (Spring 1979): 165–88.

Nathan, Maude. *The Story of an Epoch-making Movement.* New York: Doubleday, Page and Co., 1926.

———. "Women Who Work and Women Who Spend." *Annals of the American Academy of Political and Social Science* 27 (May 1906): 646–50.

National Bureau of Economic Research. *Aspects of Labor Economics.* Princeton, N.J.: Princeton University Press, 1962.

National League of Girls Clubs. *History of the National League of Women Workers, 1914.* New York: Pearl Press, 1914.

New York Bureau of Social Hygiene. *Housing Conditions of Employed Women in the Borough of Manhattan.* New York: Bureau of Social Hygiene, 1922.

New York Conference of Charities and Correction. *Proceedings, 1912.* Albany, New York: J. B. Lyon, 1912.

Nye, F. Ivan, and Hoffman, Lois Wladis. *The Employed Mother in America.* Chicago: Rand McNally, 1963.

Oettenger, Katherine Brownell. "Maternal Employment and Children." In *Work in the Lives of Married Women*, edited by the National Manpower Council. New York: Columbia University Press, 1958.

Ogburn, William F. "The Family and Its Functions." In *Recent Social Trends in the United States*, 1:661–708. New York: McGraw-Hill, 1933.

Ohio Board of State Charities. *Twenty-third Annual Report.* Columbus, Ohio: Westbote Co., 1899.

Oppenheimer, Valerie Kincade. "Demographic Influence on Female Employment and the Status of Women." In *Changing Women in a Changing Society*, edited by Joan Huber. Chicago: University of Chicago Press, 1973.

———. *The Female Labor Force in the United States: Demographic and Economic Factors Governing Its Growth and Changing Composition.* Population Monograph 5. Berkeley, Calif.: University of California Press, 1970.

Parker, Cornelia Stratton. *Working with the Working Woman.* New York: Harper and Brothers, 1922.

Penny, Virginia. *Think and Act: A Series of Articles Pertaining to Men and Women, Work and Wages.* Philadelphia: Claxton, Remsen, and Haffelfinger, 1869. Reprint. New York: Arno Press, 1971.

Peters, David Wilbur. *The Status of the Married Woman Teacher.* Contributions to Education no. 603. New York: Columbia University Press, 1934.

Pivar, David. *Purity Crusade: Sexual Morality and Social Control, 1868–1900.* Contributions in American History no. 23. Westport, Conn.: Greenwood Press, 1973.

Pleck, Elizabeth. "Two Worlds in One: Work and Family." *Journal of Social History* 10 (Winter 1976): 178–95.

Popenoe, Paul. *The Conservation of the Family.* Baltimore: Williams and Wilkins, 1926.

Post, Emily. *Etiquette: The Blue Book of Social Usage.* New York: Funk and Wagnalls, 1935.

Powell, Aaron M., ed. *The National Purity Congress; Its Papers, Addresses, Portraits.* New York: American Purity Alliance, 1896.

Pruette, Lorine. *Women and Leisure: A Study of Social Waste.* New York: E. P. Dutton, 1924.

———. *Women Workers through the Depression.* New York: Macmillan, 1934.

Rauschenbusch, Walter. *Christianizing the Social Order.* New York: Macmillan, 1917.

Raybeck, Joseph G. *A History of American Labor.* New York: Free Press, 1966.

Rayne, Martha Louise. *What Can a Woman Do? Or, Her Position in the Business and Literary World.* Petersburg, N.Y.: Eagle Publishing, 1893.

"Report of the Committee on Vagrancy of the Conference of Charities of New York City." *Charities Review*, May 1896, p. 244.

Report and Testimony Taken before the Special Committee of the Assembly Appointed to Investigate the Condition of Female Labor in the City of New York. 2 vols. Albany, N.Y.: Wynkoop, Hallenbeck Crawford, 1896.

Rhine, Alice Hyneman. "Women in Industry." In *Women's Work in America*, edited by Annie Nathan Meyer. New York: Henry Holt, 1891.

Richardson, Anna Steese. *The Girl Who Earns Her Own Living.* New York: B. W. Dodge, 1909.

Richardson, Dorothy. "The Difficulties and Dangers Confronting the Working Woman." *Annals of the American Academy of Political and Social Science* 27 (May 1906): 624–26.

———. *The Long Day: The Story of a New York Working Girl as Told by Herself.* 1905. Reprint. New York: Century Co., 1911.

———. "Trades-Unions in Petticoats." *Leslies Monthly* (March 1904).

Richmond, J. F. *New York and Its Institutions, 1609–1872.* New York: E. B. Treat, 1872.

Richmond, Mary E., and Hall, Fred S. *A Study of Nine Hundred and Eighty-Five Widows Known to Certain Charity Organization Societies in 1910.* New York: Russell Sage Foundation, 1913.

Robinson, Harriet Hanson. *Loom and Spindle: Or Life among the Early Mill Girls.* New York: Thomas Y. Crowell, 1898.

Roosevelt, Eleanor. *It's Up to the Women.* New York: Frederick A. Stokes, 1933.

Roosevelt, Theodore. *The Foes of Our Own Household.* New York: George H. Doran, 1917.

Rosen, Ruth. *The Lost Sisterhood: Prostitution in America, 1900–1918.* Baltimore: Johns Hopkins University Press, 1982.

———, and Davidson, Sue, eds. *The Maimie Papers.* Old Westbury, N.Y.: Feminist Press, 1977.

Rosenau, Nathaniel S. "Day Nurseries." *Proceedings of the National Conference of Charities and Correction, 21st Annual Meeting.* Boston: Geo. H. Ellis, 1894.

———. "Schemes for the Self-Help of the Poor." *Proceedings of the National Conference of Charities and Correction, 13th Annual Meeting.* Boston: Geo. H. Ellis, 1886.

Rothman, Sheila M. *Woman's Proper Place: A History of Changing Ideals and Practices, 1870 to the Present.* New York: Basic Books, 1978.

Rupp, Leila J. *Mobilizing Women for War: German and American Propaganda, 1939–1945.* Princeton, N.J.: Princeton University Press, 1978.

Russell, Thomas H. *The Girl's Fight for a Living: How to Protect the Working Woman from Dangers Due to Low Wages.* Chicago: M. A. Donahue, 1913.

Salmon, Lucy Maynard. *Domestic Service.* New York: Macmillan, 1897.

Sanger, William. *The History of Prostitution: Its Extent, Causes and Effects throughout the World.* 1858. Reprint. New York: Eugenics Publishing, 1939.

Schaffer, Rudolph. *Mothering.* Cambridge, Mass.: Harvard University Press, 1977.

Schiffman, Jacob. "Marital and Family Characteristics of Workers, March 1960." *Monthly Labor Review* 84 (April 1961): 355–64.

Schneider, Eric C. "In the Web of Class: Youth, Class and Culture in Boston, 1840–1940." Ph.D. dissertation, Boston University, 1980.

Scoresby, William. *American Factories and Their Female Operatives, with an Appeal on Behalf of the British Factory Population, and Suggestions for the Improvement of Their Condition.* Boston: William D. Ticknor, 1845.

Scott, Joan W., and Tilly, Louise A. "Women's Work and the Family in Nineteenth-Century Europe." *Comparative Studies in Society and History* 17 (January 1975).

Shreve, Anita. "Careers and the Lure of Motherhood." *New York Times Magazine*, November 21, 1982.

Simms, Mary. *The Natural History of a Social Institution: The Young Women's Christian Asso-*

ciation. New York: Women's Press, 1936.

Sklar, Kathryn Kish. *Catharine Beecher: A Study in American Domesticity*. New Haven: Yale University Press, 1973.

Smith-Rosenberg, Carroll, and Rosenberg, Charles. "The Female Animal: Medical and Biological Views of Woman and Her Role in Nineteenth-Century America." *Journal of American History* 60 (September 1973): 332–56.

Smuts, Robert W. *Women and Work in America*. 1959. New York: Schocken, 1971.

Sorokin, Pitirim, and Zimmerman, Carle C. *Principles of Rural-Urban Sociology*. New York: Henry Holt, 1929.

Spencer, Anna Garlin. *The Family and Its Members*. Philadelphia: J. B. Lippincott, 1923.

––––––. "What Machine-Dominated Industry Means in Relation to Women's Work: The Need of New Training and Apprenticeship for Girls." *Proceedings of the National Conference of Charities and Correction, 37th Annual Meeting*. Fort Wayne, Ind.: Archer Publishing, 1910.

––––––. *Women's Share in Social Culture*. 1912. Reprint. Philadelphia: J. B. Lippincott, 1925.

Stansell, Mary Christine. "Women of the Laboring Poor in New York City, 1820–1860." Ph.D. dissertation, Yale University, 1979.

Steinfels, Margaret O'Brien. *Who's Minding the Children?: The History and Politics of Day Care in America*. New York: Simon and Schuster, 1973.

Stewart, William Rhinelander. *The Philanthropic Work of Josephine Shaw Lowell*. New York: Macmillan, 1911.

Stigler, George. *Domestic Servants in the United States, 1900–1940*. New York: National Bureau of Economic Research, 1946.

Stokes, Rose H. Phelps. "The Condition of Working Women, from the Working Woman's Viewpoint." *Annals of the American Academy of Political and Social Science* 27 (May 1906): 627–37.

Stoltz, Lois Meek. "Effects of Maternal Employment on Children: Evidence from Research." *Child Development* 31 (1960): 749–82.

Straub, Eleanor. "United States Government Policy toward Civilian Women during World War I." *Prologue* 5 (Winter 1973): 240–54.

Sum, Andrew M. "Women in the Labor Force: Why Projections Have Been Too Low." *Monthly Labor Review* 100 (July 1977): 18–24.

Suransky, Valerie Polakow. *The Erosion of Childhood*. Chicago: University of Chicago Press, 1982.

Sutherland, Daniel E. *Americans and Their Servants: Domestic Service in the United States, 1880–1920*. Baton Rouge, La.: Louisiana State University Press, 1981.

Sweet, James A. *Women in the Labor Force*. New York: Seminar Press, 1973.

Taeuber, Conrad, and Taeuber, Irene. *The Changing Population of the United States*. New York: John Wiley and Sons, 1958.

Talcott, Mrs. H. B. *Madge; Or, Night and Morning*. New York: D. Appleton, 1863.

Tentler, Leslie Woodcock. *Wage-Earning Women: Industrial Work and Family Life in the United States, 1900–1930*. New York: Oxford University Press, 1979.

Terhune, Mary Hawes [Marion Harland, pseud.]. "Counting-Room and Cradle." *North American Review*, September 1893, pp. 334–40.

Thernstrom, Stephen. *Poverty and Progress: Social Mobility in a Nineteenth-Century City*. Cambridge, Mass.: Harvard University Press, 1964.

Thurston, Henry W. *The Dependent Child*. New York: Columbia University Press, 1930.

Tilly, Louise A. "Urban Growth, Industrialization, and Women's Employment in Milan, Italy, 1881–1911." *Journal of Urban History* 3 (August 1977): 467–84.

Tolman, William Howe, and Hemstreet, Charles. *The Better New York*. New York: Baker and Taylor, 1904.

Trattner, Walter L. *Crusade for the Children: A History of the National Child Labor Committee and Child Labor Reform in America*. Chicago: Quadrangle Books, 1970.

Travis, Anthony R. "The Origins of Mothers' Pensions in Illinois." *Journal of the Illinois State Historical Society* 67 (November 1975): 421–28.
Tyson, Helen Glenn. "The Fatherless Family." *Annals of the American Academy of Political and Social Science* 77 (May 1918), pp. 79–90.
———. "The Professional Woman's Baby." *New Republic*, 7 April 1926.
Valesh, Eva McDonald [Eva Gay, pseud.]. *St. Paul Globe*, 26 March 1888–3 August 1891.
Van Duzer, Adelaide Laura. *Everyday Living for Girls.* Philadelphia: J. B. Lippincott, 1936.
Vanek, Joann. "Time Spent in Housework." *Scientific American*, November 1974, pp. 116–21.
Van Vorst, Mrs. John, and Van Vorst, Marie. *The Woman Who Toils: Being the Experiences of Two Ladies as Factory Girls.* New York: Doubleday, Page and Co., 1903.
Wagner, Richard Roland. "Virtue against Vice: A Study of Moral Reformers and Prostitution in the Progressive Era." Ph.D. dissertation, University of Wisconsin, 1971.
Wald, Lillian D. "The Immigrant Young Girl." *Proceedings of the National Conference of Charities and Correction, 36th Annual Meeting.* Fort Wayne, Ind.: Archer Publishing, 1909.
Waldman, Elizabeth, et al. "Working Mothers in the 1970s: A Look at the Statistics." *Monthly Labor Review* 102 (October 1979): 39–49.
Walsh, Mary Roth. *Doctors Wanted: No Women Need Apply: Sexual Barriers in the Medical Profession, 1835–1975.* New Haven: Yale University Press, 1977.
Wandersee, Winifred D. *Women's Work and Family Values, 1920–1940.* Cambridge, Mass.: Harvard University Press, 1981.
Ware, Norman Joseph. *The Industrial Worker, 1840–1860: The Reaction of American Industrial Society to the Advance of the Industrial Revolution.* 1924. Reprint. New York: Quadrangle Books, 1964.
Watson, John B. *Psychological Care of Infant and Child.* New York: W. W. Norton, 1928.
Weiner, Lynn. " 'Our Sister's Keepers': The Minneapolis Woman's Christian Association and Housing for Working Women." *Minnesota History* (Spring 1979): 189–200.
"Widows' Pension Legislation." *Municipal Research* 85 (May 1917).
Wiebe, Robert H. *The Search for Order, 1877–1920.* New York: Hill and Wang, 1967.
Williams, Robin M. "Rural Youth Studies in the United States." *Rural Sociology* 4 (June 1939): 166–78.
Wilson, Elizabeth. *Fifty Years of Association Work among Young Women, 1866–1916: A History of Young Women's Christian Associations in the United States of America.* New York: Young Women's Christian Association, 1916.
Wisconsin Bureau of Labor and Industrial Statistics. *Third Biennial Report of the Bureau of Labor and Industrial Statistics, Wisconsin, 1887–88.* Madison, Wis.: Democratic Printing, 1888.
———. *Tenth Biennial Report of the Wisconsin Bureau of Labor and Industrial Statistics, 1900–1901.* Madison, Wis.: Democratic Printing, 1901.
Wisconsin Bureau of Labor Statistics. *First Biennial Report of the Bureau of Labor Statistics of Wisconsin, 1883 and 1884.* Madison, Wis.: Democratic Printing, 1884.
Wishy, Bernard. *The Child and the Republic: The Dawn of Modern American Child Nurture.* Philadelphia: University of Pennsylvania Press, 1968.
Wolcott, Louise. "Discussion: Poor Widows with Dependent Children." In *Proceedings of the National Conference of Charities and Correction, 15th Annual Meeting.* Boston: Geo. H. Ellis, 1888.
Wolfe, Albert Benedict. *The Lodging House Problem in Boston.* Harvard Economic Studies. Boston: Houghton Mifflin, 1906.
Woods, Robert A., and Kennedy, Albert J. *Young Working Girls: A Summary of Evidence from Two Thousand Social Workers.* Boston: Houghton Mifflin, 1913.
Wright, Carroll D. *The Working Girls of Boston.* 1889. Reprint. New York: Arno and the New York Times, 1969.
Wylie, Philip. *Generation of Vipers.* New York: Farrar and Rinehart, 1942.

Yans-McLaughlin, Virginia. *Family and Community: Italian Immigrants in Buffalo, 1880–1930.* Ithaca, N.Y.: Cornell University Press, 1977.

Yates, Gayle Graham. *What Women Want.* Cambridge, Mass.: Harvard University Press, 1975.

Zimmerman, Carle C. "The Migration to Towns and Cities." *American Journal of Sociology* 32 (November 1926): 450–55.

Index

DATE DUE

1-25-93			